The French Prophets

The French Prophets

The History of a Millenarian Group in Eighteenth-Century England

Hillel Schwartz

University of California Press
Berkeley • Los Angeles • London

University of California Press
Berkeley and Los Angeles, California
University of California Press, Ltd.
London, England
© 1980 by The Regents of the University of California

Library of Congress Cataloging in Publication Data

Schwartz, Hillel, 1948-
   The French prophets.

   Based on the author's thesis Yale, 1974.
   1. Millenialism—England. 2. Millenialism—
France. 3. Huguenots—England. 4. Huguenots—
France. 5. England—Church history—18th century.
6. France—Church history—18th century.
I. Title.
BR758.S34   284'.5'0941   78-65459
ISBN 0-520-03815-0

Printed in the United States of America

1 2 3 4 5 6 7 8 9

To Roger & Sandra

Contents

List of Illustrations ix
Acknowledgments xi
Abbreviations xiii
Notes on Style and Dating xvi

    Introduction   1

I. The Desert   11
    The First Prophets   17
    The Camisards   22

II. The English Setting   37
    England and the Millennium   37
    The Huguenot Community in London   54
    The Movement for Spiritual Reform   62

III. The French Prophets in London, 1706-1707   72
    The *Inspirés* and the Refugees   72
    English Contacts   79
    The Ascendance of the English   85
    The Shaping of the True Church   98
    The Second Trial   104

IV. The Legacy of Dr. Thomas Emes   113
    Prophecies Fail   113
    The Reunion of the Two Alliances   125
    The Rise of False Prophets   130
    The Role of Women   134
    Orders for Assemblies   146
    An Overview   150

V. Distant Piety: Scotland and the Continent 154
    The French Prophets in Scotland 154
    The Impact of Quietism 162
    Missions to the Continent 169
    Prophecy and Pietism in Europe 181

VI. Toward the Female Embassy 191
    1715-1730: The Silence 191
    Hannah Wharton 194
    The Evangelical Revival 202
    The Female Embassy 210

VII. Seekers, Citizens, Scientists 216
    The Seekers 217
    The Citizens 219
    The Scientists: Motion 233
    The Scientists: Salt 242
    The Wild and the Walled 251

Conclusion 279
    Appendices 293
    Bibliography of Manuscript Sources 331
    Index 343

Illustrations

Map 1	Simplified map of southeastern France and Switzerland, c. 1700	25
Map 2	Simplified map of London, c. 1708	59
Map 3	Great Britain	137
PLATE I	Music to Psalm LXVIII as sung by 17th-century Huguenots	13
PLATE II	Map of the Cévennes, from Antoine Court, *Histoire des troubles des Cévennes* (Villefranche, 1760)	24
PLATE III	Map of London, from Edward Hatton, *A New View of London* (1708)	58
PLATE IV	First leaf from Fatio's calendar of events, BPUG	74
PLATE V	Woodcut from broadside, *Pillory Disapointed, or, the False Prophets Advancement* (1707)	111
PLATE VI	Marie Huber's drawing of a beast seen in the skies in 1718, BPUG	187
PLATE VII	Engraving by Francis Hoffman for Richard Roach's *The Imperial Standard of Messiah Triumphant* (1728)	195
PLATE VIII	Portrait of Nicolas Fatio de Duillier, from BPUG	224
PLATE IX	Portrait of Francis Moult, from Stack Collection	226
PLATE X	Portrait of Charles Portales, from Stack Collection	227
PLATE XI	View of London from Islington, by T. Bowles (1730)	264
PLATE XII	Engraving by Simon Gribelin for Fatio's *Fruit-Walls Improved by Inclining Them to the Horizon* (1699)	270

PLATE XIII	Frontispiece to *Quand vous aurez saccagé, vous serez saccagés* (1714)	271
PLATE XIV	Old Bawn plaster chimney piece, National Museum (Dublin)	274
PLATE XV	Reconstructed ground plan of Sir Richard Bulkeley's ancestral home, Old Bawn	275

Plates I, III, VII and XII reproduced courtesy of the William Andrews Clark Library (UCLA). Plate V reproduced courtesy of the Bodleian Library (Oxford).

Acknowledgments

I am indebted first and foremost to T. Lindsay Stack and Shirley Stack. Not only did they grant me the privilege of using their family papers; they also prepared a typescript of one of the manuscripts, arranged for photographs of portraits of Stack ancestors Charles Portales and Francis Moult, and supplied me with tea at all the right hours. This book is poor recompense for their profuse hospitality.

I am grateful too for the hospitality and informed conversation of Dr. and Mrs. David Pariente, Prof. and Mme. Philippe Joutard, and Pasteur Frank Christol. Prof. John Walsh, Prof. John Sommerville, Prof. E. J. Hobsbawm, Dr. David F. Musto and Prof. Margaret C. Jacob have been consistently helpful. I am especially obligated to Professor Walsh for references and discussions, and to Professor Jacob for the opportunity to read prepublication copies of her book and several articles. I must thank M. de Tocqueville for permission to use the microfilm copy of the Fonds Lamoignon in the Chartrier de Tocqueville at the Archives Nationales (Paris), and Eva Murray-Browne for permission to cite from the Lloyd-Baker papers in the Worcester Record Office. Arnold H. J. Baines and G. Reid Doster III were kind enough to provide me with information on the French Prophet Isaac Hollis, William McMenemey on Worcester and the eighteenth-century medical profession, Prof. Edwin Welch on the registration of dissenters' meetinghouses, Harry R. Schwartz and Herbert C. Katz on the composition of *Sal volatile oleosum*, and Peter Walsh on Sir Richard Bulkeley's now-demolished ancestral home near Dublin. Others who have spent considerable time and thought answering my queries include Edouard Allut, Harry Carter, Olive Goodbody, Rev. Roger Hayden, Ann Hyde, Louis Hyman, Theodore E. Johnson, Rolf Loeber, Daniel Vidal and Rev. Canon A. R. Winnett. Charles Domson (d. 1973) was more helpful than I had any reason to expect or deserve.

I can think of few instances when librarians and archivists have not been extraordinarily courteous and imaginative. Irene Scouloudi secured me access to the Archives of the French Protestant Church, Soho Square, and Rev. N. S. Moon to the Broadmead Baptist Church archives in Bristol; both demonstrated remarkable kindness and patience. Arthur E. Barker, Rev. W. D. Cooper, Lt. Col. Alan Faith, Arthur H. Frost, Rev. G. Rusling, C. W. Schooling, W. H. Spyvee, and Prof. Barry White were also very gracious custodians of archival materials. The staffs of the following libraries deserve special mention: in England, the Bodleian, the Friends House Library (London), Guildhall (London), Dr. Williams's Library, Moravian Church House, and the British Museum; in Scotland, the Mitchell Library (Glasgow) and the National Library of Scotland; in Ireland, Trinity College Library (Dublin); in Paris, the Bibliothèque de la Société pour l'Histoire du Protestantisme français; in Switzerland, the Bibliothèque publique et universitaire (Geneva); in the United States, the Boston Public Library, the John Hay Library of Brown University, the William Andrews Clark Library (UCLA), and the Beinecke Rare Book Library at Yale. To the archivists in record offices throughout England (particularly Worcester, Essex, Chester and Bristol) my heartfelt thanks.

This book is based upon a Yale dissertation (1974). Parts of the first chapters in this book have appeared previously in much abbreviated form in my monograph, *Knaves, Fools, Madmen and that Subtile Effluvium: A Study of the Opposition to the French Prophets*, University of Florida Social Science Monograph Series, 62 (Gainesville, 1978).

I typed the manuscript myself.

H. S.

Del Mar, California

Abbreviations

AE	Archives des Affaires Etrangères (Paris)
AH	Archives Départementales de l'Hérault, Montpellier
BCUL	Bibliothèque cantonale et universitaire de Lausanne
Bibl. Nîmes	Bibliothèque municipale [Bibliothèque Séguier], Nîmes
BM	British Museum
Bodleian	Bodleian Library, Oxford
Bost 1921a,b	Charles Bost, "Les 'prophètes' du Languedoc en 1701 et 1702: le prédicant-prophète Jean Astruc, dit Mandagout," *Revue historique* 136 (1921) 1-36 and 137 (1921) 1-31
Bost 1925	Charles Bost, "Les 'prophètes des Cévennes' au XVIIIe siècle," *Revue d'histoire et de philosophie religieuses* 5 (1925) 401-30
BPUG	Bibliothèque publique et universitaire de Genève
Brand	Samuel Keimer, *Brand pluck'd from the Burning* (1718)
BSHPF	Bibliothèque de la Société pour l'Histoire du Protestantisme français, Paris
BSHPF	*Bulletin de la Société pour l'Histoire du Protestantisme français*
CSPD	Great Britain, *Calendar of State Papers Domestic*

Abbreviations

DNB	*Dictionary of National Biography*
Dutton-Cuninghame Corr.	Mitchell Library (Glasgow), MSS Slains Collection 562590, Correspondence between Thomas Dutton and James Cuninghame, 1709-40, copied and commented upon by Alexander Falconar
Fatio Calendar	Nicolas Fatio de Duillier, unfoliated calendar of events, 1706-10, in BPUG, MSS fr. 601
Fatio Notebooks	Dr. Williams's Library, MSS 28.33-34, Nicolas Facio, Notes on French Prophets, 2 volumes
HAL	Archives of the Library of the French Protestant Church, Soho Square
Historical Relation	"A Historical Relation of the workings and operations of the Holy Spirit concerning the everlasting Covenant which Jesus Christ comes to establish upon the Earth with his People. To be left as a memorial for ever unto his universall Church upon the Earth, 1710," in Stack MSS 1j
HMC	Great Britain, *Historical Manuscripts Commission, Reports* (1870-)
HSL	Huguenot Society of London
Kingston	Richard Kingston, *Enthusiastick Impostors No Divinely Inspired Prophets* (2 parts, 1707, 1709)
Lacy, *Warnings*	John Lacy, *The Prophetical Warnings of John Lacy, Esq; pronounced under the Operation of the Spirit* (3 vols., 1707; third volume with variant title, *Warnings of the Eternal Spirit by the Mouth of his Servant, John, sirnamed Lacy*)
MMM	Charles Bost, ed., *Mémoires inédits d'Abraham Mazel et d'Elie Marion sur la guerre des Cévennes 1701-1708* in *HSL Publications* 34 (1931).
NLS	National Library of Scotland (Edinburgh)
PRO	Great Britain, Public Record Office
RO	Record Office
Roach Diary	Diary of Richard Roach, 6 volumes, December 21, 1706-June 8, 1730, in Bodleian Library (Oxford), Rawlinson MSS D. 1152-1157

Stack MSS Private manuscript collection of Mr. T. Lindsay Stack, London
TS F.-Maximilien Misson, comp., *Le théâtre sacré des Cévennes; ou, récit de diverses merveilles nouvellement opérées dans cette partie de la province de Languedoc* (1707)

Notes on Style and Dating

All spellings except those in poetry and titles have been modernized. Italics are never my addition. Unidentified translations are mine. Dates are in Old Style unless marked for the continental Gregorian calendar (N.S.). The Gregorian year began on January 1, the English year on Lady Day, March 25. English dates are traditionally given with both years for the period January 1-March 24. In footnotes only the new year is given; thus in the text, February 3, 1708/09, and in footnotes, 2/3/1709 (American system: month/day/year).

Place of publication is London unless otherwise noted. All libraries and archives are in London unless otherwise noted or obvious. Entries are short-titled after their first appearance in each chapter. Cumbrous eighteenth-century titles have been severely abbreviated for the sake of economy. Full titles (and locations, if not in the BM) may be found in the bibliography to my dissertation (Yale, 1974).

Introduction

Historians give an (imperfect account);
yet the world believes them; and won't
believe matter of Fact, of my immediate
Proceedings upon the Earth.
>—a warning of the Eternal Spirit,
spoken by John Lacy, August 7, 1707

From mountain roads that wind through groves of chestnut trees, I can see in the valleys below the sheep and the vineyards that have supported the people of the Cévennes for centuries. Some of the roads are as narrow now as when the government began building them in the late seventeenth century. The Abbé du Chayla, supervisor of those new roads, was supervising the penetration of royal power into the remote parts of a fiercely independent region—where today I read, splashed on the rock walls of this hard land, the slogan "Tourisme = Prostitution." Caves in which Protestant rebels may have hidden to escape royal troops during the Camisard revolt (1702-04) are now signposted; the home of the guerilla leader Roland is a museum; much of the wild Hautes Cévennes is a national park. But the people here in northern Languedoc are still poor, are still farmers, shepherds and artisans, living in villages and small towns, used to climbing the hillsides to gather the precious chestnuts.

I can walk for an hour or more from Charing Cross in London, where the Sign of the Camisards once hung above the doorway of an inn, but I will find no hillside of chestnut trees, only the suspect irregularity of English gardens. In 1706, of course, London was smaller, a city of some half-million people, and Sir Joseph Tiley could walk from his chambers in

Whitehall near Charing Cross through the graceful Pall Mall to pasture grounds and Hyde Park, a deer preserve, in less than half an hour. Dr. Thomas Emes might wander from his home in Old Street Square to Bunhill Fields nearby and then through open land just north to suburban Hoxton in a short stroll after dinner. But if the city was more open than it is now, if the center was slightly less congested after the great fire of 1666 than it has come to be, people like Hugh Preston still lived underground, and Sir Christopher Wren lost his battle to rebuild the city on the same principles as informed his elegant church architecture. The poor lived in tenements or in basements, and everyone knew the darkness of the London air, those "fameuses fumées de Londres," as F.-Maximilien Misson wrote in 1719.

What happened to a tradition of millenarian prophecy, geographically and culturally specific to southeastern France, when three Cévenol prophets arrived in the London of 1706? What conflicts and compromises were there as a new prophetic group developed, more English than French? How did their millennial vision slip and shift as believers confronted an ever-delayed Second Coming? How did people who relied upon prophetic inspiration for a perspective on human events come to terms with false prophecy and apostasy? Such questions underlie this study of the early eighteenth-century millenarian group known as the French Prophets.[1]

To answer these questions, I have adopted the approaches of both Emile Durkheim and Max Weber. With Durkheim I have asked, "How is this related to society as a whole?" With Weber I have asked, "What meaning does this have for the people involved?"[2] I also borrow much from anthropologists—Kenelm Burridge, Mary Douglas, Victor Turner—in order to trace the interplay of belief, ritual and social organization. For the social and affective worlds of the millenarian are complex, and a millenarian group has much more than an eschatology; it has an ethos, a distinguishing mood, tone and pattern to its expectations of the world's end.[3]

---

   1. Whatever their nationality and whether inspired or not, members of this group were referred to by contemporaries as French Prophets. I adopt this usage here. Lowercase references to "prophets" will always be to those men and women who actually laid claim to the act of prophecy.
   2. Peter Berger makes this distinction in *The Precarious Vision* (New York, 1961) 107.
   3. My use of "ethos" is similar in scope to that of Theodore Schwartz, "Cult and Context: Paranoid Ethos in Melanesia," *Ethos* 1 (1973) 153-74.

The French Prophets and their sympathetic contemporaries moved within a Christian universe of four kinds of millenarian ethos: the ethos of judgment and its inverse, the ethos of pentecost; the ethos of cataclysm and its inverse, the ethos of the New Jerusalem. Religious groups must always deal with two kinds of problems, social and symbolic. They must struggle to define the range of personal autonomy compatible with their desires for social cohesion; they must struggle to devise a symbolic system—a way of classifying and explaining phenomena—sufficiently clear that it may be shared, and yet neither so narrow nor so diffuse that it is ineffective. Each millenarian ethos represents a different solution to these two basic problems.[4]

The ethos of judgment lays emphasis upon God's role as judge and upon the situation of the penitent society. One anticipates the millennium as a squaring of accounts between God and humankind.[5] Society is valued for its stability, and sin is penultimately the transgression of social rules. Religious language is the language of law and status, condemnation, confession, and reprieve. Authorities labor to establish orders and ranks of

---

4. The following discussion is based upon a reworking of the model proposed by Mary Douglas in *Natural Symbols: Explorations in Cosmology* (2nd ed.; New York, 1973). She proposes that one may plot religious behavior along two axes. The horizontal axis is a measure of the degree of personal autonomy or social control. The vertical scale is a measure of the degree to which people share a symbolic system. Along this latter scale, as one proceeds from bottom to top, ways of classifying and explaining phenomena become increasingly public— one gains a common context. At the very top and the very bottom, the symbolic system may be equally articulated and condensed, but at the top it will be widely accessible, at the bottom as inaccessible as a private language. Douglas locates characteristic forms of religious interplay in each of the four quadrants formed by the intersection of the axes. Where, for example, there is both a coherent, shared classification system and a dominant cohesive group, she would expect to find an emphasis on ritual, hierarchy, and a fear of loss of control (emotional, physical, political). Where there is entire personal autonomy and a private symbolic system, she would expect to find ecstatic religion and personal revelation. I call the former, in millenarian terms, the ethos of judgment, the latter the ethos of pentecost. I have done some violence to her model in making it specific to the analysis of millenarianism. For a schematic representation, see Appendix X.

5. Throughout this study, "millennium" refers to the thousand-year period during which faithful Christians are to reign in the Kingdom of God with Jesus while Satan is bound up, as described in the Book of Revelation 20. St. John's vision includes two judgments, one preceding the millennium, and one after Satan has been loosed and then defeated forever. For most Protestants of the seventeenth and eighteenth centuries, the millennium lay in the future, so Judgment Day logically meant the first judgment; for orthodox Roman Catholics, the Council of Ephesus (431 A.D.) had established the doctrine that the millennium corresponded to the life-span of the Christian Church, not to any future period, and Judgment Day meant the second judgment. Cf. James P. Martin, *The Last Judgment in Protestant Theology from Orthodoxy to Ritschl* (Grand Rapids, 1963).

being. Those within the ethos of judgment therefore restrict personal autonomy in favor of the security of social cohesion. Similarly, the symbolic system is highly articulated and legalistic. Time itself is seen as a series of precedents and *exempla*. One may piece together scriptural clues to the chronology of the millennium precisely because the key to scripture is a systematic analysis of precedent and prefiguration. The church is both the creator and arbiter of a widely shared system for interpreting events, and as long as it conforms to precedent it will be the worthy instrument of judgment.

The inverse ethos is that of pentecost. Not church but a spiritualized self becomes crucial; faith is a creative, not a recreative process. One anticipates the Second Coming of Jesus as the spread of the spirit that informs the son of God. One relates personally to God and values the spontaneity of forms or worship. The proof of true religion is not in the well-being of the state or group but in the well-being of the individual, against whose religious sensations there is no argument. Here social cohesion is secondary to personal autonomy. Similarly, the symbolic system is private, sometimes inaccessible to other members of the group. One may speak in holy paradoxes; language may become a string of contrary predicates resolving into silence. Either in silence or in inspired talk, possessed or meditative, one is able to pierce the secrets of the Book of Revelation because one has disclosed oneself to an intimate God.

Within the ethos of cataclysm, people share a way of looking at and explaining the world, but they have lost the social cohesion necessary to ensure a prized personal security. The external world is precarious, and one looks ahead to a time of cataclysm which may be a time of renewal. Human nature suffers a general downward progress, much as the natural world does, but the faithful cannot act together successfully to avert the final moral erosion. Instead, modelling the group upon the original apostolic church, they work to redeem themselves as the elect. Redemption in such a desperate world is balance. It may be found in the establishment of social or sexual equivalence, or in balanced economic relations, or in the solution of generational conflicts, for reciprocity in the external world is a sign of reciprocity between human and deity.[6] During the search for balance, the quality of things becomes inextricable from the quantity of things, and numbers assume great importance. As one

6. On reciprocity, see Kenelm Burridge, *Mambu: A Melanesian Millennium* (1960) and his *New Heaven, New Earth: A Study of Millenarian Activities* (Oxford, 1969); Andrew Strathern, "Cargo and Inflation in Mount Hagen," *Oceania* 41 (1971) 255-65.

measures wealth, one measures social progress, religious processes and time itself. The millennium is announced as much because it comes at the end of the divine calculus as because it holds promise of prosperity.

The inverse ethos is that of community, New Jerusalem.[7] Here people remain closely bonded but lack a coherent, articulated code for assessing behavior. Either they are jealous of their prerogatives, for fear that their prerogatives are not universally recognized, or they are broadly ecumenical and assume few prerogatives. Whichever behavior is evident, the interior person is at risk. One prepares for the millennium as a means of relieving pressure upon the self, for in the millennium the group will be a world community and all action will be authentic—less by virtue of a shared symbolic system than by virtue of the universality of the group. Millennial dreams, however, resist analysis as mere defense mechanisms. In the ethos of the New Jerusalem, the emphasis is upon the creative expansion of human nature toward its outer limits, where miracles educate humankind as to the extraordinary possibilities of collective faith. Redemption is not the opposing of contraries, not balance between poles, but unanimity; one's own redemption remains incomplete without the redemption of others. The sage and the scientist combine forces to uncover the philosopher's stone which at the same time purifies and doubles. This is the missionary's amulet too. Worship, like science, makes and then generalizes the connections between primitive elements. Time too is a collection of incidents whose meaning becomes clear in the process of accretion.[8] Since the walls of the New Jerusalem rise around an immense place, one will have to sacrifice some of the power of a shared symbolic system in order to accommodate a world of people so various and yet so hopeful.

The schema I have just set out relies very little on the traditional binary terms common to studies of millenarian movements: optimistic-pessimistic, active-passive, rational-irrational, premillennial-postmillennial, prepolitical-political, conservative-radical.[9] No millenarian group fits neat-

---

7. Cf. Victor Turner, "Passages, Margins, and Poverty: Religious Symbols of Communitas," in his *Dramas, Fields, and Metaphors: Symbolic Action in Human Society* (Ithaca and London, 1974) 231-71.

8. Cf. the summary pages on monochronic and polychronic time in Edward T. Hall, *The Hidden Dimension* (Anchor ed.; New York, 1966) 173-74; J.G.A. Pocock, "Modes of Political and Historical Time in Early Eighteenth-Century England," *Studies in Eighteenth-Century Culture* 5 (1976) 87-102.

9. An extended critique of these binary terms appears in my review article, "The End of the Beginning: Millenarian Studies, 1969-1975," *Religious Studies Review* 2,3 (1976) 1-15. "Pre-

ly into a single ethos, and tensions within a millenarian group may best be understood as tensions between the varieties of millenarian ethos. Millenarianism is, paradoxically, a way of looking back at the world from its end; millenarian moods and perceptions change as believers battle to keep their footing.

Throughout this book I will not follow strictly a cognitive or functionalist view of society. One may find at different points that a given millenarian ethos determines or is determined by social processes and/or symbolic systems. Just as prophecies of a Second Coming may be a response to political oppression or cognitive dissonance, so also they may shape wide social boundaries or enrich perceptions of the natural world, or, indeed, they may be dysfunctional. When the center of gravity of time has been shifted to the moment before the apocalypse, people may not be consistent, or they may be too consistent, strangely regular in their behavior. No single set of analytic tools will avail the historian of a millenarian group.[10]

Having briefly situated my approach along the methodological axis of millenarian studies, I should now identify my position along the historiographical axis. This book explores the strength and extent of a millenarian movement alive in England at a period when, according to much previous scholarship, millenarian activity should be at its lowest ebb. My account of the French Prophets is thus an account of the survival of the millenarian impulse between mid-seventeenth-century English sectarians and mid-eighteenth-century Methodists and Shakers.

---

millennialism" refers most simply to the expectation that Jesus will appear on earth again before the millennium begins; "postmillennialism" is the belief that the Second Coming takes place after the millennium has begun. Although historians have made much of the theological and behavioral implications of each belief, present scholarship has become critical of any absolute dichotomy, especially before the nineteenth century. See the valuable article by J.F. Maclear, "New England and the Fifth Monarchy: The Quest for the Millennium in Early American Puritanism," *William and Mary Quarterly* ser. 3, 32 (1975) 223-60.

Sociologists will notice that I also avoid the sect-church typology so forcefully developed by Ernst Troeltsch sixty years ago in *The Social Teaching of the Christian Church* (German ed., 1911). Despite modern adjustments of this typology by Bryan Wilson (*Religious Sects* [1970]) and Richard T. Vann (*The Social Development of English Quakerism 1655-1755* [Cambridge, Mass., 1969]), I have chosen to describe the French Prophets in their own terms as a dispensation and the True Church.

10. Cf. Vittorio Lanternari, *The Religions of the Oppressed: A Study of Modern Messianic Cults*, trans. Lisa Sergio (1963); Leon Festinger, Henry W. Riecken, and Stanley Schachter, *When Prophecy Fails* (New York, 1956) on cognitive dissonance. For works stressing the creative dynamism of millenarianism, see Frances R. Hill, "Millenarian Machines in South Vietnam," *Comparative Studies in Society and History* 13 (1971) 325-50; John G. Gager, *Kingdom and Community: The Social World of Early Christianity* (Englewood Cliffs, 1975).

Historians have chronicled (though less successfully explained) the blossoming of eschatological speculation in England under the early Stuart monarchs. Influenced by the writings of John Foxe, Joseph Mede, J. H. Alsted, and Thomas Brightman, laypeople and clergy of almost all persuasions adopted an apocalyptic attitude toward national and personal crises.[11] Among them were men and women who, during the Civil War and Commonwealth periods, insisted upon radical political reorderings of English society, based upon prophetic texts in scripture and often upon personal revelation. Few historians have challenged the traditional assumption that the millenarian impulse died away in England after the defeat of the hopes and plans of those politically radical chiliasts. After the Restoration of Charles II to the Stuart throne in 1660, millenarianism as a creed or program of action is assumed by many to have lost its political thrust, its vitality and its wide appeal. By the time of the Glorious Revolution of 1688-89, so the tradition goes, millenarians had become introspective, or exponents of a secular notion of progress, or mildly insane.[12] Historians, fascinated by the politically active chiliasts of the midcentury—Fifth Monarchists, Levellers, Ranters, Diggers—have often neglected those millenarians of minor political engagement, such as the French Prophets, for they have been more concerned to determine the roots of political theory and action than to investigate all facets of a millenarian's world.[13] They have focused upon political failures, not upon the social or affective continuity of a millenarian ethos.

11. See Michael Walzer, *The Revolution of the Saints* (Cambridge, Mass., 1965); William L. Lamont, *Godly Rule: Politics and Religion 1603-60* (1969); John F. Wilson, *Pulpit in Parliament: Puritanism during the English Civil Wars 1640-1648* (Princeton, 1969); J.A. De Jong, *As the Waters Cover the Sea: Millennial Expectations in the Rise of Anglo-American Missions 1640-1810* (Kampen, 1970) 8-78; Peter Toon, ed., *Puritans the Millennium and the Future of Israel* (Cambridge and London, 1970); Tai Liu, *Discord in Zion: The Puritan Divines and the Puritan Revolution 1640-1660* (The Hague, 1973)—perhaps the clearest exposition of a confusing era; Paul Christianson, *Reformers and Babylon: English Apocalyptic Visions from the Reformation to the Eve of the Civil War* (Toronto, 1978).
12. See Arthur L. Morton, *The World of the Ranters: Religious Radicalism in the English Revolution* (New York and London, 1970); Norman Cohn, *The Pursuit of the Millennium* (3rd ed.; New York, 1970); P.G. Rogers, *The Fifth Monarchy Men* (1966); George Juretic, "Digger No Millenarian: The Revolutionizing of Gerard Winstanley," *Journal of the History of Ideas* 36 (1975) 263-80; Christopher Hill, *Antichrist in Seventeenth-Century England* (1971); Ernest Lee Tuveson, *Millennium and Utopia: A Study in the Background of the Idea of Progress* (Berkeley and Los Angeles, 1949).
13. One example of an article which goes beyond politics is Lynnewood F. Martin, "The Family of Love in England: Conforming Millenarians," *Sixteenth-Century Journal* 3 (1972) 99-108.

I hope to demonstrate in this book that the French Prophets appealed to an astonishing variety of people who drew upon types of millenarian ethos common to men and women of the early seventeenth century. The first significant group of English followers of the Camisard prophets were Philadelphians, whose theosophical and prophetic lineage can be traced back to the 1640s and the popularity of the mystical writings of Jakob Boehme. Another important group to join the movement were Scottish quietists whose spiritual guides were Antoinette Bourignon and Madame Guyon, women who had read deeply in the confessional, apocalyptic literature prevalent during the Thirty Years War (1618-48). From the anguish and dislocation of that brutal war came also the reflections of Philipp Jakob Spener, whose pietist disciples in Germany and Switzerland would be much affected by the French Prophets. Indeed, the relationship between the two would remain close throughout the early years of Methodism; the French Prophets momentarily attracted the members of the small Moravian meeting from which would come John Wesley's first London Methodists.

Scholars have recently discovered millenarian ideas in the papers and programs of some of the most prominent figures of later seventeenth-century English society: Robert Boyle, Thomas Hobbes, Sir Isaac Newton, and the latitudinarian bishops. The new scholarship argues that images of the world's end had lost neither their intellectual attraction nor their political thrust some forty years after the Restoration.[14] I argue in this work that an entire millenarian way of life flourished in England between 1660 and 1740. The French Prophets were not the source but the sign of its vitality.

14. See J.E. McGuire and P.M. Rattansi, "Newton and the 'Pipes of Pan,'" *Notes and Records of the Royal Society of London* 21 (1966) 108-43; David C. Kubrin, "Providence and the Mechanical Philosophy: The Creation and Dissolution of the World in Newtonian Thought," Ph.D. thesis, Cornell University, 1968; J.G.A. Pocock, "Time, History and Eschatology in the Thought of Thomas Hobbes," in J.H. Elliott and H.G. Koenigsberger, eds., *The Diversity of History* (Ithaca, 1970) 149-98; Bernard S. Capp, *The Fifth Monarchy Men: A Study in Seventeenth-Century Millenarianism* (1972); Frank E. Manuel, *The Religion of Newton* (Oxford, 1974); Margaret C. Jacob, *The Newtonians and the English Revolution 1689-1720* (Ithaca, 1976); J.R. Jacob, *Robert Boyle and the English Revolution* (New York, 1977). Similar arguments for the continuity of millenarianism in colonial New England are advanced by Sacvan Bercovitch, "Horologicals to Chronometricals: The Rhetoric of the Jeremiad," *Literary Monographs* 3 (1970) 1-124; Stephen J. Stein, "Cotton Mather and Jonathan Edwards on the Number of the Beast: Eighteenth-Century Speculation about the Antichrist," *Proceedings of the American Antiquarian Society* 84 (1974) 293-315.

I will follow a millenarian movement from origin to end, looking at it from within as much and as often as possible.[15] By concentrating on the group's internal conflicts and responses to events in the larger social arena, I will in effect be examining transformations in millenarian ethos during the reign of Queen Anne and after. Not inadvertently, my sketch of the French Prophets may serve as the foreground to a landscape of general religious life in late Stuart and early Hanoverian England.

15. Consequently, I will refrain from the use of intrusive legalisms when describing the behavior of the French Prophets. Thus, "Lacy levitated," rather than, "the group claimed that Lacy levitated." Were I to constantly interrupt the narrative with the suspicions of an outsider, the reader might lose that sense of the inner workings of the group which is important to this book. A recent study with some of the same concerns (and methodological problems) as mine is B. Robert Kreiser, *Miracles, Convulsions, and Ecclesiastical Politics in Early Eighteenth-Century Paris* (Princeton, 1978).

CHAPTER I

The Desert

When the French Prophets in London composed their own history in 1708, they began with an account of the persecution of Huguenots in Languedoc and Dauphiné.¹ This study too begins in southeastern France and travels, as did the original prophets, to England, Scotland, and then back to the continent.

By 1560 rural artisans had brought Protestant ideas to the most inaccessible parishes of Languedoc. The people of the Cévennes, a mountainous area in northern Languedoc, embraced Reform as perhaps no other group in France. Protestantism became for them an all-encompassing culture, uprooting earlier folkways. In the 1590s, after thirty years of religious wars between French Protestants (Huguenots) and Catholics, Protestantism—of Calvinist temperament and form—was firmly planted in Languedoc, most especially in the rocky soil of the Cévennes. Although the Edict of Nantes in 1598 assured Huguenots of religious liberty and legal equality, not until the end of another war in the Cévennes in 1630 did Huguenots of Languedoc have peace enough to enjoy their freedom.²

   1. Historical Relation, f. 1.
   2. David S. Hempsall, "The Languedoc 1520-1540: A Study of Pre-Calvinist Heresy in Languedoc," *Archiv für Reformationsgeschichte* 62 (1971) 225-43; Raymond A. Mentzer, Jr., "Legal Responses to Heresy in Languedoc, 1500-1560," *Sixteenth-Century Journal* 4 (1973) 19-30; Henri Hauser, "La Réforme et les classes populaires en France au XVIe siècle," *Revue d'histoire moderne et contemporaine* 1 (1899) 24-37; Robert M. Kingdon, *Geneva and the Consolidation of the French Protestant Movement 1564-1572* (Madison, 1967) 15, 202; Emile-G. Léonard, *L'établissement (1564-1700)* (Paris, 1961) ch. 3; Emmanuel Le Roy Ladurie, *Les paysans de Languedoc* (Paris, 1966) I, 334-56, 410, 613; Michel Richard, *La vie quotidienne des Protestants sous l'Ancien Régime* (Paris, 1966) 13-15, 63.

Protestant worship in France, like that of puritans in England, drew its strength less from ceremony than from a direct encounter with the word of God. Huguenots read the Bible and listened to others read it aloud, sang the psalms as set to music by Marot and Goudimel, recited prayers and heard their ministers expound scripture. Children memorized sermons and psalms, took part in church responses from the age of ten. Much church activity was conducted by laymen, and the consistories which guided their temples were primarily lay bodies. Men and women, segregated in the temple, shared in the religious upbringing of their children, and the family cult was a valued aspect of Huguenot life. Ministers or not, the faithful were intimate with God's Word.[3] (See Plate I.)

Between 1630 and 1660, many Huguenots altered the manner in which they understood God's Word. Concurrent with a similar issue in the Catholic world and the debate over Arminianism in the Netherlands, French Protestants strove to interpret correctly the meaning of faith and grace. Moise Amyraut, early a student of the Scot John Cameron at the Huguenot academy at Saumur, proposed a shift of emphasis to allow for reason in faith, for mercy in God's judgment. Challenging the theological rigidity of Calvin's successors at Geneva, Amyraut defended John Cameron's view of faith as an operation of the understanding rather than of the will alone. He stressed the universality of grace (Jesus's redemption as applicable to all) and the element of choice (howsoever limited) before God condemned the unbelievers. Amyraut's theology was most strenuously opposed by Pierre du Moulin, a theologian at the academy of Sedan. By 1650 Amyraut's position was predominant except around La Rochelle and in Languedoc.[4]

As Louis XIV renewed the persecution of Huguenots after 1660, French Protestants in Languedoc strengthened their attachment to the theology of Pierre du Moulin and Genevan orthodoxy. In the years of suffering that followed, the Calvinist doctrine of redemption for the elect and du Moulin's particular millennial vision of history would have wide appeal to those who remained in southeastern France. Between 1660 and 1685, despite their continued royalism,[5] Huguenots faced over three hundred

3. Paul de Félice, *Les Protestants d'autrefois* (Paris, 1896) I, 64-117.
4. Brian G. Armstrong, *Calvinism and the Amyraut Heresy* (Madison, 1969); Guy H. Dodge, *The Political Theory of the Huguenots of the Dispersion* (New York, 1947) 167; Walter Rex, *Essays on Pierre Bayle and Religious Controversy* (The Hague, 1965) 9-20, 88-97; Roger Zuber, "Calvinisme et Classicisme," *XVIIe siècle* 76-77 (1967) 20; Pierre Chaunu, "Le XVIIe siècle religieux. Réflexions préalales," *Annales: é.s.c.* (mars-avril 1967) 279-302.
5. Dodge, *Political Theory*, 5 Solange Deyon, *Du loyalisme au refus* (Lille, 1976); Hartmut Kretzer, *Calvinismus und französische Monarchie im 17. Jahrhundert* (Berlin, 1975).

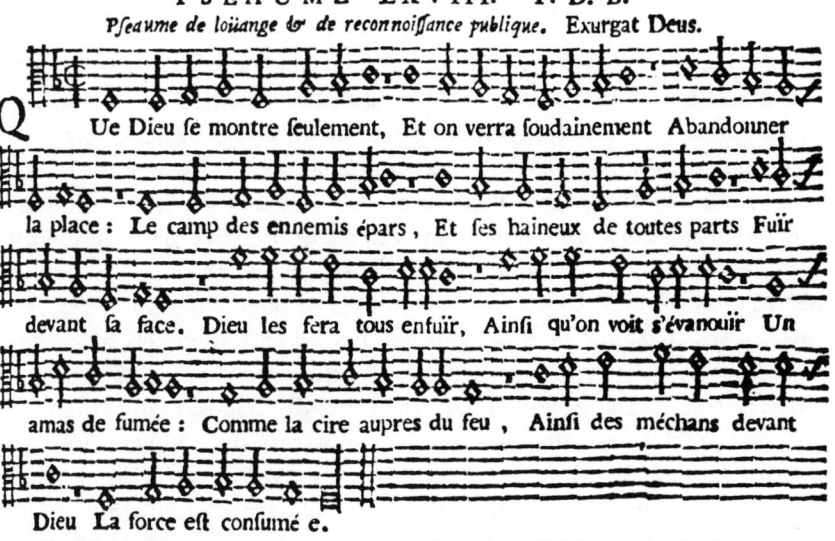

PSEAUME LXVIII. T. D. B.
Pseaume de loüange & de reconnoissance publique. Exurgat Deus.

Que Dieu se montre seulement, Et on verra soudainement Abandonner la place : Le camp des ennemis épars, Et ses haineux de toutes parts Fuïr devant sa face. Dieu les fera tous enfuïr, Ainsi qu'on voit s'évanouïr Un amas de fumée : Comme la cire auprés du feu , Ainsi des méchans devant Dieu La force est consumée.

¶ Cependant devant le Seigneur
Les justes chantent son honneur
En toute éjouïssance :
Et de la grand' joye qu'ils ont
De voir les méchans qui s'en vont,
Sautent à grand' puissance.
  Chantez du Seigneur le renom,
Psalmodiez, loüez son Nom,
Et sa gloire immortelle :
Car sur la nuë il est porté,
Et d'un nom plein de majesté,
L'Eternel il s'appelle.
¶ Réjouïssez-vous devant lui,
Qui est des pauvres sans appui
Le pere debonnaire :
Qui le droict des veuves soustient,
Devant Dieu, dis-je, qui se tient
En son saint Sanctuaire.
  Dieu fait avoir pleine maison
A ceux qui ont longue saison
Sans nuls enfans soufferte :
Delivre les siens enferrez,
Tient les rebelles enferrez
En leur terre deserte.
✱✱✱ 1 ¶ Lors que ton peuple tu menois,
O Dieu, & que tu cheminois
Par le desert horrible,
Les cieux fondirent en sueur :
La terre trembla de la peur
De ta face terrible.
  Le mont de Sion ébranlé,
Dieu, Dieu d'Israël a branlé
Regardant ton visage :

C'est toi, puissant Dieu, qui as fait
Degoutter la pluye à souhait
Dessus ton heritage.
¶ Quand il a esté mal en poinct,
Tu l'as redressé de tout poinct,
Là les troupeaux demeurent :
Tu l'emplis de biens infinis,
Dont les plus pauvres tu fournis,
Que sans secours ne meurent.
  C'est toi, Seigneur, par ta bonté,
Qui as l'argument presenté
A l'armée pudique
De nos pucelles qu'on ouït,
Lors que l'ennemi s'enfuït,
Prononcer ce cantique :
¶ Or s'en sont fuïs les grands Rois,
Les grands Rois, dis-je, & leurs arrois
S'en sont fuïs grand' erre :
Celles qui n'avoient point sorti
De la maison, ont departi
Et leurs biens & leur terre.
  Quoi que ternis & bazanez
Des ennuis qu'on vous a donnez,
Vous ne diffriez gueres
De ceux que l'on voit tous noircis
D'avoir esté toûjours assis
A l'ombre des chaudieres.
¶ Vous reluirez comme feroit
L'aile d'un pigeon qui seroit
De fin argent brunie :
Dont le pennage estincelant
Fait sembler l'aile en l'air volant
De plus fin or jaunie.

PLATE I. Psalm LXVIII, a favorite of the Camisards, from *La Bible, qui est toute la Sainte Escriture du Vieil et du Nouveau Testament . . . Avec les Pseaumes de David, mis en rime Françoise par Cl. Marot & Theod. de Beze. Imprimée par l'approbation de Ministres de l'Eglise Françoise de la Savoye et de celle de Londres* (1687).

decrees that eroded their religious freedom and personal liberties. After 1678 and Louis XIV's conversion to a vehement Catholicism, the pace of attack quickened and Huguenots lost political and economic power: the government disbanded special bipartisan chambers of justice in Guienne, Languedoc and Dauphiné; Protestants were denied the right to practice various professions and could no longer be masters of trades. Other measures encouraged the conversion of those who obstinately adhered to the "*Religion Prétendue Réformée.*" In 1681 began the *dragonnades*: royal troops were quartered in Huguenot homes and permitted acts of violence. Protestant schools were boarded up. Temples were pulled down.[6]

By the time of the Revocation of the Edict of Nantes, many Huguenots had fled into exile, abandoning their possessions. Others, often the wealthy, chose to convert; they bore the name *Nouveaux Convertis* (New Converts), a term of opprobrium to both Protestants and Catholics.[7] The Revocation itself, in October, 1685, proscribed all exercise of the "R. P. R." Parents were not allowed to raise their children as Protestants, and pastors who refused to convert were ordered into exile within a fortnight. All others of the "R. P. R." forfeited their right to emigrate. Protestants remaining in France became, under severe pressure, nominal Catholics, *Nouveaux Convertis,* constantly interrogated to determine whether they attended mass, went to confession and took communion.

Despite surveillance, the Huguenots tried to preserve their religious tradition. Accustomed to the family cult, they perpetuated in secret the familiar forms of private worship. What they missed was the visible church and the preaching of the word of God. In Languedoc and Dauphiné, as nowhere else in France, arose lay preachers (*prédicants*) to meet the needs of 150,000 Huguenots bereft of a regular ministry. The *prédicants* convened the faithful in illicit assemblies whose format was that of the Protestant service: a psalm, scriptural exegesis, a sermon. In their sermons the *prédicants* urged the congregants to repent of their conversion to idolatry, passive or active, politic or sincere. The assemblies were held late at night in wilderness places where the singing of psalms might not carry to prowling royal troops. Such was the origin of the "Desert," a metaphor at once for the spiritual desolation of Huguenots in southeastern France and

6. See Jean Orcibal, *Louis XIV et les Protestants* (Paris, 1951); Warren C. Scoville, *The Persecution of Huguenots and French Economic Development 1680-1720* (Berkeley and Los Angeles, 1960) 64-97.

7. On the social rank of converts, see Paul Romane-Musculus, "Les abjurations de Protestants à Toulouse entre l'Edit de Nantes et la Révolution," *Annales du Midi* 71 (1959) 283-95; Georges Frêche, "Contre-Réforme et dragonnades 1610-1789," *Actes du 95e Congres national des sociétés savantes, Reims, 1970; Section d'histoire moderne et contemporaine* (1974) II, 275-91.

for the geography of their assemblies, the last sign of their visible church.[8]

Sustained by Desert meetings, Huguenots were also consoled by the possibility that their trials were part of God's scheme for the coming of the millennium. Early in the century, Pierre du Moulin, whose books were nearly as popular as the psalms of Marot, had examined St. John's Revelation for clues to the divine chronology. From Revelation 13:5 it was clear to du Moulin that the Beast would endure for 1260 years (42 months = 1260 prophetic days = 1260 years), and from other passages it was equally clear to him that the Beast was linked with the Pope. Dating the Papal Kingdom from 755 A.D., there remained (in 1611-12) 404 years to the end of the Beast and the Second Coming of Jesus. Of more immediate interest, du Moulin ascertained that the persecution of the True Church by the Beast (the Pope) would end with the resurrection of the two witnesses of Revelation 11 in 1689.[9]

Amyraut had written a treatise against such millennial speculations, and Huguenot ministers generally needed special permission to discourse upon Revelation, but even so Huguenots of the Desert were familiar with and fond of St. John's visions. They found that he had foreseen their exact situation. By 1685, the *Eclaircissement sur l'Apocalypse de St. Jean* had shown them that the Revocation of the Edict of Nantes signalled the death of the two witnesses, who would lie unburied for three and one-half years and then rise in 1689. Near Pont-de-Montvert in 1686, a Cévenol carpenter declared that the persecution would last but three years more. A popular Languedoc poem in 1687 looked forward to 1689. The intendant of Languedoc, Nicolas Lamoignon de Bâville, was quickly aware of du Moulin's influence and the Huguenot millennial interpretation of the Revocation.[10]

The winters of 1684/85 and 1685/86 were hard ones, and in the summer of 1685 a plague of grasshoppers swept along the Mediterranean coast as

---

8. Samuel Mours, "Essai d'évaluation de la population protestante réformée aux XVIIe et XVIIIe siècles," *BSHPF* 103 (1958) 17-19, and his *Essai sommaire de géographie du Protestantisme réformé français au XVIIe siècle* (Paris, 1966); Charles Bost, *Les prédicants protestants des Cévennes et du Bas-Languedoc 1684-1700* (Paris, 1912) II, 367-81; S. Deyon, "La résistance protestante et la symbolique du Désert," *Revue d'histoire moderne et contemporaine* 18 (1971) 237-49.

9. Pierre du Moulin, *Accomplissement des prophéties* (La Rochelle, 1612) 239-41. On du Moulin's influence, see Bost, *Les prédicants,* I, 44, 49, 51, 178-80.

10. Moise Amyraut, *Du regne de mille ans, ou de la prospérité de l'Eglise* (Saumur, 1654); Richard, *La vie quotidienne,* 48-49; Bost, *Les prédicants,* I, 179, 219, and his "Poésies populaires huguenotes de Vivarais," *BSHPF* 89 (1940) 225; Le Roy Ladurie, *Les paysans de Languedoc,* I, 616. Philippe Joutard, *La légende des Camisards: Une sensibilité au passé* (Paris, 1977) 46 *et passim,* would not place the same emphasis on millenarian prophecy as I do. Cf. Philippe Joutard and Henri Manen, *Une foi enracinée: La Pervenche* (Valence, 1972) 66.

far west as the Rhône. The *dragonnades* in Languedoc continued. Bâville feared a revolt in the Cévennes. Under such circumstances the Huguenots of the Desert first made acquaintance with the work of du Moulin's grandson, the pastor Pierre Jurieu, exiled in Rotterdam. Jurieu resumed the millennial themes of his ancestor in the *Accomplishment of Scripture Prophecies* and in the famous *Pastoral Letters* of 1686-88, which circulated clandestinely in Languedoc. Like du Moulin before him, Jurieu attributed special importance to the year 1689; like Huguenots of the Desert, he identified the Revocation with the death of the two witnesses and tentatively proposed April of 1689 as the month for the resurrection of the witnesses and the True Church.[11]

The marvels that would likely accompany the downfall of the Beast or Antichrist had already begun, Jurieu noted, with extraordinary storms and fires falling from heaven. Huguenots of the Desert were also aware of the signs, for they had begun to hear angelic choirs. Where before had stood their temples, now razed, they hearkened to voices in the wind, "a Harmony bearing much Resemblance to the Singing of our Psalms." There were as well some less pleasant sounds: plaintive songs, tambourines beating as if soldiers marched to their rhythm, a trumpet announcing the charge of an army. The heavenly noises persisted through 1687, while Huguenots were imprisoned, transported to America or sentenced to the galleys for attending illicit assemblies. The celestial psalms seemed to serve a double purpose, as prelude to other promised rewards for the steadfast and as goad to repentance for those who had wavered. If God punished the Huguenots, wrote the French Prophets in retrospect, "he comforted them also and . . . his mercy did not depart from them since he did send unto them Thousands of Angels to declare unto them the Song of their Deliverance."[12]

Transformation and endurance were the conflicting motifs of Desert life. On the one hand, the faithful sought a continuity in religious experience; on the other hand, the casualties of persecution encouraged them in their hopes that any break in continuity was a sign of imminent spiritual revolution. In the context of millennial hopes given additional impetus by the remorse of the *Nouveaux Convertis*, in the context of a

11. [Pierre Jurieu], *Apologie pour l'accomplissement des prophéties* (Rotterdam, 1687) 8-9; Dodge, *Political Theory*, 35; Rex, *Essays*, 217-25; Bost, *Les prédicants*, I, 41, 219-22; Le Roy Ladurie, *Les paysans de Languedoc*, I, 34; A.M. Boislisle, ed., *Correspondance des contrôleurs généraux des finances avec les intendants des provinces* (Paris, 1874-98) I, 184-85.

12. Pierre Jurieu, *Lettres pastorales addressees aux fideles de France, qui gemissent sous la captivite de Babylon* (Rotterdam, 1686) 27-56; O. Douen, *Les premiers pasteurs du Désert (1685-1700)* (Paris, 1879) II, 42; Historical Relation, f. 5.

Calvinism of severe judgment and strict mercy, the faithful by their very suffering were participants in the necessary fulfillment of scripture prophecy.

The First Prophets

When the first prophets appeared among them in 1688, the people of the Desert exulted, for truly, then, were these the last days and persecution could not last much longer. The prophets were messengers half-expected, and they were only children.

They prophesied while asleep. The physical act of prophecy was, like the Desert, a metaphor: in the dead-but-not-dead state of the two witnesses of Revelation, in the full repose of the innocent, the prophets were figures of the True Church; as deliverance drew near, their bodies became agitated. The ecstasy of the first prophet, a sixteen-year-old shepherdess in Dauphiné, seemed at the beginning to be "a sort of Apoplexy, or Natural Lethargy, into which she fell without any appearance of a violent motion." Her father a *Nouveau Converti*, her mother dead, Isabeau Vincent had been baptized as a Catholic but now she returned to the original faith of her parents. On the night of February 3, 1688 (N.S.), asleep in the home of an uncle with whom she lived, she suddenly cried out and began to sing the Ten Commandments. Each night thereafter when Huguenots sat in the room, she sang, preached and prayed while asleep. Physicians examined her while she talked; men sat by to copy down her words. Her room became a temple where the faithful might hear the Word spoken eloquently and where they themselves might worship while they waited. Accounts of the prophet included detailed descriptions of her physical symptoms, for these were half the miracle and half the metaphor. Isabeau lay on her back and fell asleep swiftly. She sang the Ten Commandments in rhyme, then a psalm. After a pause, she preached fluently. Her gestures were as rapid as her speech, and sometimes the "Natural Lethargy" gave way to full agitations. She woke in the morning refreshed and did not remember what had occurred during the night.[13]

In her nights of prophecy, Isabeau exhorted all to repent, for suffering was the result of disrespect for God's Word. Persecution would last,

13. Valentin Esprit Fléchier, *Lettres choisies* (Paris, 1752) I, 383, 389 (quote), 394; Justin Brun-Durand, "Vincent (Isabeau) dit la Bergère de Crest," *Dictionnaire biographique et biblio-iconographique de la Drôme* (Grenoble, 1901) II, 403-04; E. Arnaud, *Histoire des Protestants du Dauphiné aux XVIe, XVIIe et XVIIIe siècles* (Paris, 1876) III, 71-72; Pierre Jurieu, *The Reflections of the Reverend and Learned Monsieur Jurieu, upon the Strange and Miraculous Exstasies of Isabel Vincent* (1689); Bost 1925, 403-04, 418-19.

echoing Revelation, forty-two months, but the faithful would have eternal life. "It is not I that speak, but the Spirit that is within me," she proclaimed, reciting the prophecy of Joel which is repeated in Acts 2:17: "In the latter days your young People shall prophesy, and your Old Men shall dream Dreams." Celebrated and persuasive, Isabeau was a threat to the Catholic government as both a new sort of Huguenot minister and an older but powerful sort of visionary. Imprisoned by royal officials in June, 1688, the shepherdess soothed the distraught: others younger than she would take her place.[14]

Within six months younger (and older) prophets had indeed appeared in Dauphiné and Languedoc, fulfilling the words of Joel. The new prophets had physical symptoms which hinted at the emotional setting in which their visions flourished. Like Isabeau Vincent, they would be passive but agitated, asleep but awake, unconscious but perceptive, exhausted but refreshed. Their sermons and predictions betrayed a similar strain, a tension between mercy and judgment. The child prophets were symbolic figures for the complex anxieties of the Desert, for the spiritual conflict of the *Nouveaux Convertis*, for the wrenched relations between the faithful and the apostate, for whatever shame or guilt lay between fearful parents and accusing children.

The prophets were also a symbolic solution to the conflicting desires of the people of the Desert. The inspired children were proof of religious continuity, yet they were equally the mark of a new era of spiritual transformation. Prophecy was consequently more than a substitute for traditional preaching; it was a step toward and an implicit part of the millenarian ethos.

After the bountiful harvest of 1688, children were prophesying throughout Dauphiné. In the village near the home of Isabeau Vincent, more than sixty had received the Holy Spirit by the year's end. By January, 1689, as prophecy spread from Dauphiné into Languedoc, the *inspirés* became more public, more violent and apparently more irresistible. With judgment looming in this apocalyptic year, the preliminary agitations of the inspired matched in violence the anticipated sorrows of the wicked and victory of the faithful. Enemies who perceived plots and artifices said that a glassmaker taught children to "beat their hands on their heads, to throw themselves down on the ground on their backs, to close their eyes, to puff

14. BPUG, Ba 1910 vol. 31, MS bound in *Recueil de diverses pièces imprimées,* "Lettre écrite à S. Daniel Dumond par M. Combet de la ville de Crest, du premier mai 1688"; Arnaud, *Histoire,* III, 73-74, 416-19; Jurieu, *Reflections,* 3-5, 52-64; *Copie d'une lettre écrite de Genève touchant les enfans qui prophétisent en Dauphiné, en date du 25 décembre 1688* (The Hague, 1689) 5.

up their stomachs and throats, to rest unresisting [*assoupis*] in this state for some moments, and then, waking with a start, to spout out anything that came to their mouths." The myth of the glassmaker shaping children into prophets as one might blow glass has been discredited, but the description of physical symptoms was accurate. Shaking, falling, choking and convulsions would characterize future *inspirés* and also the prophets in London.[15]

Soon a farmer's wife would be found asleep, flailing her arms and legs, shouting "Mercy, mercy." She predicted that the world would end for the wicked in three months, but the faithful would reign on earth with Jesus for one thousand years. Another woman, her eyes blindfolded, saw William, Prince of Orange (Jurieu's favorite for the Davidic role) as warrior of the apocalypse. Some had already concluded that Isabeau Vincent's promise of a September (1688) deliverance had been redeemed by William's entry into England and the flight of King James II. Now, in the vision of Jacquette Ranc, an angel transported William to France, the deliverer suspended by his hair. With him in the skies were 100,000 Christian soldiers.[16]

Visions proliferated as April's Judgment Day approached, and the uninspired too fell to the ground in Desert congregations. The *évanouissement* or swoon of the Dauphiné prophets became a general symbol of personal spiritual travail among the uninspired, and a social act of repentance. In Languedoc the prophets themselves—more numerous, often awake and appearing in public—were no more public than their audience, who arrived in large numbers (1500 in some assemblies) "as if they were processions, and at Noon day."[17]

"But their Apostate Brethren and those of the Communion of Rome not being able to hear that Voice which did Condemn them and which Called

---

15. *A Relation of Several Hundreds of Children and Others that Prophesie and Preach in their Sleep* (1689) 16-17, 25, 27, 28 *et passim; Copie d'une lettre de Genève,* 6-7; *Histoire admirable de ce qui est arrivé dès le 12 novembre 1688 à Mornas en Dauphiné* (n.p., 1689); Bost 1925, 405; David Augustin de Brueys, *Histoire du fanatisme de notre tems,* I (1692) reprinted in F. Danjou, ed., *Archives curieuses de l'histoire de France* (Paris, 1840) 2nd ser., XI, 347 (quote); Fléchier, *Lettres choisies,* I, 341-56, which is taken from the letter by the priest Mongé in Bibl. Nîmes, MSS 186 (15). The glassmaker myth is disproved by Cilette Blanc, "Genève et les origines du mouvement prophétique en Dauphiné et dans les Cévennes," *Revue d'histoire suisse* 23 (1942) 234-49, but for the metaphor see Ronald Knox, *Enthusiasm* (Oxford, 1950) 358.

16. Bibl. Nîmes, MSS 186 (15) pp. 393-94. Cf. Charles Bost, "Le prophétisme en Dauphiné à la fin de 1688," *BSHPF* 56 (1907) 535, and his "Poésies populaires," 231. On the Davidic image of William of Orange, see Rex, *Essays,* 216-24.

17. Bibl. Nîmes, MSS 186 (15) pp. 393, 398 and cf. 400, 407, 409; cf. Bost, "Le prophétisme en Dauphiné," 534-35; *Relation of Children,* 30, 33.

unto them, Repent, Repent, did stir up a Dreadful Persecution," wrote the French Prophets years later. Early in the spring of 1689, royal officials hunted down the prophets, sent the younger ones to convents or prison-hospitals, and condemned others to death. This the prophets had foreseen, the short but cruel peak of persecution that would herald final deliverance. In April, 1689, with most prophets silent or secret, Judgment Day did not arrive, but William and Mary were crowned joint Protestant sovereigns of England, just three and one-half years after the Revocation of the Edict of Nantes. A month later England entered the League of Augsburg against France.[18]

Huguenots of the Desert had known too many of the predictions of the *inspirés* to come true to be dumbfounded by a world that continued into 1690 just as it had been. Perhaps they had not well comprehended the precise sense of the inspirations. Wrote one correspondent from Geneva, "No other Prophecies are to be looked upon as well reported, but only those that have had their Accomplishment. . . . [I]f anything does not happen, 'tis because the Prediction was not well taken nor understood." Pierre Jurieu in Rotterdam rearranged his prophetic chronology and put forward alternate dates for the end of the Beast's reign, one of which was 1690.[19]

Neither chiliasm nor prophecy disappeared from the Desert in the subsequent years. To the successes of William III and the League of Augsburg were attached dreams of the defeat of French forces and the restoration of Huguenot freedoms. The few prophets who remained, hidden in the mountains of the Cévennes or in the Vivarais to the north, preserved the rhetoric and hopes of the inspired of 1688-89. Even after the disappointment of the Treaty of Ryswick (1697) by which France made peace with the League but was not compelled to make provision for Huguenot liberty, Matthieu Boissier in Dauphiné could still attend a prophetic assembly in which a young girl promised, "after a manner very powerful, exact, and pressing," that Protestantism would be reestablished in France.[20]

Late in 1700, Daniel Raoux discovered that God had "transfused into him" the spirit of the Old Testament prophet Daniel. Through Daniel and

18. Historical Relation, f. 7; Bibl. Nîmes, MSS 186 (15) pp. 414, 420; Bost 1925, 405. On England's part in the War of the League of Augsburg, see David Ogg, *England in the Reigns of James II and William III* (2nd ed.; Oxford, 1966) 345-48, 373-74.

19. *Relation of Children*, 35 (quote); Jurieu, *Lettres pastorales* (Rotterdam, 1688/89) 492-517 (Letter XXI, July 1, 1689); Dodge, *Political Theory*, 38-39.

20. Bost 1925, 406, and Bost 1921a, 10; François-Maximilien Misson (comp.), *Le Théâtre sacré des Cévennes* (1707) 9-11. English translation from that made by the French Prophets, *A Cry from the Desart* (1707) 10 (quote).

others in the Vivarais, the prophetic tradition was reasserted so widely that by the autumn of 1701 there were literally hundreds of prophets, many of whom were of the same generation as the children who preached while asleep in 1688.[21] Many, perhaps the majority, could not recall a time before the Desert. Often they had not heard the preaching of the Word by an ordained Huguenot minister. "Those whom the Lord visited with his Spirit," wrote the French Prophets in their history, "were for the most part Young people of both Sexes of the most Simple, most abject, most Ignorant." After their conversion, they "ran with Eagerness to the fields and the woods and all the several places of their Assemblies, whether in the night or the Day. Whatsoever Danger there was, nothing was able to stop them."[22] The children of Cruviers howled like wolves and cried in public, "We are in the latter days; brothers, sisters, repent!" François Pierre, sixteen, foresaw a time when Protestant temples would be built in the middle of the road.[23]

In addition to recurrent millennial themes announced more boldly and vividly than ever before, the Desert was a backdrop for miracles more dramatic than voices in the sky or sermons from infants. Pierre Chantagrel walked barefoot but unharmed over burning coals; newborn infants spoke up to refuse Catholic baptism; Jeanne Bonnisolle promised that she would die and then rise an hour later. (She fainted but did not die.) In September, 1701, Marie Boîteuse wept tears of blood. An *inspiré* said that the blood was a demand for repentance and a sign that the world would soon come to an end.[24]

The inspired also became more aggressive. Isabeau Dauphinenche, terrifying the witnesses who testified against her as a *fanatique*, prayed in court for the conversion of her judges. Women and children of Valérargues rescued a captured *inspiré* from three priests. Led by him to the village church, they destroyed the altar and smashed the crucifix.[25]

21. Bost 1921a, 11-12; Le Père Louvreleuil, *Fanaticism Revived: or The Enthusiasm of the Camisars* (trans. from 2nd edition of the French, 1707) 5, 6, 8.
22. Historical Relation, f. 10.
23. AH, MSS C. 180, f. 180v. and MSS C. 181, f. 3; Bost 1925, 407, and Bost 1921a, 14-15.
24. AH, MSS C. 180, ff. 321v., 328v.-329 and MSS C. 181, ff. 28v.-30, 116, 125v., 128, 168; Bost 1921a, 8, 31 and 1921b, 2.
25. AH, MSS C. 180, f. 415 and MSS C. 181, ff. 505, 520; Bost 1921a, 17, 20, 26; Ernest Roschach, ed., *Histoire générale de Languedoc* (Toulouse, 1872-1905) XIV, pièces justificatives, DLXIX, 1537-41. David Flotard in the *TS* (p. 62) claimed that the designation *fanatique* was arrived at by the medical faculty of the University of Montpellier after an examination of the *inspirés*. There is no evidence for this. The word *fanatique* had been current for more than thirty years before the appearance of the prophets as a description of what the English called an "enthusiast." See Wälther von Wartburg, "Fanatisme" and "Fanatique," *Französisches Etymologisches Wörterbuch* (Berlin, 1934) III, 409; Paul Robert, "Fanatique,"

By November, 1701, as more prophets arose in the plains of Bas-Languedoc and in the Cévennes, over 350 *fanatiques* were in prison, and the Intendant Bâville had condemned some forty prophets to slavery in the galleys. Nonetheless, a royal officer that month could happen upon the inhabitants of Ayguesvives dressed for a holiday on a normal workday, standing in the road and listening to a fourteen-year-old boy sing psalms and preach.[26]

The Camisards

Early in 1702, an itinerant band of *inspirés* and companions had gathered in the mountains of the Cévennes, fugitives from the deadly justice of priests and soldiers. They brought the breath (*souffle*) of the divine spirit with them as they toured the countryside, and they prophesied harshly against their enemies. Among the prophets was Abraham Mazel, twenty-four, who for several months had been warned by the Holy Spirit to prepare to take up arms against his implacable enemies. On July 22, 1702 (N.S.), under frantic agitations, he pronounced the divine order to rescue Huguenots imprisoned at Pont-de-Montvert. Other *inspirés* confirmed the order. On July 24, twelve days after France had entered the War of the Spanish Succession against England and her Protestant allies, some forty to sixty Huguenots, carrying an assortment of guns and makeshift weapons, marched into Pont-de-Montvert singing psalms. They freed the prophets locked in the cellar of a house occupied by the Abbé du Chayla and his few soldiers, and killed du Chayla, a zealous Catholic missionary detested by the Huguenots for his active and cruel persecution of the unconverted.[27]

The next day, scrupulously following divine orders, the band killed the curé of Frugières and destroyed the images and altar of the Catholic church. "I did this in every detail as I had been commanded," wrote Mazel later. Within a week, the band had shot the curé of another village and castrated the local schoolteacher who kept a mistress. They burned the château of a man who had thrown young *inspirés* into his pigsty to prevent

---

Dictionnaire alphabétique et analogique de la langue française (Paris, 1955) II, 1909.

26. Bost 1921a, 19-21; Boislisle, *Correspondance*, II, 83; Roschach, *Histoire générale*, XIV, pièces justificatives, DLXXX, 1555-56 and DCXIII, 1608; Archives Nationales (Paris), AN 154 Ap II 120, Fonds Lamoignon de Basville, pièce 37, letter of November 4, 1701 (N.S.).

27. *TS*, 85-87; *MMM* 5-11; Bost 1921b, 3, 16-17; Historical Relation, f. 13; Mme. de Merez, *Mémoire*, ed. E. Marie (n.p., 1874) "Résumé des événements survenus dans les Cévennes et le Diocèse de Nîmes de 1688 à 1704," 130-131.

their prophesying. Always they took care to confirm the directions of the Holy Spirit.[28]

So began the revolt of the Camisards.[29] Their numbers increased slowly, mounting to five hundred by September, with eighty under the command of the famous twenty-year-old prophet, "Colonel" Jean Cavalier. Among the thousand or more men and women who entered the guerilla ranks in 1703 were three whose names will figure prominently among the French Prophets in London: Durand Fage, Elie Marion, and Jean Cavalier of Sauve (not to be confused with the "Colonel"). By 1704 the Camisards had a force of perhaps two thousand men and women.[30]

The war proper lasted more than two years, from the summer of 1702 through much of 1704. Twenty thousand royal troops did not have immediate success against these bands of village Huguenots who knew the mountains, caves and footpaths of the Cévennes as they knew their psalms. Moreover, the soldiers were battling against people who believed themselves to be divinely warned of traitors, guided to their camps at night by celestial lights, and protected from ambush by guardian angels.[31] Many of the Camisard leaders were themselves prophets; uninspired commanders relied upon prophets among their troops. In December, 1702, more than two hundred Catholic churches in the Cévennes put to flame, Camisard generals addressed a letter to the Intendant Bâville from their *Camp de l'Eternel*. While making known to him that they desired simply the restoration of their religious liberties, they vaunted the redeeming role of the prophets among them. Had the Lord not had compassion upon His children, Protestantism might have disappeared completely, for the young knew little about true religion and the old had been forced to convert; "but the father of mercy, having seen the cowardice of our fathers, has spread his spirit upon his manservants and maidservants as he promised us by the

---

28. *MMM*, 11-12 (quote); de Merez, *Mémoire*, 131; Bost 1921b, 15-16n. Cf. Le Roy Ladurie's psychiatric explanation of sexual assault in *Les paysans de Languedoc*, I, 626-27. I will later use the analysis by Natalie Zemon Davis, "The Rites of Violence: Religious Riots in Sixteenth-Century France," *Past and Present* 59 (1973) 58-60.

29. The term "Camisard" derives either from the word for "night attack" (obs. Fr. *camisade*) or from the patois for a white shirt (*camisole*): *MMM*, 30. Bost insists that the Pont-de-Montvert incident was not a signal for revolt and that immediately subsequent actions were not premeditated. The Intendant Bâville regarded the affair as kindred to the earlier (June) rescue of an *inspiré* by armed Huguenots: Bost 1921b, 29-30. Cf. Frank Puaux, "Origines, causes, et conséquences de la guerre des Camisards," *Revue historique* 129 (1918) 212, 235; Roschach, *Histoire générale*, XIV, pièces justificatives, DLXXXIII, 1558.

30. *TS*, 87; *MMM*, 21-24; Marcel Pin, *Jean Cavalier* (Nîmes, 1936) 6-8.

31. *TS*, 28, 34, 38, 107; *MMM*, 18, 20, 30.

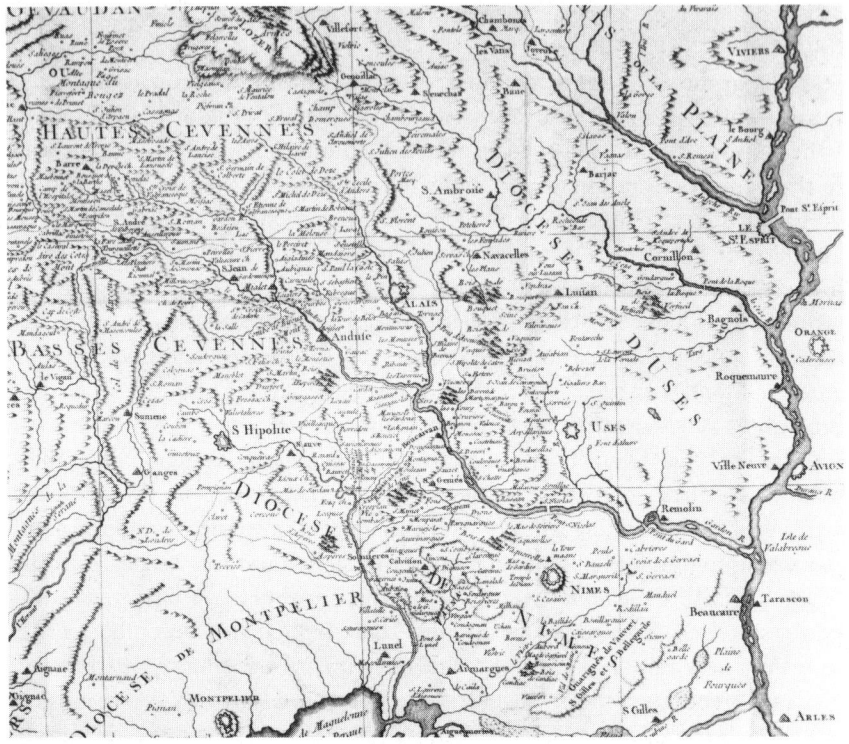

PLATE II. Map of the Cévennes, the Vivarais, and Bas Languedoc, from Antoine Court, *Histoire des troubles des Cévennes* (Villefranche, 1760).

mouth of his prophet Joel, in order to teach us to return to the bosom of his Church, which we had abandoned out of the fear of men."[32]

Led by young men and advised by young prophets, the Camisards gained a series of small victories in 1703. By October they seemed the masters of the plains of Bas-Languedoc as well as of the mountains of the Cévennes. Encouraged by the miracle of Pierre Claris, who walked safely through flames, and by the promises of David Flotard, an agent of the English and Dutch who brought news of a fleet sent in support of the rebels, the Camisards fought pitched battles against royal troops, not without success.[33] (See maps, Plate II and Figure 1.)

32. Roschach, *Histoire générale*, XIV, pièces justificatives, DCXXIII, 1624-25; de Merez, *Mémoire*, 133; *MMM*, 18.

33. *MMM*, 29-38, 46-52, 110-12; *TS*, 52, 73, 114-16; de Merez, *Mémoire*, 36, 134-42. The English fleet under Admiral Shovel hazarded only two ships off the Languedoc coast and failed to make contact with the Camisards, who knew nothing about the signal code. Charles

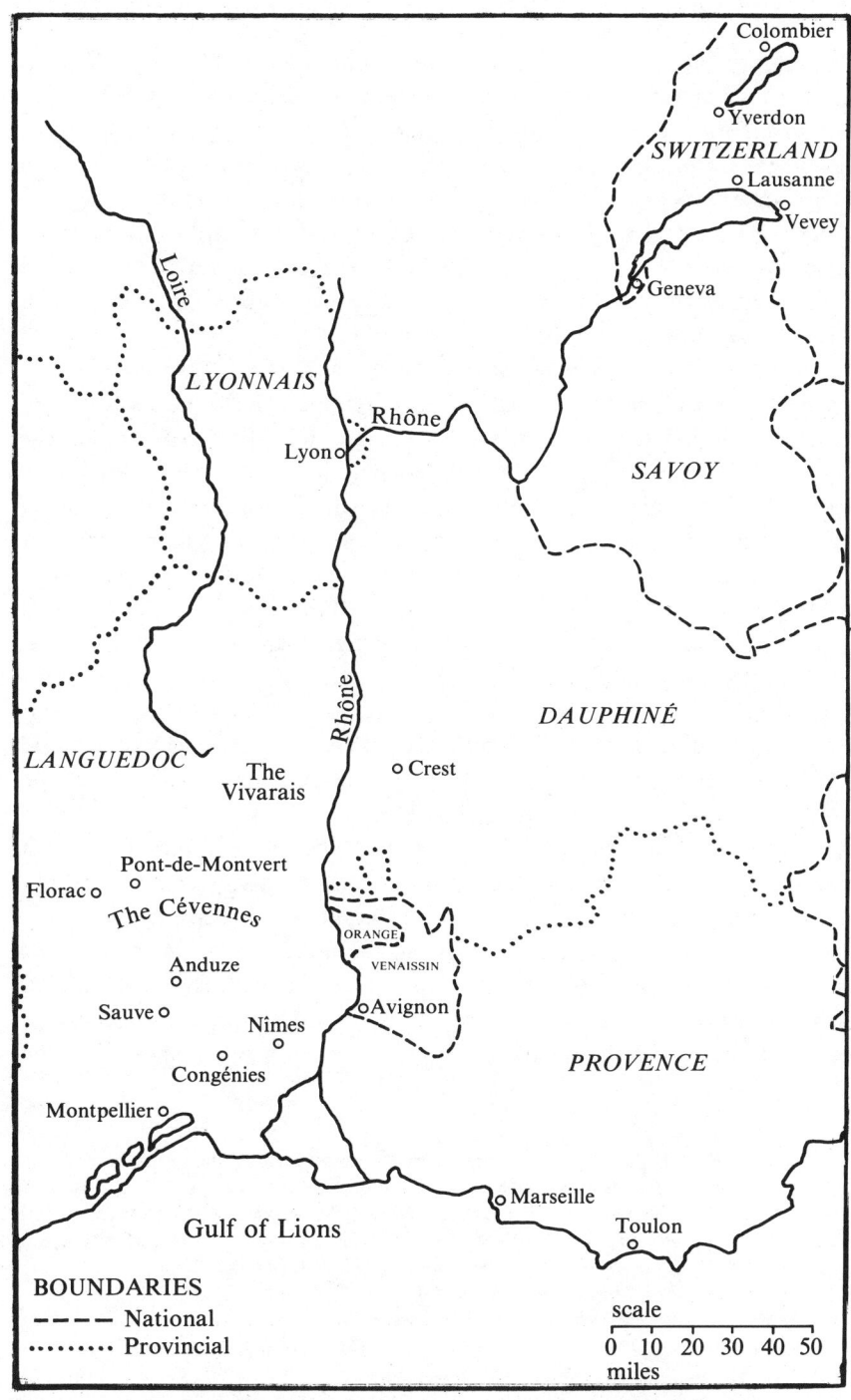

Map 1. Simplified map of Southeastern France and Switzerland, c. 1700.

Intendant Bâville responded by imprisoning entire village populations that were sympathetic to the Camisards and in the fall of 1703 undertook the systematic devastation of settlements in thirty-one parishes in the Cévennes. Camisards had occasionally burned villages and would burn others most opposed to their cause, but in less than three months Bâville's military razed 466 Cévenol villages. The Camisards only fought more doggedly and exercised less restraint on their acts of reprisal. Guerilla bands formed throughout eastern Languedoc, and early in 1704 a revolt began in the previously peaceful Vivarais.[34]

Fearing the consequences of this prolonged revolt, especially since nearby Savoy had in October allied itself against France, Louis XIV sent the distinguished Claude Louis Hector, duc de Villars, to replace the Maréchal de Montrevel as commander in Languedoc. Villars arrived in April, 1704, several days after "Colonel" Cavalier's forces had sustained a severe defeat including loss of stores and ammunition. Villars promptly offered a general amnesty to all rebels who would surrender, then combined diplomacy with wholesale imprisonment of the parents and relatives of the remaining guerillas, a strategy which proved effective. Finding the Cévennes ravaged, their families jailed, their supplies exhausted, their prophets shot, and fresh professional soldiers always at their heels, band after band of Camisards surrendered between May and November, 1704. Elie Marion and fellow prophets sought the advice of the Spirit, but none came. For some time they had prophesied that the True Church would not be restored by material powers, but they could not abandon a divinely inspired war without a specific divine edict. At length Marion and his companions understood the silence of the Spirit as itself a directive, and they too signed a treaty in the fall of 1704, unaware of the Duke of Marlborough's recent victory over the French at Blenheim. Abraham Mazel, however, predicted that the Lord would soon regather the Camisards or, as they called themselves, the *Enfants de Dieu* (Children of God).[35]

Portales, later French Prophet, was secretary to the marquis de Miremont, who had long pushed for such an expedition; Portales was aboard one of the two ships. *CSPD* 1703-1704, 126-29 and cf. 202; Abel Boyer, *The History of the Reign of Queen Anne, Digested into Annals. Year the Second.* (1704) 101-05. Cf. Henry L. Snyder, ed., *The Marlborough-Godolphin Correspondence* (Oxford, 1975) I, 169, 185, 210-11, 262, 287.

34. *MMM*, 53-60; de Merez, *Mémoire*, 134-42.

35. *MMM*, 61-104; Charles Alméras, *La révolte des Camisards* (Paris, 1960) 175-86; Historical Relation, ff. 19-20; Bibl. Nîmes, MSS 57 (6) ff. 249-53: Relation de ce qui s'est passé à Calvisson; Claude Louis Hector, duc de Villars, *Mémoires,* ed. le marquis de Vogüé (Paris, 1884-1904) II, Appendix, 319; Antoine Court, *Histoire des troubles des*

Unlike most, Elie Marion did return from exile in Geneva to fight once more. Financed feebly by England and the United Provinces, the Camisards who continued the battle achieved little. The duc de Berwick, successor to Villars, caught many of the remaining prophets and rounded up a large circle of supporters in Nîmes. Marion capitulated a second time and returned to Switzerland in August, 1705, with Durand Fage and Abraham Mazel. Stray bands of rebels and *inspirés* yet hid in the Cévennes "as a leaven," and Mazel himself would engage in sporadic guerila actions until his death in 1710, but the harsh war was over.[36]

The war had not been against tyranny, for indeed one of the Camisard rallying cries was "Fin du clergé, vive notre bon Roy," and some Huguenots nourished a belief that Louis XIV was uninformed of the plight of his Protestant subjects.[37] Nor had the Camisards, most of them weavers and peasants, risen against feudal levies and state taxation. Royal officials feared the conjunction of *fanatisme* and the widespread hatred of taxes, but the Camisards never promoted their cause as an antifiscal revolt. Although they interrupted the collection of the clerical tithe to insure themselves of supplies for the winters, the Camisards did not use millennial texts in support of a program of social change. Unlike the Levellers in England fifty years before, the *Enfants de Dieu* did not make egalitarian currency out of passages from Revelation, nor did they make

---

Cévennes (Villefranche, 1760) III, 123-29; Philippe de Courcillon, marquis de Dangeau, *Journal,* ed. Soulié et al. (Paris, 1854-60) IX, 492-93 and X, 135, 210; C.G. Sturgill, *Marshall Villars and the War of the Spanish Succession* (Lexington, Ky., 1965) 61. According to Sir James Fitzjames Stephen, "Cavallier [sic] and the Camisards," *Edinburgh Review* 104 (1856) 152, Villars had gained a military as well as diplomatic victory: "At the crisis which succeeded to the battle of Blenheim, even a small additional impetus might have produced extraordinary results. If the Camisards had held out a very few months longer, they would have thrown open the whole of the south of France from the Rhône to the Atlantic to a foreign invasion."

36. *MMM,* 105-42, 196-200, 206-14; Historical Relation, f. 21; Alméras, *La révolte des Camisards,* 223-25.

37. Philippe Joutard, "Les Camisards: 'Prophètes de la Grande Révolution' ou derniers combattants des guerres de religion?" *L'esprit républicain, Colloque d'Orléans, 4-5 septembre 1970* (Paris, 1972) 113-16. Wrote Bâville in 1701, "Croiriez-vous que les Prophètes disent que le petit fils du Roi est de leur parti . . . ?" Archives Nationales (Paris), AN 154 Ap II 120, pièce 35, letter of March 7, 1701 (N.S.) and also cited in J.-R. Armogathe and Philippe Joutard, "Bâville et la guerre des Camisards," *Revue d'histoire moderne et contemporaine* 19 (1972) 61n. Pierre Jurieu in Rotterdam did defend the uprising with antiroyalist rhetoric: Dodge, *Political Theory,* 159-65; Rex, *Essays,* 215-24; Elisabeth Israels Perry, *From Theology to History: French Religious Controversy and the Revocation of the Edict of Nantes* (The Hague, 1973) 99-103, 193-98; Gerald Cerny, "The Crisis in Late Seventeenth-Century French Protestant Thought: Jacques Basnage and the Moderate Huguenot Refugees in Holland," (Ph.D. thesis, University of California, Berkeley, 1974) 166-73, 204.

common cause with all of the downtrodden in southern France.[38] Like other popular uprisings of the era, the Camisard revolt was not radical.[39]

The war had been one of spiritual crisis, with social and economic overtones. Persecution had affected all areas of Huguenot life, so that the rebels and their community had endured economic and social hardship as well as distress of conscience. Their prophets had in addition suffered from the general impoverishment of the social strata from which they came (peasantry, artisans, small landowners), a result of the economic depression in Languedoc after 1680. Yet the prophets did not ordinarily come from the poorest homes or the most depressed regions, and prophecy was not just a symbol or symptom of socioeconomic deprivation.[40] The shaping force of prophecy within the millenarian ethos of the Desert was manifest as the prophets became the articulate dramatists of spiritual

38. The fears of royal officials were exaggerated by their own perduring inability to collect the assessed taxes and fulfill the financial obligations imposed upon them by a state engaged in increasingly expensive wars. The capitation tax, for example, was so far in arrears for 1701 and 1702 that Bâville wrote a memorandum showing the impossibility of collecting the tax proposed for 1703. Since 1688, less than five per cent of the tax collectors in the province had been voluntarily employed at the unpopular occupation. The problems with the tithe (*dîme*) during the war in the Cévennes were only a special case of the more general tendency of the rural populace to avoid taxation. Le Roy Ladurie argues that the revolt was politically radical, but his evidence is all from royal sources who tended to see any protest as not only threatening to the state but motivated by desires to undo that state. See Joutard, "Les Camisards," 117-18; Patrice L.-R. Higonnet, *Pont-de-Montvert: Social Structure and Politics in a French Village 1700-1914* (Cambridge, Mass., 1971) 39-43; de Merez, *Mémoire*, 10, 107; Roschach, *Histoire générale*, XIV, pièces justificatives, DCXII, 1605-07; Le Roy Ladurie, *Les paysans de Languedoc*, I, 603, 627-29.

39. Cf. J. Bastier, "Une résistance fiscale du Languedoc sous Louis XIII: La quérelle du franc-alleu," *Annales du Midi* 86 (1974) 253-74; André Leguai, "Les 'émotions' et séditions populaires dans la généralité de Moulins," *Revue d'histoire économique et sociale* 43 (1965) 45-65; François Hincker, *Les français devant l'impôt sous l'Ancien Régime* (Paris, 1971); William H. Beik, "Two Intendants Face a Popular Revolt," *Canadian Journal of History* 9 (1974) 243-62; Léon Bernard, "French Society and Popular Uprisings Under Louis XIV," *French Historical Studies* 3 (1964), reprinted in Raymond F. Kierstead, ed., *State and Society in Seventeenth-Century France* (New York, 1975) 157-79.

40. Cf. Louis Mazoyer, "Les origines du prophétisme cévenol," *Revue historique* 197 (1947) 30-31, 52; Le Roy Ladurie, *Les paysans de Languedoc*, I, 571-72, 614; Bost, *Les prédicants*, II, 300; Marie-France Chaumet, "De la Révocation de l'Edit de Nantes à la guerre des Camisards," Mémoire de Maîtrise, Université de Paris à Nanterre, 1970, 11, 14, 16, 99. The thesis that oppression gives rise to millennialism and prophecy was early proposed by Bost, who believed that an "exaspération du pays" produced a state where Huguenots "n'étaient plus maîtres ni de leurs esprits ni de leur corps." (Bost 1921a, 4.) The most interesting scheme involving deprivation theory is presented by Charles Y. Glock. "The Role of Deprivation in the Origin and Evolution of Religious Groups," in Robert Lee and Martin E. Marty, eds., *Religion and Social Conflict* (New York, 1964) 24-36. The most careful studies are I.M. Lewis, *Ecstatic Religion* (1971); Peter J. Wilson, "Status Ambiguity and Spirit Possession," *Man* 2 (1967) 366-78.

problems and translated the experience of the Desert into a millennial idiom through which each Huguenot might make sense of events.[41]

Desert society recognized the dynamic role of prophecy during the war, developing a system of prophetic ranks and corresponding functions. Huguenots perceived a hierarchy of divine gifts and spiritual functions appropriate to each of four ranks of prophets. The first stage was the gift of prayer, one small remove from the uninspired act of fervent worship; prayer functioned as exhortation, leading the faithful to a frame of mind and heart in which to receive the prophetic Word. The second stage was the dual of the first, the gift of general prediction, an answer to prayer in the form of a promise of eventual triumph for the True Church. The third stage, specific prophecy and judgments, was the gift of Camisard leaders and advisors; they had the power to pierce the consciences of their audience, they discerned traitors, they distributed communion to the truly faithful and baptized children in the Desert. Those who had attained the third stage were usually granted the final gift of fluent preaching, and in this last stage the prophets realized the dream of the Desert that the almost mythical ministry return to preach to their people. As preachers, the inspired were proof of religious continuity and the Desert assemblies became legitimized images of the True Church. Yet the prophets were more than stand-ins for the ordained ministry, more than inspired replicas of *prédicants*. Prophets created a vocabulary of emotional experience, models of religious behavior, centers of spiritual authority; in so doing they restored a sense of communal integrity. In turn, believers had available to them a wider gamut of acceptable spiritual response by which to ensure the vitality of the community and a new church framework in which to worship.[42]

The mimetic violence and peace of the act of prophecy had been since

---

41. The second wave of prophets promised redemption for 1705, 1706 or 1708, as before the prophets had concentrated on the year 1689. *TS*, 30, 33; Roschach, *Histoire générale*, XIV, pièces justificatives, DCL, 1682-83.

42. *TS*, 64, 70-71, 104; Roschach, *Histoire générale*, XIV, pièces justificatives, DCLXXVII, 1747; de Brueys, *Histoire du fanatisme*, I, 376-77. For differences between prophets and *prédicants*, see Bost 1921b, 10. Sources for my analysis of the prophets include Johannes Fabian, "Genres in an Emerging Tradition: An Anthropological Approach to Religious Communication," in Allan W. Eister, ed., *Changing Perspectives in the Scientific Study of Religion* (New York, 1974) 249-72; Gary Schwartz, *Sect Ideologies and Social Status* (Chicago, 1970); Kenelm Burridge, *Mambu: A Melanesian Millennium* (1960) and his *New Heaven, New Earth: A Study of Millenarian Activities* (Oxford, 1969); Erika Bourguignon, "The Self, the Behavioral Environment, and the Theory of Spirit Possession," in Melford E. Spiro, ed., *Context and Meaning in Cultural Anthropology* (New York and London, 1965) 39-57.

1688 a figure for the spiritual agitation of individual Huguenots, for the ambivalence of Calvinist mercy and judgment, for the social predicament of the Desert. With the outbreak of the Camisard rebellion, the physical motions of the prophets served as prototypes for social violence: just as heavy breathing, gasping and choking, flailing of limbs, convulsions and falling as if dead were premonitory signs of true inspiration, so the grim battles of the Children of God were a necessary prelude to the restoration of the True Church. The prophets reversed the direction of the ritual of the earlier inspired children—from an inward reflection of the body politic through the medium of the physical body, to direct interference with the body politic through the instrument of militant prophecy. Abraham Mazel, Elie Marion and others thus had in themselves, and in the respect accorded them by the community, momentum to break the taboo against large-scale violence which in the forms of royalism and pacifism had prevailed in Languedoc since 1630.[43]

What the prophets mobilized was not random violence against a persecuting majority but the violence of the surgeon. Their intent was purification, not annihilation. While Camisards burned Catholic churches and laid waste to offensive, idolatrous images on florid altars, Elie Marion wept cleansing tears of blood. Pierre Claris, to show that he was clear of all association with the traitors he had just denounced, stood in a purifying fire until the flames disappeared. Abraham Mazel had his troops "purified" by the prophet Couderc, who stared into the face of each guerilla and determined the faithful. The discernment of traitors merged with the discernment of faith as prophets exercised their gifts in ceremonies against pollution. The impure were obligated to a display of atonement as exhaustive as that of the penitent *Nouveaux Convertis*, whose prayers and confessions stressed abasement, defilement. Jean Cavalier of Sauve digressed in his testimony for the French Prophets in London to recite an otherwise irrelevant story linking *ordure* with social ostracism and the devil, making literal the link between pollution, treason, and spiritual waywardness. The prophets in their capacity as ministers penetrated to the very soul of the uninspired and sought to remove the stains of pride from each person; as warriors they attempted to remove that which polluted the body social of French Protestantism. The burning of churches, the discriminating murder of only the more hostile priests, the castrations were all part of a cleansing of the world before the millennium. Persecu-

---

43. Cf. Mary Douglas, *Purity and Danger* (1966) 128 ff.; Peter L. Berger, *The Sacred Canopy* (New York, 1967) 38-40.

tion and defeat were regarded by the Camisards as reminders of moral imperfection among the elect.[44]

The youth of the *inspirés*, their illiteracy or idiocy, their unsophisticated habits and rural background stood as proof of purity for Huguenots of the Desert. The prophets whose mouths were the passive organs for divine inspiration had to be clean instruments of the Lord's will. Spectators in 1688 had emphasized the innocence of the sleeping children, whose inability to recall what happened under agitation convinced them that the inspirations were unblemished by human meddling. Similarly, after 1700, sympathetic reporters were impressed by the telling simplicity of the prophets when not inspired, and they retailed anecdotes of thirteen-month-old infants who prophesied.[45]

Like contemporaries, Protestant historians have made much of the youth of the *inspirés* after 1700, most of whom were born shortly before the Revocation. Reared secretly in the Protestant faith, the inspired had known little but persecution and bitterness, despair over forced conversions. Historians have "explained" prophecy in terms of the resilience and impressionability of the young, for whom the preaching of repentance was a method of redeeming their own parents.[46] But in many ways the young prophets were meeting adult expectations, entering a vocation prepared for them by their elders. To find a child prophesying was confirmation for Desert society that a new generation—for which adults felt both responsible and guilty—had survived untouched. Young prophets capped parental hopes that, though themselves defiled, their children were yet pure, unaffected by Catholic education or propaganda. The ritual of atonement demanded of adults by children was at once the expression of relief that the young had endured (by the grace of God) and an acknowledgment that the old had not suffered in vain. The call to repentance and the promises of a church restored had meaning in both millennial and generational contexts.

44. *TS,* 35, 52-54, 69-70, 110-13; Historical Relation, ff. 18-19. For examples of prayers of *Nouveaux Convertis,* see Edward D. Seeber, ed., *Choix de pièces huguenotes (1685-1756)* (Bloomington, 1942) 15-22. Cf. Douglas, *Purity and Danger,* and Davis, "Rites of Violence," 58-61.

45. *TS,* 15-16, 23, 32, 109.

46. Chaumet, "De la Révocation de l'Edit de Nantes à la guerre des Camisards," 88-90; Emile-G. Léonard, "La part de la jeunesse dans la restauration du Protestantisme au XVIIIe siècle," *Revue de théologie et d'action évangéliques* (October, 1944) 345-64; Bost 1921b, ll; Puaux, "Origines," 16-17, citing Villars, "Tout ce qui est révolté est né dans la religion catholique car c'est la fleur de la jeunesse et cependant plus huguenot que leurs pères." A list of prophets with approximate ages appears in *MMM,* 181-88.

Although participants in the millenarian ethos of the Desert, young men and women accepted the prophetic vocation on their own terms, and after 1700 engineered a shift in the ethos itself. Coming to the role of prophet during a period of personal flux, unmarried but able to marry, not yet at the age of majority but able to live independently, they took advantage of their fluid social status and the flexibility of their calling.[47] They did not merely adhere to the conservative tasks outlined by their elders but opened a wider millennial arena.

Between the Revocation and the war in the Cévennes, the millenarian ethos of Desert society moved from judgment to cataclysm. While maintaining a common structure of beliefs in a resurrected True Church and a fallen Whore of Babylon, Huguenots had lost much of that sense of familial cohesion played upon by the sleeping children of 1688. Instead of situating themselves within the emotional architecture of hearth and temple, Camisard prophets spoke from a freer and more personal space in which the bond between child and parent was less important than the bond between leader and tribe. Significant action was transposed from public confession within the community to assertion beyond it. The social anonymity of most early *inspirés* was superseded during the war by the reputation of individual prophets who had assumed or been granted defiant new sobriquets and military titles. For the image of God's House was substituted God's Camp, and in that camp miracles protected and renewed the warriors as before they had guaranteed the purity of prophetic speech.

The shift in millenarian ethos was most evident in the changing position of female prophets within the group. Until the Camisard revolt, the majority of prophets had been female.[48] Given the significant, perhaps dominant role which Protestant women played in the covert religious training of children after the Revocation, the leadership claimed by young *inspirées* strongly reflected the conditions of Desert life.[49] Prophecy was an

47. Cf. Dorothy Emmett, "Prophets and Their Societies," *Journal of the Royal Anthropological Institute* 86 (1956) 13-23. Average age at marriage in Languedoc was 29 for men, 25 for women. Men did not reach majority until age 30, though women might marry from the age of 12 and men from the age of 14. Le Roy Ladurie, *Les paysans de Languedoc*, I, 557-58; de Félice, *Les Protestants d'autrefois*, I, 198-99.

48. Chaumet, "De la Révocation de l'Edit de Nantes à la guerre des Camisards," 87-90. There is no evidence to suggest that this predominance of females was simply a reflection of sex imbalance in the Huguenot population or in the age distribution of the population at large: Louis Henry, "The Population of France in the Eighteenth Century," in D.V. Glass and D.E.C. Eversley, eds., *Population in History* (Chicago, 1965) 434-56.

49. "Les plus ardentes Camisards, il faut le remarquer, furent des fils de veuve, dont la mère avait seul dirigé l'éducation." Marcel Pin, *A côté des Camisards* (Uzès, 1944) 7.

act whereby women could deliver the Lord's Word in the absence of ordained ministers without violating the injunction against female preachers in I Corinthians 14:34.

Females also had more leeway than males to pursue a prophetic career. They benefitted, ironically, from the current assumptions about the feminine "character." Just as prophecy itself was an ingenious (if not ingenuous) sidestep to biblical laws against women preaching and civil laws against Protestant worship, so the inspirations of young women were doubly difficult for royal authorities to handle. Betraying their beliefs that women, like children, were more susceptible than men to the emotional sway of *fanatisme* and therefore (since involuntary) less culpable, judges punished *inspirée* less severely than *inspiré*. Though in the fall of 1701 the Intendant Bâville decreed that females would be treated with the same rigor as male *fanatiques*, he wrote in May of 1702, "I am embarrassed only about the punishment of women, finding nothing on this article but what presents great inconveniences." The only solution, he added, was to transport them all to America (and out of the way). Despite Bâville's ordinance, more often than not male prophets were executed while female prophets were jailed.[50]

Psychological discomfort with aggressive female *fanatiques* had social roots. Desert society was at first willing to recognize the equal stature of prophets of both sexes. French Catholic officialdom was immediately disturbed by evidence of female leadership. For the Huguenots, respect for the Spirit and belief in the purity of its vehicles supposed some equivalence between male and female. The familiarity of Huguenot women with the Bible and their role in religious education, as well perhaps as their increased community power in a milieu of broken families, had accustomed Huguenot men to a degree of female independence and authority. Catholics, directed by a male ministry and government, reacted fiercely to a notion of prophecy that allowed women such authority, and they declaimed with especial venom against the female prophets. They

---

50. Bâville, May 29, 1702 (N.S.): "Je ne suis embarassé que de la punition des femmes, ne trouvant rien sur cet article qui n'ait de grands inconvéniens." Archives Nationales (Paris), AN 154 Ap II 120, pièce 42. Cf. Bost 1921b, 18; A. Bonnemère, *Les dragonnades sous Louis XIV* (2nd ed.; Paris, 1869) 134-35. In medical literature women were considered as more pliant and imaginative than men and susceptible to hysteria, a disease with supposed sexual origins. See Jean Chastelain, *Traité des convulsions* (Lyon, 1691) 120, 198; Philippe Hecquet, *Le naturalisme des convulsions dans les maladies de l'épidémie convulsionnaire* (Soleure, 1733) I, 15-16, 45, 73, 151, 176, 193; Ilza Veith, *Hysteria: The History of a Disease* (Chicago, 1965). Le Roy Ladurie noted that the Camisards themselves said that "chez les jeunes prophétesses, l'inspiration dure autant que la virginité; et elle disparait avec le mariage." *Les paysans de Languedoc,* I, 627. I do not subscribe to his conclusions.

used sexual innuendo, trying to undercut the legitimacy of the *inspirées* by challenging their purity. The numerous sexual accusations included by Catholics in their descriptions of the prophets were characteristic of the response of a society ill-accustomed to feminine leadership, let alone bravado or audacity.[51]

But from the onset of the Camisard revolt, Huguenots too seemed to believe that command was the prerogative of males. *Inspirés* dominated the war, and guerilla leaders were always men. Although each band usually had a cohort of influential female prophets and companions, the strategic decisions, the determination to proceed or surrender, and the eventual bargaining with royal agents were within the exclusive purview of the *inspirés*.[52]

Part of the change in the status of *inspirées* may have been due to Huguenot attitudes toward the revolt and common patriarchal opinions. Ambivalent about the violence of the revolt, ever-careful to seek agreement from several prophets for each surgical murder or larger campaign, the Camisards themselves hinted that the war verged on the impure, like the practices of the physician which could easily become those of the cutthroat barber-surgeon. Regarding young women, like children, as innocent of violence (sexual or social), Desert society may have wished to remove female prophets from the threat of contamination to which they, more than males, were deemed susceptible.

A far greater part of the change in the status of *inspirées* was due to the underlying shift in the millenarian ethos of the Desert. Millennial ideas do not necessarily entail social or sexual equality, and the millenarian ethos of judgment as it appeared in the Desert allowed for traditionally female activity to become extended more in style and scope than in essence. Isabeau Vincent and her successors had been welcomed by their community as precocious children within a larger family. Older female prophets, whether praying or predicting, looked forward to redemption through a male figure and restoration of the Temple in order to restore the

---

51. On the position of women in French society, see Jeffry Kaplow, *The Names of Kings: The Parisian Laboring Poor in the Eighteenth Century* (New York, 1972) 55-65; Georges Ascoli, *Essai sur l'histoire des idées féministes en France du XVIe siècle à la Révolution* (Paris, 1906-07); Gustave Fagniez, *La femme et la société française dans la première moitié du XVIIe siècle* (Paris, 1929); A. Abbiateci et al., *Crimes et criminalité en France 17e-18e siècles* (Paris, 1971) 106-07, 141, 234-35, 237, 259; Carolyn C. Lougee, *Le Paradis des Femmes: Women, Salons, and Social Stratification in Seventeenth-Century France* (Princeton, 1976). For examples of sexual accusations, see Bibl. Nîmes, MSS 186(15) esp. pp. 399, 403-05; de Brueys, *Histoire du fanatisme*, I, 361.

52. *TS*, esp. 107, and *MMM*, 177n.

Home. They painted judgment in terms of scenes between parents and children. Whether or not they used domestic images in their prayers and sermons, they functioned as leaders of an invigorated family cult.[53]

As the ethos of judgment shifted to the ethos of cataclysm through the dreams and prophecies of the hunted men in the Cévennes, female prophets lost their social footing. Their traditional roles did not extend to the world of combat. This is not to say that they were unequal to the battle, for indeed many were renowned guerilla fighters; rather, visions of the millennium in the Cévennes never completely obscured or undermined the structure of inherited social relationships. The flouting of rules of sexual conduct by young women (and men) in the guerilla bands may have been an occasional radical step for people in a Calvinist environment, but neither the prophecies nor promiscuity of women upset the basic lines of power in Camisard tribes. Men, accustomed to the theater of war through the images and tales of more than a century of Huguenot history, became the leading prophets of cataclysm.[54]

Most difficult to pinpoint is the source of the shift in millenarian ethos. I would suggest that in 1698, confronted with the disheartening news of the Treaty of Ryswick, with renewed persecution and further *dragonnades*, with the hanging of the most esteemed of the *prédicants*, Claude Brousson, people of the Desert were induced to relocate themselves psychologically.[55] Unable to secure a territory of their own, alive in a Desert which had not blossomed, they gradually made their home within chronology rather than geography. The ethos of judgment, if insistently apocalyptic, had been primarily the ethos of a community which hoped to remain intact by reclaiming its place in France. The ethos of cataclysm would be the ethos

---

53. Of the more than twenty *prédicants* between 1685 and 1688, only one had been a woman. While the *prédicants* in the early period had both authority and mobility, the prophets were more or less geographically fixed and consequently home- and village-centered. For a list of the first *prédicants*, see Douen, *Les premiers pasteurs*, II 5-7, 33-38, 44.

54. Cf. Natalie Zemon Davis, "Women on Top," in her *Society and Culture in Early Modern France* (Stanford, 1975) 124-51.

55. On Brousson, his fame and his controversy with royalist Huguenot ministers exiled in Geneva, see Douen, *Les premiers pasteurs,* II, 178-86, 235-38, 246, 283, 379; Bost, *Les prédicants,* I, 227, and II, 178-82, 199-202, 308, 387-94; Napoléon Peyrat, *Histoire des pasteurs du Désert* (Paris, 1842) I, 237; Fléchier, *Lettres choisies,* I, 405-09; AH, MSS C. 191, ff. 354-55 and 418-21; Claude Brousson, *La manne mystique du Désert* (Amsterdam, 1695); Eugène Haag and Emile Haag, *La France Protestante, ou vies des Protestants français* (Paris, 1846-58) III, 23-36; Henri Vuilleumier, *Histoire de l'Eglise réformée du Pays de Vaud sous la régime bernois* (Lausanne, 1927-33) III, 153-65, 205-09; Elie Merlat, *Le moyen de discerner les esprits* (Lausanne, 1689). On the year 1698 and Huguenot reactions, see Bost, *Les prédicants,* II, 199-202, 308; Bost 1925, 406; Dodge, *Political Theory,* 158; Philippe Joutard, ed., *Journaux Camisards* (1700-1715) (Paris, 1965) 109-10.

of a community which was increasingly sensitive to its social and political weakness and which could not establish itself securely except within God's millennial time. Instead of anticipating a near but fixed and geographically focussed judgment, the loyal remnant could become dynamically involved in the process and momentum of millennial events.[56] So the Daniel of dreams could be transformed into the David who rose, unlike William of Orange, from within the Desert. So the Old Testament tribe and pure apostolic church of the New Testament might emerge as a composite model for social organization—a model which gave men pride of place. Confident of their standing within an explosive divine chronology, the Camisards might be the elect agents of that cataclysm which precedes judgment.

From the diffuse apocalyptic speculation of Pierre du Moulin early in the 1600s to the Camisard uprising in 1702, Huguenots in southeastern France had shared millennial beliefs and feelings which affected at first their theology, then their religious worship, and finally their entire social fabric. The history of the French Prophets is the history of what happened when three *inspirés* left the Desert and made their way to London, to another culture, another society, and a different life.

56. Cf. Sacvan Bercovitch, "Horologicals to Chronometricals: The Rhetoric of the Jeremiad," *Literary Monographs* 3 (1970) 1-124, and Edward T. Hall, *The Hidden Dimension* (New York, 1966) on relationships between territory and time. See also Lucienne Roubin, "Male Space and Female Space within the Provençal Community," in Robert Forster and Orest Ranum, eds., *Rural Society in France,* translators Elborg Foster and Patricia M. Ranum (Baltimore and London, 1977) 152-80, originally published in *Annales: é.s.c.* 25 (1970) 537-60. When war entered the Desert, did the Desert become a primarily male space?

CHAPTER II

The English Setting

England and the Millennium

England in 1706 was no stranger to prophecy or to millennial speculation. The Camisard prophet Elie Marion arrived in London just twelve years after Jesus had appeared there to Barbara Cadell, twelve years too since Jesus had announced the millennium in person to Rev. John Mason of Water Stratford.[1] In 1706, according to Thomas Beverly, the world was seven years along the apocalyptic finish to time.[2] If the Fifth Monarchist Mary Cary and the Baptist William Sherwin had their figures correct, the millennium should have already begun around 1700; Francis Mercurius van Helmont, Kabbalist and Quaker, dated the reign of the Philadelphian Church (immediate precedent to the Second Coming) from 1702.[3] For Bishop William Lloyd, vicar William Allen, mathematician William Whiston, the world in 1706 had yet a little respite before the end—some ten, twenty or thirty years at most.[4]

These were not slipshod estimates by whimsical people. Stirred by the Reformation identification of Antichrist with the Papacy, serious Protestant scholars of the seventeenth century looked for other identities

---

1. On Cadell see Lambeth Palace, MSS 953, f. 124; on Mason see below.
2. Thomas Beverly, *Indiction or Accounting by Fifteens: The Great Style of Prophetic Time* (1699). Cf. Beverly's letter in Ambrose Barnes, *Memoirs,* ed. W.H.D. Longstaffe (Durham, 1867) 246-47.
3. Doris Stenton, *The English Woman in History* (1957) 172; D.P. Walker, *The Decline of Hell* (1964) 146; William Sherwin, *The Times of Restitution of All Things* (1675) frontispiece.
4. William Allen, *Of the State of the Church in Future Ages* (1684) 317; E.S. de Beer, ed., *The Diary of John Evelyn* (1955) V, 26, 321-22; W.G. Hiscock, ed., *David Gregory, Isaac Newton and their Circle* (1937) 16; Humphrey J.T. Johnson, *Anglicanism in Transition* (1938) 24.

between biblical symbols and historical persons or events. Reviving early Christian beliefs in a future millennium, Joseph Mede, Thomas Brightman, Johann Heinrich Alsted, and James Ussher, Archbishop of Armagh —to name only the men most influential in England—had combed scripture for clues to the approach of apocalypse. Mede, for example, interpreted the fourth vial of Revelation 16:9 as the Thirty Years' War (1618-48) and put the millennium in 1716; Alsted computed it for 1694. English Protestants in the 1620s and 1630s, in an era of eschatological hopes and political unrest that culminated in the Civil War, found these calculations neither surprising nor unwelcome. Whether Jesus would return to earth to introduce the thousand years of peace for the faithful (premillennialism) or would come in glory only at the end of those years (postmillennialism), it was assumed by a wide range of men and women that contemporary events were rapidly fulfilling the signs of the latter days.[5]

From the puritan pulpit and through their own reading or discourse, people learned to search for the groundplan of the New Jerusalem in the English nation itself. Threatened by the high churchmanship of Archbishop Laud and his "Arminian" party of bishops, whose attitude toward ritual and church governance approached that of Roman Catholics, and clumsily intimidated by the high-handed Charles I as he pushed for alliance with France and tolerance for Catholics, a great number of English Protestants gradually refused to acknowledge either King or Laudian clergy as the Lord's agents toward the establishment of Zion. By 1642, after ecclesiastic, economic, legal and parliamentary crises, civil war had come. By 1646 Parliament had abolished episcopacy and Cromwell's New Model Army had routed most royal forces. Thereafter, with the execution of Charles I in 1649 and the creation of the Barebones Parliament in 1653, the overriding issue was how best to achieve a Kingdom of Saints. Although the two increasingly distinct parties, Presbyterians and Independents, shared visions of a direct immediate relationship between the spiritual state of believers and the state of the nation, each set those visions within a different structure. Presbyterians,

5. Peter Toon, ed., *Puritans the Millennium and the Future of Israel: Puritan Eschatology 1600 to 1660* (1970) introduction by Toon and article by Robert G. Clouse, "The Rebirth of Millenarianism," 42-65; also Clouse, "Johann Heinrich Alsted and English Millennialism," *Harvard Theological Review* 62 (1969) 189-207; Christopher Hill, *Antichrist in Seventeenth Century England* (1971) 4-32, 108-20; R. Buick Knox, *James Ussher, Archbishop of Armagh* (Cardiff, 1967) 105-06, 157-59; Bernard Capp, "The Millennium and Eschatology in England," *Past and Present* 57 (1972) 156-62; Melvin B. Endy, Jr., *William Penn and Early Quakerism* (Princeton, 1973) esp. 35.

committed to a corporate system, hoped for religious conformity under an orderly national association of churches. Independents, deferring to personal spiritual progress, hoped for a nation of separate congregations wherein the faithful gathered for their common advance on the millennial path, however diverse their routes. Even with the Army's initial support and the Barebones Assembly of Saints, the Independents failed to inaugurate the Christian kingdom for which they had pressed, and the English Commonwealth became Cromwell's Protectorate until his death in 1658. Two years later, royalists and Presbyterians working together, the Stuart monarchy was restored.[6]

Despite diplomatic feints toward a policy of religious compromise and a presbyterian church order, Charles II and his advisors promoted a religious settlement which led away from a comprehensive national church. By the Act of Uniformity (1662) and subsequent legislation, Presbyterians and Independents were forced out of the established church into "dissent," and numerous "nonconforming" ministers were ejected from their livings. Episcopacy returned, though bishops had less political clout than under Laud, and the Church of England became again a force for the preservation of social hierarchies. Fifth Monarchists who had struck an easily parried "Blow for King Jesus" in 1661 did not exploit the London fire, plague, or indeed the numeric symbolism of 1666.[7]

Chiliasts of the Civil War and Commonwealth periods had earned for millennial doctrines, especially premillennialism, social calumny. Ranters and Fifth Monarchists in the late 1640s and 1650s had interpreted the end of the world in utopian and sometimes antinomian terms. Relying often upon private inspirations, they advocated and actively sought to implement a set of egalitarian social values which they anticipated would be the norm for the coming Kingdom. Politically radical, eager to slough off the burdensome social distinctions which made wealth or title the determinant of political power, they had failed noisily in their attempts to adjust English society to the Christian order of the approaching millennium. They had also frightened many who benefitted from traditional social

6. The most pertinent accounts of events 1640-60 occur in Tai Liu, *Discord in Zion: The Puritan Divines and the Puritan Revolution 1640-1660* (The Hague, 1973); Charles Webster, *The Great Instauration: Science, Medicine and Reform, 1626-1660* (New York, 1976); John F. Wilson, *Pulpit in Parliament: Puritanism during the English Civil Wars, 1640-1648* (Princeton, 1969); William L. Lamont, *Godly Rule: Politics and Religion, 1603-60* (1969).

7. See Robert S. Bosher, *The Making of the Restoration Settlement: The Influence of the Laudians 1649-1662* (Westminster, 1951); Walter G. Simon, *The Restoration Episcopate* (New York, 1965); P.G. Rogers, *The Fifth Monarchy Men* (1966) 110-33. The number 1666 included the traditional number of the Beast of the Book of Revelation (666) and the millennium (1000).

ranking, and they had scarred the memories of churchmen who feared that private inspiration might replace all church structures.[8]

Nonetheless, millennial beliefs did not wither at the Restoration. Rather, there was a strong tendency on the part of those who adhered to the views of Alsted and Mede to dissociate themselves from the ethos of cataclysm as shaped by the more radical Christian groups. The millennialism of the later Stuart era most often conveyed a socially and politically moderate eschatology. Millenarian clergymen were anxious for a reasonable stability and toleration in the church. Millenarian laypeople —scholars, scientists, virtuosi by no means plebeian—were as eager as the clerics to assure a significant role for the English Church in the preparation of Christian society for the coming Kingdom. These men and women found clues to the progress of the latter days in natural, historical, and scriptural sources, not in new personal revelation.[9] They tended to divorce the ethos of the New Jerusalem from the ethos of cataclysm, the ethos of judgment from the ethos of pentecost.

Concerned with the sinews of community, many of the millenarians after 1660 were religious moderates, broad churchmen (latitudinarians) willing to cut away the ideological bracken from Christian essentials and admit to the national church a variety of Protestants whose differences over church governance and liturgy were ultimately minor. Critical on the one hand of religious groups that cherished personal inspiration, and on the other hand forsworn enemies of the Roman Catholics who had the sympathies of Charles II and his successor James II, latitudinarians paddled through their own rapids toward a comprehensive church. Their efforts were rocked and jarred less by fear of Protestant dissenters than by fear of Popery. Charles and James each issued Declarations of Indulgence

---

8. Bernard S. Capp, *The Fifth Monarchy Men: A Study in Seventeenth-Century English Millenarianism* (1972) 229-32; Alfred Cohen, "The Fifth Monarchy Mind: Mary Cary and the Origins of Totalitarianism," *Social Research* 21 (1964) 195-213; Arthur L. Morton, *The World of the Ranters* (1970); Christopher Hill, *The World Turned Upside Down* (New York, 1972); James F. Maclear, " 'The Heart of New England Piety Rent': The Mystical Element in Early Puritan History," *Mississippi Valley Historical Review* 42 (1956) 621-52; Endy, *Penn,* 16-49; Gertrude Huehns, *Antinomianism in English History* (1951) which does not distinguish utopians from millenarians. See also Capp's review, *"Godly Rule* and English Millenarianism," *Past and Present* 52 (1971) 106-11, and William L. Lamont's response, "Richard Baxter, the Apocalypse, and the Mad Major," *Past and Present* 55 (1972) 68-90.

9. See Barbara J. Shapiro, "Latitudinarianism and Science," *Past and Present* 40 (1968) 16-41; Lotte Mulligan, "Civil War Politics, Religion and the Royal Society," *Past and Present* 59 (1973) 92-116; Christopher Hill, "Newton and His Society," in Robert Palter, ed., *The "Annus Mirabilis" of Sir Isaac Newton 1666-1966* (Cambridge, Mass., 1970) 26-47; Margaret C. Jacob, *The Newtonians and the English Revolution 1689-1720* (Ithaca, 1976). See also chapter seven on The Scientists.

which might have eased the strict boundaries of the established church, but the Declarations were rightly suspect to Parliament as means to relax restrictions on Catholics. In response to the Declaration of Indulgence of 1672, Parliament passed a Test Act (1673) which further narrowed the rights of all dissenters by demanding religious conformity of officeholders. Up to his deathbed conversion in 1685, Parliament remained at odds with Charles, who throughout his reign braided together the interests of the French, his monarchy, his own Catholic inclinations, and the foreign involvements of England. Welcomed at first, James II soon showed Catholic colors in his appointments for high civil and military offices and his concurrent disregard of the Test Act. Having prorogued Parliament in late 1685, having thrust Catholics into university posts, James issued two Declarations of Indulgence, the second of which, in May, 1688, was ordered read from every pulpit. Seven bishops—and most of the English clergy—publicly defied the order. While the trial of the bishops was being set, the Queen gave birth to a healthy male (and Catholic) heir, James Edward. By mid-July, the bishops acquitted, another seven highly placed men had invited the intervention of the Protestant William of Orange, husband to Mary, the elder daughter of James. Abandoned by his Protestant younger daughter Anne, too disconcerted to mount a coherent political or military campaign against William, James was allowed to escape to France with his wife and infant son. There he would die, his son and later his grandson to be troublesome Pretenders to the English throne. At the end of December, 1688, William entered London.[10]

Among the first to pledge themselves to the new monarchs were the broad churchmen who saw in the Glorious Revolution a sign of England's prominent role in the union of Protestantism and who urged the passage of an act that would ensure a comprehensive church. What they managed was a Toleration Act (1689) which granted limited legal status to organized Protestant dissent and required of all clergy an oath of allegiance to William and Mary.[11] With this lame bill the latitudinarians

10. Simon, *Restoration Episcopate,* esp. ch. 11; Geoffrey F.A. Best, *Temporal Pillars* (Cambridge, 1964) 36; Jacob, *Newtonians,* ch. 1; John Carswell, *The Descent on England: A Study of the English Revolution and its European Background* (New York, 1969) esp. 130-51; Stephen R. Baxter, *William III and the Defense of European Liberty 1650-1702* (New York, 1966) 193-242; David Ogg, *England in the Reigns of James II and William III* (2nd ed.; Oxford, 1966) chs. 5-8.

11. Five of the seven bishops who had defied James, and about 400 other clergy, refused to take the oath of allegiance. Known as nonjurors, they were generally deprived of their livings for upholding strictly the doctrine of nonresistance. George Hickes, "bishop" of the nonjurors, would be among the most vocal of opponents to the French Prophets. On the Revolution and the clergy, see Gerald M. Straka, *Anglican Reaction to the Revolution of 1688* (Madison,

would have to be content for the next decades, whatever their personal conviction that, as Walter Garret would show in 1706 in a discourse on Revelation 4 and 5, "the Church of England by Law Established, has the Special Approbation of the Spirit of God in Prophecy; and (consequently) that she is Set-forth as for a Pattern for All other Churches, and the Center of their Peace and Union."[12]

Like the *inspirés* of the Desert who had looked toward England for immediate deliverance in 1689, so too millenarian churchmen recognized the eminence of the English Church in the scheme of redemption. A French gentleman from Languedoc, reminding his English readers that Archbishop Ussher himself had foreseen the persecution in France, pleaded with them to keep their land a sanctuary of Protestant peace for fleeing Huguenots. In turn, like Pierre Jurieu, millenarian churchmen were disposed to regard the persecution in France as a hallmark for the completion of scripture prophecy. In 1689 Bishop William Lloyd identified one of the two witnesses of Revelation with the Cévenol Protestants. In 1690 he believed that the witnesses had been resurrected by the Duke of Savoy, who switched loyalty from Catholic France to English allies and so saved the Huguenot remnant in the Vaudois. English divine Thomas Burnet wrote the next year that "the Resurrection of the Witnesses goes on very well in Savoy and Dauphiné, and that [is] another argument to hope all will end well." Thomas Beverly awaited wondrous appearances in France that might clinch the relationship between Huguenot persecution and the final deliverance.[13] With deep interest, then, would these men read the numerous published accounts of Huguenot suffering.[14]

1962); Jacob, *Newtonians,* ch. 2; G.V. Bennett, "King William III and the Episcopate," in Bennett and John Walsh, eds., *Essays in Modern Church History* (1966) 104-31; Edward Carpenter, *The Protestant Bishop: Being the Life of Henry Compton, 1632-1713 Bishop of London* (London, New York and Toronto, 1956) 140-75; Thomas Lathbury, *A History of the Nonjurors* (1845). For a list of dissenting groups which had registered their meetinghouses by 1713 under the terms of the Toleration Act, see C.E. Fryer, "The Numerical Decline of Dissent in England Previous to the Industrial Revolution," *American Journal of Theology* 17 (1913) 235n.

12. Walter Garret, *The Testimony of the Spirit of Prophecy Concerning the True Church At this Day* (1707) final part of title.

13. *A French Prophecy; or an Admonition to the English, concerning their near approaching Danger, and the Means to escape it* (1690 or 1691) reprinted in J. Somers, ed., *A Collection of Scarce and Valuable Tracts* (1748) IV, 440-45; de Beer, *Diary of John Evelyn,* IV, 636, and V, 25-26, 321-22; Bodleian, Tanner MSS XXVI, f. 44, Burnet to John Patrick, cited in Jacob, *Newtonians,* 124; Beverly, *Indiction, 41.*

14. Among these accounts published between 1689 and 1706 were K. Pineton de Chambrun, *The History of the Persecutions of the Protestants by the French King in the Principality of Orange* (1689); *Account of the sufferings and dying words of several French protestants* (1699);

The year 1689 had a special significance to another man within the fold of the Church of England. John Mason, rector of the small village of Water Stratford near Buckingham, had a fine reputation as a pious cleric. One of the first to compose original hymns instead of versifying the Psalms, as author of the *Spiritual Songs* (1683) he had an enduring popularity with Anglicans, Moravians and Methodists into the middle of the next century.[15] He had given thought to the Book of Revelation, and he had read Alsted and Ussher, but it was not until 1689, a year after his wife's death, that Mason had intimations of the coming of the Kingdom.[16] In 1689 a divine messenger declared to Mason that "the Lord would have a kingdom in this World, and the time draws near." Mason began to hear voices and had visions of the New Jerusalem. He saw the signs of deliverance for the figurative church of Philadelphia, that faithful church which would be present at the Second Coming (Revelation 3:7-10). Believing himself inspired, he began to preach extempore, and in 1691 his popular sermon, *The Midnight Cry*, was published.[17] One of Mason's critics, unhappy about the rector's influence, tried to explain the appeal of his sermon:

> and though there appeared (to several at least) nothing extraordinary in that Discourse, more than to quicken up all sorts to an earnest Expectation of, and Preparation unto Christ's speedy Approach to Judgment, (Mr. Mason's Modesty not prefixing any limited Time, etc.) yet it became of such Universal Acceptation with the more pious sort [who under this late Great *Revolution* throughout the Christian World (and more especially in these Kingdoms) have been waiting for some extraordinary Things immediately Antecedent thereunto] that the Book soon spread.[18]

Elias Neau, *An Account of the sufferings of the French Protestants Slaves on board the French King's Galleys* (1699); *The History of the Persecutions of the Reformed Churches in France, Orange and Piedmont* (1699); A. D'Auborn, *The French Convert.... To which is added, A Brief Account of the present Severe Persecutions of the French Protestants* (2nd ed.; 1699). Jean Claude's *A Short Account of the Complaints and Cruel Persecutions of the Protestants in the Kingdom of France* (1686) was ordered burned by James II upon the request of the French ambassador. It had a third edition in 1708.

15. Christopher Hill, "John Mason and the End of the World," in *Puritanism and Revolution* (Panther ed.; 1969) 311-23; John L. Myres, "John Mason: Poet and Enthusiast," *Records of Buckinghamshire* 7 (1897) 20-21; Bedford RO, MSS MO 607, p. 1, Thomas Pierson's Memoirs.

16. Hill, "John Mason," 316; Myres, "John Mason," 16; a Reverend Divine, *Some Remarkable Passages in the Life and Death of Mr. John Mason* (1694) 26; John Mason (grandson of rector), *Select Remains of the Reverend John Mason* (2nd ed.; 1742) xv.

17. John Mason, *The Angels Oath, Time is no longer* (1694) 10, 12, 17-23, 30, 34; Henry Maurice, *An Impartial Account of Mr. John Mason* (1695) 31.

18. *The Tryal and Condemnation of Two False Witnesses* (1694) 3-4.

When Mason, like Alsted, eventually fixed upon 1694 as the year for the millennium to commence, he had a receptive audience, and his congregation that spring swelled considerably. The Presbyterian Elias Pledger even wrote to him from London in January for more details of his predicted "desolating judgment" to befall London and environs.[19] At last, about 1:00 A.M. on Easter Monday, April 16, 1694, in the midst of the dancing and singing of the faithful at Water Stratford, Jesus appeared in person to John Mason. He promised that on Whitsunday (Pentecost) He would gather together all the saints on the holy ground of the small Buckinghamshire village and inaugurate the millennium.[20]

Men and women flocked to the holy ground to await the Kingdom and "to live in imitation of the primitive Saints," with all possessions in common and continuous praising of the Lord. The clergyman Henry Maurice, come to interview Mason, found believers running up and down, "one while stretching his Arms upwards to catch their Saviour in his coming down, others extending them forwards to meet his embraces, a third with a sudden turn pretends to grasp him and a fourth clapping their hands for joy they had him." By April 26, more than eighty danced around Mason's rectory. Hundreds came to watch the celebration and to hear Mason prophesy from his balcony.[21]

John Mason was ill. Through his two witnesses, Thomas Ward and Valentine Evans, and his sister-in-law Margaret Holms, messages from him were brought to the faithful in the weeks before Pentecost. They announced that judgment neared and God's decree against the impenitent had been irrevocably issued. Mason declared that time was no longer and that the kingdoms of this world were become the kingdoms of the Lord (Revelation 10:6, 11:15). Water Stratford was the new Zion and Mason himself the new Elias.[22]

In mid-May, having prophesied his own resurrection, John Mason died. On May 28, certain followers claiming to have seen the risen minister,

19. Dr. Williams's Library, MSS 28.4, Pledger diary, ff. 60-62v.
20. Browne Willis, *The History and Antiquities of the Town, Hundred, and Deanry of Buckingham* (1755) 344; Maurice, *Impartial Account*, 4-7; [Mr.] Pickfat, *A Letter from a Gentleman in Buckinghamshire* (1694) 4. Cf. de Beer, *Diary of John Evelyn*, V, 177-178.
21. Maurice, *Impartial Account*, 8; *Strange News from Bishop's Stafford near Buckingham* (1694) broadside. Even though the faithful lived with goods in common, they did not seek to extend levelling principles to the wider society and turned away the poor who came to benefit from their property sharing, according to Pickfat, *Letter*, 6-7. Cf. BM, Add. MSS 34274, 07, letter to Mr. Mellefont (?) from W.C., 5/20/1694.
22. Mason, *Angels Oath*, preface, 4, 38; a Reverend Divine, *Some Remarkable Passages*, 3-6; *Tryal and Condemnation of Two False Witnesses*, 11.

Margaret Holms wrote optimistically that "we expect a most glorious issue of this seeming Dark Providence: Not that his Death is a step backward." A band of believers lingered at Water Stratford to witness the completion of prophecy. The succeeding rector disinterred Mason to convince the faithful that their prophet had been an ordinary mortal, but for another fifty years men and women would meet on the holy ground near the rectory to sing, dance and proclaim the millennium.[23]

Those who intended to republish Mason's hymns in 1707 also awaited the millennium and identified with the figurative church of Philadelphia.[24] Nearly all Anglicans, they called themselves Philadelphians, believing that the time allotted for the purification of Christianity would shortly expire. Theirs was not a new church but a "Religious Society for the Reformation of Manners, for the Advancement of an Heroical Christian Piety, and Universal Love towards All." Their society centered upon personal inspiration and theosophical principles current since the Civil War. They were the most important millenarians within the Church of England to precede and then to acclaim the Camisard prophets.[25]

The history of the Philadelphians winds and turns through the religious geography of seventeenth-century England like a rambling antiquarian who finds something of value along every path. The story might begin with the eminent antiquarian and astrologer, Elias Ashmole, who granted Dr. John Pordage (1607-81) the clerical living at Bradfield (Berks.) sometime before 1650. Pordage, a student of medicine and alchemy, had a wife who was a spirit medium, and he was ejected from his living in 1654 for convoking spirits and claiming the power to bestow gifts of the Spirit upon whom he pleased.[26] Thenceforth he concentrated on the elaboration of a

---

23. Maurice, *Impartial Account,* 8-9; a Reverend Divine, *Some Remarkable Passages,* 6-7, 10-11; Willis, *History of Buckingham,* 344-45; Myres, "John Mason," 40. Mason's critics associated him with the Fifth Monarchists, not without some cause (biographical rather than political), as Hill points out, "John Mason," 318-21. Cf. *HMC* 22: 11th R.: Leeds (Bolton Papers) 151; *Memoirs of Literature* 4 (1714) 60.

24. Richard Roach, Mr. Hoffman and Mr. Bridges, Philadelphians who later became French Prophets, agreed on June 15, 1707, to publish an edition of Mason's hymns, but there is no record of any edition of Mason's *Spiritual Songs* between 1704 and 1718. The *Midnight-Cry* was reprinted in 1707 with two added hymns. Roach Diary, I, ff. 18, 59.

25. Philadelphus, *State of the Philadelphian Society* (1697) 7 and advertisement *re* 27; *The Principles of a People Stiling themselves Philadelphians* (1687) esp. 2, which accuses them of singing hymns of their own making. On the rarity of hymn singing before 1700, see Michael R. Watts, *The Dissenters* (Oxford, 1978) I, 308.

26. Bodleian, Rawlinson MSS D. 833, Roach Papers, f. 63; Serge Hutin, *Les disciples anglais de Jacob Boehme aux XVIIe et XVIIIe siècles* (Paris, 1960) 69, 82-83; D.P. Walker, *The Decline of Hell: Seventeenth-Century Discussions of Eternal Torment* (1964) 218-19; Dr.

theosophy closely aligned to that of the German mystic Jacob Boehme (1575-1624), many of whose writings, translated during the 1640s, had impressed English chiliasts.[27]

Boehme had propounded a theosophy—a system deriving knowledge of things divine from mystical insight and contemplation—which emphasized the different aspects of divine energy. He perceived the divine spirit operating on many levels, and evil itself was simply spiritual imbalance, an elemental part of divine energy out of harmony with the rest. The dualism inherent in this perception was made explicit in his hypothesis of an original androgynous human who reflected the double nature of the godhead. Androgyneity and harmony would be restored by the return of Jesus, but Boehme was hesitant to posit more than the spiritual advent of the Lord at the millennium. He did contemplate a seventh period in human history, when all would be happy and peaceful; this he called, after the example of the patriarch, the Enochian time.[28]

Whether or not John Pordage first consulted the works of Boehme to pry loose alchemical secrets, he came away with a slightly different treasure: the image of the Virgin Sophia, or Wisdom, female counterpart to male divinity. Borrowing from the syncretic writings of the sixteenth-century German physician Paracelsus, Boehme had accepted the alchemists' three fundamental elements of nature—sulphur, salt and mercury—only to add an organizing principle akin to light. Pordage embroidered upon Boehme's image of Sophia, discerning a role for Wisdom as an organizing force in human progress toward the millennium.[29]

Mrs. Jane Lead, central figure of the Philadelphians, first met Pordage in 1663. In 1674, widowed, she came to lodge with the theosopher in London. She was fifty, he was sixty-seven. During the remaining years of his life, Pordage transmitted to Jane Lead an image of Sophia and desires for the restoration of universal harmony which were deeply woven into her mystical visions. At Pordage's death in 1681, she assumed leadership of his small circle of seekers.[30]

Williams's Library, MSS 24.109 (9)a, Henry Dodwell to Francis Lee, 8/23/1698, referring to Christopher Fowler's *Daemonium Meridianum* (1655) for information on Pordage's spirit contacts. Elias Ashmole presented (the future bishop) William Lloyd for the living vacated by Pordage: A. Hart Tindal, *William Lloyd 1627-1717* (1952) 15.

27. Nils Thune, *The Behmenists and the Philadelphians* (Uppsala, 1948) 31-49, 52, 81; Richard Roach, *The Great Crisis* (1725 [sic for 1727]) 98-99; Hill, *Antichrist*, 104.

28. Thune, *Behmenists and Philadelphians*, 31-40, 77-78; Désirée Hirst, *Hidden Riches: Traditional Symbolism from the Renaissance to Blake* (1964) 93; A. Koyré, *La philosophie de Jacob Boehme* (Paris, 1929).

29. Hirst, *Hidden Riches*, 87-91, 103-09; Thune, *Behmenists and Philadelphians*, 49.

30. Thune, *Behmenists and Philadelphians*, 60-61, 77, 81; Walker, *Decline of Hell*, 218-19.

Though she immeasurably strengthened the millenarian inclinations of the group and gradually turned her own thoughts toward the possibility of universal salvation, Jane Lead still recognized an agreement between her theosophy and that of Boehme. She retained, too, some of the alchemical imagery so dear to her mentor and described a process of initiation into heavenly mysteries which corresponded to the alchemical apprenticeship of the adept.[31]

Until 1697, the Philadelphians convened privately at Jane Lead's house in Hoxton or at the homes of Joanna Oxenbridge and Ann Bathurst in Baldwins Gardens, London. Their meetings were subdued, begun with prayer and scripture readings and followed by that silence, familiar to Quakers, in which the inspired might speak. The privacy of their meetings was due in part to their respect for the integrity of inner spiritual life, in part to their belief in stages of spiritual enlightenment, such that the uninitiated might mistake the significance of revealed words. "I cannot, I must not make known to you," wrote Ann Bathurst in her diary, "how the spirit operates, it is only to be known to the Children of the Kingdom." Earlier she had confided, with some apprehension at being misunderstood, that her soul was as a Pentecost and immersed in the Ocean of Love:

> But I must shut my mouth so often when I begin to declare, because Ears are not fit to hear it. If I should launch into the Ocean of it: it's well, if some did not think it's by learning and say much learning has made me mad. I have learned it indeed, but not of man: but seeing the Deeps and feeling the infinite Love in my Self.

Pordage's followers included Edmund Brice and Thomas Bromley, graduates of All Souls' College, Oxford; Herbert Philip, second earl of Pembroke; Ann Bathurst and Joanna Oxenbridge: Bodleian, Rawlinson MSS D. 833, f. 63, and cf. Dr. Williams's Library, MSS 24.109 (9)a, Dodwell letter, 8/23/1698. Most of the Dr. Williams's material on the Philadelphians was printed by Christopher Walton in his ungainly and unhandy book, *Notes and Materials for an Adequate Biography of the Celebrated Divine and Theosopher, William Law* (n.p., 1854) 188-258.

31. It was not by chance that in August, 1693, a group of visionaries calling themselves "true Rosicrucians" should spend time with the Philadelphians in London. Deriving from the "theosophical fraternity" founded by Johann Zimmerman, these German Protestant separatists had in common with Jane Lead's group a boundless admiration for Boehme's works. They shared also a belief in an interior, personal New Jerusalem, which the Germans located, by the summer of 1694, on the quiet shores of the Wissahickon in Pennsylvania. Contact with these Rosicrucians was neither the first nor the last Philadelphian link with continental Protestantism. By 1697, Philadelphian circles had gathered in Holland, Germany and Switzerland. Hutin, *Les disciples anglais de Boehme*, 99-100, 119; Thune, *Behmenists and Philadelphians*, 78, 125-26; Julius F. Sachse, *The German Pietists of Provincial Pennsylvania 1694-1708* (Philadelphia, 1895) 4, 15; Walker, *Decline of Hell*, 219, 231-44; BCUL, MSS TH 1194 B. 10 and B.16 on Swiss connections; Bibliothèque Nationale (Paris), MSS f.f. 24190, Mémoires concernant la nouvelle secte des Piétistes ou Quiétistes ou société philadelphique répandue dans les Cantons suisses. See also chapter six.

Certainly, as Quakers had learned, the doctrine of an inner revelation was subject to harsh criticism from the established ministry, who would be quick to see the danger in such a statement as this by Ann Bathurst: "*the kingdom of heaven is within me and the breath of God, Christ,* is in us, what need we go to a Symbol?" Jane Lead was equally specific: "Is Christ to be conceived, and born in every one for Salvation so Intrinsically? Yea surely."[32]

Stirred by Lead's inspiration that there was "much to be done in the Kingdom of this World by a more plentiful Effusion of the Spirit than yet hath been," the Philadelphians in 1697 prepared to give public, open testimony to their private faith and their Enochian walk into the "Celestial Globe of Eternity." They moved many of their meetings to Hungerford Market and Westmoreland House, which they duly licensed as places of religious worship under the terms of the Toleration Act. In addition, the group was bolstered by the recent active involvement of two Oxford graduates, the nonjuring physician Francis Lee (son-in-law to Jane Lead) and the Anglican rector Richard Roach, who began to publish the short-lived *Theosophical Transactions,* a miscellany of often abstruse articles, some dealing at length with the intricacies of Jewish mystical thought (Kabbala).[33]

According to the Huguenot Henri Misson, who in 1697 had difficulty distinguishing it from the Society of Friends, the new society of Philadelphians seemed to advertise itself as

> the Germ of the commencement of the sole true Church, Virgin Bride of Jesus Christ, whose Members, dispersed among the diverse Religions of the World, are soon to appear and unite with them, in order to form this pure and holy Church, such as the church of Philadelphia was at the birth of Christianity.[34]

32. Bodleian, Rawlinson MSS D. 1263, Bathurst diary II, 7/2 and 10/20/1693; Jane Lead, *The Enochian Walks with God* (1694) 36; Walker, *Decline of Hell,* 221. A list of Jane Lead's published works appears in Walton, *Notes,* 148.

33. Lead, *Enochian Walks,* 6, 32; Bodleian, Rawlinson MSS D. 832, f.53 and D. 833, ff. 65-66; Walker, *Decline of Hell,* 219-20; *Theosophical Transactions* (1697) esp. 25-43, 108-31, 160, 169-92. Philadelphians accepted Boehme's postulate of an androgynous godhead and of the feminine principle of divine wisdom, both of which had close parallels in Lurianic Kabbalism with the figure of Shechina. If, as Walker suggests (p. 225), the Kabbalistic contributions to the *Transactions* came from F.M. van Helmont, he may have been linked to the Philadelphians through another man who will appear in the following chapters: Benjamin Furly, a former Quaker living in Rotterdam. See Gershom G. Scholem, *Major Trends in Jewish Mysticism* (New York, 1961) 237-38 and n. 101; Thune, *Behmenists and Philadelphians,* 84, reading "Furley" for "Finley"; William I. Hull, *Benjamin Furly and Quakerism in Rotterdam* (n.p., 1941) 82-83.

34. [Henri Misson], *Mémoires et observations faites par un voyageur en Angleterre* (The

In their own statement of purpose, the Philadelphians announced that their public assemblies would keep the spirit of love burning and would nourish apostolical faith. Despite the various degrees of spiritual gifts and mystical knowledge attained by their members, the Philadelphians represented themselves as the devout guardians of the sacred temple fires during the gradual but hastening universal redemption. If they agreed with the Quakers on the "Internal Principle of a Light within," they were more careful than the Quakers to assert their basic conformity with the Church of England, for "We design not to set up any Form, or to lay any Burden either upon our Selves, or upon others; but to maintain the Evangelical Liberty of Prophesying, to all those that are, or shall be, Anointed with the Spirit of Christ."[35] At a time when the "Reformation and Re-union" of religion were soon to be accomplished, wrote the apologist Philadelphus, it could not be naive to expect divine assistance, effusions of the Spirit, signs and wonders.[36]

Philadelphus had taken up his pen to answer critics who had already compared the new society to chiliasts like the Fifth Monarchists who hoped to turn the world upside down for King Jesus. The *Theosophical Transactions* and now Philadelphus insisted on the orderliness of prophecy and the exclusively spiritual concerns of the society. (He did not mention that the suspicion of social radicalism was hardly justified, given Jane Lead's own appreciation of the social order. Most members of the society were well-off, and she had recognized that spiritual disciplines required an unusual freedom from material worries. She advised the "lower Ranks," who could not be "so much at leisure to wait the Motions of the Heavens," simply to have faith.) Some in England evidently distrusted seraphic love, peaceful prophecy and millennial expectations. "Our good God extricate you out of the snares of Enthusiasm and seducing Spirits wherein you are engaged," wrote the nonjuror Henry Dodwell to his friend Francis Lee. Ruffians disturbed the meetings at Westmoreland House and forced the abandonment of Hungerford Market assemblies.[37]

Philadelphus was not daunted, for the history of the Philadelphian church was well known, "having at first but a little Strength, Power or Splendor, and so obliged to pass through a most severe Probation, beyond

---

Hague, 1698) 369. The book was edited by F.-Maximilien Misson, his brother and soon a French Prophet: J.-M. Quérard, *Les supercheries littéraires dévoilées* (Paris, 1869) III, 980e.

35. *Theosophical Transactions*, 221 (part of the Philadelphian Constitution, pp. 221-24) and cf. 85-90, 195-97, 203-10; Philadelphus, *State of the Philadelphian Society*, 15.

36. Philadelphus, *State of the Philadelphian Society*, 10.

37. *Ibid.*, 5; Bodleian, Rawlinson MSS D. 832, f. 53 and D. 833, f. 66; Dr. Williams's Library, MSS 24.109 (9)b, letter of 8/23/1698; Lead, *Enochian Walks*, 3.

all others, and to undergo all manner of Contempt and Ignominious Treating, even from those who profess themselves to be Christians."[38] In the next ten years, the society would undergo that trial of faith. Removed to Lorimer's Hall, the Philadelphians were prevented from meeting there after 1699. They slowly retreated from public view. In 1701, after three years of neglect by the learned and buffetting by the mob, the Philadelphians saw the work of judgment once more overcome the work of mercy. Just as their public testimony had begun in tandem with the Peace of Ryswick, now the War of the Spanish Succession coincided with the decline of their evangelism. Having withdrawn to the suburb of Hoxton, the society turned to the law and appealed to the chief magistrate of London for a warrant to suppress the "Tumults and Profaneness" which "Wicked and Dissolute Persons" still committed against them. "Let us watch, one and all," wrote Francis Lee in 1702, "for snares and nets are spread everywhere; on all sides there are the stratagems of the Prince of Evil." The Great Storm of 1703 seemed another vindication of the increasingly judgmental outlook of the Philadelphians.[39]

By the end of 1703, Jane Lead, blind for some years, was confined to her bed; a missionary was making rounds in Germany with a newly composed creed and forty-four articles defining the hierarchy, methods and purposes of the society; and the group had published a "*Protestation* against the Infidelity, Supineness and Degeneracy of the Age," intuiting new judgments at hand. Upon Jane Lead's death on August 8, 1704, the Philadelphians ceased to hold public meetings but continued to gather in private. Lee wrote of his mother-in-law's concern that none be staggered by her death or incline to doubt previous spiritual experiences. During her last illness she had charged Lee to encourage Philadelphians "with the assurance of the Unchangeable Truth of God, notwithstanding all the present Clouds and Darkness."[40]

---

38. Philadelphus, *State of the Philadelphian Society*, 9.

39. *The Declaration of the Philadelphian Society of England, Easter-Day, 1699* (1699); Roach, *The Great Crisis*, 36-37; *The Vindication and Justification of the Philadelphian Society* (1702); Thune, *Behmenists and Philadelphians*, 97, 115-17; Walker, *Decline of Hell*, 250; Dr. Williams's Library, MSS 186.18(2), Francis Lee epistles to Peter Poiret, 1st Epistle (quote) and 2nd Epistle. There had been one bright spot: Thomas Beverly's prediction of the millennium coincided with the beginning of the public testimony of the Philadelphians in 1697. Roach claimed that Beverly, after conferring with the Philadelphians, revised the date for the millennium to 1700. A Philadelphian in Germany was so impressed by Beverly that he translated the *Indiction* into German. Roach, *The Imperial Standard* (1727) xix, xvi; Thune, *Behmenists and Philadelphians*, 127; F. Ernest Stoeffler, *The Rise of Evangelical Pietism* (Leiden, 1965) 176.

40. Roach, *The Great Crisis*, 36; Walker, *Decline of Hell*, 251; Thune, *Behmenists and*

Notwithstanding Lead's precautions and Lee's perseverance, the society lost much of its energy in 1704 and 1705. Fissures which had appeared before at the deaths of other charismatic individuals—Dr. Gilman, Ann Bathurst—became schisms. The prominent Behmenist, Dionysius Andreas Freher, was driven to address his fellow Philadelphians in almost desperate language: "What is the Reason, why there is breach made after breach? Why we cannot agree and unite in the one only Spirit of Jesus, when we all pretend to be led by the same?"[41] Jane Lead's visits in spirit form to Joanna Oxenbridge and Richard Roach could not forestall the divisions. Roach, who assumed nominal leadership of the majority of English Philadelphians, read in vain an inspired manifesto of unity to reclaim the schismatics. By 1706 Rebecca Critchlow would write a friendly yet faintly distressing letter to Roach, rejoicing in his spiritual progress but too eager to mention that "though in some circumstances you may in this [work?] differ from us, yet I am well assured we are engaged in the same work and that the unity that is amongst us in the general and most particular shall never be broken."[42]

That unity would disappear, but Roach, Critchlow and other Philadelphians would keep to their beliefs, often as followers of the Camisard prophets, but drawing upon the strength of English millenarian traditions which had survived the Restoration. And if millennial beliefs continued within Anglican ranks, they were sure to do so among nonconformists whose roots were in the eschatological visions of Civil War Independents.

Lodowick Muggleton himself did not die until 1698. A tailor, he had withdrawn from all public worship in 1647 at the age of thirty-eight. Three years later he was attracted by the Ranter prophet John Robins, who esteemed himself one of the Trinity and expected his wife to give birth to a new Jesus. Muggleton soon deserted Robins, "the last great Antichrist," and received his own revelations. In 1652 he and his cousin John Reeve, the two witnesses, had composed the *Transcendent Spiritual Treatise*, a book commissioned by the Lord for the final dispensation. From this and other inspired writings would believers read to each other for two centuries after Muggleton's death.[43]

Philadelphians, 115, 117-118; Lambeth Palace, MSS 1559, Copies of Letters from Francis Lee, ff. 19, 21, 23, 24v.; similar letters in Dr. Williams's Library, MSS 186.18(2).

41. Bodleian, Rawlinson MSS D. 1341, f. 2 and D. 833, f. 28v. Freher had his own following in London: Charles A. Muses, *Illumination on Jacob Boehme* (New York, 1951); Walton, *Notes,* 141n., 258-328.

42. Bodleian, Rawlinson MSS D. 832, f. 37 and D. 833, ff. 27, 28-28v., 57v.-61v., 69.

43. *DNB,* XIII, 1161-64; John Reeve and Lodowick Muggleton, *A Transcendent Spiritual Treatise* [1652] esp. 5-9, 34; George C. Williamson, *Lodowick Muggleton* (1919); John

Early Quakers had been reluctant to assign a decisive date to the millennium, but they had a powerful sense of the approaching apocalyptic conversion of the entire world. They accepted miracle and prophecy as further signs of the direct operation of the Spirit in the latter days. Founder George Fox and schismatic James Naylor had both worked the miracle cures which accompany inspiration in scripture examples; Naylor was supposed to have resurrected a woman in 1656, and in 1657 Susanna Pearson tried but failed to raise William Pool from the dead.[44]

The Spirit guiding men and women during these few years before the Kingdom did not depart from the Quakers even as their hopes declined for a rapid worldwide Christian conversion. Prophecy and ecstatic religious behavior continued among Quakers long after they had tempered their millennialism to allow for the solid establishment of church societies.[45] As their eschatology changed, so did the nature of their prophecies, from forecasts of the onset of the Kingdom to promises of judgment upon the wicked. Prophecy became an expression of the missionary impulse that had sent Mary Fisher to Constantinople to convert the Sultan, or Thomas Holmes running naked through the streets as a sign to the unrepentant. "I therefore," wrote the fresh convert James Jackson in 1674, "in the powerful Constrainings of this Love, am unwilling to eat my Morsel alone, or to hide my Talent in the Earth." During the same decade, Mary Adams and James Parke warned London of impending judgments. After 1690, the majority of Quakers now opposed to public prophecy, John Love and Thomas Mudd stubbornly pronounced warnings in the streets of Bristol. In 1705 James Jackson's friend Anne Steed prophesied in London.[46]

Gratton, *Journal* (1720) 23-25, 72-74; Barry G. Reay, "The Muggletonians," *Journal of Religious History* 9 (1976) 32-49.

44. Endy, *Penn*, 55, 84-89; Geoffrey F. Nuttall, *Studies in Christian Enthusiasm Illustrated from Early Quakerism* (Wallingford, 1948) 47 and his *The Holy Spirit in Puritan Faith and Experience* (Oxford, 1946) esp. 181-84; Henry J. Cadbury, *George Fox's "Book of Miracles"* (Cambridge, 1948); T.L. Underwood, "Early Quaker Eschatology," in Toon, *Puritans the Millennium and Israel*, 91-103.

45. Cf. Richard T. Vann, *The Social Development of English Quakerism 1655-1755* (Cambridge, Mass., 1969) 122-23, 168. The most famous instance of ecstatic religious behavior among later Quakers was at Waltham Abbey in 1679, where the entire congregation, swayed by the children, broke out in tears and trembling: Christopher Taylor and Francis Taylor, *A Testimony to the Lord's Power and Blessed Appearance In and Amongst Children* (1680). Similar behavior was noted in the church of the Independent minister, Richard Davis, in the 1690s: Norman Glass, *The Early History of the Independent Church at Rothwell, alias Rowell, in Northamptonshire* (Northampton, 1871) 85-87.

46. Vann, *Social Development of English Quakerism*, 113-14; [Charles Leslie], *A Defence of a Book Intituled, The Snake in the Grass* (1700) 47; James Jackson, *The Strong Man Armed Cast Out* (n.p., 1674); Russell S. Mortimer, "Warnings and Prophecies," *Journal of the*

Whether within or beyond the confines of the Church of England, men and women continued to hold millennial beliefs. After 1660 or so, however, these beliefs were sustained outside of the ethos of cataclysm, and the axis of millenarianism rested upon the ethos of the New Jerusalem and the ethos of judgment, both of which demanded social allegiance and coherence. Broad churchmen who were millenarians lived within the context of the New Jerusalem, and in their scientific as well as clerical enterprises they evinced an ecumenism which had at its basis a desire for the apocalyptic union of Protestantism. For them the act of prophecy had much less to do with inspiration than it did with clear perception, clear and common discourse.[47] John Mason's holy ground at Water Stratford was no cataclysmic territory but one which had been settled along the borders of pentecost and New Jerusalem; for him and his followers, the act of prophecy was the act of witnessing, public, joyous, assured. Philadelphians and Quakers, sadly conscious of a receding New Jerusalem, obstinately used that image of universal spiritual change as the focus for the tensions in their circles between judgment and pentecost. Millenarian Quakers shouted and published their judgments of a world which had allowed the New Jerusalem to slip away. Prophecy for the Philadelphians split in all directions and could accommodate nearly any model; for this reason among others they would be the first major group of English followers of the Camisard *inspirés*.

Although their critics would identify the French Prophets most often with the early Quakers and John Mason's adherents, followers would include Sir Richard Bulkeley, who with his friend Bishop William Lloyd was moved to the study of scripture prophecy by Bishop John Fell at Oxford,[48] and Rev. John Foster, prebendary of Salisbury Cathedral. Some followers would resemble Laurence Clarkson, who dared a remarkable but not unique religious voyage through seventeenth-century England, having been in sequence a Presbyterian, an Independent, a Baptist, a Seeker, a Ranter and finally a Muggletonian.[49] For others, the

---

Friends Historical Society 44 (1952) 14-20; James Parke, *A Warning to London in Particular* (1676); Henry Pickworth, *A Charge of Error* (1716) Anne Steed's Account, 329-33.

47. On contemporary attempts to unite Protestant churches throughout Europe, see Norman Sykes, *William Wake Archbishop of Canterbury 1657-1737* (Cambridge, 1957) II, ch. 6; Carpenter, *The Protestant Bishop,* 281-374; on reform activities see below. On language see James Downey, *The Eighteenth Century Pulpit* (Oxford, 1969) 22-27; Michel Foucault, *The Order of Things: An Archaeology of the Human Sciences* (New York, 1970) 78-87.

48. Lambeth Palace, MSS 931, f. 14, Lloyd letter to Tenison, 11/19/1712; Sir Richard Bulkeley, *An Answer to Several Treatises lately Published on the Subject of the Prophets* (1708) 94.

49. Morton, *World of the Ranters,* 115.

French Prophets would be no prophetic port of call but a home away from home, the final dispensation of the True Church.

There would be furious opposition to the *inspirés* and their followers, for the original Camisard rhetoric and ethos of cataclysm were not congenial to an England which, despite an Act of Settlement (1701) denying the throne to James' sons, and Anne's peaceful succession in 1702, still was jealous for the security of the Protestant kingdom. But just as millenarian broad churchmen had severed the relation between cataclysm and New Jerusalem, just as Quakers and Philadelphians played the New Jerusalem against inspiration and judgment, so the first English followers of the *inspirés* would transform the millenarian ethos of the Camisards. The New Jerusalem would come to mean something different in London than in the embattled Cévennes, and warring prophecy would encourage a different sort of martyrdom.

Appealing as frequently to Anglicans as to dissenters, the French Prophets would confront English society with a turbulent and menacing millenarianism. The potential power of the French Prophets lay in their unusual ability to attract millenarians of all persuasions and from every ethos. Fear of this power, as well as of the original ethos of the Camisards, was a major factor in the English reception of the *inspirés*. The sentiments of English society, unlike those of Desert Huguenots, were not squarely behind prophets of an imminent, vengeful judgment.

The Huguenot Community in London

A second factor in the soured reception of the prophets was the complex of tensions within the Huguenot refugee community in England. Aided and supported in the main by broad churchmen and royal grants, the Huguenots were at pains to define for themselves a respectful role vis-à-vis the established church. Huguenot clergy dissociated themselves from religious "enthusiasm" as zealously as the Huguenot Meric Casaubon had described and explained it.[50] Huguenots in England had therefore pragmatic if not theological scruples about prophets who might upset the working relationship between the non-episcopal French Protestants and their episcopal Anglican benefactors.

Huguenot reliance upon the good will of the established church led indirectly to an important schism within the exile community, particularly in London where the large majority of emigrants settled. Before 1660,

---

50. Meric Casaubon, *A Treatise concerning Enthusiasme* (1655).

there existed two major French Protestant churches in the capital, one at Threadneedle Street (founded 1550) and a second in the chapel of the former palace of Savoy (founded 1641). Both Threadneedle Street and the Savoy adhered to the liturgy and ritual of French Calvinism. After the Restoration, Charles II insisted on the reconstitution of the Savoy as a church conforming to Anglican ritual and answerable to the Bishop of London. Henceforth, Calvinist Threadneedle Street and conformist Savoy would represent variant styles in Huguenot religious accommodation to English life. The fifty thousand refugees who arrived between 1660 and 1706 ranged themselves on both sides of the split and so firmed the dichotomy. Of the new London Huguenot churches, half were Calvinist, half conformist; elsewhere the government policy favoring conformist churches was more pronounced.[51]

The expansion of the exile community in London, especially in Soho (with ten new churches or annexes) and Spitalfields (with seven), produced a welter of stubbornly independent congregations. They acknowledged no central authority among themselves and set up no comprehensive system of jurisdictions such as had existed in France before the Revocation. Younger churches resented the attempted dominion of the Savoy, and the Savoy itself engaged in contests with Anglican authorities.[52] The disunity of the proliferating churches was aggravated by the surplus of Huguenot ministers. Nearly one hundred pastors scavenged for positions in London after the exile from France in 1685. Huguenot churches, even those which created nonresident ministerial appointments in order to cope with the problem, found themselves host to the jousting and scuttling of men anxious for place and bitter over their loss of status in exile.[53]

51. Fernand de Schickler, *Les églises françaises de Londres après la Révocation de l'Edit de Nantes* (1886) and his "Un chapitre de l'histoire des églises du refuge de langue française en Angleterre après la Révocation de l'Edit de Nantes. Les Deux Patentes," *HSL Proceedings* 6 (1901) 269-71; Robin D. Gwynn, "The Distribution of Huguenot Refugees in England," *HSL Proceedings* 21 (1969) 435. It is significant that the first new London congregation, formed by Dr. Pierre Allix in 1686, was conformist. Allix was a devoted millenarian; his willingness to practice Anglican ritual stemmed probably from his own dependence upon and connections with the millenarian broad churchmen William Lloyd and Gilbert Burnet. Hart, *William Lloyd,* 68-71; Cambridge University, Add. MSS 2608, XII, Allix's Treatise on Antichrist; **Pierre Bayle,** *Dictionnaire historique et critique* (4th ed.; Amsterdam, 1730) I, 658n., article "Braunbom"; Jacob, *Newtonians,* 129.
52. Francis H.W. Sheppard, "Huguenots in Spitalfields and Soho," *HSL Proceedings* 21 (1969) 357-59; Carpenter, *The Protestant Bishop,* 338-40.
53. Phyllis Bultmann and William A. Bultmann, "Claude Groteste de la Mothe and the Church of England, 1685 to 1713," *HSL Proceedings* 20 (1959) 90-91; David E.A. Agnew, *Protestant Exiles from France* (3rd ed.; 1896) II, 361. I have not seen Robin D. Gwynn, "The Ecclesiastical Organization of French Protestants in England in the Later 17th Century, with **Special Reference to London,"** Ph.D. thesis, University of London, 1973(?).

On only two occasions before the arrival of the *inspirés* did the Huguenot churches of London act in concert. Both actions had come under pressure from English authorities. In 1691, hoping to put an end to contemporary fears that Huguenot pastors brought Socinian doctrines with them from the France of sceptics as well as Catholics, Henry Compton, Bishop of London, asked the refugee ministers to declare unanimously their belief in the Trinity denied by Socinians. They did so. In 1706, implying that the refugees were more sympathetic to their French homeland than they were enemies of Roman Catholicism, Secretary of State Harley provoked the Huguenot churches to a common declaration of support for the conduct of the war against France.[54] Compton, a Whig and broad churchman, had hoped to protect the Huguenots from Tory attack; Harley, a Tory in 1706, was subtly pursuing his party's strategy of undermining Whig support. It was the necessity of remaining in the good graces of the Whigs, rather than any issue of church doctrine or organization, that stimulated these two otherwise negligible but united gestures.[55]

Huguenot attachment to the congealing Whig party was particularly important as emigration increased and Huguenots hoped for general naturalization acts. Since 1681, the refugees could apply, free of charge, for denizenship, but denizens had restricted rights and were unable to bequeath landed wealth. Bills granting full citizenship for Huguenot refugees were several times laid before Parliament, but none was passed until 1709. Before the Glorious Revolution, opponents had based their arguments upon fears of Popery, wary of the coincidence between royal

---

54. Bultmann and Bultmann, "Claude Groteste de la Mothe," 90-91; HAL, MS 8, Threadneedle Street Church, Livre des actes de 1692/93 à 1708, pp. 494-96; Carpenter, *The Protestant Bishop*, 328.

55. Properly speaking, there were no full-fledged parties in the reigns of William III or Anne. Contemporaries did identify interests which seemed to oppose one another more often than not: normally, those called Whigs supported both the political principles of the 1688 Revolution and its consequent religious compromises, while Tories accepted the Revolution but would allow it little bearing on the established church or the integrity of local government. Whigs therefore tended to defend a modicum of religious toleration while Tories attacked dissent. Perhaps the briefest, clearest discussion of a topic so thoroughly covered by historians who disagree is in Christopher Hill, *The Century of Revolution 1603-1714* (New York, 1961) 280-84. See also Geoffrey Holmes, *British Politics in the Age of Anne* (1967). Holmes believes that the two parties sharpened their contours during Anne's reign. For a good account of the confusing turns in the relationship between political parties and religious allegiances, see G.V. Bennett, *The Tory Crisis in Church and State 1688-1730: The Career of Francis Atterbury Bishop of Rochester* (Oxford, 1975); J.P. Kenyon, *Revolution Principles: The Politics of Party, 1689-1720* (New York, 1977).

support for naturalizing French aliens and royal sympathy for the Catholic French monarchy. After 1688, high churchmen, unwilling to recognize fully the Calvinist Huguenots, combined with Tory leaders to fend off all Whig attempts at the passage of a citizenship act. The failure of broad churchmen and Whigs to secure much earlier a general naturalization act was one source of another division within Huguenot ranks, that between denizen and citizen. While the poor might become denizens if they had time to register, those Huguenots with wealth and influence could yet become full citizens by having their names listed on private naturalization bills, several of which were passed before 1709.[56]

Citizenship problems were just a small part of the social and economic tensions among the refugees, tensions which reached their height in London. By 1696, possibly twenty thousand Huguenot weavers, most of them poor and, that year especially, in great economic distress, had settled in Spitalfields and adjoining areas in northeastern London. None too prosperous in the best of times, journeyman weavers (and the more prosperous master weavers) were resented by native Englishmen who could not compete with the superior techniques of the French. English weavers suspected the foreigners of working for lower wages and diverting the country's wealth from honest English labor. Only in 1703 did the Weavers Company of London relax its regulations to admit alien weavers as masters.[57] (See Plate III and Figure 2 for London maps.)

On the other side of London, in Soho, lived most of the wealthier refugees. Between 1685 and 1710, more than 150 goldsmiths, silversmiths, jewelers and watchmakers had set up shop in the city. They usually flourished; Huguenot merchants exploited their overseas contacts with other exiles in Holland and Brandenburg. Others had managed to escape with their wealth before the Revocation. Whatever the sources of their

---

56. Caroline Robbins, "A Note on General Naturalization under the Later Stuarts and a Speech in the House of Commons on the Subject in 1664," *Journal of Modern History* 34 (1962) 168-77; Roy A. Sundstrom, "Aid and Assimilation: A Study of Economic Support Given French Protestants in England, 1680-1727," Ph.D. thesis, Kent State University, 1972, 185-88, 204-05; William A. Shaw, ed., *Letters of Denization and Acts of Naturalization for Aliens in England and Ireland 1603-1700* in *HSL Publications* 18 (1911) introduction, and lists of private naturalization bills; Malcolm R. Thorp, "The Anti-Huguenot Undercurrent in Late Seventeenth-Century England," *HSL Proceedings* 22 (1976) 569-80; Keith Feiling, *A History of the Tory Party 1640-1714* (Oxford, 1924) 373, 377, 403 ff.

57. Ogg, *James II and William III*, 292; Ephraim Lipson, *The Economic History of England* (1931) II, 34, 101-02 and III, 52; P. Thornton and N. Rothstein, "The Importance of the Huguenots in the London Silk Industry," *HSL Proceedings* 20 (1964) 87; W.S. Holdsworth, *A History of English Law* (1938) XI, 420; E.H. Varley, "The Occupations of Protestant Refugees in the 17th Century," *Geography* 24 (1939) 131-34.

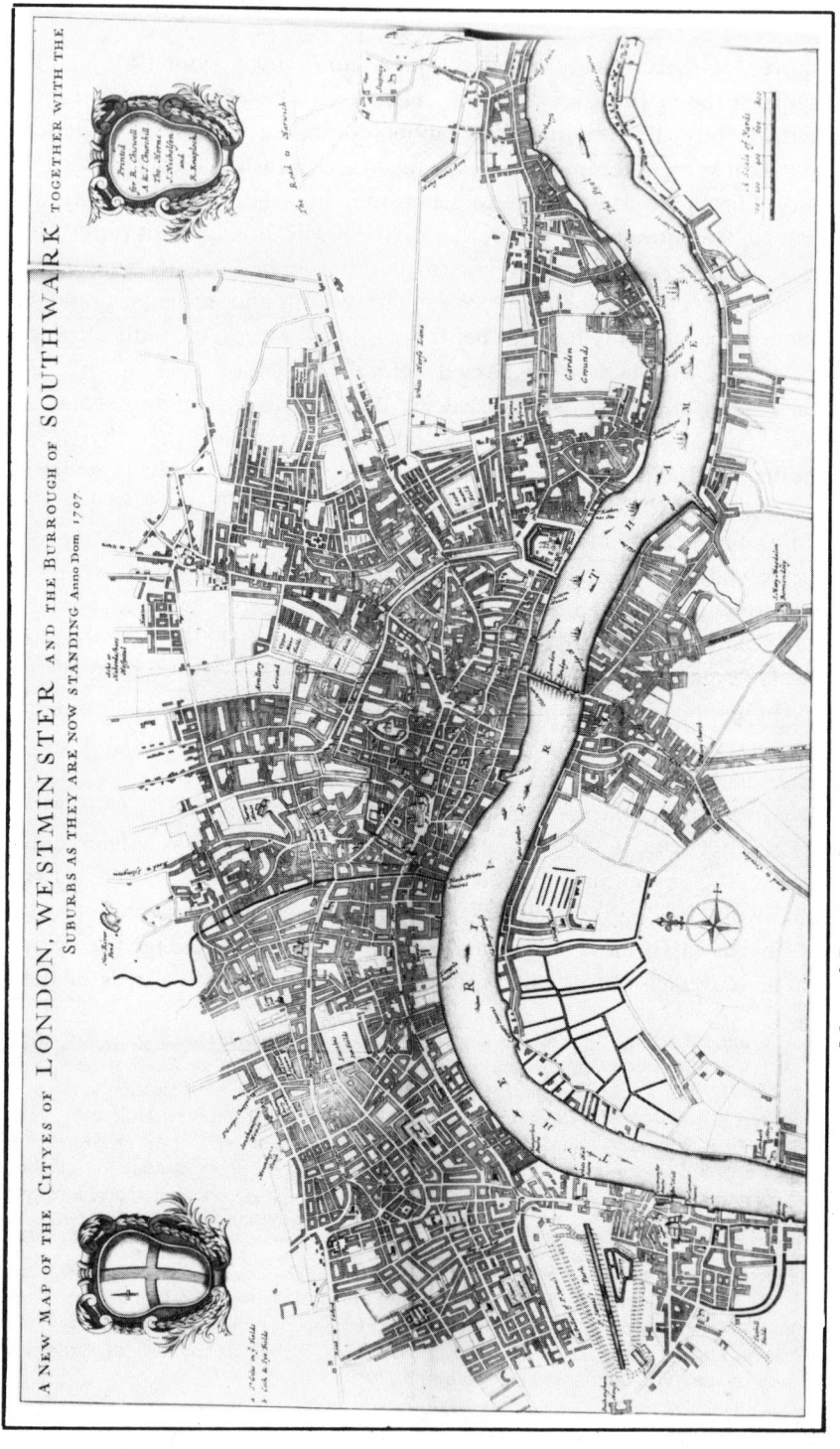

PLATE III. Map of London, from Edward Hatton, *A New View of London* (1708).

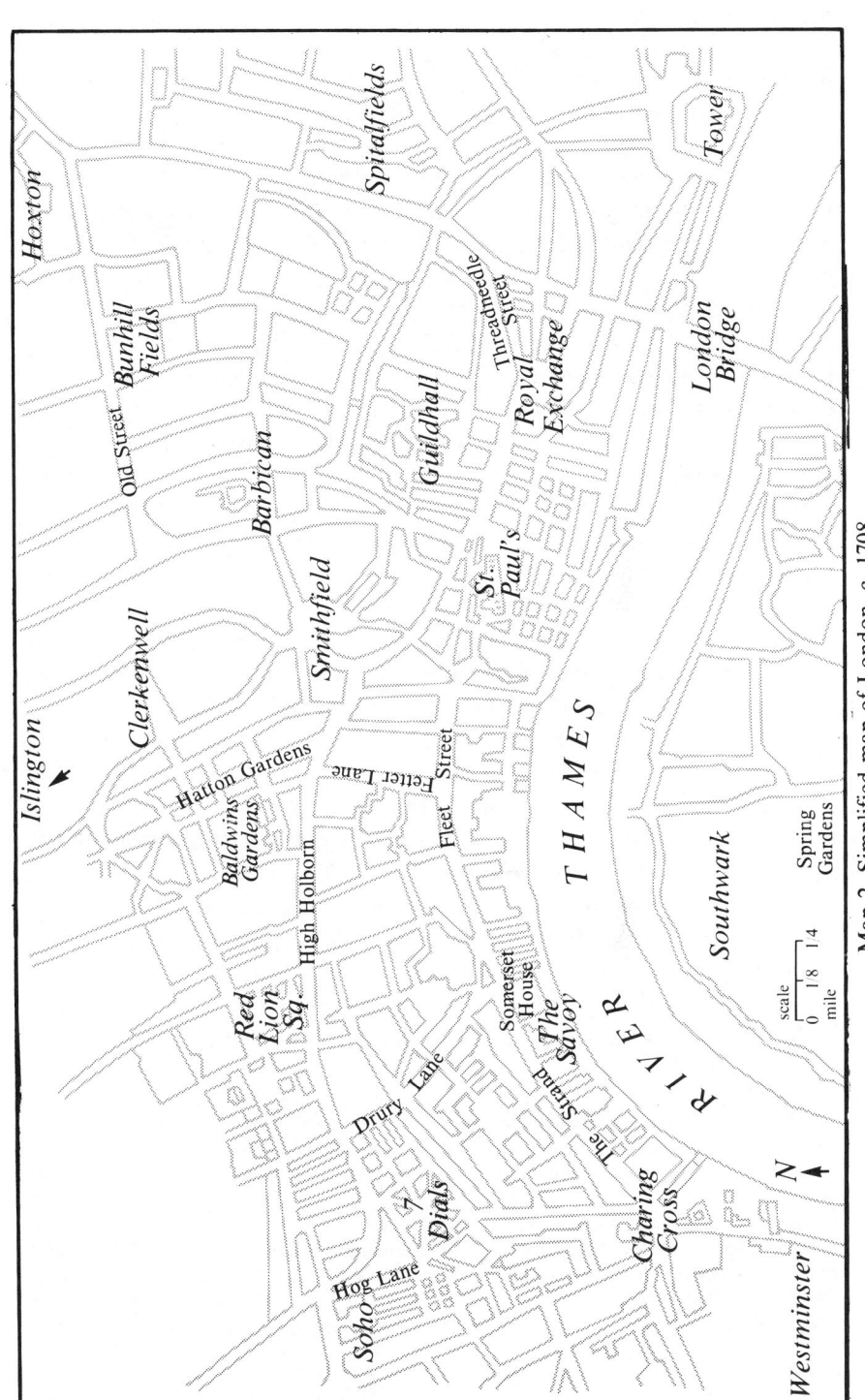

Map 2. Simplified map of London, c. 1708.

livelihood, ten per cent of the investors in Bank of England stock during this period were Huguenot refugees or their children.[58]

The gap between weavers and investors had more than economic import. Due to the nature of Huguenot emigration, economic differences were bound to social differences that penetrated the entire community. Those refugees who resumed their trades and prospered in England—goldsmiths, lawyers, merchants—were more likely to have urban backgrounds and to feel more at ease in London than originally rural weavers. Also, weavers found the status of their occupation significantly lower than it had been in France, while Huguenot gentlemen might profit from their education as tutors in the houses of Whig nobility. The disparity between rich and poor was a disparity between urban and rural, socially acceptable and unacceptable.[59]

Royal and national charity for the poor refugees did not reduce tensions in Spitalfields and Soho. Although Charles II and James II had authorized collections which netted £85,000, and though Parliament under William and Mary voted £15,000 per year after 1696 for Huguenot assistance, the monies were distributed in such a way as to emphasize social distinctions. The French Committee which administered the national charity assigned aid according to social rank. This encouraged emigrants who in France had wealth and social standing to retain their social standing without the corresponding wealth. For example, in 1705 the gentleman Olivier de Brossard des Preaux and his wife, both in their forties, received £16 in aid; the same year the common people Jean Guillemot, 65, "fort incommode," and his wife Susanne, 46, received £1.15.[60] The distribution enforced a social hierarchy inherited from France and not altogether functional in English surroundings. From 1705, the French Committee was accused of fraud by men who held that the common people did not receive their proper share of the charity monies. The imbroglio of accusations was so tangled that even the Camisard *inspirés* would be cited by one author as

---

58. Alice C. Carter, "The Huguenot Contribution to the Early Years of the Funded Debt, 1694-1714," *HSL Proceedings* 19 (1955) 21-41; Warren C. Scoville, *The Persecution of Huguenots and French Economic Development 1680-1720* (Berkeley and Los Angeles, 1960) 324-35.

59. Cf. Sundstrom, "Aid and Assimilation," 164.

60. William A. Shaw, "The English Government and the Relief of Protestant Refugees," *English Historical Review* 9 (1894) 346-51; E.S. de Beer, "The Revocation of the Edict of Nantes and English Public Opinion," *HSL Proceedings* 18 (1950) 380; Comitté François, *Estats de la distribution de la somme de douze mille livres sterling* (1705) 1, 31. All four emigrants became French Prophets.

part of the scheming of the Committee; such controversy was symbolic of the socioeconomic problems within the Huguenot community.[61]

Huguenot clergy were caught up in the web of tensions as rich congregation connived against poor and conformist against Calvinist. Of all refugees, the ministers were under the most psychological strain. Beside ministerial jealousies and financial straits, beside Anglican-Huguenot disputes, ministers had a discomforting ambivalence toward their own exile. On one hand they regretted leaving their French congregations destitute of spiritual support; between 1686 and 1688 exiled ministers in London had considered sponsoring forty among themselves to return to France and preach in secret to the faithful. On the other hand, they sought to justify their forced emigration on spiritual grounds, intuiting some divine purpose in the persecution and exile of the faithful. They could not but resent Huguenots who had lived for years as *Nouveaux Convertis*, who had not abandoned everything to continue in the open practice of their faith. They would have difficulty expressing sympathy for the unordained *prédicants* who replaced the pastors in Languedoc and who reminded the ministers of their own (too hasty?) departure. How much less sympathy might they have for the *inspirés*, neither ordained nor well educated, who were rumored to have administered the sacraments?[62]

The gulf between ministers and prophets had been fashioned by time and geography. The London ministers had not preached in France for at least twenty years. Their vision of that country and their experience of Huguenot worship in France pre-dated the Revocation. Further, had they stayed, the majority of them would not have shared the Cévenol experience. Like most of the London refugees, the ministers came primarily from northwestern France.[63] If the years of exile and different geographical origins were not enough to distance the ministers from the prophets, age completed the separation. Huguenot clergy in London were on an average thirty years older than the prophets; an entire generation and sometimes two stood between them. Minister and prophet sang the same psalms, but each worshipped in a context foreign to the other.

The Huguenot community in London to which the *inspirés* made their

---

61. *Les malversations du comitté françois* (1708) 10-11; Sundstrom, "Aid and Assimilation," 132-65; Jean Claude, *Short Account of the Persecutions* (3rd ed.; 1708) preface, 30-31. Carpenter, *The Protestant Bishop,* 336; Michael Malard, *The Proselytish Hercules Against the Mystery of Iniquity* (1720) 9-10; *English Post* No. 1328 (April 4-6, 1709).
62. Cf. O. Douen, *Les premiers pasteurs du Désert* (Paris, 1879) I, 134, 160-61.
63. Charles Weiss, *History of the French Protestant Refugees,* trans. Henry W. Herbert (New York, 1854) 248-49.

first appeal was veined with the tensions of exile. Followers of the prophets would come from the wealthy and the poor, from natives of Normandy as well as of Languedoc; they would be gentlemen and they would be weavers, living in Soho or Spitalfields. But others would oppose the prophets, be they gentlemen, weavers, or ministers. By virtue of their personal conflict with the ministry, the prophets in London would become a focal point for the emotions of a fragmented refugee society. The sentiments of London Huguenots, unlike those of the Desert, were not squarely behind the new prophets.

The Movement for Spiritual Reform

The nature of popular religiosity and religious controversy among English Protestants was a third factor in the reception of the *inspirés*. Although jeremiads about the decline of piety were abroad throughout the seventeenth century as each faction applied its own favorite criteria of Christian behavior, after 1689 Protestants of many persuasions came to agree that theirs was peculiarly an age of irreligion. "How much is the world and many the highest Pretenders to Religion in it, alienated and changed from True Religion, and the Scope and Design thereof, in its primitive Purity and Plainness?" lamented the "Deist turned Christian" Thomas Emes in 1698.[64] This general sense of decline was in one regard a delayed reaction to the supposed immorality of the Restoration period, its profane theater, its libertine court, its all-too-Catholic monarchs.[65] In another regard, it was a reaction to the influential principles of deism.

Deism was itself a movement to restore the possibility of belief in an era that witnessed profound challenges to the Christian faith. Biblical scholars armed with elaborate textual apparatus were uncovering the numerous mistranslations from original scripture, errors and substitutions barnacled by centuries of tradition to the pristine Word. Science, under the sway of Newtonian mechanics, seemed to reveal the natural laws by which, without mystery or miracle, the universe was regulated. People had new respect for the wisdom of the East, the Turkish philosopher and Chinese sage who had lived moral lives without the aid of Christianity.[66]

---

64. Thomas Emes, *The Atheist Turned Deist, and the Deist turned Christian: or, the Reasonableness and Union of Natural, and the True Christian Religion* (1698) 185.

65. See David Foxon, *Libertine Literature in England 1660-1747* (New Hyde Park, 1965), but cf. Peter Laslett and Karla Oosterveen, "Long-term Trends in Bastardy in England," *Population Studies* 27 (1973) 255-86.

66. Frank E. Manuel, *The Eighteenth Century Confronts the Gods* (Cambridge, Mass., 1959) 35; Paul Hazard, *The European Mind: The Critical Years (1680-1715)*, trans. J. Lewis

Deists responded to these challenges by advocating the primitive plainness of religion itself. Accepting the probability that scripture accounts were historically unreliable, accepting too the assumptions of experimental science about the natural order of the world, the deists proposed to measure all revelations, natural or divine, by the inch-marks of reason. "For as 'tis by reason we arrive at the certainty of God's own existence," wrote John Toland in his famous deist manifesto, *Christianity not Mysterious* (1696), "so we cannot otherwise discern his revelations but by their conformity with our natural notices of him." Since, as commonly believed, the gifts of miracle and prophecy had ceased after apostolic times, good people, Christians or not, must conduct themselves in accord with the moral principles which biblical miracle and prophecy had simply highlighted.[67]

Resort to reason, the universal human faculty, could reawaken popular religion. True Christianity—no mirage of supernatural events—was well within the scope of the poor and the illiterate, for, as Toland wrote, "the uncorrupted doctrines of Christianity are not above their reach or comprehension, but the gibberish of your divinity schools they understand not." Each person, according to the deists, had something within that enabled an appreciation of morality, if only humans were not led astray into thickets of wonder stories, meaningless ceremony and theological wrangling.[68]

Churchmen and nonconformists alike took offense at this approach to the renewal of religion, for it exalted human reason to the detriment of scripture and church order. To some, indeed, deists seemed to imply that Christian institutions and hierarchy had only a social value. To others, the deist interpretation of the Bible verged upon heretical views of the Holy Writ. Detractors associated deism with one of two heresies: Arianism, which denied Jesus' full divinity, and Socinianism, which disregarded the authority of scripture and denied completely the divinity of Jesus. The

---

May (New Haven, 1953). The French Prophet Charles Portales would note in his commonplace book, " 'Tis said, There is Thirty Thousand various Readings which are owned to be crept in[to] the New Testament," Stack MSS 11. Cf. Benjamin Hoadly, *A Brief Vindication of the Antient Prophets* (1709) 21-22.

67. John Toland, *Christianity not Mysterious* (1696) 30, 36, 158-73; Manuel, *Eighteenth Century Confronts the Gods,* 71; Hazard, *European Mind,* 255; Roger Lee Emerson, "English Deism 1670-1755: An Enlightenment Challenge to Orthodoxy," Ph.D. thesis, Brandeis University, 1962, esp. 37, 43; Ernest C. Mossner, *Bishop Butler and the Age of Reason* (New York, 1936) 53; cf. Margaret C. Jacob, "Newtonianism and the Origins of the Enlightenment: A Reassessment," *Eighteenth-Century Studies* 11 (1977) 1-25.

68. Toland, *Christianity not Mysterious,* 147; Manuel, *Eighteenth Century Confronts the Gods,* 59, 61.

similarity between deists, atheists, Arians and Socinians, in the opinion of the orthodox, lay in their simplistic desire to avoid the incomprehensible.[69]

Replying to Toland, Peter Browne asked whether "there be not some things in the Gospel concerning which we are bound to believe that there is much more in them than we are now able to comprehend." The standard orthodox answer to deism was that human reason was too feeble to understand all revelation, that true Christianity was not as easily or as commonly recognized as deists claimed. Finding people swamped by the "mysteries" of Christianity and deluged by theological jargon, however, deists wished to renew religion by exposing people to the bare bones of belief, devoid of those elements incompatible with reason.[70]

Those who rejected deist strategy and philosophy had still to deal with the religious decadence which they saw mirrored in the deist critique of revealed religion. They opted for societies for religious reform. Operating upon the belief that declining piety was the result of ignorance of God's Word, they sought to spread scriptural knowledge to the most humble. They had hopes too of returning to the spirit of the early Christians. John Lacy, member of the Societies for the Reformation of Manners, wrote in 1704,

> In the Primitive Ages of Christianity they say, there was, under Variety of Administrations, an illustrious Union of Affections; Light and Love were not so disjoined; Humility made them willing to stoop mutually to one another; but is the Report hereof to be disowned, or has that one, Uniting, Spirit, the Coelestial Dove, withdrawn from this Relapsed and Apostate World.[71]

---

69. Roland N. Stromberg, *Religious Liberalism in Eighteenth-Century England* (1954) 9-10, 34, 50; Walker, *Decline of Hell*, 9, 16, 26; Rosalie L. Colie, "Spinoza in England, 1665-1730," *Proceedings of the American Philosophical Society* 107 (1963) 183-219 and her "Spinoza and the Early English Deists," *Journal of the History of Ideas* 20 (1959) 23-46; John Redwood, *Reason, Ridicule and Religion: The Age of Enlightenment in England 1660-1750* (Cambridge, Mass., 1976). In October, 1710, the millenarian William Whiston was expelled from his professorship of mathematics at Cambridge for defending Arian positions; see Eamon Duffy, " 'Whiston's Affair': The Trials of a Primitive Christian 1709-1714," *Journal of Ecclesiastical History* 27 (1976) 129-50.

70. Peter Browne, *A Letter in Answer to a Book entitled Christianity not Mysterious* (Dublin, 1697) excerpted in E. Graham Waring, ed., *Deism and Natural Religion: A Source Book* (New York, 1967) 28; Stromberg, *Religious Liberalism,* 22, 69.

71. John Lacy, *A Letter to Sir H. Mackworth, Concerning His Treatise About the late Occasional Bill* (2nd ed. [?] 1704) 12. Lacy, a Presbyterian, was defending the right of dissenters to establish nominal conformity with the established church by attending Anglican services occasionally. Tories throughout Anne's reign would push for and eventually achieve an Occasional Conformity Bill that would prevent civil officials from meeting their obligations toward the established church in such a nominal way that they could be conscientious

In this "Relapsed and Apostate World," the Societies for the Reformation of Manners (founded 1691) shut down five hundred houses of ill fame, though hampered by the overzealous activities of reformer Sir Richard Bulkeley. They also sponsored the publication of sermons, such as one by the Presbyterian minister Thomas Cotton, who was so far above religious controversy that he could say, "The many Differences, that there are in the World about Religion, speak it Excellent." The Society for Promoting Christian Knowledge (founded 1696) printed and gave away thousands of Bibles and worked closely with the Society for the Propagation of the Gospel in Foreign Parts (founded 1701) to extend Christian brotherhood to American Indians.[72]

What effect the deist debates and the societies for reform had upon the common people is as questionable as the influence of all revival efforts upon the religiosity of England's urban laborers and country cottagers. How typical were the people of the Isle of Axholme in this epoch, "so extreme ignorant that not one in twenty can say the Lord's Prayer right, not one in thirty the Belief?"[73] Perhaps a "*Little* Opera, Called the Old *Creation of the World* Newly Revived," affords some clues to the nature of popular religious belief. The opera, current early in the reign of Queen Anne, played at Bartholomew Fair, a raucous and crowded holiday fair in London for the amusement and enrichment of the poorer folk. If the contents of the opera be any indication of what the common people understood by the Protestant faith, then biblical vengeance and heavenly justice were uppermost in their minds. The opera opened with the creation of Adam and Eve, who were driven from Paradise by Lucifer's "intrigues."

---

dissenters. For a summary of this controversy, see John Flaningam, "The Occasional Conformity Controversy: Ideology and Party Politics, 1697-1711," *Journal of British Studies* 17 (1977) 38-62.

72. W.K. Lowther Clark, *A History of the S.P.C.K.* (1959); Dudley Bahlmann, *The Moral Revolution of 1688* (Hamden, 1968) 19-21 on Bulkeley; Christopher Hill, "Propagating the Gospel," in H.E. Bell and R.L. Ollard, eds., *Historical Essays 1600-1750 Presented to David Ogg* (1963) 35-59; Eamon Duffy, "Primitive Christianity Revived: Religious Renewal in Augustan England," in Derek Baker, ed., *Renaissance and Renewal in Christian History,* Studies in Church History, 14 (Oxford, 1977) 287-300; W.A. Speck, "Mandeville and the Eutopia Seated in the Brain," in Irwin Primer, ed., *Mandeville Studies* (The Hague, 1975) 66-79; C.F. Secretan, *Memoirs of the Life and Times of the Pious Robert Nelson* (1860); [Edward Fowler], *A Vindication of an Undertaking of Certain Gentlemen, In Order to the Suppressing of Debauchery, and Profaneness* (1692); T. Sharp, ed., *Life of John Sharp* (1825) I, 174-78; Thomas Cotton, *A Sermon Preached to Societies for Reformation of Manners* (1702) 14.

73. Samuel Wesley, writing in 1702, cited in W.H. Hutton, *The English Church from the Accession of Charles I to the Death of Anne 1625-1714* (1903) 307. Axholme was in Lincolnshire, near Epworth, where John Wesley was born in 1703.

Cain killed Abel, Abraham offered up his son Isaac, and (immediately after) the Three Wisemen worshipped the infant Jesus. Joseph and Mary fled to Egypt, King Herod persecuted Jesus, rich Dives spurned Lazarus and both died. At the apocalyptic finale, spectators found "Rich Dives in Hell, and Lazarus in Abraham's Bosom, seen in a most glorious Object, all in machines, descending in a Throne, Guarded with multitudes of Angels, with the Breaking of the Clouds, discovering the Palaces of the Sun, in double and treble Prospects."[74] Was this how the majority of people made sense of the Old and New Testaments—original sin as part of a plot, the faithful suffering divine trials time and again, and at last a marvelous reward for the downtrodden Lazarus?

Such an episodic history of Judaism and Christianity conformed to anti-Catholic attitudes which best characterize the wide spectrum of English Protestantism in the late seventeenth century. Scarcely escaped from the perils of a Catholic monarchy, menaced by Jacobite schemes to undo the Glorious Revolution, informed of Catholic Herods and Protestant stamina by the enduringly popular *Book of Martyrs* compiled by John Foxe, all levels of English society could share a hatred of Catholicism. This negative expression, and possibly definition, of Protestant faith was scarce bolted to any theology; rather, anti-Catholicism was a political and social attitude. With doubts as to his parishioners' theological grounding, one "Country-Parson" had warned them to refrain from argument with Catholics and to answer "That you understand very little of the Privileges of the Church of Rome. That to know the State of any Foreign Church, required more Skill and Reading than can be expected from Persons of your mean Condition."[75] It took little skill or reading to make Catholic plotters into the agents of Lucifer (or of Antichrist), and to interpret the travails of the Civil War and the Restoration as part of a continuing martyrdom preliminary to the vision of the "Palaces of the Sun." Beyond this possible glimpse of the plebeian version of Christianity and the common image of Popery, I cannot well describe the religious beliefs or piety of the lower ranks of English society.[76]

---

74. Playbill reproduced in John Ashton, *Social Life in the Reign of Queen Anne* (1882) I, 256-57; cf. the puppet shows described in George Speaight, *The History of the English Puppet Theatre* (New York, 1955) 165.

75. W. Assheton, *The Country-Parson's Admonition to his Parishioners* (1686) 8-9. Cf. O.W. Furley, "The Pope-Burning Processions of the late Seventeenth Century," *History* 44, 30 (1959) 16-23.

76. But see Christopher Hill, "Plebeian Irreligion in 17th Century England," in Manfred Kossok, ed., *Studien Uber die Revolution* (Berlin, 1969) 46-61; Norman Sykes, *Church and State in England in the Eighteenth Century* (2nd ed.; Hamden, 1962); Keith Thomas, *Religion*

The English Setting 67

Among the literate, which by 1700 would include urban artisans and tradespeople as well as merchants and gentry, works on religion and religious devotion were the most widely sold books. Between 1660 and 1711, more than a thousand different titles on religion required reprinting. Whether people practiced what the books preached I do not know, but the most popular books stressed a reliance upon scripture rather than reason, upon revelation rather than tradition. That people preserved their faith despite the obscurity of some biblical passages proved, to the authors of these books, that Christianity was strong and healthy.[77] But the literate might not maintain their healthy religion in a church framework; London, for example, in 1711 had less than forty churches to serve the more than 400,000 Anglicans in the city.[78]

Literate or not, many in England needed no special piety to hope for a

---

and the Decline of Magic (New York, 1971); Alan D. Gilbert, Religion and Society in Industrial England: Church, Chapel and Social Change 1740-1914 (New York, 1976); Peter Burke, "Popular Culture in Seventeenth-Century London," London Journal 3 (1977) 143-62; C. John Sommerville, Popular Religion in Restoration England (Gainesville, 1977); Deborah M. Valenze, "Prophecy and Popular Literature in Eighteenth-Century England," Journal of Ecclesiastical History 29 (1978) 75-92.

Whatever the criteria for popular religiosity—church attendance, alms-giving, knowledge of scripture, sexual morality, adherence to fast days, prevalence of religious prologues to wills—no data is yet complete enough to permit generalization. Most scholars, like Hill and Sykes, believe that church-related practices were declining among the majority (the poor) in England. This may be little more than the obverse of the standard view that Anglican clergymen were not meeting their parochial obligations. Cf. Natalie Zemon Davis, "Some Tasks and Themes in the Study of Popular Religion," in Charles Trinkaus and Heiko A. Oberman, eds., The Pursuit of Holiness in Late Medieval and Renaissance Religion, Studies in Medieval and Reformation Thought, 10 (Leiden, 1974) 307-36.

77. I am borrowing much from Sommerville, Popular Religion. On literacy see also R.M. Wiles, "Middle-Class Literacy in Eighteenth-Century England: Fresh Evidence," in R.F. Brissenden, ed., Studies in the Eighteenth Century (Toronto, 1968) 49-65; Lawrence Stone, "Literacy and Education in England, 1640-1900," Past and Present 42 (1969) 69-139; Margaret Spufford, "Schooling of the Peasantry in Cambridgeshire 1575-1700," Agricultural History Review 18 (1970) supplement, 145-47; Victor E. Neuburg, Popular Education in Eighteenth Century England (1971) esp. ch. 5; R.C. Richardson, "The Diocese of Chester: Religion and Reading in the late Sixteenth and Early Seventeenth Centuries," Local Historian 11, 1 (1974) 14-17; Richard T. Vann, "Literacy in Seventeenth-Century England: Some Hearth-Tax Evidence," Journal of Interdisciplinary History 5 (1974) 287-93; Kenneth Lockridge, Literacy in Colonial New England (New York, 1974); David Cressy, "Literacy in Pre-Industrial England," Societas 4 (1974) 229-40, and idem, "Levels of Illiteracy in England, 1630-1730," The Historical Journal 20 (1977) 1-24.

78. By comparison, Huguenot refugees had 25 churches to serve their London community of 40-50,000: G.M. Trevelyan, England under Queen Anne (1930) I, 58; Esther de Waal, "New Churches in East London in the Early Eighteenth Century," Renaissance and Modern Studies 9 (1965) 98-114; Robin D. Gwynn, "The Distribution of Huguenot Refugees in England. II. London and Its Environs," HSL Proceedings 22 (1976) 509-68.

68 *The English Setting*

Protestant uprising against Louis XIV. Firm enemies of the Papacy, and political opponents of French dominion in Europe, the English public could eagerly support a rebellion that subverted the chief Catholic power on the continent. Plans for the invasion of Languedoc by refugee Huguenot regiments had been afoot among the Protestant allies soon after the start of the War of the League of Augsburg in 1688. French officials by 1690 feared a revolt in the Cévennes as part of the strategy of the League.[79] When the revolt finally broke out in 1702, shortly after Anne succeeded to the throne, English opinion was heavily on the side of the Camisards. Camisard prayers and manifestoes, evidence of a "sublime zeal and piety," had several editions in London, and proposals for the relief of the rebels were widespread.[80] Although efforts to furnish the Camisards with munitions, money and shoes somehow always fell short, the guerilla bands had the favor of the English public.[81]

Rumors of Camisard miracles would add to their appeal. For millenarians, the miracles might confirm the Camisards as one of the witnesses of Revelation; for Huguenot refugees, miracles might prove the divinely ordained nature of their trials in France; for others, miracles could be used

79. P.J. Shears, "Armand de Bourbon, Marquis de Miremont," *HSL Proceedings* 20 (1963 for 1962) 408; L.A. Robertson, "The Relations of William III with the Swiss Protestants, 1689-97," *Transactions of the Royal Historical Society*, 4th ser., 12 (1929) 137-62; Louis de Rouvroy, duc de Saint-Simon, *Mémoires*, ed. A. de Boislisle (Paris, 1895) XI, 66-67, n. 1; Ernest Roschach, ed., *Histoire générale de Languedoc* (Toulouse, 1876) XIV, 1347-48; A.M. de Boislisle, ed., *Correspondance des contrôleurs généraux des finances avec les intendants des provinces* (Paris, 1874) I, 279.

80. There were diverse editions of *The Lawfulness, Glory and Advantages of Giving Immediate and Effectual Relief to the Protestants in the Cévennes* (possibly by Abel Boyer), the third edition of which added *A Form of Prayer, used by the Cévenois in their Assemblies* (1703); a Doctor of the Civil Laws, *A Compleat History of the Cévennes* (1703) included a Camisard manifesto and form of prayer, 196-216. On the English response, see George H. Healey, ed., *The Letters of Daniel Defoe* (Oxford, 1955) 20-21 and n.; Defoe's *Review of the State of the English Nation* III, 59 (May 16, 1706) 34; the quote is from Gilbert Burnet, *History of His Own Time* (1734) II, 357.

Ambivalence about the right to revolt split the Huguenot exile community in Holland and in England. The English were presented with arguments supporting the Camisards as loyal subjects abused as were English Protestants by James II: wrote Boyer(?), the Cévenols "ought not with English Men, and Protestants, to pass for Rebels, since they act upon the same principle, by which the late Revolution was happily accomplished" (pp. 5-6). In turn, scepticism of Camisard piety and miracles was usually limited to those who denied their right to rebel, especially George Hickes and Nathaniel Spinckes, nonjurors. See *Daily Courant* (January 13-20, 1707); *The Cévenois Relieved, Or Else, Europe Enslaved* (1703); Guy Dodge, *Political Theory of the Huguenots of the Dispersion* (New York, 1947) 40-41, 81, 232.

81. *CSPD 1702-03*, 698-705, 710, and *1703-04*, 126-202; *Calendar of Treasury Papers 1702-07*, 562; *Manuscripts of the House of Lords*, new ser., V, 517, 519; "Arris, Robert," *Biographia Navalis*, ed. John Charnock (1794-98) III, 120-24. See also note 33, chapter one.

as evidence against surly atheists and deists who chipped away at the foundations of Christianity. Moreover, an appreciation for the miraculous was not absent from a country which had undergone so much civil and religious strife and come through it all with a few flags flying. Robert Fleming in 1693 reflected this appreciation of the wondrous affairs of England when he wrote,

> it's such in this Age, that the State of Britain and Ireland hath been a Theatre of such Amazing Concussions and Changes, as no History past can bear a Resemblance thereto, in such Surprizing Various Scenes as have been acted therein; nor can any suitable Reflection be on the same, without Admiration, to this day, how these Nations have not been swallowed up, and got safe out of all these Civil Storms that have successively followed each other. . . .[82]

There were as well some less earthshaking miracles in England: between 1693 and 1695 a spate of miraculous cures took place in and near London. Mary Maillard, a Huguenot, was cured of lameness in 1693 by the power of prayer and the reading of scripture. With her example in mind, the husband of the lame Elizabeth Savage read aloud from the Bible and praised the Lord "for showing his Power in so wonderful a manner, at such a time as this, when Atheism and Infidelity so much abound." Shortly, Mrs. Savage too was restored to perfect health. In the following year, Baptists Lydia Mills and Susannah Arch were cured by wonderful religious means. The cures were written up, published, and widely disseminated. Early in 1694, the Presbyterian Elias Pledger recorded in his diary that he was "much affected with the late miracles wrought upon Mary Malliard [sic] a French refugee, and Mrs. Savage in Moorfields, and David Wright a Shepherd at Hitchin."[83]

The Camisard prophets entered a London in which the illiterate had sympathies for the victims of Catholic persecution but suspicions of Frenchmen; in which the literate, aware of controversy over prophecy and miracles, had not forsworn the possibility of either but wanted a vital

---

82. Robert Fleming, *The Present Aspect of our Times, And of the Extraordinary Conjunction of Things therein* (1694). Fleming, however, saw the miraculous teetering of the English nation as a sign of the nearness of apocalyptic catastrophe.

83. *A True Relation of the Wonderful Cure of Mary Maillard* (1694); *The Happy Damsel* (1693) reprinted with discussion in Hyder E. Rollins, ed., *The Pack of Autolycus* (Cambridge, Mass., 1927) 229-34; *A Narrative of the Late Extraordinary Cure Wrought in an Instant upon Mrs. Elizabeth Savage* (1694); *A Relation of the Miraculous Cure of Susannah Arch* (1695); *A Relation of the Miraculous Cure of Mrs. Lydia Hills* (1695); Dr. Williams's Library, MSS 28.4, Pledger diary, f. 60v. Cf. Roach, *The Great Crisis,* 11. There was another cure in Colchester in 1705; two of the four witnesses (Hicks and Todd) would become French Prophets: *Narrative of the miraculous cure of Anne Munnings* (reprint; Totham, 1847).

national church; and in which the campaigning reformers deplored the immorality of the age but wished to renew religion through scripture. The common people might regard the new prophets as Protestant guerillas and miraculous survivors of Catholic violence, or as Frenchmen, likely Jesuit plotters in an intrigue against Church and Queen. In the face of new prophecy and wonder-working, opponents of deism could choose to exalt the prophets as evidence of the primacy of revelation or could determine to defend Christianity from those who, like deists, made a mockery of original revelation. Reformers might acclaim the prophets' blasts against English religious "deadness" as welcome evangelism for religious revival, or as superfluous and exaggerated sermons undermining the credibility of true evangelical endeavors. Thomas Emes, John Lacy, Sir Richard Bulkeley, and in the beginning Thomas Cotton would believe the new prophets to be possessed of the genuine apostolic spirit; Cotton would later decide, with many other reformers, that the prophets subverted Christian piety.[84]

Whatever the social or theological context, there were latent in English society convictions that ran counter to one another, that might lead one person to follow the prophets and another, of the same social standing or general religious beliefs, to detest them. Responses to the prophets were as various as the many natures of popular religion. The notoriety of the prophets would be due in good measure to the fact that their claims to prophecy and miracle put them in the center of heated controversies about the role of the church, reason, and revelation.

So it was that in 1706 in London, prophets from the Cévennes, predicting an imminent Second Coming, could expect a mixed reception. They might anticipate a sympathetic audience from diverse parts of society—from Anglican prelates to the linen draper and the tinplate-worker's wife who signed affidavits for Elizabeth Savage, from poor and illiterate Spitalfields weavers with relatives in Languedoc to the Huguenot diplomat, the marquis de Miremont. If the Camisard prophets were not

---

84. Another man early involved with the French Prophets, although probably not as committed as Thomas Cotton, was also very active with the Society for Promoting Christian Knowledge: Sir John Philipps. Philipps was the sponsor of the Welsh evangelist Griffith Jones and would later be a strong Methodist supporter. See Thomas Shankland, "Sir John Philipps; The Society for Promoting Christian Knowledge; and the Charity-School Movement in Wales, 1699-1737," *Transactions of the Honourable Society of Cymmrodorion Session 1904-5* (1906) 74-216; John McLeish, *Evangelical Religion and Popular Education* (1969) 6-7, 15-17, 29; Honourable Society of Cymmrodorion, *The Dictionary of Welsh Biography Down to 1940* (1959) 755.

greeted as warmly as they hoped, it was because the millennium and prophecy had a distinctly different sense in England than in the mountains of Languedoc.

The *inspirés* arrived in England during the reign of Queen Anne, whose death in 1714 would signal the end of the Stuarts and the beginning of Hanoverian times. By 1706 the War of the Spanish Succession against France has lasted four years and would last six years more, conducted by the Duke of Marlborough. In 1706 the English did not yet dominate the seas, and they had but recently grasped the key to financial stability. Industrial progress lay ahead, foreshadowed in 1705 by Thomas Newcomen's steam engine for pumping water at coal mines, but people were more impressed by the textile looms and papermaking techniques brought to light by Huguenot refugees.

Through London, the prophets' main port and harbor, religious currents ran with especial confusion past the meetinghouses of Quakers, Baptists, Muggletonians, and Philadelphians. One-fifth of the city's population was composed of dissenters and Huguenot refugees. The "mobile" tumbled through city quarters, shouting the slogans of the "Church in Danger." Men in the new and numerous coffeehouses leafed through deist pamphlets and orthodox repartee. London's increasing wealth and dominance as a financial center for the country permitted the architect Christopher Wren some leeway in the design and materials for the fifty new churches proposed for the city. The reform societies, all based in the capital, included not only eminent Anglicans and dissenters, but also local constables and common informers. Durand Fage, Jean Cavalier, and Elie Marion would find themselves in 1706 in a city larger than they had ever known and in a religious milieu more complex than anything they had encountered before.[85]

London's ambiance fostered the rivalries between millenarian churchman and inspired chiliast, between Calvinist and conformist Huguenot, between deist and reformer, between English citizen and alien. The history of the French Prophets weaves through all of these divisions and others just as powerful, just as perplexing.

85. On the increasingly urban focus of English life in the eighteenth century, see Alan Everitt, "The Food Market of the English Town, 1660-1760," *Third International Conference of Economic History* (Paris, 1968) 57-71; Peter Borsay, "The English Urban Renaissance: The Development of Provincial Urban Culture c. 1680-c. 1760," *Social History* 5 (1977) 581-604. On London's economic centrality, see P.G.M. Dickson, *The Financial Revolution in England* (1967); E.A. Wrigley, "A Simple Model of London's Importance in Changing English Society and Economy 1650-1750," *Past and Present* 37 (1967) 44-70.

CHAPTER III

The French Prophets in London, 1706-1707

The Inspirés *and the Refugees*

When the Camisard prophet Elie Marion arrived in London on September 16, 1706, he was assured of a sympathetic audience. Another *inspiré*, Durand Fage, had reached the city three months earlier. Since June, Fage had delivered the Lord's message to a small band of men who recorded his inspirations. Although the first signs of his prophetic gift had appeared in the Cévennes in 1703, he had not prophesied frequently then or attracted much attention. In England now after imprisonment and escape, after a journey through Switzerland and Holland, the twenty-five-year-old Fage stood momentarily at the center of what would become the French Prophets.[1]

In August, Jean Cavalier of Sauve had joined him. The only son of a Languedoc cloth merchant, Cavalier had become inspired in 1701 at the age of sixteen. He achieved notoriety less for his inspirations than for questionable dealings with a French judge. Suspected of betraying fellow Huguenots, he left for Switzerland. In Geneva he had met Fage, taken up stocking weaving, then departed for Holland to enlist in a regiment formed by the famous Camisard "Colonel" Cavalier. He did not sail with the regiment when it left for Portugal but went instead to London, where his cousin Jean Allut had settled. By August 10, Cavalier had pronounced two warnings or *avertissements*; within a week, Allut had opened his house in Soho to all interested in the prophets. On August 20, at his rooms in Somerset House on the Strand, Cavalier's host was the marquis de

1. Fatio Calendar, June-July 1706; *MMM*, 116, 120, 137, 142, 154-55.

Miremont, through whose efforts the English expedition to relieve the Cévennes had been organized.[2]

Fage receded into the background. Assemblies which had occurred with less publicity at the home of the Presbyterian minister Thomas Cotton moved to Allut's house near the French Protestant church called The Greeks (an annex of the Savoy Church). The two original secretaries, Jean Daudé and Charles Portales, found a third in Nicolas Fatio de Duillier. A warning spoken by Fage on September 3 reflected the gathering momentum of the group: "My Child, you have but to speak openly. You must openly announce my Wonders."[3]

The stature of their followers increased the appeal of Fage, Cavalier and (soon) Marion. Jean Daudé was a lawyer from Nîmes. Charles Portales, a lawyer's son, acted as secretary to the marquis de Miremont. Chaplain to the noble Russell family in Bloomsbury, Thomas Cotton was a respected nonconformist minister. Nicolas Fatio, scion of a bourgeois Huguenot family of Geneva, had established an international reputation as a mathematician, a Fellow of the Royal Society and a friend of Sir Isaac Newton. These men all had close ties to the Huguenot refugee community in London, but none more so than Thomas Cotton, who had witnessed the persecution of Huguenots at Poitiers and Saumur and returned to England with an active concern for their plight. As scribes and hosts awaiting the inspirations of the prophets, these men contributed a distinct formality to the assemblies and a gravity to the physical agitations which preceded the warnings.[4]

During the summer months before Marion's arrival, the two *inspirés* and their adherents established much of the apparatus and procedure for meetings that would prevail in the years ahead. Two or three scribes in the drawing room of a house would note the place and those present. One of

2. Fatio Calendar, August 1706; *MMM*, 154n., 157; Historical Relation, f. 24; *TS*, 38-60; P.J. Shears, "Armand de Bourbon, Marquis de Miremont," *HSL Proceedings* 20 (1963 for 1962) 405-18.

3. Fatio Calendar, August 1706; Historical Relation, f. 24; Lambeth Palace, MSS 934, f. 52, "Préciz du Discours de Mr. Durand Fage d'Aubaye prononcé sous l'opération de l'Esprit: à Londres, le 3e septembre 1706, à 8 ou 9 heures du matin. S[tyle] V[ieux]."

4. On Portales and Daudé, see *MMM*, prefatory note by Francis M.E. Kennedy and 159n. On Cotton, see Walter Wilson, *The History and Antiquities of Dissenting Churches and Meeting Houses, in London, Westminster, and Southwark: including the lives of their Ministers* (1814) IV, 376-88. On Fatio, see Frank E. Manuel, *A Portrait of Isaac Newton* (Cambridge, Mass., 1968) ch. 9; Charles A. Domson, "Nicolas Fatio de Duillier and the Prophets of London: An Essay in the Historical Interaction of Natural Philosophy and Millennial Belief in the Age of Newton," Ph.D. thesis, Yale University, 1972. For brief data on all French Prophets mentioned hereafter, see Appendix I.

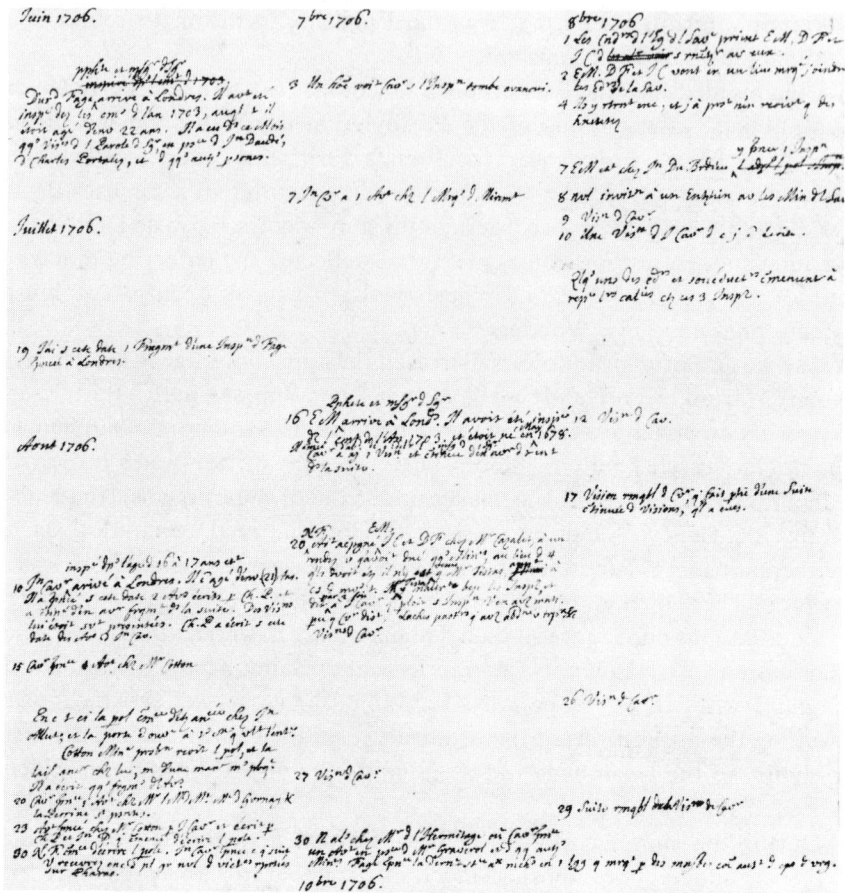

PLATE IV. First page from Nicolas Fatio's calendar of events concerning the French Prophets, BPUG, MSS fr. 601. The calendar is in an abbreviated hand. The first entry begins, "Durand Fage, prophète et messager du Seigneur [crossed out: inspiré depuis le commencement de 1703] arrive à Londres. Il avait été inspiré des les commencements de l'an 1703, auquel temps il étoit agé d'environ 22 ans. Il a eu dans ce Mois quelques Visites de la Parole du Seigneur en présence de Jean Daudé, de Charles Portales, et de quelques autres personnes."

the prophets would succumb to agitations—shaking, jumping, gasping, convulsions—and eventually begin to speak. The scribes, jotting comments on the manner of agitation, would render in shorthand a faithful account of the inspiration. At the end, Fage or Cavalier silent and physically restored, the scribes would initial their accounts and compare them for discrepancies. Later each of the first three scribes testified "That not foreseeing, at first, whither these Warnings would tend, I did apply my self to take them in Writing, chiefly with a Design to preserve them, and to have by me some accurate Memoirs, which might, some time or other, help to determine, whether indeed they proceeded from God."[5] Such concern for accuracy hinted at the semipublic nature of the memoirs as scrupulous documents of the presence of the Holy Spirit among the prophets. From the same desire for witness, the group welcomed onlookers, spread news of meetings, and circulated copies of particularly impressive warnings.[6]

It was an auspicious time for prophecy. Late that spring, the Duke of Marlborough had led English and allied forces to a convincing victory over French troops at Ramillies, causing the French to withdraw from their major strongholds in the Netherlands. By July, English and Portuguese soldiers occupied Madrid. Londoners were enjoying a new commercial prosperity that would last until 1709. Threatened neither by military defeat nor by economic recession, the English might welcome Camisard veterans and inspired refugees to their free and, for the nonce, bountiful land.

Elie Marion however was accustomed to adversity. At Lausanne in July, uncomfortably and poorly rewarded for his campaigns in the Cévennes, he had received a divine command to go to England, and once there he delivered a harsh message from the Lord. Three years had passed since he had become a prophet, three years during which he had fought Catholic troops, surrendered and returned to fight again. Now at the age of twenty-eight the oldest of the three *inspirés*, well used to positions of command, he supplanted Cavalier as the leading figure.[7]

Cavalier's inspiration on September 3 had promised that God would come quickly to heal the sick, console the afflicted and revive the weak.[8] Marion's warning of September 18 changed the tenor of prophecy to the warlike tones appropriate to his familiar Desert:

> The Trumpet is ready to sound. Fire, Lightnings and Thunderbolts are prepared for thine Enemies. Since there are many Persons who come only out of a Spirit of Curiosity, I will not have my Word manifested to such People. Prepare thy self to depart within a short time out of this Country, and go to thy Brethren, to fight there more than ever.

---

5. Elias Marion, *Prophetical Warnings* (1707) Oath of 4/1/1707, xi.
6. Cf. Lambeth Palace, MSS 934, f. 52 on scribes recording the effects of the prophets on the audiences.
7. *MMM*, throughout; *TS*, 43-45, 72-93.
8. Lambeth Palace, MSS 934, f. 52, "Préciz du Discours de Mr. Jean Cavalier de Sauve."

His second message, two days later, throbbed with vengeance: "Oh what Tempests are preparing for the Wicked! . . . No Peace for the Wicked; He must be destroyed."[9] Before Marion's warnings, there had been little evidence of violent judgment in the inspirations, no trace of hostility toward the spectators in London. Marion's warnings retained the belligerent values of the Camisard ethos of cataclysm, and he applied them in English surroundings. The discontinuity between the Desert and the situation of Huguenot refugees in London would shape decisively the early history of the French Prophets.

Just before Elie Marion arrived in London, "certain pretended *inspirés* who are trying to lead astray some of our members and who undertake as well to predict events of moment to the State" had come to the notice of the French Protestant church in Threadneedle Street. The consistory directed four envoys to entice the prophets, "whose vocation is more than suspect," back to the fold. On September 20, Fage, Cavalier, Marion and Nicolas Fatio met with one of the envoys, Pierre Testas, a minister of the church. Testas was confronted with erudite debate from Fatio and inspirations from Jean Cavalier, who now echoed Marion's angry pitch. Testas considered the inspirations as "nothing but very violent and convulsive movements of the chest and head, with general prophecies of the destruction of Babylon and Antichrist, and some exhortations equally general to prayer and repentance, spoken in a manner very unworthy of the Spirit." Moreover, Testas complained, Fatio's prophets had not performed any validating miracles. Fatio offered the example of the victory of allied troops at Turin some weeks past, foretold by Cavalier. Testas declared that he himself had predicted that victory before the prophets ever set foot in England. At this point Cavalier had an inspiration accusing the Huguenot ministers in London of cowardice for having abandoned their congregations in France. Testas, sensitive to this accusation as were other refugee ministers ambivalent about their exile, reprimanded Cavalier for speaking under a spirit of deceit, exhorting him to abandon his shameful pose as a prophet of the Lord.[10]

The evident intransigence and enmity of this meeting would mar most

---

9. Marion prophesied in French. All English translations of his warnings come from the translation prepared by the French Prophets, *Prophetical Warnings* (1707). These quotations are from pp. 1-2.

10. HAL, MS 8, Threadneedle Street Church, Livre des actes de 1692/3 à 1708, 499, 501, and printed in the English translation which I have used in Kingston, II, 197-200, Letter to the Lord Bishop of London [Henry Compton] from the Threadneedle Street French Church; Fatio Calendar, 9/20/1706.

other contacts between the refugee ministry and the prophets. Despite a few feints toward reconciliation, dialogue would remain at roughly the same level of threat and bitter counter-threat. Suspicion of the prophets' physical symptoms, criticism of the style of their warnings, demands for miracles as proof of divine commission, reports of imposture would constantly accompany the pastors' general disinclination to regard the Cévenol tradition of prophecy as valid in Soho or Spitalfields. The *inspirés* in turn would come to define their group in opposition to the French Protestant churches, and they would stress the importance of the prophetic gift for the true Christian ministry. Their millennial vision would include a scene of triumph over all who discounted the role of the Holy Spirit in Christian teaching. On September 30, in the presence of several Huguenot ministers, Fage pronounced final sentence on the wicked.[11] But the trials of the prophets had only begun.

Alerted by the Calvinist Threadneedle Street Church, the leaders of the conformist Savoy Church requested a meeting with the *inspirés*. During a series of five interviews in October, the prophets felt their reception at the Savoy grow perceptibly cooler. After the first interview, Marion repeated that the prophets would shortly depart for France, yet a month passed and they were still in London, attracting larger audiences. Throughout the month, Cavalier and Marion pronounced judgments and had visions of the annihilation of the wicked. The Savoy consistory cautioned the prophets in a last interview that they had made influential enemies.[12]

The interviews concluded, Marion had two inspirations. In one the judgment theme returned, in the other a new theme opened: "My Child, I assure thee that this Day there have been mischievous Contrivances plotting against you." News of ministers and Savoy leaders speaking ill of the prophets in public confirmed this warning. Convinced of the duplicity of the Savoy consistory, the prophets refused to attend another series of interviews, denying the authority of that conformist church over members of the church of the Desert.[13]

In response to revelations of plots and powerful enemies, the group stressed the millennial elements in prophetic messages. Fatio introduced his friend, the scientist David Gregory, to the prophets at the end of

11. Fatio Calendar, 9/30/1706.
12. Marion, *Prophetical Warnings*, 5-6; Fatio Calendar, October, 1706; *MMM*, 157; *TS*, 143-46; Kingston, II, 200. The Savoy consistory reported the outcome of the meetings to the Bishop of London, who had asked for a report: Bodleian, Rawlinson MSS C. 984, ff. 248-249v.
13. Marion, *Prophetical Warnings*, 7; Fatio Calendar, 10/12?/1706; *TS*, 145-46. Cf. N. N., *An Account of the Lives and Behaviour of the Three French Prophets* (1708) 13-14.

October. Gregory found them concerned exclusively with the marvelous history and promising future of Huguenots in France; they predicted "the Peace of the Church to follow upon the ruin of Rome," more continental victories against French forces, and the approaching restoration of Protestantism in France.[14] On November 4, Marion received a divine command to begin a three-day fast and immediately prophesied the "Burning of a great City" within "a few days." After secret conference with the Lord, after an inward warning and agitations but no speech, Marion prophesied, "My Kingdom is at hand; my Kingdom upon the Earth. I will come to reign visibly before Men. I will descend in a visible Form before my People." Soon there would be "Overturnings of whole States, I tell thee. I will overturn them upside down."[15]

Marion's private communion with the Lord and public warnings vindicating the *inspirés*, alternate measures of retreat and attack, would recur as a pattern of group behavior whenever opposition was strong. It was the pattern of guerillas who struck quickly and then disappeared, and it was ultimately the pattern for the millennial kingdom, which lay hidden but would come, swift and sudden. Just as Marion resorted to the rhetoric of the Desert, he fell back upon habits of behavior acquired in the Desert. Marion's fasting, inward inspiration and secret messages (acts themselves in the nature of plots) were matched by a concerted group effort to hallow the miracles in the Cévennes which sanctioned the authority of the *inspirés*.

Sometime in November, François-Maximilien Misson, Huguenot gentleman, son of a refugee minister and author of the popular *A New Voyage to Italy*, paid a visit to Fage and Marion, who lived near his house in Tower Street. He was impressed, failing to find in them any signs of imposture or self-seeking. By midmonth he had begun to record the experiences of Huguenot émigrés who had witnessed prophecy and miracle in the Cévennes. The sessions lasted for more than three months, and seventeen refugees gave testimony. Five of them were or would become followers of the prophets.[16] The project involved a sustained effort

---

14. Royal Society, Gregory MSS f. 63, memorandum of 10/26/1706, cited by Margaret C. Jacob, *The Newtonians and the English Revolution 1689-1720* (Ithaca, 1976) 256; Edinburgh University, Gregory MSS, Folio c. DC. 1.61, f. 707, entry for 1/19/1707, supplied by Professor Jacob.

15. Marion, *Prophetical Warnings*, 11-22.

16. F.-Maximilien Misson, *Meslange de litérature historique et critique sur tout ce qui regarde l'état extraordinaire des Cévennois, appelez Camisards* (1707) Au Lecteur. The witnesses who became followers were Sara Dalgone, Claude Arnassan, David Flotard, **Isabeau (Elisabeth) Charras,** and Matthieu Boissier.

on the part of Misson and others to seek out people. The texts were consciously destined for publication. Here was the first extended missionary endeavor of the followers: they sought support for their faith in the prophets outside their small group; they had to convince former inhabitants of Languedoc and Dauphiné to testify to the miracles; they devoted many hours to transcribing and proofreading the accounts; they prepared themselves for a more public commitment to the prophets. In April, 1707, the combined texts would appear as *Le théâtre sacré des Cévennes; ou, récit de diverses merveilles nouvellement opérées.*

By December, 1706, the dozen or so members of the prophetic community had deeply integrated the values and ideals of Desert millenarianism and Camisard inspiration. Their focus on the Cévennes gave them a strength of purpose with which to proclaim the coming of the Kingdom and a sense of continuity with which to blunt the edge of criticism. But while the *inspirés* in the mountains of Languedoc could rely upon widespread communal sympathy, in England they had either to recreate the atmosphere of the Desert or to reinterpret the function of prophecy and the meaning of the millennium. As the group expanded, it became more and more difficult to perpetuate an English Desert. So began the English transformation of the Camisard tradition.

English Contacts

Between December, 1706, and April, 1707, the *inspirés* attracted more than twenty new followers. Among them was John Lacy, Esq., who exhibited the first signs of inspiration on March 1. This was the very day on which he handed to the printer the English translation of the *Théâtre sacré (A Cry from the Desert)* which had occupied him since January. Lacy, a well-to-do English Presbyterian, age forty-two, would become the foremost English prophet.[17]

Lacy's long-time friend, Sir Richard Bulkeley, second Baronet, holder of estates in Ireland and Surrey, entered actively into group affairs during these same months. Bulkeley, who knew well the millenarian Bishop William Lloyd and other latitudinarian churchmen, was a moderate Anglican and, like Lacy and Thomas Cotton, involved in the Societies for

17. Fatio Calendar, 3/1/1707; *TS*, iii; Lacy, *Warnings*, I, iii-iv. For biographical material on Lacy, see Edmund Calamy, *An Historical Account of My Own Life*, ed. John T. Rutt (1829) II, 76-78, 94-99, 113-14; House of Lords RO, MSS 2519, Lacy's Estate Act, ff. 51-74 and Committee Book, Minutes 24 October 1704-5 April 1710, ff. 337-38. The *D N B* article on Lacy is drawn from Calamy and Lacy's *Warnings* and is unsatisfactory.

the Reformation of Manners. He was forty-six, well educated, and a member of the Royal Society in Ireland.[18]

The social standing of Lacy and Bulkeley contributed to the group's initial respectability beyond Huguenot circles, but it hinted too at the changing context for Cévenol prophecy. By mid-April, there were more than thirty people in the group that came to be known in general (regardless of nationality or the actual gift of prophecy) as the French Prophets; the English among them, like Cotton, Lacy, Bulkeley, Richard Roach and Sir John Philipps, were older and wealthier than the Camisard *inspirés*.[19] Theirs was an urbane and literate culture whose values, by no means always coherent, would eventually clash with the cultural values of the Desert.

The growth of the French Prophets flouted the intent of the "Acte Noir" published by the Savoy consistory on January 5, 1706/7. Consistory ministers announced from the pulpits of their three churches (the Savoy, the Little Savoy and the Greeks) that

> the Agitations of these pretended Prophets are only the Effect of a voluntary Habit, of which they are entirely Masters, though in their Fits they seem to be agitated by a Superior Cause. . . . But the Way in which they make the Spirit speak, is still more unworthy of him, which is by perpetual Hesitations, Childish Repetitions, unintelligible Stuff, gross Contradictions, manifest Lies, Conjectures turned into Predictions, already convicted of Falsehood by the Event; or some moral Precepts, which may be heard every day much better expressed, and have nothing new but the Grimaces, with which they are accompanied.[20]

Misson reported that this Act inflamed the Huguenot populace in London, who insulted the French Prophets in public, spattered them with mud, and assaulted them on their doorsteps. But had not Fage long ago prophesied, "There will be some who will suffer Martyrdom for the sake of my Word"? And did not Marion say under inspiration, "Let them utter Blasphemies and Curses against thee; I will have it so, my Child"? The

---

18. On Bulkeley, see G.E. Cockayne, ed., *Complete Baronetage*, IV, 207; K. Theodore Hoppen, *The Common Scientist in the Seventeenth Century* (1970) *passim*; Dudley W.R. Bahlmann, *The Moral Revolution of 1688* (Hamden, 1968) 19-21; *DNB*, III, 233 (which gives the wrong birthdate).

19. See Appendix I for ages, and Appendix IX on education.

20. The original French announcement is in the Bodleian, Rawlinson MSS C. 984, ff. 242-242v. and is printed in full in *MMM*, 160. This translation comes from N.N., *Account of the Three French Prophets*, 9-10, who says (p. 17) that Bishop Compton approved of the *Acte*. Misson denied this in his *Plainte et censure des calomnieuses accusations publiées par le Sieur Claude Groteste de la Motte* (1708) 49.

same day that the consistory published the "Acte Noir," Marion received divine orders to publish the irate warnings which he had spoken since his arrival.[21]

The active hostility of the Huguenot ministry created in effect a London replica of the Desert. The influence of the Desert image during the early months of 1707 was apparent in the otherwise strange sadness and frustration of some of the inspirations:

> My Child, I tell thee, Faith and Truth are dead upon the Earth: There is nothing Left of them, I tell thee. But behold the Day of Vengeance and Indignation, upon the Men of the Earth, My Child. I would rest my Head upon Earth; (but) I have no Place of Abode. I have no Habitation upon the Earth: I am driven away from all Places: I am wandering, I tell thee, like the things of nought.[22]

Concurrently, however, the influence of the English milieu, literate and prosperous, made itself felt: the publication of warnings and accounts of miracles had not been integral parts of the Camisard tradition.[23] The faithful in Languedoc and followers in London might share millennial hopes, but their responses to martyrdom began to set them apart.

During the winter of 1706/7, as the French Prophets prepared two sets of manuscripts for the press (Marion's *Avertissemens*, the *Théâtre sacré* and their English translations), they enjoyed a sense of direction distinct from any original motive for group formation, such as support for the refugee cause or for the Camisards in particular. New prophecies by Marion enhanced this sense of the group in London as more than an adjunct to the Camisards, for Marion prophesied that some of the London followers would themselves receive miraculous gifts. He was granted a vision of a new Pentecost and promised signs and miracles in answer to those who demanded proofs of his divine commission. "I have Three Days to work visibly upon the Earth," declared Marion in late January (as usual, in God's persona); on February 19 he warned followers: "My Children, I have great Gifts, great Presents to make to you. Be my loyal followers: I have trials to send you, in a few days."[24]

---

21. Misson, *Plainte et censure,* 52; Lambeth Palace, MSS 934, f. 52; Marion, *Prophetical Warnings,* 117, 131; Fatio Calendar, 1/5/1707.

22. Marion, *Prophetical Warnings,* 105, 111, 122.

23. Publication required wealth not available to the Camisards. The amount spent on publications in April was rumored to exceed £40: *Account of the Apprehending and Taking Six French Prophets, Near Hog-Lane in Soho* (1707) broadside. The BM copy of Marion's *Prophetical Warnings* is numbered, in Fatio's (?) hand, 1425, indicating a large edition at a time when a normal press run was 1000 copies. Cf. Arnold Lloyd, *Quaker Social History 1669-1738* (1950) 147-54.

24. Marion, *Prophetical Warnings,* 72, 95, 128.

The new trials materialized on March 30, when the Savoy consistory banished the three *inspirés* from Holy Communion. The new Pentecost began upon the publication of Marion's *Avertissemens* on April 8. In the subsequent week seven French men and women discovered their prophetic gifts. The presence of the new prophets called for constant attention on the part of all followers and for more time spent with the group. Both the millennial state and the evidence of the Holy Spirit now had London referents, and continuing persecution in England helped mold the French Prophets into a religious group with traditions of its own, separate from the Cévennes.[25]

Benefitting from the internecine dispute over consistorial authority among Huguenot churches, the *inspirés* did receive Easter Communion, at the hands of the French minister Daniel Chaise de la Place.[26] But ten days later a mob in Soho, enraged by reports of men who wished to set up a new gospel and destroy the foundations of the Church, started to harass the French Prophets. The next day, the mob forced Cavalier and Allut to abandon their house and flee to Misson's. Bulkeley, Lacy and several others also suffered the insults of the crowd.[27] On April 24, the *inspirés*, the three secretaries, and three of the new prophets (Jeanne Cavalier, Jean Allut and his wife Henriette) departed by divine command for Northfleet, near Gravesend, eighteen miles from London. There the Spirit came upon several "in a very extraordinary manner," brought them "consolations and assurances of the Love of God," joined Charles Portales to Elie Marion in a bond of spiritual fellowship, and encouraged them to return to the city to continue their ministry. Back in London, Marion and Portales walked boldly down the streets, showing themselves openly lest their retreat be interpreted as a victory for their enemies.[28]

25. *MMM*, 161; *TS*, 146; Fatio Calendar, April, 1707. See also Appendix VI. A copy of the act of excommunication is in *MMM* and also in manuscript in HSL Library, Registre des Actes du Consistoire dans l'Eglise dans West Street St. Giles, 1690 Jusquà 1741, 117.

26. *MMM*, 162; Fatio Calendar, 4/13/1707. Daniel Chaise de la Place was suspended from the pulpit for six weeks for giving the prophets communion: HSL Library, Registre des Actes du Consistoire dans l'Eglise dans West Street St. Giles 1690 Jusquà 1741, 116-19.

27. *MMM*, 158, 162; *TS*, vii; Fatio Calendar, 4/22 and 4/23/1707; *Account of the Apprehending and Taking Six French Prophets* (1707) broadside; Kingston, II, 219-20. According to the "Relation historique de ce qui s'est passé à Londres au sujet des Prophètes Camisards," *Nouvelles de la république des lettres* (February, 1708) 132-33, there were twice as many English as Huguenots in the Soho mob. On mobs as a conservative force in the community, see E.P. Thompson, "The Moral Economy of the English Crowd in the 18th Century," *Past and Present* 50 (1971) 76-136.

28. Fatio Calendar, 4/24/1707; Misson, *Plainte et censure*, 46-47; *MMM*, 162; Historical Relation, f. 28.

The pattern of riot, refuge and publication was repeated on their return. On Sunday, April 27, several French ministers condemned the prophets from their pulpits. The next day, Lacy and Bulkeley, with a warrant from Chief Justice Holt, arrested some of the participants in the late riot, who were bound over to the next Quarter Sessions. The legal action by the two followers was enough to provoke a second riot, more violent than the first, during which Marion, Portales and Cavalier were escorted by constables to a justice of the peace to ensure their safety. Upon a confrontation between the justice and the mob, the three men had to flee by a back way to a neighboring house. The next day, at Fatio's lodgings, Marion and Portales received orders to fast in private. Others obeyed a command to retire again to Northfleet.[29]

Those who left London were Jean Cavalier and his recent wife Jeanne, Jean and Henriette Allut, Elisabeth (Isabeau) Charras, Anne Voyer, Durand Fage, David Flotard—agent of the marquis de Miremont—, Nicolas Fatio, Jean Daudé and his wife. The number of women in the list is remarkable, for the records of the French Prophets until then pointed to an almost exclusively male society.[30] The apparently sudden change in the status of women in the group could have been due in part to a failure by male secretaries to account for female followers, especially wives. Inspired women, however, whose inspirations the scribes would be morally obliged to record, began to speak only in April. By the year's end, there would be twenty-three prophets in addition to the three *inspirés*; of these, fourteen would be female. In April, four of the seven newly inspired were women; three of them (Henriette Allut, Jeanne Cavalier, Anne Voyer) went to Northfleet.[31]

The April retreats ceremonially recognized new relationships within the group: Portales to Marion, old secretaries to new prophets, male to female followers. Not one of the English followers (Lacy, Bulkeley, Rebecca Critchlow, Elizabeth Gray) participated. The inner core of the group remained for another month completely French. Yet the influx of wo-

29. *TS*, vii; *MMM*, 163-65; Fatio Calendar, 4/28 and 4/29/1707; Historical Relation, ff. 29, 30; "Relation historique," *Nouvelles de la république* (February, 1708) 133; Abel Boyer, *The History of the Reign of Queen Anne Digested into Annals. Year the Sixth.* (1708) 368.

30. Rebecca Critchlow, who hosted meetings, may have been the only woman centrally participant in group affairs before April; see also Appendix I. The low percentage of women among early followers is consistent with findings for early Quakerism: Richard T. Vann, *The Social Development of English Quakerism 1655-1755* (Cambridge, Mass., 1969) 81-82.

31. Charras, who had earlier given testimony for the *TS* (95-104), later also became a prophet. On Flotard see *MMM*, 143-53 *et passim*.

men among the inspired was a clue to the growing influence of the English milieu among Huguenots close to the Camisard tradition of male leadership.

On April 30, as the Northfleet circle returned and the fasts of Marion and Portales came to a close, the French Prophets published the English translation of Marion's *Avertissemens (Prophetical Warnings)*.[32] On May 5, Marion, Daudé and Fatio presented themselves before Chief Justice Holt in Queen's Bench Court, accused at the instance of the Savoy consistory of publishing prophecies filled with blasphemy and sedition. In the warrant, Marion was described as a "pseudo-prophet, an abominable, detestable and diabolic blasphemer, a disturber of the peace, heretic and impostor, publisher of false, scandalous and seditious libels." Fatio and Daudé were accused of helping Marion to deliver his messages against the Queen, the established church, and the people of London.[33]

The trial of the three men dragged on through November, the accused appearing in court at least ten times. Nevertheless, the group expanded in May and June as never before, opening itself up, asserting itself publicly. The "Jubilee" began, Elie Marion delivered the first divinely inspired individual promises known as blessings, and, on May 25, Jean Cavalier received the millennial sign of the Restitution of the Great Scepter. Public assemblies commenced on May 28.[34]

Under the pressures of legal prosecution begun in May, believers sought and found social devices to secure the faith of all French Prophets. Exposure in public assemblies raised the level of commitment required of veterans and initiates alike. Blessings effectively bonded followers: the ceremony demanded a formal demonstration of respect for the prophets and, since the blessings were often predictions, stimulated personal interest

---

32. Fatio Calendar, 4/30/1707. The translation of the *TS* appeared on May 6 as *A Cry from the Desart: or, Testimonials of the Miraculous Things lately come to pass in the Cévennes, Verified upon Oath, and by other Proofs.*

33. Fatio Calendar, 5/5/1707; *MMM*, 165; Georges Ascoli, "L'affaire des prophètes français à Londres," *Revue du XVIIIe siècle* 3 (1916) 85, cites the warrant, which I have not located. I have translated the warrant's description of Marion from Ascoli's French. The warrant was based on the statute of Elizabeth I.15, "An act against fond and fantastical prophesies." On May 11, deputies from Huguenot churches in London approved of the Savoy's prosecution of the French Prophets, and the Savoy appointed several of its ministers to publish a refutation of the *TS*. Numerous affidavits were signed to prove that the *TS* testimonials were either false or misleading. N.N., *Account of the Three French Prophets*, 17; HAL, Threadneedle Street Livre des actes 1692/3 à 1708, 519; AE, Corr. politique, Angleterre, vol. 222, f. 245; [Claude Groteste de la Mothe], *Examen du théâtre sacré des Cévennes;* Kingston, II, 38-53.

34. Fatio Calendar, 5/23 and 5/25/1707; Historical Relation, f. 30.

in the fulfillment of prophecy.³⁵ The retreats, the publications, the open assemblies and personal blessings helped the group achieve a substantial measure of integration. Enabled to accept new members by the coherence of the "Small Number who had been already gathered together by the Spirit," the French Prophets brashly entered the domain of English religious groups competing for the allegiance of men and women in all of London.

The Ascendance of the English

The spring and summer of 1707 were flooded with reports of the severe English defeat at Almanza in Spain and the possibility of a war in the Baltic that might disrupt English naval supplies. Parliament had passed the bill for the union of Scotland and England, which came into effect on May 1. Despite economic prosperity, London experienced a mild financial panic and a sharp increase in bankruptcies. Political dissatisfaction with the conduct of the war against France was mounting, and in a moment with unforeseen consequences for both Whig and Tory, Sarah Churchill introduced Abigail Hill (Mrs. Masham) to Queen Anne.³⁶ In this atmosphere of political maneuvering which would strengthen the Tory hand against nonconformists and Protestant refugees, the French Prophets were on trial; in this atmosphere of social anxiety the French Prophets had their first considerable successes among the English populace.

From the diaries of Richard Roach, Anglican clergyman and Philadelphian, heir to Jane Lead and the theosophy of Jakob Boehme, comes much of the information on the new English converts. As early as March, Roach and other Philadelphians had met with the French Prophets. Marion especially made a lasting impression, and the first public assembly of the French Prophets was hosted by Rebecca Critchlow in the same

---

35. Blessings also clarified the status of followers by indicating to each the route of personal progress toward inspiration; if, for example, followers had agitations but did not prophesy, they would be promised speech. Bulkeley described the ceremony: those pronouncing blessings had their eyes shut and were in a dark corner of the room, so positioned that the pertinence of the blessing could not possibly be the result of the prophets' acquaintances with those seeking blessings. The prophets blessed casual observers as well as followers and aroused antipathy for their disregard of the patterns of social deference (the poor blessing the rich, women blessing men). See Bulkeley's *An Answer to Several Treatises lately published on the Subject of the Prophets* (1708) 95-99; *The Rehearsal of the Observator*, Dec. 3, 1707.

36. T.S. Ashton, *Economic Fluctuations in England 1700-1800* (Oxford, 1959) 116; Geoffrey Holmes, *British Politics in the Age of Anne* (London and New York, 1967) 210-16.

rooms where the Philadelphians convened. From then on, Philadelphians frequently appeared in connection with the French Prophets. On June 3, convinced of a parallel between the recent union of England and Scotland and the prospective union of Camisards and Philadelphians, Roach wrote of "the 1 Triumphant Progress; in Public; upon the Union Whitsun Tuesday. Camisards met with us in the School room." The Philadelphians were deeply affected, Roach noted:

> Mr. King took me by the Hand in a Sweet Power and told me he had now received abundant Conviction.
> Mrs. Wells declared that she was sick when she came; and presently found a Good Justice that scattered all her Illness and so declared after the meeting that she believed it was of God.
> Mr. Kemp declared to me; his thought that it was God's Answer to Souls under [illegible] vindication Power and came out of the meeting and humbled and prayed.[37]

At least ten Philadelphians would enter the ranks of the French Prophets while other English followers also came to the fore, as the Lord finally opened John Lacy's mouth on June 12 "and little by little opened the mouths of others of the same nation." Between June and December, twelve of fifteen new prophets would be English, as would three-quarters of the total new membership.[38]

The shift from Huguenot to English majority within the group had important implications for the future, but it did not immediately imply a shift from the Camisard ethos of cataclysm. The Camisard tradition was of one piece and had the strength of consistency. English followers as a whole had no single millenarian ethos. Early followers—Bulkeley, Lacy, Cotton, Sir John Philipps and probably Elizabeth Gray—were Anglicans or moderate Presbyterians with the New Jerusalem ethos of evangelism and reform, hoping for a comprehensive universal church; they were joined by such as John Hooke, founding member of the S.P.C.K., and Timothy Byfield, son of a prominent Presbyterian clergyman who had written of the *Gospel's Glory* in 1659.[39] On the other hand, most English converts in 1707—and, likely, the majority of new English prophets that year—were

37. Roach Diary, I, ff. 32, 52v., 55, 57; Fatio Calendar, 5/28/1707.
38. Fatio Calendar, 6/12/1707 and see Appendix II and Appendix VII.
39. On Hooke, see Bahlmann, *The Moral Revolution*, 57; *DNB*, IX, 1174-75. On Byfield, see H.F. Water, *Genealogical Gleanings in England* (Boston, 1901) I, 115, and II, 1394-96; "Byfield, Richard," *DNB*, III, 565, and the discussion in chapter seven. Bulkeley claimed that more Anglicans than dissenters joined the French Prophets: *Preface to the Reader of Warnings of the Eternal Spirit, Spoken by the Mouth of the Servant of God, Abraham Whitro* (1709) 69.

either Philadelphians, Quakers or Baptists, familiar with the pentecostal ethos surviving after the Restoration, intent more on personal than on universal faith.[40] Changes within the entire group were complicated by the variety of forces it contained or, eventually, could not contain. Slowly, however, as the English learned to take the pulse of the group, the Camisard ethos was adapted to the traditions of the English contingent.

One influence of the English followers which quickly became apparent was a new formalistic, legal tenor. In June, Lacy rented the Barbican, a building formerly used by Presbyterians, to serve as an officially licensed meetinghouse for the French Prophets.[41] This attempt at respectable equivalence with dissenters attracted much notice. Although the French Prophets continued to meet as well in private houses, the Barbican would be the focus of public outrage. The weekly newspaper, *Humours of a Coffee House*, written in dialogue, revealed the degree to which the French Prophets, by virtue of encounters with the law, had gained notoriety:

> *Bohee.* You must know that these Camisards were taken up, and admitted to Bail.
> *Hazard.* Great News Indeed! As if our Ears had not been Deafened with them, and their Proceedings at a *Half Penny a Piece.*
> *Bohee.* But my neighbour *Yea* and *Nay*, the Quaker, was here just now, and has given such a Relation of them as is altogether *New*. They were no sooner got out of the Justice of Peace his Hands, by being Bailed, but they took a Shop of *Inspiration* (as they call it) in Barbican, which, by their way of managing themselves, might be called the *Club-Room of Ugly Faces*. And here they whined and screwed themselves into such Postures, that several People, I won't say as *Great Knaves*, but *Wise as themselves*, became their Proselytes.[42]

Bohee was referring to John Lacy and Sir Richard Bulkeley, who did most to establish legal respect for the French Prophets; they had pursued in

---

40. Of the 52 French Prophets who joined between June and the end of December, 1707, 11 were Philadelphians, 8 Quakers, 7 Baptists, 5 Anglicans, one possibly a Roman Catholic, and 11 were Huguenots (with twenty unknown). Of the new prophets, there were 4 Baptists, 1 Philadelphian, 1 Quaker, 1 Anglican, 3 Huguenots (with 5 unknown).

41. *MMM*, 165. Rebecca Critchlow registered her house in Baldwins Gardens as a place of worship for Independents in July, 1707: Greater London RO (Middlesex) MSP 1707 July /74. The group had also rented a house from Quakers in [Red] Lion Square: AE, Corr. politique, Angleterre, vol. 222, f. 307. Lacy may have hired the Barbican in response to the trial, but it was also a place where the prophets might be public and yet control the environment. Lacy warned on June 20, "I will move some, my Child, to follow thee, instead of sending for thee." *Warnings,* I, 22, 24-25.

42. *Humours of a Coffee House*, II, 6 (June 25-July 2, 1707). Cf. Bulkeley, *Answer to Several Treatises*, 90.

court the French rioters, an act which had prompted the second riot. In mid-June, by order of the Queen, the legal process against the rioters was stopped by a *nolle prosequi* (unwillingness to prosecute). John Lacy went (or wrote) to Chief Justice Holt with the information that Holt had been commanded by the Lord to order a similar *nolle prosequi* for Marion, Fatio and Daudé. Holt objected that the command could not have been divine, for surely the Lord would know that Holt was legally powerless to obey it, since he could issue no order whatsoever for a *nolle prosequi*.[43]

As substantial property owners, Lacy and Bulkeley were more accustomed to litigation than Huguenot followers.[44] The legal protection afforded English dissenters contrasted with the intolerance of the Desert, and resort to the courts as a method of attack was peculiar to English followers. Not surprisingly, juristic metaphors first surfaced in Lacy's warnings. On the way to a conference with the attorney general on June 17, Lacy prophesied:

> I am he that sits in the chief Place of Judicature. I will make it known that I am the only Judge of the Earth. I will plead my own Cause.... I never appointed any Magistrates to oppose me, from the beginning of the World to this Day. If any do it, so far they Usurp over me.... They think they have Power, but they have not. I can put a *Noli presequi* [sic] to their Power, as well as they to mine Honour.[45]

Such balanced language and refined argument differed much from the prophecy of the *inspirés*, who rarely employed extended metaphors or spoke in elevated tones. Uninspired London followers (Misson, Bulkeley, James Jackson, Francis Moult) also used the rhetoric of law; they wrote elaborate briefs for the French Prophets, and their arguments frequently hinged on a legalistic concern for the details of criticism.[46] Action at law, ritual formality, familiarity with the niceties of debate reflected the social

---

43. John Humfrey, *An Account of the French Prophets* (1708) 14; John Lacy, *A Relation of the Dealings of God* (1708) 18; Fatio Calendar, 6/17 and 6/18/1707; "Holt, John," *DNB*, IX, 1099, with erroneous information; and in many primary and secondary reports. The French Prophets may have feared a trial before Holt, who had a stiff view of sedition, as in his decision in Rex v. Tutchin: see W.S. Holdsworth, *A History of English Law* (2nd ed., 1937) VI, 266.

44. According to Calamy, *Life*, 76-77, 111-13, Lacy had been despondent over the loss of a lawsuit judged by Holt in 1706. Lacy also had a petition up before the House of Lords in 1708: House of Lords RO, MSS 2519, Lacy's Estate Act, ff. 51-74. (The Act was given Royal Assent April 21, 1709: *Journal of the House of Lords* XVIII [1708-09] 724.) Bulkeley's legal antics had been reprimanded in 1691: W.J. Hardy, ed., *Calendar of the Sessions Books 1689 to 1709* (Middlesex County Records, 1905) 57, 60.

45. Lacy, *Warnings*, I, 18-19 and cf. 29, 39-41, 54.

46. James Jackson, *The Great Question Answered* (1707); Francis Moult, *The Right Way of Trying Prophets* (1707). (Works by Misson and Bulkeley have already been cited.)

habits of London gentleman rather than refugee weavers. The establishment of a public meetinghouse in a section of London not densely populated by Huguenots was further clear evidence of the impact of the English believers.

Less clear were the effects of changing membership upon the group's religious thought. From the beginning, the French Prophets administered no admission tests to members and had no rigorous definition of membership. Until their own churches excluded them, followers did not disclaim their previous religious affiliations. The theological demands of the group were simple and sufficiently slack to allow for a wide variety of viewpoints generally manifesting belief that the millennium was nigh, belief in the probability of widespread divine inspiration during these last days, and confidence that prophets within the group were divinely inspired. In the course of controversy with churchmen, the French Prophets would defend their Christian orthodoxy and discuss their beliefs in more detail, but even then they would not construct a coherent doctrinal system. Their seemingly indiscriminate acceptance of members made the French Prophets look very suspicious to critics; one wrote that

> the whole *Gang* of them, generally speaking, are composed of *Atheists, Papists, Quakers, Anti-Scripturists, Socinians, Ranters, Muggletonians,* and *Debauchees*; for though other Sects and Factions have some *Terms* and *Qualifications* requisite to the Admission of Members into their Societies; these pretended Prophets have none at all, but Tag, Rag, Knave or Fool, Rich, or Poor, young Children, or superannuated Dotards, as soon as they have come among them, are *blessed, admitted,* and immediately set up for Prophets; so that, instead of admiring (as some do) that there are so many of them, I wonder there are no more, since, like *Hell,* they refuse none.[47]

Since the group harbored English followers of diverse backgrounds, the lack of a complex theology was functional and may itself be interpreted as evidence of the impact of changing group membership. In order to accommodate such diversity, the French Prophets did not impose upon followers the strict Calvinism of Huguenots of the Desert or develop a tight schedule for events preceding the millennium.

47. Kingston, II, 132-33 and cf. Appendix V. Although I find no Muggletonians or Ranters in the group, and "Atheists," "Anti-Scripturists" and "Debauchees" are probably general terms of reproach, there is evidence that Thomas Emes had once been a Socinian: Regents Park College (Oxford), Angus Library, Cripplegate (London) Baptist Congregation Church Book 1699-1724, f.8 (September, 1694). Fatio, also accused of Socinianism, wrote to his brother in December, 1707: "Je suis convaincu que la Doctrine des Unitaires approche moins de la vérité que ne fait la Doctrine connu sur la Trinité, quand elle est bien entendue." BPUG, MSS fr. 602, f. 115. Lacy claimed that diverse Socinians had been converted by the prophets (*Warnings,* I, 12).

"This Mission brings no new Doctrine with it, nor advances any thing dissonant from the Scriptures," wrote Lacy in the preface to his first published volume of warnings. The purpose of the French Prophets was to broadcast news of the coming Kingdom. The Lord through Lacy justified to the English the need for extraordinary messengers—messengers who had required little justification in the desolate Cévennes:

> You say there was no need of such a mission here, as in France, where no Ordinary Ministers did remain; But I see and know that your Ministers here do not teach nor proclaim my approaching Kingdom. As to that Point, they are totally silent, shamefully silent. Therefore I think fit to publish this Mission here, as in France; and not here only, but over all the Earth.[48]

If people hearkened to the warnings of the prophets, they would prepare themselves, they would lead pious lives; all could be saved, but those who hardened their hearts would be judged severely.[49] The faithful were promised a heavenly Kingdom, but it was not certain whether it would actually be on the earth as presently known. The sequence of the Second Coming, the millennium and the judgment was also vague. Unlike other readers of Revelation, few of the French Prophets had struggled with its clues to the exact mechanisms of the end of the world.

What distinguished the French Prophets was not eschatology but the fact of the inspired among them. They would define heresy and apostasy not so much in terms of doctrine as in terms of the nature of prophecy; they designed guidelines to the style of true inspiration rather than theological rulebooks. Their faith was a millennial faith, but above all it was faith in the prophets who brought word of the millennium.

That faith had endured throughout a full year of prophecies. Between, June, 1706, and June, 1707, the *inspirés* had engineered an environment of imminent judgment, but they had refrained from time-specific predictions. Until late July, 1707, in a warning by the English prophet John Lacy, few if any predictions held a real possibility of being disconfirmed. One source claimed that Marion had the previous November predicted the burning of

---

48. Lacy, *Warnings,* I, 58 and cf. 36.

49. Belief in the universal *possibility* of salvation is what Melvin B. Endy, Jr., calls "universalism": *William Penn and Early Quakerism* (Princeton, 1973) 70 and note. Some of the English followers, notably the Philadelphians, believed in the *eventuality* of salvation for all, whether after purification in hell or through a potent manifestation of the spirit before the millennium: D.P. Walker, *The Decline of Hell* (1964) 218-63. Whether "universalists" or believers in universal salvation, the English followers undermined the Calvinist soteriology of the Camisards; the necessarily irenic position of Huguenot refugees in England also tended to reduce the vitality of the notion of a small elect group to be redeemed.

London within three weeks, but when Marion's *Avertissemens* were printed, someone had substituted the usual "in a few days." Another quoted Marion prophesying the release of Huguenot galley slaves by the end of 1707. A third discussed the French Prophets' belief that the winter of 1706/7 would bring "pestilential Fogs or Mists, that should sweep away, like a Plague, a vast Number of the inhabitants" of London.[50] Despite these examples, the group did not yet seem bothered by the problem of failed prophecy. Marion often referred to "three days' time," but followers like Fatio were inclined to regard such figures as divine metaphors similar to the "three and one-half days" during which the two witnesses of Revelation lay dead in the streets of Sodom.[51] Perhaps the successful prediction of heavy trials for the children of God overshadowed the judgments which had, in the opinion of their enemies, failed. Perhaps the group did not consider the time-specific predictions pointed out by opponents to be crucial to the inspired status of any given prophet. Certainly, none of the prophecies that had "failed" demanded significant personal investment on the part of group members, and the advent of English followers proved that for some the powers of the *inspirés* were not in doubt.[52]

English followers and the prophet John Lacy also strengthened group beliefs in the inevitable martyrdom of divine messengers and the imminence of signs and wonders. These beliefs were intertwined, for signs and wonders would be decisive proof to their persecutors of the divine call of the prophets. In June, Cavalier was supposed to have said in a warning, "My Child, My Child, I tell thee, that those Miracles which were done by Jesus Christ and his Apostles, are nothing in comparison of what will be done in a few natural Months, and your Feet shall be dyed with the Blood of your Enemies, in the Place where you shall be publicly assembled."[53] In this millennial design, reminiscent of Desert assemblies where Huguenots

---

50. Kingston, I, 21 and II, 213-15, and cf. Marion, *Prophetical Warnings*, 11-16, 111-12 and his *Avertissemens*, 10-14, 101-2; *An Appeal from the Prophets to their Prophecies* (1708) 5, 7.

51. There is some suggestion that followers interpreted the "three days" as years and hoped for the millennium in 1709. Calamy, *Life*, 72-73; Kingston, I, 23, 94; Humfrey, *Account*, 24; Josiah Woodward, *Remarks on the Modern Prophets* (1708) 49-50.

52. Cf. Leon Festinger, Henry W. Riecken and Stanley Schachter, *When Prophecy Fails* (New York, 1964); J.A. Hardyck and M. Braden, "Prophecy Fails Again: A Report of a Failure to Replicate," *Journal of Abnormal and Social Psychology* 65 (1962) 136-41; John Lofland, *Doomsday Cult* (Englewood Cliffs, 1966). All three stress the role of personal commitment in maintaining group integrity when prophecy seems to fail.

53. Kingston, II, 211-12.

were surprised and massacred by French dragoons, Cavalier fashioned the link between martyrdom and miracle that Lacy would repeat five days later: "It is not any Man, nor any Thing that you do, that does produce Change in the Souls of Men. How should it be? I know the People of the City will not believe, till they see Signs and Wonders. They shall not be long without them. Only I try my People, to see the Degrees of their Faith."[54]

Followers therefore relied upon the prophets when faced with opponents whose biases made them immune to logic. The Lord outlined the strategy for a confrontation with sceptics on July 2: "I would have thee and thy Friends appoint a Meeting with those that once send to thee for it. Leave them to choose their own Company and Place. Be concerned about no Argument and Reasoning; for that is not the way that I intend to convince the World. I will be with you."[55] John Chamberlayne, gentleman, founding member of the S.P.C.K. and close friend of a vociferous critic of the French Prophets, the Huguenot minister Claude Groteste de la Mothe, reported of the meeting:

> Sir Richard [Bulkeley], who seems to be their advocate General, was about to read a Paper, but was prevented by Mr. Marion's falling into one of his Fits, or *Inspirations*; who after a few *Sighs*, *Sobs*, and *Hiccups*, broke Silence; but every Word almost being accompanied with a Gulp, or a Hiccup, and violent Agitations of the Head and Body, which seemed to be *Affected*, and all his Sentences so broken and incoherent, that I could scarce understand, much less bear in Mind the Particulars he discoursed.[56]

Similar responses from other unbelievers promoted the feeling among followers that human reasoning was useless where people blinded themselves to divine arguments (signs and wonders). The English, particularly the Philadelphians, had experienced this situation before and could accept this aspect of the Camisard heritage of martyrdom and miracle. The cynical stubbornness of critics encouraged all French Prophets to anticipate persecution, but the English especially looked for new miracles.

54. Lacy, *Warnings*, I, 22-23.
55. *Ibid.* I, 38.
56. Kingston, I, 54. At this meeting were the Anglican ministers Josiah Woodward and White Kennet, the Presbyterian ministers John Spademan and Mr. Turner, John Chamberlayne and others whose names have been disguised: Mr. Y[a]tes, Mr. W[oodc]ock, Mr. H[od]ges, Mr. H[u]nt, Mr. K[ei]th, Mr. T...g, Mr. G..ton, dissenters. AE, Corr. politique, Angleterre, vol. 223, f. 37. For more detail on the interplay between prophets and their opponents, see my *Knaves, Fools, Madmen and that Subtile Effluvium: A Study of the Opposition to the French Prophets*, University of Florida Social Science Monograph Series, 62 (Gainesville, 1978).

On July 2, two days before the major trial of Marion, Daudé and Fatio, John Lacy spoke in tongues (Latin) for the first time. On July 3, Bulkeley wrote to John Chamberlayne about this amazing event:

> If Mr. Lacy had spoken any *modern* Language, Men would then have objected, that he had learned it perhaps by *Travel*, or by Converse with those of that Language; and now that he has spoken in a Language which no Country speaks, it will be objected, that the Spirit of Wisdom would not be the Author of a *Miracle* to no Purpose, to make a Man speak a Language that none other speak, or may be converted in. Thus do Men fight against even all the sensible Demonstrations of the Goodness of God to them.

So followers learned to expect instant rejection. "If Men will not believe us," wrote Bulkeley in the same letter, "we have the testimony of our Consciences, to approve to us our Sincerity."[57]

On the eve of the trial the French Prophets had already developed attitudes toward the law and toward opposition that would make it easier to accept any outcome of legal prosecution. Lacy and Bulkeley had registered a meetinghouse for the group and had sought to maintain the credit of the group in the courts with warrants against rioters. Lacy at the same time had denied the jurisdiction of courts over divine messengers and predicted renewed persecution for the faithful. The French Prophets saw their efforts to impress critics thwarted by an unsympathetic handling of divine signs, and Bulkeley contended that no argument and no wonder could induce belief if people had hardened their hearts against the Lord.

On July 4, Marion, Daudé and Fatio appeared upon bail at Queen's Bench Court in Guildhall. The three men had received considerable encouragement from Lacy's Latin inspirations.[58] They were glad too that, ostensibly, the French Prophets as a group were not on trial. (Cavalier and Fage, as well as the new prophets, had not been charged at all, and the active secretary Charles Portales, though sworn as a witness, was not mentioned in the indictment.) Finally, as a result of the prophetic

---

57. Fatio Calendar, 7/2/1707; Lacy, *Warnings*, I, 56-57; Kingston, II, 75. Cf. the reactions of the ministers to their meeting with the French Prophets on July 2: "Mr. Y[at]es had not altered his Mind, upon the uttering of Latin. Mr. K[eit]h had more to say to lessen the Credit of the supposed *Inspirations* being from the Spirit of God. Mr. W[oodcoc]k also was scandalized at Mr. Lacy's *Whistling*, when under his Ecstatic Motions." Kingston, I, 61.

58. Lacy spoke his first French inspiration on the fourth, during the trial: "Tant plus qu'ils vous persécutent, tant plus de Joie intérieure je te donnerai." Lacy, *Warnings*, I, 63. The next day, Anthony Ashley Cooper, third earl of Shaftesbury, heard Lacy pronounce a warning in Latin (Fatio Calendar, 7/5/1707). The eventual outcome was Shaftesbury's famous *A Letter Concerning Enthusiasm* (1708), for a discussion of which see my *Knaves, Fools, Madmen and that Subtile Effluvium*, 53-54.

guarantees of the last months, they were secure in their roles as men suffering from the plots of the ungodly.

Prosecutors for the Queen, informed by the French consistories, denounced six articles in Marion's *Warnings*, one for blasphemy and five for tendency to sedition.[59] Misson vouched for the sincerity of the accused and spoke against the injustice of the accusations. Portales, next to testify, said succinctly that it was the voice of God or an angel which spoke through Marion. The counselor-at-law for the three men, probably John Hooke,[60] showed that none had impugned Marion's integrity. He explained that the suspect expressions from the *Warnings* were to be understood in a mystical sense, in the style of Old Testament prophets. The expressions did not refer to specific civil or ecclesiastic authorities. Fatio reviewed the true meanings of several of the more "profane" warnings: "Thunderbolts are preparing," "You have not to continue long in the Country—but I will destroy the World," "All shall be destroyed."[61] He also enjoined the Chief Justice to reflect upon the dangers of rejecting a message which claimed to come from God, reminding Holt of the fate of the Jews who spurned Jesus.

After a trial of almost three hours, the jury returned a verdict of "Guilty of printing and publishing the Book."[62] Since the verdict was rendered outside the legal term, Holt had to delay sentencing to the next term, and the defendants were released upon bail to appear again in November. The French Prophets interpreted the verdict as a victory: the jury had not judged Marion's *Warnings* explicitly profane or seditious.[63] As obvious

---

59. Misson, *Meslange de littérature*, 30. The following account of the trial is drawn primarily from the "Récit abrégé" (Stack MSS lg) written by the French Prophets, and from the hostile but reasonably complete *Account of the Tryal, Examination and Conviction of Elias Marion, and other of the French Prophets* (1707) broadside.

60. Kingston, I, 50, but Hooke may have been simply a consultant to one James Mazel (relative of the Camisard Abraham Mazel?): un Particulier, *Lettres à Monsieur Misson, l'honnête homme* (1707-08) Letter 5, 13-14.

61. "Lettre écrite d'Angleterre," *Nouvelles de la république* (September, 1707) 340; *Tryal, Examination and Condemnation of the French Prophets* (1707) broadside; Marion, *Prophetical Warnings*, 1, 7, 60.

62. Fatio Calendar, 7/5/1707; Stack MSS lg: Récit abrégé, f. 26v. *Account of the Tryal, Examination and Conviction of the Pretended French Prophets* (1707) broadside, reports that the prophet and his companions were also "forbid their Tumultuous and Disorderly Assemblies."

63. "Relation historique," *Nouvelles de la république* (February, 1708) 135; Misson, *Meslange de littérature*, 31; Stack MSS lg: Récit abrégé, f. 26v. Jean Lions, a Huguenot minister friendly to the French Prophets, said, "la justice ne les a point condamné d'imposture Mais seulement pour avoir fait imprimé et publié un livre." HAL, Misc. Papers 105, MSS of the Eglise de l'Artillerie, Oct. 9, 1707.

reward for their perseverance, the French Prophets attracted more followers. Lacy had prophesied before the trial, "'Tis strange to you, that you should have more Friends, after you are in Custody, than you have had before. Your Sufferings shall turn to my Glory." Public assemblies continued unabated; important new prophets—John Potter, Mary Keimer, Abraham Whitrow, Mary Beer—appeared in July and August. The faith of followers was not shaken.[64]

Wonders happened. Lacy now spoke in Greek and performed automatic writing.[65] In the evening of July 19, a sign came from the heavens. A careful eyewitness wrote: "The most remarkable thing has happened just now, as ever was known in my Memory—It is now about 7 a clock in the Evening—for this half hour it has Rained Flies all over London, in a most prodigious manner; the streets are all covered with them, People's Hats and Cloaks are full of them." The *Observator's* Countryman remarked that "There's my Neighbour, Goody Prattle, says, she will go to the new Prophets at the Barbican, and enquire of them the Meaning of it." The French Prophets may have triumphed in the event; it answered well to a prophecy that "all of a sudden the Air shall be covered with thick darkness."[66]

In this milieu Lacy proclaimed unusual judgments. On July 15 he prophesied "A terrible overthrow of Buildings in this City," and on July 26 he said, "How, how, how, there's the Tower Guns will roar in a few days, before this day seven-night." The month culminated in miracles and visions: Lacy glided ten feet across the floor, Betty Gray prophesied the gift of healing for Lacy, and she herself had a vision of a golden bird.[67]

The gift of tongues and the gift of healing had not been granted to *inspirés* in the Desert, and the Tower Guns prediction was the first openly time-specific prediction made by any French Prophet. Less than two

64. Lacy, *Warnings*, I, 52; Roach Diary, I, ff. 60-60v.
65. Fatio Calendar, 7/6 through 7/12/1707; Lacy, *Warnings*, I, 67-68. On July 11, "J.W." [Josiah Woodward] wrote to Dr. White Kennet, "I spake with Sir R Bulkeley yesterday, who solemnly affirms that there is a gift of languages among them, and that specimens will be printed; and that they shall speedily have the gift of healing. I would desire you to refrain printing anything against them for a while; for if these (truly miraculous) are manifest, they will demand an awful Regard." BM, Lansdowne MSS 938, f. 39, cited in John Henry Blunt, *Dictionary of Sects* (new ed., 1886) 100-101.
66. Letter to Daniel Defoe's *Review of the State of the English Nation*, IV, 80; *The Observator*, VI, 42 (7/23-7/26/1707); *Clavis Prophetica: or, a Key to the Prophecies of Mons. Marion, and the other Camisars* (2 parts, 1707) I, 37-38 and II, 36. Defoe gave an accurate explanation: these were flying ants mating in mid-air and then falling to the ground.
67. Fatio Calendar, 7/30/1707; Lacy, *Warnings*, I, 100 and II, 21-22, 26-27, 39-40, 64-66.

months after Lacy had spoken his first prophecy, one month after Betty Gray had become a prophet, they and other English prophets had begun to draw upon distinctively English millenarian traditions. Tongues and healing were part of the New Jerusalem ethos of wide evangelism and regeneration, certainly not of the Camisard ethos of cataclysm and battle. The English prophets were accepting the miracles and martyrdom of the Cévennes only to invert them, linking martyrdom to missionary activity and miracle to the restoration of the self. The function of the prophets within the group changed as the nature of their powers changed, and the increasing status of the English prophets threatened the position of the *inspirés*. Latent conflicts between the old and the new prophets, between English and Huguenot, soon were manifest.

The first volume of Lacy's warnings was printed on July 18. A week later, Bulkeley received a divine order to write a brief advertisement to be cried in the streets but was cautioned, "Ay and then, then leave them to themselves. Nobody must know when you go, nobody, not your own Friends, and Families." During the month, Lacy had warned of plotting enemies and given directions to maintain a degree of secrecy hitherto unnecessary. By July 25 a number of followers had received commands to go on a very private retreat.[68]

When Lacy, Bulkeley, Fatio, Gray and the Alluts left for Bushy (near St. Albans) on July 28, even Elie Marion was surprised. The retreat excluded the three *inspirés* and two of the foremost scribes (Portales and Daudé). The core of the group was changing, taking into account female and English prophets. Lacy's warnings in July revealed an acute concern with hierarchy: "And I will make it known, that the Prayers of the Servants I especially choose, shall prevail in behalf of others. I will have them all mutually dependent. No superiority among them. If any one glorifies himself, I will take away what he glories of." On July 10 he repeated, "I have said, there should be no Superiority among my Children." And again, in Bushy where Lacy levitated: "Let none think of another the better, nor of himself; for I don't intend to exalt any one. I may give Distinction, but wherever I see an assuming of Self-ascription, I'll take away. The Order of my Government requires some Difference, but none for themselves, their sake, for their Honour." Yet there was an air of superiority about the clique that went to Bushy. In July Lacy had promised Gray and Fatio the gift of healing, and he had also renamed

---

68. Fatio Calendar, 7/18-7/25/1707; Lacy, *Warnings,* I, 81 and II, 34-38, 49-50.

them. Fatio was the patriarch Isaac; Gray was Sarai, meaning "No more Bondage." The renaming was a valuable gesture, as Lacy explained under inspiration: "I pronounce thee his selected Servant, and received into his House more solemnly this Day, to be a resplendent Pillar."[69]

Marion, in a letter to Fatio dated August 5, showed a wounded awareness of the secrecy and distinction assumed by the six people on retreat. Cautiously, he tried to ensure that the retreat would not cause any split among followers:

> We were much surprised as well as all your brothers by your departure, not knowing whether it was by fear or by commandment. . . . If it is by commandment, he who believes he has received it from God should not hide the commandment from his brother . . . because the spirit of God has no partialities. . . . I must assure you, my very dear brother, that I make these enquiries of you neither through envy nor through any design to contradict some commandment of God if one there was.[70]

Marion had good reason to believe that the retreat was inspired more by fear than by God. The Tower Guns prophecy was subject to clear disconfirmation, and the retreat coincided nicely with the time of its supposed accomplishment. (The guns were to roar before August 3; Lacy was on retreat from July 28 to August 8.) Lacy, Gray and Jean Allut had been involved in agitated signs and warnings which dealt with the Whore of Babylon (whose defeat was performed in mime) and the morning star (whose brightness was embraced by Lacy). These representations of judgment and reward became notorious, and sexual innuendo against the prophets appeared in enemy tracts.[71] Lacy's recently printed *Warnings* might well draw the same prosecution as Marion's *Warnings* in April. By late July the staunchest believers might have expected trouble.

Even so, those who went to Bushy and then on to St. Albans had hesitated. Fatio, in an unsent answer to Marion, wrote:

> We left by an order, announced long ago and repeated diverse times by different people. And for greater certainty, having prayed for the order to be repeated if it was the will of God, and to determine that no mixture of foreign spirits and human passions entered into it, there came a precise order from the mouths of two of our brothers, to one of whom it was said that he would be exterminated

---

69. Fatio Calendar, July 1707; Lacy, *Warnings*, I, 68, 83 and II, 22, 25-26, 67. Fatio was also promised the gift of discerning spirits, Gray the gifts of tongues and elegance in speech: II, 21, 27.

70. BPUG, MSS fr. 601, ff. 241-241v.

71. Kingston, I, 65-66; Lacy, *Warnings*, II, 7-8 and III, 6-7. Homosexual innuendo was directed against Jean Cavalier in Kingston, II, 210 and the *Clavis Prophetica*, II, 34.

if he did not obey, and to the other, that he should depart alone, if we did not wish to follow him.[72]

The care taken to confirm the order for departure, the need to ascertain that no alien influences had entered the prophecies, these would become group habits as prophet pulled against prophet and the danger of divisions increased. This retreat bore the first signs of cracks within the group. Through Lacy's warnings and the special graces bestowed upon those at Bushy, followers were sensitized to the problems of hierarchy and differences between prophets and between nations. By August, 1707, the French Prophets faced unconfirmed predictions, insinuations of immorality and possible schism. The influx of English followers and prophets had aggravated the first two problems and created the third.

The Shaping of the True Church

An appreciation of the strains within the group may have sparked those at Bushy toward a closer relationship. Their retreat, as others before, knitted them together in solemn ceremony. But there was more; this retreat involved the reassertion of the family as a model for community. The Camisard ethos of cataclysm had substituted the tribe for the broken families of the Desert; now, men and women who had not been part of that war returned the millennial vision to the hearth which had been central to the *petits prophètes* just after the Revocation. Jean Allut's inspiration on August 2 ended, "My Children, great Blessing is going to fall upon you. You are my Family; the Family well-beloved of the Eternal." On August 6, the four men and two women celebrated a type of communion service, never before celebrated among the French Prophets. Lacy, inspired, passed around a plate symbolic of the Bread of Life and a cup symbolic of the Wine that rejoices the Heart of Man.[73]

Appropriately, during the retreat Lacy had a vision of the True Church, "a large luminous Chapel, filled with a thin lucid Smoke; People in the Side-Aisles worshipping; no Roof; but a Circle of Angels in the Air over it." It was the universal church of the New Jerusalem ethos, a second model of community: large, roofless, blessed. If inspiration within such a community might be frighteningly diverse, this too would be overseen; before the retreat ended on August 8, the circle of six received a promise

---

72. BPUG, MSS fr. 601, ff. 242-242v.
73. Lacy, *Warnings*, II, 75, 102-10.

that God would always make it known when an evil spirit spoke among the French Prophets. As a family, as a True Church, as men and women freed from anxiety over true inspiration, the people at Bushy located a sense of community and integrity. The retreat had served as ritual purification: they had fasted, they had found a more elevated communion with the Eternal, and they learned that angels protected the True Church. They returned to London with confidence during the second week of August, to confront the spectres of failed prophecies and the taunts of mobs.[74]

The Tower Guns had made no noise whatsoever. Lacy explained in an inspiration in London:

> They know not what to make of the Words, *little time, speedily, shortly, suddenly, soon*. They would have me define the Time, in the Prophecies of my ancient Servants. Yet those Predictions carried in them my authority, and were fulfilled soon enough, for those, that suffered under them. . . . I have seen it best, not to assign the punctual Times, by their Definition among Men; that I might keep Men always, in their due distance, and reverential Fear of invading what I reserve, in secret, to myself. . . . The Tower-Guns are the *Tormenta e Turre aethera*, with which this City I have declared should be battered. . . . I have not yet given a Key to Time in this Revelation.

The prophecy was a metaphor for storms and thunders to arrive in due course according to a mysterious providential plan. Of course, critics would harp on the failure of the literal prophecy, but the same critics refused to believe that Lacy had cured Elizabeth Gray of temporary blindness while at Bushy. Lacy warned on August 14, "I know the other Signs of Healing will be doubted of, and disbelieved too." Followers interpreted predictions and miracles as symbols meant primarily for members of the True Church.[75]

Sunday, August 17, a miracle was promised to Elizabeth Gray. Lacy, said Gray under inspiration, would heal her. Presently she choked and seemed to be suffocating. Lacy prayed for the healing gift while onlookers argued over the nature of her illness. Lacy did not receive the gift, and Gray came out of her ordeal by herself. Some followers claimed that the miracle had occurred: Gray would have died had not the Holy Spirit rescued her. Lacy thought the miracle had not happened. Dr. Timothy Byfield, French Prophet and vendor of the panacea *Sal volatile oleosum*, reconciled the

74. *Ibid.*, II, 73-74, 117, 135. The image of the group as *the* church was new, but the image of a nascent true church had appeared before: Lacy, *Warnings*, I, 54 and Marion, *Prophetical Warnings*, 3, 121-23, 185.
75. Lacy, *Warnings*, II, 171-72, 178.

dispute. His explanation became the prototype for later defenses against unconfirmed prophecy:

> Although God might intend in the Morning to work a Miracle by the Hand of his Servant, for the Strengthening the Faith of his Children, and the Convincing of others of his Power and Glory; yet, there coming in a Mixed Multitude, a Medley sort of People, with Obdurate Hearts, and Hearts set against it, and Spirits prepossessed, and resolved not to believe: Now [consider], whether God might not withdraw his Spirit for a time, because of the Unbelief and Want of Faith in these People.

An inspiration delivered by Gray after her recovery stressed the importance of extended faith which does not rely upon a single miracle as its source; she too said that prophecy required faith: "As to Accomplishments of Predictions, 'tis as unreasonable to expect the fulfilling of every one of those Predictions, before you believe any one of them; and not believe the Predictions of any thing till you see it passed, that's not believing at all."[76]

These double-edged arguments reflected the ambivalence of the French Prophets toward unbelievers. One hoped to convince sceptics, but they were more than likely impossible to convince; God's signs and wonders were dedicated to the conversion of sceptics, but they should not be expected to sway the obdurate. Persecution was a true outward sign of true prophets, who throughout history were slighted; on the other hand, persecution was a divine trial of the faithful. Everything giving outward testimony to the prophets' powers might be perceived as an inward testimony to the faith of followers. As the French Prophets expanded, ambivalence toward unbelievers became more painful, for the group could sustain itself without further recourse to the unredeemed, and yet, with so vital a message as the coming of judgment, how could followers— especially those imbued with the ethos of the New Jerusalem—forbear witnessing to sceptics?[77]

The problem of faith in the midst of unfulfilled or coded predictions disturbed not only the relationship between believers and nonbelievers, but also the loyalties of members within the True Church. Elizabeth Gray's deferred miracle, Fatio noted, had shocked several believers. On August 22, Lacy's warning dealt with fears that the group was losing cohesion:

> Indeed, this shaking of all Things, before they are renewed, how should it else be? it must be attended with Confusion of Tongues, and loud Clamors: and I'll

---

76. *Ibid.*, I, ii, vii-viii; [Mr. Collett], *The Honest Quaker, or, The Forgeries and Imposture of the Pretended French Prophets and their Abettors Exposed* (1707).

77. "They would hang you if they could, yet you are concerned for them," prophesied Lacy on July 20. *Warnings*, II, 6-7.

divide them. There will be offences too, among my People; . . . . But there shall nothing happen, among my faithful Followers and Expectants, but what will be found, in the Consequence, overruled by my Wisdom, to have tended to the Good of the several Persons exercised. And all the seeming Disagreement will, by my Art, be directed to form the Beauty of the Piece.[78]

Like the controversy over the deferred miracle, group disputes were another part of a divine test; in perspective they would make elegant sense.

Another development in August exposed group efforts toward consensus. Spurred in part by tracts published against them, the French Prophets began collecting and preserving materials intended for an impartial history of the group. On August 7 the Lord commanded Lacy to "give the History, as it lies on my side," and he was directed to keep a diary of extraordinary events among the followers. By 1710, the French Prophets had compiled seven historical reports for posterity.[79]

The men sitting as scribes had established the historical importance of the French Prophets, although their task had been primarily to furnish accurate transcriptions of the warnings. Lacy's August commands gave a more formal recognition to the group as an historical phenomenon. In the context of the changing composition of membership, the desire for a careful history was an expression of the need to document the group's essential continuity from the Cévennes to London, from the *inspirés* to English prophets. Moreover, the histories might prevent dissension and encourage a uniform interpretation of events. Historical thinking—with a serious attempt to link contemporary happenings to the heralds of the millennium—would place the True Church in its proper setting. Followers, like the Philadelphians before them, soon discovered convincing parallels between the actions of the French Prophets and the universal progress of the Spirit. The commission to prepare histories was also a recognition that the end of the world would probably not occur tomorrow. Some little time was left for the establishment of the True Church and for chronicling its miraculous birth in France and growth in England. As followers tempered their millennial vision—as they looked less for cataclysm than for the foundations of the New Jerusalem—they adopted an historical perspective on their own millenarian group.[80]

78. Fatio Calendar, 8/17/1707; "Signe de suffocation sur Eliz Gray lequel rebute plusieurs." Lacy, *Warnings*, III, 17-18.
79. Lacy, *Warnings*, II, 127, 174; of the seven works noted in *MMM*, 167, four are extant: two in the *MMM*, the Historical Relation and the Récit abrégé in Stack MSS 1j and 1g.
80. Elizabeth Isichei suggests that recourse to writing history is an attempt at group revival: "From Sect to Church among English Quakers," *British Journal of Sociology* 15 (1964) 220. On seventeenth-century ideas of history and prophecy, see J.G.A. Pocock, "Time,

The histories had value, as well, as sources of information for followers in a group too large for the activities of all members to be commonly observed. Lacy's demand for witnessed accounts must be viewed in the light of a spreading religious movement. Between mid-August and mid-September, nine more English followers had inspirations. Six of them were female, three were under the age of twenty. For the first time there were more females than males inspired, more English than French in the group. The number and variety of prophets meant that no individual could keep in constant touch with them all. Fears of false prophecy, calmed at Bushy, came again to the surface. Jean Cavalier reprimanded Thomas Dutton (an English newcomer to the group) for "having forced the Spirit."[81] Lacy on September 28 tried to weld perceptions of group size to an argument in favor of numerous prophets; he prophesied, ostensibly toward the critics:

> Why; if I had sent a Prophet alone to predict; you would have more easily suppressed him. You won't believe the many. And, if they were more, you won't believe them; though they do testify one to another, and not contradict one another, and this without Consultation. . . . They are separate in Habitations. They are different, in Condition in the World. They are Persons never knowing one another before. And yet these all agree, being dictated to, by the same Spring.[82]

This prophecy made of the group's increasing variety a virtue. Like persecution, the gathering of strangers was painful but necessary, a proof of the energy of the Holy Spirit in the last days. The historians would present the evidences of the Spirit in their bewildering variety, since variety itself was God's sign to the world of the approach of the Kingdom.

The True Church was apprised of its true home on the fourth of September, when Elie Marion identified London with the New Jerusalem. An important feature of the New Jerusalem was, despite its size, its complete and invincible purity. On September 5, one day after the publication of Lacy's second volume of warnings, ten French Prophets left the New Jerusalem for a retreat to the northern suburb of Hoxton, where perhaps they had a better perspective: "Behold my Jerusalem. Walk round about her. Behold her Towers. Tell the Number of Her Palaces. My Mountains are round about Her. . . . Her Gates are Magnificent: her Fortresses Inaccessible. And for Her sake I will renew this World. No

---

History and Eschatology in the Thought of Thomas Hobbes," in J.H. Elliott and H.G. Koenigsberger, eds., *The Diversity of History* (Ithaca, 1970) 149-98.
81. Fatio Calendar, 9/11-9/12/1707 and see Appendix VII.
82. Lacy, *Warnings*, III, 127-28.

poisonous Thing shall creep within her Precincts."[83] The retreat mixed Huguenots (Marion, Fatio, Portales, the Alluts) and English (Gray, Bulkeley, Thomas Emes, Benjamin Jackson—a good friend of Bulkeley's), new and old followers, new and old prophets, male and female, young and middle-aged. It demonstrated how well the True Church might entertain many differences, many palaces, and yet stand whole and magnificent, free from poisonous things. Their vision hinted too at inclinations to merge the ethos of cataclysm and the ethos of the New Jerusalem, the mountains of the Cévennes and the mansions of London.

The day of the retreat to Hoxton, the French Prophet Marie Le Tellier gave birth to a child. When she and her husband Daniel presented the child for baptism at the French Protestant church called the Artillery, the minister d'Argenteuil agreed to baptize the child only if godparents "of our Communion" presented it. Jean Lions, another Huguenot minister, acted as advocate on behalf of the Le Telliers, to no avail. The child was not baptized in a French Protestant church.[84]

This incident, as well as the suspension of several followers from the Threadneedle Street and Artillery churches, furthered the group impulse to regard themselves as the True Church.[85] Discontent with the established ministry had been building for a long while; now the prophets would be God's ministers. Elizabeth Gray had recently warned: "Yes, deceitful Hypocrites. They are afraid you should come and put down all their Learning, all their Doctrine. . . . Yes, these are a parcel of fine righteous Folks in their own Conceits: but you shall be my minister; you shall preach to my People very shortly." On September 8, Lacy was promised the ability to explain scriptures. By the end of September, the prophets had delivered blessings, celebrated communion, expounded scripture, and offered up prayers for the assembled. As ministers to the last dispensation, the inspired could simultaneously pronounce judgments, spread the

---

83. Fatio Calendar, 9/5/1707; Lacy, *Warnings*, III, 48.

84. The Le Tellier child was eventually baptized by Daniel Le Tellier himself in 1709. Jean Lions's refusal to sign a declaration denouncing the French Prophets led to his suspension from the pulpit and engendered a heated controversy. Among the mass of manuscript and printed material on Jean Lions, see esp. [Claude Groteste de la Mothe], *Relation de ce qui s'est passé sur l'affaire de Sieur Jean Lions Ministre (1707)*; Jean Lions, *Relation de ce qui s'est passé entre Jean Lions ministre et les consistoires* (1707) and his *Apologie* (1708); [Pierre Rival], *Réfutation de la prétendue apologie* (title page missing: 1708?).

85. On August 10, Isaac Havy had been the first follower to be cut off from any organized religious body—the Threadneedle Street Church. In September, Jeanne and Madeleine Raoux were excommunicated from the same church, and Pierre Dubuc suspended from the Artillery Church. HAL, MS 8, Threadneedle Street Livre des actes de 1692/3 à 1708, 530-35, and MS 187, Registre des actes du consistoire de l'Eglise de l'Artillerie, 62-63.

"Gospel of Peace," and fulfill the ceremonial requirements of any Christian community.[86]

The state of Christianity (disparate, dominated by "Sects") and the importance of the "Way of universal Union" were predominant prophetic themes in September. "So it becomes me to unite all things in one," prophesied Lacy. "The Jew and the Gentile Church are now to be united: the Heathen to be called, which has never been done fully yet."[87] The call to unite; the creation of a church, a ministry and a history; the collaborative reinterpretation of time-specific prophecy and deferred miracle—all muffled the tensions of growth. New powers and gifts were accompanied by the development of an image of the group as a family and a church. Followers responded to the possibly divisive influence of new English prophets by recalling and codifying the history of the group, its continuity, its unified mission. Historical perspective established a firmer group identity. Most crucial, French and English prophets both shared in the shifting of millennial perspective, slowly, awkwardly, from warfare to evangelism, so that martyrdom was not the warrior's reward but the missionary's burden, and the tribe striking in the mountains became the communicants in a "large, luminous Chapel."

The Second Trial

With the true Church founded and the prophets become ministers, with miracles understood and historians hard at work, followers seemed to think that things were coming to a head. Fatio asked his family in Geneva to suspend judgment on the French Prophets: "A few months, a few years will clarify all things. Your patience need not wait three years [to be satisfied], perhaps not even three months."[88] In October, Lacy and Thomas Emes, concerned still with the cataclysm that would precede the New Jerusalem, warned of fire and brimstone to rain down upon London, "quickly, in a few Days. And ye here present shall see it, or feel it, one of the two." On October 12 Lacy intimated that God's servants would raise the dead; *that*, Jean Lions believed, would be the decisive proof of the new

---

86. Lacy, *Warnings*, II, 66 and III, 31, 36, 49, 60. The delay in administering baptism was indicative of group hesitance to depart entirely from "established" churches. Only a few children born of Huguenot parents were denied baptism.

87. Lacy, *Warnings*, III, 70, 75, 88. Marion in late November, 1706, had prophesied, "I will have my Word to go forth to the four Corners of the World," but this sense of mission in his prophecies was not frequent. *Prophetical Warnings*, 36.

88. BPUG, MSS fr. 602, f. 114 (9/5/1707).

dispensation.⁸⁹ Mary Keimer appealed to her audience to repent before the opportunity was lost: "Oh, ye will never have done scoffing; no, till I send my Judgments: Then ye will repent, when it is too late."⁹⁰

The accelerated growth of the French Prophets in the autumn of 1707 was taken as a sign that millennial expectations had become more general. In late October Lacy wrote of "50 or 60 English in London" who had the preliminary marks of inspiration. Sometime in November an observer noted: "The Prophets continue to furnish out the talk of the town, they multiply against all opposition, about a hundred having the gift of the preparatory symptoms."⁹¹ The French Prophets met at the Barbican and elsewhere, in public and in private. In late November they attracted English followers from outside London for the first time. Jonathan Taylor, a young Birmingham cutler, went to see the prophets in London and received a blessing. He returned in December with two others, inaugurating the Birmingham circle of French Prophets which would in the 1730s play a crucial part in the history of the group.⁹²

In the light of imminent judgment and the numbers flocking to the last dispensation, the continued trial of Marion, Fatio and Daudé appeared to followers as a symbol of foolish human stubbornness.⁹³ The three men presented themselves at Westminster for sentencing on November 6. On the tenth, due to a clerk's error which would normally void proceedings, the judges ordered the case retried. There was a definite element of victory for the French Prophets in the dismissal of charges and the opening of a new trial.⁹⁴

Only the day before, November 9, the prominent Presbyterian minister Edmund Calamy had preached against the French Prophets in London and

---

89. Lacy, *Warnings*, III, 118, 169-70; *A Collection of Prophetical Warnings of the Eternal Spirit* (1708) 73, 78; HAL, Misc. Papers 105, MSS of the Eglise de l'Artillerie, 10/9/1707. Cf. also Lacy's warnings of a fiery tempest for London (July 31): *Warnings*, II, 68, 70.

90. *Collection of Warnings*, 98-99. This appeal to repent quickly only marginally conflicted with the group's developing historical sense; what was imminent was less the end of the world than the end of divine patience with unbelievers.

91. Lacy, *Warnings*, III, 5-6; *HMC* 15: Portland IV, 462, letter from William Mace to Edward Harley. Some followers first mentioned in the list of 1/19/1708 (Appendix I) had probably joined the group in late 1707.

92. Nathaniel Spinckes, *The New Pretenders to Prophecy Re-examined* (1710) 24.

93. The Huguenot consistories had decided not to drop the case, although some motions in that way had been forwarded: HAL, MS 8, Threadneedle Street Livre des actes de 1692/3 à 1708, 540-41; *Clavis Prophetica*, II, 39; un Particulier, *Lettres à Monsieur Misson*, Letter 4, 17-18; *HMC* 15: Portland IV, 462, Mace says that Justice Holt did not like the proceedings.

94. Fatio Calendar, 11/6-11/10/1707; un Particulier, *Lettres à Monsieur Misson*, Letter 4, 17-19; Narcissus Luttrell, *A Brief Historical Relation of State Affairs from September 1678 to April 1714* (Oxford, 1857) VI, 231-33.

Dr. Offspring Blackall preached against them before the Queen. A week before, William Whiston had dedicated his final Boyle sermon to the false modern prophets. By mid-November more than twenty-five tracts, broadsides and newspaper articles critical of the French Prophets had been published in London.[95] Prophetic warnings occasionally addressed themselves to specific opposition writings.[96] In answer to theological arguments and scriptural debate, prophets during November fleshed out the group's skeletal beliefs in judgment and the millennium, just as they were being compelled to define their relationship to the state in the legal arena.

On November 9, Thomas Dutton warned believers to take literally the promises of scripture that there would be a glorious church on earth where all partook of the Holy Spirit:

> I have said, that my Spirit shall be poured out upon all Flesh: That I will instruct immediately: That my Law shall be written on the Heart of each one: That he shall have no need to enquire of his Neighbor: to ask his Pastor, or his Teacher, which is the Way of the Lord: for he shall know it by my immediate Teaching. ... And almost all have interpreted these Prophecies of this glorious State of this Prince of Peace, in a metaphorical Sense. They have clouded the most glorious Part of my revealed Will. They have overlooked the principal Part of my Revelation.

Lacy said that present-day churchmen robbed the Lord of his Second Coming, which was a "very different thing from sleeping in Jesus, every one as he dies." Inspired, Lacy portrayed the judgment day and the Second Coming in premillennial terms; both would occur on a familiar earth at the end of but still within time. Judgment would be as real as that upon Marion, Fatio and Daudé, but for eternity. Humans would enter into the millennial church on earth by their present faith. The salvation which the Lord promised was not what others saw as the salvation of the soul at the death of the body; it was a material, terrestrial salvation. When the gates of the New Jerusalem shut, the faithless would understand how literal were scripture prophecies.[97]

It is noteworthy that Lacy and Dutton, English prophets, were the ones

---

95. Offspring Blackall, *"The Way of Trying Prophets." A Sermon Preached before the Queen at St. James's, November 9, 1707* (1707); William Whiston, *The Accomplishment of Scripture Prophecies* (1708) Sermon 8; N.N., *Account of the Three French Prophets*, 16. For a complete bibliography of opposition works, see my *Knaves, Fools, Madmen and that Subtile Effluvium*. Cf. Jacob, *Newtonians*, ch. 7.

96. Lacy, for example, prophesied directly against Richard Kingston: *English and French Prophets Mad or Bewitched* (1707) broadside.

97. *Collection of Warnings*, 25-26, 111-12, 115, 117. Lacy later denied (an afterthought or change of sentiment?) that the French Prophets threatened unbelievers with eternal damnation: *The Scene of Delusions, By the Reverend Mr. Owen of Warrington, At his own*

to elaborate the millenarian beliefs of the French Prophets. The English, accustomed to close definition and exposition, were taking doctrinal control of the group; as they did so, they tended to see the ethos of the *inspirés* less as that of cataclysm than of judgment. What they were doing—and had been doing, since the translation of the *Théâtre sacré*—was situating the origins of the group in the familial social tradition of the *petits prophètes* anterior to the war in the Cévennes. So the English, through their prophets and literate controversialists like Bulkeley and Moult, worked in two ways to reshape their heritage from the *inspirés*: they inverted the context of such Camisard values as cataclysm, martyrdom and rescue by referring them to the New Jerusalem, and they identified the group not with the Camisards directly but with the ethos of judgment from which the war had broken. Doctrinal consistency could scarcely be established during this process of translation and transposition. Whether or not followers were aware of the group metamorphoses, they were becoming increasingly aware of the theological and behavioral consistency expected of them by both friends and enemies.[98]

English prophets in November were particularly conscious that the group itself was on trial. As they had defended group beliefs, now they defined group behavior. In a curious set of warnings at the Barbican on November 13, the Lord told followers to act with decorum in public assemblies, lest spectators judge them adversely: "Don't break my Order, *Oh! Oh! Oh!* for how shall public Assemblies be to my Honour, if you do not Obey me, as God, with Fear? . . . The more public, the more care, and fear is incumbent on you. I command to you such Prudence, as don't disturb me, *Ya, Ya,* nor betray any shame you have of my Word." On the fourteenth, Elizabeth Gray was struck dumb by Lacy for disobeying divine orders.[99] The French Prophets were learning to see themselves as a group with problems of group prestige and as a church with defined postures of worship. The process of unification escalated the degree of commitment required of followers. They had a True Church to embrace, a more complex theology of salvation to accept, a higher standard of religious

---

Earnest Request, Considered and Confuted (1723?) 66-67. Cf. Thomas Emes, *The Atheist turned Deist, and the Deist turned Christian* (1698) 186-87. On the significance of Lacy's reference to sleeping in Jesus, see George H. Williams, "Socinianism and Deism: From Eschatological Elitism to Universal Immortality?" *Historical Reflections* 2 (1975) 265-90. Were the prophets simply warning people to repent, or did they expect all the repentant to join their group? Cf. A.D. Nock, *Conversion* (Oxford, 1961) 1-16.

98. Some critics and followers were aware of certain doctrinal changes concerning the consciousness of the prophets under inspiration; see chapter four.

99. *English and French Prophets Mad or Bewitcht,* broadside; Roach Diary, I, f. 92; Lacy, *Relation of the Dealings of God,* 24.

behavior with which to conform. There were also heavier pressures on members of the True Church to testify publicly to their faith.

On November 15, Lacy told Richard Roach that he had miraculously restored James Jackson's sight and that God "was here going forth to do wonders: Cures on the streets of the City." By November 16, Roach, with healing powers, had restored prophet Gray's voice. Perhaps it was she, perhaps another who that morning went on the first literal mission of the French Prophets. An inspired woman stripped in the shadows of the Sardinian (Roman Catholic) Chapel in Duke Street and ran naked up to the altar after mass, "where she appeared in several Strange and Indecent Postures, and being seemingly full of the pretended Spirit, she did hold forth in a Powerful manner; and could by no means be prevailed upon to desist; but on the contrary, told them she was come to Reform the People, and bring them to a right understanding." She refused clothing and spoke for fifteen minutes, then dressed and left.[100]

Six days later, on November 22, a second jury again found Marion, Daudé and Fatio guilty. Mary Beer, age thirteen, prophesied: "Woe to those that now condemn me, without searching the Cause, which I now lay before them. I am the Judge of all; and as they judge me, so shall I judge them. . . . But, my Children, I suffer them to rise up against me, for their greater Condemnation." She appended a comforting note: the children of God would shortly triumph worldwide, for "'tis not to this Nation alone, that I send my Spirit; but it shall be spread over all, in a short time."[101] The second trial and sentence were not, as the first were, hedged by retreats but rather imbedded in an equation of martyrdom with missionary purpose. The French Prophets looked outward to the widened task of crying the midnight cry to other nations, to heathens and Jews. The prophets had new gifts, followers anticipated more heavenly signs, the True Church encompassed people from many Christian "Sects" and was growing. How could persecution deter men and women (and children) who campaigned not for earthly honors but for God?

In their history of the second trial, the French Prophets depicted Marion, Fatio and Daudé as brave martyrs wounded to the quick by the arrogance of humankind. Asked if the defendants had anything to say before sentence was pronounced, Fatio recapitulated his arguments, showing the justices the danger in which they placed themselves and the

---

100. Roach Diary, I, f. 92; *The French Prophetess turned Adamite* (1707) reprinted by W. Sparrow Simpson in "Lincoln's Inn Fields: The French Prophetess," *Notes and Queries,* 6th ser., XI (Jan. 10. 1885) 21-22. This was the first incident of prophesying outside the group.
101. Fatio Calendar, 11/22/1707/; *Collection of Warnings*, 6-8.

people of the kingdom by pretending to judge a cause which was not theirs to judge. One justice cut him short, eager to get on with other business. The sentence was pronounced: the three men were to stand twice on a scaffold (once at Charing Cross, the next day at the Royal Exchange), wearing papers explaining their crimes. They were to pay a fine of £20 each and to give sureties for their good behavior for one year.[102]

The three men reacted to the sentence with joy; their account merits citation at length for its tone as well as its detail:

> The sentence pronounced, we testified to the entire assembly the pleasure with which we received it; and that we esteemed ourselves honored by what Christ found us worthy to suffer in his Name. Also we received this Sentence with a joyful air, which corresponded to the liberty and contentment of our hearts. We answered them only, that we appealed our cause before the King of Kings, the Judge of Judges, who must judge us all one day. After that, we were handed over to the officers of the law who removed from two of us, namely J Daudé and N Facio, the swords which we were wearing at our sides; and had us pass all three as if in triumph before our Enemies.[103]

This was a notable day, for precisely one year ago had begun "our Solemn Engagement with Jesus Christ, our true King and Master, who we desire to follow and to serve, through the Aid which he promised us by his Holy Spirit." On November 28, 1706, through Elie Marion, God had given them the horns of his altar to hold and to keep, as a safeguard and sword.[104] What matter if the swords of Fatio and Daudé were taken by law officers, when French Prophets had the sword of the Lord with them always?

November 28, 1707, was an equally important day for John Lacy, whose third and final volume of *Warnings* appeared for sale. In the preface, Lacy made a personal commitment that assumed much significance within and without the group. Rumors of the commitment had circulated in London since the preface was signed on October 29. The next day, Bishop Burnet's Presbyterian cousin, James Johnston, had written to the elderly Sir William Trumbull, "Lacy has printed that unless God attest all solemnly

102. Stack MSS 1g: Récit abrégé, 47-48; Fatio Calendar, 11/28/1707; *Post Boy*, No. 1956 (Nov. 27-29, 1707); Luttrell, *State Affairs*, VI, 239; Boyer, *Annals. Year the Sixth*, 371. That the men did not, as often reported, stand in the pillory but on a (less shameful) scaffold is emphasized in *English Post*, No. 1119 (Dec. 1-3, 1707); BPUG, MSS fr. 602, f. 115; Greater London RO (Middlesex) Acc 1017/2, Diary of the Quaker Peter Briggins, 1706-09, 2:xth month: 1707. According to the *Clef du cabinet des princes de l'Europe* 8 (February 1708) 130, the £20 fine was later remitted by the Queen due to the poverty of the defendants.
103. Stack MSS 1g: Récit abrégé, 48. They would also have rejoiced to hear that the deputies from the Savoy would be rebuffed by the court in their request to change the sentence to exile: HAL, Threadneedle Street Livre des actes de 1692/3 à 1708, 547.
104. Marion, *Prophetical Warnings*, 34; Stack MSS 1g: Récit abrégé, 68.

within six months, he will own himself in a delusion."[105] Lacy actually committed himself to something less exact: "but as it were preposterous, to have expected the fulfilling of Denunciations, before they are fully published; so this Volume being the Completion of them, if within six months now to come, the might Power of God does not attest, they were from him; I shall before all the World acknowledge my Delusion."[106] In one respect, Lacy was offering himself up to human judgment just as Marion, Fatio and Daudé confronted human law, with an appeal to a higher court. In a second respect, Lacy's commitment bolstered group confidence. Human judgments upon followers would be returned in full measure by the judgments (fire and brimstone, earthquake, heavy clouds) yet to fall on London.

On November 29 the French Prophets had another cause to rejoice. Lacy completed the cure of Hugh Preston, whose boil had intimidated many a physician. Preston was the first person to be cured who had not been a follower beforehand. His cure demonstrated the happy connection between prophetic gifts and the missionary impulse of the True Church. Lacy's success implied that the Lord was already counteracting the legal decision against the group.[107]

Officers led Marion, Fatio and Daudé onto the scaffold in Charing Cross around noon, Monday, December 1, 1707. They attached a paper to Marion's hat. The paper read, "Elias Marion, Convicted for falsely and profanely pretending himself to be a true prophet in printing and uttering many things as dictated and Revealed unto him by the Spirit of God to terrify the Queen's people." Fatio and Daudé wore papers announcing their conviction "for abetting and favouring Elias Marion in his wicked and counterfeit Prophecies." The three men stood for an hour before a large crowd which pelted them with mud and stones. They would have suffered much more had not the Duke of Ormond instructed law officers to prevent inordinate abuse, because Fatio had been a tutor to his brother, the earl of Arran.[108] As it was, despite a cordon of guards around the

105. Fatio Calendar, 11/28/1707; HMC 75: Downshire I, part II, 854.
106. Lacy, *Warnings,* III, 8. Cf. Lacy's later *Letter to the Reverend Dr. Josiah Woodward* (1708) 11, denying that the mission should be proved "by many unquestionable Miracles" before April 29, 1708.
107. Bulkeley, *Answer to Several Treatises,* 113-14. On the role of healing as a missionary device for millenarian groups, cf. Susan Naquin, *Millenarian Rebellion in China: The Eight Trigrams Uprising of 1813* (New Haven and London, 1976) 28-32, 104-06.
108. Stack MSS 1g: Récit abrégé, 62; Historical Relation, f. 32; Fatio Calendar, 12/1/1707; *Post Boy,* No. 1957 (Nov. 29-Dec. 2, 1707); Luttrell, *State Affairs,* VI, 240; Edmund Chishull, *The Great Danger and Mistake of all New Uninspired Prophecies* (1708) 42-43. Fatio wrote to his elder brother on December 19, 1707, "J'ai eu des raisons pour ne pas donner ma

PLATE V. Woodcut from broadside, 1707.

scaffold at the Royal Exchange next day, the throng managed to spit on Marion and Daudé and covered all three with ordure. Marion was wounded in the face.[109] (See Plate V.)

The three men on the scaffold recorded how they felt: "Our tranquility even on the scaffold, and the full assurance of confidence and joy which

---

consentement qu'on intercédat pour me disposer de cette punition." BPUG, MSS fr. 602, f. 115. All three men had evidently refused to acknowledge their error and so avoid public humiliation: AE, Corr. politique, Angleterre, vol. 223, ff. 252-252v.

109. Stack MSS 1g: Récit abrégé, 67; Fatio Calendar, 12/2/1707;BPUG, MSS fr. 602, ff. 115-115v; *Pillory Disapointed, Or, the False Prophets Advancement* (1707) broadside. Marion, in *MMM*, 166, said that the French Prophets had constantly been subject to "Une grêle d'ordures, de chiens, de chats morts et pourris (tout ce qu'ils pouvaient trouver de plus sale et de plus puant) et souvent de pierres dont plusieurs ont été blessés." In *Purity and Danger* (1966), Mary Douglas suggests that such action is a response to social ambiguity or anomaly. The French Prophets were viewed as a pollution of the body politic where the power to curse and to bless usually resides in recognized political authorities. Opponents also saw the French Prophets as a pollution of the social body and implied that they were unnatural in their sexual acts. It is impressive in this context that several men convicted of sodomy, scheduled to humiliation on the same scaffold immediately before Marion, Fatio and Daudé, had their punishment delayed to December 3. *English Post*, Nos. 1120-1121 (Dec. 3-5, 5-8, 1707). Cf. Natalie Zemon Davis, "The Rites of Violence: Religious Riot in Sixteenth-Century France," *Past and Present* 59 (1973) 57-60; Randolph Trumbach, "London's Sodomites," *Journal of Social History* 11 (1977) 1-33.

God put in our hearts and which appeared on our faces, drew tears from some people." Elisabeth Charras, under inspiration in a nearby house, warned "Today is the day of Triumph." The French Prophets held a public assembly at the Barbican, and others came to the prison to hear the word of the Lord through Marion. In the Whitehall Coffee House near Charing Cross, debating with an opponent, Sir Richard Bulkeley promised that "Though there is at present not above two or three hundred of the Inspired, yet before a Twelve-Month comes about, there will be more than ten thousand of them." Tuesday night, Richard Roach dreamed of an extraordinary escape. He was "up at the top of the Great Hall in Guild Hall Hanging by one Hand. After finding Power of Moving gradually down did so by the wall & Cavalier met me." On December 5, Elizabeth Gray consoled those that suffer for the sake of Jesus, "for they shall be great in his Kingdom." On the sixth, a newspaper advertisement made it known "to all the world" that the three men had been prosecuted at the expense of the Huguenot churches of London.[110]

The group response revealed the extent to which the French Prophets had become self-reliant. Followers had developed a private perspective on (and history of) external events. The gestures of the group were a form of denial: what happened in the eyes of the outside world was not what happened in the eyes of the messengers of God. The inner meaning of events which various followers had sought throughout their lives— Richard Roach in his dreams, Timothy Byfield in elemental medicine, the persecuted Huguenots in the prophecies of Revelation—was being unveiled. And it was being unveiled not in the context of the Desert but in London, primarily by English prophets, to a group that was preponderantly English. Martyrdom was understood as prelude to the New Jerusalem and an ever-expanding True Church. The True Church, once established amidst the tensions of growth and cultural diversity, had resilience. It would endure for more than thirty years.

In the fervor of the moment, the French Prophets exulted. The anxieties of the past months did not disappear, but a strange joy obscured them. A new series of prophecies in December would be a fit climax to the celebration. John Lacy, said several of the inspired, would raise the dead.

110. Fatio Calendar, 12/2-12/6/1707; Stack MSS 1g: Récit abrégé, 67; Kingston, II, 26; *Collection of Warnings*, 92-93; Roach Diary, f. 95v. The total cost of the prosecution to the consistories was £136. HAL, MS 8, Threadneedle Street Livre des actes de 1692/3 à 1708, 535-36, 548-49.

CHAPTER IV

The Legacy of Dr. Thomas Emes

Prophecies Fail

About the time that crowds pressed against the scaffold on which stood three French Prophets, Dr. Thomas Emes fell sick. On December 6, Lacy prophesied, "if thou diest, I will raise thee; or if thou remainest, for some time, as thou art, I will restore thee." On the fourteenth, Jean Cavalier told the group that within five natural months the Holy Spirit would raise several followers from the grave. Emes died a week later, on the twenty-second. Rumors flew that the French Prophets expected him to rise on Christmas Day, but on Christmas afternoon John Potter prophesied: "I'll give now undeniable proof, that this is my Word: That these distracted Motions are caused by the Operation of my Spirit, in my Children. The Restoring of the Blind, the Healing of the Sick, the raising of the Dead shall decide it, after some Months being interred. Will not this do?" Followers buried Emes that evening in Bunhill Fields.[1]

Dr. Thomas Emes, chemist, "Atheist turned Deist, and Deist turned Christian," was the first prophet the group had lost.[2] His death challenged the hope that the present believers would be participants in the coming Kingdom. How far off was judgment if an inspired man might die before it had come? Was this new dispensation truly the last?

The group mourned Emes in a week of meetings until the prophets had completed an elaborate picture of his return, assuring followers that the

---

1. *Predictions concerning the Raising the Dead Body of Mr. Thomas Emes* (1708) 1-2; John Humfrey, *A Farther Account of our Late Prophets* (1708) 38; *A Dissuasive against Enthusiasm* (1708) 89-90; Fatio Calendar, 12/25/1707.

2. Some uninspired French women may have become apostates before Emes's death: Kingston, II, 216-23.

group was not vulnerable to the ravages of time. The funeral became a celebration. Indeed, Emes would rejoin the group "more fat, and more fair than ever he has been before." John Potter designated Lacy as the one to raise Emes, who would emerge from his grave sitting up and without breaking the ground. One might believe that he had never been gone.[3]

The funeral and fête for Emes climaxed on January 1, 1707/8. Apprentice printer Samuel Keimer had a preview of the day's glory as he and his family journeyed from Southwark to the meeting of the French Prophets at the Three Foxes Inn in Holloway. In the coach, the Spirit seized his sister Mary, who said that this day they would learn when Emes should rise. The Keimers arrived to find the English assembled in one room, the French in another. Soon John Potter entered crying "Grace, Grace, Grace," and put a paper on the table. The paper read, "Here's your Pardon purchased by the Blood of the Lamb, for all your Sins past to this Day. Signed and Sealed by the Great Jehovah. I AM." Followers began to cry for joy, jump and dance. Potter, who had been resisting his instrumental role in announcing the exact day for the resurrection, finally blurted it out: "Know ye the Day in which my Servant was Interred? Five Months from that Day, the Twenty-Fifth Day of May, you shall behold him rise again. One Month above the Number of Days that Lazarus was in his Grave." The conjunction of the pardon and the dating of the resurrection was instructive. In a sense the pardon was from Emes: none was to blame for his death; Emes forgave everyone. Not only did Potter identify Emes with Lazarus; he nearly confused him with Jesus: "But pray that your Faith may not fail. Many, at his Appearing, will deny any Appearance. Look to your selves. I say, some in this Room, will deny that it was the Appearance of God: Therefore look to your selves." Emes became a powerful symbol of faith, his resurrection part of a creed of miracles which the group upheld and which in turn upheld the group. The divine promise for Emes, coming as it did at the end of a full month of public martyrdom and commitment, provided followers—especially the English—with a surer footing in the outer world.[4]

The impact of Emes's death was felt beyond London. Three young men of Birmingham, Jonathan Taylor, Richard Wharton, and Stephen Halford, had visited the French Prophets at Christmastide. They returned to

3. *Predictions concerning Emes*, 1-7.
4. *Brand*, 22-25; Fatio Calendar, 1/1/1708; Abraham Whitrow, *Warnings of the Eternal Spirit* (1709) 204; *Predictions concerning Emes*, 8. Keimer (*Brand*, 25) states that French followers had among them a woman whose son had lately died and had also been promised resurrection, but this is confirmed in no other source; Keimer himself makes no further mention of a matter which would certainly require commentary.

Birmingham in January with vivid impressions of the group's concern for Dr. Emes. Gathering a small circle in their own town, Taylor and Halford found themselves inspired. In the last week of January, Halford predicted that he would die at the next assembly (Tuesday, February 3), lie unburied three days (as had Emes), and rise from his churchyard grave on February 20. Stephen Halford's brother Thomas, a steadfast Quaker who twice that week saw the devil's apparition assume his brother's shape, sought to keep Stephen from the Tuesday assembly. Finally, Thomas obtained a warrant to detain his brother and so preserve him from the rowdy mob that waited about the house of one Mrs. Roberts, where Stephen was to die and lie exposed to public view. On February 3, constables confined Stephen in the baliff's house; after a long day and night, he acknowledged that he would not die and had been deluded by the devil. Others who had experienced agitations also admitted their delusion. A few Birmingham believers, however, remained loyal to the French Prophets—Jonathan Taylor, William Humphreys, Richard Wharton. For more than twenty-five years, Taylor and Wharton's wife Hannah would rank among the most prominent prophets.[5]

A second example of Emes's posthumous influence came in February, when the French Prophets undertook the first of their missions outside London. Although Elie Marion had earlier spoken of missions to the four corners of the earth, it had always been with reference to a departure for the Cévennes. Now English prophets and scribes advanced into the English countryside, with the promise of the resurrection and Mary Beer's prophecy of a worldwide spiritual conquest to sustain them.

The prelude to the first mission was more publicity. The prophets held meetings all over London: Kingston Gravel Pits, Holloway, Hatton Gardens, the Barbican, Southwark.[6] *Predictions Concerning the Raising the Dead Body of Dr. Thomas Emes* was published on January 21 and may have helped fill out the meetings. The tract certainly increased the public commitment of known followers, although authorities seized most of the copies.[7] Bishop William Lloyd found events come to such a pass that on February 10 he temporarily set aside his project to convert Roman Catholics and wrote his old friend Sir Richard Bulkeley a worried letter.

---

5. G.P., *The Shortest Way with the French Prophets* (1707 or 1708); Nathaniel Spinckes, *The New Pretenders to Prophecy Re-examined* (1710) Appendix I, 24-29, letter from Thomas Halford; *The Postman and the Historical Account*, No. 1876 (Feb. 19, 1707/8) advert.; *Censura Temporum*, I, 111 (March, 1707/8) 94.

6. Fatio Calendar, January, 1708.

7. Spinckes, *Pretenders Re-examined*, 2; *The History of the Works of the Learned*, XI, 10 (October 1709) 626.

Lloyd had dipped into the *Predictions* and was shocked to discover Emes's resurrection favorably compared to that of Lazarus. "In short this is either a new Book of Divine Scriptures or a Devilish Heap of Impostures," Lloyd declared. Bulkeley wrote back, "O quench not the Spirit, despise not prophesyings, but prove all things and hold fast that which is good etc.— Prophecy has anotherguess Energy than ordinary Pastoral breathing."[8]

With "anotherguess" energy and the momentum of recent prophecies, the English inspired went to Enfield, ten miles north of London, on February 17. They had considered taking a license for a meetinghouse there, as Lacy had done for the Barbican, but a prophet warned them not to be worldly wise. Trusting in the Lord, they prophesied judgment and mercy at Enfield and Enfield Chase. Abraham Whitrow bestowed blessings on one hundred people, but he and others were arrested for provoking tumult and riot. Francis Moult bailed the prophets, otherwise in danger of being pressed into the Queen's service. On February 22, the Anglican minister of Enfield preached against the French Prophets, and in turn Whitrow's warning to the people of Enfield was printed for everyone to read. The Lord was impatient with fencesitters:

> 'Tis not their saying we will suspend our Judgments, and say nothing till we see Miracles wrought. 'Tis not that that pleases me. No, my Delight is in the Diligent Inquirer of me. For know, he that is not for me, is against me. Many shall go to see the Dead rise, thinking to believe at their pleasure; but I will consume them [along] with the open Blasphemers of my Name.[9]

The conviction which followers expressed in Emes's rising became the touchstone or stumbling-block of new English prospects. One dared not wait upon a decisive miracle to make one's commitment; one could not be dainty about belief. The predictions about Emes were public; so also must be the dedication of French Prophets.

Whitrow's inspired wife Deborah, Francis Moult and a few others straggled back from Enfield, bruised but undaunted. On March 8, the Baptist church at Colchester, whose membership included witnesses to the miraculous cure of Anne Munnings three years earlier, invited Lacy to speak to the congregation. Lacy, Thomas Dutton, Elizabeth Gray and other English prophets delivered warnings at the meetings of Colchester Baptists, Quakers and Independents. Pursued by a mob which accused

---

8. Worcester RO, Lloyd Papers, BA 5230, Appendix II.14, 2030-31, 2038.
9. Richard Bulkeley, *An Answer to Several Treatises lately published on the Subject of the Prophets* (1708) 103; Fatio Calendar, 1/17-1/24/1708; Historical Relation, ff. 40-41; Francis Hutchinson, *A Short View of the Pretended Spirit of Prophecy* (1708) 40, 59-60; Abraham Whitrow, *A Prophetical Warning . . . to the People of Enfield* (1708) broadside.

them of being traitors, some of the missionaries were obliged to swear oaths of loyalty before local magistrates. At the same time, French missionaries approached the Huguenot congregation in Colchester. Turned away at the door, they retreated to London after publishing a warning "of Reproof, of Complaint, of Exhortation." Five English missionaries traveled to Ipswich, leaving behind a written warning to Colchester magistrates, containing "the promises of the Kingdom, the Threatenings of Judgments and the near Restitution of all things." Ipswich innkeepers would admit no French Prophets. After prophesying in the streets, the last inspired returned to London.[10]

English followers now had troubles in their own churches. Edmund Calamy preached against the French Prophets while Lacy sat listening in a pew.[11] Quakers of the Peel Meeting (London) dissociated themselves from James Jackson, whose vision Lacy had restored.[12] The missions and the well-known prophecies about Emes had contributed much to the public recognition of the English set of French Prophets. Of the six prophets who had spoken concerning Emes, four were English. (Durand Fage delivered one short warning, and Jean Cavalier acted as John Potter's shadow and echo.) Huguenots of the Desert had identified with the witnesses of Revelation and calibrated their sufferings with the timetable for resurrection; like the sleep of their *petits prophètes*, resurrection was a social metaphor. The Camisards had spoken of resurrection as the revival of the Protestant community in France.[13] In England, resurrection was both metaphor and medicine. English Protestants could recall early Quaker

10. *A Collection of Prophetical Warnings of the Eternal Spirit* (1708) 147, 150; Fatio Calendar, 3/8-3/16/1708; Historical Relation, ff. 41, 42, 44; James Jackson, *An Appeal to Country Friends* (1708) 3; [Claude Groteste de la Mothe], *Examen du théâtre sacré des Cévennes* (1708) i-ii.

11. Edmund Calamy, *An Historical Account of My Own Life*, ed. John T. Rutt (1829) I, 99; Richard Bulkeley, *Preface to the Reader of Warnings of the Eternal Spirit, Spoken by the Mouth of the Servant of God, Abraham Whitro* (1709) 68-69. Lacy protested, "I am utterly ignorant that our Inspiration ever gave an order, to those who were pleased to hear us, that they should quit the sacred Ordinances and regular Ministry; on the contrary, it has acknowledged both. And I am very confident, most of our Followers have frequented those several forms of Congregations, to which their Inclinations before used to lead them." Lacy, *A Relation of the Dealings of God* (1708) 17.

12. Jackson, *Appeal to Country Friends*, 4-5, 7; Fatio Calendar, 2/25/1708; Friends' House Library, typescript Dictionary of Quaker Biography, "James Jackson." Other French Prophets to have trouble with their standing among Quakers included Anne Steed, Mary Willis, Samuel Shaw and Henry Pickworth: William Beck and T. Frederick Ball, *The London Friends' Meetings* (1869) 253; Henry Pickworth, *A Charge of Error* (1716).

13. Chapter one notes the single instance of a predicted resurrection among the Desert Huguenots—Jeanne Bonnisolle prophesied her own death and resurrection; she fainted and was restored.

attempts to raise the dead, or the reports that Rev. John Mason of Water Stratford would rise again. English tracts proclaimed the wonder of those who lay as dead for several nights and then awoke with marvelous heavenly visions to describe.[14] In the millenarian ethos of English followers, resurrection was the evangelical healing of the person, just as missions were the means to a universal healing, a union of the faithful in the New Jerusalem.

There were no further missions until June, for followers had enough to occupy them in London. Destruction was not far off. It was nearly the end of March; the Stuart Pretender to the English throne, James Francis Edward, Prince of Wales and son of James II, was sailing to Scotland with French troops. There were signs of panic in London. Thunder crashed over the city, and two French Prophets (both English) predicted that fire and brimstone would pour down upon the wicked on March 25 (Lady Day, the beginning of the new year in the English calendar). Followers also expected a famine, some going to great expense to stock their larders. Other English prophets were commanded to leave their jobs and devote themselves entirely to prophetic tasks.[15]

These events deepened the commitment of English believers in particular, for only the English left their occupations, spent money in anticipation of famine, or openly announced their belief in the March 25 destruction and May 25 resurrection. The events also changed the nature of the commitment, for a number of English followers now had an economic stake in the powers of the prophets. Thomas Rigby and Christian Steffkins made large wagers on Emes's rising; Isaac Owen sold his estate and lived off the proceeds during the short period before the

---

14. For example, *The Norfolk Wonder, or, the Maiden's TRANCE: Being a Strange and True Relation, of one Sarah Barker of Elsom in Norfolk of Sixteen Years of Age; who on the 2d of this Instant May (being in perfect Health) fell into a Trance, and lay as Dead for Three Days and Nights together* (1708). See also Douglas Linebaugh, "The Tyburn Riot Against the Surgeons," in Douglas Hay et al., *Albion's Fatal Tree* (New York, 1975) 65-118, on popular beliefs in "resurrection."

15. Brand, 28-29, 31, 108; Fatio Calendar, 3/18?/1708; *Reflections on Sir Richard Bulkeley's Answer to Several Treatises* (1708) 42; Samuel Keimer, *A Search after Religion* (1716?) 15; W.A. Speck, "Conflict in Society," in Geoffrey Holmes, ed., *Britain after the Glorious Revolution 1689-1715* (1970) 151. Some followers did obey the command to leave their jobs: Henry Nicholson, *The Falsehood of the New Prophets Manifested* (1708) 28-29; Dutton-Cuninghame Corr., 10/2/1709, 202, "there being some who were Called from their Worldly Employments and immediately Employed in this Work, the Enemy takes Occasion from hence to Order a great many others to leave off their honest Employments—that had large families to Support, and could by their Trades not only do that, but charitably contribute to the Relief of those that Wanted."

world's end. Those who purchased food to forestall famine had made a significant investment in an era when food preservation was not efficient, and those who forsook their livelihoods had made a possibly irrevocable gesture. Other financial commitments were less clear: did the wealthy French Prophets support the impoverished with discreet charity? How were the full-time prophets maintained? Observers named some Englishmen (Whitrow, Lacy, Bulkeley, Moult, Dutton, Peter Cuff) who supposedly sacrificed their wealth for the use of the group. Enemies reported that poor French Prophets received a weekly allowance (implying that the group bribed and bought followers).[16] Bulkeley did make large outlays, but much later and in an atmosphere of intense group controversy. Both he and Lacy denied spending more than £20 each on behalf of the inspired, excluding printing costs, in 1707.[17] Whitrow, Moult, Dutton, Cuff and others must have been at considerable expense as landlords, hosts, providers of bail and charity. The money for missions (more numerous, distant and expensive by November) had to come from some coffer. As the French Prophets grew, financial obligations grew.

On March 24, surrounded by biscuit, meal, beef, pork and peas, English followers prayed and fasted. The wicked lived on, mercifully spared, into April. The Jacobite rebellion in Scotland was over quickly, the Pretender returned to France, and there was no famine in the land.

The unfavorable reception of their missions to Enfield, Colchester and Ipswich, the unconfirmed prophecies of fire, brimstone and famine, combined with new economic investments, explain much of the declining confidence of English followers in the May 25 resurrection. With Lacy's six-month moratorium for decisive miracles about to end on April 29, followers were concerned about the importance of miracles in general as proof of divine inspiration. Just as the English were trying to work out their position vis-à-vis the French, they had to examine the dual nature of their own belief in the millennium. On one hand, they agreed that they lived in the last days, that judgment and the Kingdom were impending. On the other hand, they had made specific commitments to specific prophecies of miracles which were but signs of imminent end. If such prophecies

16. *Brand*, 38, 66; Kingston, I, 73-74; J[osiah] W[oodward], *The Copy of a Letter to Mr. F. M.* (1708) 6; AE, Corr. politique, Angleterre, vol. 223, ff. 51-51v. Misson claimed that Marion, Cavalier and Fage were poor and lived on the alms of good Huguenot families: *Plainte et censure des calomnieuses accusations publiées par le Sr. Claude Groteste de la Motte* (1708) 81n.

17. Lacy, *Warnings*, III, 3; *The English and French Prophets Mad or Bewitcht* (1708) broadside; Sion College, MSS bound in pamphlet collection 47-B-5, copy of Sir Richard Bulkeley's answer to a letter from J. Field, 11/15/1707.

were not fulfilled, how might they continue to support their broad millennial faith?

John Potter interpreted predictions of destruction, like those for March 25, as metaphorical judgments,[18] just as Lacy months before had glossed the Tower Guns roaring as celestial thunder, but it was much more difficult to avoid a "natural" understanding of the Emes resurrection. Jean Cavalier had carefully indicated "natural" months, and English prophets had referred to Emes's return in practical, mundane terms.

Edmund Calamy, debating good-naturedly with Francis Moult that spring, asked about Emes. Did Moult not reckon Emes's resurrection to be "the great confirming evidence" of the French Prophets? Moult did. Calamy then promised to join up with them when Emes rose, if Moult promised to quit the dispensation should the resurrection be delayed. Moult hesitated and finally gave the argument Timothy Byfield had employed with Elizabeth Gray: "He said, he did not know how far the infidelity of the present age might provoke God to deny so public an appearance, in a way of punishment." Richard Roach too had doubts, and voices told him that Emes would not rise. On March 4 he reflected about Emes, "If their Faith keep up and Answer—But if they Decrease, and Faith not Answer, may it not be put off . . .?" Four days after the predicted judgment upon the wicked of London, Abraham Whitrow had prophesied, "And will you presume to say, that when I have declared such a time or thing, I cannot suffer that time to pass, without fulfilling the thing limited to it?" Sir Richard Bulkeley, commanded to declare publicly his faith that "open Miracles, public Attestations, from Heaven shall be given this City before May next," argued that prophets could be sent of God although their prophecies (often conditional upon repentance) might not be confirmed.[19]

Looking toward May 25, English followers felt distinctly uncomfortable. English prophets, unveiling alternatives for understanding the failure of predictions, advocated an argument from design: only God knew the logic of things, the reason for the twist of events. Since one may not call God to account, one reviewed instead the infidelity of the age, the faltering of the faithful, all the cues of human behavior which might betray the grand design. Thomas Dutton had warned in January that the seeming irregularities in God's work were a result of "scanty, bounded" human knowledge. Mary Beer in February had prophesied that God would come

18. *Collection of Warnings*, 110-11, 156-58.
19. Calamy, *Life*, I, 103-05; Roach Diary, f. 115; Bulkeley, *Preface*, 37; Bulkeley, *Answer to Several Treatises*, 87.

in his own time, in his own way, for the faithful little knew what was best for them. On April 29, Lacy humbly acknowledged himself deceived in several specific predictions which had proved false since the end of October, 1707. God alone knew, wrote Lacy, "for what ends this Chain of Providence was permitted and appointed of him; and he, I doubt not, will work his own Glory out of it." Lacy would not attend Emes's graveside on the twenty-fifth; the proper divine attestations, wrote Lacy, were incomplete. On May 23, Pentecost (Whitsunday), John Glover spoke under inspiration: "Who can find out the Almighty to Perfection? Why then are ye so anxious, my Children? You must be brought to an entire Resignation of your Wills unto mine, before I will appear for you. Therefore cease murmuring and disputing: or else my Hand shall fall upon your own Heads."[20]

Murmuring and disputing within the group did not cease. Abraham Whitrow, already reprimanded for having "forced the Spirit," commanded more than a dozen followers to appear at Bunhill Fields on May 25 and await the miracle. Whitrow's inspiration contradicted Lacy's decision not to appear, and Lacy was the one supposed to raise Emes. Whitrow nevertheless warned that followers were under divine obligation to attend upon Emes, whether or not he should rise: "What if he were not to rise? What then? Would it not look more to your dishonour, if you did not go, than if you went in obedience to That that you took to be the Command of God?" Unchastened, none but Whitrow went to the gravesite on May 25. Lacy and other English followers spent the day in the country.[21]

It was safer in the country. May 25, Whittuesday, was a public holiday. Newspapers predicted that a throng of curious and excitable people would converge on Bunhill Fields. One broadside pretended that grandstands would be erected and refreshments sold, "since it is plainly evident, that, of all the shows or wonders that are usually seen on holiday-time, this must bear the bell." Daniel Defoe, fearing mob violence, hoped that the deluded prophets would be protected by the law. Magistrates may have shared this fear; they posted two regiments of trained bands at the cemetery.[22]

20. *Collection of Warnings*, 19-21, 57, 78-80; Lacy, *Relation of Dealings*, 29-31.

21. Whitrow, *Warnings*, 219-23; Fatio Calendar, 5/25/1708; Bulkeley, *Preface*, 51. Of those commanded to come to Bunhill Fields, at least three were Huguenots: Cavalier, Marion and Abraham Verduron.

22. *The Mighty Miracle; or The Wonder of Wonders at Windmill-Hill* (1708) reprinted in William Oldys and Thomas Park, eds., *The Harleian Miscellany* (1811) VII, 94-95; *An Epitaph on the French Prophet, Who was to make his Resurrection on the 25th of May* (Edinburgh, 1709); Defoe, *Review of the State of the English Nation* (April 24, 1708); Narcissus Luttrell, *A Brief Historical Relation of State Affairs from September 1678 to April 1714* (Oxford, 1857) VI, 307.

One contemporary estimated that 20,000 people milled about Emes's grave.[23] To their disappointment there was no resurrection. According to three contemporary satirists, however, Dr. Thomas Emes rose about noon and addressed the multitudes. In one case he asked for Dr. Byfield's panacea, *Sal volatile oleosum*, and the chemist Francis Moult's *Elixir Proprietatis*.[24] In a second case he prophesied a heaven on earth (the Thames flowing with ale, roast beef sprouting in the forests) where

> The Mighty shall in Troops before ye bow,
> And you shall Reign in Pow'r as they do now:
> Those who have scorned you shall your Foot-stools be,
> And labour to fulfill my *Prophesie* . . . .[25]

Unable to date precisely these welcome upheavals, he sank again beneath the earth. A third version of Emes's address was printed and distributed to the crowd. Slanted toward the political, it insinuated that the hullabaloo of the resurrection served the interests of an evil party which intended to goad the mob against City and Court. The summary reflected a common attitude toward the French Prophets, mixing facile theology and fear of masterminded plots, a fear lingering from the Civil War and fed by continuing suspicions of Jacobite conspiracy. These and other enthusiasts were politically dangerous because so easily led astray:

> For as for the Prophets themselves, they are the Objects of Pity, not of Fury, tricked by the Devil and his Agents into unheard-of Delusions, and by a Cursed Infatuating Juggle made the Instruments of their own Misfortunes. The greater Part of them are men of Morals, Men of Principle, Men of Sense; some of them Men of good Estates, and Men of Honour. . . .
> Pity them therefore as Men that have lately suffered Shipwreck of their Senses. Pity them as People that the Devil has buffooned, as Men, that will to Morrow be ashamed of all.[26]

---

23. AE, Corr. politique, Angleterre, vol. 224, f. 248, and also *Flying Post*, No. 2040 (May 25-27, 1708); A clue to the crowd's size was the state of Mr. Nathaniel Vincent's tomb in Bunhill Fields in 1717, "much broken by the Mob (who rose on the Report of Mr. Emes's intended Resurrection)." Charles Reed, comp., *Appendix to Proceedings in Reference to the Preservation of the Bunhill Fields Burial Ground* (1867 [1717]) 79.

24. Kingston, II, 141-42, "Dr. Emes's rising Speech," by Kingston.

25. *The French Prophet's Resurrection With His SPEECH to the Multitude that behold the Miracle* (1708) broadside.

26. *A Letter from Dr. Emes to the MOB, Assembled at his Grave* (1708) 4. AE, Corr. politique, Angleterre, vol. 224, f. 248v., refers to "quelques Esprits brouillons et mal Intentionnez" who hoped to profit from the occasion to raise a mob. The political overtones were partly the result of the change in the English ministry which had been proceeding since February; by November the Whig Junto controlled Parliament. G.V. Bennett, *The Tory Crisis in Church and State 1688-1730* (Oxford, 1975) 89-101.

On the morrow, contemporaries were astonished to find the French Prophets neither ashamed nor repentant. Jonathan Swift's Isaac Bickerstaff had seen in the stars that the month of June would be distinguished by the "utter dispersing of those ridiculous deluded Enthusiasts" who had been so unwise as to make detailed prophecies for a time so near. Defoe confessed his own surprise in June at the "Prevalency of this new Delusion." Nathaniel Spinckes, nonjuror and consistent critic of the French Prophets, later wrote,

> And is it not an Amazing Consideration, that after such unquestionable demonstration of these Men's enthusiastical Blindness, or worse, that when their utmost expectation has failed them, and they have not the least hope of effecting what they had so often and so confidently promised, they should not yet be put to silence.[27]

The French Prophets had, nervously, prepared for the failure. By May 25, English followers could justify the turn of events with eloquent rhetoric and a backlog of experiences. None had deserted or reproved the prophets who predicted the famine; Lacy and Bulkeley, despite the April 29 deadline, had not broken with the dispensation. French followers had not been closely linked to the predictions about Emes, and English followers (except Whitrow) had put emotional and geographical distance between themselves and the body of Emes. John Lacy declared that the threat of public violence was the major cause of the failed (or deferred) resurrection. Lacy explained that the atmosphere of the day had been inappropriate for the accomplishment of the miracle. Followers had been threatened by "open rage, mob, fury, and even death itself," for, "had the miracle really been wrought in such a confused medley of ungovernable rabble; instead of being acknowledged as such, we had run the hazard of being torn in pieces, and perhaps occasioned a fatal and general disorder among the people." Thus Lacy turned the fear of the excitable crowd to the advantage of the group. Some French Prophets would continue to believe in Emes's eventual resurrection. Two Scottish prophets would predict it once more in 1711.[28]

27. Jonathan Swift, *Bickerstaff Papers and Pamphlets on the Church*, in *Works*, ed. Herbert Davis (14 vols.; Oxford, 1957-68) II, 146; Nathaniel Spinckes, *The New Pretenders to Prophecy Examined* (1709) 430; Defoe, *Review*, V, 33 (June 12, 1708) 131 and also V, 48 (July 17) 190, an anonymous letter thanking Defoe for his pity for the French Prophets, "and kindly accepted without doubt, by thôse who do not yet look upon themselves as proper Objects of it; but whose Faith in this Dispensation, as they call it, is stronger than it was before the 25th Day of May." Claude Groteste de la Mothe had anticipated that the failure of the resurrection would not dishearten believers: *Caractère des nouvelles prophecies* (1708) 68-69.

28. John Lacy, *Esquire Lacy's Reasons why Doctor Emes was not raised from the Dead*

As if to compensate for the disappointment of May 25, prophets forecasted a wider distribution of divine gifts. The apothecary's apprentice Nathaniel Sheppard was to heal, and messengers of the Lord would give "Ocular Demonstration" of their divine mandate. Abraham Whitrow cured a waterman, Richard Cheney, of his distemper. The gift of healing was a spiritual physic, for the Lord cured illness by winnowing the soul, just as the predicted resurrection was meant to winnow believers from sceptics. "Why is Distempers?" asked Whitrow. "Are they not Scourges for Sin? You will seldom see the healthful Soul without a healthful Body."[29]

Their faith propped by this renewal of divine regard, followers surged into the public forum, proclaiming their faith stronger than ever.[30] Samuel Keimer was to be a "Minister Extraordinary" of the dispensation, as was a newcomer, Henry Nicholson, a university man. He and others would soon go forth, said the inspired, so "the World shall know they are not ashamed to own that God to be true, who failed in the Resurrection promised, according to the literal sense of the Word." Another university man, Thomas Lardner, came into the fold in June. He met Elizabeth Gray, John and Francis Moult on the road to Coventry, whither they were sent to "publish the Approach of the time of the Restitution of all things." He acted as their scribe while they were spurned in the marketplace of Coventry and while magistrates opposed them in Stratford.[31]

On July 6, Lacy estimated that the inspired and those who had the "preparatory Symptoms of the Spirit" amounted to two hundred. In a preface to the *Collection of Warnings* of fifteen English prophets, printed on July 29, Lacy stressed the startling unanimity of forty prophets actively witnessing to the Spirit, and all agreeing in what they said. No false

---

(1708) reprinted in Oldys and Park, *Harleian Miscellany*, VII, 195-96; Dutton-Cuninghame Corr., endpaper, 9/26/1711. Cf. also *Collection of Warnings*, 3-4, 24-25, 80-83, 97-98, 142-43; *Brand*, 32-33. In 1712, Humphrey Ditton speculated on the response had Emes risen: *A Discourse concerning the Resurrection of Jesus Christ* (4th ed.; 1727 [1712]) 267-68.

29. *Brand*, 33-34; Whitrow, *Warnings*, 229-35; *Collection of Warnings*, 81-82.

30. This is consistent with some of the findings of Zygmunt; when the Jehovah's Witnesses conceded prophetic error, it was "rationalized in terms of the fallibility of human judgment, but welcomed as divinely provided lessons revealing God's purpose more fully." Proselytization increased only after the group redefined its missions and "relegitimated" its belief. Joseph F. Zygmunt, "Prophetic Failure and Chiliastic Identity: The Case of Jehovah's Witnesses," *American Journal of Sociology* 75,6 (1970) 944-45, and cf. James A. Beckford, *The Trumpet of Prophecy* (New York, 1975) 18-20; John G. Gager, *Kingdom and Community: The Social World of Early Christianity* (Englewood Cliffs, 1975).

31. *Brand*, 33; Nicholson, *Falsehood of the New Prophets*, sig. A2, 16-18; *Historical Relation*, ff. 44-46.

doctrine had proceeded from "some Thousands of Discourses, of People of different Sects, and Opinions, and Capacities." Though "mixtures" of human and divine words might occur, as they had with primitive Christians, Lacy held that "that Spirit, which, for many wise Ends, known to himself, does, sometimes, provide or foretell, or denounce such Things, as have not, or will not come to pass; that Spirit, I say is now come as Judge, to try the hearts."[32]

The hearts of English followers had been gravely tested this spring and summer of 1708. They had suffered prophetic and perhaps economic setbacks. They had encountered hostility on missions and in London and incurred a public notoriety equal to that of the French in 1707. They had managed, with a lingering pain, to comprehend and accept some of the reasons for their fate as messengers of the Lord. Many of those reasons had to do with the New Jerusalem notion that redemption comes through collective faith, that miracles point the way to the Kingdom; if Emes had not risen, then the world had better take note that it was not yet ripe for grace, that it should expect more judgments. In this way the millenarian ethos of judgment worked in tandem with the Kingdom, both oriented toward the establishment of a healthy, loyal community of believers. What English prophets and followers wished to avoid was riot, fury, cataclysm, the trauma out of which had come, two years before, the *inspirés*.

The Reunion of the Two Alliances

Throughout the spring, French followers had been involved in controversies over the *Théâtre sacré*. Huguenots in London attributed much importance to the opinions of "Colonel" Jean Cavalier, most renowned of Camisards and a prestigious figure in England. After signing a treaty with Maréchal Villars, Cavalier left France for Holland, where he raised a regiment of Huguenot refugee troops for the allies. He led his regiment into battle against the French at Almanza, in Spain, where most of his men perished and Cavalier himself was left for dead.[33] By November, 1707, Cavalier was recuperating at The Hague. A Huguenot minister in Holland, René Saunier de l'Hermitage, needled the "Colonel" into a declaration maligning the character of the three London *inspirés* and denying that they

---

32. John Lacy, *Letter to the Reverend Dr. Josiah Woodward* (1708) 17, 20; *Collection of Warnings*, vi-x, xii-xvi.
33. *Monthly Miscellany* (June, 1707) 180-81; AE, Corr. politique, Angleterre, vol. 223, f. 280; Marcel Pin, *Jean Cavalier* (Nimes, 1936); David C.A. Agnew, *Protestant Exiles from France* (3rd ed.; 1886) II, 149-59.

had prophesied in the Cévennes.[34] Cavalier signed a similar declaration for the Savoy consistory when he came to England in February, 1707/8. In a third testimonial he refused to acknowledge any connection between the miracles of the Cévennes and the prophecies in London. His opinions would later change, but meanwhile they struck at the node linking the French Prophets to the traditions of the Desert.[35]

The "Colonel" Cavalier's visit to London and other events that spring— the Threadneedle Street consistory's attack on Jean Cabanel's deposition in the *Théâtre sacré*, the death of Jean Pellet's child "of great promise," the celestial voice speaking to Jeanne Raoux[36]—diverted the attention of French followers from Emes's rising. English involvement in the prophecies about Emes was matched by a French concern for the *Théâtre sacré*. As the Emes predictions seemed critical to the status of the English prophets, so the miracles of the Cévennes seemed critical to the status of the French prophets.[37] The English were trying to create an English context for the New Jerusalem, the French were trying to cultivate their Desert. The two nations of believers were set on their own paths, drifting, if slowly, apart.

On August 12, 1708, began the Sign of the Reunion of the Two Alliances. Officially a merger of Old and New Testaments, this was equally a merger of French and English. Jeanne Raoux and Elie Marion renamed the followers and assigned them to one of the twelve tribes mentioned in the seventh chapter of Revelation as comprising the 144,000 faithful. The tribes were not complete until December and even then did not include all people friendly to the dispensation.[38] Fatio saw the tribes as a "Sign to the

---

34. Winifred Turner, ed., *The Aufrère Papers*, in *HSL Publications*, XL (1940) 63-64; Kingston, II, 202-03. "Colonel" Cavalier, who had himself been inspired in the Cévennes, carefully maintained silence on this.

35. Kingston, II, 204-05; *MMM*, 170-72; Fatio Calendar, 1/17 and 2/19/1708. By March, Cavalier had begun the reversals and diplomacy which lasted another ten years, apologizing to Misson and affirming the accuracy of the *Théâtre sacré:* Misson, *Plainte et censure*, 58n-59n; *MMM*, 170-76. For his later ties to the French Prophets, cf. BPUG, MSS fr. 605, letter from Jean Allut to Nicolas Fatio, 3/3/1719: "Le Colonel Cavalier désire que l'on s'assemble pour savoir si l'esprit concouroit avec quelque autre advertisement dans les Sévennes qui l'invitent à revenir là, pour quelque Grande entreprise," and letters of 3/14/1719 and 3/25/1730.

36. Groteste de la Mothe, *Examen du théâtre sacré*, 17-19; Misson, *Plainte et censure*, 30-32; Kingston, II, 40-42; Fatio Calendar, 3/1, 4/17 and 4/29/1708; HAL, MS 8, Threadneedle Street Livre des actes de 1692/3 à 1708, 553-54.

37. Cf. Kingston, II, 35-36, on the English version of the *Théâtre sacré*: "I am credibly informed, that the greatest Part of those that have been *abused* and *wheedled* into the dangerous *Errors* of our pretended *Prophets*, attribute their Seduction to the reading of the *Cry from the Desart*."

38. Fatio Calendar, 8/12/1708; Historical Relation, f. 37. The tribes held 160 people (two

Earth and particularly the Jews that the House of God is building again, and will be Raised from its Ruins." The tribes also put the internal House of God in order, whole and friendly: within tribes French mingled with English, male with female, prophet with novice, newcomer with veteran. In fact, try as followers did to detect the pattern to tribal assignments, the tribes seemed to hold a mysterious unity invisible to human eyes. Even the man renamed Benjamin was not in the tribe of Benjamin.[39]

As the first tribe (Levi) formed, there were other attempts to assure group integration. A few followers hosted open love feasts that brought together those who had drawn apart, jealous of the privileges bestowed unequally by the Lord.[40] On August 13, the French Prophets met in sevens, each septet with its own prophet. With hindsight, Fatio wrote in 1709, "I do not know, that the Assembling by Sevens, has been Explained, but that being the Ordinary Number of People, which is Reckoned to make up a Family, I have suspected that the Work Would be Carried on, in private families, and not in a public manner, which indeed agrees with what has been done here."[41] Fatio's reference to the family was revealing. Ironically, in the very attempt to unite, the French Prophets operated on two different models. The tribe was an allusion to the Camisard band thrown together by circumstance and refined in battle; it was part of the millenarian ethos of cataclysm that pervades the Book of Revelation, and it was consistent with Calvinist ideas of the small elect group to be redeemed. The family belonged to the millenarian ethos of judgment with which the English followers more warmly identified; it alluded to the Desert of the *petits prophètes* and, on a larger scale, to the family of nations that would worship in the New Jerusalem. The family was a social unit whose hierarchy was not imposed (as in tribal military ranks) but natural, whose existence was not temporary but basic; tribes wandered, families preserved. These distinctions would become more crucial in the next years. In August, 1708, both tribes and assemblies of seven provided sanctioned ways for people to withdraw into small groups without raising suspicion of schism.

There was a further effort at unity. On August 20, the French Prophets

---

sets of fourteen in the first tribe, twelve in the others). The first two tribes were predominantly French, the rest mostly English, but no tribes were exclusively French and only one tribe was exclusively English.

39. *Post Boy*, No. 2241 (Sept. 22-24, 1709), letter from Fatio to Thomas Lardner of 4/2/1709; BSHPF, Papiers Coquerel, MS 302, letter from Charles Portales to David Flotard, 4/22/1709, ff. 5-5v.

40. *Brand*, 29-30.

41. *Post Boy*, No. 2241 (Sept. 22-24, 1709); Fatio Calendar, 8/13/1709.

received and obeyed a divine command to wear a yard-long green ribbon in public. This, Fatio later explained, was the livery of the Lord; followers wore the ribbons "as a Mark for the destroying Angel to know us by, when he should come to execute the Judgments of the Lord." Samuel Keimer's new name, "Jonathan, of the Tribe of Asser," was written on a small scrap of parchment and sewn up in his ribbon.[42]

These demonstrations of unanimity had significance as a leave-taking gift for Abraham Mazel. The Camisard prophet, in England since January, was to return to the Cévennes. He had expressed concern about the followers, and on August 21 delivered a divine order that the French Prophets sign a declaration (of faith?). On August 25, as the inspired fasted, Mazel signed his completed memoirs of the war in the Cévennes. He left the next day for Geneva.[43] As the tribe of Levites grew, as followers flaunted their faith by means of green ribbons, Mazel might take heart and the Huguenot refugees might prove the extent of their debt and devotion to the Camisards.

The posture of French followers in public assemblies three miles north of London lends credence to this interpretation. Followers had been physically threatened since their first assemblies at Hackney Marsh. On October 7, some Frenchmen attacked Isaac Havy and pulled off his offensive green ribbon. A week later, during the last assembly at Hackney Marsh, there was a riot. Accounts differed. Fatio noted in his calendar, "Assembly at Hackney Marsh where the Spirit ordered us to put sword in hand and arrest the Assassins who had come to exterminate us. Audemar was wounded in the head and the Spirit ordered us to proceed against these Assassins at law." Ten Frenchmen, opponents, testified that fifteen minutes after the meeting had begun, Isaac Havy, recognizing unbelievers in the midst of the large assembly, stepped back and cried out, "Brothers, in the Name of the Lord follow me, and draw your Swords, for these are Enemies to our Gospel." Then the French Prophets attacked and wounded many spectators, one of whom lost a finger.[44]

---

42. *Brand*, 26, 46-47; *Post Boy*, No. 2241 (Sept. 22-24, 1709); Fatio Calendar, 8/20/1708. The green ribbon was probably intended by Marion as a reference to the green hats and green-and-red ribbons worn by the Camisards, but it had unfortunate associations in England to the sea-green ribbons worn by the Levellers, to English weavers' enmity toward Huguenot ribbonmakers in London, and to the Whig Green Ribbon Club which was active in the Exclusion Crisis in 1680. Green was also the color traditionally associated with Jesus.

43. Fatio Calendar, 8/21-8/26/1708; *MMM*, 39, 40, 99, 209ff.

44. Kingston, II, 168; *Post Boy*, No. 2111 (Nov. 23-25, 1708); Nicholson, *Falsehood of the New Prophets*, 23; AE, Corr. politique, Angleterre, vol. 225, ff. 208-208v.; Fatio Calendar, 8/14 and 10/7-10/14/1708.

Whichever report one accepts, two things stand out: a posture of belligerence hitherto unknown in the group, and the preponderance of Frenchmen in the mêlée. It was as if French followers, now with a semblance of unity, were reliving the battles of the Camisards. The first Havy incident had shown how provocative were the green ribbons, and Hackney Marsh was merely an open space, more like a parade ground or muster yard than a meetinghouse. The French efforts to restore group vitality had entailed a reassertion of the Camisard ethos.

As 1708 drew to a close, the group's attempted resolution of the split between French and English was accompanied by the tentative resolution of another problem catalyzed by the Emes prophecies. Emes left to followers a legacy of insecurity about the future which was not immediately checked by prophetic promises or permanently allayed by the tribes and green ribbons which heralded a new age. In late November, Elie Marion issued an inspired command that those followers already renamed should have their new names attached to their heads when they died. Never had there been so explicit a recognition of the tension between the approach of the last days and human mortality. Eleven months after the death of Emes, the possible deaths of other followers were much less subversive to the group's chiliasm, in part because the French Prophets were loosening their grasp on an urgently imminent millennium, in part because they had fashioned rituals to preserve the memory of the dead.[45]

On November 28 came the first order for the Sign of the Feast of the Lamb of the Lord's Supper, the most solemn of rituals yet performed by the French Prophets. On Christmas day, 1708, one year after the burial of Emes, the group celebrated the Feast of the Lamb and the taking of Holy Communion. Elie Marion, Daniel Le Tellier, Jean Allut and John Potter distributed the bread and wine, pronounced blessings, offered prayers. By January 2, 1708/9, two hundred people of seven different religious persuasions had participated in the Feast.[46]

At the end of January, in another solemn communal ceremony, Isaac Havy and Daniel Le Tellier baptized Le Tellier's two children. The self-conscious formality of the baptism, recorded as a model for posterity, was typical of the new rituals:

45. Fatio Calendar, 11/21/1708; Keimer, *Brand*, 86-87, who says that he had a belief in purgatory as a result of the manner in which the French Prophets dealt with the faithful who died. Cf. Defoe, *Review*, V, 12 (April 24, 1708) 48. See D.P. Walker, *The Decline of Hell* (1964) 34-35, for a lucid exposition of early Christian beliefs about the state of the faithful who died before the imminent millennium.

46. Fatio Calendar, 11/28 and 12/14-12/28/1708, 1/1-1/2/1709; Historical Relation, f. 38.

Daniel Le Tellier under the Operation of the Spirit of the Lord caused the Child to be brought whom he was appointed to baptize, and having caused the Top of its head and the Soles of its feet to be uncovered, took water with the Ends of his fingers and washing the head and feet of the Child, he pronounced these Words unto it: Elizabeth, I wash thee, I cleanse thee, I receive thee in the name of Jesus Christ; I wash thee I cleanse thee in the name of the Father and the Son and the Holy Spirit, those three are but One.[47]

The rituals, culminating in the baptism, tended to calm worries about how the group fit into the Lord's schedule. Followers now had established models for the fundamental rites of passage (baptism, communion, burial) which provided for group stability among the tempests of uncertain time. Rites of passage guaranteed that, while the millennium pended, the lives of believers had regular, formal, divinely ordained rhythms. Meetings themselves were to have a regular rhythm. The celestial voice arranged assemblies for Thursdays and Sundays from five to ten in the evening. The English would hold two meetings, the French three.[48]

As the prophets performed an increasing number of ministerial functions in formal settings, French and English followers reached par. The ceremonies since June had been directed by prophets of both nations, and approximately the same percentage of each nation's followers became tribe members. Although French and English met separately more often than not, the separation was no longer poorly defined or disconcerting. If, despite mutual desires, there was no relaxing nuclear family of believers, at least there was a reaffirmed kinship between French and English followers. The situation involved more than the rivalry of brothers or sisters; it included as well the problems of authority and respect between parents and children, for the French represented an earlier, Desert generation to which the English had had to pay homage while they began as a new generation to prepare for their own mission.

The Rise of False Prophets

The failed resurrection had another and enduring effect upon the French Prophets. It exacerbated a fear of false prophets which would never be completely resolved. The process of explaining the delayed resurrection entailed losses as well as gains.

Abraham Whitrow's prestige as a prophet had been stained by the Emes affair. On May 27, Whitrow had delivered a prayer, "in great Bitterness of Soul," asking for mercy for those who had hidden themselves in time of

---

47. Historical Relation, ff. 35-36.
48. Fatio Calendar, 1/4/1709.

trial. "Not one," he mourned, "appears in vindication of your Lord." His prophecies and his person were uneasy reminders of the pains to which the group had gone to anticipate the failed resurrection. Moreover, Whitrow compounded difficulties by taking to heart the "Restitution of all things." He began to advocate a widespread charity which closely resembled the doctrine of levelling, or spreading wealth equally. In June, prophets again accused Whitrow of speaking "his own Words and Imaginations in his Ecstasies," and his wife Deborah was similarly rebuked. Lacy, inspired, called on Abraham Whitrow to humble himself or be broken by the Lord, who appreciated neither pride nor levelling. Whitrow retorted that his enemies were possessed by a lying spirit. After June 23, he absented himself from all meetings. On June 25, Jean Allut dreamed that his leg was bitten by a serpent, "which he did cut asunder."[49]

Whitrow's separation was most painful to the group because Sir Richard Bulkeley stuck with him to the end. In February he had been joined to Whitrow by the Holy Spirit and ordered to "advise, esteem and love" the woolcomber prophet. A scarcely fluent companion when not inspired, Whitrow taught the baronet the virtues of humility toward the ignorant and the poor. When the French Prophets, convinced that false prophets would rise among them at the end of time, split with Whitrow, Bulkeley sided with his spiritual master. Lacy demanded that an inspired discourse against levelling be sent to Bulkeley for "Information that he was under a Delusion." On July 11, 1708, Bulkeley answered that he and Whitrow would meet no more with the French Prophets, for fear of violence.[50]

Followers persevered in their overtures to Sir Richard. Despite several invitations and a divine reprieve, granted when he refused to appear, Bulkeley lost his place in the tribes. Nonetheless, until his death in 1710, followers maintained contact with him, and he at times sought them out. The split with Bulkeley was never as clean as it was with Whitrow, whom Lacy officially denounced as an impostor in 1709.[51]

Meanwhile, Whitrow and Bulkeley had put the principle of charity into practice. They established a short-lived charity school in Chesham (Bucks.), and Whitrow, with Bulkeley's aid, purchased an estate nearby called Greencroft. Here they were supposed to have held open house for

49. Whitrow, *Warnings*, 224; Fatio Calendar, June 1709; Nicholson, *Falsehood of the New Prophets*, 18-19; Historical Relation, ff. 39-40.
50. Nicholson, *Falsehood of the New Prophets*, 19; Bulkeley, *Preface*, 33; *Brand*, 34; Fatio Calendar, 7/11/1709.
51. Fatio Calendar, Sept. and 10/10/1708, 7/6, 7/17, 9/4 and 9/7/1709.

the "simple People." Whitrow gadded about, relieving the poor, and he engaged many in spinning and weaving. By the time that his *Warnings* (with an extensive preface by Bulkeley) appeared in July, 1709, Whitrow was on his way to Ireland. Later in the year Bulkeley joined him and liberally assisted the impoverished people of Dublin.[52]

Whitrow spoke shamelessly of the inequalities between rich and poor. In a warning to gentlemen about to go on a hunt, he stormed, "For shame, for shame boast not any longer, nor insist on the Name of Gentility, while you are so unworthy, and so much differ from those you make a Scoff at; that freely distribute out of their little, to the Poor, for *Christ's* sake, who died on the Cross for you all." So Sir Richard, following the precepts of unstinted almsgiving, spent much of his wealth, for estates and bags of gold would avail him not when the Lord came "to have all things common among my People." Then, Whitrow was positive, "There shall be no more admiring of Greatness, for their having the Riches of this World; but for their Goodness, for that they have the Holy Spirit of God in them guiding and directing them to do his Will."[53]

Bulkeley insisted that none of this implied levelling, or the "confused mixing of Stocks." Rather, it was a distribution to the needy. But he forthwith furnished a dozen arguments against holding private property, foremost among them that property begat avarice, fraud, malice and a false worldly hierarchy of names and titles. Instead, the Lord bade his children sell all, that they might be refined and purified. To the objection that excessive charity would make the world run haywire, Bulkeley would reply, as Jesus to Peter (John 21:22), "What is that to thee? follow thou me."[54]

"In short," wrote an observer, the Irish philosopher, Bishop George Berkeley, "Sir Richard was resolved to sell his estate and give all to the poor. But I am told the Chancery opposed him as *non compos* [*mentis*]." He died on April 7, 1710, in his country house at Ewell, Surrey, after a sudden illness. Creditors sold his house to pay for the debts incurred by charity, and his will was hotly contested by various relatives.[55]

---

52. Kingston, II, 111; Whitrow, *Warnings*, 325, 329-30; Spinckes, *Pretenders Reexamined*, xiii, 20-22, Appendix III, 51-56; George Berkeley, *Letters*, ed. A.A. Luce (1956) 31. Bulkeley in 1699 had hoped to establish a college for Christian upbringing as an act of charity: *HMC* 1: 2nd R., Lyons, 238-40. Contrast Bulkeley, *Preface*, 147.

53. Whitrow, *Warnings*, 166, 202, 278-79.

54. Bulkeley, *Preface*, 82-83, 108-11. Cf. Whitrow, *Warnings*, 157, 202.

55. Berkeley, *Letters*, 31; Georges Ascoli, "L'affaire des prophètes français à Londres," *Revue du XVIIIe siècle*, III (1916) 100; Trinity College (Dublin), MSS 2531, letterbook of William King, 11/10/1711; Land Registry Office (Dublin), Memorials, VI, 111 (No. 1519) Sir

Unsettled by the schism with Whitrow and Bulkeley, the inspired in 1708 sought retrenchment. Three prophets, including the aggressive missionary Mary Turner, found themselves indicted by the group for speaking falsely under inspiration. John Potter cast out the evil spirit from an agitated follower. A prophet hinted to the newcomer Nicholson, soon apostate, that one must be wary of people filled with new wine.[56]

During the autumn of 1708, French followers discovered their first false prophet. By September 28, the priestly tribe of Levites was complete; both Marion and Fage were members along with eighteen other French men and women, but the *inspiré* Jean Cavalier had been omitted. That day he spoke a warning which was condemned by the Holy Spirit. Fatio in his calendar noted the day as the beginning of Cavalier's disaffection, but he had been in bad graces for some time. His signature was missing from the attestation to Mazel's memoirs in August. His wife Jeanne had received divine orders to carry the Lord's message to Holland, but Jean had been commanded to remain behind. Contrary to the divine warnings, Jean intended to go with his wife, and he tried to convince an assembly of prophets of his role in the mission. On October 2, Jeanne Raoux had a vision of a porcelain cup shattered as a sign of a prophet rejected by the Lord. Invited to a meeting of the Levites, Jean Cavalier did not come. He and his wife, poorly prepared for a Dutch winter, sailed for Holland in November.[57]

The English after May 25 had expelled a man too fond of Emes's resurrection; the French after Mazel's August departure had excluded a man too fond of missions, a man as well who of all the Huguenots had most linked himself to the Emes prophecies. Given Jean Cavalier's status as one of the original three *inspirés*, his refusal to obey divine commands resembled in impact the adherence of Bulkeley (veteran follower, baronet) to Whitrow. At times when the English and French wished to project an image of coherence, they had become infinitely sensitive to contumely and waywardness. False prophets like Whitrow and Cavalier had lost their balance on the narrow line between arrogance and despair.

Whitrow and Cavalier were also, perhaps, the first victims of a change in the group's perception of the process of inspiration. The *inspirés* in the

---

Richard Bulkeley, A Memorial of a Will to be Registered (will of 1706, likely complete before Bulkeley's exposure to Whitrow, and registered by claimants and legatees in October, 1710).

56. Nicholson, *Falsehood of the New Prophets*, 11, 18; Woodward, *Letter to Mr. F.M.*, 7-10; Humfrey, *Account*, 37; *Collection of Warnings*, 144-45.

57. Fatio Calendar, 9/28, 9/30 and 10/2-10/3/1708; *MMM*, 39 and n.; Historical Relation, f. 46.

Cévennes and the first prophets in London had claimed not to remember what they said under ecstasy. To critics in England, loss of memory and of the senses in general was less a guarantee of the purity of prophecy than it was of the animality of frenzied people. In 1707, spokesmen of the French Prophets adjusted their description of what occurred under ecstasy to include the survival of intellect and memory. The new emphasis on consciousness, a shift which did not escape the notice of opponents, left its mark on the group. Followers had weakened the position of their prophets. The faithful had more cause to fear the mixture of human and divine speech when their prophets were alert during inspiration. The emphasis on consciousness also changed the way in which believers related to one another. Unconscious prophecy required that prophets depend upon an audience to preserve the message. The prophet was then a social being. When the consensus was that prophets were aware of the content of their inspirations, prophets could begin to assert a degree of independence from their audience. The group's nervousness about false prophecy after the failure of Emes's resurrection was aggravated by the changed terms in which the French Prophets understood the prophetic act.[58]

The Role of Women

On December 4, 1708, one more false prophet sprang up. Fatio's comment was phrased with great suspicion of her pride: "Mrs. Dinah Stoddart having written to Mr. Lacy etc. And having also seen me, in order that we should receive her as the Saviour of womankind, writes at last to me also a letter of reproof still urging her Pretensions."[59] Comparable to Whitrow's expulsion at an anxious season for English followers and to Cavalier's rebellion during efforts by the French to unite the nations, Dinah Stoddart's act suggests that there were difficulties between male and female followers. Of the 160 tribe members, 107 were male, although by the end of 1708 an equal number of each sex had appeared as French Prophets. In the eminent tribe of Levi, there were 25 men and only 3 women (Jeanne Raoux, Elisabeth Charras, Anne Watts).[60] The dispropor-

---

58. *Appeal from the Prophets to their Prophecies* (1708) 17; O[swald] E[dwards], *The Shaking-Prophet Alarmed* (Dublin, 1711); *Reflections on Sir Richard Bulkeley's Answer to Several Treatises* (1708) 26; Benjamin Bayly, *An Essay upon Inspiration* (2nd ed.; 1708) 76, 398-400; and see my fuller discussion in *Knaves, Fools, Madmen and that Subtile Effluvium*, University of Florida Social Science Monograph Series, 62 (Gainesville, 1978) chapter three.

59. Fatio Calendar, 12/4/1708.

60. Of important prophets put in other tribes, three were male (Thomas Dutton, Jean Allut, John Potter) and seven were female. The missionary John Giles, Timothy Byfield, Jean

tion in the tribes, both in numbers and status of women, reflected male dominance of the ministerial functions within the group. Male prophets had a near monopoly on blessing, and they alone conducted love-feasts, worked cures, administered baptism. Among the tribes were scattered twelve male apostles, the proper officiants at communion.

Between 1708 and 1712, all schismatic false prophets were women. The particularly "extravagant" gestures or claims of inspired women may be attributed to their restricted sacerdotal roles. Excluded from the shaping of more familiar (less "extravagant") religious ceremonies, they were often inspired to perform signs that gave them center stage. So a prophet removed her clothes and preached to the horrified audience in the Sardinian chapel; so Elizabeth Gray impersonated the Whore of Babylon and began by barricading the door. "This done, she laid aside her *Manteau* and *Nightclothes, tied* up her Hair before all the Company with singular Modesty; then taking a *Peruke* and *Hat* that she found in the Room, put them on her Head, and sat down in an Elbow Chair very Majestically, with her Arms akimbo." Samuel Keimer later asked the meaning of her burning John Glover's face with a flaming handkerchief. "Or what was the meaning of her taking a Wig off a Prophet's Head and putting it on her own Head, under Agitations? What influenced one of the most eminent Prophetesses to snatch my Hat from me, and fling it upon the ground, in the Middle of the Room, and then sit down upon it?"[61]

Since sexual tensions in the group manifested themselves in such oblique ways, the breach between male and female did not immediately evoke pertinent healing rituals such as those devised for the split between English and French. There was good reason for this. The eminence and freedom already accorded women among the French Prophets was unusual in comparison with other religious groups in England. Only the Quakers and Philadelphians allowed women something approaching the same latitude and authority. To Anglican clergymen, one chief proof that the French Prophets lacked a divine commission was their tolerance (or encouragement) of female "teachers" and leaders.[62] Women prophets, if denied a fully sacerdotal character, did have considerable power. Scribes,

---

Pellet and his family were among the prominent followers absent from the tribes altogether, for no apparent reason.

61. Kingston, I, 65-66; *Brand*, 54, 109-10. Cf. Richard T. Curley, *Elders, Shades, and Women* (Berkeley and Los Angeles, 1973) 185-90.

62. The text against a female ministry is 1 Corinthians 14:34-35; 1 Corinthians 11:5 does sanction female prophets. Under inspiration, Whitrow said, "That Women prophesied they cannot deny; but that Women taught they may deny, for they were forbid to teach, but allowed to Prophesy." Bulkeley, *Preface*, 143.

most of them male, devotedly copied the prophecies of females. Followers attended assemblies convoked by women, kneeled before them occasionally to receive blessings, and accepted new names from them. Women issued inspired orders concerning the publication of books and the direction of missions; they reproached intemperate and faint-hearted believers; they healed private feuds between men.[63]

Women also made themselves noticeable by their mobility and independence. Women had a major role in the augmented missionary efforts of the French Prophets in 1709. A total of eight female and six male prophets went on sixteen different missions; six men accompanied them as scribes. Of the ten expeditions with three or more inspired persons, only two were controlled by men.[64]

The women prophets seemed more adventurous; they were the first to Cambridge, Oxford, Wales, and the first also to Scotland. The prophet Jeanne Cavalier had initiated the missions to Holland in the fall of 1708, and two women, with John Moult and John Giles, returned to Holland in 1709. When Moult and Giles voyaged to Ireland, they had barely stepped ashore (and they did not prophesy) before returning across the Irish Sea. The only other male prophets to enter new areas were John Potter and Nathaniel Sheppard, who travelled close to home (Pulham, Northampton, Norwich). According to the group's Historical Relation, however, Potter and Sheppard were chiefly sent "to such in those parts as expected the Kingdom of Christ." When four men set out for Scotland in May, 1709, they were sent by the Spirit "to confirm the faith of such as had already believed."[65]

For a variety of reasons, men were more reluctant to go on missions and less aggressive than women when finally on their way. First, male prophets

63. Anna Maria King, Mary Turner and Ann Topham, *Warnings of the Eternal Spirit to the Priest and People of Chichester* (1709) 15; Mary Beer, Mary Keimer and Ann Watts, *A Collection of Prophetical Warnings . . . To the Inhabitants in and about the City of Bristol* (Bristol, 1709) 68-69; Anna Maria King, John Moult, Mary Turner and Ann Topham, *Warnings of the Eternal Spirit, Pronounced at Edinburgh* (Edinburgh, 1709) verso of title page, 29-30, 35-38.

64. Historical Relation, ff. 41-56, gives a detailed account of the missions. The French followers Audemar, Nolibet and Mahieu received divine commands to go to the Cévennes. Two of them, Nolibet and Mahieu, departed for Holland in October. Fatio Calendar, 7/18-7/29 and 8/18/1709; BSHPF, Papiers Coquerel, MSS 302, f. 6.

65. Fatio Calendar, August 1709; Historical Relation, ff. 42, 51; King et al., *Warnings at Edinburgh*. Geoffrey Nuttall notes that early Quaker women were similarly independent and adventurous: *The Holy Spirit in Puritan Faith and Experience* (Oxford, 1946) 87-88. Cf. Patricia Higgins, "The Reaction of Women, with special reference to women petitioners," in Brian Manning, ed., *Politics, Religion and the English Civil War* (1973) 179-225.

Map 3. Great Britain. ● = towns with followers; ○ = other towns noted in text.

and scribes had more family connections than their female counterparts. The women who became well-travelled messengers for the Lord were with one exception considerably younger than the men and unmarried. The older woman (Elizabeth Hughes) was a widow whose daughter was an itinerant prophet as well. On the other hand, at least five of the missionary men had wives and children. Guy Nutt, who directed Samuel Noble to leave his family behind and go to Scotland, asked Noble's wife, "Art Thou Willing to resign thy Husband up to the Lord, now He is like to call him forth?" She answered in tears, "The Spirit is willing, but Flesh and Blood struggle hard." Nutt himself felt the strains of separation, praying the Lord to protect near and dear relations, for "It will be very hard for some to part with us."[66]

Second, men in general, and specifically those on missions, had more business entanglements than the women. This was a factor of age as well as a common feature of the society.[67] One woman, again the widow Hughes, owned a cook's shop; Anne Watts sold pies, Mary Keimer was a shopmaid. Among the men, Francis Moult was a prosperous chemist, Lardner and Sheppard were apothecaries, Giles a well-to-do merchant, Dutton a lawyer, Glover a victualler, Noble a printer. Some of them may have retired from or deserted their trades, or were wealthy (or poor) enough to suspend operations for a bit, but most had to free themselves from commercial pursuits in order to travel.

Third, magistrates were partial to arresting men. Potter and Sheppard sat in jail in Pulham, threatened with impressment as had been some of the male prophets at Enfield. Francis Moult was imprisoned and prosecuted in Monmouth. Glover and Noble, disregarding a timely divine warning, languished for several days in the Edinburgh Tolbooth (jail). Dutton, seeking to strengthen their resolve with a letter, wrote, "You are the first English called to this Way of trial [legal punishment]." English followers thus established equivalence with the French in terms of legal persecution, but men had the lopsided share in this martyrdom. There are no definite reports of inspired women similarly tried.[68]

66. Thomas Dutton, Guy Nutt and John Glover, *Warnings of the Eternal Spirit, to the City of Edenburgh* (1710) Orders 2/7 and 5/21/1709.

67. On women in English business, contrast Alice Clarke, *The Working Life of Women in the Seventeenth Century* (1919) 20-21, 32-33; Eric Richards, "Women in the British Economy since about 1700: An Interpretation," *History* 59 (1974) 337-57;, Margaret George, "From 'Goodwife' to 'Mistress': The Transformation of the Female in Bourgeois Culture," *Science and Society* 37 (1973) 152-77.

68. Historical Relation, ff. 42-43, 49, 51, 54; Dutton-Cuninghame Corr., comment on letter of 8/26/1709, 58-63, and letter of 1/12/1710, 259; Dutton et al., *Warnings to Edenburgh,* i, 52.

The degree of assertion and command manifested by women in the group was socially remarkable and remarked upon. The famous actress who played Betty Plotwell (Elizabeth Gray) in Thomas d'Urfey's "serious and moral" play, *The Modern Prophets* (performed in June, 1709) had the major role. Betty shammed inspiration to regain a lover led astray by the French Prophets. She told her secret to the audience; it was, for d'Urfey, the secret of the French Prophets: "I'm a rare Actress you must know, and perform my Rants, and my Groans, my Flights, and my Fancies with exact Method: I manage my Soap for Foaming, better than any Eastern Gipsy; and have as pretty a Trick to make my Belly swell, you would admire, my dear—." Sexual innuendo, customary with d'Urfey, prevailed. In Act III, Kate the innkeeper spoke bluntly to Betty: "Why look'e, Mistress a—— You pretend to Prophecy, and Wisdom, and Revelation, and this and that and t'other, when to be plain with you, I fancy you deal more in the Flesh than the Spirit."[69]

Contemporary public opposition to the French Prophets was predominantly male,[70] and critics often concentrated on linking hypocrisy and sexual misconduct. Opponents, struck as much by the presence of so many female prophets as by their "indecent" agitations, expressed their suspicions of women in sexual and theological terms, but their disapproval was rooted in social judgments. Women prophets were more conspicuous than men prophets because they were more obviously deserting traditional social roles. As they abandoned rules of deportment and ignored constraints on physical movement (and, sometimes, dress), they drew loud criticism, as if it were those freedoms, rather than religious inspiration, which they sought.[71]

---

69. Thomas d'Urfey, *The Modern Prophets: or, New Wit for a Husband* (1709) Act I, scene 2 and Act III. D'Urfey's play was forbidden by the Lord Chamberlain after three performances, but it caused the group some discomfort, for Fatio was at unusual pains to record the fate of the play: Fatio Calendar, 7/22 and 9/8/1709; Emmett L. Avery, ed., *The London Stage 1660-1800* (Carbondale, 1960) Part 2, I, xxix, note c, 191-92. Cf. *The Tatler* XI (May 5, 1709); *The Female Tatler* No. 4 (July 13-15, 1709) and No. 8 (July 22-25, 1709).

70. Mary Astell assumed the pseudonym William Wotton and criticized Shaftesbury's leniency with the French Prophets, but none of the other contemporary women authors entered the controversy. There is some evidence of less public opposition on the part of women. Ladies-in-waiting around the Queen, and perhaps the Queen herself, approved of Calamy's *Caveat* against the French Prophets. William Wotton [Mary Astell], *Bart'lemy Fair; or, An Enquiry after Wit* (1709); Calamy, *Life*, I, 100-101; Rev. Joseph Hunter, ed., *The Diary of Ralph Thoresby* (1830) II, 21-22. See also William Tong, ed., *An Account of the Life and Death of Mrs. Elizabeth Bury* (1720) 126.

71. See, for example, William Wycherly's letter to Alexander Pope about the new prophets, "amongst which there is one Betty Grey, so pretty and hansome a young Wench, (as they say) that she would be able to turn you to her; and communicate to you some of her

Followers were cognizant of the controversial roles adopted by women in the group. Accepting contemporary attitudes toward women, many male believers had more cause to fret about the excessive authority of women than about roles closed to female prophets. The exclusion of certain inspired women was comparable to the rejection of Whitrow for his advocacy of "levelling." Once they asserted equality in ceremony or inspiration, women were viewed as threats to structures of social deference inherited from the outer world. In 1709, the French cast out the schismatic Anna Angibert, who had physically extravagant agitations and had not humbled herself to other (male) prophets. In July of the same year, John Potter cast out Dorothy Harling as one who thought herself the imperial woman mentioned in Revelation 12:1-6, clothed with the sun, with the moon under her feet, who would bring forth the man-child to rule the nations. Harling declared that she was "actuated by the very same Spirit he and the rest were," and led a small schism of her own. In August, John Potter dealt harshly with a prophet in Pulham who made unusual promises to followers and predicted the destruction of towns and people hostile to her message.[72]

By October, 1709, Thomas Dutton was worrying about a new Scottish prophet, the Lady Abden, some of whose inspirations had already been discounted by the Spirit as "mixtures." Dutton had left followers in Edinburgh with a warning to watchfulness and prayer, for "Ye are yet *Novices*." Less than three months passed before he was troubled by Lady Abden's novitiate, by "The Multitude of Commands, and the imperious haughty Style." Here was a woman of high social status, whom one could conceivably integrate into the priestly order of prophets without upsetting patterns of deference, yet Dutton suspected that she was drifting toward Whitrow's heretical "universal charity." The Spirit had condemned such charity, "for though the Spirit highly Commends the forsaking of all, the giving all in particular Cases, . . . yet It still preserves the Economy of the Body, keeping every member in its just place." Lacy and Marion refuted most of Lady Abden's prophecies, and Dutton wrote her long letters urging patience and care. Instead, with the support of Edinburgh believers, she printed her warnings in a book disapproved by the Spirit in London. "I desire of you," wrote Dutton to a correspondent, "that on every Copy of it

---

Sanctify'd Agitations of Body, by the secret Operations of her Spirits, upon Yours . . . ." George Sherburn, ed., *The Correspondence of Alexander Pope* (5 vols.; Oxford, 1956) I, 35.

72. Fatio Calendar, 7/13-7/27 and 9/12/1709; Historical Relation ff. 29, 43-44; *Brand*, 38-39, 80, 111; Dutton-Cuninghame Corr., 10/2/1709, 203; *Post Boy*, No. 2241 (Sept. 22-24, 1709).

you meet with, you would write that it is Condemned and Rejected by the Spirit in me." This adamant disclaimer amounted to denial of Lady Abden's status as a prophet. Dutton alluded to her "lapse," hoping that she might be "recalled."[73]

In 1710 and 1711, both male and female prophets had to contend with suspicions of their warnings, but the serious problems were again with women. John Moult upbraided Ann Topham and Mary Turner for pride and rebellion; Mary Keimer refused to prophesy the recuperation of mortally ill Nathaniel Sheppard until she was soundly rebuked by John Potter. Ann Topham and Anna Maria King were turned out from meetings by Potter.[74]

Sexual tensions, sexual fantasies and advances often occur in small groups when members fear group dissolution.[75] The male attack on female prophets during these years may be interpreted in part as an unconscious response to sexual feelings whose expression would violate the group's sense of itself as morally unblemished. Indeed, not all sexual desires went unexpressed. In Manchester, a wealthy widow named Christina Pickering uttered blasphemies and bawdy words under inspiration; Dorothy Harling was accused of sadism, exhibitionism and urinating on her adherents.[76]

Explicit and inexplicit problems with sexuality were part of the larger problem of group purity. Concern for the purity of inspiration may arise in anxious prophetic groups of any millenarian ethos, but the definition of impurity will vary. In the ethos of cataclysm, impurity is betrayal of the

73. Dutton-Cuninghame Corr., 71, 74, 77, 110, 112; Dutton et al., *Warnings to Edenburgh*, 179; NLS, MS/493/73, letters of 9/16 and 11/10/1709 and Cuninghame (?) to Ramsay, 1710; George D. Henderson, *Mystics of the Northeast* (Aberdeen, 1934) 215. Lady Abden's book, *The Last Revelation*, has eluded me.

74. Fatio Calendar, 1/1/1710; *Brand*, 47-51, 63; Fatio Notebooks, I, 36, 40-41, 101; Dutton-Cuninghame Corr., 12/19/1711?, 306, and 1/21/1712, 328-39 and commentary on letter of 12/12/1711.

75. See Philip E. Slater, *Microcosm: Structural, Psychological and Religious Evolution in Groups* (New York, London and Sidney, 1966); W.R. Bion, *Experiences in Groups and Other Papers* (1970); Victor Turner, *Dramas, Fields and Metaphors* (Ithaca and London, 1974) 246-48.

76. *Brand*, 38-40; Dutton-Cuninghame Corr., 5/2/1711, 7-10. Cf. Charlotte O. Kursh, "Dirt, Pollution and Patina: A Vocabulary of Behavior Control," *The Psychoanalytic Review* 63 (1976) 5-25. The use of obscenity may also be considered part of a ritual of abasement or debasement in the process of conversion and initiation; that the French Prophets on the whole did not accept such "violent" tactics may argue for a desire on their part to keep more permeable boundaries between the inspired and the uninspired, or between themselves and the world outside. Cf. Bennetta Jules-Rosette, "The Conversion Experience," *Journal of Religion in Africa* 7 (1975) 142-45; Jacqueline Monfouga-Nicolas, *Ambivalence et culte de possession* (Paris, 1972) 126.

tribe, and one is punished for treason; in the inverse ethos of the New Jerusalem, impurity is insincerity and exclusiveness, a betrayal of the universal community. In the ethos of judgment, impurity is immorality and insubordination, the act of lying to God and denying his law; in the inverse ethos of pentecost, impurity is inauthenticity, lying to oneself. Whitrow had been cast out for betrayal and insubordination, Cavalier for insubordination—the women for insubordination and immorality. For the French Prophets, the association of women with false prophecy was intricately bound to the ethos of judgment which, in England, had particular patriarchal overtones.

The Philadelphian Richard Roach seemed to recognize this. He and the prophet Sarah Wiltshire inaugurated the Polemica Sacro-Prophetica on June 4, 1710, arguing for a new ministration as the synthesis of the imperfect Philadelphians and French Prophets. Although the French Prophets had added the sword of Power and the direct Word of the Lord to Philadelphian love and peace, they concentrated too much on destruction and judgment. Now Roach and Wiltshire, advocates of pentecost and New Jerusalem, wished to redress the balance. The Philadelphians had begun to move apart from the French Prophets prior to 1710, Roach urging his companions to reconvene private meetings and revive the Philadelphian community. Since the Philadelphians did not entirely forsake the meetings of the French Prophets, there was a conflict of allegiances. This conflict was not only theological; a prime difference between the two groups was the attitude toward women within them. The Philadelphians had a tradition of female leadership. Jane Lead and Ann Bathurst had commanded the loyalty of all in the 1690s. When Lead died in 1704, the mantle passed to the scribes Roach and Francis Lee, neither of whom received divine revelations but who kept in contact with circles on the continent whose prophetic leadership was also in the hands of women. True to this tradition, Roach, in his public crusade to unify the dispensations, relied upon the divine authority of another woman prophet. Sarah Wiltshire, a former Quaker, was conscious of her perilous status among the male-oriented French Prophets, and in February 1709/10 described herself as "set on a wall or Precipice to walk the more warily for villains ready enough to give me a push." In October, she had a revelation of a "new miraculous Effective way of Healing" and by 1711 had cured the despondent Mary Heath, a first and controversial example of a woman prophet exercising healing powers. Roach and Wiltshire endured long contests with the French Prophets, despite energetic opposition from

Mary Keimer, Thomas Dutton, John Lacy, and Louis Joyneau (who pummeled Sarah Wiltshire). By 1713, Dutton would write news of Roach, "who with his prophetess you know with all his Schemes has been frequently condemned, is now fallen into the very Abyss of Ranterism, under that Specious self-deluding Name of the Kingdom of Love."[77]

Throughout these years, men had the major part in denouncing false prophets, although women like Mary Keimer who accepted the regime of the men were vocal in combats with both men and women of questionable prophetic purity. Excommunication was the prerogative of the male prophets who assumed ministerial functions. The disproportionate number of women designated as false prophets cannot be interpreted simply as a sign of discontent among women in the group, for the identification of the impure was tied to the values and fears of the men. Esteeming a patriarchal social and religious system,[78] they feared to concede equality to female prophets lest the habits of sexual deference be eroded. Excommunication of presumptuous inspired women was an expression of the common belief that women, children and infants were easily swayed by emotions and therefore less able than adult men to distinguish the good from the bad, or the true spirit from the false.[79]

77. Bodleian, Rawlinson MSS D. 832, ff. 34v. (misdated in Bodleian catalogue), 35, 77v., 78v., and D. 833, ff. 30-35, 43v., and D. 1318, ff. 55-68; Dutton-Cuninghame Corr., 1/13/1713, 185. Cf. Walker, *Decline of Hell*, 245-63. On Mary Heath, see the Archives of the Bethlem Royal Hospital and Maudsley Hospital (Beckenham), Subcommittee Book, 1709-17, 3, and Admissions Book 1702-15, 159.

78. A system, be it noted, which could allow for some role flexibility: see Margaret W. Masson, "The Typology of the Female as a Model for the Regenerate: Puritan Preaching, 1690-1730," *Signs* 2 (1976) 304-15, and contrast Susan Gubar, "The Female Monster in Augustan Satire," *Signs* 3 (1977) 380-94.

79. On the position of women and men's attitudes toward them in the early eighteenth century, see Jean Gagen, *The New Woman: Her Emergence in English Drama 1600-1730* (New York, 1954) esp. 130-31; Keith Thomas, "Women and the Civil War Sects," *Past and Present* 41 (1958) 42-62; idem, "The Double Standard," *Journal of the History of Ideas* 20 (1959) 195-216; Katharine M. Rogers, *The Troublesome Helpmate: A History of Misogyny in Literature* (Seattle and London, 1966) ch. 5; Irvin Ehrenpreis, "Letters of Advice to Young Spinsters," in Earl Miner, ed., *Stuart and Georgian Moments* (Berkeley and Los Angeles, 1972) 245-70; John M. Beattie, "The Criminality of Women in Eighteenth-Century England," *Journal of Social History* 8 (1975) 80-116; Janelle Greenberg, "The Legal Status of the English Woman in Early Eighteenth-Century Common Law and Equity," *Studies in Eighteenth-Century Culture* 4 (1975) 171-81; Paula Backschneider, "Defoe's Women: Snares and Prey," *ibid.* 5 (1976) 103-20; Marlene LeGates, "The Cult of Womanhood in Eighteenth-Century Thought," *Eighteenth-Century Studies* 10 (1976) 21-39; Miriam Slater, "The Weightiest Business: Marriage in an Upper-Gentry Family in 17th Century England," *Past and Present* 72 (1976) 25-54; Paul Fritz and Richard Morton, eds., *Woman in the 18th Century and Other Essays* (Toronto and Sarasota, 1976) esp. essays by Katharine Rogers, F.P. Lock, and Miriam J. Benkovitz;

Whitrow's early apostasy possibly excepted, no male prophets led schisms. The only men to lead schisms were ordained ministers. The Huguenot(?) pastor Milliet published a small pamphlet in his apostasy, claiming that the French Prophets were instruments of the devil. Five of his "flock" left with him in July, 1709, among them John Hartland, a prophet and one of the twelve apostles named to the tribes.[80] Other clerics split from the group without leading schisms: Thomas Cotton,[81] Jean Lions.[82] Ministers were subject to intense social pressures from followers and from unbelievers, and their departure is not surprising.[83] The schisms with ministers highlighted the conflict between the spiritual authority acknowledged by English society and that acknowledged by the group. The schisms with women (and with Whitrow) reflected attempts to align traditional social orders with a new spiritual hierarchy.

The only male prophet to verge on schism was John Lacy, whose behavior with Elizabeth Gray disrupted the traditionalist moral code of the French Prophets. Sometime in the summer of 1711, French Prophets heard rumors that John Lacy would do "some great Things." Followers learned by the new year that he had received a divine command to leave his wife and sleep with Elizabeth Gray. Many were terribly upset and confused, for Lacy was a circumspect gentleman and principal prophet. Was this a trial such as Abraham had undergone with Isaac, where the Lord accepted the will as the deed? Jonathan Taylor thought so until Lacy and Gray actually consummated the union. None was more disturbed than Thomas Dutton, who criticized Lacy for his obedience to an evil spirit.

Cynthia S. Matlack, "'Spectatress of the Mischief Which She Made': Tragic Woman Perceived and Perceiver," *Studies in Eighteenth-Century Culture* 6 (1977) 317-30; Lawrence Stone, *The Family, Sex and Marriage In England 1500-1800* (New York, 1977); Melissa A. Butler, "Early Liberal Roots of Feminism: John Locke and the Attack on Patriarchy," *American Political Science Review* 72 (1978) 135-50; Robert H. Michel, "English Attitudes Towards Women, 1640-1700," *Canadian Journal of History* 13 (1978) 35-60; and notes 65 and 67 of this chapter.

80. Fatio Calendar, 7/12-7/21/1709.

81. For Cotton's deathbed statement about his apostasy from the French Prophets, see Walter Wilson, *The History and Antiquities of Dissenting Churches and Meeting Houses* (1814) IV, 384.

82. BSHPF, Papiers Christol (uncatalogued), unpublished manuscript, Frank Christol, "Une affaire sensationelle: le prophétisme Camisard en Angleterre," 190-205/4.

83. An illustration of both kinds of pressures is the saga of Dr. John Foster, Prebendary of Salisbury Cathedral and rector of Longbridge-Deverill in Wiltshire. He was commanded by the prophet Susannah Sanger to allow her to speak to his congregation. He publicly announced the time for the delivery of the prophetic message (late 1712), and Mrs. Sanger that day spoke a short warning in the church. Leaders of Foster's parish complained to Bishop Edward Fowler and began a prosecution against him under the Statutes of Conventicles. Fowler suspended Foster from the pulpit for six months. Dutton-Cuninghame Corr., 1/13/1713, 187; *Brand*, 66n; there is nothing in the ecclesiastical records.

Lacy published a long letter in reply. Until February (1711/12), wrote Lacy, he thought himself under temptation, but now he knew that he could no more refuse the command than deny the Lord's absolute sovereignty, having been threatened with "*Eternal Destruction and Hell-Fire* if I disobeyed."[84]

Slowly, followers were reconciled to the adultery of John Lacy. Dutton conferred with him and asked that he "not justify this Act on the foot of a general doctrine, but as a Singular Case." Lacy said that he so understood it. "Certainly," wrote Dutton, somewhat reassured, to the Scottish prophet James Cuninghame, "what you and Mr. Potter have had from the Spirit in Condemnation of Human Reasoning On the Ways of God, is right." Cuninghame had been sore distressed. By March 12, 1712, he had found consolation. He wrote to a friend:

> You cannot think how Odiously this affair of Mr. Lacy is Represented and aggravated by some: and yet my dear friend all this is little in Comparison to the Trial within, while I disquieted myself in accounting for this matter and could find no way so to do; But it has pleased the Lord in some measure, to Restore my mind to more Composure, and I can now in peace and full assurance of Faith wait quietly for the brighter displays of his Power, which I believe will suddenly break out from under this Cloud.[85]

Under "clouds of thick darkness" described by the prophet Henrietta Irvine, other followers were regaining mental composure, and Cuninghame reported that the faith of few in London had collapsed. Mary Keimer, opposed to Lacy's adultery, was seized by the Spirit and desisted from her opposition. Jonathan Taylor found relief from his perplexity in the incomprehensibility of divine commands.[86]

"It was some Time," recalled Samuel Keimer, "before many of the Believers could be thoroughly reconciled to his leaving his Wife,"[87] but neither Lacy nor Gray was expelled from the group. A number of factors account for this. Gray, less assertive in this instance than Lacy, presented no threat to the upper echelons of male prophets. She remained in the background and had already lost much of her earlier prestige, "for none of the Prophetesses were so highly Blest being set as a figure of the Church

---

84. John Lacy, *A Letter from John Lacy to Thomas Dutton, being Reasons why the former left his Wife, and took E. Gray a Prophetess to his Bed* (1711/12). For Jonathan Taylor's comments, see Baptist College Library (Bristol), MSS "A & E Gifford Remains," I, no. 44.

85. Dutton-Cuninghame Corr., 173-75, 334-35, 371, 374.

86. Baptist College Library (Bristol), MSS "A & E Gifford Remains," I, no. 44; Fatio Notebooks, II, 217, 233-34; *Brand*, 57.

87. *Brand*, 58.

and Spouse of Christ for a time and now," asked Sarah Wiltshire, "who is less than she? She's like an empty Useless Vessel though of the first the fullest . . . ."[88] Lacy, on the contrary, had unique stature within the group as the foremost English prophet, favored with the gifts of healing and speaking in tongues. He had social status as a landed gentleman. Moreover, the cautions and conditions of his adultery affirmed rather than undermined the traditional moral code to which the group owed allegiance. Lacy had moved warily and with scriptural support. He had not contradicted any other prophets, there had been no inspired condemnation of him, and he had not proposed a general negligence of the moral code.[89] He and Gray further eased the situation by settling in distant Lancashire, where they begot several children.[90] They were not constantly present in London as reminders of an unpleasant era of doubt and consternation. The group's hesitance and eventual refusal to oust Lacy and Gray was an indication that prophets were expelled only when they showed a "pride" detrimental to the male hierarchy.

Inspired men maintained their dominant position within the group by restricting sacerdotal functions to themselves and by acting as judges of true inspiration. The series of expulsions of female prophets took place as the group struggled to redeem itself after May 25, 1708. In the struggle, sexual and sex-related tensions complemented the distressing search for a coherent millenarian ethos. Emes's failed resurrection had exaggerated the differences between French and English followers, and it had led to questions not only of individual mortality but of group survival. Purity in prophetic discourse and behavior seemed, day by day, more and more the key to survival.

Orders for Assemblies

The emphasis on purity paralleled the group's tendency to contract. In 1709, Fatio had remarked that most of the activities of the French

88. Bodleian, Rawlinson MSS D. 832, ff. 34-35.
89. Some followers may have regarded the Lacy-Gray adultery as a permissive model. There are imprecise allusions to some French followers leaving their wives in *Brand*, 70, and an ambiguous memorandum on Joseph Bundy, a Bristol follower, in Baptist College Library (Bristol), MSS "A & E Gifford Remains," I, no. 44, dated London 1712. Two Huguenots committed bigamy (wives in France and in London), Anne Steed cohabited with Samuel Tomlinson, and Mary Keimer lived with a ship captain in America: BPUG, MSS fr. 605, letter of 3/3/1719; *Brand*, 71.
90. Calamy, *Life*, I, 113-14, says that Lacy and Gray were brought before the Bishop's Spiritual Court in Lancashire for their adultery. See also *Brand*, 57-58.

Prophets occurred in family-size circles, although missionaries went far and wide to find believers. In the following years, small assemblies were the rule, and the tenor of large assemblies changed. When many of the French nation met at the home of Moïse Boussac in 1711, they were formal and tentative, reading out general orders for the conduct of meetings and specific inspired directives for the present meeting. Assemblies met to discuss and confirm orders given through single inspired persons, as if one could no longer trust any individual prophet. Regular biweekly meetings had an almost inflexible format. Followers read from warnings, scripture, or letters of missionaries and then sang a psalm or two, all the while expecting to be interrupted by the inspired among them. If none was quickly inspired, followers waited in silence, sometimes for hours. The Spirit did not often disappoint them, testimony to the strong bond between the prophetic act and ritual preparation.[91]

In 1712, soon after the Lacy-Gray crisis, the French Prophets obeyed a divine command that henceforth only the inspired and select scribes were to meet together formally.[92] Casual assemblies, earlier recommended by Richard Roach as the true method of meeting in the final dispensation, did continue, and in May, James Cuninghame could report the addition of new believers. The practical effect of the restricted meetings was to enhance the prestige of the prophetic office. "All in general are much satisfied with our ministry," wrote Cuninghame, "and Testify to a very uncommon thirst after, and thankfulness, for the divine Teachings, a disposition I believe produced in them, by the Surcease of the Meetings."[93] As the prophets held themselves aloof from the uninspired and from the uneducated who could not serve as scribes, they inflated the value placed upon their inspirations. The incidence of false prophets had menaced the purity of the prophetic hierarchy; the contraction of ceremony made it doubly important that inspiration be free from "mixtures." The problem of schism and false prophets finally called forth an imperfect ritual solution: the inspired established an enclave within the group where they conferred and held court.

In August, 1712, John Potter defined a general assembly as a gathering of all those who believed in "a God who reveals himself immediately," and

91. The meetings of 1711 and 1712 are described in the Fatio Notebooks; see esp. I, 1, 25, 55, 60, 110, 119, 126, 250 and II, 199. Cf. John Lacy, *The Scene of Delusions . . . Confuted* (1723?) iii.
92. *Brand*, 74; Dutton-Cuninghame Corr., 3/27/1712, 355; Fatio Notebooks, II, 236, 257.
93. Fatio Notebooks, II, 229, Dutton-Cuninghame Corr., 3/27/1712, 335 and 5/5/1712, 341.

a private assembly of the Lord's instruments as a gathering of those by whom the Lord speaks. Ten months later, in May, 1713, as scribes began to record the *Orders for Assemblies*, these definitions were read out to eliminate the unqualified from an assembly of the inspired. Mary Keimer chased away one woman who had remained behind, thinking herself an approved scribe. In each of the inspired assemblies recorded in the *Orders* and printed in 1715 as a guidebook for the dispensation, a cleansing act similar to this occurred. The assembly had to be pure. The *Orders* themselves consisted of instructions, usually from Potter or Cuninghame, on the method of discerning true spirits from false, on the number of inspired necessary to call a meeting, on the conduct of novices. Uppermost was a concern for unblemished prophecy and the sanctity of the gathered true prophets.[94]

By 1715, four prominent French prophets (including Isaac Havy and the Levite Daniel Le Tellier) and one English prophet were expelled for refusing to acknowledge the supremacy of the inspired assembly. The prophets formulated a new hierarchy in terms of roles performed in the assembly; the assembly assumed powers which made it indistinct from a traditional consistory or board of elders. Desperate for some security of belief, the prophets were devoting themselves to consolidating the True Church. Cuninghame said that not numbers of prophets but the quality and power of the Spirit created a church, that the essence of the True Church was a theocracy, its laws descending from "the most-holy Oracle." Potter warned believers to submit to the authority of the Church and to appreciate that "nothing ordered, acted or performed by the Spirit which presides in the Church can be revoked, abolished, or overruled except by that same Authority." Schism was explicitly schism from the True Church, and its ministry supervised discipline everywhere. The prophets commissioned Jean Daudé and Louis Gervaise to report on the disobedient, and they dispatched troubleshooters to the disorderly in Bristol and in Longbridge-Deverill (near Salisbury).[95]

The surviving prophets seemed exhausted by their battles with schismatics but proud of their endurance and willing to make their battle scars

---

94. The printed Orders are entitled, *Recueil d'avertissemens touchant l'ordre des assemblées et les regles de discipline* (1715); I have not located an English edition. A much fuller copy of the third through tenth assemblies recorded in the *Recueil* is in BPUG, MSS fr. 605, Booklets numbered "III.Fr"-"X.Fr." 6/13 through 9/26/1713. Fatio later omitted descriptions of certain inspired women and expelled prophets when editing the manuscript for publication. For this paragraph see Booklets II, VI, X; *Recueil*, 94, 192-95.

95. BPUG, MSS fr. 605, Booklets II, IV, VI, VII, VIII, X; *Recueil*, 91, 116, 133, 162, 172, 180, 188.

the sign of all true prophets. Dutton had written to a friend in 1709 concerning the ambitious prophet Lady Abden: "We had our Stumblings of Dr. Emes, they at Birmingham One of the like Nature, at Pulham one as hard to bear, and now you have had yours at Edinburgh, which fulfills what the Spirit had declared, that all who received this dispensation should do it, on the same foot with us [in London]." In the assemblies of 1713, Mary Keimer disappointed an applicant to the ranks of the inspired by demanding additional knowledge and experience. Potter said that prophets had to suffer trials before they could be granted recognition. Simple true inspiration was not now enough to certify a prophet. As the end of time seemed less imminent, followers could reassert the importance of seniority and experience.[96]

The *Orders* imposed an extraordinary degree of caution toward new prophecies that effectively curtailed any widespread outbreaks of independent prophecy. Under these circumstances the group could scarcely support the pentecostal ideal—stated earlier by Potter himself[97]—that all the faithful would be inspired. The defensiveness of the prophets made it equally unlikely that the group in its present shape could promote the New Jerusalem ethos of an universal church. Nor did the group act as if cataclysm were imminent. "It requires *Faith* and *Patience*," Dutton prophesied in 1709,

> and a great Assistance of the Spirit of God; to teach and persuade the People, that, their Lord will come, according to his gracious Promise, and restore all Things, as at the Beginning: And, though the Lord should seem to *delay his Coming*, yet *not* to be *weary* of such a Waiting for Him, *nor* to *faint*, in their faith: to bear with Meekness, and Patience, knowing, the Lord will reward Them, in his Kingdom, for the Reproaches, which the *Scoffers* shall cast upon Them; saying, where, *Where is the Lord coming in his Kingdom, that you speak of?*[98]

The world had passed safely into the year 1710, despite the "three years" prophecy by Elie Marion in 1706. Faith and patience were the keynotes of the *Orders*, and the fashioning of a durable fabric of assemblies and jurisdictions suggested that the True Church had yet some earthly labors to perform.

This was a True Church anchored in the millenarian ethos of judgment. It was primarily a man's church whose Book of Discipline had been framed by men, whose rigorously defined "public ministry" was composed

---

96. Dutton-Cuninghame Corr., 89; BPUG, MSS fr. 605, Booklets III, VI; *Recueil*, 101.
97. J[ohn] P[otter], *Warnings of the Eternal Spirit* (1711?) 6.
98. Dutton et al., *Warnings at Edenburgh*, 63.

of many more men than women, whose inspired women did little more than terminate meetings and announce future assemblies.[99] Although sex-related antipathies may have been declining by 1713 (all expelled from the assemblies were male), tensions between male and female remained, linked as they were to varieties of millenarian ethos at play beneath the ritual and rule of the *Orders*. There were still strains of the pentecost and New Jerusalem in the chorus of the True Church. During the next thirty years, these would shape the dominant ethos of the group. The following chapters will trace that transformation, which was set in motion not from the very center of the French Prophets, but from their geographical, cultural and theological periphery.

An Overview

The failure to raise Dr. Thomas Emes from the dead left the French Prophets with a legacy of spiritual trials. The group had changed in response to the problems of human mortality and false prophecy. Eschatologically, they emphasized the doctrine of incomprehensible but harmonious providence, accepting some "delay" in the fulfillment of predictions and the coming of the Kingdom. Ritually, they performed ceremonies to heal divisions within the group and devised rites of passage for believers who had to live in a world whose ultimate renewal was continuously being deferred. Socially, they had gathered themselves into tribes and families. In ecclesiastic terms, they had enlarged the ministerial functions and, consequently, the status of true prophets, who in turn reconstrued the power and boundaries of the True Church.

From the Desert to London, from 1706 to 1713, the *inspirés* and their followers experienced changes in the context, scale and density of millenarian prophecy. Camisard prophecies of battle and revenge had been out of place in England in 1706. The millenarian ethos of cataclysm had been discredited during the Restoration, and the spirit of "Violence, Turbulence, Wrath and Contradiction" was, as Richard Roach remarked, "somewhat softened, as Translated from the French into the English Prophets."[100] The "softening" took several forms. Huguenot and English followers in London cooperated to redirect attention from the war in the Cévennes to the Desert of Isabeau Vincent and the sleeping prophets

---

99. A list of the "public ministry" appears in the *Recueil*, 195.
100. Richard Roach, *The Great Crisis* (1725 [sic for 1727]) 51. Cf. also Bayly, *Essay upon Inspiration*, 396: "This Matter seems much refined in England from what it was in the Cévennes."

whose miracles and visions occurred as part of an ethos of judgment, familial, collective. Through the collation of accounts for the *Théâtre sacré* and their subsequent translation and defense, the group gave a new meaning to the mission of the *inspirés* in England. The *inspirés* themselves helped in this endeavor, predicting an English pentecost, a New Jerusalem in London. Though the Camisard tradition was reasserted in the tribes and ribbons of 1708, though images of destruction were never entirely absent from inspired discourse, persecution and redemption were reinterpreted within the frame of an ethos other than cataclysm.

The transformation of the Camisard ethos into one of pentecost, judgment or New Jerusalem depended upon the social environment of the prophetic group and the individual inclinations of members. When the scale of prophecy increased in 1707 and 1708, with more prophets and more inspirations, veteran prophets chose to emphasize the *communal* value of the spread of prophecy.[101] Prosecuted at law, insulted in the streets, attacked in the press, the leading French Prophets desired most of all to present a united front to a hostile English audience. Their desire to advance their cause in the public forum derived from their personal familiarity with the style of eighteenth-century literate debate and from the legal and social devices employed by enemies to force them to a public confession.

The increase in the scale of prophecy carried with it an increase in the density of prophecy. The group had to cope with a greater volume of prophecies from a more diverse set of prophets in action at the same time and generally in the same place. The most obvious and convenient way to accommodate such diversity and intensity was to advocate the New Jerusalem ethos in which Quakers, Baptists, Independents, Presbyterians, Anglicans, Roman Catholics, and Huguenots would pull together in the last dispensation. In the years 1707-1708, the French Prophets did tend to invert the ethos of cataclysm into the ethos of the New Jerusalem: those who did battle against the world would go on missions to do battle for the hearts of the world; the church of the faithful would open out rather than close in upon itself; persecution was a sign of trial in the process of universal rather than tribal renewal; one was renamed not so much to shed an old identity as to take part in a new world; walls that tumbled down would spring up again around the "large luminous Chapel."

But the French Prophets soon drew away from the New Jerusalem, for

---

101. On the importance of scale in social change, see esp. Monica Wilson, *Religion and the Transformation of Society: A Study in Social Change in Africa* (Cambridge, 1971).

group members were accustomed to the embrace of a social hierarchy, and felt endangered by the radical openness of the universal kingdom. Lacy had warned, "Do not think there is to be Equality, in outward secular Concerns. There will be Order and Degrees."[102] The fears of false prophecy which prompted the turn toward judgment had arisen out of twin anxieties—anxieties over social autonomy and shared symbolic systems. Whitrow, Cavalier and the women prophets expelled by the group had urged the autonomy of the inspired person; Cavalier, Harling, Angibert and Pickering had also had the wildest agitations, exemplary of the divorce of ego and body, spirit and matter. Their emphasis on the pentecostal, personal aspects of millennial times was opposed by prophets and followers who esteemed more highly the integrity of the group. Suspicious of the loss of bodily control and physical spontaneity, they were concerned to suppress open signs of sexuality as well as to maintain an orderly hierarchy of the sexes. The *Orders* were issued by a millennial court of judgment eager to prove the power of group sanctions. This was the victory of those who wanted a structured environment in which individual actions had meaning only in the larger, group context.

It was also a victory for those who wanted a structured set of social interactions, so that prophets, agreeing to the preeminence of the group, knew how to behave within it toward one another. With the rejection of Whitrow's "levelling" principles, the group had begun to turn its back on the New Jerusalem. At its most positive and insistent, levelling was a proposal for idiosyncratic symbolic systems. Where all goods are no longer marketable, individual evaluations take precedence, and social interactions may become quirky, unpredictable. Or so thought Whitrow's opponents, who could not approve of a social unanimity based upon a refusal to admit class differences.[103]

Between 1706 and 1713, in an often frustrating search for group stability, the French Prophets—with much equivocation—gradually adopted the millenarian ethos of judgment, an ethos which offered the

102. Lacy, *Warnings*, III, 88.
103. For related analyses of group style, group organization and symbolic systems, see James A. Beckford, "Two Contrasting Types of Sectarian Organization," in Roy Wallis, *Sectarianism* (New York, 1975) 70-85; Bryan R. Wilson, "The Pentecostalist Minister: Role Conflicts and Status Contradiction," *American Journal of Sociology* 64 (1959) 484-504; Kurt H. Wolff, ed., *The Sociology of Georg Simmel* (Glencoe, 1950) parts one and two. For a model of group interactions based upon information theory—in which prophecy may be seen as information which is both difficult to channel and hard to recapitulate—see Tom McFeat, *Small-Group Cultures* (New York, 1974).

security of explicit law and clear social articulation.[104] The ethos of judgment was adopted in response to external and internal pressures; as the group changed, its perception of the world changed. The inspired were both responsive to group needs and agents of group change; they were no less anxious about the directions of the group than were the uninspired. After seven years, the act of waiting—of waiting on and waiting for—beset as it always is by fantasies and problems of discipline, had taken on a new style. The French Prophets waited now as if for a verdict in a series of higher courts. The waiting was, they hoped, more than ceremonial; it must be instrumental, an active element in the millennial scheme.[105] It was a nervous sort of waiting, but more orderly, and quieter, much quieter.

104. A schematic representation of this overview appears in Appendix XI.
105. My ideas about waiting have been much affected by a reading of Barry Schwartz, *Queuing and Waiting: Studies in the Social Organization of Access and Delay* (Chicago and London, 1975) esp. 33-36, 168 ff.

CHAPTER V

Distant Piety: Scotland and the Continent

The French Prophets in Scotland

By 1712, two years after the final uprising in the Cévennes,[1] the French Prophets had adherents scattered across England. There were circles with prophets at Bristol, Birmingham, Manchester, Colchester, Pulham (Norfolk), Sleaford (Lincs.), and Deverill-Longbridge near Salisbury; isolated followers lived in Cambridge, Northampton, Enfield, and Eye and Great Yarmouth (Suffolk).[2] The dispersal of the French Prophets ran generally true to the typical map of earlier puritan centers: London and environs, southeast England, corporation towns. Missionaries had no success in northern England, and Wales proved a barren country.

Ireland too had been severe on the missionaries. Dublin so intimidated John Moult and John Giles that they had departed without inspirations, and Thomas Dutton remarked that later audiences were "impenetrable as Rocks." A few Anglicans clung to the dispensation, overcoming doubts raised by the Bulkeley-Whitrow affair. In 1711, twenty-one people were blessed by the prophets, but, wrote Dutton, "the Cowardice of the people in this Island is very great, and they require Strong Cords not only to draw them in any measure towards this Work, but also to move them, each Step they took in it." Some prophets approached the Quakers, and Dutton himself addressed some young Jews, but the Friends forced Guy Nutt and his party from the Meath Street (Dublin) meeting, and the Jews were courteous but distant.[3]

---

1. Abraham Mazel died in the revolt, which was easily put down: *MMM*, 208-15; Emile Bonnet, *Les Anglais en Languedoc juillet 1710* (Montpellier, 1915).
2. See lists in Dutton-Cuninghame Corr., 3/27/1712, 335; Winifred Turner, ed., *The Aufrère Papers*, in *HSL Publications* XL (1940) 70.
3. Dutton-Cuninghame Corr., 5/2/1711, 1-15 (quote, p. 3); Cambridge University, Add.

154

Enclaves of French Prophets in the English countryside and Ireland were small, with ten or fifteen members at most. Anglicans, Baptists, Quakers, they followed the lead of the group in the capital, and they added little to the conventions of the French Prophets. Another enclave, however, would place its indelible stamp upon all followers, for the largest circle outside London was in Scotland, and these men and women were quietists, avid readers of Jakob Boehme, Mme. Guyon and Antoinette Bourignon. They had meditated upon the hidden mysteries of scripture; they had watched for signs of the millennium; they had desires for a spiritual inward life. Like the Philadelphians, they were disposed to welcome others who had the promises of the Spirit which they themselves had so long sought.

Followers in Scotland were mostly Episcopalian gentry and Jacobites, dedicated to the cause of the Stuart Pretender to the English throne. Suffering under the Revolution Settlement which did away with episcopacy and established Presbyterianism as the state religion in Scotland, they drew apart from the preaching and formal liturgy of the church toward a personal and family religion of worship and prayer. If they maintained contact with the church (particularly in the northeast where Presbyterians had the least sway), they directed most of their religious concerns toward the divine light within themselves.[4]

Antoinette Bourignon's life and teachings had much in common with the experiences of these Scottish Episcopalians. Persecuted in France and the Netherlands for her religious beliefs, she retired to Hamburg in 1678, and was hounded by church authorities until her death in 1680. She had visions and dictated to her secretary, Pierre Poiret, spiritual treatises which stressed abandonment of church forms for the work of inner regeneration. She taught "that we have but one Master, Christ; and that he teaches us inwardly, and that we ought to listen to him within, for which all outward Instructions are our Monitors." True regeneration was accomplished through the guidance of the Spirit in each person. Formerly a Roman Catholic, Bourignon did not encourage a change of church connection, hoping that all might labor to effect the union of churches "in true Primitive Christianity." Everywhere was visible a universal corruption; from that, her Scottish translator reasoned, "we may all discover that

---

MSS 5, ff. 160-160v., letter from Jane Bonnell to J. Strype, 10/25/1709 (for which reference I thank Margaret Jacob); O[swald] E[dwards], *The Shaking-Prophets Alarmed* (Dublin, 1711); Fatio Notebooks, I, 184-85; John Moult, Guy Nutt and John Parker, *Warnings of the Eternal Spirit to the City of Dublin* (Dublin, 1710) iii-iv esp.

4. The Jacobite-quietist connection has been admirably described by George D. Henderson, *Mystics of the Northeast* (Aberdeen, 1934).

we live in the last Times."⁵ Her doctrines were popular among Episcopalians in Scotland, where Presbyterian general assemblies condemned them in 1701, 1709, and 1710.⁶

When the French Prophets arrived in Edinburgh, proclaiming the last days and prophesying against lifeless religion, they and the Episcopalians shared a history of religious persecution and a wish to avoid the sterile "Party spirit" of corrupt Christianity. Late in 1709, a Scottish gentleman wrote that he found the French Prophets foretold by Antoinette Bourignon. The conversion of John Forbes of Pitfichie was described by a friend who saw millenarianism as the meeting point of the two ways: "He was a good man, and had been very serious of a while before he joined the prophets, believing these to be the last times.... In this view he respected much Madam Bourignon, as giving an alarum of these things and with great Simplicity laying down Ways for people to prepare themselves against that great Event." Forbes was seized with agitations at the first prophetic assembly which he attended, and later in Aberdeen he spoke under inspiration. Andrew Michael Ramsay wrote to a friend in 1709 that "there is not one person in or about Edinburgh that read the Writings of A[ntoinette] B[ourignon] but what are more or less under the agitations except [George Lundie and James Cuninghame]."⁷

Some Scots, attracted too by the works of Mme. Guyon (Jeanne Marie Bouvier de la Mothe), wavered between her doctrine of complete resignation and the French Prophets' agitated warnings. In retirement at Blois in France after her beliefs had finally been cleared of heterodoxy by the Gallican theologian Bossuet, Mme. Guyon presided over a number of English and Scottish admirers "like a mother with her children." She saw no need for new prophets in this last age, and before her death in 1717 she wrote against the French Prophets for their impetuosity, for speaking in God's person, and for mistaking external marks of inspiration for the

---

5. Antonia Bourignon, *A Collection of Letters*, preface and translation by George Garden (1708) vii; Bourignon, *A Warning Against the Quakers*, preface and translation by Garden (1708) vi.

6. A.R. MacEwen, *Antoinette Bourignon, Quietist* (1910) 96-97; Pierre Bayle, "Bourignon (Antoinette)," *Dictionnaire historique et critique* (4th ed.; Amsterdam, 1730) I, 651ab; J. Orcibal, "Les spirituels français et espagnols chez J. Wesley et ses contemporains," *Revue de l'histoire des religions* 139 (1951) 89n.

7. Dutton-Cuninghame Corr., 1/14/1710, 125, and commentary by Alexander Falconar preceding two letters from Forbes of Pitfichie, 210; NLS, MS/493/73, letter of 11/12/1709. Cf. John Anderson, *A Defence of the Church-Government, Faith, Worship, and Spirit of the Presbyterians* (Glasgow, 1714) 300; James Hog, *Notes about The Spirit's Operations* (2nd ed.; Edinburgh, 1709).

simple, intimate peace of the Lord. The true "interior silence" never promoted bodily agitation, she explained, no matter how violent one's inner turmoil. Yet some of her admirers showed an enduring interest in the French Prophets. A few—George Middleton, Lady Jane Forbes, perhaps James Ogilvie (Lord Deskford, later second earl of Seafield)—became followers. Mme. Guyon, answering Ogilvie's troubled letters, advised that he relax his will and express love rather than ambition; he must not apply his mind or feelings to the achievement of internal silence.[8]

But what if one were entirely passive and loving and then knew for certain that the Spirit was plunging one into agitations and prophecy? Thomas Middleton, cousin to the Bourignonian George Garden and himself an avid reader of Guyon, perceived just such a link between quietism and prophecy, for he could "agitate himself when he pleases, by making himself passive."[9]

This was essentially the path to conversion trod by James Cuninghame, laird of Barns (Fife), between thirty and forty years old in 1709 and soon the most prominent of nearly a dozen Scottish prophets. Recuperating from an illness at the waters of Bath in the spring of 1709, he had time for reflection and the reading of Augustine Baker's *Sancta Sophia*, a work with manifold guidance for the contemplative. On May 21 he wrote that he was "recovered to a miracle" and scarcely knew himself "to be the same man I was some weeks ago." His restored health was a divine gift, and he desired "henceforth to be a Child of Providence, to live no longer but to God and to employ none of that time (which in a strict sense is his) upon my own selfish Ends." From Bath, having perhaps seen the prophets then at Bristol, Cuninghame wrote home for more news of them. By August, he compared them with a "Scheme about prophets" in Bourignon.[10]

A new man, Cuninghame returned to Scotland, observing the Prophets in Edinburgh and noting the good influence they had on several acquain-

---

8. Henderson, *Mystics*, 5-20, 86, 89, 100-01, and his *Chevalier Ramsay* (1952) throughout; George Balsama, "Madame Guyon, Heterodox," *Church History* 42 (1973) 350-65; Jean Marie Guyon, *Lettres chrétiennes et spirituelles* (new ed.; 1767-68) III, 231 (lettre LIII) and IV, 479-99 (lettres CXXIV-CXXV); BCUL, MSS T.P. 1155, Recueil de divers traités sur les dernières années de Madame Guyon, 6-7. Bourignonians also wrote against the French Prophets; see Garden's preface to Bourignon's *A Warning against Quakers*, vii, xix-xxi; Henderson, *Mystics*, 214, 246; Episcopal Theological College (Edinburgh), Forbes MSS (Old Catalogue), Letter in Latin from Pierre Poiret, concerning the Prophets in England.

9. Robert Wodrow, *Analecta* (Glasgow, 1842) II, 304 (October, 1715).

10. NLS, MS/493/73, letters of 5/21/1709 (quote) and 6/27/1709?; Henderson, *Mystics*, 198-200; Dutton-Cuninghame Corr., 8/9/1709, 221. The Bourignon *Tombeaux* reference is to part one, 8th letter (1669-1672).

tances. He learned that some of his closest friends had become followers, "and some actually agitated." Critical, he turned to the mystics, particularly St. John of the Cross, for advice, and he continued his spiritual exercises during which he felt the first motions "to something that was more silent." He chanced to hear the warnings of Lady Abden, who herself had been immersed in quietist literature. Cuninghame was struck by the pertinence of her inspirations:

> The precept given is this: that every man and woman retire, and enter into their closets, humble themselves as in my sight, hold their peace, silence their thoughts, be careful that their imaginations do not interpose, that they may be altogether still; when they are in such a disposition, then will I pour my Spirit into their souls.

After other apt warnings, Cuninghame felt his prejudices against the French Prophets vanish. By November, 1709, he had a degree of conviction about the dispensation which allowed him to disregard its history of failed predictions and the split with Abraham Whitrow. "The more silent my prayer was," he wrote to his friend George Garden, "and the less mixture of any thing of my own, the stronger was my conviction.... It was now no longer in my power to doubt that this was the voice of God unto my soul calling it powerfully inward." So did James Cuninghame validate the French Prophets in quietist terms. To him the two were complementary. Of Thomas Dutton's sceptical approach to the mystics, Cuninghame wrote, "He is but little Acquainted with the Mysteries, or he would find all to flow from the same spirit."[11]

At the beginning of 1710, Cuninghame was sure of his belief and would not admit to deception unless the mystics whose methods he had practiced had themselves practiced to deceive. Having tried the spirit of the French Prophets "in the most pure unbiased manner," he had, like others, found internal evidence for them. "And the strength of this argument cannot be evited [evaded], unless we deny the certainty of all inward feelings, and so unhinge the foundation on which all revelation is grounded, overthrow the doctrines of divine calls and impulses on which all the mystic writings do depend, and so bring us back to the outward, the letter which killeth." George Garden realized that there was no persuasive against powerful internal conviction, but he gave Cuninghame some reasons why others disliked the French Prophets. Cuninghame dismissed them all: violent

11. Henderson, *Mystics*, 200-04, 249; Dutton-Cuninghame Corr., 12/6 and 12/27/1709 and 1/14/1710 (pp. 121, 129, 245). Cf. NLS, MS/493/73, letter of Cuninghame to Ramsay, 11/10/1709 and letter of Sir Thomas Hope to Ramsay, 9/16/1709.

agitations were not a fatal flaw in the dispensation but a sign by which flawed men and women knew that they spoke God's perfect word; the prophets may have been strangers to mystical literature, but all confessed that their agitations produced "this introversion and passivity; and the like effects follow from reading or hearing the warnings, or being present at their meetings." Nor did the French Prophets sow strife in the Christian community. Just as they were essentially quietists, so partisans of the inner light were essentially followers of the dispensation:

> There is a certain sympathy, communion, and if I dare use the word, homogeneity, between light and light, the spirit in others and that within our selves by which alone we can judge. There is no need of joining outward Societies in order to be in this dispensation. All who constantly attend unto and follow their inner light are as to their essential part already so; and when 'tis God's will and time shall be so in another manner.[12]

By dint of personality, wide reading and lengthy meditation, James Cuninghame had integrated two religious systems far more successfully than Richard Roach. Although Philadelphians in London had been attracted to the French Prophets for many of the same reasons as Scottish quietists, the Scots had a theology more consistent with the ethos of judgment than was the Philadelphian belief in a merciful divinity. If John Lacy in 1710 had said that God was love, in 1712 he railed against the Philadelphian theme of universal salvation. "Who is it," Lacy snarled, "Presumes Now, to Fill up that Book of LIFE, with the Names of the ABOMINABLE?" Roach and Sarah Wiltshire wrestled against "the Ministration of Judgment" in public debates, where, Roach noted, "They threat doing Terrors and Judgment, and we proclaiming the Mercies of God."[13]

The Scots, on the other hand, accepted the Ministration of Judgment. Cuninghame prophesied, "They, who have not felt *the Spirit of Christ* in them, as a Vital Principle; must be cut off, as putrefied Members, and be thrown into the Flames of everlasting Perdition." John Forbes of Pitfichie, inspired in the manner of Old Testament prophets, began, "Thus sayeth the Lord God: have not I declared myself to be the Lord Gracious and Merciful, long suffering and slow to wrath? . . . But now I do declare that also I am a Just sin-revenging God." The Scot Henrietta Irvine defended

12. Henderson, *Mystics*, 229, 230, 234 and cf. 213, 224, 233.
13. John Lacy and John Potter, *Warnings of the Eternal Spirit, Pronounced in and about London* (1711) 14; Bodleian, Rawlinson MSS D. 1318, ff. 67, 68v. (printed in D.P. Walker, *The Decline of Hell* [1964] 257, 260) and D. 832, ff. 77-77v., and D. 833, f. 31v.

the French Prophets from Richard Roach by tearing up several of his letters.[14]

In this judgmental vein, Lady Abden had warnings of "great Mortality" to fall upon Edinburgh in 1709. Cuninghame was of the mind that, in a spiritual sense, the prediction had been accomplished. He himself, in September, 1710, prophesied judgments to fall upon Edinburgh within forty days. Imprisoned in the Tolbooth that month for prophesying in the streets, Cuninghame addressed a letter to the city Provost, warning him to act to avert the "just Indignation of the Most-High," and portraying himself as a latter-day though less obscure Jonah. At liberty in November, judgments postponed or invisible, the prophets Cuninghame and Dutton, with Dutton's wife Mary and the scribe Kennet Gordon, travelled to Stirling and Glasgow. One observer was so impressed by the tenor of the inspirations that he wrote in his journal, "Cuninghame of Barns does not pretend to prophecy, but only to denounce judgments."[15]

After another year of missions around Scotland in the company of the prophet Margaret Mackenzie, after further days in jail and numerous escapes from mobs, Cuninghame went to London. There he also behaved in accord with a Ministration of Judgment. Evening services concluded on Sunday, July 6, 1712, congregants in St. Paul's Cathedral heard James Cuninghame speak in a voice louder than the cathedral organ: "Thus saith the Lord, to the Inhabitants of this City, Repent, Repent and turn from the Evil of your Doings." At first stunned, the people became furious and attacked the prophet, dragging him through the streets toward a horse pond. They were luckily diverted to the house of the Lord Mayor, who dismissed the throng and engaged Cuninghame in some refined conversation, then let the prophet slip away with a warning against similar public displays. Cuninghame stayed in London through August, nursing his wounds, gaining the respect of the central group of French Prophets. He returned to Scotland in the fall, prophesying along the way in Northamp-

---

14. James Cuninghame and Margaret Mackenzie, *Warnings of the Eternal Spirit to the City of Edenburgh* (1710) 17; NLS, MSS 5166, religious verse and sermons 1710-11, by James Cuninghame, 219; Bodleian, Rawlinson MSS D. 1318, f. 66.

15. Dutton-Cuninghame Corr., 12/20/1709, 236-37 and endpapers, letter of 9/26/1711; James Cuninghame, *Warnings . . . during his Imprisonment in the Tolbooth of Edinburgh* (1712) attestation, 52-53; NLS, Wodrow MSS, Letters II, No. 114, 9/04/1710; Robert Wodrow, *Correspondence*, ed. Thomas McCrie (Edinburgh, 1842) I, 169-70, and quote from idem, *Analecta*, I, 309; Robert Calder, *A True COPY of Letters Past betwixt Mr. R.C. Minister of the Gospel and Mr. James Cuninghame of Barns* (Edinburgh, 1710) v-vi, 72; James Cuninghame and Margaret Mackenzie, *Warnings . . . to the City of Glasgow* (1711) ix-xiii.

ton and York. Mary Keimer was with him, encouraging and consoling him.[16]

He had need of someone, for despite his public bravado, he was not immune to despair. The nature of his despair and the vocabulary in which it was cast demonstrated other facets in the synthesis of quietism and prophecy. He was not sad about his perpetual harassment; that was an external rite of sanctification to which the quietists were accustomed as part of their spiritual regimen. In 1709, after but three or four months' exposure to the French Prophets, Kennet Gordon had written that "we're all of us pretty well inured to the lash of tongues and to the names of fools, crackt, light, mad and the like." The Lord told Cuninghame and Dutton in Edinburgh Tolbooth that their sufferings were destined "for mortifying the Irregularities of your Nature, for restraining the Impetuosity of your Temper, for breaking your Stubborn Wills." Outward persecution could only drive a quietist onward in the search for God's grace.[17]

Rather, Cuninghame was depressed by the "delay" in the Lord's judgment, for he understood this delay in personal terms. In 1710 he had prophesied that God's promises would not be tied to human time, and counseled followers, as was his wont, in inspired verse:

> See that ye faint not in your Minds
> Tho' God seems to delay;
> And his most mighty Power appears
> Put off, from Day to Day.

Believers should "draw some new Encouragement of approaching unto God" from every event and divine order, for until the faithful drew close as possible to God, humble and passive, the millennium would not come.[18] Delay was therefore an indication of prolonged human divorce from God. In the winter of 1712/13, Cuninghame felt the delay as the absence of the Lord's Spirit, an inner emptiness. Time and again Mary Keimer pro-

---

16. Dutton-Cuninghame Corr., 5/27 and 9/18/1711, 317, 380 and commentary on letters of 8/8/1711 and 6/24/1712, 314-17, 321-22; NLS, MSS 2686, ff. 271-72; Fatio Notebooks, II, 210-12, 236, 298, 305; Brown University (Providence, R.I.) MSS PR1191/S3, Sacred Poems 1712-1713, by James Cuninghame, 4-18; Jean Allut et al., *Plan de la Justice de Dieu sur la terre* (1714) 213-18, 228; James Cuninghame, *A Warning of the Eternal Spirit . . . June 25, 1712* (1712?); *Brand*, 54-56.

17. *Post Boy*, No. 2241 (Sept. 22-24, 1709) Gordon-Lardner letter; Cuninghame and Mackenzie, *Warnings to Edenburgh*, 9-10, 34; Cuninghame, *Warnings . . . during his Imprisonment in the Tolbooth*, 10, 11, 24, 347.

18. Cuninghame and Mackenzie, *Warnings to Edenburgh*, 25-26; Cuninghame, *Warnings . . . during his Imprisonment in the Tolbooth*, 208, 310, 542.

nounced blessings of encouragement. Cuninghame responded, spoke under inspiration, but retreated once more. In reply to one blessing:

> And I did once believe this Work begun,
> Yea that it quickly should be fully done.
> But ah! I now no Hope thereof descry;
> I can discern naught but Obscurity:
> We seem bewilder'd now in darkest Night:
> We can discern no more thy sacred Light.

Three days before Christmas, Cuninghame was so disconsolate that

> I cou'd not trace of Providence the Chain;
> I lost some Links, & there for sought in vain
> To reconcile those Things, which seemed to be
> So distant, yea & so unlike Thee.

Soon the troubled mood spread to others, and the Scottish company was in the throes of a despair equivalent to that wrought upon the English by the failure of Emes's resurrection. Cuninghame prayed that the Lord would renew his covenant with him. God's light had withdrawn, and though the withdrawal might not be punitive but designed mysteriously for the progress of the Word, believers had need of some visible assurance of the powers of the True Church. Spiritual desolation led to physical disease; by April, 1713, Cuninghame was ill. Exhorted by the Spirit "to an absolute Resignation, even to natural Death," he prepared for the end in London. On April 9, 1713, he experienced an attack of ague which lasted more than a day and disappeared only after a hymn whose opening words were, "O Death, where is thy sting?" A new man again in this his second resurrection (the first at Bath), Cuninghame participated fully in the assemblies of the inspired and delivered some of the *Orders*. He returned in high spirits to Edinburgh at the end of July.[19]

The Impact of Quietism

While Scottish quietists assimilated the inspirations and agitations of the French Prophets, the latter, less consciously, assimilated quietist attitudes toward worship and prophecy. Scottish followers affected the nature of group assemblies, the notion of false prophecy, and the relationship between male and female prophets.

---

19. Edinburgh University, MSS La. III.708, 248 religious hymns and prophetic poems by James Cuninghame, 279 (quote), 307-16, 333 (quote), 350, 382, 403-04, 440, 446-50, 458, 468, 470; Brown University, (Providence, R.I.), MSS PR1191/S3, 62.

James Cuninghame and his friends were familiar with, if not at some time part of the coterie of men and women living together at Rosehearty, devoted to the principles of Antoinette Bourignon. By 1711, French Prophets in Scotland had formed a similar congregation at Montrose. Prophets had missions to Montrose, and Mrs. Keith of Caddam, the commanding figure, was constantly in touch with Cuninghame. Congregants met together twice daily for sessions two or three hours long; they also "waited in private" for two hours in the morning and in the afternoon. Alexander Falconar described the more public "waiting on God," where followers would be "sitting in silence for a while, and looking up to God for an answer." This waiting became increasingly common in the meetings of the French Prophets in London. It was a waiting compounded of caution and silent prayer, fear of "mixtures" and hope for revelation. The Scots added to this the motif of inward reflection, a "waiting on God" which was personal, mystical. One could be agitated or actively inspired, or (now the option was more clearly present) one could be in close silent communion with the Lord.[20]

Such a model of worship was well suited to the restricted assemblies in London. Emphasizing submission to the *Orders* and subordination to the inspired assembly, prophetic leaders could consider silence doubly golden. Indeed, there was a close relationship between the posture of the believer and the nature of prophecy. Aware that false prophets might deceive "*the very Elect*" in Scotland (as Whitrow had deceived the pious Bulkeley), Scottish prophets believed that complete passivity was the sole insurance against "mixtures." Had they not achieved certainty of their own inspiration through quietist exercises? Did not other prophets admit to a feeling of inner peace when speaking the Lord's Word? If one waited properly upon the Lord, one could never introduce selfish words into inspiration. False prophets were too assertive, incompletely passive.[21]

French Prophets in London began to employ quietist terms. Admonitions to passivity became more frequent as Scottish influences made themselves felt. In 1712, after a warning by the Scot Thomas Arpwood ("Resist thou not, but yield up thy will and body, that the Lord may do by thee as seemeth good"), John Potter said, "Be ye always passive except in opposing what opposeth my truth." In other *Orders*, Potter warned those under agitations to make all imaginable efforts to abandon themselves to the Lord. "It is not by a notion of the Spirit, or by the Spirit operating and

20. Henderson, *Mystics*, 35 and idem, *Chevalier Ramsay*, 18-24; Dutton-Cuninghame Corr., 5/2/1711, 11, and commentary on 5/27/1711, 293.
21. Cuninghame and Mackenzie, *Warnings to Edenburgh*, 8, 29-30, 38.

influencing the Understanding that you must be instructed, but by an interior Sentiment," said Potter. "Under this operation, be passive." A year later, in 1714, Potter raised the dictum to a dogma: "Note this, and receive it as a general rule with no exceptions: If the Knowledge which you have of things Spiritual does not produce in your soul a true Humility, a Resignation to the Will of God, and a Renunciation of your own Will, this Knowledge in no way comes from a Divine source." This *Order* had roots in older warnings against pride, but the Scottish quietists had contributed a psychological explanation to the problem of false prophecy. The inspired now commanded those who spoke impurely to retire to their prayer closets and spiritual meditation. It was no longer necessary to exclude all suspected of exalting their own words. Just as there were grades of assemblies, there were grades of knowledge and spiritual awakening.[22]

Scottish followers elaborated the system of grades which had developed within the London group since the naming of the tribes. Some had thought from the beginning that inspiration provided a key to hidden mysteries; the quietists, like the Philadelphians, embraced a tradition which assigned these mysteries to a hierarchy of spiritual growth. Katharine Orme in Scotland spoke a strange, unintelligible language when inspired; Cuninghame conjectured that she had been vouchsafed the "language of nature" mentioned by Jakob Boehme as one of the steps of revelation. Cuninghame even believed that the French Prophets had access to a higher level of spiritual knowledge than the first Apostles: "It is plain, that, this clearer Manifestation of all Truth was not given to the Apostles: They *knew*, still, *but in part*." Prophets had often warned against mere rational understanding as means of entry into the spiritual realm, and Lacy in 1713 wrote that "it is unreasonable to expect, that every Thing in the secret Operations of Vision, should be accountable for by Reason." The French Prophets could easily accept that part of the quietist tradition which stressed the necessity of inspired spiritual knowledge and gradual revelation of scriptural mysteries. Given such a scheme of religious development, prophets could achieve optimum authority and prestige as sources of the highest knowledge, and the leading prophets could justify doctrinally the functional hierarchy of the inspired upon which they insisted.[23]

---

22. Fatio Notebooks, II, 260, 262; BPUG, MSS fr. 605, Assemblées Booklets VII, VIII, IX; *Recueil d'avertissemens touchant l'ordre des assemblées et les regles de discipline* (1715) 127. Cf. the difference between "regenerative gradualism" and enthusiasm proposed by Keith Thomas, *Religion and the Decline of Magic* (New York, 1971) 302-06.

23. Dutton-Cuninghame Corr., 12/13/1709, 231-32; NLS, MSS 5166, f. 215; Cuninghame, *Warnings . . . during his Imprisonment in the Tolbooth*, xii; John Lacy, *The General Delusion of Christians* (1713) 61 and cf. 12-13.

Followers also readily accepted the implications of spiritual grades, and in the *Orders*, John Potter spoke formally of "novices." Dutton in 1709 had warned believers in Edinburgh that they were but novices, yet it is doubtful whether he realized the importance of the term for quietists, to whom a novitiate was almost as formal as a mystic's apprenticeship to an alchemist in seventeenth-century literature. Scots expected that, like the sorcerer's apprentice, there would naturally be religious novices, spiritually inept, overanxious. In 1710, Cuninghame sang a hymn about the Israelites crossing the Red Sea:

> But yet, God's Ways they did not know:
> Even then, but Novices they were:
> Their over-heated Fancies, did
> Suggest they were already there.

They needed instruction and patience, for which they marched forty years through the Sinai. Alexander Falconar, commenting on a letter of 1711, suggested that the problems caused by some of the inspired were due to their spiritual youth; the Spirit had come upon several at Montrose, and "they being all Novices, disorders arose among them." John Potter began to use the term in 1711, casually, in a warning to followers to determine between the merely preternatural and the supernatural. In his *Orders* for 1714, the idea of a novitiate was formalized. Potter, addressing two inspired Irish missionaries who had disappointed the group, commanded them to return to Ireland, "not in the capacity of Messengers, but as Novices." Among the categories of people admitted to inspired assemblies was one designed for the novices, those admitted as potential prophets. They attended in the role of apprentices or students. The prophets saw themselves as spiritual directors, and Potter in 1713 referred to the *Orders* as instructions, "as if this had been in a school." James Cuninghame wrote a dissertation on the colleges of prophets in the time of Samuel, proposing that "these Schools of the prophets were formed to Instruct the New Inspired (even by the good Spirit) of the way of the Operation of it upon man, and what behaviour on their part was suitable unto it, for that new Inspired are apt to Run into disorders and need Rules and Intendency." While Thomas Dutton continued to be suspicious of "Over-refined Spiritual Constructions and Solutions of things so as It is no longer an Aid to discern Truth from falsehood," the French Prophets were absorbing some of those constructions and solutions. When, much later, the prophet Hannah Wharton announced a teaching dispensation as the outcome of twenty years' prophecy, her vocabulary and many of her assumptions were those of Scottish quietists and Philadelphians. If she confused things, garbled syntax, repeated herself, it was only that she too, a teacher of novices, had not yet been granted final grace.[24]

The sum of these Scottish influences was to temper further the chiliasm of the French Prophets. Inner "waiting upon God" had eschatological implications: patience, a belief in a more gradual appearance of the Lord. Having accepted stages of spiritual insight, the French Prophets had laid extensive groundwork for a long-term dispensation. Novices needed time to adjust to their new gifts. False prophets had resented the waiting and spoken without inner assurance. Cuninghame's spiritual crisis over the delay in the millennium had been resolved not by a divine promise that the time was short but by a renewal of personal acquaintance with the Holy Spirit.

At the end of 1713, with missions curtailed and the London assemblies deliberately narrowed, Cuninghame prayed,

> Since Men reject those whom thou dost inspire
> Permit them now in silence to retire.
> Permit them to work out what doth belong
> To their own Peace, deliver'd from the Throng
> Of Rebels, whom they have in vain invited long.

The Lord responded,

> The Methods of my working here below
> Are slow, and gradual . . . .[25]

Followers in Scotland were particularly withdrawn, preoccupied with other matters. The Hanoverian succession secured at the death of Queen Anne on August 1, 1714, dashed Jacobite hopes for the peaceful accession of the Stuart heir (James Francis Edward, son of James II) to the English throne. In 1715, James Cuninghame entertained thoughts of joining the Jacobite rebellion which began that summer. Cuninghame asked the Spirit's advice, interpreted silence as consent, and participated in the attempt (the "scalade") on Edinburgh Castle. Visits of the Spirit became more frequent after he had joined the rebellion and, as he wrote to Mrs. Keith, "I never think I enjoyed its presence in a more comfortable and Ravishing manner, than when Standing One Night as a Sentry upon my post with a musket in

---

24. Cuninghame, *Warnings . . . during his Imprisonment in the Tolbooth*, 49; Dutton-Cuninghame Corr., 186, 309, 328; Fatio Notebooks, I, 139; BPUG, MSS fr. 605, Assemblées Booklet VIII; *Recueil*, 132. On the functional hierarchy of the inspired, cf. L.F. Martin, "The Family of Love in England: Conforming Millenarians," *Sixteenth-Century Journal* 3 (1972) 101.

25. Edinburgh University, MSS La. III. 708, pp. 547-49.

my hand." Captured after the battle of Preston, Cuninghame spent months in a cell in Chester Castle, distributing money and food collected by friends on the outside. He contracted rheumatic fever in November, 1716, after nearly a year's imprisonment, and asked for communion from a nonjuring minister. He died declaring his regard for the Church of England and singing a hymn.[26] Other followers with Jacobite involvements (Falconar, Lady Jane Forbes) survived, except John Forbes of Pitfichie, who drowned while fleeing the country after the rebellion was put down.[27]

The 1715 uprising taught the French Prophets a lesson in mystery, for while the London group had begun with the inspirations of three men who detested the French regime, Cuninghame had been assured by the Spirit that action on behalf of the Pretender, supported by France, was a worthy cause. The Scots presented the group with the model of a believer whose silent suffering was part of a beneficial engagement with mysterious contradictions.[28]

The 1715 uprising also brought to light another contribution of the Scottish followers. The quietists, like other Jacobites, accorded women respect. The Jacobite cause had been advanced by the intrigues of Scottish women, just as the quietists drew wisdom and support from the inspirations of Bourignon and Guyon.[29] Of known Scottish followers, twenty were men and ten women; significantly, only four of the men became prophets, while seven of the women were prophets. More significantly, like

26. Dutton-Cuninghame Corr., 6/27/1716, 344, 348 and commentary, with letters, 344-68; NLS, Adv. MSS 29.9.9(iii), ff. 24-24v., 26, letters from Cuninghame, 12/11/1715 and 1/30/1716; PRO, KB 8/66 Part I MS page 38, A List of the Prisoners Rebells at Wiggin [Wigan]; William Nicolson, "Diary," *Transactions of the Cumberland and Westmoreland Antiquarian and Archaeological Society* n.s. 5 (1905) 6-7.

27. Dutton-Cunninghame Corr., commentary, 210-11. Alexander Falconar, second husband to Lady Errol, is mentioned with his wife as a reliable Jacobite in *HMC* 56: Stuart VI, 356. The Presbyterian minister Robert Wodrow believed that the French Prophets' threats of destruction might be part of a Jacobite plan: "The frank joining in of several Jacobites with them hath brought a fancy in my head, that they know somewhat more than you about Edinburgh do of the Pretender's designs, otherwise, perhaps, they would not limit their judgments upon the good town to the term of forty days." *Correspondence*, I, 169-70 (Sept. 20, 1710). See also *HMC* 60: Mar, 555, referring to John(?) Forbes of Pitsligo.

28. Adding to the mystery, John Lacy probably had a Whig vision against the Pretender: *The Vision of John Lacy, Esq; and Prophet, On Thursday the 9th of June, 1715* (1715), unless the attribution is spurious, as it surely is in two Tory pamphlets published by Morphew—John Lacy, *The Steeleids or the Tryal of Wit* (1714), and John Lacy, *The Ecclesiastical and Political History of Whig-Land, of Late Years* (1714).

29. See Andrew Lang, *A History of Scotland* (Edinburgh, 1907) II, 84-85, 428, and IV, 138, 174.

the Philadelphians, the Scottish quietists granted women complete equality of inspiration, accepting their leadership. Cuninghame owed much of his status to his strong bonds with the London prophets; when he journeyed through Scotland, he was accompanied by inspired women—Margaret Mackenzie, Henrietta Irvine—who shared his willingness to pronounce judgments on the wicked. The readiness of the Edinburgh followers to sponsor Lady Abden's book of prophecies despite protests from the English revealed a difference in attitude toward inspired women in general. By shifting the problem of false prophecy to the sphere of inadequate spiritual preparation, the Scots weakened the group's tendency to identify social and sexual threats with false inspiration.

Finally, the quietist link to continental figures was extended by the Jacobite alliance of Scottish and French conspirators in the 1715 uprising. Bourignonians such as George Garden maintained their political and religious loyalties in European exile after 1715, affording Scottish quietists new continental contacts. Since they read widely in European theology, the quietists acknowledged the influence of German pietism and, like the Philadelphians who had adherents in Holland and Germany, saw many similarities between themselves and religious movements on the continent.[30] Through their missions to Scotland, the French Prophets had inadvertently established a relationship with a widely diffused European movement for spiritual regeneration.

Scottish quietists proved a rich quarry for the French Prophets. The contemplative tradition had its own strengths, and the merger of quietism and prophecy affected equally the mystic and the prophet. Quietists acquired the physically expressive vocabulary of agitations and mime integral to the prophetic act in London. They learned to be vocal about the impending judgments on humankind and so could express anger through the impartial voice of the Lord. Scottish followers in turn added weight to the concept of a spiritual hierarchy and a more gradual but still imminent apocalypse. With the Philadelphians, they offered a model of devotion to consummate female leadership. Able to maintain a footing in both the millenarian ethos of judgment and the pentecostal ethos, a gift perhaps of their Scottish Protestant heritage, they were far more effective than the Philadelphians in directing the religious practices of the French Prophets toward the peace of the inner spirit. Most importantly, they were skillful

30. Henderson, *Chevalier Ramsay*, throughout; Walker, *Decline of Hell*, 218-44, and Nils Thune, *The Behmenists and the Philadelphians* (Uppsala, 1948) give good accounts of Philadelphian links to the continent.

interpreters for the French Prophets of a continental movement toward heart-felt Christianity.

Missions to the Continent

The interplay between Scottish and English followers was, writ small, a sample of the French Prophets' exchange with continental Protestantism. Given that the major successes of the French Prophets had been with English Philadelphians and Scottish quietists, it was hardly coincidence that missionaries to the continent would find pietists most responsive to their message.

Stirred as were English millenarians by the exhausting Thirty Years War (1618-48) on the continent, some Protestants in Germany responded to the confusing shift of territorial borders and the ensuing shifts in church establishments by seeking true Christianity in the personal relationship between God and the individual. This experiential religion bypassed the politically wearying problems of Lutheran, Calvinist and Roman Catholic conflicts within the domain of the Holy Roman Empire. Influenced by Johann Jakob Arndt's devotional works, a Lutheran pastor at Frankfurt-am-Main published his *Pia desideria* in 1675. Philipp Jakob Spener thus gave a name and a creed to a growing movement toward spiritual reformation in lands subject to that unbending orthodoxy which only war and uncertain authority can inflict upon the devout. He proposed colleges of piety (*Collegia pietatis*), or small groups of worshippers, as the means to renew the integrity of Christian life. These colleges would allow the laity a share in spiritual governance. Members would be intent on communal study of the Bible and personal sanctification. The Christian life depended primarily on one's inner spiritual state and a full, if gradual, conversion to a self-denying intimacy with the Spirit of the Lord.[31]

Through the University at Halle (Prussia), founded in 1694, Spener and August Hermann Francke spread the ideals of the pietists over the continent. Like the French Prophets, pietists sought to affirm the simple and fundamental Christian principles which lay behind religious divisions. Like Philadelphians and quietists, they believed in the practice of religious

---

31. On pietism see F. Ernest Stoeffler, *The Rise of Evangelical Pietism* (Leiden, 1965); Martin Schmidt, *Wiedergeburt und Neuer Mensch: Gesammelte Studien zur Geschichte des Pietismus* (Witten, 1969); Jean-B. Neveaux, *Vie spirituelle et vie sociale entre Rhin et Baltique au XVIIe siècle de J. Arndt à P.J. Spener* (Paris, 1967); Michel Godfroid, "Le piétisme allemand a-t-il existé? Histoire d'un concept fait pour la polémique," *Etudes germaniques* 26 (1971) 32-45.

introspection. European influences on the French Prophets would strengthen trends within the group toward an emphasis on one's inner state, on silent worship, and respect for guidance by women. The French Prophets would on their part bring to the continent the dynamic of inspiration and the still-bold call to repentance in the face of an approaching judgment.

Searching for "signal tokens of grace," the French Prophets had not neglected news from the continent. Along with their enemy, the latitudinarian minister Josiah Woodward, they rejoiced to hear of the Silesian children who had formed assemblies for prayer and repentance in 1708. Hundreds of children gathered daily in the duchy of Lignitz to pray and sing songs such as "The Time of the Appearance of the Son of God, the second Time, is certainly at hand." They read from Arndt's tract, *The Garland of Paradise*, and prayed for the restoration of the Lutheran Church to its original purity. Woodward, early impressed by August Francke's pietist orphanage at Halle, and now by the modest behavior of the Silesian children, amassed twenty reasons why the widespread events might be thought divinely guided. His reasons were familiar to the French Prophets as elements of their own divine commission. "What is befallen in Silesia," wrote John Lacy, "is pursuant to the Tenor of the Prophetic Voice in London." By the year's end, that voice had crossed the Channel. Jeanne Cavalier and her husband Jean (disobeying divine commands) departed for Holland on the first continental mission.[32]

Awaiting them in Rotterdam were Pierre Jurieu, his wife, Hélène, and Benjamin Furly. The exiled Huguenot pastor Jurieu, whose *Lettres pastorales* had carried numerous accounts of the miracles and prophecies of the Desert, had a penchant for millennial calculations. He and his wife, both grandchildren of Pierre du Moulin, had not discarded their hopes for a Protestant uprising in Languedoc as a token of the downfall of Antichrist. Pierre acted as a paid informant on French activities for the English, and both Pierre and Hélène assisted allied agents on their journeys to Savoy and the Cévennes. The Jurieus did not conceal their

32. Josiah Woodward, *Praise out of the Mouth of Babes* (1708); August Hermann Francke, *Pietas Hallensis*, translated by Anton Wilhelm Boehm, preface by Woodward (2nd ed.; 1707); Richard Roach, *The Great Crisis* (1727) 9; Richard Bulkeley, *An Answer to Several Treatises lately published on the Subject of the Prophets* (1708) 116-18, printed in French in Misson's *Le nouvel hosanna des petits enfans* (1708); "Fernere Nachricht wegen der Schlesischen Religions-Begnadigung," *Unschuldige Nachrichten von Alten und Neuen Theologischen Sachen* (1708) 59-61; *Historische Nachricht von dem Zustand der Religion in Schlesien* (n.p., 1707).

interest in the French Prophets, and they died staunch believers in the dispensation.[33]

Benjamin Furly (1636-1714), in 1709 a man of "no special religion," had been a prominent Quaker at Colchester, where his family still had Quaker attachments. In his late twenties he had settled at Rotterdam, and in 1677 he accompanied the Quaker luminaries George Fox and George Keith through Holland and Germany as their interpreter. A wealthy merchant, Furly hosted influential English and French thinkers, most of them deists or republicans (Locke, Shaftesbury, Algernon Sidney, Jacques Basnage de Beauval, Pierre Bayle), and the Street-Light Club of Huguenot exiles met at his house. Like Jurieu, Furly aided English envoys, and his son Arent had been secretary to the Earl of Peterborough, commander of English troops in Spain. Furly had translated into Dutch excerpts from the *Théâtre sacré* and Marion's *Avertissemens*. He corresponded with Maximilien Misson, but his closest tie to the French Prophets was through Sir Richard Bulkeley, whom he had met in the 1680s while the baronet was touring the continent.[34] When the Cavaliers arrived in Rotterdam, Whitrow and Bulkeley had already split with the French Prophets, placing Furly in a delicate position. He had not lost respect for Bulkeley, whose arguments in favor of Whitrow seemed convincing, but he wished also that the cause of true Christianity should prosper in Holland, regardless of events in London.

Furly and the Jurieus welcomed the missionaries with open houses and open wallets, anxious to receive and transcribe the divine message. Unfortunately, the Cavaliers' mission to Holland was a fiasco, and for a moment even Furly was on the verge of snapping his tenuous association with the French Prophets. Neither Cavalier was inspired, and the pair got themselves into financial straits despite the subsidies of Furly and Hélène Jurieu. The prophets in London early in 1709 withdrew support from Jeanne Cavalier as they had at the beginning from Jean, while implying

33. Elisabeth Labrousse, *Pierre Bayle* (The Hague, 1963-64) I, 143, 206, 209, 231n.; Frederik R.J. Knetsch, *Pierre Jurieu Theoloog en politikus der Refuge* (Kampen, 1967) 346-50; Turner, ed., *Aufrère Papers*, 66-67; BM, Add. MSS 28,916, f. 196, and Stowe MSS Fr. 223, f. 345; BSHPF, Papiers Coquerel, MSS 302, f. 5; Fatio Notebooks, II, 271.

34. Labrousse, *Pierre Bayle*, I, 210-14; Julius F. Sachse, *Benjamin Furly "An English Merchant at Rotterdam"* (Philadelphia, 1895) esp. 3-18; Thomas I.M. Foster, *Original Letters of Locke, Algernon Sidney and Anthony Lord Shaftesbury* (1830); H. de B. Gibbins, "The Furly Family of Essex," *Essex Review* 8 (1899) 86-95; William I. Hull, *Benjamin Furly and Quakerism in Rotterdam* (n.p., 1941) 76, 147; *DNB*, VII, 770; Gemeente Archief (Rotterdam), MSS 2469f and notarial documents; BM, Add. MSS 31,135, f. 233; John Locke, *Correspondence*, ed. E.S. de Beer (Oxford, 1976-) III, 39-40 *et passim*.

that Rotterdam sympathizers had something to do with the stifling of the Spirit. Furly composed a furious answer, half in defense of Bulkeley, half perplexed by the Cavaliers. What was he supposed to do? Should he have exhorted the missionaries to run hither and thither prophesying, merely because they had been inspired in England? Did the prophets in London know what they were doing, or were they misled by a deceiving Spirit, as seemed to be the case in their disgraceful expulsion of Whitrow and Bulkeley?[35] By 1710, if not before, Jean Cavalier had deserted the dispensation; his wife went back to England and did not enter into group affairs.[36] No one had felt the grace of God or heard the Word.

Somehow the damage done by the Cavalier mission was swiftly repaired. Furly's temper had cooled sufficiently for him to welcome three other missions in 1709 and 1710. This was fortunate, for Furly, like Fatio, would act as a linchpin between nations and between men of differing religious outlooks. His linguistic abilities permitted him access to audiences the French Prophets might not otherwise have reached. His eclectic religious reading and his circles of friends also brought continental influences to bear upon the French Prophets.[37] Both Fatio and Furly were crucial to the exchange between the French Prophets and the continent.

This exchange, almost aborted with the Cavaliers, was with one exception the domain of Huguenot followers. In the spring of 1709, Elizabeth Hughes and her daughter Elizabeth, John Moult and the scribe John Giles spent two months in Rotterdam, The Hague, Amsterdam and six other Dutch towns.[38] The group treated this first and last English mission to the continent with comparative indifference. There is no record of an elaborate farewell or sober communion before departure, and unlike all subsequent European missions, no book of prophecies resulted from their travels. Just as the Scottish and Irish missions had been exclusively English, so continental missions were the prerogative of French followers. Continental encounters were in one sense an attempted reconciliation between exiled Huguenots, in another sense a symbol of the residual influence of the French followers in London.

35. BPUG, MSS fr. 609, letter from B.F., paginated 9-32.
36. Turner, ed., *Aufrère Papers*, 64-65; BPUG, MSS fr. 605, letter from Furly, 10/30/1710 (N.S.), f. 2; BM, Stowe MSS Fr. 223, f. 345.
37. See Fritch and Bohn, auctioneers' catalogue, *Bibliotheca Furliana* (Rotterdam, 1714: Auctio fiet die 22 Octobris 1714). It is interesting that Furly had the friendship of the man most actively campaigning within Huguenot circles against Jurieu's vision of the Refuge—Jacques Basnage de Beauval—while he and Jurieu worked together for the French Prophets.
38. Fatio Calendar, 7/10/1709; *Historical Relation*, ff. 46-47 says that Durand Fage was with them.

The mission from which was drawn the *Discernement des ténèbres d'avec la lumière* began in July, 1710. During the months before the missionaries sailed from England, the prophet Jeanne Raoux, her daughter Madeleine, the child prophet Marthe Vergnon and her parents had settled in Rotterdam, so there were familiar faces to greet Elisabeth Charras, Jean and Henriette Allut, and the scribes Fatio, Daudé, and Jaques Portales (brother to Charles). At the Raoux house on July 2 (N.S.), Jean Allut warned that the only true ministers of the Lord were those who were inspired. Within the week, a mob ran through the quarter of the city in which the missionaries lodged, and Charras announced that the Spirit had come bringing war, not peace. She restricted the French Prophets to private meetings and let it be known that powerful men conspired against them.[39]

She was correct. Two ministers of the Huguenot consistory asked for an interview with the three scribes. Daniel de Superville and Jean Brutel de la Rivière met with them for several hours of quiet discussion. That night Charras described the ministers as ravaging wolves who would chase the prophets from the city. The following afternoon, the consistory sent a letter to Hélène Jurieu. She was asked to refrain from taking communion in her husband's church until she had repented of her fondness for the French Prophets.[40] This was the harbinger of future persecution, and, like the denunciation of the *inspirés* by the Savoy consistory in London in 1707, foreboded legal action. Two police commissioners summoned the missionaries to appear before them on July 19 (N.S.). They summoned also Jeanne and Madeleine Raoux, the Vergnon family, and David Nolibet, another follower resident in the city, so that all formal members of the dispensation were judged at once. Motivated by a concern for public order or respect for the French ministry, the commissioners directed the defendants to leave the city within twenty-four hours. Before they left, they made written copies of a warning to the people of Rotterdam, who had preferred to remain in darkness (*ténèbres*) rather than follow the great light of God's Word.[41]

---

39. Allut et al., *Discernement des ténèbres d'avec la lumière* (Rotterdam?, 1710) 1, 4, 13, 16-17, 41-44, 82; NLS, MS/493/73, letter of 7/15/1709 (N.S.).
40. Allut et al., *Discernement des ténèbres*, 50-56; Gemeente Archief (Rotterdam), Actes du Consistoire de l'Eglise Wallonne de Rotterdam, B, ff. 337-39, partially printed in J.W. Marmelstein, "Het Profetisme onder de Camisards," *Stemmen des Tijds* 29 (1940) 302-303n.; Turner, ed., *Aufrère Papers*, 67.
41. Allut et al., *Discernement des ténèbres*, 3, 71-80, 82; BM, Stowe MSS Fr. 223, f. 345; BPUG, MSS fr. 605, letter from Furly, 10/30/1710, f. 1.

The French Prophets would experience the enmity of Huguenot clergy throughout Europe. Although they continued for a time to use Huguenot contacts as centerpoints for their travels, the missionaries did not make much headway in Huguenot communities. Their inclination to distrust ministers, their emphasis on inspiration to interpret scripture, their broad disregard of "party" divisions among Christians set them apart from other Huguenots. For the most part, Huguenots in exile shared the reactions of the young Antoine Court, who by 1715 had formed a synod in the Desert in order to reestablish the regular ordained male ministry. Court himself had been a spectator at meetings in the Cévennes where the inspired spoke, yet he did not acknowledge the French Prophets or the Cévenol *inspirés* as divine messengers, and he abstained from millennial speculations. Like "Colonel" Cavalier, he publicly denied the connection between truly miraculous events in the Desert and the marvels performed by prophets in England. He repeatedly urged Huguenots to return to the habitual forms of church worship.[42] Huguenots in Holland and Germany were even more strongly impressed with the need for sobriety, fearing reprisals from the generally tolerant communities in which they were allowed to live.

English prophets had made an alliance with quietists in Scotland; now French prophets, stymied by the opposition of most fellow Huguenots, would find themselves bound to the continental counterparts of the quietists. English missionaries had gone north and discovered Montrose; the French went east and discovered Halle.

Charras, the Alluts and the scribes passed another two months at Delft and The Hague, holding private meetings, editing the Rotterdam warnings for publication in French and Dutch. Allut prophesied in August that soon would come a baptism of the Holy Spirit over the entire earth. Authorities in The Hague were dubious, for they imprisoned the missionaries. The Court of Aldermen examined them for proof of treachery and called in the apostate Jean Cavalier for testimony. Cavalier allowed that he had misgivings about some unfulfilled prophecies and that some actions of the prophets shocked him, but he refused to impugn the integrity of the missionaries. Five of the six were released after two weeks, and Fatio remained a month in jail.[43]

42. See Jules Chavannes, "Les prophètes des Cévennes," *Le Chrétien évangélique* 12,5 (1869) 262; Antoine Court, *Histoire des troubles des Cévennes* (Villefranche, 1760) esp. III, 293; BPUG, Papiers Court.
43. Allut et al., *Discernement des ténèbres*, 80-81; Jean Allut et al., *Eclair de lumière* (Rotterdam?, 1711) 7-8, 59, 85-89, 97, 143; Sachse, *Benjamin Furly*, 20-21; BPUG, MSS fr. 605, letter from Furly, 10/30/1710; Fatio Notebooks, I, 88.

The *Discernement des ténèbres d'avec la lumière* was available for distribution when Fatio was released, and scribes were at work on a second collection of prophecies, the *Eclair de lumière*. Furly wrote prefaces to both books. His perspective on the teachings of the French Prophets reveals the manner in which bridges were built between them and pietists. Furly said that he had scrutinized the prophets and saw nothing contrary to "la Morale Chrétienne." They simply and stubbornly preached that the time was near when the Lord would come, not in the flesh but in the spirit, to wreak vengeance upon the wicked. In any case, Furly argued, one could not go wrong in admiring the message of the French Prophets unless one could repent too much.[44]

Furly then introduced pietist names and ideas. Instead of trying to discern the source of the French Prophets' inspiration, he wrote, rather "examine, in searching your heart by that Light which illumines every Man coming into the World, if you are in a state to receive . . . the true Witness of the Spirit." He referred readers who wished to know more about the coming judgment to the works of two German visionaries, Johann Tennhardt of Nuremberg and Johann Maximilian Daut.[45] The writings of Tennhardt were pietist favorites, and a Swiss pietist, François Magny, later sympathetic to the French Prophets, had translated Tennhardt's *Two Treatises* into French by 1712. Furly himself had translated Daut's *The Approaching Judgments of God upon the [Holy] Roman Empire* in the months before he wrote the preface to the *Eclair de lumière*. English followers in London, acting upon inspirations, had decided by April of 1711 to sponsor the printing of the Daut translation.[46]

Daut, shoemaker of Frankfurt-am-Main, first inspired in 1709, glorified the Lord for revealing things to the simple which were hidden from the wise. Opposed by the ministers to whom he brought his message, and by Senate members who refused to believe in the coming judgment, he was locked up in the city orphan-house. The Lord advised Daut to preach only the essentials necessary to salvation and to conceal the rest, frightening as it was. Forbidden to speak in public, Daut printed his warnings. He had prophesied that the Turks and the Swedes (led by God's new David, Charles XII) would be instruments of God's wrath upon impenitent Germany. The Lord would chastise the "Popish-Priest-Whores" among the "Three Sects" (Catholic, Lutheran, Calvinist) who had diverted the

---

44. Allut et al., *Eclair de lumière*, preface and 170-71; Allut et al., *Discernement des ténèbres*, preface; Fatio Notebooks, I, 156, 168, 183.
45. Allut et al., *Eclair de lumière*, preface.
46. Fatio Notebooks, I, 198.

faithful from true religion. A great "religion-fire" would sweep across Europe, and the Lion from the North (Charles XII) and the great Bird from the East (the Caliph) would cover the land in thick clouds. The grip of persecution would last the familiar three and one-half years of Revelation, after which would appear the Redeemer.[47]

The French Prophets were thinking along similar lines. Their three missions to the continent after the publication in English of Daut's *Approaching Judgments* were to Germany and Vienna, where they called down judgments upon the capital city of the Holy Roman Empire; to Sweden, with a message for Charles XII; and through Germany to Turkey, with warnings for the Caliph.

On January 8, 1710/11, an assembly of prophets met in London to consider the order received by Daniel Le Tellier that he should prepare for a voyage to Brandenburg. By June, Daut's book in press, the mission to Brandenburg was confirmed, but Le Tellier was not to be among the missionaries. Four of the most prestigious Huguenots would go: Elie Marion, Jean Allut, Nicolas Fatio, Charles Portales. These old friends, veteran prophets and scribes, represented the group—and in particular the French followers—on the major missions to the continent. Of the thirty-five people attending their farewell ceremonies, more than thirty were French, and all prophecies for the mission had originated with the French. The missionaries left London in late June, four men whose names were written on the corners of the scroll of judgment, conducted by "The Ark of the Alliance of the Holy Spirit" in Ezekiel's chariot.[48]

The prophets did seek the union of alliances. Where there was no unity, they predicted destruction. Reaching Berlin on July 23, 1711 (N.S.), the missionaries were opposed by Huguenot ministers and were expelled from the city after a riot among the French populace. They did enjoy some success, for they left behind several believers, chiefly Roman Catholics, and a larger number of supporters, French and German pietists. After a week in Berlin, Fatio or Portales had written,

---

47. Johann Maximilian Daut, *The Approaching Judgments of God upon the Roman Empire*, trans. Benjamin Furly (1711) i-ii, 2, 4, 7, 11, 25-26, 28, 32, 39-47, 103-04. Charles XII of Sweden had an illustrious career as a Protestant conqueror, but he was defeated in 1709 by Peter I of Russia and fled to Turkey. In 1710, when Daut was prophesying, the Alliance of The Hague established the neutrality of Swedish possessions in Germany, but the war between Russia and the Swedish-Turkish alliance continued to 1713. That year the Turks turned on Charles and imprisoned him. The bird and the lion were images from Daniel 7:4.

48. Fatio Notebooks, I, 60, 291, 298-99 and II, 48-49; Jean Allut and Elie Marion, *Cri d'alarme* (Amsterdam?, 1712) 12.

as to the Work of Sanctification, It seemed that several persons here, especially amongst the Pietists, are further advanced than we, or our brethren. God grant that we may be affected by their Example and good Conversation [behavior]. They seemed several of them to be entered into the Kingdom of God, and if it should please God to Raise up amongst them some select Instruments, we have hopes, they'll prove patterns of all Manner of Virtues.

Impressed, the missionaries eagerly noted the scantest signs of good will among such people, who "Conclude their Conversation with us in wishing they may be made sensible that a New duty Rises up Incumbent upon them from that Instant, that a Voice Speaking in the Name of God, begins to Sound in their Ears."[49]

From Berlin the prophets and scribes made straight for the pietist center at Halle. The pietist leader Francke, along with André Kock, inspector of the famous orphanage, had been estranged from the dispensation by news of the failed resurrection of Dr. Emes. Fatio had a long conversation with Francke, and after their stay in Halle, the four missionaries believed that they had restored the affection of Halle pietists for the French Prophets.[50]

They spent the latter half of August, 1711, in Leipzig, where "the Pietists in general seem well affected." As they continued through Germany to Vienna, the pattern of Huguenot hostility and pietist support was repeated in Coburg, Erlang, Schwabach. In Schwabach, however, they had the good fortune to run across some who had witnessed miracles in the Cévennes and some who had been inspired. These gave loud testimony in favor of the French Prophets, but the Huguenot minister preached against them. The missionaries travelled on to Ratisbon, seat of the Diet of the Holy Roman Empire, where they conferred with agents of the various

---

49. Fatio Notebooks, II, 57-102; Dutton-Cuninghame Corr., 12/19/1711, report of letter from Berlin, 301-05; Thomas S. Penny, "French Prophets of 1711," *Baptist Quarterly*, n.s., 2 (1924) 171-72, introducing Stack MSS 1e, probably by Charles Portales but attributed by Penny to Jean Allut.

50. Fatio Notebooks, II, 103; Penny, "French Prophets of 1711," 173; Dutton-Cuninghame Corr., 12/19/1711. Cf. Paul Ernest Jablonski, *Institutiones Historiae Christianae* (2nd ed.; Frankfurt-an-der-Oder, 1766-67) III, 381. The French Prophets had good reasons to believe that Francke would be friendly. Furly knew of Francke's admiration for the Erfurt prophet Anna Maria Schuchart and that the *Eigentliche Nachricht von Begeisterten Mädchen* had appeared under Francke's signature in 1692. Francke's female assistants, particularly Mlle. Charbonet, were themselves probably involved with the French Prophets. Julius F. Sachse, *The German Pietists of Provincial Pennsylvania 1694-1708* (Philadelphia, 1895) 303-06; Gustav Kramer, *August Hermann Francke* (Halle, 1882) II, 162-63; Johannes Wallmann, *Philipp Jakob Spener und die Anfäng des Pietismus* (Tübingen, 1970) 283-330 on pietist interests in millenarian schemes, and cf. James P. Martin, *The Last Judgment in Protestant Theology from Orthodoxy to Ritschl* (Grand Rapids, 1963) ch. 2.

German princes. On October 11, 1711 (N.S.), Marion warned his companions to press forward, for, said the Lord, "I pass by like a Man riding Post, Crying *Babylon is fallen! She is Fallen: Her Ruin draws near.*"[51]

In Vienna, at the climax of their journey, the four men kept to their room at an inn and saw no one. Although they had letters of introduction to men in the city, they obeyed divine commands to remain sequestered: "We were sent in this City to be a Sign unto it, as when a King sends spies in a place He would surprise with its Inhabitants." The prophets warned of the imminent destruction of Vienna by the Turks and then, after only three days in the city, they departed and were back in Rotterdam a month later. They arranged the warnings and prayers of their mission for publication as the *Cri d'alarme*, which appeared in 1712 in French and German editions and spread widely throughout Europe.[52]

The second of their missions began in the spring of 1712 as James Cuninghame anointed Allut and Marion as the Lord's messengers. English followers participated in the preliminaries to this mission, and when Marion specified the date for departure, the shadow of Emes lay still upon the group: the prophets and scribes, said Marion, would leave for Stockholm, "the Levant of the North," before May 25, fourth anniversary of the failed resurrection. On May 22, the missionaries and four others (Daudé, Cuninghame, Francis Moult and Louis Gervaise) sat down to the Celebration for the Proclaiming of the Eternal Gospel of Heaven. They partook of a communion where the cup of wine stood balanced on the Bible at the junction of the Old and New Testaments. Marion announced that a new alliance would be forged in a few days, since the old alliance of the Lord with humankind through Jesus had been broken by human faithlessness.[53]

In June, the servants of the Lord were in Holland, unveiling part of the *Plan de la justice de Dieu sur la terre*. In July they arrived in Stockholm to find God's instrument Charles XII absent from his capital. Allut uttered judgments against Roman Catholics and Swedish Lutherans, but he had not the gift of tongues, and Fatio did not know Swedish. Allut ordered that the book of warnings from this mission (the *Plan*) eventually be

51. Fatio Notebooks, II, 104-87; Penny, "French Prophets of 1711," 173-77; Dutton-Cuninghame Corr., 12/19/1711, 305.
52. Fatio Notebooks, II, 187-96; Penny, "French Prophets of 1711," 178-79. There was no English edition of the *Cri d'alarme*.
53. Fatio Notebooks, II, 308; Allut et al., *Plan de la justice*, 21, 37, 57, 61, 68-80. On the theme of the Everlasting (Eternal) Gospel, see A.L. Morton, *The Everlasting Gospel: A Study in the Sources of William Blake* (1958); Walker, *Decline of Hell*, 226-27, 236, 247, 261, 263.

translated into Latin, so that more might understand the Lord's message. He prayed for the courage to accept the Lord's incomprehensible justice, "for thou hast led us to a People, who do not understand at all the Language by which thou makest us to speak, and further, among whom thou dost not make thy Word to manifest itself." The Lord replied with orders for a mission to the East, and to Rome.[54]

On September 10, 1712 (N.S.), on the road through Polish Prussia, the missionaries were arrested as Swedish spies by officers of the Polish army. The four men languished in prison for eight months. By the time of their release in May, 1713, the Peace of Utrecht had been established between France and the Protestant allies, ending the War of the Spanish Succession and once more revising national (and religious) borders. The Peace of Rastatt between France and the Holy Roman Empire, however, would not be signed until 1714, so the political situation on the continent was uncertain. Without money or passports, but with the draft of the *Plan* miraculously safe, the missionaries rode hastily to their haven in Halle.[55]

They passed the June of 1713 very profitably in the pietist center. August Francke was friendly, and the cathedral preacher, Theodor Knauth, accepted the prophets with enthusiasm. Jean Allut had inspirations almost daily, discoursing against sect divisions, against the spiritual Desert which reigned among the nations, against the worldly wise who had caused both. He entitled the book of prophecies which had begun with the Polish imprisonment, *Quand vous aurez saccagé, vous serez saccagés* (literally, When you will have sacked, you will be sacked). This referred to the rampages of the wicked upon the earth and their subsequent divine punishment. The pietists of Halle were touched by the prophecies, not least by Allut's new emphasis upon the Spirit working within the soul to effect a true Christianity. When the missionaries departed in July, 1713, thirty-one followers bade them well.[56]

The time was ripe to search for the Star of the Orient, which shone with

54. Allut et al., *Plan de la justice*, 94, 153, 155, 162, 169-70, 181-84.

55. Jean Allut and Elie Marion, *Quand vous aurez saccagé* (Rotterdam?, 1714) 1-9, 102; BCUL, MSS TH 1194 B, letter 7a, 5/10/1713 (N.S.), printed in part in Eugene Ritter, "Magny et le piétisme romand 1699-1730," *Mémoires et documents publiées par la Société d'Histoire de la Suisse romande*, 2nd ser., III (1891) 314-15. The Peace of Utrecht, like the Peace of Ryswick in 1697, disappointed Huguenots; it had no significant provisions for easing the oppression of Protestants in France.

56. Allut and Marion, *Quand vous aurez saccagé*, 13, 24, 39, 43, 64-65; Max Goebel, "Geschichte der wahren Inspirations-Gemeinden von 1688 bis 1850," *Zeitschrift für die historische Theologie* (1854-57) in 5 parts, part 1 (Band 24, Heft 2) 303-04. Henceforth cited as Goebel, "Geschichte," referring always to part 1.

news of Israel's recreated glory. In Bude and Belgrade, awed perhaps by the solemnity of their mission, Allut advised humility and silence unless assured of one's words. Come at last to the largest city they would ever see, heart of the Ottoman Empire, Constantinople, the prophets—as in Vienna and Stockholm—saw no one and spoke only in private. Allut directed warnings to the Caliph, chosen by God as an instrument of vengeance but himself in danger of judgment until he repented of his pride. Allut also had a message for Charles XII of Sweden (prisoner of the Turks), for, said the Lord, "There is something of good in You." After five days in the capital of the Bird of the East, the missionaries traveled to Smyrna in the helpful company of a servant of the English ambassador. Allut informed Smyrna of her unpleasant fate, then the four men boarded a ship and set sail for Rome.[57]

It was the fall of 1713. Elie Marion had not been inspired since May. He was mortally ill from a fever caught in prison in Poland, and he died on the way to Rome in Leghorn (Livorno) on November 29, 1713 (N.S.). Fatio, Portales and Allut sadly completed their mission to Rome, which would, predicted Allut, experience severe judgments worked by the "Pagan Eagle of the South" seen by Marion two years earlier. By December 10, 1713 (N.S.), the final general mission to the continent had been achieved. Portales and Allut returned at once to England, where London followers mourned for Marion. Fatio remained in Holland, to see the last books of the missions (the *Plan, Quand vous aurez saccagé*, and their Latin translations) through the press.[58]

The French Prophets established ties with continental pietism in the same period that Scottish quietism was filtering into the group's liturgy and eschatology. Attacked by French mobs in Berlin and Rotterdam, denounced by Huguenot clergy in Holland and Germany, missionaries turned with relief to the pietists. The insular peace at Halle and the external violence of Huguenot communities created a situation in which the normally ambivalent response of the prophets was exaggerated: where persecution was anticipated or disappointment likely, Marion and Allut spoke harsh judgments in private; where the audience was sympathetic, they spoke in public of mercy and the ways of the Spirit. The pattern of riot, refuge and publication, notable from the first years in London, prevailed on the continental missions, but now refuge had spiritual

57. Allut and Marion, *Quand vous aurez saccagé*, 61, 82-99; BM, Sloane MSS 4043, ff. 307-307v. letter from Fatio to Sir Hans Sloane, 10/26/1714.
58. Allut and Marion, *Quand vous aurez saccagé*, 107-17; Allut et al., *Plan de la justice*, 8-9; *MMM*, 217-18.

connotation as an inturned mode of worship. How followers in London were affected by the contact with pietism will be the subject of the next chapter. What had the French Prophets brought to the continent?

Prophecy and Pietism in Europe

Shortly after the missionaries left Halle in the spring of 1713, five pietist followers became inspired. Maria Elisabeth Mathes, age eighteen, and her father, Francke's secretary at the orphanage, had visions and spoke warnings. Three brothers, students at the University, also received the gift of inspiration. With their widowed mother, the brothers Pott formed the nucleus of the Halle circle. Francke and other pietist leaders meanwhile had lost their tolerance for the new dispensation, which seemed to them divisive. Francke dismissed his secretary Mathes, and Theodor Knauth was deprived of his duties at the Halle cathedral for espousing the cause of the French Prophets.[59]

The brothers Pott and the Mathes pair brought the Lord's message to Berlin in the summer of 1714, stirring up a hornet's nest of pamphlets against them and all French Prophets.[60] They headed next for Wetteravia, an area of relative religious freedom in central Germany in which had settled many Protestant separatists and pietists. Four new prophets from Amsterdam also made their way to Wetteravia in 1715. They came from an energetic circle of followers who were printing Lacy's first book of warnings in Dutch. Passing through Halle in 1714, they attracted forty people to their meetings, despite Francke's opposition.[61]

In 1715, men and women in Wetteravia began to experience the

---

59. Goebel, "Geschichte," 304-05; Kramer, *August Hermann Francke*, II, 161-70; Dutton-Cuninghame Corr., 12/19/1711, commentary, 302; Johann Michael Heineccius, *Schrifftmassige Prüffung Der sogenannten Neuen Propheten* (Magdeburg, 1715) 34-37. For some clues to Francke's change of heart, see *Der Briefwechsel Carl Hildebrand von Cansteins mit August Hermann Francke*, Texte zur Geschichte des Pietismus, Abt. III, Band 1 (Berlin and New York, 1972) 590-93, 621, 634-35, 641, 653, 673.

60. Goebel, "Geschichte," 271-83, 305, and see also *Der Briefwechsel Carl Hildebrand von Cansteins*, op. cit. Heinrich P.K. Henke, *Allgemeine Geschichte der Christlichen Kirche nach der Zeitfolge* (Braunschweig, 1806) Part IV, 508-09, lists 15 contemporary works against the French Prophets published in Germany, most after the visit of the brothers Pott to Berlin. Before this, Germans had been kept abreast of the movements of the French Prophets since 1708 by articles and reviews in Ernst Löscher's *Unschuldige Nachrichten von Alten und Neuen Theologischen Sachen* (Leipzig).

61. Goebel, "Geschichte," 306 ff.; Penny, "French Prophets of 1711," 175; Kramer, *August Hermann Francke*, II, 160; Dutton-Cuninghame Corr., 1/13/1713. On Protestant separatists in Wetteravia, a generally clear English account is Donald F. Durnbaugh, *European Origins of the Brethren* (Elgin, 1958) 107-110 and throughout.

agitations common to the French Prophets. Johann Friedrich Rock, the Lutheran minister Eberhard Ludwig Gruber and others became prophets. Gruber formed a "Community of True Inspiration" (*Wahrinspirations-Gemeinde*) in 1718 in the Marienborn area near Himbach and Büdingen, and a similar community arose in Schwarzenau (Wittgenstein). Rock printed his own warnings for more than thirty years and prophesied widely. Nicolaus Ludwig, the Count von Zinzendorf, godson of the pietist P. J. Spener, and later leader of the Moravians, would find Rock prophesying under convulsions at Büdingen. The French Prophets still corresponded with German supporters in 1719 and, as will be seen, appealed to New World pietists well into the 1730s.[62]

Relatives of Nicolas Fatio helped transfer the prophetic impulse from England and Germany to Switzerland. Demoiselle Berger (née Fatio) in Geneva, friendly with the Swiss pietist François Magny, had found the Lord in 1711. Magny too was familiar with the French Prophets and had read the *Eclair de lumiére* with pleasure. He wrote to a relative in 1712 that at first the conduct of the French Prophets had given him pause, but having closely examined their character and doctrine, and the character of their adversaries, he recognized the London inspired as true prophets. There were, he confided, "some places a little obscure and confused which the profane call nonsense, but at bottom they manifest with very great energy and evidence the universal defection from Christianity among all the sects." Magny was most favorably impressed by the unanimity of their doctrine and its conformity with pietist beliefs and with the books of Johann Tennhardt. "Now, my dear brother," asked Magny, "from whence can come this uniformity and conformity between men who have never had the least communication with each other?" Such a question epitomized the attitude of many pietists toward the French Prophets: surprise and gratitude for God's gift of making diverse people sensible to the same spiritual task. Magny discerned among the London inspired the very ideals of a pietist community. "They live among themselves with a marvelous union and communion of the Heart. They are frequently at fasting and prayer; they are patient and debonnaire toward their own persecutors." As

62. Karl Scheig, "Die Wetterauer Inspiranten Bewegung. Ihre Entwicklung und Ihre Bedeutung," *Beitrage zur Evangelische Theologie* 6 (1941) 73-106; BPUG, MSS fr. 605, letter of 3/3/1719; Donald F. Durnbaugh, *The Believers' Church* (New York, 1968) 122-24; idem, *European Origins of the Brethren*, esp. 148-57; Heinz Renkewitz, *Hochmann von Hochenau (1670-1721)* (Witten, 1969) esp. 97-100, 289-94; F. Bovet, *Le Comte de Zinzendorf*, I, 224, cited by Chavannes, "Les prophètes des Cévennes," 140; Gottfried Mälzer, *Die Werke der Württembergischen Pietisten des 17. and 18. Jahrhunderts* (New York and Berlin, 1972).

additional proof of true inspiration, the fruit of the French Prophets' message had been the conversion of Magny's cousin Montet, his wife and daughter, in spite of persecution from a "fat and oily Epicurean" minister.[63]

The movement in Switzerland spread from these pietists to others, such as Magny's spiritual student, Mme. Ursule de Warens, dominating figure of the Vevey circle of pietists. Through letters from the ever-active Benjamin Furly, and through personal association with Durand Fage and Jean-Jacques Doladille (an itinerant prophet soon accepted in the London assemblies), the Swiss had close relations with the inspired. Both Fage and Doladille were prophesying in Switzerland in 1713, and they caught the attention of continental quietists at Yverdon near Lausanne. Their minister, Samuel Lutz (spelled also Loutz, Lucius), commuted between Germany, Switzerland and France, linking students of Bourignon at Yverdon with a variety of other religious societies. By 1714, there was news of self-proclaimed prophets among the devotees of Bourignon.[64]

Not far away, in Lyon, lived other relatives of Nicolas Fatio. The Huber family had removed from Geneva in 1711 to settle in the village of Millery. Five years later, influenced by their reading of the books of warnings sent them by their great-uncle Fatio, and by the occasional presence of the prophets Fage and François Pagez, two of the Huber daughters began to have inspirations. Fatio cautioned his great-nephew Jean that novices had much to fear from the misinterpretation of the Lord's signs. Fatio was also disturbed by the zeal of Pagez and insisted that all commands issued by Pagez be submitted to the consideration of other prophets, according to the Book of Discipline (the *Orders*). Nevertheless, Fatio's great-niece Deborah, age eleven, had agitations and delivered prophecies which

63. Ritter, "Magny," 264, 273, 277-82; Fatio Notebooks, I, 240.
64. Ritter, "Magny," 258-59, 292; Henri Hennebois, *Pierre Laporte dit Rolland et le prophétisme cévenol* (Geneva, 1881) 121n-122n.; P.-L. Ladame, "Un prophète cévenol à Genève au XVIIIe siècle: Procès criminel de Jean-Jacques Doladille, mystique ératomane," *Archives de l'anthropologie criminelle* 26 (1911) 835; BCUL, MSS TH 1194 B1, letters 5, 6b, 9: F. Trechsel, "Samuel Lutz . . . ," *Berner Taschenbuch* 7 (1858) 73-129.

The prophets in Switzerland are so well covered that there is no need here to elaborate on the very rich sources. See Paul Wernle, *Der schweizerische Protestantismus im XVIII. Jahrhundert (Tübingen, 1922-25)* I, 111-468; Henri Vuilleumier, *Histoire de l'Eglise réformée du Pays de Vaud sous le régime bernois* (Lausanne, 1927-33) III, 200-466; W. Hadorn, "Die inspirirten des XVIII Jahrhunderts mit besonderer Berücksichtigung ihrer Beziehungen zur Schweiz," *Schweizerische Theologische Zeitschrift* 17 (1900) 184-223; Geoffrey Rowell, "The Marquis de Marsay: A Quietist in 'Philadelphia,'" *Church History* 41 (1972) 61-77. There is a need for a broadly interpretive essay based on these and other works.

described agitations as signs of the Lord's presence. And Marie Huber, twenty-one, obeyed an order from Pagez to deliver warnings in Geneva.[65]

Esteemed later as a thoughtful writer of books carrying arguments for universal salvation, Marie Huber went to Geneva in 1716 carrying the *Cri d'alarme, Quand vous aurez saccagé*, and a manuscript prophecy by Pagez. She was received none too genially by the Geneva ministry, which for years had been sporadically dealing with prophets coming from southern France. Although the Huber parents expressed their consternation when confronted with Marie's mission, by 1718 another daughter, Marthe, was reporting in detail on the progress of the Spirit in Europe, especially as she learned of it in the letters of her correspondent, the minister Lutz of Yverdon. He wrote to them of the Geneva pietists and of the German inspired who were "a living Copy of the First Christians." There was talk of new *inspirés* in Languedoc, and Daniel Roussière had come from London to southern France on another independent mission. Marthe surmised from the letters of her cousin Emilie that she had "already well entered into that interior path which will disabuse her of those prejudices she formerly had against the extraordinary workings of the Lord."[66]

This religious eclecticism was not unusual. More remarkable was the variety of religious groups and spiritual regimens which Marthe Huber accepted with equanimity as examples of dedication to the "interior path." A manuscript circulating in Lower Languedoc around 1715 provides a clue to Marthe's equanimity. The manuscript, entitled the "Book of the Spirit," claimed that God the Father and Jesus the Son had finished their work and now was the time of the Spirit.[67] As the Spirit's presence became more pervasive, more devout people, regardless of church connection,

---

65. Gustave-A. Metzger, *Marie Huber (1695-1753)* (Geneva, 1887) 13-14; BPUG, MSS fr. 601, ff. 211-212v., letter of 3/25/1716 (N.S.) and MSS fr. 602, ff. 116-117v.; J.-B.-G. Galiffe, *Notices généalogiques sur les familles genevoises* (Geneva, 1829-57) IV, 44-46.

66. Metzger, *Marie Huber*, 13-14; BPUG, MSS fr. 601, ff. 213-214v., 215v.-216v., letters of 4/5/1716 and 4/30/1718; Charles Tylor, *The Camisards* (1893) 431; Walker, *Decline of Hell*, 261; C. Du Bois-Melly, *Les moeurs genevoises de 1700 à 1760 d'après tous les documents officiels* (2nd ed.; Geneva and Basle, 1882) 331-32; Dutton-Cuninghame Corr., 5/2/1710, 168 and see the works noted in footnote 64.

67. Tylor, *Camisards*, 237. This notion of a third age derives from the twelfth-century abbot, Joachim of Fiore, whose millenarian ideas have been traced by Marjorie Reeves down to the seventeenth century and, with less care, by Clarke Garrett to the French Revolution; Marjorie Reeves, "History and Eschatology: Medieval and Early Protestant Thought in Some English and Scottish Writing," *Medievalia et Humanistica*, n.s., 4 (1973) 99-123; Clarke Garrett, *Respectable Folly: Millenarians and the French Revolution in France and England* (Baltimore and London, 1975).

would own the same truths and the same belief in an inner light. Continental followers of the French Prophets tended to believe that once-parallel paths to God were now converging. In Germany, Switzerland and southern France, prophets appeared in disparate social and religious contexts—among communitarian pietists in Wetteravia, among urban quietists in the Swiss canton of Vaud, among rural descendants and neighbors of the early *inspirés* in the Cévennes. Beyond a point it is mere speculation as to which of the continental prophets were professed adherents of the London group and which were participants in a corresponding European movement toward spiritual renewal. The majority of continental French Prophets applied quietist or pietist criteria to the act of prophecy and developed systems of spiritual discipline which had already begun to affect the French Prophets through the influence of Scottish believers. They did not quail at the possibly incomplete synthesis of judgment and mercy, public warnings and private devotion, agitations and passivity.

Of those who had started off with definite bonds to the French Prophets, Doladille and Magny in Switzerland continued longest as leaders of prophetic groups. The Geneva consistory learned that the number of pretended prophets had multiplied considerably in 1717, and that assemblies of thirty to forty people met in the suburbs to hear the prophets. "There are two sorts of bands," said a report in 1718, "those of the Cévennes in which the *inspirés* are particularly followed, and those others in which Magny presides." The minister Lutz was suspected of wielding great influence over both groups, and the list of authors read by the faithful included Mme. Guyon, Antoinette Bourignon, Johann Tennhardt and the French Prophets (the *Eclair de lumière*). In the 1720s, while Lutz devoted himself to a pietist commune in Switzerland, German prophets visited Geneva. In 1727, J. F. Rock and two fellow prophets stayed at the pietist colony led by Mme. de Warens in Vevey.[68]

About the year 1727, praying constantly to the Lord, at least five women in Doladille's entourage received the gift of inspiration. Sensible of a greater love for the Lord, the women under agitations occasionally exchanged sexual caresses with Doladille, whose wife was also a believer. In 1731, interrogated and condemned for "detestable acts and opinions" committed under the guise of pietism, Doladille adamantly defended

---

68. Hennebois, *Pierre Laporte*, 122n.; Ladame, "Doladille," 847; Ritter, "Magny," 296-97; Jean Picot, *Histoire de Genève* (Geneva, 1811) III, 241-42; BCUL, MSS TH 1191 B1 letters 23, 39, and B4 letter 40.

himself. Prayer and devotion were the source of his prophecies, he said, and the ways of the Lord were mysterious. He asserted that he had consistently resisted those familiarities with women which were, in the eyes of unbelievers, indecent; that he had openly opposed the prophets in London who thought themselves inspired to leave their wives and take other women; and that he had prophesied against them everywhere he went, until at last he too was overpowered by the Spirit and performed what was most evidently the Lord's will. Doladille was sentenced by the court in Geneva to public penance and life imprisonment. In 1738 his own house was made his cell; there he sustained a religious circle until his death in 1761.[69]

Swiss opposition to the French Prophets arose in other quarters. A professor of theology wrote against those "systematic fanatics" (*Fanatiques à Système*) who believed themselves inspired because they believe that all noble thoughts come directly from God. Some pietists began to suspect the French Prophets of haphazard commitment to inner spiritual growth. Louisa Brandt, future wife of the English Moravian James Hutton, was proud that she had resisted the inspired men who attempted her spiritual "seduction" around Yverdon in the 1720s. An anonymous pietist during these years wrote a treatise on the *inspirés*, directed against prophets who had their origins in the Cévennes and in London. They were led unwittingly by the malicious souls of the dead, wrote the pietist author, and their millennial warnings implied no thoroughgoing reformation of the soul. On the other hand, the author admitted the difficulty of explaining how malicious spirits might have guided prophets to their exemplary moral conduct. The pietist case against the French Prophets was by no means incontestable, and pietist opposition had not persuaded people such as Mme. de Warens, who saw no reason to deny that the French Prophets were truly inspired.[70]

In France, the Hubers adopted pietist and quietist tenets. Marie Huber sent Fatio a drawing of the Beast of Revelation, seen in the sky for twelve days by friends of minister Lutz. (See Plate VI.) Communication between Huguenots in France and Swiss pietists was maintained by Fage, Pagez

---

69. Ladame, "Doladille," 854-938. Of those named as members of Doladille's circle between 1718 and 1730, there were ten women, eight of whom became inspired, and perhaps six men, none inspired.

70. Samuel Turrettini, *Preservatif contre le fanatisme ou, réfutation des prétendus inspirés des derniers siècles* (Geneva, 1723) esp. 53; Daniel Benham, ed., *Memoirs of James Hutton* (1856) 520; BCUL, MSS TH 1195 B3 No. 73; Ladame, "Doladille," 934. Cf. Benedict Pictet, *Lettre sur ceux qui se croyent inspirez* (Geneva, 1721).

PLATE VI. The pietist minister Samuel Lutz sent Marie Huber a description of a beast seen in the skies over Switzerland in 1718. Marie drew a picture of it for her great-uncle Nicolas Fatio. From a letter of 2/3/1719 N.S., BPUG MSS fr. 601, f. 217v.

and Roussière, prophets who sometimes crossed into Switzerland on their solitary missions. Four Cévenol prophets toured the area west of Nîmes in 1720, recounting visions and performing cures.[71]

By 1721, after the signal drought in southeastern France, the plague at Marseille, and the national bankruptcy which followed the failure of John Law's monetary scheme, a large number of Huguenots (many of them *Nouveaux Convertis*) had gathered in Montpellier to await the millennium. They worshipped formally but secretly in the house of Mme. Verchand, a good friend of the Huguenot gentleman Benjamin Du Plan. Du Plan (who will make a more dashing entrance later in the history of the French Prophets) was but one of several hundred members of this group which became known as the Multipliants. The prophets Jean Huc and Jean Vesson led the group; they had split with the conservative Antoine Court in 1715 and formed a band of *inspirés*. Three men of Pont-de-Montvert, where the Camisard uprising had started, established a larger following around Huc and Vesson in Montpellier. The Multipliants, whom Court called "the most extravagant sect which the human spirit had perhaps ever invented," were a peculiarly fine example of the possibilities of religious eclecticism. They combined Jewish mysticism (Kabbala), Christian chiliasm and elaborate oriental ritual in an atmosphere of Calvinist inspiration. Mme. Verchand's rooms for ceremony were inscribed with Hebrew and Latin letters; trees of life, ornamented with fruits and cakes, were dispersed about the floor; branches of laurel, ribbons and fruit decked the walls. Followers wore white damask bonnets and hoods, their leaders long tunics like albs decorated with stars and mirrors. The Multipliants fasted on Thursdays and Sundays, practiced a baptism of repentance, and recorded in a book the names of those who had received the favors of the Holy Spirit and now awaited the advent of the Messiah. In 1723, having met covertly for more than two years, they were discovered by royal authorities. Three male prophets and one female prophet were hanged, five others sent to the galleys, and seven women imprisoned for life in the Tower of Constance.[72]

71. BPUG, MSS fr. 601, ff. 217-218v. and MSS fr. 605, letters of 11/20/1718 and 9/19/1719; Alfred Dubois, *Le prophètes cévenols* (Strasbourg, 1861) 133-34. Jean Allut attempted a mission to France in 1719 but was turned back at Calais: BPUG, MSS fr. 605, letter of 3/19/1719 and cf. MSS fr. 602, f. 116v.

72. Mme. de Merez, *Mémoire et journal*, ed. Edouard Marie, comte de Barthélemy (n.p., 1874) 5-7; Bost 1925, 432; Dubois, *Les prophètes cévenols*, 127-41 and Court quote, 132; A. Germain, *Nouvelles recherches sur la secte des Multipliants, d'après les manuscrits autographes, encore inédits* (Montpellier, 1857); BPUG, Papiers Court 17 G, ff. 26, 133v.; Hennebois, *Pierre Laporte*, 139-46, which may be found in BPUG, Papiers Court 17 R, ff. 49-55; Turrettini, *Preservatif*, 237-40.

The florid syncretism of the Multipliants was an extreme example of the way in which the Desert traditions of millenarian prophecy were susceptible to external influences. It was also an instructive example of a Huguenot attempt to provide a context other than the Desert for prophecy and millenarian hopes. The *inspirés* Fage, Cavalier and Marion had faced this problem when their refuge in London was prolonged. Warnings to London, public prophecy which inflamed their audiences, the compilation of the *Théâtre sacré* had been means of renewing the Desert in England. Now, after Antoine Court's effective campaign against them, *inspirés* faced the identical problem in Languedoc. How might prophetic traditions linked to the Desert survive in a different setting? One solution, that of the Multipliants, was to surround prophecy with the trappings of a luxuriant church, true successor to the spare wilderness. Another solution, chosen by people in Congénies (near Nîmes) was to make the Desert and its silence an ongoing interior spiritual experience.

According to the people of Congénies, a schismatic prophet named Lucrèce had, about 1715, led a band of admirers to her own house when other *inspirés* tried to stifle the Spirit in her. Her home became the center for religious meetings in which men and women sat in silence worshipping the Lord and waiting for the Spirit. In the 1740s, these meetings spread to neighboring villages. Although these *Gonfleurs* ("pouters," "inflaters") later recognized in themselves a Huguenot parallel to English Quakers, their early meetings were similar to those of pietists in Switzerland and quietists in Scotland.[73]

The Multipliants, the *Gonfleurs*, and the Huber family demonstrated each in their fashion the various possibilities for a change in the Desert traditions. Just as prophetic chiliasm might instigate the formation of communities of inspired Protestants in pietist Germany, just as prophecy and quietism might merge in the Vevey colony guided by Mme. de Warens, so Huguenots in Languedoc might be influenced by the practice of introspective religion. So, too, Huguenots might posit for men and women an equality of spiritual status that had been missing from the Camisard ethos but which was common to pietists and quietists elsewhere on the continent. The inspired women around Doladille, the charismatic Mme. de Warens, the prestigious women assistants at Halle had their counterparts in active and creative Huguenot women like Mme. Verchand

---

73. Dubois, *Les prophètes cévenols*, 142; Tylor, *Camisards*, 431-36; Martha Braithwaite, comp., *Memorials of Christine Majolier Alsop* (1881) 1-24, 245-47; Henry van Etten, *Chronique de la vie Quaker française de 1750 à 1838* (Paris, 1938). Is Lucrèce the prophet mentioned in *MMM*, 72?

and the *inspirée* Lucrèce. Camisard images of destruction might be referred to internal spiritual change; intimations of an impending judgment were also intimations of the arrival of the Messiah. The ethos of cataclysm was, for the Hubers and the Multipliants, convertible into the New Jerusalem ethos: the beast in the sky would lead diverse people to a recognition of the same vital religious feelings. The ethos of judgment was, for pietists, quietists, *Gonfleurs*, convertible into the pentecostal ethos: sincere repentance led to a sensibility of the influx of the Spirit. If, like some German and Swiss believers, one were fortunate enough to live in an isolated communal environment where a balance might be struck between personal autonomy and group sanctions, then too the distance between pentecost and New Jerusalem was not unbridgeable. The narrative comes full circle now, for as the French Prophets quickened the prophetic and millenarian impulses on the continent, they took back with them to England the idioms of continental pietism.

CHAPTER VI

Toward the Female Embassy

1715-1730: The Silence

The England to which the missionaries returned in 1714 was celebrating the Peace of Utrecht and the recovery of import trade. Upon the succession of the Hanoverian King George I (1714-1727), Whigs took control of the government, a control that was battened down by Sir Robert Walpole. In the financial panic of 1720, the stock of the South Sea Company in which many, including several French Prophets, had made considerable investments, fell steeply; Walpole, the reputed wizard who rescued the nation from economic disaster, soon assumed the political leadership that he would not relinquish until 1742. Walpole's era was one of cheap gin for the poor, tea and sugar for the wealthy. The cost of living continued to fall, new territorial possessions gained at Utrecht were exploited, and the colony of Georgia was founded.[1]

Like the weather of the mid-eighteenth century, as Europe heaved past the Little Ice Age and the particular cold of the 1690s, the religious climate in England was also more temperate. By 1718 the Whigs had repealed the Tory Occasional Conformity Bill directed against the nominal Anglicanism of English dissenters in public office. Although deists and freethinkers still prickled the conscience of the orthodox and the raw fear of Catholicism might erupt in riots, the government had befriended the France of Louis XV (the Sun King, Louis XIV, died on the eve of the Jacobite rebellion in Scotland). The pious throve not within a vital church

1. T.S. Ashton, *Economic Fluctuations in England 1700-1800* (Oxford, 1959) 64; A.H. John, "War and the English Economy, 1700-1763," *Economic History Review* 7 (1955) 330-36; Dorothy Marshall, *English People in the Eighteenth Century* (1956); J.H. Plumb, *The Growth of Political Stability in England 1675-1725* (1967) and *Sir Robert Walpole* (1956).

community but through the personal exercises of faith. Family worship was enlivened by the popular hymns of the nonconformist Isaac Watts, and in 1728 William Law's *Serious Call to a Devout and Holy Life* beckoned many to a world of quiet religious devotion. The number of dissenting congregations dwindled, and the Anglican establishment suffered as the political giftbag of an administration that settled its debts with ecclesiastical appointments. Progress, not apocalypse, was the theme of the country's ruling oligarchy, despite the public lectures of the indefatigable William Whiston, who expected the millennium in 1736.[2]

In this fallow period, the French Prophets too avoided the clamor of their earlier years. Their group structure and manner of worship, influenced by Scottish and European quietists and pietists, encouraged disengagement. Not trumpets but the gentle music of the soul would hail the coming Kingdom.

Subtly and very slowly, the influence of the European missions was at work. The assemblies of the inspired admitted for the first time prophets whose primary allegiance was continental: Doladille, Pagez, Roussière. Marie Hélène de Ridder, a Dutch *inspirée* instrumental in the assemblies, chose to remain in London. The French Prophets continued to heed the quietist ideal of passivity and silence which was strengthened by pietist convictions. Devotion to the interior path as a means of combatting prophetic "mixtures" had been accepted. Fatio's advice to his nephew Jean Huber revealed an increasing scepticism of inspiration; Jean Huber, with the perplexity of a novice, lamented his ignorance of all the "different orders of Spirits." In 1716 Henriette Allut reported only an interior warning, and in succeeding years Jean Allut had as many prophetic dreams as public warnings. Charles Portales in 1719 understood one inspiration by John Potter as a command to "silence and fear," lest human words be taken as divine.[3]

A general decline in the cohesion of the London group accompanied the "silence and fear" and may explain the delayed impact of continental pietism. By 1718, personal feuds, geographical dispersion and death had

---

2. Norman Sykes, *From Sheldon to Secker: Aspects of English Church History 1660-1768* (Cambridge, 1959); C.E. Fryer, "The Numerical Decline of Dissent in England Previous to the Industrial Revolution," *American Journal of Theology* 17 (1913) 232-39; Russell E. Richey, "Effects of Toleration on Eighteenth-Century Dissent," *Journal of Religious History* 8 (1975) 350-63; Arthur O. Lovejoy, *The Great Chain of Being* (Cambridge, Mass., 1964[1936]); H.H. Lamb, "Britain's Changing Climate," *The Geographical Journal* 133 (1967) 445-68.

3. BCUL, MSS TH 1194 B 1 letter 6b; BPUG, MSS fr. 601, ff. 213v.-214, and MSS fr. 602, f. 116v., and MSS fr. 605, letters of 2/5, 3/17 and 6/13-6/14/1719.

sundered the remaining unity of the French Prophets. The deaths of Cuninghame and Marion had loosened the bonds of Scottish and Huguenot followers to the English with whom both prophets had some close ties. In Rotterdam, Pierre Jurieu died in 1712 and Benjamin Furly in 1714; Hélène Jurieu died in England in 1714.[4] The strongest personal links to the continent had been broken.

During these same years, Dr. Timothy Byfield had a bitter falling-out with his business partners Francis Moult and Dr. Daniel Critchlow. Moult, worried about his financial state, disputed with his fellow apothecary, James Craven. Samuel Keimer, his effects seized by John Potter and Thomas Dutton, was forced to sell even his silver shoebuckles and go to debtors' prison; he soon turned apostate. Jean Allut and Mary Beer disputed at length with Hannah Wharton and Jonathan Taylor over the criteria for true inspiration. Fatio and the Alluts moved to Worcester, and the prophet Mary Keimer departed for Pennsylvania. In 1718, only half of those mentioned in the *Orders* were yet in London.[5]

Between 1715 and 1730, the French Prophets maintained an often tenuous relationship with one another. Wharton, Taylor and a few other prophets rode from circle to circle, prophesying, rarely drawing in new believers. Followers in London had small assemblies around the prophets John Potter and Mary Beer.[6] Fatio, Moult, Benjamin Jackson, Benjamin Steele, Charles Portales and Robert Eaton corresponded on scientific matters and shared business interests. They computed lottery probabilities and watched sadly as their investments in the York Buildings Company produced no dividends.[7]

4. On the Jurieus see Frederik R.J. Knetsch, *Pierre Jurieu Theoloog en politikus der Refuge* (Kampen, 1967) 378-80; Gemeente Archief (Rotterdam), Actes du Consistoire de l'Eglise Wallonne de Rotterdam, B, ff. 400, 407, 410, 411, and notarial documents for 1713, series 1506, 1508, 1509, 1510, 1550, 2314; PRO, PCC Administration Act Books, PROB 6/97 ff. 2v-4, will of Hélène Du Moulin, registered 1721.

5. *Brand*, 76-77, 81-103, 124; BPUG, MSS fr. 602, f. 120, and MSS fr. 605, letter of 3/3/1719; Byfield will printed in H.F. Waters, *Genealogical Gleanings* (Boston, 1901) II, 1396; Guildhall, MSS 8201/8, Court Book of the Society of Apothecaries, Nov. 1715-May, 1721, entry for 12/5/1716; Stack MSS 11, Portales Notebook and Commonplace Book, entry 9/11/1715.

6. BPUG, MSS fr. 605, letter of 3/14/1719; Broadmead Free Baptist Church (Bristol), MSS church records 1655-1784, 11/10/1720 and 1/12 and 12/31/1721, 171-72, 177; Dutton-Cuninghame Corr., endpapers, letter of 7/16/1737.

7. BPUG, MSS fr. 601, f. 278, and MSS fr. 602, ff. 137, $63-64, and MSS fr. 605, letters of 1719; Stack MSS 1c, notes of Portales in a French almanac. The York Buildings Company in 1719 purchased forfeited estates in England and Scotland; in 1728 the stock was at 11½ (compared to East India Company stock at 172): *Sam Farley's Bristol Post Man*, Feb. 10, 1728. See also the next chapter.

Family connections held some of the French Prophets together. Charles Portales had married one niece of Francis Moult, John Potter the other. Marie Brunelle married a follower named Durand, and Joseph Steel married the prophet Mary Aspinal.[8] Further deaths offset these in-group relationships. Misson and the prophet Mary Waller died in 1722, Byfield in 1723, the wives of Charles Portales and John Potter (Moult's nieces) in 1726. Moult wrote emotional letters to Dutton and Fatio, trying to square their deaths with the dispensation. "Should the children of wisdom weep and mourn," he asked, "at the gathering in the number of the Elect of God to their proper centers?" He mused to Fatio, "If no one can trace the ships of men in the Deep waters of this world, who shall then search out the Almighty's ways in the unfathomable ocean of his wisdom?" Moult hoped finally that the deaths might stir followers to prepare for God's rays of light. "This will show," he concluded, "of that paradisical anointing which we wait and hope for to find in the enjoinments of the new covenant Blessings etc." Sarah Critchlow died in 1728, Richard Roach and John Lacy in 1730. Fatio refused to consider Lacy's death, at the age of sixty-six, "otherwise than as a Memorandum of our common Mortality."[9]

Fatio's muted tone was characteristic of the French Prophets between 1715 and 1730. Their only publication was John Lacy's *The Scene of Delusions, By the Reverend Mr. OWEN . . . Confuted*, in 1723, a learned criticism of a book ten years old. Lacy in his critique made no reference to more recent events and defended the slowness with which the dispensation progressed. In 1727, Jean Allut remarked that the dispensation seemed to be making no visible progress at all, except for a few visits of the Spirit.[10]

Hannah Wharton

Only Richard Roach retained the vitality of the early years. In the 1720s he kept up contacts with French Prophets, with mystics, with Philadelphians in London and on the continent. He published two books complete with diagrams of the cycles of time leading to the millennium. (See Plate VII.)

---

8. *Brand*, 64, 74-75; *MMM*, Tableau Généalogique, vii; Stack MSS 12g, page ll; *Recueil d'avertissemens touchant l'ordre des assemblées* (1715) 140.

9. *The Historical Register*, chronological diaries for 1722 (p. 7) and 1723 (p. 49); Stack MSS 11 and 2a, Moult letters; Robert Hovenden, ed., *Registers of St. James Clerkenwell, vol. VI* in *Harleian Society Publications, Register Series* 20 (1894) 18; BPUG, MSS fr. 605, letter of 5/5/1730, postscript; Roach Diary, V, 3/17/1728.

10. BPUG, MSS fr. 605, letter of 172[7]. Although I have not found Owen's book, a review of it appears in *Unschuldige Nachrichten von Alten und Neuen Theologischen Sachen . . . auf das Jahr 1713* (1713) 1072.

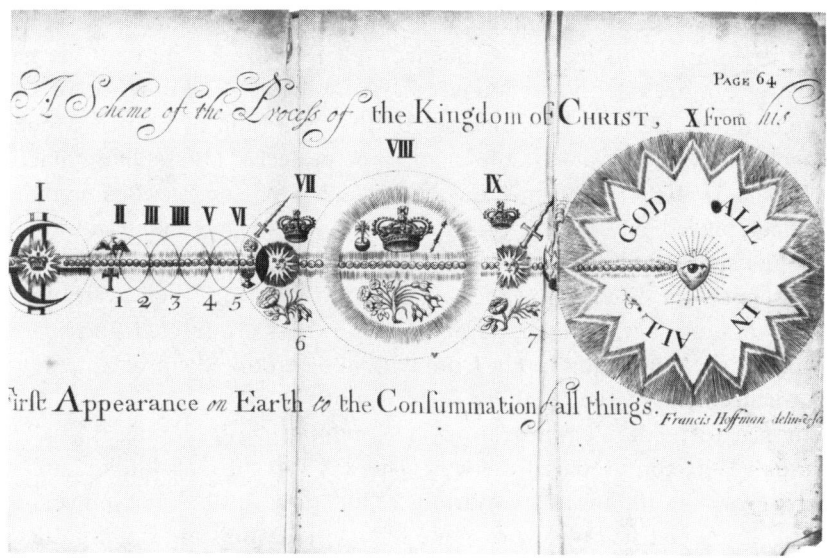

PLATE VII. Engraving by Francis Hoffman for Richard Roach's *The Imperial Standard of Messiah Triumphant* (1727 [sic] for 1728). Explanation: arabic numerals represent the seven church states (Ephesus, Smyrna, Pergamus, Thyatira, Sardis, Philadelphia, Laodicea); Roman numerals represent the stages of Christ's progress from birth to his coming in glory at the end of the world. The Philadelphian state (6) begins with the rise of the Two Witnesses (candlestick and olive tree), then enters the darkness of Judgment Work which leads into the Davidic kingdom and then (VIII) the Millennium. Conflagration and Final Judgment precede the Last Coming (X).

His friend Sarah Wiltshire spoke her last prophecies in January, 1722/23, and that year Roach wrote *The Imperial Standard of Messiah Triumphant*, comparing former testimony to the Spirit—judgments, cries in the wilderness, theosophy—with the more mature Philadelphian testimony which made a systematic and clear exposition of God's grace. In his second book, *The Great Crisis*, Roach explained that the French Prophets were false prophets because their predicted judgments necessarily failed in an epoch of increasing grace, but true prophets because they testified publicly to the immediate operation of the Spirit. Roach understood the present silence of the French Prophets and the divine prohibition against their meeting in public as a confirming sign of grace prevailing over judgment. The revival of the Philadelphian church was thus a "Conquering and *holding fast* the *Love* which Ephesus lost, and thereby proceeding on into the Millennial State and Kingdom." Exulting, Roach sought the merger of the dispensations of mercy and justice. After an illness and an "Internal Call to a more silent Attendance on the Powers of the Work of the Kingdom" in 1728, and encouraged by the friendship of Francis Moult, Roach believed that at last the chance for perfect synthesis had come.[11]

It had. In 1730 the inspirations of Hannah Wharton, the Birmingham prophet, played back the rhetoric and theology of Philadelphians, quietists and pietists. Although delayed, the impact of continental religious movements upon the French Prophets in England was confirmed by Hannah Wharton's message, by the kind of new followers she attracted, and by the nature of the opposition to her from within the group. She proclaimed the commencement of the teaching dispensation.

In her forty days' ministration at London (April 23-June 2, 1730), Hannah Wharton prepared the way. The way was through Philadelphian mercy, through the inward sensations of quietists, through the indwelling Spirit of the pietists. Wharton spoke of "spiritual moisture," "outgoings" and "indwellings" of the Spirit, "centers of fulness," the "Blessing of Power," the Gospel of "Power, Wisdom and Love." Her language resembled the English translations of Boehme's works, the *Theosophical Transactions* of the Philadelphians, the letters of James Cuninghame. Her theology was that of continental pietism: divine communications enriched personal movement toward God; where the indwelling Spirit was known, it was more and more desired.[12]

Richard Roach may have attended one of Wharton's assemblies shortly before his death. He who filled his diary with allusions to powers and internal waiting would have been pleased by what was said:

> This indwelling Power which is Spirit, which is the Revelation of Jesus, as each one must have to Witness to the Revelation, and know that the Witness in them is indeed that of the Spirit, which Spirit is Life and Power, and it is to be known an indwelling Power, notwithstanding this inward Life knows not at all times the

---

11. Roach Diaries, II-VI, *passim* and Bodleian MSS D. 832, ff. 92-93, Roach to Moult, 10/8/1728; Roach, *The Great Crisis: or, the Mystery of the Times and Seasons Unfolded* (1725 [*sic* for 1727]) 7-8, 14, 35-41; Roach, *The Imperial Standard* (1727 [*sic* for 1728]) 20-21, 31, 36-37, 56-58.

12. Hannah Wharton, *Some Manifestations and Communications of the Spirit* (1730) 3, 12, 22-26, 96, 99-101, 103, 212. On the significance of pietist language, see Michel Godfroid, "Le piétisme allemand a-t-il existé?" *Etudes germaniques* 26 (1971) 40-41; August Langen, *Der Wortschatz des deutschen Pietismus* (Tübingen, 1954). Cf. Daniel Vidal's analysis of the language of the earlier French Prophets: "L'ablatif absolu (De quelques textes prophétiques)," mimeograph, Centre d'Etude des Mouvements Sociaux, Ecole Pratique des Hautes Etudes, VIe section, (Paris), 1974.

same Exercise of Power in itself, but yet the Witness remains, and this Witness which is of God holds all the Senses and Faculties of the inward Mind in that Conformity of a passive humble waiting as that every Moving of divine Power may be known.

Roach would have been especially pleased by the shift in Wharton's theology from judgments she had pronounced a dozen years before to the perseverance she now taught. Although these were the very last days, the personal reappearance of Jesus would be made known mildly at first and to the inward self. Like her syntax, introverted and complexly repetitive, the Lord's workings also demanded considerable patience of the faithful. Each disciple was to wait "until in waiting he finds the Increase of this Power, which is the putting on Knowledge as a Garment." There was now a "Blessing of Waiting" in which the Spirit operated as it had never done before, even in apostolic times.[13]

The next year, 1731, in a series of Revelations, Exhortations, Intercessions and Praises from Birmingham and Worcester, Hannah Wharton often discoursed on the passive disposition appropriate to Waiters in Zion. "How wonderful is it, O mighty God," she said, "that thou shouldst be delighted with the Waiting of thy Children!" The Lord had not forsaken his Work. Because there were degrees of preparation, stages of spiritual knowledge to be attained, the work progressed slowly while the faithful learned about the Lord. By meditation, believers might know the Lord on earth as He was in heaven.[14]

Followers must have been aware of the similarities between Wharton's doctrine and that of continental pietism. Wharton's fervent admirers were aligned either with Richard Roach or directly with continental religious figures.[15] Francis Moult, his nieces, and Benjamin and Elizabeth Steele were warm friends of Roach. Their associations with the continent through him were clear, for in his last years Roach actively extended his European correspondence. He was in regular communication with the Amsterdam translator of Philadelphian works, Loth Fischer, and in 1729 he wrote his first letter to the Baron Dodo von Knyphausen, minister of finance in Brandenburg, sponsor of the German translations of Jane Lead's books,

---

13. Wharton, *Some Manifestations*, 69, 169, 286. The "R.R." noted as present on May 24, 1730, could have been Richard Roach or Robert Richardson. For Wharton's earlier tone, see Jonathan Taylor and Hannah Wharton, *Warnings of the Eternal Spirit Spoken at Birmingham* (1711).

14. Hannah Wharton, *Divine Inspiration* (1732) 15 et passim.

15. A list of Wharton's followers, omitting Jonathan Taylor, appears on the title page of her *Divine Inspiration*.

and patron of the chiliast couple Johann and Johanna Petersen. In his *The Imperial Standard*, Roach published an extract from Johann Petersen's defense of the German prophet Rosamunde von Asseburg. To complete this fascinating religious circuit, Petersen had met the French Prophet missionaries in Germany and claimed to have converted two of the men to the doctrine of universal salvation.[16]

Francis Wynantz and William Weintraub, friends of Moult, were also followers of Hannah Wharton. Wynantz, born in Dantzig, was naturalized as an English citizen in 1732, but he fostered continental liaisons and hosted the Moravian leader August Spangenberg in London in 1735. (Spangenburg had found pietist life at Halle too worldly and had involved himself in the Herrnhut Moravian colony on Count Zinzendorf's estate in lower Saxony. He was on his way to the Moravian settlement in Georgia.) It was at Wynantz's house in February, 1738, that John Wesley, who had met Spangenberg in Georgia, now met Peter Böhler, a Moravian who deeply marked the course of Wesley's life. Two months later, Francis Wynantz married Marguerite Portales, daughter of Charles Portales and Mary Portales (née Moult).[17]

Contrary to Roach's hopes and Wharton's prophecy that "All Ministrations stand in Unity, and do not oppose one another or condemn one another," there was a sharp division in the group as continental doctrines took root. The controversy around two prophets to appear in 1732 revealed the texture of the opposition to Hannah Wharton and her supporters. In the first mission to come *from* the continent since Marion's arrival in 1706, the French Prophets showed some willingness to recognize similarities between themselves and inspired pietists, but it was Charles Portales who was sceptical of Jean Philippe Arnould, and Isaac Hollis who defended him. Arnould had spent his last few years in Schwarzenau among a variety of German pietist groups. With a long dirty beard and a torn blue cloak, he had come from Copenhagen claiming to be inspired. He sought out Portales at Baker's Coffee House; Portales did not take this

16. Roach Diaries, II-VI, esp. V; D. P. Walker, *The Decline of Hell* (1964) 219, 231-44, 261-62; Roach, *The Imperial Standard*, 205-17; Walter Nordmann, "Im Widerstreit von Mystik und Föderalismus. Geschichtliche Grundlagen der Eschatologie bei dem pietistischen Ehepaar Petersen," *Zeitschrift für Kirchengeschichte* 50 (1931) 146-85. Petersen's hymms were later used in America by the Amana Society which derived from Gruber's "Wahrinspirations Gemeinde" in Wetteravia.

17. Stack MSS 12g, page 6; Henry Wagner, "The Huguenot Family of Portales," *The Genealogist*, n.s., 22 (1906) 50-51; J. Taylor and K.G. Hamilton, *History of the Moravian Church* (n.p., 1967) 76, 78; John Wesley, *The Journal of the Rev. John Wesley, A.M.*, ed. Nehemiah Curnock (1938) I, 437 and VI, 469.

as a compliment, writing Fatio that the new prophet had already been chased from the doorsteps of the mighty after receiving alms. Isaac Hollis, a Baptist friend of Richard Roach, thought Arnould well meaning and no impostor. The prophet from Schwarzenau undertook a mission through England, travelling from one enclave of French Prophets to another.[18]

When Jean Michaut departed London on October 1, 1732, on a prophetic mission in pursuit of Arnould, the Fatio-Portales-Allut triangle was obviously swerving from Hannah Wharton's London-Birmingham alliance. There was no mistaking the division between followers: Michaut was expelled from the London assemblies and suspected by Hollis of speaking the devil's words, but he was embraced by the loyal old Huguenot Abraham Mahieu and welcomed by Fatio in Worcester. Michaut, unlike Arnould, pronounced judgments, promising that Babylon would fall and Zion rise, that soon there would be a wedding in Canaan. He used the rhetoric of the original *inspirés*; his inspirations were prefaced with the distinctive "I tell thee, my child" address of Camisard prophets. Michaut's impact upon Fatio was extraordinary. Twice while in Michaut's presence, Fatio felt the Spirit move him, a rare event, and the second time Fatio threw his arms around the prophet and embraced him.[19] Michaut was appealing to the veteran Huguenots who still associated judgments and missions with the Camisard ethos of cataclysm and battle, while Arnould was appealing to the English who sought the New Jerusalem in a final union of Christians.

Despite his years of missionary travels, Jean Allut had been vehemently resisting the Roach synthesis, the all-inclusive teaching dispensation supported by Wharton's claims to "the Highest Peak of Revelation." In 1732 Allut wrote a scorching letter to Jonathan Taylor, "Concerning the Report spread at London by George Wharton that the Dispute concerning the Birmingham Doctrine was at an end by Mr. Allut's having owned that he was deceived." The doctrine under debate was the right of Hannah Wharton as a prophet to control the temporal possessions of believers. Francis Moult and Timothy Ireland had already acquiesced to the doctrine, so the matter was not theoretical. Allut, in a letter to Moult, stated that neither reason nor soul nor scripture could justify such a doctrine. Moult persisted, and when he died he left the greater part of his

18. BPUG, MSS fr. 601, ff. 261-62 and unfoliated letter, 10/3/1732, and MSS fr. 605, notes on letter of 10/10-10/11/1732; Wharton, *Some Manifestations*, 45.

19. BPUG, MSS fr. 601, 10/3/1732 and f. 239, 9/12/1732 and MSS fr. 605, letter of 10/10-10/11/1732. Louis Joyneau, who expelled Michaut from the London assemblies, had had business troubles with Jean Allut in the 1720s: BPUG, MSS fr. 602, f. 135.

wealth to the prophet and her husband. Charles Portales, with a perhaps temporal interest in his father-in-law's possessions, wrote Fatio that Moult's attachment to the "oracle and Paraclete" of Birmingham reminded him of Bulkeley's attachment to Whitrow.[20]

If the lines of battle were not yet unmistakable, by 1736 the prophet Simon Saudignan made them so. Figuratively and literally, the Desert lay between the camps of Wharton and Allut. "This faith thou hast," warned Saudignan in an inspired letter to Wharton, "is not tried by the Fire of Afflictions." He accused Wharton of manipulating the wealth of followers for her own pleasure. She was selfish in another and more alarming way, for she broadcast God's mercy because she was not rigorous in her own conduct. "Mercy glorifieth herself above Condemnation," Saudignan admitted; "But Condemnation without Mercy, is going to manifest itself upon thee if the Mercy of God is not quickly manifested by having Compassion of those who are in need." Wharton returned Saudignan's letter unopened, having previously committed one of Allut's letters to the flames and posted a divine sentence against him. Saudignan, like Michaut, was a prophet of the Camisard tradition, a prophet who in one inspiration announced that Elie Marion was present within him. He proclaimed a new manifestation which was to be the "*Plan de ma Justice*," the "*Cri d'alarme*." He prophesied love, peace and charity, but the brunt of his message was judgment against the haughty. Portales, Fatio, Allut, Jean Pellet and Mme. Delbose studied his words. He also had an inspired letter for the Camisard "Colonel" Jean Cavalier.[21]

The group was breaking up along the line of an old fracture, that between Huguenots looking back toward the seventeenth century and English Protestants looking around at the eighteenth century. This was not a simple fracture between the ethos of cataclysm and the ethos of the New Jerusalem or, as Roach had put it, between advocates of judgment and advocates of mercy. For the French themselves changed their outlook, reinterpreted the Camisard experience. They drifted toward the ethos of judgment when purity and law were most vital to them, toward the New Jerusalem when they needed broad social approval and a sense of return from exile. They sent four men on European missions to restore the

---

20. BPUG, MSS fr. 601, ff. 261-62, and MSS fr. 605, letters of 3/25, 3/26 and 5/5/1730, 10/30/1731. There were differences between Allut, Taylor and Wharton as early as 1718 (or, possibly, 1715): BPUG, MSS fr. 605, letters of 3/3, 3/4 and 3/17/1718 and MSS fr. 602, note in f. 116v.; Stack MSS 11, Portales notebook, page 2, 9/11/1715.

21. BPUG, MSS fr. 605, papers of March, 4/19, 5/4, 6/16-6/17/1736.

integrity of the Huguenot refugee community only to have them received much more warmly by a more diverse set of continental pietists and quietists. So the missionary prophets had prophesied judgments upon their recalcitrant Huguenot family, a universal awakening and wideflung church for their new friends. Now, Portales, Fatio and Allut seemed to act paradoxically, setting themselves against the pietism of Hannah Wharton, returning to the narrower Camisard ideas about salvation. But they had gone on their missions twenty years before, at a time of grave concern over the viability of the French Prophets, as if support from the continent would ensure the group's survival in England. By 1730 their concern was primarily with the purity of those who had survived. Accustomed to an English isolation, they needed the vows of loyalty more than renewed predictions of a bountiful Spirit and a new kingdom. Prophets who identified explicitly with the Desert tradition were foci for professions of faith in a group "tried by the Fire of Afflictions."

Hannah Wharton's dispensation was a blend of the pentecostal ethos and the ethos of the New Jerusalem, but she had not forsworn the judgmental tones of earlier prophets and roundly condemned Allut. Unlike the French, however, she was certain that judgments could be regularly delayed by the Lord's merciful hand. Judgment was for her another method of instruction, and what she offered English followers was in essence a pietist *collegia* in which the Spirit was more openly and constantly active.[22]

The silence of the French Prophets between 1715 and 1730 marked a period of personal, social and theological retrenchment. "Waiting in Silence" also affected group eschatology, both Wharton and Allut arriving at a belief in progressive revelations which might not end in their own time. The varieties of millenarian ethos were not compressed by the urgency of the apocalypse—as they had been at moments during the first years of the French Prophets—into a tense, vibrant but whole anticipation of the millennium. The world might hover on the brink of salvation or destruction (that could be argued: it was a matter of degree), but whatever millennial urgency remained was personal.[23] Hannah Wharton's success was a measure of the change in group sensibilities. She promoted a social environment for personal stocktaking rather than self-assertion, for companionship rather than hierarchy. Introspection was offset by the pietist image of a silent but powerfully spreading universal church.

22. For Wharton's judgments, see her *Divine Inspirations*, 62, 169, 288, 346.
23. BPUG, MSS fr. 605, letters of 4/6, 4/15 and 6/17/1736.

As Scottish quietists and German pietists realized, introspection could lead one to a public ministry. When Hannah Wharton resumed at large the Lord's work, English and some French followers seemed nearly strong enough again for the strains of energetic witnessing. Some had worked through quietist logic to link meditation with mission; others had never lost the missionary urge but had lost nerve, distressed by the deaths of friends or the problem of false inspiration. Hannah Wharton had no quick answers, but her tone was comforting, her manner resilient. "Come," she said, "let us now tell one another [about] the Establishment and Strength of such Bands that did keep and hold together even in a Time the Band did not speak with so loud a Voice." She spoke too of holy boldness. The Lord's children would not only congregate and talk of God, "but shall be able to proclaim the Name of the Lord in the Assemblies of different Nations."[24]

Even with such encouragement, no missions or public appearances of prophets come to notice until 1738. A dreary letter written by Thomas Dutton in 1737 was indicative of the condition of the French Prophets. Dutton was writing to a Scottish friend after many years' lapse. Subdued, he recited a litany of deaths among followers (Francis Moult, Joseph and Beata Tovey, Guy Nutt, John Glover, Mary Beer, Thomas Lardner) and noted that "The Spirit in its public Manifestations has gradually withdrawn." He extended best wishes to Lady Clara Gordon, David Spence and other Scottish believers, if they were alive. With no last fanfare he ended praying that "God keep you and all of us in the true faith, and in the direction and sanctification of his Holy Spirit."[25]

The Evangelical Revival

Though weak, the pulse of the group still beat. In 1738, the voices of the French Prophets were heard again in the land. Significantly, the news came from Bristol. Thomas Whitehead, a Quaker and long a believer in the dispensation, hosted two women prophets in the spring. At the end of the well-attended Friary Yearly Meeting of Bristol Quakers, one of the women prophets sitting in the gallery stood up. Removing her outer clothing, she appeared in a sackcloth gown, strewing ashes on her head, and began "such a raving, with Postures so frightful, that the Meeting broke up immedi-

24. Wharton, *Divine Inspirations*, 329, 363, 371.
25. Dutton-Cuninghame Corr., endpapers, letter of 7/16/1737.

ately." Thrust from the building, Whitehead and the prophets were mobbed and stoned.[26]

Bristol as a location was significant for two reasons. First, Bristol followers were allied to the Birmingham ministration, and one of the prophets was possibly Hannah Wharton. The last active missionaries of the French Prophets were those who had been influenced by quietist and pietist religious forces. Second, the initial success of John Wesley as a Methodist missionary in England would occur in Bristol less than a year later. Two religious groups whose leaders had absorbed substantial continental influences found the same town for their coming-out.

Coincidental or not, Methodists and French Prophets shared more than an interest in Bristol. They also shared an interest in the London Moravian societies. While French Prophets made concerted efforts to attract Moravians to the dispensation, Wesley would discover his companions at the Fetter Lane religious society in London frequenting the French Prophets. The relationship between the three groups draws attention to the importance of continental forces which shaped the dispensation in its later years.

A small band of Protestants, spiritual descendants of Bohemian and Moravian congregations that emphasized the study of scripture and apostolic discipline, had been invited by Count Zinzendorf to take refuge in a corner of his Saxony estate. Fleeing persecution in their homeland, the Moravians had settled at Herrnhut by 1722, practicing a personal and Christ-centered religion. Their community was fashioned into a church by Zinzendorf and his assistant, August Spangenberg, both of whom had pietist backgrounds. Zinzendorf and Spangenberg encouraged an evangelical Christianity that overlooked denominational distinctions and sought to spread the gospel as widely as possible. The Moravians or *Unitas Fratrum* carried on their missionary work in London, Georgia and Pennsylvania. Their love feasts at the Aldersgate Street and Fetter Lane societies in London, their emphasis on the inner workings of the Spirit, their insistence upon a religion of the heart attracted those French Prophets who had already responded to continental pietism.[27] Two followers regarded the common ground between the French Prophets and the Moravians as so extensive that they converted. Each of their stories

---

26. Abel Boyer, ed., *The Political State of Great Britain*, Aug., 1738, pp. 145-47, with numerous references to Bristol followers surrendering their possessions to the French Prophets, suggesting an association with Hannah Wharton. The incident is misdated by Elie Halévy, *The Birth of Methodism in England*, trans. and ed. Bernard Semmel (Chicago, 1971) 69.

27. Taylor and Hamilton, *History of the Moravian Church*.

illuminates the interplay between continental and English religious forces.

Jean Pellet, a French Prophet for thirty years, was a member of the Fetter Lane society by 1742. As late as 1736, Pellet had been active among those of the Camisard tradition in London; yet, like the people at Congénies in France, Pellet was admitting quietist influences, for he raised his grandson to be familiar with Antoinette Bourignon's *An Admirable Treatise of Solid Virtue* (1698). Moravians esteemed Jean Pellet and referred to him as "Old Father Pellet, the Simeon of our Congregation."[28]

A second follower's history is much more complex. In 1693, a group of German pietists originally formed by the Behmenist Johann Zimmerman and known as the "true Rosicrucians" had travelled from Holland to London, where they made friends among English Philadelphians. Continuing their journey in 1694, they settled in Germantown, Pennsylvania. Among them was Daniel Falkner, soon expelled for his defense of several female prophets, especially of the Erfurt prophet Anna Maria Schuchart. Falkner left America but returned in 1700 under the auspices of Benjamin Furly, who sent out another business agent named Johann Heinrich Sprogel. (Sprogel's father, a Philadelphian pastor at Quedlinburg near Erfurt, had had as a servant one of the prophets admired by Falkner.) By 1720, Johanna Christina Zeidig, granddaughter of pastor Sprogel, niece of Johann Heinrich Sprogel and niece also of the pietist church historian Gottfried Arnold, had come to Pennsylvania. At first she associated with pietists from Schwarzenau known as Dunkards (German Baptist Brethren). Between 1730 and 1740, she adhered to some French Prophets (possibly offshoots of Mary Keimer's mission to Pennsylvania in 1718). In the 1740s, caught up in the evangelical revival, she left the French Prophets for the Moravians. There, among August Spangenberg's people, she remained.[29]

---

28. Daniel Benham, ed., *Memoirs of James Hutton* (1856) 93; Moravian Church House: MSS, Fetter Lane Diary IX, Feb. 2, 1757; Minutes of "Elders and Wardens" of Fetter Lane Elders Conference, 1A, April 20, 1743; Extracts from the London Archives of the United Brethren, 214, 374 (all dates in N.S.). Cf. Jean Orcibal, "Les spirituels français et espagnols chez J. Wesley et ses contemporains," *Revue d'histoire des religions* 139 (1951) 59.

29. Julius F. Sachse, *The German Pietists of Provincial Pennsylvania* (Philadelphia, 1895) 4-27, 124-25, 171, 258-59, 303-15; Nils Thune, *The Behmenists and the Philadelphians* (Uppsala, 1948) 125-26; Donald F. Durnbaugh, *The Believers' Church* (New York, 1968) 121-25; John B. Frantz, "The Awakening of Religion among the German Settlers in the Middle Colonies," *William and Mary Quarterly*, 3rd ser., 33 (1976) 272-74; Pennsylvania Historical Society (Philadelphia), MSS Martha Lawrence Collection, Benjamin Furly papers; John W. Jordan, "William Parsons," *Pennsylvania Magazine of History and Biography* 33 (1909) 343-44. Johanna Zeidig married Parsons in 1722; Jordan's valuable references are untraceable.

The spiritual odysseys of Jean Pellet and Johanna Christina Zeidig had parallels among those of the Fetter Lane society interested in the French Prophets. John Wesley's own life illustrated the possibilities. In the month and year that the two female prophets in Bristol performed the drama of repentance for the Quakers, John Wesley was deeply committed to the theology of Peter Böhler, the Moravian whom he had met through Hannah Wharton's follower, Francis Wynantz. On May 24, 1738, after attending the Moravian Aldersgate Street meeting, Wesley experienced his full Christian conversion. (His brother Charles, the hymn-writer, had undergone his conversion three days before.) That summer, John Wesley spent several months at the Moravian colony at Herrnhut. Six days after he returned to London in September, 1738, he was having tea with Isaac Hollis of High Wickham, former Baptist and now French Prophet. John Wesley met twice more in October with Hollis, and by December Charles Wesley was also at High Wickham. Charles lodged with Hollis, who at night was seized by the Spirit, had agitations and "gobbled like a turkey-cock." Charles began to exorcise Hollis, who calmed down; himself unsettled, Charles did not sleep well "with Satan so near me."[30]

On January 28, 1738/39, John Wesley, "having been long importuned thereto," visited the French Prophet Mary Plewit. He and some friends hoped to observe her inspirations. They were not disappointed, for the young woman quickly fell into convulsions and then prophesied. As described by Wesley, her inspiration was evidently in the manner of the English, pietistic French Prophets:

> She spoke much (all as in the person of God, and mostly in Scripture words) of the fulfilling of the prophecies, the coming of Christ now at hand, and the spreading of the gospel over all the earth. Then she exhorted us not to be in haste in judging her spirit to be or not to be of God; but to wait upon God, and He would teach us, if we conferred not with Flesh and blood. She added, with many enforcements, that we must watch and pray, and take up our cross, and be still before God.

Although Wesley himself reserved his opinion, friends John Bray and Lydia Sellers were much impressed with the prophet. Before long, the society at Fetter Lane would find itself embroiled in arguments with her supporters.[31]

30. John Wesley, *Journal*, II, 76d, 86d, 93d; Charles Wesley, *The Journal of the Rev. Charles Wesley, M.A.*, ed. Thomas Jackson (n.d.) I, 138; Charles W. Towlson, *Moravian and Methodist* (1957); John Telford, articles on the two Wesleys, *Encyclopaedia Britannica* (1961 ed.) XXXIII, 515-58.

31. John Wesley, *Journal*, II, 136-37.

John Wesley went to Bristol in February, leaving his brother Charles to cope with problems at Fetter Lane in the spring of 1739. John Bray, Lydia Sellers, Shepherd Wolf, Mr. Fish, Mr. Bowers, Mr. Shaw and probably others, swayed by the spirit of prophecy among the French Prophets, began to espouse a priesthood of the Spirit which implied lay preaching and a lay ministry. Charles Wesley, a high churchman who always upheld the necessity of proper ordination for clergy, and who never deserted the Church of England, fought hard against lay preaching and its advocates. He was curt with another French Prophet, a woman named Lavington, who prophesied in favor of the possibility of absolute spiritual perfection. In June, with many in the Fetter Lane society "pestered by the French Prophets, and such-like *pretenders* to inspiration," Charles Wesley brought the matter to a head. He took depositions against the immoral conduct of prophet Lavington, who had cohabited with Mr. Wise, and forced the Fetter Lane membership to divide against her followers. Asking, "Who is on God's side? Who for the old Prophets rather than the new?" he led the faithful away from Lavington, John Bray and the others. On June 11, 1739, in the presence of John Wesley (back temporarily from Bristol), the society expelled Mr. Shaw and Shepherd Wolf. Bray, Bowers and the rest disowned Lavington.[32]

John Wesley had also encountered the French Prophets in Bristol. His was a curious position, for since April many in his audiences had been subject to convulsions similar to those of the inspired. Some felt strong pain and had to "roar for the disquietness of their heart," others dissolved into "strong cries and tears." One man suffered a fit as if "fallen raving mad." On June 6, when Wesley visited the prophet Mrs. Cooper, it was with such episodes in recent memory that he remarked, "Her agitations were nothing near so violent as those of Mary Plewit are." Prophet Cooper told Wesley that he was yet in darkness, but the veil would soon lift. Wesley thought "The words were good," and he reserved judgment once again. Later that month he called upon Thomas Whitehead, baptized by the Methodist George Whitefield at Gloucester but still mingling with the French Prophets. Now Wesley appeared to disapprove in general of the group, and at Bristol's Weavers' Hall, he tried to point out the French Prophets in the crowd "and earnestly exhorted all that followed after

---

32. Charles Wesley, *Journal*, I, 147-53; Benham, *Memoirs of James Hutton*, 39; J.K. Foster, *Life and Times of Selina, Countess of Huntingdon* (1840) I, 35-36. The names of Bray and Bowers later appear in Moravian records. See Moravian Church House: MSS Fetter Lane Elders Conference, Minutes, EC 1, Aug. 18, 1743; Minutes of "Elders and Wardens" IA, Jan. **26,** 1742/43; Fetter Lane Diary, II, Aug. 19, 1743 (all dates N.S.).

holiness to avoid, as fire, all who do not speak according 'to the Law and the Testimony.'" The next year in Bristol, Wesley preached against enthusiasts who imagine that they have divine gifts.[33]

The French Prophets did not stop pestering the Methodists. In 1742 they approached both John Wesley and the Calvinist Methodist preacher, Howell Harris (a man also influenced by German pietists). The envoys were received without love. But a Methodist ambivalence toward the French Prophets became evident if it was not so already, for in 1741 Wesley had returned to have tea with Isaac Hollis, and Howell Harris was "humbled much in hearing of one James Cuninghame that went through England, Scotland and Wales preaching in 1710, 1711 and 1712." Wesley chose to visit another prophet in 1746 who denounced the clergy and spoke in poor Latin. Harris occasionally heard reports of the French Prophets and in 1749 visited Isaac Hollis, who showed him the printed warnings of John Lacy. In 1750 John Wesley was reading with approval Lacy's *The General Delusions of Christians*. Wesley's comments reveal the common ground upon which both Methodists and French Prophets could stand. Lacy had defended the Montanists (a second-century Christian prophetic millenarian group) as true Christians, for the French Prophets had often been slightingly compared to them. By reflecting on Lacy's book, wrote Wesley,

> I was fully convinced of what I had long suspected, 1. That the Montanists, in the second and third centuries, were real, scriptural Christians; and 2. That the grand reason why the miraculous gifts were so soon withdrawn, was not only that faith and holiness were well nigh lost; but that dry, formal, orthodox men began even then to ridicule whatever gifts they had not themselves, and to decry them all as either madness or imposture.

Apprehensive of condemning all manifestations of the Spirit as false, and loving the true Christian enthusiast, Wesley condemned the French Prophets but often accepted their tenets. What they had in common was the pietist dissatisfaction with stultified spiritual life among the orthodox and quietist confidence in some flickering internal light.[34]

33. John Wesley, *Journal*, II, 180, 186, 190-91, 214-15, 226-27, 234d; John Wesley, *Standard Sermons*, ed. Edward H. Sugden (7th ed; 1968) II, 92-93 and also 84.
34. John Wesley, *Journal*, II, 440d, 474d, and III, 49-50, 239, 490; Tom Beynon, trans., "Extracts from the Diaries of Howell Harris," *Bathafarn* 9 (1954) 31-37; idem, ed., *Howell Harris's Visits to London* (Aberystwyth, 1960) 47-48, 68, 228; idem, ed., *Howell Harris Reformer and Soldier (1714-1773)* (Caernarvon, 1948) 18; Geoffrey F. Nuttall, *Howell Harris 1714-1773* (Cardiff, 1965) 26-27. For Wesley's condemnations of the French Prophets, see his *Standard Sermons*, II, sermons XXXI, XXVII; *London Magazine* (1760) 652; John Telford, ed., *Letters of John Wesley* (1931) II, 24.

The continental influence absorbed by English followers of the French Prophets made them especially attractive to early Methodists who themselves had Moravian connections. In turn, French Prophets regarded the Moravians as likely converts. There were more than theological and liturgical similarities between them: in the 1740s prophets arose among Moravian societies in England. A Moravian-linked prophet, Ann Lawrence, aroused the religious fervor of many in Wiltshire in 1741, and her auditors succumbed to the agitations characteristic of the French Prophets. In 1742, a Methodist compared the eccentric behavior of the Moravian preacher John Cennick to the antics of the French Prophets. The next year, the ubiquitous Isaac Hollis was conversing earnestly with London Moravians, and the "lazy" Mrs. Inks of Fetter Lane had become a prophet. With such evidence disposing them to believe the Moravian tradition consonant with their own, French Prophets presented themselves at Fetter Lane public services in the summer of 1744. (One missionary was Lydia Sellers, former Methodist.) On July 15, 1744, worshippers in the Moravian chapel heard the muffled voices of inspired women who stood outside, refused entrance. The worshippers paid no heed and preserved themselves in "Stillness and Grace." They were ignoring the last traces of evangelism by a vanishing religious group known as the French Prophets.[35]

It is difficult to gauge the success of the final public testimonies of the dispensation, for there are few remaining records. Thomas Dutton, in a second letter to his Scottish friend in 1740, sounded more sanguine than before. Though Jean Allut, John Potter and Dutton's own son, age nineteen, had all recently died; though few attended the meetings of the inspired in London, since the new prophets had no authority to speak in general assemblies; and though there had been of late little sign of the Spirit, something stirred Dutton to close his letter on a long inspirational note:

> Thus it has pleased God to remove most of those by whom he was pleased In an Eminent Manner to Manifest Himself yet has not left himself without Witness both as to outward appearances and also the Inward Testimony of his Holy

---

35. Benham, *Memoirs of James Hutton*, 153; John Cennick, "Memorable passages relating to the Awakening in Wiltshire which began in the year 1740," *Moravian Messenger* (1874) 10-18, 335-45, 372-79; Moravian Church House: MSS, Diary of the English Provincial Pilgrim House, July 27, 1743-Oct. 30, 1748, trans. by E. Klesel (1905-06) pp. 575-78, 585, 592-95; Minutes of "Elders and Wardens," IA, June 1, 1743; Diary of Fetter Lane Congregation, I, Jan. 10, Feb. 24 and July 7, 1743 (all dates N.S.); John Rylands Library (Manchester), Eng. MSS 897, R. Cruttenden to Mr. Godwin, 9/6/1742, for which reference I thank Prof. John Walsh.

Spirit in the Hearts of the Faithful. Let us not therefore doubt; but he that has begun this Work will Carry it on. And though perhaps not altogether in our way yet so as Shall Certainly accomplish the Glorious Prophecy concerning our Lord's Kingdom.[36]

But the French Prophets had not quite finished their course in 1740 or in 1744. Their meetings in Hatton Gardens and just north, in Clerkenwell, were listed in 1745,[37] and they found at least one new believer in 1746. His name was Benjamin Du Plan, former Multipliant. He had connections with Swiss *inspirés* and pietists, and he had faith that in these last days many would receive the gifts of the Holy Spirit. In London he was occupied with soliciting funds for Huguenot relief on the continent. By 1746 he was frequently the host of the remaining French Prophets. Two years later he angered influential London Huguenots who thought that his relationship with the French Prophets hampered his effectiveness as a fundraiser. Despite his Cévenol background, his association was with the English camp of the French Prophets, and he was most influenced by a Scotsman who prophesied favorable things in Du Plan's future. Cleared of charges of confiscating funds, Du Plan retired to Kentish Town (northeast London) in 1749 and did not marry the Princess Amélie or become King of Scotland.[38]

Some of the faithful survived past mid-century: Jaques and Charles Portales, Francis Wynantz, Isaac Hollis—and Nicolas Fatio, who died in 1753. As late as 1748, Fatio had reaffirmed his beliefs, for Providence, he wrote, had "more and more persuaded me that God manifests himself in our days by the immediate Operation of the Spirit." Charles Portales, writing his will in 1755, made careful provision for his archive on the French Prophets. To his daughter Frances Belchier he left "ten papers and manuscripts kept apart by themselves, both Families [of sons-in-law

36. Dutton-Cuninghame Corr., endpapers, letter of 6/28/1740.
37. *The Universal Pocket Book* (5th ed., 1745), which may simply repeat the list of religious society meetings in William Maitland, *The History of London* (1739) 517. Slightly better evidence for continued activity of French Prophets is in Thomas Chubb, "The Author's Farewell to His Readers," *Posthumous Works* (1748) I, 365n.; George Wilhelm Alberti, *Briefe betreffend den allerneuester Zustand der Religion und der Wissenschaften in Gross-Britannien* (Hanover, 1752) I, 219.
38. D. Bonnefon, *Benjamin Du Plan, Gentleman of Alais* (1878) 139, 248-54; Frederic Gardy, *Correspondance de Jaques Serce*, in *HSL Publications* 43 (1952) 139, 204, 214, which letters are complete in BPUG, Archives du Comité genevois pour le Protestantisme français, C.F. no. 2, liasse E, ff. 137-138e and see also Papiers Court, no. 9, pp. 241-42; Charles Tylor, *The Camisards* (1893) 243, 268, 329-31; BM, Add. MSS 32,799 ff. 33, 105, 335, and Add. MSS 32,802, f. 247. On Du Plan's early connections see A. Germain, *Nouvelles recherches sur la secte des Multipliants* (Montpellier, 1857) 20-25; BCUL, MSS TH 1191 B1 letter 23.

Francis Wynantz and William Belchier] to have the use of them and at last left to their prudence." It was a clear sign of the end of the dispensation when later (how much later?) someone prudently scratched out the names of Moult and Portales from those cherished records of the French Prophets.[39]

The widespread movement for spiritual reform in the early eighteenth century eventually encompassed Calvinist *inspirés* in Languedoc, Lutheran children in Silesia, Protestant separatists in Wetteravia, Episcopalians in Scotland, and devout Anglicans, like the Wesleys, in England. The French Prophets disappeared from view in the midst of an evangelical revival that stretched from Moravia to Georgia, from Bristol to the Rev. Jonathan Edwards's Connecticut Valley. Where the French Prophets left off, Methodism had only begun.

The Female Embassy

The prophets through whom the dispensation finished its course were almost all women. After the deaths of Allut and Potter, the only inspired men are the anonymous prophet visited by John Wesley, and the Scot at the side of Benjamin Du Plan. And the women were new prophets, not simply those who, like Hannah Wharton, had outlived the men of the early years. Mary Plewit, Cooper, Lavington, Lydia Sellers had not been named into tribes or taken part in the assemblies of inspired that promulgated the *Orders*. They appeared in the 1730s and were, in effect, a second generation of followers.

The predominance of female leaders among the last French Prophets was the final enduring impress of pietist and quietist influences. Philadelphians offered the model of devotion to Jane Lead and Sarah Wiltshire. Philadelphians and Scottish quietists shared the venerable images of Antoinette Bourignon and Mme. Guyon. The Scots had formed a community around Mrs. Keith at Montrose. Swiss pietists at Vevey were held together by Mme. de Warens. Unknown to the English, descendants of the Camisards clustered about the prophet Lucrèce at Congénies, turning silent and inward.

By 1715, the climate of relationships between men and women among the French Prophets had shifted. After that, no women were expelled as

---

39. BPUG, MSS fr. 602, f. 182; Stack MSS 12g, notebook with copy of Charles Portales will [PRO, P.C.C. "Simpson" Sept. 18, 1764, 363-64] pp. 20-22; see Stack MSS 1e and 1j for erasures.

false prophets. As English followers accepted Scottish and continental religious forms, female prophets among them were soon granted an equality never apparent among Huguenots. Mary Beer, Hannah Wharton and Mary Keimer achieved an eminence far surpassing that of their nearest French parallels, Elisabeth Charras and Henriette Allut. When Jean Allut opposed Hannah Wharton in the later years, it was an opposition between the Huguenots whose leaders had always been men and the English who had come to be led by women.

Richard Roach in *The Great Crisis* had sensed the "Female Embassy" by which the end of time was blessed. He had in mind the tradition of Bourignon, Guyon, Lead, Rosamunde von Asseburg, Sarah Wiltshire.[40] That tradition continued among the French Prophets after Roach's death. As people in Manchester might have known them in their twilight years, the French Prophets would have been gathered silently around inspired women, awaiting agitations and eager to hear prophecies that combined judgment, instruction and mercy, warnings which jumbled the language of Boehme and Bourignon, Lacy and Wharton.

If, as American Shakers claimed, their Mother Ann Lee transformed a group based upon the French Prophets into the Millennial or Second Christian Church, she would not have had too difficult a task. They shared dispositions, religious beliefs and forms of assembly. They looked back at Christian history from nearly the same perspective. They both knew the appeal of the evangelical revival.

According to the Shaker ministry in Ohio in 1808, the two witnesses chosen by God to prepare the Second Coming and the Second Christian Church were the Quakers and the French Prophets. Both had been faithful and inspired witnesses. The Quakers lost their light as they compromised with secular society. The French Prophets awakened many, and the Spirit in them produced its "principal Effect" upon James and Jane Wardley. The Wardleys, tailors in Bolton near Manchester, had supposedly been Quakers who joined the French Prophets in the 1740s and worshipped thereafter in private. They had visions of the Second Coming, of the downfall of Antichrist, and of the rise of the Church in transcendent glory. The Wardleys moved to Manchester and lived with John Townley, a wealthy bricklayer whose wife rapidly gained the gift of prophecy. By 1747 there had emerged a society of thirty people whose religious work Townley

---

40. Roach, *The Great Crisis*, 97-98, 111. See also Joyce Irwin, "Anna Maria Van Schurman: From Feminism to Pietism," *Church History* 46 (1977) 48-62.

financed. Their manner of worship resembled that of the later French Prophets:

> Sometimes after assembling together and sitting a while in silent meditation, they were taken with a mighty trembling, under which they would express the indignation of God against all sin. At other times they were affected, under the power of God, with a mighty shaking; and were occasionally exercised in singing, shouting or walking the floor, under the influence of spiritual signs, shoving each other about,—or swiftly passing and repassing each other like clouds agitated by a mighty wind.[41]

In 1758, at the age of twenty-two, the unlettered Ann Lee joined the Wardley society. She had worked in a cotton factory, then as a cutter of hatters' fur, then as a cook in the Manchester infirmary. Married in 1762 to an Anglican blacksmith, Ann Lee arrived at powerful spiritual insights by the end of 1766, after her fourth child (as had all three earlier) died in infancy. She experienced a conversion in which her soul broke forth to God, "which I felt as sensibly as ever a woman did a child, when she was delivered of it." Convinced that celibacy and moral discipline were the true paths to salvation, she became more active in the group. As relatives of Townley and her own friends and family joined the group, Ann Lee began to direct the Shakers, for she had the greatest "light and power of God." Like Jane Wardley before, Ann Lee was called Mother, and Shakers began to confess their sins to her, since they could not "rest short of complete salvation from all sin." Each dispensation had its own church forms; the Shakers distinguished theirs by restoring the primitive confession of sins.[42]

What truly distinguished the Shakers, however, was the work of God in

---

41. [Benjamin S. Youngs], *The Testimony of Christ's Second Appearing* (Lebanon, Ohio, 1808; approved by the Shaker ministry) 18-21, quoted or paraphrased by most later works on the Shakers. Edward Deming Andrews and Faith Andrews, *The People Called Shakers* (new ed.; New York, 1963) add some detail on the early history of the Shakers, most of which had already been supplied by William E.A. Axon, *Lancashire Gleanings* (Manchester, 1883). I have been unable to confirm any Wardley attachment to the Quakers or the French Prophets. Cf. Mary L. Richmond, *Shaker Literature: A Bibliography* (Hanover, 1977) xix, and entry 1469.

42. Andrews and Andrews, *People Called Shakers*, 4-9; [Youngs], *Testimony*, 20,22; Axon, *Lancashire Gleanings*, 82, 156, 160, 181; Thomas Brown, *An Account of the People called Shakers* (Troy, 1812) 312; F.W. Evans, *Ann Lee* (4th ed.; 1858?) 111, 116. On the confession of sins, see esp. New York Public Library, MSS, Angell Matthewson Reminiscences, Letter III (1782). The new followers included John Partington and John Hocknell, whose supposed French Prophet and Methodist connections I cannot confirm, although there was a Methodist Mary Hocknell in the Chester Circuit in 1790, and John Hocknell did have a daughter Mary: Francis F. Bretherton, *Early Methodism in and around Chester 1749-1812* (Chester, 1903) 276.

Mother Ann Lee, for the marriage of the Lamb had come and with it a new covenant and a new spiritual woman. Arrested and imprisoned for willfully disturbing the congregation of Christ Church, Manchester, Ann Lee met and merged with the Spirit while in prison. Released from her cell, as before she had been released from childbearing, she announced what was in effect her second conversion, for now she was Ann the Word, Christ's spiritual bride. Quakers and French Prophets had had hints of a new covenant, but only through Ann Lee was woman restored to her original equality with man. Thus humankind could at last attain perfection, celibate and pure, for divinity had been invested in a woman as well as in a man.[43]

Although Shakers found precedents for most of their own beliefs, including the doctrine of spiritual perfection,[44] they did not search for precedents to their attitude toward Ann Lee. The tradition from which the French Prophets drew much of their later rhetoric and theology was not incompatible with the image of a new spiritual woman. Antoinette Bourignon, Jane Lead and the Philadelphian Gichtel (translator of Jakob Boehme) had affirmed the importance of Adam's original androgyneity and the necessary spiritual equality of the sexes. Boehme's works were themselves not hidden from the Manchester public. In 1752 Joseph Harrop, editor of the *Manchester Mercury*, was printing by subscription Boehme's *The Way to Christ Discovered* and hoped to print others of Boehme's writings. Richard Roach was even closer than Boehme to Shaker theology when he wrote in *The Great Crisis* that females who before had tempted man to his fall would now tempt and "draw the Male Upwards, in Order to the Recovery of Paradise again, even on earth."[45]

---

43. [Youngs], *Testimony*, 440 *et passim*; Andrews and Andrews, *People Called Shakers*, 11-12, who note as American antecedents of the Shaker celibate community the colony of Johannes Kelpius and the Ephrata order founded by Johann Konrad Beissel. Kelpius and his pietist "true Rosicrucians" had stayed with the Philadelphians in London in 1694; Beissel was a schismatic from the major party of German Baptist Brethren at Schwarzenau; both groups have been noted in connection with Johanna Christina Zeidig.

44. Brown, *Account of the People Called Shakers*, 309. John and Charles Wesley had excoriated the French Prophet Lavington for espousing this doctrine, and it was one of the doctrines which caused their split with the Moravians.

45. Serge Hutin, *Les disciples anglais de Jacob Boehme aux XVIIe et XVIIIe siècles* (Paris, 1960) 19, 27; Thune, **Behmenists and Philadelphians**, 122; Roach, *The Great Crisis*, 97; *Manchester Mercury*, March 13 and May 4, 1752, advertisements. Androgyneity in the godhead or in the original human state had also been postulated by Jewish mystics and the Cambridge Platonists, the latter supposing that souls are born of the marriage of the Father with the Word. The prophet Joanna Southcott would by 1800 make public her belief in the feminine counterpart to the Immortal Father. Walker, *Decline of Hell*, 115-16; Désirée Hirst,

By returning to the archetype of the androgyne, Ann Lee resolved those sexual tensions which underlay the French Prophets' earlier fears of powerful inspired women. The complete human was celibate because spiritually whole; sexuality was no longer a threat because entirely dissociated from the body. The ritual of confession was a means toward a purer desire for the purer Spirit. The Mother of the Shakers struck a balance between the ethos of judgment and the ethos of pentecost, restoring a primitive family where lines of authority were clear and purity essential, yet modelling behavior upon the companionship of trance and contemplation. The image of the androgyne was also the image of the healed person in a healed world, and it was this evangel that Ann Lee and seven followers took with them to America on the ship *Mariah* in 1774.

If the Shakers belong to the history of the French Prophets, they belong as much to the first Desert of virginal *petits prophètes* eliciting confessions as they do to the Birmingham of Hannah Wharton weighing the wealth of the New Jerusalem against the authenticity of the person.[46] Ann Lee was the virgin whose purity gave force to inspirations in the Desert, the mother in whose embracing wisdom Jane Lead found Sophia, the lover in whose marriage to the Spirit Elizabeth Gray and John Lacy found the Morning Star. Hannah Wharton had not claimed to be more than a teacher and administrator in the New Jerusalem; the code and architecture of the spiritual world were to some degree still inaccessible to her. Ann Lee widened the entry into the New Jerusalem, for what she promised was the secret of her self. Earlier prophets had given James Cuninghame and Sir Richard Bulkeley proof of their divine mission by seeing into their souls. Ann Lee offered to disclose her own invested humanity. It was the hope for spiritual perfection that powered the confessions of Shakers, and it had been the absence of such intimate disclosure that made the French Prophets so terrified of false inspiration. Not until the 1730s did the French Prophets constantly identify the lagging of the millennium with their own personal unpreparedness; before, they had seen the end delayed by a doubting world, each delay an outward test of their perhaps faltering but accurate faith.[47]

Hidden Riches: Traditional Symbolism from the Renaissance to Blake (1964) 41, 165-72; R.A. Baldwin, *The Jezreelites* (Orpington, 1962) 12, 40. On the social and theological functions of androgyneity as a religious image, see Wayne A. Meeks, "The Image of the Androgyne: Some Uses of a Symbol in Earliest Christianity," *History of Religions* 13 (1974) 165-208.

46. See *A Relation of Several Hundreds of Children and Others that Prophesie and Preach in their Sleep* (1689) 3.

47. As a group the French Prophets never fully developed an apparatus for confession,

Since 1709 the French Prophets had had to come to terms with the passage of a time that always seemed pregnant with apocalypse. French followers had sought to sustain the group by adding to its numbers through continental missions. In the 1730s they had given up this desire for a public sign of victory and sought instead to renew the group internally by reference back to their historical Cévenol origins. The English followers had sought to reassure themselves of the validity of the message through the *Orders* and assemblies of prophets. In the 1730s, influenced by quietist and pietist ideas, they knew that waiting was the root metaphor of religious experience.

Continental religious forces had guided the French Prophets to a new understanding of the millennial timetable. Accustomed to a ritual waiting in worship, to a slow internship through the stages of illumination, to images of growth rather than cataclysm, they coordinated the millennium with internal rather than external events. Hannah Wharton had therefore come to teach, to show the road. Ann Lee, however, came to confide, to explain that the internal event upon which the millennium hinged had happened in her. The waiting was over.

---

either of sins or of the experience of grace. Since it was assumed by the group that those who were truly inspired were also on the path to salvation, prophecy became a prime vehicle for attesting to one's spiritual state, and public defense of the prophets became a prime vehicle for individual narratives of conversion. But there was little opportunity for the confession of sins within the group, even when the assemblies of the inspired assumed the policing role, so prophecy could and did result in a series of assertions and counter-assertions difficult to resolve because they hinged as much on the spiritual state of the prophet as on the tenor of the inspirations themselves. The group had no lower-level apparatus by which error might be dealt with separately from the threatening problems of false prophecy and mistaken eschatology. Quietist insistence on grades and stages of spiritual growth did provide some mechanisms for the defusing of error, but quietist ceremony, unlike Shaker ceremony, tended to drive the celebrants back into themselves and into self-doubt. The use of confession as a legitimating device was, in Protestant worlds, characteristic of early puritan and later revivalist movements, both Methodist and Shaker. It would also be characteristic of late eighteenth-century romantic autobiographies, in which self-exposure is a means to redemption. See esp. Jerald C. Brauer, "Conversion: From Puritanism to Revivalism," *Journal of Religion* 58 (1978) 227-43; John Bossy, "Holiness and Society," *Past and Present* 75 (1977) 124-25. Cf. Paul Delany, *British Autobiography in the Seventeenth Century* (London and New York, 1969); Georges Gusdorf, "Conditions et limites de l'autobiographie," in G. Reichenkron, ed., *Formen der Selbstdarstellung* (Berlin, 1956) 105-23; J.R. Jacob, *Robert Boyle and the English Revolution* (New York, 1977) 41-42; Thomas C. Oden, *The Intensive Group Experience: The New Pietism* (Philadelphia, 1972), which argues cogently for a close parallel between pietist *collegia*, Methodist band meetings, and modern encounter groups.

CHAPTER VII

Seekers, Citizens, Scientists

From first inspiration to last, more than five hundred people became French Prophets.[1] What disposed each of them to join the group? What conditioned their sympathies for new prophecy and millenarian promises? I have devoted the last four chapters to the French Prophets as a religious group. In this chapter I look at individual biographies. What follows is inadequate. I cannot do justice to the complex personalities of those for whom I have much information, and the obscure suffer as always from the monochrome of statistics.[2] I can only suggest alternatives that may account, though never completely, for the faith of believers. Whatever alternatives I propose, I am not the hunter of a wounded animal: I have not assumed that millenarian beliefs are the product of spiritual malaise, socioeconomic deprivation or psychological festering.[3] On the other hand,

---

1. See appendix I for all followers in Great Britain (including also Johanna Christina Zeidig and those who had definite English ties—Furly, the Jurieus, Doladille, etc.). Adding anonymous references, there may have been as many as 600 followers. On the continent were another 50 to 75 sympathizers, most of them men.

2. A few followers have found biographers: Charles A. Domson, "Nicolas Fatio de Duillier and the Prophets of London," Ph.D. thesis, Yale University, 1972; Frank E. Manuel, *A Portrait of Isaac Newton* (Cambridge, Mass., 1968) ch. 9 on Fatio; Julius F. Sachse, *Benjamin Furly* (Philadelphia, 1895); Stephen Bloore, "Samuel Keimer: A Footnote to the Life of Franklin," *Pennsylvania Magazine of History and Biography* 54 (1930) 255-87, and in the same journal, C. Lennart Carlson, "Samuel Keimer: A Study in the Transit of English Culture to Colonial Pennsylvania," 61 (1937) 357-86; George D. Henderson, *Chevalier Ramsay* (Edinburgh, 1952).

3. On deprivation theories, see esp. Norman Cohn, *The Pursuit of the Millennium* (3rd ed.; 1970); Vittorio Lanternari, *The Religions of the Oppressed*, trans. Lisa Sergio (1963); David F. Aberle, "A Note on Relative Deprivation Theory as Applied to Millenarian and other Cult Movements," in Sylvia Thrupp, ed., *Millennial Dreams in Action* (New York, 1970) 209-14.

people who feel uncomfortable may seek comfort through religious means. There is evidence to support both positive and negative definitions of the faith of French Prophets.

The Seekers

The reader has already been introduced to believers who led their spiritual lives in a series of different religious settings. James Jackson (Independent turned Quaker), Isaac Hollis (Baptist, Philadelphian), Johanna Christina Zeidig (pietist, Moravian) became French Prophets at one time in their long spiritual quest. They were seekers. They had a personal history of shifting allegiances, a habit of spiritual transfer.[4] Another seeker was Marie Sterrill, originally Huguenot, who with her husband had been among the inner core of Philadelphians. After her husband's death she joined the Quakers, moving within short periods to three different Friends' meetings. By 1708 she was among the French Prophets but the next year chose to follow the prophet Anna Angibert into apostasy.[5] Samuel Keimer was another experienced seeker. Educated as a Presbyterian, influenced by the Independent minister Joseph Jacobs, Keimer became a Baptist, wandering from congregation to congregation. At nineteen he became a French Prophet and retained his faith for nearly ten years. In debtors' prison at the instance of several fellow believers, Keimer verged on Catholicism and soon after, again in prison, announced his conversion to Quakerism. He was not yet thirty years old.[6] At least fourteen followers belonged to three or more religious societies in the course of their lives.[7]

This sort of seeking does little to explain the particular attractions of the French Prophets. But there was another sort of seeking among believers which carries more explanatory force. Some believers were disposed to

---

4. Cf. William R. Catton, Jr., "What Kind of People Does a Religious Cult Attract?" *American Sociological Review* 22 (1957) 561-66; John Lofland, *Doomsday Cult* (Englewood Cliffs, 1966) 7-10; H.T. Dohrman, *California Cult* (Boston, 1958) 102-19; Robert W. Balch and David Taylor, "Seekers and Saucers: The Role of the Cultic Milieu in Joining a UFO Cult," *American Behavioral Scientist* 20 (1977) 839-60.

5. Bodleian, Rawlinson MSS D. 832, f. 95, and D. 833, f. 92; Friends' House Library, MSS, Wandsworth Monthly Meeting Minutes, I, 4th of 10th month, 1706, and 1st of 11th month, 1706/07, and also St. Albans Monthly Meeting Minutes for 1703-24, 1st of 9th month, 1706; Fatio Calendar, 7/21-7/27/1709. A book by "Mary Sterrell" was entitled *A New Years Gift, or a Token of Love to all Persons of what Perswasion soever*: advert., Philadelphus, *State of the Philadelphian Society* (1692) 32.

6. *Brand*, 76-104, and Keimer's *A Search After Religion* (1716?) 9-14.

7. Seven men and seven women, numbers 48, 49, 50, 61, 62, 82, 156, 166, 181, 186, 189, 505, 510, 519 in Appendix I (later allegiances not listed).

examine all events in a spiritual light. Sir Richard Bulkeley was one such; in a moment of nostalgia, he wrote, "When I was a Child and bred up under a Religious Grandmother who took Occasion from everything to discourse of Providence or other Religious Subjects, I remember her to have often said when the hedges were full of haws, *See the good Providence of God which provided so great store for the birds against a hard winter*."[8] How many followers had this upbringing I do not know,[9] but Bulkeley had one thing in common with others of the same disposition, such as Nicolas Fatio, James Cuninghame and John Lacy. In each of their lives, illness played a major role, leading them to seek the meaning behind daily providences. Like the Reverend John Mason, the prophet Barbara Cadell, William Freke the "Great Elijah," all of whom underwent a "divine sickness" before changing their spiritual course, Fatio, Lacy, Cuninghame and the Lady Jean Forbes had survived illnesses which deeply affected their religious outlook.[10] The physical crisis was a prelude to spiritual conversion and change in behavior: Fatio, previously a sceptic, absorbed himself in scripture prophecies; Lacy, Cuninghame and Forbes, within months of recovery, became prophets. For Sir Richard Bulkeley, humpbacked, afflicted with sciatica, "hectic fevers" and gonorrhea, life was perpetual crisis. He was the model of the hypochondriac, struggling with headaches or fevers one day in three, often bedridden, writing to his physician Dr. Martin Lister, "It will be in vain for me to complain to you of my great want of health, [since] you are resolved to believe it to be only fancy; but I that feel it know it to be real." Reframed, was this not one of his arguments in favor of the French Prophets? In 1697 he felt so ill "that except in some Intervals I am become a useless Creature, with a *jactitatio* and *anxietas mentis* for whole days together." Worried about his blurred

    8. Bodleian, MSS Lister 36, f. 44, letter of 2/15/1693.
    9. I cannot determine whether many followers had a heritage of "left-wing" Christianity. Timothy Byfield was the son of a moderate Presbyterian and nephew of a puritan divine (*DNB*, III, 565); Isaac Owen was probably a son of the Presbyterian minister James Owen (1654-1706) and grandson of an Anglican royalist (Charles Owen, *Some Account of... Mr. James Owen [1709]*; *Brand*, 38); Sir Richard Bulkeley was the great-grandson of the Archbishop of Dublin, Lancelot Bulkeley (1568-1650) and the grandson of Archdeacon William Bulkeley, and his father had been a pious man who read church service in house twice each day: *DNB*, III, 231; *HMC* 36: Ormonde, new ser. VII, 19-20.
    10. *DNB*, VII, 687 (Freke); Lambeth Palace, MSS 953 f. 124 (Cadell); John Mason, *The Angels Oath* (1694) 34; Manuel, *Portrait of Newton*, 194, 199-202 (Fatio); Kingston, I, 39 (Lacy) confirmed by Edmund Calamy, *An Historical Account of My Own Life*, ed., John T. Rutt (1829) I, 94-95; NLS, MS/493/73, letters of 5/21 and 6/5/1709 (Cuninghame and Forbes). Sir Joseph Tiley was also quite ill when he met the French Prophets: Isaac Newton, *The Correspondence*, eds. H.W. Turnbull, J.F. Scott, A. Rupert Hall and Laura Tilling (Cambridge, 1959-78) IV, 501.

vision, he pleaded with the imperturbable Lister, "as a friend and as a Christian I entreat your Answer, i.e., your judgment, whether this Symptom be fatal."[11]

No wonder that Bulkeley would testify on behalf of the healing powers of the inspired, or that cures would be described so meticulously by John Lacy. Physical healing had spiritual reverberations, and those miraculously cured often became believers—James Jackson, Hugh Preston, John Moult (brother of Francis), William Spong, Sir Joseph Tiley.[12] It was not simply the powers of the prophets or the relief of illness that brought these healed men into the group; it was also the spiritual drama of the cure. The experience of physical disruption and restoration could contribute positively to an awareness of the spiritual side of life. Prophecy and miracle promised to meet the desire for an understanding of that providence through which one had been so singularly blessed. When Cuninghame recovered at the waters of Bath, he had written, "I know not if I make myself understood, but I'm persuaded that this new Lease of Life is given me for some particular End and I can't hinder myself often to beg of my blessed Redeemer to let me know it."[13]

Some seekers, then, were on a mission to discover the perfect religious society. Others, healed, purified, found in the French Prophets the meaning of their renewed sense of mission.

The Citizens

Too obvious, too banal, yet of all socioeconomic factors most demonstrable, a pre-existing web of social relationships underlay the group. Probably half of all followers had personal relationships with other followers that pre-dated their association with the French Prophets. Either by kinship or marriage, by business compacts or previous religious life, the normal follower had a good chance of finding an acquaintance, relative or spouse already in the group. Endogamous marriages, business enterprises, shared lodgings and the terms of wills sustained this network as the French Prophets expanded.[14]

Personal relationships were an important source of group integrity.

---

11. Bodleian, MSS Lister 3, ff. 35, 38-42, 46-48, 51-52, 54, and MSS Lister 36, ff. 44v., 182-182v., 213-14.

12. John Lacy, *A Relation of the Dealings of God* (1708) 24-27; Sir Richard Bulkeley, *An Answer to Several Treatises lately published on the Subject of the Prophets* (1708) 210-14.

13. NLS, MS/493/73, letter of 5/21/1709.

14. The wills of Francis Moult, F.-M. Misson, Joseph Tovey and Charles Portales mentioned twenty other French Prophets. Cf. Lofland, *Doomsday Cult*, 60.

Most of the prophets expelled or excluded from meetings—and all of the prominent female false prophets—had few discernible relationships with other followers. Ultimately, however, personal bonds may have been the undoing of the group. Except for Nicolas Fatio and Charles Portales, Huguenot and English followers did not mix socially. Never was the group as a social whole more than an amalgam of cliques, affines and religious affiliates. That the French Prophets did not erect an extensive theological system or a standard initiation ceremony was symbolic of their inability to unify membership. The boundaries of the group, carefully patrolled on the perimeters of the inspired, remained vague beyond. For an individual believer, the lack of definition might lead to anxieties over one's status—anxieties forestalled by adopting a specific role in the group (scribe, host, missionary) and moving closer to the center. Or, peripheral imprecision could be exploited by those like Richard Roach who had concurrent membership in several religious societies. Lack of integration implied that loyalty to the group need not subsume personal loyalties.

The separate networks of personal relationships proved more decisive in the eventual decline of the French Prophets than any differences between members of conflicting millenarian ethos. Indeed, with regard to age, wealth, social status and sexual composition, there was a remarkable homogeneity between Huguenot and English followers. What the French Prophets could not overcome were the knots of personal loyalty, rooted in cultural differences.

However detrimental in retrospect, personal bonds were in the beginning a major appeal of the French Prophets. For Huguenot refugees, the French Prophets might reduce the emotional isolation of exile. The group could mediate between life in the large city and life in the countryside for those who found themselves awkwardly placed in a foreign urban environment. By scheduling a continuous series of intimate social events in which people could assume that they shared many feelings and hopes, the French Prophets might blunt the sharp transition from rural to urban, from cottage to tenement, from feudal obligations to window taxes, from village temple or Desert assembly to bickering churches five minutes' walk apart. It was not so much exile *per se* as the fact of exile in London which established the appeal of French Prophet assemblies. Huguenots in the smaller towns of Norwich, Canterbury and Bristol paid little attention to the Camisard *inspirés* in England. Most Huguenot believers might have been comfortable in towns the size of Bristol or more likely Canterbury (pop. 10,000), but only Pierre Allix, his wife, and the Missons, familiar with Paris, had any extended acquaintance with a city comparable in size to

London (pop. 575,000). Perhaps a third to a half of Huguenot believers came from very small towns or villages in Languedoc and Dauphiné, had been in London five years or less by 1706, and lived in crowded Spitalfields. For them especially, the French Prophets could play a supportive role, in the manner of mutual benefit societies or similar lay fellowships conspicuously absent from the London refugee community.[15]

Not all Huguenot followers, many of whom adjusted well and independently to London commercial life, needed the French Prophets as a provincial confraternity.[16] But the group could function as a community of friends for many who had other reasons to believe themselves in exile— Scottish quietists whose Episcopalian church had been disestablished after 1689, English dissenters whose legal privileges were constantly threatened with new restrictions, and the followers whose claims to scientific prowess were slighted. Quietists, dissenters and scientists, however, had other and equally convenient alternatives for sympathetic gatherings. The possibly exclusive reliance of recent emigrants from Languedoc and Dauphiné upon the French Prophets for mutual reassurance may explain the tenacity of Desert images in the history of the French Prophets.

Of no less importance to the English than to the Huguenots was the group's ability to attenuate the problems of life in an increasingly urban society. The French Prophets met in London during an era when the city commanded ten per cent of the nation's population and most of the nation's finances; prophets dispersed on missions through England at a time when smaller cities and market towns were coming to dominate the distribution of food, clothing and information in the countryside. Although the majority of English people still lived in country settlements of five hundred inhabitants or less, these too felt the impact of urban growth as middlemen weaseled themselves between farmers, weavers and the marketplace, as field enclosures spread in widening circles around urban areas, and as urban tastes shaped consumption patterns.[17]

15. Of the 55 Huguenot believers for whom I have data, 27 came from Languedoc and Dauphiné; this is significant, since most London refugees came from northwestern France (Normandy, Brittany, Picardy, Guienne): Charles Weiss, *History of the French Protestant Refugees*, trans. H.W. Herbert (New York, 1854) I, 248-49. On differences between rural and urban cultures, see Charles Tilly, *The Vendée* (Cambridge, Mass., 1968) 16-26, 53-65; John B. Holt, "Holiness Religion: Cultural Shock and Social Reorganization," *American Sociological Review* 5 (1940) 740-47.

16. The Misson circle of followers, for example, had a wealthy community of their own which they transposed into the group. Most of them had come from Normandy and had been in England longer than other refugee believers, so they had had time to establish themselves.

17. P.G.M. Dickson, *The Financial Revolution in England* (1967) 11, 32; Alan Everitt, "Food Market of the English Town, 1660-1760," *Third International Conference of Economic*

If the French Prophets were primarily an urban phenomenon, and if the large majority of English believers were born in London, Bristol and Birmingham, this did not mean that they sponsored the culture of the city.[18] From their warnings against worldly sophistication, city vanities and scepticism, and from their exasperation with and judgments upon London, there emerges an image of the French Prophets as advocates of rural or pastoral values. Followers responded to the *Cry from the Desart* not as satisfied citizens but as city dwellers who wanted London to be something other than it was. English believers seemed to hope that the Desert would bloom in and transform London. John Lacy, reared in the small Essex village of Saffron Walden, described the New Jerusalem as "no noisy City; no dirty one. Canals and Walks abound in her." He glimpsed the millennial kingdom in a "delicious Prospect of florid Fields and stately Buildings in a fine Country," and the Lord's mansion was surrounded by gardens. The New Jerusalem had "No hurtful Air, no Thief, no Beast, no Nauseous Insect," and the True Church resembled a "fruitful Garden thick planted, and everything thriving in it."[19] The most prominent London meetings took place in Baldwins Gardens and Hatton Gardens, adjoining neighborhoods of the city in which the well-to-do attempted to lead a country life and where lived at least nine of the French Prophets, among them the prestigious Francis Moult, Richard Roach, Charles Portales, Rebecca Critchlow and Abraham Whitrow. Sir Richard Bulkeley on his estates in Ireland and in Surrey experimented with dozens of varieties of plants and trees in his well-tended orchards; Nicolas Fatio wrote a mathematical treatise on the construction of fruit-walls to give fruit trees maximum sunlight.[20] Fatio and the Alluts moved to Worcester,

---

History (Paris, 1968) 57-71; H.J. Habakkuk, "English Landownership, 1680-1740," *Economic History Review* 10 (1940) 2-17; Gordon Philpot, "Enclosure and Population Growth in Eighteenth-Century England," *Explorations in Economic History* 12 (1975) 29-46; Ray B. Westerfield, "Middlemen in English Business, Particularly Between 1660 and 1760," *Transactions of the Connecticut Academy of Arts and Sciences* 19 (1915) 111-445; Peter Laslett, *The World We Have Lost* (New York, 1965) 55-57; David Ogg, *England in the Reigns of James II and William III* (2nd ed.; Oxford, 1966) 405.

18. A few English believers had been born in the countryside—Thomas Dutton, John Lacy, Timothy Byfield and probably Abraham Whitrow—but all had taken up residence in London before 1700. There is a basic bias in my data, for I know less about country followers, and nothing at all about anonymous believers in Norfolk, Suffolk and Wiltshire.

19. Lacy, *Warnings*, II, 63-64, 69-70, 73-74. Cf. Arthur J. Weitzman, "Eighteenth-Century London: Urban Paradise or Fallen City," *Journal of the History of Ideas* 36 (1975) 469-80.

20. Bodleian Library (Oxford), MSS Lister 3, f. 51, and MSS Lister 35, f. 116, and MSS Lister 36, f. 61; Fatio, *Fruit-Walls Improved By Inclining Them to the Horizon* (1699).

at the end of Foregate Street, with open country and orchards on their doorstep. These are hints that believers other than Cévenol refugees might have come to the French Prophets with the desire to preserve contact with the countryside, or with what they imagined the pastoral life to be.

Yearnings of London citizens were conditioned by economic factors. The French Prophets, especially scribes and hosts, were generally people of substance: prosperous artisans, innkeepers, apothecaries, merchants, professional men and gentlefolk.[21] With the exception of John Lacy, Thomas Dutton, Sir Richard Bulkeley and most Scottish followers, their wealth came from the city, not from land but from commerce and investment in securities, from professional and mercantile activities which in their prevalence distinguished the city from the village and London from all other cities. In an epoch when country gentlemen could scarcely hold their own against large landowners and when minor gentry were, like Lacy, slipping away from their landed tenures, the wealthier French Prophets represented the new urban gentry.[22] "How unlike an Ambassador of God," wrote Samuel Keimer of Francis Moult, but how like a leisured city gentleman for Moult to build "a costly magnificent House" and adorn his garden with naked statues.[23] Although none of the French Prophets could lay claim to membership in the emerging urban patriciate that would govern England in the eighteenth century, the wealthier believers could pose as elegant hosts and patrons, recreating open spaces for the Lord's audiences in a closed city.[24]

Connections within the group reflected a discrimination of status

21. See Appendix IV, which is designed to correspond to Table 4 in Richard T. Vann, *The Social Development of English Quakerism, 1655-1755* (Cambridge, Mass., 1969) 59-60.

22. On the decline of the lesser gentry and the appearance of urban "pseudogentry," see Alan Everitt, "Social Mobility in Early Modern England," *Past and Present* 33 (1966) 56-73; Christopher Clay, "The Price of Freehold Land in the Later Seventeenth and Eighteenth Century," *Economic History Review*, 2nd ser., 27 (1974) 173-89, and idem, "Marriage, Inheritance, and the Rise of Large Estates in England, 1660-1815," *Economic History Review*, 2nd ser., 21 (1968) 503-18; J.P. Cooper, "Social Distribution of Land and Men in England, 1436-1700," *Economic History Review*, 2nd ser., 20 (1967) 428; F.M.L. Thompson, "The Social Distribution of Landed Property in England since the 17th Century," *Economic History Review*, 2nd ser., 19 (1966) 505-17; Habakkuk, *op. cit.*; Keith Wrightson, "Aspects of Social Differentiation in Rural England, c. 1580-1660," *Journal of Peasant Studies* 5 (1977) 33-47; G.E. Mingay, *The Gentry: The Rise and Fall of a Ruling Class* (1976).

23, *Brand*, 113-14.

24. The wealthiest non-noble follower may have been Jeanne Perrot, who died worth more than £3700. Charles Portales's daughter Frances married into the urban patriciate; her banker husband was M.P. for Southwark, William Belchier. PRO, Prob. 11.622, f. 158, Jean Perrott will, 1728; Stack MSS 12g, page 6. On the urban patriciate, see J.H. Plumb, *The Growth of Political Stability in England 1675-1725* (1967).

PLATE VIII. Pastel portrait of Nicolas Fatio de Duillier (artist unknown), from BPUG Salle des estampes.

pertinent to the gentry model. The most elaborate connections (Misson, Fatio, Moult-Portales) uniformly encompassed the higher levels of French Prophet society. By and large the poor had no visible ties with other than their immediate family unless, like Anne Steed, they had former religious friendships. If a baronet rubbed shoulders with watermen and weavers in prophetic assemblies, if wealthy ladies met shopmaids and servants as equals before the Lord, the prosperous and the impoverished did not meet together outside of the ritual contexts. When Bulkeley upset the balance between spiritual equality and social hierarchy, he and the woolcomber were repudiated—and by whom? by the English gentlemen-prophets John Lacy and Thomas Dutton.

The French Prophets appealed to Huguenots and English, to rich and poor, on basically the same terms, as an entrancing image of rural vitality and as a rare social opportunity. The leisured and the laboring followers responded to prophecy in different ways and with different roles, but for each the promise of the millennium was a promise of return or renewal. Other factors combined to make the leisured numerically superior, for they had more time to devote to the group, more effective ways of sustaining relationships within the group, and more resources to defend themselves from social reprisals by enemies. Socioeconomic deprivation could in practice work against popular chiliasm as much as it might in theory inspire millennial dreams.[25]

Due not only to the demands of their trades or stations but also to the demands of London life, most French Prophets, of whatever economic standing, were literate. Richard Roach, in the capsule biographies footnoting his satiric poem on the wedding of Lacy and Gray, thought Elizabeth Hughes's illiteracy remarkable enough to record as a distinctive personal trait; widow Hughes was the only adult follower I know to have been illiterate. The prevailing literacy of believers was characteristic of London citizens and had bearing upon their approach to the French Prophets.[26]

The Desert experience had been above all an oral and visual experience. Prophecy, the singing of psalms, memorized prayers and sermons had not demanded literacy. Londoners had the urban propensity for written records, publicity and printing. The people who became followers were impressed by the oral tradition of the Desert. Only in London did people act methodically to preserve on paper the Camisard tales; the *Théâtre sacré*, the memoirs of Mazel and Marion, the Historical Relation with its account of persecution in the Cévennes were compiled and carefully edited

25. Gary Schwartz, *Sect Ideologies and Social Status* (Chicago, 1972) suggests that attitudes toward and experiences of socioeconomic mobility are important factors in millenarian outlook. The economic status of believers before they became French Prophets is interesting but follows no pattern. Charles Portales, Francis Moult, Timothy Byfield had become wealthier, Pierre Valette and John Glover had just fallen bankrupt. *Brand, passim*; *London Gazette*, No. 4302 (Jan. 30-Feb. 3, 1707) and No. 4305 (Feb. 10-13, 1707) on Glover, and No. 4343 (June 23-26, 1707) on Valette.

26. Forty per cent of male followers and thirteen per cent of female followers left behind proof of literacy beyond that of simple alphabetism. On literacy in England, see chapter 2, footnote 77. On oral versus literate cultures, see Jack Goody and Ian Watt, "The Consequences of Literacy," in Jack Goody, ed., *Literacy in Traditional Societies* (Cambridge, 1968) 27-68; Henri-Jean Martin, "Culture écrite et culture orale, culture savante et culture populaire dans la France d'Ancien Régime," *Journal des savants* sér. 5 (1975) 225-82; Walter J. Ong, "World as View and World as Event," in Paul Shepard and Daniel McKinley, eds., *Environ/mental: Essays on the Planet as a Home* (Boston, 1971) 61-79; Elizabeth Eisenstein, *The Printing Press as an Agent of Change*, 2 vols., (Cambridge, 1979).

PLATE IX. Francis Moult.

Reproduction by Photographia (Cheapside) Ltd. from a miniature in the Stack Collection.

in London. The early prophecies of Fage, Cavalier and Marion were transcribed by at least two secretaries, and the prophetic words (to be sure, the Lord's Word, but with a haunting Cévenol timbre) were treated with caution and reverence. As if they had found scarce country birds singing in their city gardens or on tenement roofs, people hurried to witness the auspicious omens, signs perhaps of a spiritual urban renewal. For those who became believers, even the impoverished French of many warnings was evidence of purity and the simplicity of the countryside.[27]

The first divine commands to print warnings were issued not in the Cévennes but in London. The transition from Camisard *inspiré* to French Prophet involved a transition from an oral culture to a nation of readers.

27. See, e.g., *An Impartial Account of the Prophets* (1708) 8.

PLATE X. Charles Portales, age 63.
Reproduction by Photographia (Cheapside) Ltd. from a miniature in the Stack Collection.

Seldom had the Desert Huguenots pored over written prophecies from Camisard *inspirés*, but people in England and Scotland could read the prophecies of John Lacy and James Cuninghame and never hear them speak.[28]

Yet how many became believers upon the reading of a book? With their missions and public assemblies, the French Prophets aimed at personal contact and affirmed that religion did not come from books. Although the intellectual truth of prophecy might be captured by the printed work, its

---

28. Some Camisard prayers did circulate in written form, and perhaps a few prophecies: *MMM*, 215; Philippe Joutard and Henri Manen, *Une foi enracinée: La Pervenche* (Valence, 1972) 64-78. See Philippe Joutard, *La légende des Camisards. Une sensibilité au passé* (Paris, 1977) for an extended discussion of oral tradition in the Cévennes, 281 ff.

visual and verbal impact was dulled. So the French Prophets struggled to convey, in little prefaces describing the tone of voice and the nature of the gestures, the physical aspect of the prophecies which were printed. Their attempt to set the scenes for many of the published warnings was an example of the importance they assigned to the physical act of prophecy. There was some necessary balance to be fixed between the remote word and the personal witness, just as one must assay scripture with inner spiritual experience. To some followers, the agitated prophets were exciting signs that vital physical religion could survive in an urban, book-bound culture.

The most literate of the French Prophets, those who had gone to grammar school and to university, were especially concerned to stress experimental religion. John Lacy, Thomas Dutton and Thomas Lardner had extraneous motives in their dislike of the dead-letter religion of the wise. All of Lacy's brothers had gone to Cambridge, but Lacy as the youngest son had not. Though sons of gentlemen of means, Lacy and Dutton had simply finished grammar school, like the much less secure Samuel Keimer. Lardner never completed his university education, begun both at Oxford and Cambridge, due to various escapades.[29] It would be vain to search the careers of the other university-educated believers for clues to resentment of university wisdom. Sir Richard Bulkeley, graduate of Trinity College, Dublin, and Christ Church College, Oxford, or John Caswell, long with Wadham College, Oxford, and appointed the university's Savilian Professor of Astronomy, had no disenchantment with the university. Still, these men seemed partial to the prophecies of the least educated: the barely literate Whitrow drew Bulkeley apart from his erudite friends; untutored Elizabeth Gray attracted John Lacy; Jean Cavalier was well received by a large number of Philadelphians, including the Oxford graduate Richard Roach, who thought Cavalier's language crude but his manner refreshing and his message vigorous. The most educated prophets —Lacy, Dutton, Cuninghame, all country-bred—were also the most prone to attack the religion of the highly literate: wise men and scholars would be befuddled, they warned, by the wisdom of the Lord proceeding from the

---

29. See Appendix IX. On Lacy, his *Warnings*, I, ix, and John Venn and J.A. Venn, *Alumni Cantabrigienses* (Cambridge, 1922-27) Part One, III, 33 (the John Lacy noted is almost certainly the prophet's son); on Dutton, Bulkeley, *Answer to Several Treatises*, 93; on Lardner, Thomas Hearne, *Remarks and Collections*, ed. C.F. Doble (Oxford, 1886) II, 243. Many believers who were apothecaries and "Doctors" had reason to resent university men, since they were excluded from the Royal College of Physicians for the lack of a university education: Bernice Hamilton, "The Medical Professions in the Eighteenth Century," *Economic History Review*, 2nd ser., 4 (1951) 141-69.

mouths of the ignorant. Missions to the university towns were composed not of male prophets refined by school training or, indeed, of men at all, but of young women such as Anna Maria King, Mary Turner and Elizabeth Hughes, daughter of the illiterate widow. The French Prophets challenged the literate urban culture of Cambridge, Oxford and London with the vitality of an oral tradition and rural values. Spiritual renewal would come to the urbane just as the Desert had come to the city.

The wild physical movements of the inspired recalled the countryside. Agitations were, after all, good exercise, like the exuberant, sometimes violent and disorderly pastimes of rural England. City women who experienced agitations were able to escape social restraints on physical expression as well as the physical restraints of customary dress. Educated men equipped themselves with a new vocabulary in which they could be happily simple-minded and yet eloquent of body. The wealthy and status-conscious could wrest themselves away from the increasingly professionalized, disciplined and spectator-oriented sport of the city. At a time when opportunities for physical recreation in urban environments were disappearing, the French Prophets opened up a space in which believers were at liberty to play and to involve the body in play. So there could be a holy laughter, a joyful dialogue at which opponents might be shocked. Over the years, the agitations developed a style which may have been akin to dance, just as the shaking of Ann Lee's followers became the circle dances of nineteenth-century Shakers. But it was always the country dance, the active, energetic expression of release.[30]

The majority of dancers were young, perhaps because the urban culture afforded little chance of leadership to apprentices, servants, students. Fage, Cavalier and Marion were, like most other Camisard prophets, in their twenties when they came to London. The people they first attracted were ten to twenty or thirty years their elders. The majority of the believers whose ages can be estimated were over thirty years old in 1708; the majority of prophets were less than thirty years old when the Spirit came upon them.[31] Slightly poorer and noticeably younger than the average

30. Dennis Brailsford, *Sport and Society: Elizabeth to Anne* (1969) esp. 252. On holy laughter see D.P. Walker, *The Decline of Hell* (1964) 256-57; Kingston, II, 123; Henry Nicholson, *The Falsehood of the New Prophets Manifested* (1708) 21-22. Cf. Alan Lomax, *Folk Song Style and Culture*, A.A.A.S., 88 (Washington, D.C., 1968) 233-36.

31. See Appendix VIII. I have systematically underestimated ages, allowing for marriage at an average age of twenty, although most evidence indicates a median age at first marriage above twenty-four. See R.B. Outhwaite, "Age at Marriage in England from the Late Seventeenth to the Nineteenth Century," *Transactions of the Royal Historical Society* 23 (1973) 55-60. Age data on the prophets is more accurate than that on other followers because the group carefully noted the ages of the inspired.

follower, the prophets matched the experience of the Desert. Like their counterparts in the Cévennes who had only a child's knowledge of the anguished years immediately before and after the Revocation of the Edict of Nantes, most English prophets could have but scant appreciation for the major events through which their elders had passed: the Restoration, the ejection of dissenting ministers, the fire and plague of London, the political blunders of two kings with Roman Catholic attachments, and the Revolution of 1688. What life experiences the prophets had in common, or what it was among those under thirty that may have engineered a disproportionate ability to prophesy, I do not know.[32] The usual accompaniments of age, such as marriage and children, increased wealth and social responsibilities, may have inhibited some older followers from pursuing the exhausting life of a prophet.[33] Whatever the explanations for the differences in ages between inspired and uninspired, followers were aware of and moved by the dynamic role played by the young in their midst. Precocity seemed to them another sign of the imminence of the millennium and was therefore assurance that they would live to see it.[34]

Age did not deter John Lacy or James Cuninghame or Hannah Wharton from dominating the group. As prophets in their forties, they were symbols of the possibility of spiritual renewal for others beyond adolescence. It is instructive in this context that Lacy maintained a master-apprentice relationship with the teenager Elizabeth Gray, that Cuninghame scurried about his missions in the company of young female prophets (Margaret Mackenzie, Henrietta Irvine, Mary Keimer), that Hannah Wharton had begun as a young prophet in tandem with her young companion Jonathan Taylor. The shift from Camisard *inspiré* to French Prophet was more than a shift from rural to urban, from oral to literate culture; it was also a shift from youth to middle age. Like the other changes, this was accomplished in small steps, with much rocking back

---

32. Cf. Alan B. Spitzer, "The Historical Problem of Generations," *American Historical Review* 78 (1973) 1353-1385.

33. Of those of marriageable age for whom I know marital status, three-quarters of the uninspired and less than half of the inspired were married before they became followers.

34. *Impartial Account*, 11-15; Bulkeley, *Answer to Several Treatises*, 90-91, 107, 109. On the role of adolescents in religious movements, see Richard C. Trexler, "Ritual in Florence: Adolescence and Salvation in the Renaissance," in Charles Trinkaus and Heiko A. Oberman, eds., *The Pursuit of Holiness in Late Medieval and Renaissance Religion* (Leiden, 1974) 200-64; John Bossy, "Holiness and Society," *Past and Present* 75 (1977) 124-26; Steven R. Smith, "Religion and the Conception of Youth in Seventeenth-Century England," *History of Childhood Quarterly* 2 (1975) 493-516.

and forth between the Huguenot past and the English present, between Desert and city.[35]

For female citizens, as for the young, the group offered chances for leadership and a latitude of behavior far less constricted than what was common in English society. This may explain in part why, throughout the history of the French Prophets, more females than males were inspired.[36] The group entire always had a majority of males, but the number of new female prophets equalled or exceeded the number of new male prophets in every year from 1707 to 1713 and again in the 1730s. From the very beginning the relatively energetic role of women in the group may have been an important attraction to other women whose opportunities for social gathering were limited or whose position among friendly peers was not exalted. For some women, particularly for those who became prophets, the group beckoned as a viable alternative to social passivity and intellectual isolation. Others, urban or suburban hosts like Mrs. Critchlow, Mrs. East, Mrs. Moreton, Mrs. Blandford and Mme. Boussac, may have longed for a pastoral revival of religion while performing as gracious ladies in gentle surroundings.[37]

35. In France, the young prophets' lives were at stake; in England, older prophets may have had an acute sense of their own natural mortality. Cf. Steven R. Smith, "Growing Old in Early Stuart England," *Albion* 8 (1976) 125-41; Peter Laslett, *Family Life and Illicit Love in Earlier Generations* (Cambridge, 1977) 160-213.

36. See Appendix VII. There may have been a slight preponderance of females in England: D.V. Glass, "Two Papers on Gregory King," in Glass and D.E.C. Eversley, *Population in History* (Chicago, 1965) 166, 206-07. R. Thompson, "Seventeenth Century English and Colonial Sex Ratios: A Postscript," *Population Studies* 28 (1974) 155, speculates on social and psychological effects of imbalanced ratios, but his categories are arbitrary. Herbert Moller, "Social Causation of Affective Mysticism," *Journal of Social History* 4 (1971) 305-08, argues that emotional mystical religiosity was the product of psychological reactions to a surplus of women in certain parts of Europe. His statistics are negligible, and he imposes Freudian assessments of the "character" of women on his meagre evidence; his conclusions are not useful.

37. I have little data on occupations of female French Prophets: two Huguenot and four Scottish women were gentlewomen; one English woman owned a cookshop, two were servants, one a housekeeper, one a shopmaid. My discussion of the role of women in prophetic religious movements has been informed by the following: James B. Christensen, "The Adaptive Functions of Fanti Priesthood," in William R. Bascom and Melville J. Herskovits, eds., *Continuity and Change in African Cultures* (Chicago, 1959) 257-78; Max Gluckman, *Politics, Law and Ritual in Tribal Society* (Chicago, 1965) 216-67; Peter J. Wilson, "Status Ambiguity and Spirit Possession," *Man* 2 (1967) 366-78; John Beattie and John Middleton, eds., *Spirit Mediumship and Society in Africa* (New York, 1969) esp. essays by Robin Horton, Elizabeth Colson, John Middleton, and F.B. Welbourn; I.M. Lewis, *Ecstatic Religion* (1971); Jacqueline Monfouga-Nicolas, *Ambivalence et culte de possession* (Paris, 1972); Pamela Constantinides, " 'Ill at Ease and Sick at Heart': Symbolic Behaviour in a Sudanese Healing

The average male French Prophet was a citizen, a married man in his late thirties, a prosperous and literate London artisan or professional with an annual income over £50. He was a Whig and probably an Anglican.[38] He was not inspired, did not go on missions and rarely was mentioned in printed accounts of the French Prophets. He had relatives or friends in the group. Judging from his profile, contemporary observers would have been hard pressed to pick him out from the daily crowds in a London coffeehouse. He was not, in socioeconomic terms, an extraordinary man.[39]

If there were extraordinary men among the French Prophets, these were

---

Cult," in I.M. Lewis, ed., *Symbols and Sentiments: Cross-cultural Studies in Symbolism* (New York and London, 1977) 61-84; Joyce Irwin, "Anna Maria Van Schurman: From Feminism to Pietism," *Church History* 46 (1977) 48-62; Richard T. Curley, *Elders, Shades, and Women: Ceremonial Change in Lango, Uganda* (Berkeley and Los Angeles, 1973); Judith Hoch-Smith and Anita Spring, eds., *Women in Ritual and Symbolic Roles* (New York and London, 1978) esp. the critique of Lewis, Beattie and Middleton by Anita Spring, 167-70. In an important article, J.G.A. Pocock suggests that England in the eighteenth century saw the "renewed feminization of time," that is, the renewed association of time with woman as symbol of chance, fortune, and dynamic change, during an era of growing credit finance and lotteries. In this respect women prophets would have been symbolic links between capitalism, notions of providence, and the romantic imagination. See Pocock's "Modes of Political and Historical Time in Early Eighteenth-Century England," *Studies in Eighteenth-Century Culture* 5 (1976) 97-98.

38. Data on the political loyalties of believers is scarce. My assumption of Whig loyalty is based upon the general preferences of the religious groups. Huguenot refugees were devoted to the Whigs, and Huguenot gentlemen like Misson and Fatio served as tutors to the sons of Whig nobility. Presbyterians, Quakers and Baptists relied upon the Whigs to protect legal dissent. Anglicans like Bulkeley were also disposed toward the Whigs, perhaps because of their latitudinarianism. Urban interests, including the majority of followers, were often Whig but less consistently. Two French Prophets may have been Tory at one time: Sir Joseph Tiley, who fled England in 1683 for fear of being implicated in the Rye House Plot, was later to return from exile and with the patronage of the Whig Duke of Shrewsbury became an M.P. for Exeter; Edmund Everard, a friend of Tiley's in Holland, went into exile after revealing details of another supposed Popish plot in 1681, but he wrote in defense of Huguenots. See G.M. Trevelyan, *Illustrated English Social History* (1950) III, 16; W.A. Speck, *Tory and Whig: The Struggle in the Constituencies 1701-1715* (1970) 65-67, 118-20. On Bulkeley see Francis Higgins, *Mr. Higgins's Case* (Dublin, 1711) and John Allen et al., *Mr. Higgins's Printed Case . . . Proved Notoriously False and Scandalous* (Dublin, 1711); also Surrey RO, Somers MSS L/16 Nos. 342-43, Bulkeley letter to Lord Somers, 11/27/1695. On Tiley, see BM, Add. MSS 41813 f. 202 and 41819, ff. 159-60, 121-25, and Sloane MSS 2717, f. 27. On Everard, see his *Discourses on the present state of the Protestant Princes of Europe* (1679) and *The Great Pressures and Grievances of the Protestants in France* (1681); *Depositions and Examinations of Mr. E. Everard* (1679); *HMC:* MSS of the House of Lords, I, 272-73, 278; BM, Add. MSS 41819 *passim,* esp. f. 58v., and 41818 *passim.*

39. For lack of data I have been unable to consider some socioeconomic factors: position as eldest, middle or youngest child; fortunes of family in preceding generations; loss of parents at an early age.

the Scientists. Slightly older and wealthier than the average follower, they were the key uninspired believers, the men with most intra-group connections, the men who composed nearly all of the published defenses of the French Prophets.

The Scientists: Motion

The baroque ambiance of science in late seventeenth-century England encouraged rather than discouraged speculative religion. Current was the sympathetic fallacy by which natural prodigies might still be believed to reflect the human condition. Natural and supernatural impinged on one another without disconcerting the natural philosophers. Scientists, engrossed in the process of collecting and classifying data, had come to no consensus on what lay beyond their reach. Scottish quietist George Garden (spiritual counselor to James Cuninghame) could send the Royal Society such random information as an account of "two monstrous Children lately born at Aberdeen," details on the proboscis of the bee, and a discourse on "the Formation of Animals." Leading scientists like Sir Isaac Newton and Robert Boyle—who distrusted analogies from chemical to human properties—could write theological treatises insisting upon God's eminent role in the mechanical universe laid bare by Cartesian and then Newtonian principles.[40]

Virtuosi, investigators of natural phenomena, were heir to two scientific modes: the hermetic and the Cartesian. Like John Pordage, physician and alchemist, mentor of Jane Lead and founder of the Philadelphians, virtuosi could adopt the Renaissance hermeticism that blended alchemy, astrology, Jewish mysticism, Christian theology and magic. Or, like the Cambridge Platonist Henry More, who wrote a major book against religious enthusiasm, they could adopt the Cartesian principles of clear and consistent proof, plain talk about things not mysterious. Most virtuosi did not completely abandon hermeticism, if only to retain a sense of themselves as Christian adepts whose scientific investigations were, according to the botanist Nehemiah Grew, an act of worship. The study of

---

40. Bodleian; MSS Ashmole 1811, Minutes of the Philosophical Society of Oxford, ff. 16, 44; Keith Thomas, *Religion and the Decline of Magic* (New York, 1971); Charles Webster, *The Great Instauration: Science, Medicine and Reform 1626-1660* (New York, 1976) esp. ch. 5; Frank E. Manuel, *The Religion of Newton* (Oxford, 1974); J.R. Jacob, "Boyle's Circle in the Protectorate: Revelation, Politics and the Millennium," *Journal of the History of Ideas* 38 (1977) 131-40.

nature led to God, and by means of curiosity, diligence, logic and faith, the fortunate virtuoso ascended the spheres of religious illumination.[41]

Millenarian ideas flourished at the very hub of this scientific community. Discerning an appropriate role for divinity in the newly discovered world of natural physical laws, the mathematician William Whiston, the astronomer Edmond Halley and Newton himself relied upon ideas of providence that had direct bearing upon millennial beliefs. With Whiston, Dr. Pierre Allix and his friend Bishop William Lloyd entertained millennial hopes for the year 1736, not only as a result of their scriptural studies but because of the number of eclipses expected then. John Craig, in his *Theologia Christianae Principia Mathematica* (1699), applied Newton's inverse square law to derive an estimate for the year of the Second Coming.[42]

Less hardy than Craig and as much adepts as Newtonian apostles, the Scientists unraveled the religious implications of the new physics, chemistry, astronomy, geology, anatomy and medicine. Improvements in the microscope and telescope, Boyle's chemical experiments and Newton's study of the prism all revealed a universe surprisingly full of objects very small or very distant, so that Sir Richard Bulkeley could write, "I imagine it not at all absurd to imagine the whole atmosphere continually full of vegetable and animal seed." Impressed by the absence of a perfect vacuum anywhere in the universe, Bulkeley, like the Cambridge Platonists before, attributed to the divine Spirit a spatial presence no less extensive than van Leeuwenhoek's microscopic "animal seed." Had not the Holy Spirit come to fill all things? "There's no Vacuum or empty Space in Nature," he wrote in the margin of a letter to Bishop Lloyd; "why should we plead for one in Grace?"[43]

41. See Frances A. Yates, *Giordano Bruno and the Hermetic Tradition* (1964) and idem, *The Rosicrucian Enlightenment* (1972) 171-205; Webster, *The Great Instauration*, esp. ch. 2; Frederic R. Burnham, "The More-Vaughan Controversy: The Revolt against Philosophical Enthusiasm," *Journal of the History of Ideas* 35 (1974) 33-49; Richard S. Westfall, *Science and Religion in 17th Century England* (New Haven, 1958) 27; Joseph M. Levine, *Dr. Woodward's Shield: History, Science and Satire in Augustan England* (Berkeley and Los Angeles, 1977).

42. Craig's treatise appears in partial English translation in *History and Theory*, Beiheft 4 (1964), see 26-27; David C. Kubrin, "Providence and the Mechanical Philosophy: The Creation and Dissolution of the World in Newtonian Thought," Ph.D. thesis, Cornell University, 1968, xii, 30, 301; M.A. Hoskin, "Newton, Providence and the Universe of Stars," *Journal for the History of Astronomy* 8 (1977) 77-101; Margaret C. Jacob, *The Newtonians and the English Revolution 1689-1720* (Ithaca, 1976) *passim*; Simon Schaffer, "Halley's Atheism and the End of the World," *Notes and Records of the Royal Society of London* 32 (1977) 17-40.

43. Bodleian, MSS Lister 35, f. 121; Worcester RO, B.A. 5230, Lloyd Papers, Appendix II.14, miscellaneous, p. 2036, note in margin; Edward A. Burtt, *The Metaphysical*

Newton and his friend and disciple Fatio affirmed divine presence in the world more indirectly, through the notion of providence. Though the universe contained an "infinite Multitude of infinitely small Quantities," both men acknowledged that the world was still incredibly empty, since physical bodies were relatively distant from one another. Space was at once so full and so empty that the collision of particles and their distribution in space could not be explained in terms of simple proximity. Even the postulate of gravity, supposing a relationship between bodies far apart, could not account for all motion. Delighted that he was rediscovering and refining ancient knowledge, Newton surmised that God, if not the immediate source of gravity, acted providentially to prevent the otherwise inevitable universal slowing down due to friction. The millenarian themes of decay and renovation of the world appeared as integral parts of physical scientific theory. Newton, Whiston and Halley, contemplating the recently established periodicity of comets, regarded these energetic celestial bodies as possible instruments of divine intervention, restoring or redirecting the complex harmony of masses in motion. Dr. George Cheyne, reader of Jakob Boehme, influential friend of James Cuninghame, Richard Roach and Nicolas Fatio, described motion itself as dependent upon God's will. For many Newtonians, God was the guarantor of the orderly behavior of particles. Because God was ultimately the force behind motion, the vital principle which translated matter through space, God was present to (but, skirting pantheism, not necessarily part of) all things in space.[44]

Fatio, in one of several attempts to modify Newton's hypotheses, described an ether consisting of the most minute and resilient particles imaginable, highly agitated and dispersed throughout nature. The vibration of the particles produced all of the effects of gravity and maintained in equilibrium the sum of universal motion. God, whose methods were eternally consistent with economy and simplicity, did not need to supervise

---

Foundations of Modern Physical Science (New York, 1927) 129-49; J.E. Power, "Henry More and Isaac Newton on Absolute Space," *Journal of the History of Ideas* 31 (1970) 289-96. Cf. Domson, "Nicolas Fatio," 108-26 and his Appendix A.

44. Kubrin, "Providence and the Mechanical Philosophy," 130, 273-78, 289-93; Burtt, *Metaphysical Foundations*, 238-92; F.F. Centore, "Mechanism, Teleology, and 17th Century English Science," *International Philosophical Quarterly* 12 (1972) 553-71; Jacob Viner, *The Role of Providence in the Social Order* (Philadelphia, 1972) ch. 1; Gerald M. Straka, "The Final Phase of Divine Right Theory in England, 1688-1702," *English Historical Review* 77 (1962) 638-58; Michael J. Buckley, *Motion and Motion's God* (Princeton, 1971) esp. 169, 200-02; Arthur O. Lovejoy, *The Great Chain of Being* (Cambridge, Mass., 1964 [1936]) 181-82; Newton, *The Correspondence*, III, 308; *Gentleman's Magazine* 6 (1737) 440.

each particle because, by Fatio's calculations, the Lord had devised a system that compensated internally for friction. To Fatio, motion was not a sphere of God's particular (individual) providence; rather, by the astonishing elegance of the mechanics of gravity, one could not fail to recognize the general providence of God, who formed the hard small particles and sent them spinning.[45]

Newtonian physics, advanced mathematics, astronomy and corpuscular chemistry provided the Scientists with keys to universal mysteries, with evidence of divine presence and of the pervasiveness of spiritual elements in nature. The Scientists perceived themselves as initiates in an epoch when the veils had begun to fall, and they found themselves participating in revelation. Fatio, writing late in life about his discovery of the sun's parallax, which supposedly disproved Newton's ideas on the subject, was pleased

> that adorable Providence so overrules all Things, to let Mankind know by my means (though most unworthy of such a Distinction) that exceeding Great and most Useful secret, Although the Greatest Philosophers and Mathematicians and Astronomers were altogether in the dark and greatly mistaken about it, and could not see what is now rendered perfectly easy and intelligible, even to Mr. A[llut] our Friend, nay to the meanest Capacities of Men, Women and Children.[46]

Fatio's certainty about the immediate cause of gravity was closer to inspiration. The precise notion of the ether had come to him during a meeting of the French Prophets; there, "whilst I was lost in thought, it struck into my mind, like a sudden gleam of light, all at once."[47]

Science as the unfolding of secrets through technical expertise, reason and revelation was fully compatible with religion as personal revelation. Not the state of contemporary science but the special tenor of their

---

45. Bernard Gagnebin, ed., "De la Cause de la Pesanteur; Mémoire de Nicolas Fatio de Duillier Présentée à la Royal Society le 26 février 1690," *Notes and Records of the Royal Society of London* 6,2 (1949), and cf. J.E. McGuire, "Force, Active Principles, and Newton's Invisible Realm," *Ambix* 15 (1968) 154-208. Mocking Fatio, "N.N." wrote, "They say, that in his System he explains Prophecy by the Exaltation of Matter to a certain Degree, in which it has the Virtue even of foretelling things to come." *An Account of the Lives and Behaviour of the Three French Prophets* (1708) 34.

46. BPUG, MSS fr. 602, f. 177 and MSS fr. 609, "Notes diverses non classées," notes on "The Beauty and Reasonableness of my New System." Fatio itched to be out from under Newton's shadow and so was glad to "overthrow the Newtonian System," as he expressed it in the *Gentlemen's Magazine* 8 (1738) 352, and see, on the solar parallax, 7 (1737) 412-14, 547-48, 611-15, and 8 (1738) 95-96. Cf. Lovejoy, *Great Chain of Being*, 111, 145.

47. Joseph Spence, *Anecdotes*, ed. Samuel W. Singer (1820) 56-57.

intellectual curiosity governed the Scientists' love for the French Prophets. True wisdom, they believed, would pop up in strange places, under strange guises that the collector, the chemist or the practitioner of calculus had willy-nilly to take in. Only Dr. Thomas Emes among the Scientists ever spoke an inspired word, but the rest marveled as the "secret and hidden Keys of Divine Wisdom" were shown them by children and ignorant adults.[48] So the Scientists willingly humbled themselves to the unlearned, not sanctimoniously worshipping holy stupidity but in the conviction that the repository of truth extended far beyond the walls of the prejudiced world of educated men. In part this was the urban gentleman's regard for country virtues; in part this was a highly personal perspective on the scientific establishment as cruel and sterile. By 1706, Fatio's close friendship with Newton had been broken, and he taught mathematics in Spitalfields rather than tutoring the sons of nobility. His recent venture into the making of jewelled watches fared poorly, and he would later write, "I believe never so excellent an Invention did meet with so much Opposition and Calumnies, and Contempt or Insults."[49] Dr. Timothy Byfield, the proud possessor of the panacea *Sal volatile oleosum*, had found to his dismay that "indeed a Person gets no Reputation in this World, if he aims above outward Forms of Things." He continued:

> For whatever Medicine transcends the Apothecary's Skill, and can't be made out of Shop-Goods, the Author is called a Quack, the Alarum is given, all Mouths are open, to cry down the Man and his Medicine. To such a Trade is Physic come.
> Here I speak feelingly. For such Treatment have I had ever since I became Professor of this S.V.O.[50]

Sir Richard Bulkeley and Benjamin Jackson also felt the slurs of the scientific community.[51] The Scientists could respond warmly to the prophetic denunciation of wisdom without divine guidance. "Ah, Science, Science all used against me," wailed the prophet Lacy. "What shall I do?

---

48. Fatio's preface to *A Collection of Prophetical Warnings of the Eternal Spirit* (1708) xi, and cf. Royal Society, MSS R.B.C. 9.77-78, letter from Benjamin Furly, 3/25/1701 (N.S.) presented by John Locke.

49. BPUG, MSS fr. 603, manuscript original of his *Navigation Improved* (1728), f. 30; Manuel, *Portrait of Newton*, ch. 9; Louis T. More, *Isaac Newton: A Biography 1642-1727* (New York, 1934) 574n.; *Reasons of the English Watch and Clockmakers Against the Bill to Confirm the Pretended New Invention of using Precious and Common Stones about Watches, Clocks and other Engines* (1705). See also footnote 56.

50. Timothy Byfield, *Directions Tending to Health and Long Life* (1717) 26.

51. On Jackson see Kingston, II, 105-06; on Bulkeley, E.S. de Beer, ed., *The Diary of John Evelyn* (Oxford, 1955) IV, 483-84.

... Learning! Learning that confounds the true knowledge of me! Multitude of Reading to make Men stupid!"[52]

While they denounced scientific knowledge pursued for its own sake, the prophets pledged to reveal quickly the spiritual knowledge that would enable followers to perceive the perfect harmony of the universe. This was the key for which the Scientists had been waiting. How easy was it for them to take in stride the petty arguments of rational men who saw nothing in the prophets but discrepancy and incoherence. "Where is Man's Reason? Is it not lost, in my Almighty Power?" asked the inspired Thomas Dutton.

> So, in like manner, can I make beauteous and harmonious, in the twinkling of an Eye, Things, that, to Man's Judgment, appear impossible or altogether improbable. This is not like the Work of God, say they. Wisdom shines not in this. This is an absurd Way; and that Piece can never appear beautiful, in my Structure. But I, who found a Place, for every Particle in the Universe to be in, and appear beautiful there; will make every Part, every Stone in my Temple, however it may appear to the Eyes of Men, shine with Brightness in the Building.[53]

The prophet Simon Saudignan dreamed that Jean Allut, while inspired, held in his hands a mirror that reflected the movements of the heavens and revealed knowledge of all things.[54] The author of the *Impartial Account* (possibly Francis Moult) had already, by 1708, been enriched by the prophets, who had given him the key to millennial doctrine and "since I have had this Key, can scarce dip anywhere into the Old and New Testaments; but I find something pointing at this restitution of all things."[55]

The intricate weave of millenarianism and scientific virtuosity was apparent in the Scientists' fascination with celestial mechanics and earthly machines. Fatio united with the De Bauffre brothers in the crafting of a watch that was in miniature a solution to the problem of universal friction. By inventing a method for piercing precious and semi-precious stones, Fatio introduced the jewelling of the holes of escapements for watch pivots, thus reducing wear and ensuring a more trustworthy timepiece. Isaac Newton had compared two of Fatio's watches to his pendulum clock

---

52. Lacy, *Warnings*, I, 29 and cf. III, 148.
53. *Collection of Warnings*, 59.
54. BPUG, MSS fr. 609, letter dated 1736, and see MSS fr. 605, letter of 3/3/1719 for a prophecy by Allut referring to Newton's prism.
55. *Impartial Account*, 29.

for a month and was satisfied with their consistency.[56] Regularity, the guarantee of precision measurement of time, was a fundamental requirement of Newtonian mechanics, but it was this very consciousness of clockwork moments that contributed to the sense of a world running down, of time as quanta rather than continuum. Fatio noted the exact duration of the prophecies at meetings of the inspired. Simon Saudignan while inspired used the analogy of the clockwork universe popularized by Robert Boyle. Addressing the watchmaker Mr. Clay, Saudignan warned "There is no Motion without Springs, nor Springs without Motion: and none of the Natural Men, have, as yet, known What that is, Motion, and What the True Spring is, which makes to move the Whole Machine of the universal World."[57]

In 1713 watchmaker Benjamin Steele had devoted himself to the discovery of a perpetual motion machine, one powerful step toward an understanding of the springs of movement. Virtuosi had long dreamed of an autonomous engine which, like Fatio's ether (and with the same general intent as Fatio's jewelled watches), internally compensated for friction. Steele was sure of success because the Holy Spirit itself had started him on his quest. Only through prophetic insight might one construct a device that otherwise excluded divine assistance; one could make a supreme breakthrough in mechanics only with the Lord's help. The perpetual motion machine, if it somehow incorporated a spark of divine agency among its counterbalances, was truly the millenarian's quest, a discovery that would inaugurate a new scientific age. In 1719, after receiving reports of "Self Moving Engines" whirring along in Germany, Benjamin Jackson, Daniel Critchlow and Francis Moult expressed enthusiasm for Steele's project. Moult wagered fifty guineas that Steele would soon unlock the secret of perpetual motion.[58]

56. PRO, Patent Rolls C66/3445; W.G. Hiscock, ed., *David Gregory, Isaac Newton and their Circle* (Oxford, 1937) 17, 21-22; Henry Ellis, ed., *Original Letters of Eminent Literary Men* (1843) 317-18; Ferdinand Berthoud, *Histoire de la mésure du temps par les horloges* (Paris, 1802) II, 8-10; L. Defossez, *Les savants du XVIIe siècle et la mésure du temps* (Lausanne, 1946) 283-86; David Glasgow, *Watch and Clock Making* (1886) 110-11; H.L. Nelthropp, *A Treatise on Watch-work* (1873) 92-93.

57. Fatio Notebooks; BPUG, MSS fr. 605, letter of 5/4/1736. Contrast Thomas, *Religion and the Decline of Magic*, 620-23, 643.

58. Saudignan warned watchmaker Clay that "there is no perpetual Motion unless it is, respecting those, who being continually moved by their Lust excite a perpetual Motion in their hearts where is no true Rest!" BPUG, MSS fr. 602, f. 123, and MSS fr. 601, ff. 259-259v., and MSS fr. 605, letters of 2/5/1719 and 5/4/1736; Stack MSS 11, p. 3. Other references to Fatio's and Caswell's interest in perpetual motion occur in R.T. Gunther, ed., *Early Science in Oxford*

At the age of twenty-six, Sir Richard Bulkeley had invented or located an equally marvelous machine, an engine "which promises to perform all that's wanting in the doctrine of mechanics." Like the other Scientists, he too was preoccupied with motion. At twenty-four he had contrived an air pump for ships that Fatio would later improve upon. In 1685 and 1686, Bulkeley and Benjamin Jackson collaborated on the design and testing of a coach that could overturn without harm to the occupants. Bulkeley's testimony for the coach resembled his testimony for the French Prophets twenty years hence: "I myself have been once overturned, and knew it not till I looked up and saw the wheel flat over my Head, and if a Man went with his Eyes shut he would imagine himself in the most Smooth way." He also experimented at length with a coach on brass rollers, riding for days despite his illnesses.[59] Benjamin Jackson, continuing his own inventive career, patented a swimming machine or mechanical life preserver for people thrown from overturned boats.[60] Might not millenarian prophecy be another sort of machine for preserving the overturned?

The Scientists' interest in machines entailed a desire for precision that was necessary as well to the study of celestial mechanics. During his youth, Fatio had demonstrated his genius with a mathematical analysis of the zodiacal light, a recurrent column of light on the horizon after sunset. In his essay on *Fruit-Walls Improved* (1699), Fatio attributed the change in weather since 1683 to a decline in the frequency of sunspots (virtually absent between 1645 and 1715). Matter from the sunspots had dispersed into space, wrote Fatio, spreading a mist between sun and earth that affected terrestrial weather. Aided by Charles Portales and Jean Allut, Fatio made astronomical measurements throughout his later life as a French Prophet, culminating in a proof, at the age of seventy-two, that Saturn was smaller than the earth.[61] John Caswell, like Fatio a Fellow of the Royal Society, astronomy professor at Oxford, made improvements

---

(Oxford, 1923-45) X, 191 and XII, 247; on Steele, see Newton, *The Correspondence*, VI, 391-92 and cf. VII, 143-44.

59. Bodleian, MSS Ashmole 1811, f. 9, and 1813, ff. 349v., 354, and MSS Lister 35, f. 123; Royal Society, MSS L.B.C. 10, 162-63, 242; Gunther, ed., *Early Science in Oxford*, XII, 161-62, 196-97.

60. Bennett Woodcroft, comp., *Alphabetical Index of Patentees of Inventions* (1854) 298; BM, Sloane MSS 4047, f. 9. French Prophet Peter Rochfort, inventor of the mock-trumpet (*Brand*, 66), founded a society to bring together "the Ingenious Men of Great Britain," advert. in *The Postman*, No. 1778 (May 8-10, 1707).

61. "Lumière zodiacale," *Encyclopédie ou dictionnaire raisonné des sciences, des arts, et des métiers* (Neufchastel, 1755) IX, 722b-723a; BPUG, MSS fr. 601, f. 258; Fatio, *Fruit-Walls Improved*, vii, 113-17; BM, Sloane MSS 4045, f. 27.

on the telescope and developed the barometer as an efficient instrument for measuring altitude. He shared Fatio's appreciation for accurate clockwork, especially for the approximation of longitude at sea, which demanded a reliable index of the time spent sailing.[62]

Concern for accuracy, which did not end when the Scientists became French Prophets, characterized their religious pursuits as much as their inventions. As they grappled with complex machines and difficult mathematics, the Scientists simultaneously labored over precise scripture chronologies. Like Newton and Whiston, Fatio and Bulkeley culled scripture as well as nature in order to ferret out the few tidy basic laws of motion and matter. Followers often protested that their belief in the prophets, like their belief in gravity, rested upon the strict application of familiar scientific principles: close observation, the trial of hypotheses, logic. And just as the inspired among the French Prophets quickened hopes for a glimpse of universal secrets, so the Scientists employed their new methods and knowledge to substantiate new miracles.

Most susceptible to investigation were the physical symptoms of the prophets. The author of the *Impartial Account* was impressed by what he considered to be medically (physiologically) impossible. He described a prophet who endured violent agitations for eighteen hours but was fresh and lively at the end, "which (I thought) nothing but a supernatural assistance could perform." Bulkeley, from his miserably intimate acquaintance with the frailty of the human body, was convinced that the physical behavior of the inspired exceeded physical laws.[63] But the Scientists did not rest content with superficial evidence. Several of the French Prophets, including Dr. Byfield, took the pulse of Elizabeth Gray as she sputtered and choked during a divine illness. A week before, prophet Gray had had another attack of suffocation; someone timed the different phases of her cure, perhaps with one of Fatio's watches. At 2:27 P.M. Henriette Allut had an inspiration, at 2:34 P.M. Lacy prayed under inspiration, and at 2:58 P.M. Elizabeth Gray rose restored to health. When Gray went temporarily

---

62. J.E.B. Mayor, *Cambridge Under Queen Anne* (Cambridge, 1911) 392-94; Fatio, *Navigation Improved* (1728); *Transactions of the Royal Society* 24 (1704-05) 1597-1603; Cambridge University, Keynes MSS 99, letter to Flamsteed, 10/14/1694; Bodleian, MSS Ashmole 1811, ff. 34, 50, 51; Hearne, *Remarks and Collections*, III, 114, 344, 412. Benjamin Steele collaborated with Fatio on making the sea watches, and the marquis de Miremont presented King George II with a copy of Fatio's book: BPUG, MSS fr. 602, f. 137, and MSS fr. 601, f. 278.

63. *Impartial Account*, 15; Bulkeley, *Preface to the Reader of Warnings of the Eternal Spirit, Spoken by the Mouth of the Servant of God, Abraham Whitro* (1708) esp. 12-14.

blind, men made diverse experiments to determine the extent of her blindness, dangling their fingers "within a quarter of an Inch of the Edge of her Eyelids," yet prompting no reflex action. She was examined for twenty minutes, then prayed at her bedside for seventeen minutes; eight minutes later John Lacy was seized with the Spirit, agitated for four minutes and then he cured her. The elaborate measurement and timing of the event include an acute observation of the blind prophet's pupils: "the Iris, where the Black of the Eye begins, was not terminated by an uniform circular line; but by a line uneven and undulating, not only in the Figure thereof, but also in some sort of a loose waving Motion.... An undoubted Token that the animal Spirits did not discharge their Function."[64] This report by Lacy and Fatio can stand as a paradigm of the scientific temperament among the French Prophets. In such a detailed and thorough manner did the admirers of Newton's *Opticks*, watchmakers and inventors, profoundly curious men with an urge to record their minute perceptions, display the scientific methods and Christian virtuosity of their time.

The Scientists: Salt

Modern as the Scientists were, devout students of the new mechanics and microscopic biology, they did not recoil from the hermetic tradition to which virtuosi were heir. Many of them would have agreed with Richard Roach, who wrote in his diary, "Divines and Physicians, Literal and Mystical. There is a World of Science, the Soul of Science, unknown to the former."[65] To some French Prophets, physics was not free from metaphysics, astronomy from astrology, chemistry from alchemy. The great Newton himself compiled many alchemical manuscripts, and the mystic William Law would later make bold claims that Newton's principles of attraction and repulsion derived from the works of Jakob Boehme.[66] In their search for a key to underlying universal principles, in their self-regard as partially illumined adepts, in their respect for inspiration, the Scientists

---

64. [Mr. Collett], *The Honnest Quaker* (1707) 4-6; Lacy, *Warnings*, II, 110-11, 146-50, 195. Wavy-lined pupils were in fact medical proof that Gray could not have willed her blindness. Drugs such as belladonna do cause that condition, but there is no other evidence or indeed allegation of drug-taking among the French Prophets.

65. Roach Diary, II, f. 304v.

66. Henri Talon, ed., *Selections from the Journals and Papers of John Byrom* (1950) 221-22; Manuel, *Portrait of Newton*, ch. 8; J.E. McGuire, "Transmutation and Immutability: **Newton's Doctrine of Physical Qualities,"** *Ambix* 14 (1967) 69-95; cf. Yates, *The Rosicrucian Enlightenment*, ch. 14.

could as easily retort the mystical salt as compute the radius of Saturn. Alchemist or astrologer, one might use mathematical expertise and rigorous analysis to achieve the mystical solution. Neither science nor Christianity seemed to exclude the Scientists' quest for the philosopher's stone.

For the Philadelphians, for Fatio, the search began with the Kabbala, the lore of Jewish mysticism that had burrowed deep into English religious thought by the middle of the seventeenth century. Margaret Cavendish, Duchess of Newcastle, had even asked in her *Description of a New Blazing World* (1668) whether the Kabbala was a work of natural reason or divine inspiration and whether it was a sin to be ignorant of it.[67] Readers of Boehme recognized his philosophical kinship with Lurianic Kabbalism, and Philadelphian attempts to uncover scripture mysteries combined the techniques of both. Kabbala became synonymous with all esoteric doctrine. Roach and Francis Lee published a long defense of the Kabbala in their *Theosophical Transactions*, distinguishing the true and the false, the divine and the planetary Kabbala. Inquirers into Revelation would find themselves at sea without an understanding of its Kabbalistic code. One article mentioned "St. John, whose Revelations are no other than a certain Divine Cabbala delivered to him from Christ." The Kabbala, by virtue of Jesus's initiation as an adept, ran through the entire New Testament; one author found 1500 passages incapable of being understood without knowledge of the Kabbala.[68]

The twin path of Behmenism and Kabbalism led the Scientists to a spiritual comprehension of the natural world. By 1706, Fatio had determined that Ezekiel's visions (Ezekiel 1 and 10) were a veiled description of the Aurora Borealis; he composed a treatise on the subject "too full of Jewish Philosophy" to publish and thought that one particular appearance of the Aurora signalled the approaching universal judgment.[69] Charles Portales, who read the *Miroir d'astrologie* and corresponded with Fatio

---

67. Margaret Cavendish, *Observations upon Experimental Philosophy To which is added, The Description of a New Blazing World* (2nd ed.; 1668) 67-68; Harold Fisch, *Jerusalem and Albion* (1964) 191-213; Gershom G. Scholem, *Major Trends in Jewish Mysticism* (New York, 1961 [1941]) esp. 237-38.

68. *Theosophical Transactions of the Philadelphian Society*, 160; Walker, *Decline of Hell*, ch. 8. Kabbalistic works are referred to by Lacy, preface to Elie Marion's *Prophetical Warnings* (1707) xx, and by F.-M. Misson, *Sentimens désinteressez* (1710) 172n.

69. Hiscock, *David Gregory*, 39; BPUG, MSS fr. 602, f. 120, and Fatio Calendar, 4/5/1707. See also BPUG, MSS fr. 603, ff. 33-61, Fatio's "Notes sur la cabale," which includes a drawing of a naked, inspired youth (the *puer aeternus*?) holding grapes, a caduceus, and a brand of fire and urinating into a stream. Below the sketch is written, "Lavez vos yeux ternis, lavez les dans cette EAU."

about meteors, respected Boehme's prophetic (i.e., figurative) interpretation of Joshua 10:12-13, in which the sun stood still. Portales wrote in his commonplace book, "The sun and the moon and all the Parts of material, or Elementary Creation, are the real Images, Representations and Characters, of the Spiritual. Whoever takes it otherwise, lies in darkness."[70] From this to the plain astrology of James Craven, rushing to inform Roach about the important "Conjunction of Jupiter with the Moon in the Heart of the Lion," was a small jump. The planets were wreathed in a spiritual glow.[71]

The Scientists knew that the minerals of the earth also had Christian dimensions. The Philadelphian Francis Lee reported to the Bourignonian Pierre Poiret that an experienced London chemist (James Craven?) gained "more profit and real science from one of [Boehme's] books than from a hundred (more or less) books of other authors."[72] Boehme, and alchemists after him, suffused chemical transformations with Christian mystical meanings; physical secrets were Christian mysteries, and alchemists were religious seekers, distilling a substance that was at once matter and spirit. Boehme, the first to identify the philosopher's stone with the Holy Spirit (true agent of all transformation), emphasized the piety and purity requisite of the alchemist as an intermediary between the natural and the supernatural. The alchemist worked to redeem gold from dross, the soul from corruption.[73]

The Scientists did not become prophets but they did function in another domain as spiritual mediums and would recognize the parallel between alchemy and prophecy. Unearthing concealed or forgotten knowledge, studying the properties of enigmatic elements, they had their own revelations. In this they had not resigned the integrity of experimental science; like Newton and others of the Royal Society who looked for the transmutation of metals, the Scientists yearned for a clear vision of the fundamental structure of the created world.[74]

70. Stack MSS 11, notes on Edward Taylor's translation of Boehme, *Theosophick Philosophy Unfolded* (1696); BPUG, MSS fr. 605, letters of 3/7/1719 and 6/16/1736.
71. Roach Diary, I, f. 23. Cf. Thomas, *Religion and the Decline of Magic*, 303-77.
72. Dr. Williams's Library, MSS 186.18 (2), First Epistle.
73. A.E. Waite, *The Secret Tradition in Alchemy* (1926) 6-10, 338; Fisch, *Jerusalem and Albion*, 201-05; Thomas, *Religion and the Decline of Magic*, 189-228; Carl G. Jung, *Psychology and Alchemy*, trans. R.F.C. Hull (1953) 234, 255, 293-304, 408.
74. J.E. McGuire and P.M. Rattansi, "Newton and the 'Pipes of Pan,' " *Notes and Records of the Royal Society* 21 (1966) 108-43; Yates, *The Rosicrucian Enlightenment*, 171-205; John Read, *Prelude to Chemistry* (1936) 307-08. In 1685 the Royal Society listed among its "Catalogue of some of the Arcana and Desiderata in Chemistry" the problem of

In 1693 Fatio offered to show Newton a "metallic putrefaction and fermentation which lasts for a great while and turns to a vegetation producing a heap of golden trees." Some thirty or forty years later, Fatio was still so preoccupied with the arcana of chemistry that he wrote into his will a chemical legacy for Francis Moult. It was the secret of a process for preparing "a Vegetable Menstruum, by which both the yellow and the green, or the celestial and the terrestrial essence of any plant are at once extracted."[75] Moult himself, respected apothecary for Jonathan Swift, discoverer of a process for separating and reducing black tin into white tin, often discussed with Charles Portales the secret of the philosopher's stone. In 1721 he had a vision of the stone or "Powder of Projection" which confirmed his faith in alchemy and inspired a poem:

> I saw then as I said a Powder so
> Encreast in Virtue (Scarce to be believed)
> That so small a Quantity, as scarce would shew
> In Bulk a Grain nor weighed much more indeed
> Which yet to Gold so great a Quantity
> Could well transmute as may be deemed a lye.
>
> No Man by Art its Number could attain,
> So Great it was, yet was the Tincture Sound
> For On One Ounce projected was that Grain
> In which Perfection did so abound,
> That all was Essence made, of which one Grain
> Was cast upon Ten Times as much again.

Richard Roach shared Moult's respect for "This noble Art so useful & so just," as Moult wrote later in the poem. Roach experimented with spirits of barley and copied out two recipes for the doubling of gold. From his Philadelphian friends he learned that "A Drop of the Fixed Indissoluble Oil given of Grace unto the Evil Angels will Maintain Life and Multiply in them to their Restoration." He must have been delighted that his forays into alchemy yielded knowledge of the process whereby universal salvation extended to the entire spirit world.[76]

Alchemy promised both material and spiritual riches. The Scientists

---

transmuting metals and making a universal medicine: Bodleian, MSS Ashmole 1810, ff. 99-102.

75. Newton, *The Correspondence*, III, 265-66; T. Nash, *Collections for the History of Worcestershire* (1782) II, Supplement, 101.

76. Stack MSS 11, p. 3, dated 7/10/1721; Woodcroft, *Index of Patentees*, 390; Jonathan Swift, *The Journal to Stella 1710-1713*, ed. F. Ryland (1913) 373; Roach Diary, I, ff. 52v., 92v., 296.

used alchemy in their quest for funds but also for the key to the transition of all things, lead to gold, matter to spirit. Behind their quest lay a vague belief in the basic unity of creation, a belief that might take the form of Philadelphian universal salvation or the millenarian ethos of the New Jerusalem. The ultimate goal of the true alchemist was not gold itself but the intuition of the laws of synthesis.[77]

In theory the philosopher's stone would demonstrate the crucial simplicity of the natural world. As a universal solvent, it could reduce all matter to its primitive element; as a universal projector, it could combine all matter into one. For the Scientists, chemical salts were the emblem of this unity.

Paracelsus, from whom Boehme had drawn extensively, had added salt as the third of the "hydrostatical principles." Mercury represented the realm of the supernatural, sulphur the realm of the natural, and salt the body in which the two were fixed by illumination. Wrote the Philadelphian Edmund Brice about the central salt, "This is that Salt, which Christ among all created things only called good. . . . This Spirit of Salt is the *medium* of all things, by which the highest are knit with the lowest, and keep in harmony." Salt was the supreme principle by which one might fashion the philosopher's stone.[78]

The Scientists used salts as healing substances whose medical properties could restore the body's internal harmony. Alchemy had a long history of medical analogies and applications, and Charles Portales could still record a friend's prescription for asthma that merely called for equal parts of sulphur and mercury. But the Scientists were not merely appropriating drugs compounded by alchemists of earlier days. For the Scientists, the administration of basic medicines was equivalent to spiritual healing, for physical and spiritual health were mirror conditions. Themselves no prophets, the Scientists might nevertheless employ the principle of inspiration, the chemical yet cosmic salt of nature, to put right the human body and, indirectly, the human soul.[79]

77. Cf. Thomas, *Religion and the Decline of Magic*, 223-28; Webster, *The Great Instauration*, 324-35, 391-92.

78. J.R. Partington, *A History of Chemistry* (1961) II, 142, 167; Waite, *The Secret Tradition*, 20, 37, 312-15: C. G. Jung, *Mysterium Coniunctionis*, trans. R.F.C. Hull (1963) 188-92, 221n., 239-57; Read, *Prelude to Chemistry*, 26-27, 132; Edmund Brice, trans. [and author], *Centrum Naturae Concentratum Or the Salt of Nature Regenerated* (1696) 55. See also Robert P. Multhauf, *Neptune's Gift: A History of Common Salt* (Baltimore and London, 1978).

79. Stack MSS 11, pp. 16-18, 20.

In 1658, Johann Glauber synthesized sodium sulphate and called it *sal mirabile*, the universal medicine which he had first located in a mineral spring near Vienna.[80] This continental discovery did not deter Dr. Timothy Byfield from his English search for a panacea, and he too explored mineral waters. By 1687, practiced in old and new methods of medicine, at ease with alchemical theory, Byfield had liberated the universal common salt of nature, "the first *Ens* or Mother of Salts," from the waters of the balsamic wells in Hoxton just north of London. Proud of having untangled the original salt from enfolding impurities, he was rewarded by the staggering virtues of the purified water. Byfield discovered his new menstruum to be effective against consumption, gout and stones (his own complaints), dropsy, jaundice, diarrhea, dysentery, asthma, ulcerated kidneys, vertigo, migraine, gonorrhea, leprosy and vapours. He had not yet compounded the universal remedy, but already he compared his pharmacopoeia to the philosopher's stone.[81]

After more than twenty years as a "Great Seeker of Medicines," Byfield drew down from the sun and the air a host of "illuminated Sulphurs," combined them magnetically with volatile salt (ammonium carbonate) and produced the universal medicine, *Sal volatile oleosum*. This mix of salt and oil followed the traditional alchemical formula for the Grand Elixir. Byfield's description of his *Sal* revealed the extent of his debt to alchemy's blend of the religious and the scientific. By "Philosophical Management," wrote Byfield,

> the truest, purest, and most wholesome Volatile Salt may be extracted from the Air; and the first begotten Oleity in the World; which transparent radical Moisture (prior to all specific Lives) has some portion of the universal Form that animates it: And this may properly be called a luminous Sulphur, which is the root of all Oleity.

In short, *Sal volatile oleosum* was "Spirit of Air, and the best seasoning in the whole World of Animal Bodies in Life." It preserved the natural "Salino-sulphureous" human temperament, promoting the harmonious union of the soul and the celestial spark with the salts and oils of the body. The creation of the *Sal* had resembled the mystical creation of life, "For

---

80. Partington, *History of Chemistry*, II, 352, 357; Webster, *The Great Instauration*, 386-88; Robert P. Multhauf, "Sal Ammoniac: A Case History in Industrialization," *Technology and Culture* 6 (1965) 569-70.

81. Byfield, *A Short and Plain Account of the Late-Found Balsamick Wells at Hoxton* (1687) 17, 21-23, 32, 43-46; Byfield, *Two Discourses* (1685) preface, 12, 13, and cf. his *The Artificial Spaw* (1684) 19-28, 48-52.

the Salts, as well as the Sulphurs, are deeply concealed in Nature, and their Union is a great mystery, as nice as the Subtile mixtions in Life." Byfield summed up his labors as if he had operated a *mistio*, the joining together of bodies under a new form: "The Sulphurs must be spiritualized [vaporized] that mix with Volatile Salts, and be united by the mean of an Aetherial Spirit, and held to view illuminated and perfectly united." Through contemplation and experiment, always with the puzzling link of soul and body before him, Byfield had intuited the secret transactions of nature, "not understood by the generality of men, who know not the *occult*, much less to make it *manifest*."[82]

Soon patented, *Sal volatile oleosum* would supposedly save a thousand children annually from fatal convulsions, cure all diseases of the brain, heal wounds, deal gently but forcefully with any bodily ferment, and sharpen the senses. Since the *Sal* could so thoroughly redeem the body from its fallen state, Byfield had some grounds for regarding himself as no "mere Physician," but as a man guided at times by the "Heavenly Dictate." He could not, he wrote in 1717, compose a discourse on health and long life without a preliminary dissertation on the union of soul and body. In his septagenarian years he published tracts devoted exclusively to the practice of true religion.[83]

About the time that Byfield perfected his *Sal*, Francis Moult had become interested in salts and mineral springs. At the sign of Glauber's Head in Watling Street, he and his relative George Moult (Fellow of the Royal Society) sold a substance identified by the virtuoso Nehemiah Grew and soon famous as Epsom salt. Despite his success as an apothecary, Francis Moult did not cease looking for the philosopher's stone, and he contracted a partnership with Dr. Critchlow and Dr. Byfield to manufacture Byfield's *Sal*. Moult's protegé, Dr. Robert Eaton, with his sponsor's help decocted an amazing balsamic styptic for the prevention of internal

---

82. Byfield, *A Short Discourse Of . . . Small-Pox* (1695) 16-21; Byfield, *Horae Subsecivae: Or, Some Long-Vacation Hours Redeemed, For the Discovery of the True SAL VOLATILE OLEOSUM of the Ancient Philosophers* (1695) 18-19, 22-23. Antony van Leeuwenhoek examined Byfield's *Sal* under his microscope: "An Extract of a Letter," *Philosophical Transactions of the Royal Society* 17 (1693) 959. *Remington's Practice of Pharmacy* (14th ed.; Easton, 1970) identifies the *Sal* as Aromatic Ammonia Spirit, primarily ammonium carbonate, the basis for smelling salts (pp. 868-69); cf. John Kersey, *Dictionarium Anglo-Britannicum* (1708) s.v., and Leslie G. Matthews, *History of Pharmacy in Britain* (1962) 283.

83. PRO, Patent Rolls, C66/3480; advert. in *The Post-Boy*, No. 1940 (Oct. 21-23, 1707); Byfield, *Horae Subsecivae*, 25-29; Byfield, *Directions*, 1-2; Byfield, *The Christian Examiner*, Part I (2nd ed.; 1720), Part II (1721); Byfield, *A Closet Piece* (1721).

and external bleeding; the styptic too was based upon salts, probably an alum compound. In 1721, Moult talked still of the Grand Elixir.[84]

Shortly before the creation of *Sal volatile oleosum*, Nicolas Fatio had tracked down the elixir of life. Since 1690, when Fatio had been fascinated by experiments upon *sal armoniac* [*sal ammoniac*] performed by one of the Moults for the Royal Society, chemistry and medicine had excited his curiosity. Francis Willis dedicated a medical treatise to Fatio that year. After his mother's death and his own illness in 1692, Fatio turned to the detailed analysis of scripture prophecies and to earnest experiments with medicines. By 1693, Fatio had furnished Newton with twelve doses of the "first imperial powder from the first region," and a friend had offered to teach Fatio how to compound the remedy for nine diseases out of ten. Wavering between careers, with little ready money at hand and less inheritance due than he expected, Fatio mulled over the prospects of an affluent life as a vendor of the panacea and healer of the multitudes. He decided against spending the years necessary to obtain a medical degree, but he was retailing pills in 1696. When he met the French Prophets, he had a reputation for "dabbling in Physic" and for claiming knowledge of a universal nostrum. The last evidence of his chemical researches shows Fatio in serious pursuit of good if not universal medicines, which he found in salt. As late as 1731, Fatio would write to the experimenter Francis Hauksbee about fifty pounds of mineral salt which he had spent forty years gathering from distant hot springs and which Francis Moult, likely out of pique at Fatio's opposition to Hannah Wharton, had destroyed. Fatio was distraught, for he had given the salt to Moult for diverse tests, believing that the large crystals of the "most precious Salt" would prove "one of the most considerable Salts in the Materia Medica."[85]

84. H.E. Roscoe and C. Schorlemmer, *Treatise on Chemistry* (6th ed.; 1923) II, 643; Nehemiah Grew, *A Treatise of the Nature and Use of the Bitter Purging Salt. . . . With Animadversions on a late corrupt Translation published by Francis Moult, Chymist* (1697) vii; Partington, *History of Chemistry*, II, 687n.; PRO, Prob. 11.594, f. 253, Byfield Will, 11/8/1715; BM, Add. MSS 36,123, ff. 18-19, warrant for patent for Robert Eaton, and Sloane MSS 4045, ff. **126, 277,** and 4058 ff. **291, 294**; Stack MSS 11, notes dated 8/15/1720 and 7/10/1721; *Farley's Bristol News-Paper*, advert. Oct. 1, 1726 (p. 285); Gunther, ed., *Early Science in Oxford*, X, 187; John Brown, "Observations and Experiments on the Sal Catharticum Amarum, commonly called the Epsom Salt," *Philosophical Transactions* 32 (1723) 350-52. Moult's copy of Glauber's *The golden ass well managed* (**pub. with** William Cooper's *A Philosophical Epitaph* and J.F. Helvetius's *A Brief of the Golden Calf*, 1673) ended up in Bronson Alcott's library at Fruitlands, Massachusetts. For a survey of the mineral springs in London, quite popular in the early eighteenth century, see Warwick W. Wroth and Arthur E. Wroth, *The London Pleasure Gardens of the Eighteenth Century* (1896).

85. Domson, "Nicolas Fatio," 17; Newton, *The Correspondence*, III, 245, 267-68;

The Scientists' reliance on salt was in part the result of contemporary confusion over chemical classes; apothecaries labeled all acids and alkalis as salts. Accepting the iatrochemical theories that organic functions were determined by chemical processes, the Scientists looked toward salts as the primary constituents of chemical interaction and so, properly applied, as medicines. Within this school, one might choose between acid or alkali as the healing agent, and all the Scientists agreed with Byfield that acids were the "grand Enemy of Man's Health." Dr. Emes wrote two pamphlets extolling alkalis and hinting at the dismal effects of the "abounding pernicious Acid." The medicines prepared by the Scientists were alkalis meant to prevent corruption by overactive acids or, in the language of alchemy, to counteract the degenerate spirit.[86]

Many contemporary chemists were seekers of salts and advocates of alkali. What distinguished the Scientists was their attitude toward salts. They sought a tincture that would cure every disease because it was in essence a microcosm of the soul's union to the body and of God's relationship to Christians. The panacea was the apex of medicine just as the perpetual motion machine was the apex of physics. Universal perfect health, like universal perfect motion, was as close as the apocalypse, or closer.[87]

Through celestial and terrestrial mechanics, through alchemy and astrology, through medicine, the Scientists had arrived at a sense of inspiration and apocalypse before Durand Fage spoke his first warning in London. The Scientists accepted new prophets and new powers—especially the power to heal—as parts of an older vision. They would tend toward the ethos of pentecost, regarding prophets as codebreakers and

---

Manuel, *Portrait of Newton*, 193, 204-05; Bodleian, Rawlinson Letters 109, f. 28; BM, Add. MSS 28,536, f. 238, letter to Hauksbee, 8/12/1731 [not 1737]; *Clavis Prophetica* (1707) II, 10; Christian Huygens, *Oeuvres complètes* (The Hague, 1911) IX, letters 2523, 2582. In Vevey, Mme. de Warens, the pietist leader, was working in alchemy and making *sal ammoniac*: Eugène Olivier, *Médecine et santé dans le pays de Vaud au XVIIIe siècle 1675-1798* (Lausanne, 1939) I, 413.

86. Partington, *History of Chemistry*, II, 283-84, 287, 290, 678; Robert P. Multhauf, *The Origins of Chemistry* (1966) 282, 296-97, 308; Byfield, *Horae Subsecivae*, 11; Thomas Emes, *A Dialogue between Alkali and Acid* (2nd ed.; 1700) esp. 62. Contrast Robert Boyle, *Reflections upon the Hypothesis of Alcali and Acidum* (1675) 26. On the controversy see Marie Boas, "Acid and Alkali in Seventeenth Century Chemistry," *Archives internationales d'histoire des sciences* 9 (1956) 13-28.

87. See J.R. Jacob, "Robert Boyle and Subversive Religion in the Early Restoration," *Albion* 6 (1974) 275-93; Webster, *The Great Instauration*, ch. 4; Peter Gibbons, "The Medical Projectors, 1640-1720," *Journal of the History of Medicine* 24 (1969) 247-71; Walter Pagel, "Religious Motives in the Medical Biology of the XVIIth Century," *Bulletin of the History of Medicine* 3 (1935) 97-128, 213-31, 265-312.

worship as personal experiment, and toward the ethos of the New Jerusalem, hoping for a glimpse of those universal laws whose understanding would bring nature and all people into right relationships. As adepts, they had striven toward the image of the divine intermediary, and at last they found the French Prophets. They would, each and every one, remain faithful to the dispensation for the rest of their lives.

The Wild and the Walled

I have shown how the French Prophets as a group may have answered personal needs for autonomy or companionship, medical attention or physical exercise, cultural renewal or social respect. This is essentially a functionalist response to the questions posed at the beginning of this chapter: people were attracted to the French Prophets because the group did something useful for them, provided services which only a group could provide.[88]

I have also shown how acts of prophecy and healing were congruent with the intellectual and religious preconceptions of the most articulate believers, the Scientists. This is essentially a cognitive/structural response. The symbolic system of the Scientists, the way they looked at and understood the world, was structurally similar to the lattice of assumptions underlying group behavior and group beliefs.[89]

A third approach is to ask how the French Prophets may have been expressive of the personal tensions of believers. This is to reverse the direction of analysis: instead of looking at individuals for clues to the nature of the group, I will look at the group for clues to the nature of the individual members. I will consider the French Prophets as a theatrical company whose repertoire of plays and whose style of performance may reflect (sometimes hyperbolically) the personal concerns of the actors and actresses.[90]

---

88. On functionalism in the social sciences, see Piotr Sztompka, *System and Function: Toward a Theory of Society* (New York, 1974) esp. ch. 4, and cf. a critique of functionalist explanations of certain millenarian movements (cargo cults) in I.C. Jarvie, *The Revolution in Anthropology* (Gateway ed.; Chicago, 1969).

89. Cf. Claude Lévi-Strauss, *Structural Anthropology* trans. C. Jacobson and B.G. Schoepf (New York, 1963) Part 3; Manuela Carneiro da Cunha, "Logique du mythe et de l'action: Le mouvement messianique canela de 1963," *L'homme* 13,4 (1973) 5-37; Nathan Wachtel, "Pensée sauvage et acculturation: L'espace et le temps chez Felipe Guaman Poma de Ayala et l'Inca Garcilaso de la Vega," *Annales: é.s.c.* 3-4 (1971) 793-840.

90. My use of the theatrical simile has been much influenced by the following: James L. Peacock, "Society as Narrative," in Robert F. Spencer, ed., *Forms of Symbolic Action* (Seattle and London, 1969) 167-77; E.P. Thompson, "Patrician Society, Plebeian Culture," *Journal of*

252 *Seekers, Citizens, Scientists*

The theatrical simile, of course, would come as little surprise to the French Prophets, one of whose major publications was the *Théâtre sacré des Cévennes* (most literally, the Sacred Theater of the Cévennes). The French Prophets were conscious inheritors of the drama of the Cévennes, conscious of themselves as millennial players on the proscenium of the Charing Cross scaffold, or standing naked at the front of the Sardinian Chapel, or miming apocalyptic events in their Barbican meetings. The inspired were sure of their roles as God's actors, and the coming of the millennium as narrated in Daniel and Revelation was itself quite a theatrical *tour de force*, even when transformed into a costume drama at London fairs.[91]

If the French Prophets were aware of audience and staging, this was not due solely to their involvement with prophecy, persecution, martyrdom and the vivid scenery of apocalypse. They were also centered in a city intensely aware of public theater and the forms of social display. It was a city of ceremonial processions, charity school parades of pious children, the spectacle of state trials such as that of the vociferous high churchman Dr. Sacheverell in 1709, and the festival atmosphere of hangings at Tyburn, where the condemned themselves dressed in wedding clothes. Virtuoso fascination with the oddities of natural history was converted into the raree show, the museum of the bizarre, the curio cabinet, hodgepodges of skeletons, fossils, and monsters. In this city of fairs and licensed theater, there were simultaneous performances inside playhouses and on the streets, where the urban patriciate, appropriately costumed, made themselves carefully visible in the coaches symbolic of their social and political command. Not always careful to jump out of the way of the carriages, the London workforce of apprentices and young laborers come from the country also performed in the streets, their frequent riots having an expressive and customary force fully as defined as the powers of the Queen's Bench.[92]

Social History 7 (1974) 382-405; idem, "Eighteenth-Century English Society: Class Struggle Without Class?" *Social History* 3 (1978) 133-65; Pierre Verger, "Trance and Convention in Nago-Yoruba Spirit Mediumship," and John Beattie, "Spirit Mediumship in Bunyoro," both in Beattie and Middleton, eds., *Spirit Mediumship and Society in Africa*, 64, 167-68.

91. Henri Desroche, *Sociologie de l'espérance* (Paris, 1973) 228-29, has called attention to the possible theatricality of the inspirations of the French Prophets.

92. See Thompson, "Patrician Society, Plebeian Culture"; Peter Burke, "Popular Culture in Seventeenth-Century London," *London Journal* 3 (1977) 144-49; Geoffrey Holmes, "The Sacheverell Riots: The Crowd and the Church in Early Eighteenth-Century London," *Past and Present* 72 (1976) 55-85; L.W. Cowie, "Holy Thursday," *History Today* 27 (1977) 513-

Theater, then, was a reciprocal relationship. London was a place where perforce strangers met, and they had to have a public language of gesture and a public rhetoric of emotions so that each in turn could be audience to the other's tale. London had specific forums, intermediate between the playhouse and the street, for the telling of tales and the meeting of strangers. These were the inn, the coffeehouse, the mineral spring and spa, the pleasure garden, and the museum. Inns had particular connections with those parts of the outlying country whose main roads led past their stables; consequently, inns were stages for regional news and commercial advertisement. Like the coffeehouses, inns were also sources of rumor, and reports of highwaymen came first to the inns, then, perhaps, to justices. Coffeehouses, regardless of their newspapers, were the sounding houses of opinion rather than the counting houses of fact—the gathering place for clubs, the origin of pamphlets and debates. Mineral springs and spas, with their various prices of admission, probably sifted out the various social strata a bit more carefully than inns or coffeehouses, but there too the apprentice might walk for a moment with an alderman's daughter. The healthful waters, as well the owners knew who brought in entertainers, were excuses for a slightly contrived society of conversations. The more elegant spas, like those at Bath, were clearly marriage arenas, designed for the manufacture of that polite drama of courtship which accompanied negotiations for marriage contracts. London proprietors hired patrols to keep rowdy youth from the broad alleys and lovers' mazes of their pleasure gardens, yet they often failed to prevent the intercourse of strangers of different social backgrounds. Other gardens and parks, less formal, less open to vista and prospect, were filled with the nightly pantomimes of rendezvous between young noblemen disguised as sailors and the London whores they patronized. In all these forums one might remark a rather unassuming and unrepentant theatricality. To be theatrical was not necessarily to be hypocritical or insincere; it was simply to be public in a place of strangers. Perhaps the museums, which made the strange both the object of discourse and the vehicle for meeting others, were paradigmatic of London experience. Museums were collections of artifacts none of which was native to the showroom itself; the artifacts were out of place and usually strangers to one another. Museum owners put the artifacts

---

19; Peter Linebaugh, "The Tyburn Riot Against the Surgeons," in Douglas Hay et al., *Albion's Fatal Tree: Crime and Society in Eighteenth-Century England* (New York, 1975) 65-118; Richard D. Altick, *The Shows of London* (Cambridge, Mass., 1978); Harry W. Pedicord, *The Theatrical Public in the Time of Garrick* (New York, 1954).

into an artificial order dependent as much upon the showperson's sense of theater as upon any scientific system of classification. Skill at display, at the arrangement of façades, stood behind whatever coherence the museum achieved.[93]

If all this were not reason enough for the French Prophets to be sensitive to theater, then certainly they became so after the appearance of puppet-master Martin Powell's marionette show about them and d'Urfey's play, *The Modern Prophets*. D'Urfey's prologue, interestingly, refers to the French Prophets as if they were part of the collection of a travelling zoo:

> As stroling Vagabonds in Country Fairs
> Shew Lyons, grinning Apes and foaming Bears,
> We bring a monster from the Camizars.

Elizabeth Gray, who may well have had associations with the Drury Lane theater before she became a prophet, was recast as Betty Plotwell, "a rare actress" who "can hold my Breath till I make my self as big as if I had a Tympany, turn up the Whites of my Eyes like a Quaker in a Trance, and make as many comical Faces as a Scaramouch or Harlequin . . . ." The French Prophets were themselves drama, and they were possibly conniving actors and actresses, at least to some critics. To others, the French Prophets were at best mere imitators of the convulsive madpeople in Bedlam Hospital, to which any Londoner might go for a shilling's worth of theater, complete with refreshments.[94]

It is not much of an imposition to regard the French Prophets as a theatrical company. But when one reviews their repertoire and style, one discovers that their performances were not all of one piece. The French

93. This and following paragraphs are indebted especially to Richard Sennett, *The Fall of Public Man: On the Social Psychology of Capitalism* (New York, 1977) parts one and two. For the particulars of this paragraph, see Wroth and Wroth, *London Pleasure Gardens;* J.A. Chartres, "The Capital's Provincial Eyes: London's Inns in the Early Eighteenth Century," *London Journal* 3 (1977) 24-39; [Edward Ward], *A Compleat and Humorous Account of all the Remarkable Clubs and Societies in the Cities of London and Westminster* (1745); R.S. Neale, "Bath: Ideology and Utopia, 1700-1760," *Studies in the Eighteenth Century* 3 (1976) 38-54; M. Dorothy George, *London Life in the Eighteenth Century* (New York, 1965) ch. 6; Altick, *The Shows of London*; Yi-Fu Tuan, *Space and Place: The Perspective of Experience* (Minneapolis, 1977) 194-95 on museums.

94. Thomas d'Urfey, *The Modern Prophets* (performed 1709) Act 1, scene 2 and prologue; Philip Dormer Stanhope, fourth earl of Chesterfield, *Letters* ed. Bonamy Dobrée (1932) IV, 1426 and VI, 2709; George Speaight, *The History of the English Puppet Theatre* (New York, 1955) 93-101; Sir Richard Bulkeley, *Preface to the Reader of Warnings of the Eternal Spirit, Spoken by the Mouth of the Servant of God, Abraham Whitro.* (1709) 78; Kingston I, 45; Altick, *The Shows of London*, 44-45. I have found no description of the marionette show.

Prophets had a curious ambivalence about being public. Some performances were meant to be public: their courtroom dramas, their Barbican meetings, their prophecy in the marketplaces of small towns, the *Théâtre sacré* with its witnesses and depositions, the books of warnings with their argumentative prefaces and stage directions ("Mr. L. is seized with the Agitations, and under the Inspiration is taken with a grevious Consumption-Cough, that makes him groan, and almost faint away. He sits upon the Bed's feet, leans his Head upon a Table, and moans and looks pitifully. . . .").[95] Some performances were meant to be private or familial: retreats with their ceremonies, fasting, assemblies of the inspired. Some performances, however, were confusing: histories composed to set the record straight, but never published; arduous missions to distant European and Asian cities where the prophets remained in their rooms or sent out private letters of warning; miracles meant to publicly legitimate the group, but called off because the crowds were too great or spectators too hostile; blessings performed in the dark corners of a large and public meetinghouse; the public wearing of green ribbons just as the group begins to meet in smaller and more private "families."

While the plots may have been confusing, the styles were more so. A wildly agitated prophet might issue a warning for sobriety; stuttering and gasping might produce promises of speaking in tongues or fluent exegesis. Sometimes the contraries were apposite, but sometimes the kinaesthetic message seemed to belong to a different tradition than the verbal message.[96] A prime example of ostensible conflict was the laughter that might accompany serious prophecies, and a fine instance of problems with laughter was this one:

> About two hours after the preceding Representation, Mr. L. [John Lacy] is seized with the Agitations, and under that Inspiration is taken with a grievous Consumption-Cough, that makes him groan, and almost faint away. He sits upon the Bed's feet, leans his Head upon a Table, and moans and looks pitifully. At the same time also the Spirit came upon J. A. [Jean Allut] who, with Agitations, expressing much Joy, and with exceeding great Laughter, sits down by Mr. L., and turns him about by the Arm, to laugh at him in his Face; Mr. L. with great Aversion avoiding the said insulting Mirth.[97]

95. Lacy, *Warnings*, II, 98 (8/5/1707).
96. Cf. the analysis by James L. Peacock, "Javanese Clown and Transvestite Songs: Some Relations Between 'Primitive Classification' and 'Communicative Events,'" in June Helm, ed., *Essays on the Verbal and Visual Arts* (Seattle and London, 1967) 64-76.
97. Lacy, *Warnings*, II, 98-99, and cf. Mary Aspinal et al., *A Collection of Prophetical Warnings* (1708) 174.

Allut prophesies that Lacy will soon rejoice and their enemies suffer. Lacy prophesies that the Lord's servants may have the power to heal. Are the two prophets playing one style off against another? Why was the mirth insulting?

The "exceeding great Laughter," however apt it may have been to rejoicing, violated the rules of public speech which Lacy and other English prophets had accepted as the rules for prophetic speech. This satirical advertisement appeared in *The Female Tatler* in 1709:

> Whereas several Gentlemen and Ladies have accustomed themselves to a very indecent Laugh; One hallows till People are deaf; another spatters in every Body's Face; a third Grins as if she fleered at the whole Company, a fourth screams five Notes above the Pitch; Solomon Simper, Laughing-Master, who was Prentice to Mr. Giggle, and has since improved himself under the famous Myn Heer Van Grin; is willing to instruct any Gentleman or Lady in the Rules of Laughing, according to Notes; which he thinks ought to be as Musical as Singing. . . .[98]

Behind the pretty attack on professionalism and the bourgeois education in the social graces lies a less comical concern with public decorum and gesture. As Restoration playwrights had shown, laughter could be as morally upsetting, as socially disruptive, as the wit that preceded it. It could undermine the value of oaths, the seriousness of passion, the meaning of honesty. Consider this exchange from Congreve's *The Double-Dealer* (1695):

> *Brisk*: The Deuce take me, I can't help laughing my self, ha, ha, ha; yet by Heavens I have a violent passion for your Ladyship, seriously.
> *L. Froth*: Seriously? Ha, ha, ha.
> *Brisk*: Seriously, ha, ha, ha. God I have, for all I laugh.
> *L. Froth*: Ha, ha, ha! What d'ye think I laugh at? Ha, ha, ha.[99]

Here, in this epitome of the double message, both God and love lose out to laughter.

Since laughter usually implied a social exchange (only the mad laughed by themselves) and since laughter was so powerful an agent in social conduct, a stable society had need of a Laughing-Master or at least some rules of laughing.[100] But why "insulting Mirth"? For the French Prophets,

---

98. [Mary de la Rivière Manley], *The Female Tatler*, No. 4 (July 13-15, 1709).

99. Cited in Virginia O. Birdsall, *Wild Civility: The English Comic Spirit on the Restoration Stage* (Bloomington and London, 1970) 204; the entire book is pertinent to my discussion.

100. Cf. the fine survey by Keith Thomas, "The Place of Laughter in Tudor and Stuart England," *Times Literary Supplement*, Jan. 21, 1977, 77-81.

laughter in its more exaggerated forms was too close an analogue to prophecy. Both might entail uncontrollable gesture, grimaces, convulsions, unusual sound patterns, abnormal pitches and volumes. Both depended upon the existence of a public domain. The difference was that laughter was primarily social, while prophecy was imbedded in the individual's relationship with God. For laughter to remain as a part of the group's public performance would be to suggest that inspiration was hardly more than social comedy; conversely, true prophecy would make itself manifest by a stylistic conservatism which the French Prophets grew to emphasize in their later years. Caught in the kind of paradox that could only make more harrowing their ambivalence about being public, the French Prophets encouraged decorum as proof of a private and immeasurably exciting experience of the Lord's Spirit.[101]

Were individual French Prophets experiencing a similar ambivalence about being public? So might be understood the Philadelphian Richard Roach's actions. Here was a man who published a journal to make public the secrets of the Kabbala, yet wrote most of his own diary in shorthand (and, possibly, cipher); a man who agonized over the public meetings of the Philadelphians and then over the theatricality of the French Prophets; a man who had visions but who never prophesied in the public domain. So too Sir Richard Bulkeley, a hypochondriac who viewed his body as a stage for nearly all diseases, a hunchback unafraid of public appearances (unlike his contemporary, the poet Alexander Pope).[102] Bulkeley was vocal, combative, and a do-gooder, yet he clove to a private compact with the schismatic Whitrow as if what he had sought all along from the French Prophets was not inspiration but intimacy—an intimacy probably absent from his relations with his wife, whom he rarely mentions in his letters. Timothy Byfield, advertising his *Sal volatile oleosum* and maligned in satires, proud of the secret of his process, proud of his patent, was yet eager to heal the world of its spiritual as well as physical ills; a man who spoke more to entice than to reveal; a man conscious of his queer fame who ends his life writing Christian closet-pieces, private prayers. Joseph

---

101. Cf. Robin Horton, "Types of Spirit Possession in Kalabari Religion," and S.G. Lee, "Spirit Possession among the Zulu," both in Beattie and Middleton, eds., *Spirit Mediumship and Society in Africa*, 28, 128-56, contrasting dancing with speaking roles, divining with "crying out" activities. Did certain of the prophets (Jean Cavalier in particular) adopt a jester role within the group?

102. On Pope, see Maynard Mack, *The Garden and the City: Retirement and Politics in the Later Poetry of Pope 1731-1743* (Toronto, 1969) 63. I do not happen upon Pope inadvertently. Like Bulkeley, he was a gardener and a man in touch with the governing aristocracy. Their different approaches to publicity may prove an instructive contrast.

Tiley, Edmund Everard, Pierre and Hélène Jurieu acted as spies or informants; how alert they must have been to issues of public and private, the Jurieus especially, who were scarcely inclined to hide themselves in corners. There was also Nicolas Fatio, so zealous of his master Newton's fame that he initiated a controversy with Leibniz over the priority of Newton's invention of the calculus.[103] Though a scribe, Fatio seems never to have written a public defense of the French Prophets; though a missionary, he acted only as interpreter and go-between; though exposed on the scaffold to public humiliation, a punishment he claimed he could have avoided had he chosen to exploit social connections, he continued to perceive himself as a scientific private investigator convinced of the validity of the new prophets.

François-Maximilien Misson wrote one of the most popular European guidebooks of his age. He was for his time an archetypal tourist, a gentleman exploring with equal interest the famous European cabinets of curiosities, the great cathedrals and the ruins, the gardens and the cities, the scientific and theological problems of fossils, and the historical dilemma of a female pope.[104] But he saw himself as a public man, a publicist (like his brother, who wrote a guidebook to England), precisely because he was a Huguenot in exile, his exile having "made me sensible enough, that I have no particular Country here below."[105] He too lived with an ambivalence about being public that was shared by the Cévenol refugees who testified before him for the *Théâtre sacré*: they were safe but not at home, and therefore it was impossible for them to be entirely private. The *Théâtre sacré* was a performance bristling with the ambivalence of exiled Huguenots who admired *inspirés* and Camisards for their attempts to reclaim a public territory for Huguenot worship, however often they might remind themselves that true religion was of the inner person.

---

103. To follow the controversy, see Newton, *The Correspondence*, V, 96-98, 208-09 and VI, 30-32, 286.

104. Maximilian Misson, *A New Voyage to Italy* (2nd ed.; 1699) esp. II, 167-71 on shells, and II, 55-64, 76-93 on Pope Joan. Cf. Levine, *Dr. Woodward's Shield*, 97; Geoffroy Atkinson and Abraham C. Keller, *Prelude to the Enlightenment: French Literature 1690-1740* (1971) 120-23, 152-53, 161.

105. Misson, *A New Voyage to Italy*, Advertisement to the Reader, Concerning this New Edition, a5v. It is important to note here that *Heimweh* (nostalgia for one's homeland) was first identified as a "disease" in 1688 by a Swiss physician. Did Huguenot refugees suffer from this "disease" or, like Misson, attempt a kind of geographical/emotional divorce so necessary to the tourist? Cf. David Lowenthal, "Past Time, Present Place: Landscape and Memory," *Geographical Review* 65 (1975) 1-36.

In simple psychological terms, the ambivalence about being public which I find in the French Prophets as a theatrical company was expressive of personal problems of intimacy.[106] How could one, in the urban flux and theater of eighteenth-century London, so ground oneself that intimacy—the sharing of secured identities—was possible or even desirable? Erik Erikson associates the issue of intimacy particularly with late adolescence, and there is some reason to believe that during the early eighteenth century, as middle-class housing incorporated a more private architecture of bedrooms and hallways, as fewer apprentices and servants lived either with their own families or with their masters, as young laborers were being divorced from the land but not yet fed into a factory system, young men and women would experience a greater sense of isolation than their counterparts in earlier generations.[107] To be isolated was not inevitably to suffer: one could use the isolation as an opportunity for independence, adventure, risk-taking, sexual experiments. One might, as the French Prophets discovered to their pleasure, prophesy. But for the young prophets, inspiration was as much a search for intimate relationships as a declaration of independence. This is Ann Good, ten years old, prophesying: "Fear not, my Children; for I will be your Watchman and Guardian: And my Angels shall always be with you: I will be your Master, and will teach you; none shall teach you, but me alone." And this is John Moult, fourteen: "My Children, fear not; I have set my Angels over you. Fear not what the World can say of you, as long as I am your God and Master."[108] Elizabeth Gray joined John Lacy as wife to husband sometime after he had embraced her as the morning star, an adolescent girl isolated from her family and at loose in London.

There were others—middle-aged men and women, widows—for whom the issue of intimacy or isolation may also have been acute.[109] During the early eighteenth century, notions of mature friendship and marital obli-

---

106. See Erik H. Erickson, *Identity: Youth and Crisis* (New York, 1968) 135-38.

107. Lawrence Stone, *The Family, Sex and Marriage in England 1500-1800* (New York, 1977) 124-26, 221-66, 375-95; Steven R. Smith "The London Apprentices as Seventeenth-Century Adolescents," *Past and Present* 61 (1973) 149-61; Thompson, "Patrician Society, Plebeian Culture," 386.

108. Aspinal et al., *Collection of Warnings*, 90, 144.

109. Cf. Pauline B. Bart, "Depression in Middle-Aged Women," in Vivian Gornick and Barbara K. Moran, *Woman in Sexist Society* (New York and Scarborough, 1971) 163-86; Barbara Myerhoff, "Bobbes and Zeydes: Old and New Roles for Elderly Jews," in Hoch-Smith and Spring, *Women in Ritual and Symbolic Roles*, 207-41. Although neither of these articles has a thesis which can be directly imposed upon eighteenth-century problems, they are suggestive concerning the power and publicity of domestic roles and the effects of aging.

gations were undergoing revision within bourgeois and patrician society. In response to public theatricality, to the changing economic relationships between men and women, to shifts in mortality rates and age-distribution patterns, adults sought more and more seriously an informal and affectionate privacy with friends, husbands, wives.[110] Although Alexander Pope might restrain sentiment within the private, Horatian model, his garden at Twickenham was meant to be responsive to his friends, and his friendships were meant to be, as good men are, "candid, free, sincere."[111] The essayist Richard Steele offered Pliny's sentimental letters to his wife as models for the expression of conjugal affection, and himself wrote that in marriage "there should be always an inward fondness pleading for each other, such as may add new beauties to everything that is excellent, give charms to what is indifferent, and cover everything that is defective."[112] Sentiment, "feeling," was not the sudden preoccupation of the late eighteenth century "romantic" but belonged as well to those singing the hymns of John Mason, Isaac Watts, and the Wesleys, and to those walking through the new, "English," gardens.[113] Women hoped to sustain deep friendships

110. Stone, *The Family, Sex and Marriage*, part four; Laslett, *Family Life*, 102-59; Edward Shorter, *The Making of the Modern Family* (New York, 1975) 64-65, 227; Margaret George, "From 'Goodwife' to 'Mistress': The Transformation of the Female in Bourgeois Culture," *Science and Society* 37 (1973) 152-77; Wilson Carey McWilliams, *The Idea of Fraternity in America* ch. 7; Christopher Lasch, "The Family and History [review article]," *New York Review of Books* 22 (Nov. 13, 1975) 33-38. See also a striking article which correlates the loss of royal divinity in seventeenth-century England with the increasing privacy of the royal person: David Starkey, "Representation Through Intimacy: A Study in the Symbolism of Monarchy and Court Office in Early-Modern England," in Lewis, *Symbols and Sentiments*, 187-224.

111. "To James Craggs, Esq.," line 12, in Alexander Pope, *Collected Poems* ed. Bonamy Dobrée (Everyman ed.; 1924) 108; John Dixon Hunt, "Gardening, and Poetry, and Pope," *Art Quarterly* 37 (1974) 1-30; Mack, *The Garden and The City*, 69, 89, 233. .

112. *The Tatler*, No. 149 (March 21-23, 1710), No. 150 (March 23-25, 1710); see also No. 159 (April 13-15, 1710) and, by Joseph Addison, No. 192 (June 29-July 1, 1710).

113. Cf. Bertrand H. Bronson, *Facets of the Enlightenment* (Berkeley and Los Angeles, 1968) 1-25; Donald Greene, "Latitudinarianism and Sensibility: The Genealogy of the 'Man of Feeling' Reconsidered," *Modern Philology* 75 (1977) 159-83. On hymns, see Michael R. Watts, *The Dissenters* (Oxford, 1978) I, 306-12; Martha W. England and John Sparrow, *Hymns Unbidden: Donne, Herbert, Blake, Emily Dickinson and the Hymnographers* (New York, 1966). If I had not placed the French Prophets within a millenarian tradition, they could be placed within a hymn-singing tradition running from John Mason of Water Stratford through Richard Davis (the Independent) of Rothwell, Benjamin Keach (the Particular Baptist) in London, the Philadelphians (who planned to republish Mason's hymns), the prophet James Cuninghame, the Independent Isaac Watts, the Moravians and the Wesley brothers. Conservative churchmen were as suspicious of hymn-singing as they were of agitations, for it seemed to them—not without justification—that those who sang hymns would come eventually to prophesying and enthusiasm. With the exception of Watts and a religious society in Kent which published its own hymnbook in 1724, the rest of the hymn-singers *did* tend toward prophecy and sentiment. One might argue that Methodist hymn-singing and

among themselves, independent of the men who increasingly controlled their economic and political actions.¹¹⁴ Or they sought, or under pressure accepted, as substitute a kind of domestic husbandry which was at once isolating and intimate, affectionate but disabling.¹¹⁵ Had John Lacy's marriage, between the youngest of five sons and the daughter of a wealthy city merchant, been as cold as it had been—most likely—calculating? Was his adultery with Elizabeth Gray the playing out of a personal need for intimacy? Did the middle-aged women who hosted many meetings of the French Prophets gain the right to a certain intimacy with a wider range of people than they might otherwise have had, or were they laying claim to a new emotional independence? Was Hannah Wharton's new dispensation, with its warm tonalities, an expression of the changing model of friendship and domestic love, or was it, with its demands for full commitment (the sacrifice of one's wealth, the split with old friends) a symbolic rejection of disabling intimacy?¹¹⁶

---

kerygmatic preaching had the same expressive function as the agitated prophecies among the French Prophets; like the hymn, the spoken inspiration would be a vehicle for the publication of a validated intimate experience. See Frank R. Grant, "The Revolution in Religious Rhetoric: John Wesley and the Evangelical Impact on England," *Historian* 39 (1977) 439-54; Garnet V. Portus, *Caritas Anglicana* (1912) 17.

114. I may be reading a nineteenth-century movement into the eighteenth century, but the surplus of women in London and the growing number of older unmarried women in England around 1700 may have been demographic encouragements toward sodality. See Keith Thomas, "Women and the Civil War Sects," *Past and Present* 13 (1958) 42-62; Katherine Philips, "To Rosania and Lucasia, Articles of Friendship," c. 1650-1660, printed in Mary R. Mahl and Helene Koon, eds., *The Female Spectator: English Women Writers before 1800* (Bloomington, London and Old Westbury, 1977) 157-59; Aphra Behn, "To the Fair Clorinda," printed in Louise Bernikow, ed., *The World Split Open* (New York, 1974) 77; Stone, *The Family, Sex and Marriage*, 380-86; Ann D. Gordon and Mary Jo Buhle, "Sex and Class in Colonial and Nineteenth-Century America," in Berenice A. Carroll, ed., *Liberating Women's History* (Urbana, 1976) 287. Cf. Roger Thompson, *Women in Stuart England and America* (Boston, 1974).

115. Stone, *The Family, Sex and Marriage*, 396-98, 656-57; George, "From 'Goodwife' to 'Mistress'"; Marlene LeGates, "The Cult of Womanhood in Eighteenth-Century Thought," *Eighteenth-Century Studies* 10 (1976) 21-39; Bernard Mandeville, *The Virgin Unmasked* (1709; facs. repr., Delmar [N.Y.], 1975) 127-28; Margaret Adams, "The Compassion Trap," in Gornick and Moran, *Woman in Sexist Society*, 555-75; Peggy R. Sanday, "Female Status in the Public Domain," in Michelle Z. Rosaldo and Louise Lamphere, eds., *Woman, Culture, and Society* (Stanford, 1974) 189-206; and cf. Jonathan Swift's different epistolary styles to women playing different roles in his life: Irvin Ehrenpreis, "Letters of Advice to Young Spinsters," in Earl Miner, ed., *Stuart and Georgian Moments* (Berkeley and Los Angeles, 1972) 245-70.

116. One might, applying Erik Erikson's developmental schema, associate kinds of millenarian ethos with stages of personal psychological development. For example, the ethos of judgment might be attractive to those who wish to resolve the issue of trust vs. mistrust, the ethos of cataclysm might appeal to those who must resolve the issue of initiative vs. guilt, the

I am not sure of the answers. I am not sure because publicity and intimacy were critically complex experiences for the French Prophets and their contemporaries in the first decades of the eighteenth century. Theatrical ambivalence reflected personal ambivalences which were themselves not wholly separable from the social dynamic of late Stuart England. But the theatrical simile leads to an appreciation for the depth of motives out of which individuals might become French Prophets.

In previous chapters I have tried in various ways to account for the difference between the Camisard ethos and the millenarian ethos of the French Prophets. To rephrase the problem in terms of theater: What happened when the *Théâtre sacré des Cévennes* was retitled, in English, *A Cry from the Desart*? What would that "Desart" mean to an English audience? What would it mean to set one's performance in the middle of a "Desart"?

First, some stock definitions. "Desart": "a large and wild part of a country, a Wilderness." "Wilderness": "a large Place uncultivated and unfrequented." "Wild": "fierce, furious; desert, or uninhabited; also that grows of it self, as some Trees and Herbs do."[117] Second, a proviso: "Wilderness" had denotations and connotations which escaped the standard dictionary. For the moment, however, just this question: where in England, given these stock definitions, could one find a desert?

Certainly, in this age of agricultural improvement, enclosures, country estates with expensive gardens, drainage of fens, extension of pasture, the replanting of forests, experiment with new crops from the Americas, new roads and coaches on springs, the sophistication of estate management, and the good-natured but relentless virtuoso hunt for buried antiquities, one might be at some loss to locate a fierce, furious, uncultivated and unfrequented place in the countryside. There were, to be sure, wastes where scrawny cattle grazed, forests where bands of robbers held their own, parts of the Lake Country still desolate, but these too were

---

ethos of pentecost might be advocated by those resolving the issues of identity vs. identity confusion, and the ethos of the New Jerusalem might be taken up by those perplexed by the issue of intimacy vs. isolation. Different sorts of persons would then be likely to enter the group at its different stages, and the group itself would tend to respond differently to the same problems as it proceeded through the stages. Though suggestive, such a developmental approach to millenarianism is fraught with complications: are Erikson's stages, which he himself warns against using too rigidly, historically immutable? Is it feasible to assume that one **kind of ethos is a more "mature" manifestation of millenarianism than another? Can or should** one treat groups as if they are individuals? For the stages in the life-cycle, see Erikson, *Identity: Youth and Crisis*, with chart on p. 94.

117. John Kersey, *Dictionarium Anglo-Britannicum* (1708) s.v. "Desart," "Wild"; N. Bailey, *Dictionarium Britannicum* (1730) s.v. "Desert/Desart," "Wild," "Wilderness"; *Oxford English Dictionary* III, 240 and XII, 124-25.

disappearing.¹¹⁸ Where, then, might an English audience think to find a desert? The answer: London itself, a large, furious, and—for many—lonely and uncultivated (immoral, weedy) place. To Jonathan Swift, the city isolated individuals, reduced them to currency; to Samuel Johnson and Henry Fielding, it was morally bankrupt; to Daniel Defoe, slightly more sanguine, it was still the scene of chaos, houses appearing to grow of themselves, encroaching on countryside, gardens and stately homes, and "notwithstanding we are a Nation of Liberty," London had "more public and private Prisons, and Houses of Confinement, than any City in Europe." To members of the Societies for Reformation of Manners, like Lacy and Bulkeley, London was the haven of atheists, libertines and wildness in its most desperate disguises. Due to the constant burning of sea-coal, claimed the gardener Timothy Nourse, "of all the Cities perhaps in Europe, there is not a more nasty and a more unpleasant Place [than London]." For migrants into the city, London was a wide, fierce, open and poorly marked space, difficult to "read" as a system of large swinging signs and crooked lanes, an accidental and incoherent landscape.¹¹⁹

So, as the French Prophets set their scene, they had converted the Camisard Desert into an urban phenomenon, and their cry from the new "Desart" against the Bank of England, their vision of London in flames

118. See Joan Thirsk, "Seventeenth-Century Agriculture and Social Change," in Paul S. Seaver, ed., *Seventeenth-Century England* (New York, 1976) 71-110; Edward G. Malins, *English Landscaping and Literature 1660-1840* (1966) 3; E.P. Thompson, *Whigs and Hunters: The Origin of the Black Act* (New York, 1975); Douglas Hay, "Poaching and the Game Laws on Cannock Chase," in Hay et al., *Albion's Fatal Tree*, 189-253; Norman Nicholson, *The Lakers: The Adventures of the First Tourists* (1955). Those who speculated on the density of population in the late seventeenth century tended to think of England as underpopulated but growing rapidly. See D.C. Coleman, "Labour in the English Economy of the Seventeenth Century," in Seaver, *Seventeenth-Century England*, 112-38; E.P. Hutchinson, *The Population Debate: The Development of Conflicting Theories up to 1900* (New York, 1967) 45-68, 137, 141, 146.

119. Carole Fabricant, "Garden as City: Swift's Landscape of Alienation," *E L H* 42 (1975) 531-55; John Hardy, "Johnson's London: The Country Versus the City," in R.F. Brissenden, ed., *Studies in the Eighteenth Century* (Toronto, 1968) 251-68; John B. Radner, "The Youthful Harlot's Curse: The Prostitute as Symbol of the City in 18th-Century English Literature," *Eighteenth-Century Life* 2,2 (1976) 59-64; Daniel Defoe, *A Tour Thro' London about the year 1725*, ed. Mayson M. Beeton and E. Beresford Chancellor (New York and London, 1969) 12, 53; W.A. Speck, "Mandeville and the Eutopia Seated in the Brain," in Irwin Primer, ed., *Mandeville Studies* (The Hague, 1975) 79; Timothy Nourse, *Campania Foelix* (1700) 349; Peter Borsay, "The English Urban Renaissance: The Development of Provincial Urban Culture c. 1680 - c. 1760," *Social History* 5 (1977) 597; Steven Marcus, *Engels, Manchester, and the Working Class* (New York, 1974) 98, on "reading" cities; Yi-Fu Tuan, *Topophilia: A Study of Environmental Perception, Attitudes, and Values* (Englewood Cliffs, 1974) 112 and Figure 9, on inner city as wilderness, and cf. E. Howard, *Man of Newmarket* (1678): "This Metropolitan Wilderness of Houses, called London," cited in *Oxford English Dictionary*, XII, 124.

and the Tower Guns roaring, occurred within a city due for apocalypse. But John Lacy, standing on a prospect north of London, had described the city as the New Jerusalem, mountains round about her, her gates magnificent, no poisonous thing within her precincts.[120] How could this large and wild place called London be the secure and walled New Jerusalem?

Lacy had been standing in Hoxton, a suburb which had been open ground only thirty years before and which, in 1707, was still not much built up.[121] The London he saw would have resembled the view from Islington: a city of steeples, girded not by mountains but by pond and pasture, deceptively spacious, and if free from soot and smoke, probably colorful. (See Plate XI.) The view, and Lacy's vision, corresponded to a second desert motif—the desert as refuge, the traditional ground of Christian contemplation and spiritual renewal.[122] It corresponded also to an eighteenth-century prospect of a country estate, in which wilderness had another and less estranging definition.

PLATE XI. View of London from Islington, by T. Bowles (1730). Reproduced with permission from Daniel Defoe, *A Tour Thro' London about the year 1725*, ed. Mayson M. Beeton and E. Beresford Chancellor (New York and London: Benjamin Blom, 1969).

120. Lacy, *Warnings*, III, 48.
121. Defoe, *A Tour Thro' London*, 19.
122. George H. Williams, *Wilderness and Paradise in Christian Thought* (New York, 1962) 4-6 *et passim*.

During the lifespan of the French Prophets, while estate management was being rationalized, the country house and its gardens were refashioned by wealthy men and women who sought a middle ground between the jostling, dirty city and the increasingly hedged or fenced working farmland.[123] Architects, dramatists, poets and gardeners designed estates that gradually departed from the rigorous straight-lined formality of French models like Versailles, which Sir William Chambers called a "mere city of verdure."[124] Accustomed by the methods of enclosure and land improvement to a wholesale reconstruction of local geography, patrician society shunted earth, rock and stream into a series of panoramas and thoughtful surprises which, they hoped, would be exemplary of human sensitivity to the natural world. The country house, vaguely Palladian, would sit on a slight eminence, surrounded by a distant rim of hills and overlooking a landscape which was carefully natural, with winding streams, pleasant twisting walks, unmown glades, and wildernesses.[125]

Originally, the gardener's wilderness had been that which one saw from the mount within the walled medieval garden. In the seventeenth century the wilderness itself was taken inside, placed within the protecting walls of the estate, and trimmed into a maze. This was the wilderness of Wimbledon in 1649: "many young trees, woods, and sprays of good growth, and height, cut and formed into several ovals, squares, and angles, very well ordered.... All the alleys of this wilderness, being in number eighteen, are of gravelled earth, very well ordered and maintained, the whole being compiled with such order and decency, as that it is not one of the least ornaments of the said Manor." In the walks of the Spring Gardens in London in 1700, "both sexes meet, and mutually serve one another as guides to lose their way, and the windings and turnings in the little Wildernesses are so intricate, that the most experienced mothers have often lost themselves in looking for their daughters." "I have several Acres about my House," wrote Joseph Addison in 1712, "which I call my

123. Raymond Williams, *The Country and The City* (New York, 1973) esp. 57, 123-24; Leo Marx, *The Machine in the Garden* (New York, 1964) 73-144; William Coleman, "Providence, Capitalism, and Ecologic Crisis," *Journal of the History of Ideas* 37 (1976) 27-44.
124. Chambers cited in Nan Fairbrother, *Men and Gardens* (New York, 1956) 209 and see p. 210.
125. Williams, *The Country and The City*, 25-26, 59, 106, 123-24; Nourse, *Campania Foelix*, 301 ff.; G.E. Mingay, *The Gentry*, 80-108; Christopher Hussey, *English Gardens and Landscapes 1700-1750* (New York, 1967) esp. 16; Rudolf Wittkower, "English Neo-Palladianism, the Landscape Garden, China and the Enlightenment," in his *Palladio and Palladianism* (New York and London, 1974) 177-92; William A. Brogden, "Stephen Switzer 'La Grand Manier,' " in Peter Willis, ed., *Furor Hortensis* (Edinburgh, 1974) 21-30; Derek Clifford, *A History of Garden Design* (Rev. ed.; New York and Washington, 1966) esp. 189.

Garden, and which a Skillful Gardener would not know what to call. It is a Confusion of Kitchen and Parterre, Orchard and Flower Garden, which lie so mixt and interwoven with one another, that if a Foreigner, who had seen nothing of our Country, should be conveyed into my Garden at his first landing, he would look upon it as a natural Wilderness, and one of the uncultivated Parts of our Country." "In a word," wrote Timothy Nourse, "let this Third Region or Wilderness be Natural-Artificial; that is, let all things be disposed with that cunning, as to deceive us into a belief of a real Wilderness or Thicket."[126]

This wilderness was part of the pastoral theater of eighteenth-century landowners. The gardens were theaters employing illusionistic devices (ha-has, false bridges, mirroring pools) to extend the calm of patrician grounds into the laboring plebeian world of cash crops and plow horses. The gardens could shut out the concerns of the market economy and political placemanship just as they masked agrarian capitalism with classical backdrops, hermit's caves, ruins.[127] Wild *and* walled, natural *and* artificial, the wilderness was a stage for the same problems as the "Desart" city, publicity and intimacy. The wilderness encouraged solitude but was a region demonstrative of the landowner's hospitality; it was an important index to the landowner's custodial intimacy with nature but also a sign of public stewardship of the bounties of nature.[128] Finally, the eighteenth-

126. Parliamentary Survey of Wimbledon, Survey No. 27, Nov. 1649, cited in Malins, *English Landscaping and Literature*, 13; Tom Brown, *Amusements* (1700) 54, cited in Wroth and Wroth, *London Pleasure Gardens*, 287; *The Spectator*, No. 477 (Sept. 6, 1712); Nourse, *Campania Foelix*, p. 322, cited and discussed in S. Lang, "The Genesis of the English Landscape Garden," in Nikolaus Pevsner, ed., *The Picturesque Garden and Its Influence Outside the British Isles* (Washington, D.C., 1974) 8; H.F. Clark, *The English Landscape Garden* (1948) 3-10. See also *The Spectator*, No. 160 (Sept. 3, 1711) where Addison, discussing classes of genius in literature, relates both the French Prophets and wilderness to genius of the first class (though the French Prophets are brought in only as contrast to the true divine impulse that "produces a whole Wilderness of noble Plants rising in a thousand beautiful Landskips without any certain Order or Regularity").

127. Williams, *The Country and The City*, 124-25; B. Sprague Allen, *Tides in English Taste 1619-1800* (New York, 1958) II, 151-52; Clifford, *A History of Garden Design*, 55n., 77, 80; Lang, "The Genesis of the English Landscape Garden," 19-29, which argues for a direct borrowing from theatrical scene design for the landscape settings; Tuan, *Topophilia*, 132-33; Kenneth Woodbridge, "William Kent as Landscape-Gardener: A Re-Appraisal," *Apollo* n.s. 100 (Aug., 1974) 126-37; Ronald Paulson, *Emblem and Expressionism: Meaning in English Art of the Eighteenth Century* (1975) 30.

128. Hunt, "Gardening, and Poetry, and Pope," 24; Paulson, *Emblem and Expressionism*, 21-30; Agnieszka Morawinska, "Eighteenth-Century 'Paysages Moralisés,'" *Journal of the History of Ideas* 38 (1977) 461-75; Fabricant, "Garden as City," 541-42; Howard Erskine-Hill, *The Social Milieu of Alexander Pope* (New Haven and London, 1975) 248, 266, 316, and note the straining set of contraries in the 1752 epitaph for William, Lord Digby of Geashill (cited, p.

century wilderness garden carried with it a religious valency which Timothy Nourse made explicit:

> what can be more suitable to a serious and well-disposed Mind, than to contemplate the Improvements of Nature by the various Methods and Arts of Culture: The same spot of Ground, which some Time since was nothing but Heath and Desart, and under the Original Curse of Thorns and Briars, after a little Labour and Expence, seems restored to its Primitive Beauty in the State of Paradise. . . . So that this kind of Employment may most properly be called *a Recreation*, not only from the Refreshment it gives to the Mind, but from the *Restauration of Nature*, which may be lookt upon as a *New Creation* of things; when from Nothing, or from something next to Nothing, we become the Instruments of producing, or of restoring them in such Perfection.[129]

It is in this sense, then, still a wilderness, that London could be the New Jerusalem: London as a country estate, a refuge, "no noisy City; no dirty one." As Lacy prophesied: "Behold my wandering scattered Flock shall be received into my Park, Inclosure. They shall run from all Parts into it, at the Aperture I'll make in the Fence; . . . I'll take my People within a Barrier, now, round the Mount, the Mount where I appear, and all that are without shall feel the Terror; they, they only sweet Repose." And nonetheless, the ambivalence was there in the prophecy itself, an ambivalence about intimacy and publicity, for Lacy also saw a large stately Building surrounded by gardens, of which he spoke: "My Mansions are prepared; are not like the Buildings of Men, All the Sides thereof are open, no need of Inclosure so, in that manner. No hurtful air, no Thief, no Beast, no nauseous Insect, no sort of Annoyance can attend them. . . ."[130] This matched well the vast and intimate, ambivalent world of the estate, with its secluded dells, dramatic vistas, imposing gates and illusions of openness.

Londoners themselves, men and women of less wealth, lacking country retreats, imitated as best they could the patrician landscape in their own town gardens, or betook themselves to the public gardens such as Cuper's or Kensington, where

---

148): "He was naturally enclined to avoid the Hurry of a publick Life,/Yet was careful to keep up the port of his Quality./Was willing to be at ease, but scorned Obscurity;/And therefore never made his retirement a pretence to draw/Himself within a narrower compass, or to shun such expense/as Charity, Hospitality, & his Honour call'd for . . . ."

129. Nourse, *Campania Foelix*, 2-3. This statement must be put in the context of a contemporary scientific and theological debate over the nature of the primeval and paradisical terrain, on which see Allen, *Tides in English Taste*, I, 159-61; Levine, *Dr. Woodward's Shield*, *passim*, and note 132 below.

130. Lacy, *Warnings*, II, 63-64, 69-70, 75-78 and III, 48. Cf. Aspinal et al., *Collection of Warnings*, 23.

> The Dames of Britain oft in crowds repair
> To gravel walks, and unpolluted air.
> Here, while the Town in damps and darkness lies,
> They breathe in sun-shine, and see azure skies.

These town gardens could rarely achieve the sense of space or the cultured wildness of their urbane country cousins, but they did turn the pastoral image in upon the city itself.[131]

Hence when the *Théâtre sacré des Cévennes* was retitled *A Cry from the Desart*, an English audience would have before them twin stages, neither of which closely corresponded to the Cévenol Desert. The English audience would see the wasteland of London and the cultivated wilderness of a well-managed garden. They would see the wild *inside* the walled.[132]

Opponents of the French Prophets were as affected by tensions between publicity and intimacy as the performers. They demanded of the prophets the working of miracles which would in fact be the violation of natural physical laws, but they insisted that wild agitations were, however abnormal, more akin to illness than godliness. They thought the prophets foolish in their public mimes but could not accept accounts of miraculous healing performed in private. Millenarian churchmen like William Lloyd hoped to keep knowledge of millennial chronology restricted to responsible religious leaders, fearing that the ebullient imagery of Revelation might turn men wild or witless.[133]

What of the individual French Prophets? Was the lapidary figure of the wild within the walled also expressive of their personal anxieties? In the cases of Nicolas Fatio and Sir Richard Bulkeley, it was, quite literally.

Nicolas Fatio wrote his *Fruit-Walls Improved by Inclining Them to the*

---

131. Wroth and Wroth, *London Pleasure Gardens*, 247; [T. Tickell], *Kensington Garden* (1722) 1; Stephen Switzer, *Ichnographia rustica* (1718) I, xxxix-xl, and xxxii, where he lists the cost of a small country garden at £200-400 per annum. Cf. Thomas Fairchild, *The City Gardener* (1722): "I find that almost every Body, whose Business requires them to be constantly in Town, will have something of a Garden at any rate," cited in Fairbrother, *Men and Gardens*, 194.

132. The Camisard revolt had taken place first in the mountains, in the Cévennes, to which the guerillas owed much of their success and, perhaps, the fundament of their ethos of cataclysm. In the late seventeenth and early eighteenth centuries, mountain areas were little explored and evocative of terror and cataclysm; the Cévennes was so poorly mapped that government troops could easily lose their way, and even in the 1760 map of the region (Plate II), the distances and directions of small towns to the west of Alès (Alais) were incorrect. Cf. Philippe Joutard, *La légende des Camisards* (Paris, 1977) 57-59, 68-69; Marjorie H. Nicolson, *Mountain Gloom and Mountain Glory* (New York, 1959); *The Tatler* No. 161 (April 18-20, 1710).

133. Or revolutionary. Cf. Jacob, *The Newtonians*, 126-27, 268-70.

Horizon in 1699. He was a young man of twenty-five, precocious, a protegé of Newton, making his way in England as tutor to the sons of nobility. The purpose of the pamphlet, "a mixture of Gardening and Geometry," was to apply mathematical and astronomical knowledge to the problem of growing fruit trees in the cold weather which had endured since 1683 in northern Europe. Fruit-walls were not his innovation, and they were customarily used to retain the sun's heat as well as to protect orchards from theft. Fatio, however, computed the angle of inclination best suited to English walls to compensate for "this Vail, that is spread between the Sun and us."[134]

If we turn to the engraving (Plate XII) which embodies his proposal, we find ourselves gazing at the lines of a rigorously formal garden from the portico of a mansion whose elegant column juts out to our left.[135] In the foreground there is not only a stately coach but what may be the beginning of a hunt, and in the middle distance is pasture. Though the mountain backdrop is continental, perhaps Genevan, as is the architecture of the distant houses, the winding path in the deer park is disturbingly English. But what makes the composition most disturbing is not the intrusion of so many modes of country life as the fact that all the fruit trees are growing aslant. Everything is so regular that the tiny gesturing humans are out of place, the fruit trees lifeless, the rearing horses inconsequential and posed, not poised. It is, despite the obvious efforts to the contrary, a strangely unsituated landscape; even the shadows falling to give us the position of the sun do not convince us of the sun's heat, which should be crucial to such a book as Fatio's.

Compare another engraving done under Fatio's supervision fifteen years later (Plate XIII). Here the original inspiration came from Jean Allut, who directed Fatio to have a copperplate made of a woman, four kings and four priests, one sword and one comet. The woman was the True Church, distressed and tempest-tossed, being stripped to her chemise by

---

134. Pp. vii, 113-14. On fruit-walls, see Edward Malins and The Knight of Glin, *Lost Demesnes: Irish Landscape Gardening, 1660-1845* (1976) 33; Nourse, *Campania Foelix*, 132-136.

135. The engraving was done by Simon Gribelin, b. 1661, who had come to England from Paris in 1680. Gribelin's other work, as in Elizabeth Elstob's *An English-Saxon Homily* (1709), is not as rigid, although it remains generally formal. Fatio, who may have come to hear of Gribelin through his engravings for a 1697 book of ornaments for watchmakers, was a decent draughtsman and may have provided Gribelin with initial sketches. On Gribelin, see *Bryan's Dictionary of Painters and Engravers* ed. George C. Williamson (New ed.; New York, 1903) II, 279; "Gribelin," *Allgemeines Lexikon der Bildenden Künstler*, ed. U. Thieme and F. Willis (Leipzig, 1922) XV, 19-20; *DNB*, IX, 662-63.

PLATE XII. Engraving by Simon Gribelin for Fatio's *Fruit-Walls Improved* (1699)

those that men call priests. The four kings were those of Daniel 7, and the comet became one of the horns in that passage—here, however, promising the coming of the Lord and the victory of the True Church.[136] This engraving is a bit more lively: the sword of the Lord's jealousy is descending upon the Lutheran Priest, there is tension in the muscles of the Greek (Orthodox) Priest, the raiment of the True Church is strewn in some disorder under the feet of her foes. Still, there is no backdrop, and the staging leaves us wondering where we are; indeed, the shadows are inconsistent, the source of light mysterious.

The two engravings are iconographic doubles. In both, the young and potentially fruitful are tied down and pulled aslant for their own good (the True Church is purified by her trials). In both, redemption comes from above, out of the clouds. In both, columns and geometric lines bound the struggling and thin protagonists. In both, youth has not yet any place of its own or any place to hide. There is in both an uncomfortable openness without a corresponding freedom.

The next scene comes of a private iconography: Fatio's dreams. In the sparse notes of his dreams, 1714-1732, Fatio twice recorded nearly the same incident. In one dream he is in a great house, but he is wearing an old and dirty dressing robe, and feels ashamed to go to dinner and sit thus in

---

136. Jean Allut and Elie Marion, *Quand vous aurez saccagé, vous serez saccagés: Car la lumière est apparue dans les ténèbres, pour les détruire* (Rotterdam?, 1714) 80-81. I do not know the engraver of this print, but I would argue that it was Fatio, not the engraver, who sketched in the ropes (absent from the prophetic directions given by Allut). Fatio may also have had personal interest in the frontispiece since the book had a title quite similar to the motto of Geneva: *post tenebras lux*.

PLATE XIII. Frontispiece to *Quand vous aurez saccagé, vous serez saccagés* (Rotterdam?, 1714), a collection of prophecies by Jean Allut and Elie Marion from their last mission to the continent, printed under the supervision of Nicolas Fatio.

the presence of English nobility. In a second dream, he is in the house of a nobleman, wearing a dressing gown and a dirty linen bedcap, and he is ashamed.[137] He is, in other words, unkempt within the walls of an orderly and superior world.

These dreams may reflect Fatio's worries about money, but they are also a reflection of worries about social recognition. Fatio endeavored to be a public figure but always felt restrained by the public world. Throughout his life he was waiting on people, petitioning, taking jobs which kept him bound to the whims of the boys he tutored.[138] Shame (*honte*), the word Fatio used to describe his feelings in the dreams, is a social state, a

137. BPUG, MSS fr. 602, f. 204 (3/25/1715) and f. 208 (5/10/1719).
138. See esp. BPUG, MSS fr. 602, ff. 60-60v., letter to his mother, 2/18/1690, and ff. 245-53, petition to the King (George II); Cambridge University Library, Add. MSS 4007, ff. 721-30; Manuel, *Portrait of Newton*, 193.

problem of being visible at the wrong time, an inept publicity. One feels out of place and unsightly; it is less a matter of what one has done than what one has been seen doing.[139] In his dreams, Fatio is seen or fears to be seen as wild, that is, unprepared for civil society.

His fears were not unjustified, however much they may have been shaped by his experiences as something of a prodigy. When he began to act on behalf of the French Prophets, his brother wrote to him, hoping to shame him out of his attachment by comparing him to their cousin Pierre Facio, who had been advocating popular sovereignty in bourgeois Geneva: "Surely our family would appear strangely fated if, while the lawyer Facio had found himself on the verge of entirely upsetting the Government of this State, and creating confusion, disorder and anarchy in this City, after having led a great part of the People to despise their Magistrates and ministers, you on your side should be the cause of a great trouble in the Church."[140]

Fatio as a young man was as sensitive as his young fruit trees to the "Vail, that is spread between the Sun and us"; he put the fruit trees into a position analogous to that in which he found himself, restricted, seeking light (esteem, fame). With the French Prophets he discovered a kind of vitality he admired, a liveliness which overstepped boundaries or ignored them, a wildness possible within walls. A strong sense of shame, derived perhaps from a too-early exposure in high society, kept him from imitating the prophets. He could follow them around, document their adventures, suffer with them on the scaffold and in prison, but he could not expose himself as the prophets did, revealing in public an intimate experience of the Holy Spirit. He could not, like the True Church in its chemise, stand proudly in public in a soiled dressing gown and dirty bedcap. He would be instead the best of the chroniclers among the French Prophets, almost compulsive, eager to record the agitated warnings of his young and enthusiastic friends.

For Sir Richard Bulkeley, as conscious of his rickety constitution as was Fatio of his precarious social position, there is no equivalent set of

---

139. On shame, see Erikson, *Identity: Youth and Crisis*, 109-15; J.A. Pitt-Rivers, *The People of the Sierra* (Chicago, 1961) 112-18; Carl D. Schneider, *Shame, Exposure and Privacy* (Boston, 1977); John M. Cuddihy, *The Ordeal of Civility* (New York, 1974) 58-63. On money, publicity, and shame, see Norman O. Brown, *Life Against Death* (Middletown, 1959) 179-201.

140. BPUG, MSS fr. 601, f. 145v. (letter of 6/14/1707 N.S.). Cf. Fatio's letter to his brother six months later, in which he emphasizes that he stood on a scaffold and not at a pillory: BPUG, MSS fr. 602, f. 115 (12/19/1707). At a pillory one is physically restrained; on a scaffold one is exposed but free to face the audience as one wishes.

engravings. Rather: a chimney piece (Plate XIV), modelled in plaster, depicting the rebuilding of Jerusalem by Nehemiah. The chimney piece stood in the parlor of Sir Richard's ancestral home near Dublin, Old Bawn, which had been burned down in 1641 and then rebuilt. Two armed men (only one is visible in Plate XIV) flank the central relief, in which the Jews, as in Nehemiah 4, carry weapons in one hand and labor to restore Jerusalem with the other. Sir Richard must have lived with this image just above him for much of his life. And he must have lived too with the book of Nehemiah, a book of gates and walls and the Feast of Tabernacles.

The house itself was architecturally intermediate between the defensive castle and the open eighteenth-century country villa. It was gabled and massive, with several stories, twelve chimneys and a small cupola. The chimney piece Jerusalem is probably a somewhat simplified replica of Old Bawn in the 1640s and 1650s, during which time the house and its grounds sustained a household of some thirty persons including cookmaids, brewers, footmen, stewards and gardeners. Sir Richard in 1693 had at least three or four men acting as gardeners for his nursery—which lay beyond the three-foot-thick walls and the "very large and deep moat" that protected Old Bawn—and for the orchard, gardens and pleasure ground of beech and yew trees which lay within.[141] (See Plate XV.)

In his nursery, gardens and orchard, Sir Richard experimented incessantly with new varieties of fruit and vegetables. He wanted to know how to graft walnut trees and quince trees, he wondered about potatoes and shamrock, he raised a crop of Virginia wheat and tried out maize as a substitute for white peas. He made bread out of a harvest of kidney beans, planted hornbeams and cypress trees, and was sorry that his correspondent Dr. Martin Lister was "so indisposed to so useful a part of Philosophy as husbandry, agriculture & gardening."[142]

141. H.G. Leask, *Irish Castles and Castellated Houses* (Dundalk, 1941) 149-50; idem, "House at Oldbawn, Co. Dublin," *Journal of the Royal Society of Antiquaries of Ireland* 6th ser., 3 (1913) 314-25; F. Elrington Ball, "Descriptive Sketch of Clondalkin, Tallaght, and Other Places in West County Dublin," *ibid.* 5th ser., 9,2 (1899) 103-05; idem, *A History of the County Dublin* (Dublin, 1905) III, 32-35; Trinity College (Dublin), Archbishop of Dublin's MSS 132 No. 1, "The Lordship of Tallagh latlie belonging to the Bishope of Dublin, c. 1650-1660"; Bodleian, MSS Lister 35, f. 116, letter of 3/19/1686. On the gardens and grounds which Sir Richard would have seen in his vicinity, see Desmond Fitz-Gerald, "Irish Gardens of the Eighteenth Century. 1. The Baroque. 2. The Rococo," *Apollo* n.s. 88 (Sept. 1968) 185-97, 204-09; Malins and The Knight of Glin, *Lost Demesnes*.

142. Bodleian, MSS Lister 3, ff. 50-51v., MSS Lister 35, f. 121v., and MSS Lister 36, ff. 43, 46; Sir Richard Bulkeley, "The Extract of a Letter... concerning the Improvement to be made by Maize," *Philosophical Transactions of the Royal Society* 17 (1693) 708-10, and see also 971.

PLATE XIV. Chimney piece, modelled in plaster, from the parlor of Old Bawn, in National Museum, Dublin.

Horticulture intruded as metaphor into other areas of his life. When he proposed to erect a full-scale college in Dunlavan, it was "to give mankind a politer education to diffuse [and so be(?)] the vehicle of many blessings, but especially (as I intend it) to send forth more laborers [unto the (?)] Lord's harvest." He also proposed to endow a public Latin school in the same town, "for a nursery" to the college. His grandmother, as he chose to recall, had seen hedges full of haws as a parable of God's providence. And with that seventeenth-century sense of a museum as a place to make apparent God's providences, Sir Richard interested himself in the foundation of a museum of natural history.[143]

How could this man, who so loved to cultivate and domesticate. who had grown up within walls and moat, whose new college would have a

143. *HMC* 1: 2nd R., Lyons, 239; Bodleian, MSS Lister 36, ff. 44-44v.; BM, Add. MSS 15,857, f. 158.

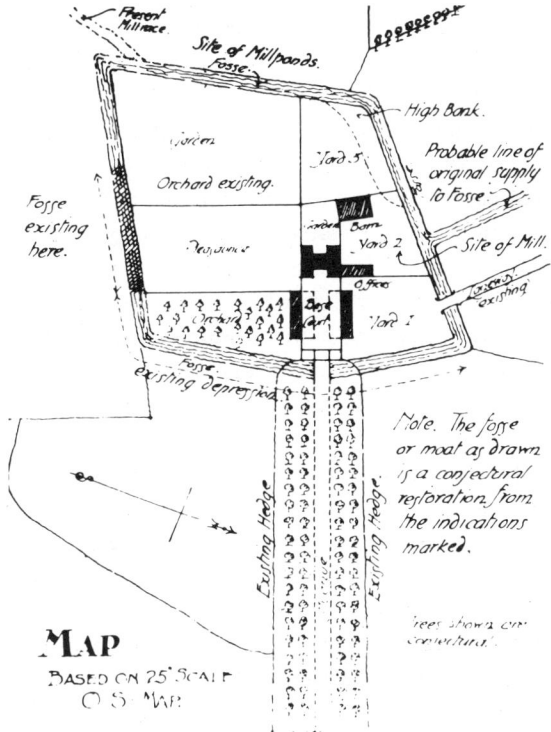

PLATE XV. Reconstruction of ground plan of Sir Richard Bulkeley's ancestral home near Dublin, Old Bawn. From H. G. Leask, "House at Oldbawn, Co. Dublin," *Journal of the Royal Society of Antiquaries of Ireland* 6th ser., 3 (1913) 320.

Photographs for Plates XIV and XV supplied by Peter Walsh.

discipline "most strict, . . . for I take discipline to be the life of a society that consists of subordinate ranks," how could such a man first join the French Prophets and then go off with the wild levelling prophet Abraham Whitrow?

For the answer we must return to Nehemiah and the chimney piece. It is curious that after Nehemiah has finally managed the rebuilding of the walls of Jerusalem, he resurrects (or claims to resurrect) the celebration of the Feast of Tabernacles. During this harvest festival, the Jews must live not within their solid masonry but under shelters of boughs and branches, to remind themselves of the sanctuary in the wilderness of Sinai. Nehemiah, like the chimney piece with its soldier-builders, insinuates a memory of wilderness and wildness into the fortress of the Lord's people.[144]

This pattern of the wild within the walled, iconographic, scriptural, had powerful resonances for Sir Richard Bulkeley. It had resonance in what he called, referring to his illnesses, "my crazy life," a life of dilapidation, physical constraint and irregularity. His illnesses kept him within walls, inactive but ill at ease: "I write you this from my bed to which I am almost confined, though not quite so much out of necessity as choice, it being the only place where for these 3 weeks past I could have ease, from a most acute pain (or rather Smart) which I suffer when I am up, without intermission. . . . But I am under this unhappy Dilemma, that while I am out of bed, which is a few hours in the day, I am miserably pained, & while I am in bed, my thighs legs & feet sweat continually, so that I am much wasted."[145]

The pattern had resonance in his scientific pursuits—his fascination with the Giant's Causeway, a natural formation on the Irish coast which resembled a series of classical pillars, a wild architecture in the sense that it grew "of it self"; his invention of a coach to travel mountain roads; his experiments with wild grasses.[146]

And it had particular resonance in his relationship with Abraham Whitrow. As part of his attack on aristocracy, Whitrow spoke of Jesus as a carpenter; Jesus was a laborer, not a man of leisure, and he "was born poorly, and lived poorly, working with his own hands." In one of his very few prophecies which left room for images of happiness, Whitrow's images were agricultural:

> My Children, my Harvest is near, and I will send forth Labourers to gather it in. I'll gather my Wheat into my Barns, and the Chaff I'll burn with unquenchable fire; nay, and the Stubble even to the Root, Root and all. . . . Some of you here present I'll send forth for Labourers, to reap and gather into my Barn. I say you must and shall have Trouble, before I'll provide Pleasure for you. Support one another. Comfort one another, and I will be comfortable to you all."[147]

Whitrow's performance, even more than that of the other prophets, was a marvelous embodiment of the men rebuilding Jerusalem, trowel in one

144. Nehemiah 8 and 9; Leviticus 23:39-43. Cf. Williams, *Wilderness and Paradise*, 15, 46, 65.

145. *HMC* 1: 2nd R., Lyons, 239; Bodleian, MSS Lister 3, f. 35.

146. Sir Richard Bulkeley, "Part of a Letter . . . concerning the Giants Causway in the County of Atrim in Ireland," *Philosophical Transactions of the Royal Society* 17 (1693) 928-30 (*sic* for 938-40); Bodleian, MSS Lister 35, f. 123, and MSS Lister 36, ff. 43, 55-56.

147. Abraham Whitro, *Warnings of the Eternal Spirit* (1709) 167, 209, 277-78, 284. Both Bulkeley and Whitrow were also grandsons of clergymen: Bulkeley, *Preface to the Reader*, 20.

hand, sword and fire in the other. His levelling, his emphasis on charity and humility, were a tabernacle language for Sir Richard Bulkeley. Bulkeley, with his predispositions for charity and nurture, with his sense of the furiously mortal substance that was his body, found in Whitrow's prophecies not a solution to his problems but a repetition of a pattern. Perhaps, too, Whitrow was the agent by whom Bulkeley could recognize that pattern or know it as a divine geometry.

When the *Théâtre sacré des Cévennes* became *A Cry from the Desert*, the prophetic arena shifted from mountains to a peculiar English desert of wilderness within walls. As a theatrical company, the French Prophets expressed the social and personal tensions inherent in the experience of such a desert. Wilderness could make for intimacy or for the publicity of "insulting Mirth." Walls could be restraining or supportive, overwhelming or comforting. One's habits of social intercourse, one's desires for intimacy or publicity, one's sense of shame might determine the role one would play as a French Prophet. This might have been so in particular for Fatio and Bulkeley, not because they were models for the group but because there is—by the inordinate bias of past archivists for the personal papers of the literate, famous and wealthy—more information about them. But the figure of the wilderness within walls was probably equally potent for many other French Prophets: if only more were known about Francis Moult's city garden with its "naked" statues, or the estate of James Cuninghame, or the homes of the women who hosted meetings; or more about the adulteries in Bristol and London among French Prophets.[148] Did Timothy Byfield think that he was bottling something essentially wild, and therefore healing, when he sold his *Sal volatile oleosum*? Were the Scientists, with their interests in the Kabbala, physics, and mineral salts, searching for that which "grows of it self," something wild at the center of a universe of laws and mechanical motions?

The appeal of the French Prophets cannot be explained by resorting simply to age, sex, wealth, or occupational data. Illness, exile, the London

148. The city with its storied buildings and gates may have been a wilderness within walls for women especially, who seem to have been socially freer in London than in the countryside. Cf. this excerpt from George Farquhar's *The Beaux' Stratagem* (1707), one of the most popular plays of the eighteenth century: *"Mrs. Sullen:* . . . when a man would enslave his wife he hurries her into the country, and when a lady would be arbitrary with her husband she wheedles her booby up to town. A man dare not play the tyrant in London because there are so many examples to encourage the subject to rebel. O, Dorinda, Dorinda, a fine woman may do anything in London . . . ." (Act II, scene 1, lines 119-21 in the edition by Charles N. Fifer [Lincoln, 1977]). See also Maximillian E. Novak, "Margery Pinchwife's 'London Disease': Restoration Comedy and the Libertine Offensive of the 1670's," *Studies in the Literary Imagination* 10 (1977) 1-23.

life of confused streets and public theater, personal demands for self-expression all contributed to the attraction of prophecy and miracle. If followers were most concerned with making the world regular once more, their millennium would be one of judgment and law, a public world. If they were concerned with personal vitality, their millennium would be one of pentecost, intimate. If they were concerned with a world universally at peace, their vision would be of the New Jerusalem, itself a place of tension between the intimate and the public. The New Jerusalem, either as country estate or pastoral city, would be the most difficult ethos to sustain, riddled as it was by the ambivalences of a wilderness within walls. This may explain, from the point of view of the individual believer, why the French Prophets acted according to several scripts, moving from one ethos to another, and back, and back again. Rarely did believers hold to a single vision or a single aspect of that vision, partly because they wanted different things at different times, partly because they were humanly inconsistent, partly because the society of the early eighteenth century was neither static nor simple.

I have asked about men and women what Newton and Fatio asked about the particles of the universe: what are the conditions by which they can move?[149] Less successful than Newton or Fatio, I have seen some patterns but uncovered no basic laws. The believers did not always proceed in straight lines, and far too many travelled in complete obscurity. Faith is a strange force, as the believers knew and the historian soon finds out. Nothing in this chapter can fully account for it.

149. Buckley, *Motion and Motion's God*, 169.

Conclusion

Isaac Hollis was the last French Prophet. At his death on June 25, 1774, Ann Lee and her Shaker companions had already sailed for America, John Wesley still rode the Methodist circuit, and in Devonshire a young Anglican maidservant attended a few Methodist meetings. That maidservant would later receive the gift of divinely guided automatic writing, identify herself, Joanna Southcott, as the second Eve, and so inaugurate the largest millenarian movement of nineteenth-century England.

The Shakers and the Southcottians yet survive, in small numbers. What happened to the French Prophets? Why, after little more than fifty years, did they disappear?

A religious group that has no formal membership requirements, that designs no self-perpetuating administrative system, that engenders no closeknit communal structure, that is skittish of new prophets yet attaches paramount importance to prophecy, such a group may still subsist beyond the lifespan of its original members if their children carry on the corpus of ritual and belief. Despite high regard for inspired children, offspring played no significant role in the later life of the French Prophets. Children of the prominent couples Jean and Henriette Allut, Daniel and Marie Le Tellier, Thomas and Mary Dutton, Thomas and Mary Emes, whatever the honors bestowed upon them in youth, whether baptized as French Prophets or named into tribes, did not participate in the dispensation as adults. Only the children of Hannah Wharton appear as believers after 1730.[1]

---

1. Hannah Wharton, *Divine Inspiration* (1732) title page, noting Joseph, Mary and Sarah Wharton, probably Hannah's grown children. In her *Some Manifestations and*

Infant and child mortality, sterility or miscarriages may explain to some degree the absence of second-generation believers. Six of the eight children born to Mary Portales died in their first year. John Potter and his wife Margaret buried several young children. Thomas and Mary Dutton lost at least two infants and their last son died at nineteen, leaving them with two unmarried daughters. Sir Richard Bulkeley and his wife Lucy, Timothy and Dorothy Byfield, Joseph and Beata Tovey, F.-M. Misson and his wife Françoise were all childless.[2]

In addition, four of the most influential French Prophets—Nicolas Fatio, Richard Roach, Francis Moult, Elie Marion—were confirmed bachelors. Although the group did not place a premium on celibacy, such as that justified by Revelation 14:4 or that established by the Shakers, there was perhaps an element of millenarian fervor in the lack of serious group efforts to rear children as French Prophets. With the Second Coming so close, children might lead the way into the Kingdom, but God rather than Christian parents would set them on the road.[3]

Nevertheless, more than one hundred French Prophets had children who might have entered the group,[4] and some followers understood the importance of children to the group's survival. James Cuninghame discussed the problems of a spiritual education with his friend Andrew Michael Ramsay, tutor to the children of Sir Thomas Hope. Cuninghame was convinced that "there are few Children who have not at some time felt somewhat of immediate Divine Influence, and if they were so happy as to receive and entertain these, it would then be true in a literal sense that of

---

Communications of the Spirit (1730) 225, 311, appear "J.P. jr." and "J.T. jr.," possibly sons of John Potter and Jonathan Taylor. One of John Lacy's daughters may have become a Baptist preacher: Baptist College Library (Bristol), MSS A & E Gifford, Remains, I, piece dated 1712. (The pertinent Eagle Street churchbook which might confirm this seems to be missing from the Baptist Church House Archives in London.)

2. Stack MSS 12g, "Portales Family" notebook, p. 6, and note on cawl enclosure; Chester County and Diocesan RO, MSS EDB/97, Bishops Transcripts, Great Budsworth Parish Church Register, child buried May 21, 1710, and child born April 2, 1711, to Thomas and Mary Dutton; Dutton-Cuninghame Corr., endpapers, letter of 6/28/1740.

3. In 1710, one follower's father seemed to believe "that the faith of this Work being of God dissolves all the bonds of Natural affection, that Children no more regard their Parents but from that time cease to Love them." Dutton-Cuninghame Corr., April, 1710, 171-72. Cf. Richard T. Vann, *The Social Development of English Quakerism 1655-1755* (Cambridge, Mass., 1969) 168; Barry Levy, "'Tender Plants': Quaker Farmers and Children in the Delaware Valley, 1681-1735," *Journal of Family History* 3 (1978) 116-35.

4. Forty French Prophet couples, eight French Prophets who were widows, and twenty-seven French Prophets whose spouses were not believers had children listed as members. Only three couples and eight single-parent followers had children not listed as members, so far as I can tell.

such is the Kingdom of Heaven."[5] Sarah Wiltshire warned in 1722, "Let the Younger learn my Statutes, that there may be Order and not Confusion amongst you."[6] Believers may well have raised their children in a milieu of scripture prophecy and printed warnings by Lacy or Cuninghame or Marion. They had also been provided with devices for the introduction of children into the group; baptism, tribal naming and blessing of the young entailed group responsibility for the child's religious upbringing.

But the position of children was vague. It was never clear to what extent children were automatically part of the group or to what extent some independent sign of commitment was later required of them. Rarely certain of its boundaries, rent by schisms and false prophecy, the group did not fashion any stable machinery for guiding a child from baptism to some conversion experience (such as inspiration) or explicit affirmation of belief (such as missionary activity). When followers no longer projected a definite timetable for the advent of the millennium, when they attended meetings where the inspired had no mandate, or refrained from meetings for that very reason, the young had few means at their disposal by which to maintain a lively sense of the group. They had the written histories of past events, the printed prophecies, the *Orders*, but these put the French Prophets little beyond artifact. They had the prophetic novitiate under the direction of the assembly of the inspired, but this corps of veteran prophets exercised such caution that it effectively limited the growth of the group, denying legitimacy to a significant number of inspired persons. By 1714 inspired children might fidget and squirm under the slow tutelage of the prophetic assembly, and uninspired children like Fatio's great-nephew Jean Huber would be confused by the fine discriminations necessary to understand aright the Lord's messages. So devoted were the French Prophets to the primacy of inspiration that as it disappeared behind a thicket of rules, as prophets died or grew silent, as authoritative assemblies met with less frequency, the group lost its focus and the children their footing.[7]

5. NLS, MS/493/73, letter of 6/18/1709.
6. Richard Roach, *The Imperial Standard* (1728) 52.
7. Cf. H. Richard Niebuhr, *The Social Sources of Denominationalism* (Hamden, 1954) 54-55 and criticism by Bryan Wilson, *Religious Sects* (1970) 233-42; Robert G. Pope, *The Half-Way Covenant: Church Membership in Puritan New England* (Princeton, 1969). In terms of information theory, highly relevant to the problem of generations of prophecy, the French Prophets failed to so phrase the content of their group culture that it was learnable by succeeding generations. Perhaps this was due to an exaggerated respect for the uniqueness of the original group experience, perhaps to a pious insistence on the spontaneity of prophecy. See Tom McFeat, *Small-Group Cultures* (New York, 1974) esp. 114.

The French Prophets failed to integrate their children into the group because, ultimately, they failed to integrate the traditions of the *inspiré* and the traditions of English prophets. What was reality in the Cévennes —persecution, battle, repentance for temporary apostasy as *Nouveaux Convertis*—was only an apt metaphor to most English followers. Urban, literate, generally prosperous, the English at first understood the call to repentance in its most amorphous terms, applicable to the almost universal decline of piety. They admired the *inspirés* as symbols of a rural, oral and youthful tradition that might renovate their own; they acclaimed the *inspirés* as literal proof that Christian renewal was at hand. Both Huguenot refugees and the English responded warmly to a vision of exile and return. Huguenots, however, appreciated the specific referents of these images; English and Scottish followers knew them only as images.

From the very beginning, by recording accounts of the miracles in the Cévennes and formalizing the situation in which new prophecies were delivered, London followers transformed the tenor of inspiration. No matter how strenuously they tried to preserve the vital qualities of Camisard prophecy, they set them in a literate urban structure. They put the group into historical perspective, regarding themselves as members of a new dispensation, final heirs of a long spiritual progression that included Quakers and Philadelphians as well as Huguenots. They sought theological underpinning and scientific demonstration for prophetic acts and millenarian beliefs which before, in the Desert, had been justified primarily on communal, social grounds.

This change in millenarian style was part of what I have been calling transformations in millenarian ethos. To track these transformations is to appreciate the conflicts from which the French Prophets never freed themselves.

The Revocation of the Edict of Nantes had immediately threatened not the lives but the livelihoods, worship and family structure of Huguenots. They lost their economic security, their ministry, their churches, and they had their children taken from them to be reared or at least educated as Catholics. In the years after the Revocation, Huguenots had to cope with a fourfold problem of secrecy: the guilt of the *Nouveaux Convertis* who continued secretly in the Protestant faith; the anxiety of those who participated in secret family cults or illicit assemblies in order to maintain the semblance of Protestant worship; the risk of death, imprisonment or galley slavery for those who tried secretly to perpetuate the Huguenot community as a social entity; the confusion of those who ached to understand the secret purpose of the Lord during these years of persecution. Millenarian prophecy by the *petits prophètes* of Languedoc and Dauphiné, provinces from which proportionately fewer Huguenots had gone into exile than elsewhere in France, promised to solve the problem of secrecy. The emphasis was on the ethos of judgment, on secrecy as communal intimacy. The little prophets were preachers sensitive to lines of authority and the importance of the home, both literal and figurative. They themselves were signs of the restoration of proper relationships between parents and children, and they elicited confessions which were in effect a ritual return to the community. The millennium would bring justice and security to the faithful. There was of course a pull toward the ethos of pentecost, for the government's attempt to isolate believers from one another could be reinterpreted as the Lord's concern with personal faith and self-interrogation. But the prophets' prayers and sermons tended to a concern with the community of worshippers and the ordering of relationships. The Lord's secret purposes, revealed by the young prophets in their trances, had to do with the church and the faith of the entire body of believers. In the realm of the secret, children had become privy to the words of the Lord; through precocious speech, penetrating talk, lofty prayer, the *petits prophètes* were holding together the social and symbolic systems of pre-Revocation Huguenot society.

For the Camisards, life itself was in jeopardy, openly threatened by the unusually violent *dragonnades* of 1698-1700 and subtly threatened by the fatigue of living out the years as a fugitive in one's own land. The millennium had not come in 1689, relief had not come with the Peace of Ryswick in 1697, and few of the *prédicants* remained to offer the faithful an experience of traditional worship. The Desert was both home and exile—home because it was a particularly familiar wilderness, exile because it was a precarious world haunted by royal troops. It was the more precarious for the loud hymn singing of the hidden assemblies, the increasingly public daylight assemblies in remote glens. As guerillas, the Camisards were public and secret, a reflection of Desert tensions between open martyrdom and hidden faith. Camisard millenarian prophecy was consequently that of cataclysm, the sudden opening of the hidden crack in the earth, the discovery of a new home in the ruins of the old, the glorious temple built upon the charred remnants of the small chapel. One put oneself at the very crevice between this world and the new world, one acted boldly with divine assurance of rescue. Unable to establish oneself in a place, one established oneself in time.[8] Unable to rely upon the degree of

---

8. This paradigm comes from Edward T. Hall, *The Hidden Dimension* (Garden City, 1966) 29.

social cohesion present in the Huguenot community twenty years before, the Camisard *inspirés* took as their model the tribe rather than the family, a looser aggregate of persons with loyalties to their Protestant heritage, however little they might have experienced of a Protestant society.

From the hearth to the battlefield, from sleep to ambush, but always in a familiar place. When the *inspirés* came to London, they were on pilgrimage through unfamiliar territory to hopefully familiar faces. In England, however, the *inspirés* were kept in limbo by the cold reception from their own church and the uninviting strangeness of the city. They did not find the kind of support they expected because they had neither social nor symbolic context. The agitations of Jean Cavalier, the prophecies of destruction by Marion may be understood as their first efforts to restore symbolic context: there *was* cataclysm hanging over the Bank of England, the country *should be* quaking, this place was not so different from the Cévennes. Their sense of an unaccomplished pilgrimage may account too for prophetic misdirections, the commands to return to the battlefield as they lingered in the English drawing rooms.

Their first followers were most impressed by the fact of inspiration. They thought of inspiration as a prelude to spiritual renewal in a country where reference to disasters must be primarily a reference to spiritual decline. Aware of cultural differences between French and English, chased by mobs and persecuted by the Huguenot consistories, followers in 1706 and 1707 acted to maintain group coherence through retreats, group projects, public assemblies requiring public commitments. The French followers worked to legitimize the prophets in England by publishing the *Théâtre sacré*. This was a double legitimation, for it made sense of the Huguenot exile while publicizing the Lord's direct involvement in the Huguenot cause. To the French, London became a new Desert with a new set of prophets persecuted by new enemies. English followers appreciated this image, but they hoped too for a New Jerusalem, a universal church that would ensure social coherence without pressuring for strict doctrinal conformity. As refugees, the French needed both symbolic and social articulation; the English were grounded well enough to accept latitude in belief.

By late 1708 the two nations together sought a shared symbolic system anchored to a system of strong group sanctions. English followers had endured the millennial embarrassments of the famine and Emes's resurrection. French followers had fought for the integrity of the *Théâtre sacré* in the presence of "Colonel" Jean Cavalier and the Camisard Abraham Mazel. It was then, inclining toward the ethos of judgment, unhappy with contradictory prophecy, that the English disputed with Abraham Whitrow and the French with Jean Cavalier. Still, the nations did not effect a complete conciliation, for the millenarian axis of the French ran from judgment to cataclysm, and the English axis ran from judgment to the New Jerusalem. The prophets Raoux and Marion named the group into tribes and gave them green ribbons, English prophets went on missions into the countryside; French followers drew their swords against hecklers at Hackney Marsh, English followers prepared love feasts.

Between 1709 and 1714, the group was torn internally by fears of false prophecy, by schism with Philadelphian advocates of a peaceful New Jerusalem, by the distressing Lacy-Gray adultery. English followers reconsidered their attitude toward inspiration, establishing a court of jurisdiction for prophecy and gradually accepting quietist ideas about stages of spiritual growth. French followers supported continental missions intended to unite the scattered Huguenot refugees of Europe. Seeking to preserve the group, the English identified insubordination with personal inauthenticity; this they learned from the Scottish quietists, whose ethos of pentecost was linked to judgment. Seeking to revitalize the group, the French went among the Huguenot tribes in exile.

The years 1715-30 were penumbral years, years of death and leave-taking, relationship by correspondence, sparse prophecy. When Hannah Wharton made waiting the root metaphor of religious experience, she gave new significance to the silence and uncertainty of the past years. Her English believers needed confidence in themselves and others; the incessant rule-making of the *Orders* was replaced by more generous instruction, and the bond between prophet and follower was that of teacher to student, not parent to child. As the English worked out the path between contemplation and evangelism, pentecost and New Jerusalem, French believers reviewed their own background of pilgrimage and refuge. Jean Allut, the prophets Michaut and Saudignan, identified themselves as French Prophets by explicit reference to a common history. Spurned by most other Huguenots in exile in England and on the continent, French believers clung to a codified history, an origin in a time and a place called the Desert. The Desert was as much conceptual as geographical; it was the grid upon which all meaningful action occurred. English followers located themselves in a broad community of the pious and inspired whose variety was intrinsic to the glory of the New Jerusalem; prophecy and millenarian hopes had a center toward which all moved to the wonder of Germans at Schwarzenau, Swiss at Vevey, Moravians at Herrnhut, the Hubers near Lyon.

Although Huguenots like Jean Pellet would respond to the call for personal sanctification and a universal church, although English prophets like Thomas Dutton would be queasy of mystical language and ecumenical posturing, in the most general terms the two nations had operated along different axes of millenarian ethos. The French had provided the group with a vital but narrow history derived from their experience in the Desert. The English had provided the group with a social context and sense of community. In this dynamic, the Philadelphians, the Scottish quietists, the continental pietists had been brokers who insistently put the *inspirés* of the Cévennes into broader historical perspective. Fatio may have been awed by the spiritual progress of pietists, but Allut resisted any erosion of the spiritual and historical uniqueness of the Desert. As French and English followers finally parted in the 1730s, the French lost their external social footing and the English lost that special history which had made for much of the excitement of 1706. The French sacrificed the vitality of community for the sanctity of memory. The English sacrificed historical uniqueness for ongoing spiritual companionship. For both, the millennium receded; it was still to be expected, but no longer was it firmly hooked to one event or one dispensation. The French Prophets did not disappear from view because the millennium seemed constantly deferred; they disappeared because they were no longer recognizable, no longer distinct.

Seen from a wider angle, the decline of the French Prophets followed the pattern of other contemporary millenarian groups. The Ranters and the Fifth Monarchists turned from active political radicalism to passive attendance upon the Second Coming. The Quakers shed their beliefs in an immediate apocalypse and codified instead the evidence of their inner light. Believers in Muggleton and Mason conquered their impatience for the millennium and celebrated the memory of their inspired leaders. The millennial errand of New England puritans had become the pious study of apocalyptic prophecy. The faithful did not resign their millenarian hopes, but they held to them with a different energy and in a different mood, with more investigation of the self. By the 1730s, the French Prophets and the Wesleys had both found in personal sanctification the same pivot for their faith. Whatever momentum the French Prophets then had was in good measure absorbed by the Moravians and Methodists.[9]

---

9. See Joe Lee Davis, "Mystical Versus Enthusiastic Sensibility," *Journal of the History of Ideas* 4 (1943) 310-14; F.M.B. Bullock, *Evangelical Conversion in Great Britain 1696-1845* (St. Leonards-on-Sea, 1959); Melvin B. Endy, Jr., *William Penn and Early Quakerism* (Princeton, 1973) 183; John D. Walsh, "The Origins of the Evangelical Revival," in Walsh and G.V. Bennett, eds., *Essays in Modern English Church History* (1968) 138, 157. For the thesis

In evangelical religion, the social functions of prophecy were once again taken over by charismatic preaching, miracles were replaced by the marvel of the conversion process itself, and millennial fervor was directed toward the universal spread of religion which must precede the Kingdom. The interplay between the last prophets and the first London evangelicals argues for a recognizable kinship, if not sibling rivalry.[10] Methodists, with much the same exuberance of the early French Prophets, created a bold ministry which, assisted by the Holy Spirit, brought to each individual a sure feeling of the power of pure Christianity.

One might depict the French Prophets as ancestors of the evangelical revival or, conversely, Methodism as the issue of early eighteenth-century millenarianism, but this sort of causal connection does justice neither to the French Prophets nor to the Methodists. Both shared rather in the tensions of the baroque world in which the crafted symmetry of reason and the unconfined expressions of sentiment played upon one another. The French Prophets often applied scientific methods to prove God's presence in the natural world and to discover in prophetic acts the forms of God's love. Marie Huber, Fatio's inspired great-niece, later arrived at a belief in universal salvation through careful logic linked to an inner confidence that none could be perfectly happy in heaven if others were known to be suffering eternal damnation. From Marie Huber and from Mme. de Warens, Jean-Jacques Rousseau drew some of the basic principles for a spiritual education that blended the intellect and the emotions.[11] The Wesleys split from the Moravians on a complicated theological argument over the means of grace and the nature of Christian perfection. They later built plain chapels whose Augustan tones belied the Methodist religion of the heart. John Lacy and John Wesley wrote learned treatises demonstrat-

---

that political radicalism and millenarian religion were divorced from each other soon after the Restoration, see Christopher Hill, *Antichrist in Seventeenth-Century England* (1971). Middlekauf describes the first three New England puritan generations in much the same fashion, tracing their sense of being the saving remnant, their subsequent sense of errand, and their final, quieter, study of prophecy: Robert Middlekauf, *The Mathers: Three Generations of Puritan Intellectuals 1596-1728* (Oxford, 1971); cf. William L. Joyce and Michael G. Hall, "Three Manuscripts of Increase Mather," *Proceedings of the American Antiquarian Society* 86 (1976) 113-23.

10. Note also the role of Huguenots in early Methodist and Moravian life: Walsh, "Origins of the Evangelical Revival," 157; Donald Davie, "Old Dissent, 1700-1740," *Times Literary Supplement* (Nov. 26, 1976) 1492; Moravian Church House Archives, MSS, Fetter Lane Elders Conference, Minutes of "Elders and Wardens," I.A, entry for 4/20/1743 (N.S.).

11. Gustave-A. Metzger, *Marie Huber (1695-1753)* (Geneva, 1887); D.P. Walker, *The Decline of Hell* (1964) 261; Albert de Montet, "Madame de Warens et le pays de Vaud," *Mémoires et documents publiées par la Société d'Histoire de la Suisse romande*, 2nd ser., 3 (1891) 1-254.

ing the adverse effects of learned religion. The French Prophets and the Methodists, drawn to and drawing upon German pietism, supposed a precarious continuity between the rational and the irrational, a continuity full of risk but promising revelation.

Millenarian prophecy and evangelical preaching were similar responses to the prevailing but not exclusive eighteenth-century vision of humans bounded in an unbounded universe. Baroque artists and architects reacted to this vision by designing churches and cities with wide open spaces and lush detail; scientists admired the immensity of heavenly spaces and studied teeming microscopic life. Prophets and preachers, speaking in open fields or crowded rooms, described formal religion as the hollow shell of a fulfilling Christianity. Both the French Prophets and the Methodists valued the tension between the closed and the open, the rational and the irrational, in order to transcend the limits of a purely intellectual or merely habitual religion. Both partook of the eighteenth-century undercurrent of resurgent emotionalism, not so much as a "retreat from reason" as another and crucial step toward unbounded faith.[12]

So apt was the comparison that the example of the French Prophets came to the mind of many revival opponents during the Great Awakenings of the 1730s and 1740s. Bishop Lavington in England recalled in no favorable light the agitations of the Camisard *inspirés* and their English heirs, concluding that the new enthusiasm of the Methodists had no more substance. In Scotland, enemies of the Kilsyth and Cambuslang revivals circulated copies of John Lacy's *Scene of Delusions . . . Confuted* to demonstrate the deplorable similarity between the prophets and the Scottish evangelists. The same year, 1742, the *Wonderful Narrative* was published in Glasgow, anonymously but with the help if not authorship of American anti-revivalists. The *Wonderful Narrative* was devoted entirely to an analogy between the emotionalism of the revivalists and the excesses of the French Prophets. The Calvinist evangelical George Whitefield had already heard revivalists compared to Ranters, the Quakers and the French Prophets by the Anglican commissary of Charleston, South Carolina, in 1740. Perhaps because the comparison had occurred to many others, the *Wonderful Narrative* was widely read in America. Probably conversant with the book, and possibly acquainted with the unflattering

---

12. Cf. Harold E. Pagliaro, ed., *Irrationalism in the Eighteenth Century* (Cleveland, 1972), esp. Bertrand H. Bronson, "The Retreat from Reason," 225-38; Lewis Mumford, *The City in History* (New York, 1961) 351; Arthur H. Lovejoy, *The Great Chain of Being* (Cambridge, Mass., 1964 [1936]) 183-226; Walsh, "Origins of the Evangelical Revival," 148-49.

report of the female prophets at Bristol which had appeared four years earlier in the *Boston Evening Post*, the American revivalist Jonathan Edwards felt compelled to deny in print the validity of the suggested parallels between the agitations of the French Prophets and the agitations of Great Awakening converts.[13]

As a religious force in England for forty years, as a spectre haunting subsequent evangelical efforts, the French Prophets had been etched in many memories. The country folk around Salisbury in the 1740s called one group of ancient barrows the "prophet's barrows" because, years before, some French Prophets had set up a standard on the largest of the barrows and addressed a crowd. The English deist Peter Annet in 1749 used the example of the miracles performed by John Lacy to assault the credibility of the miracles performed by Jesus. In 1795, the favorable *Impartial Account of the Prophets* was reprinted in connection with the new English prophet Richard Brothers, whose disciples would soon acclaim Joanna Southcott.[14]

Quaker memories of the French Prophets would continue into the nineteenth century. Confronted with the missions of Anne Steed and Mary Turner, involved in controversy with Henry Pickworth, shocked by the figures in sackcloth in Bristol in 1738, Quakers had had to deal with the French Prophets at especially close range over a long period. Friend Thomas Story was another of the many to converse with Isaac Hollis about the prophets, and ignoring their differences they parted "in friendship." Thomas Whitehead managed as both a French Prophet and a Friend (as had earlier Joseph and Beata Tovey) until his death in 1748. Is it so astonishing, then, that the Quaker Joseph Woods in 1804 should be reminded of the French Prophets when discussing the New Lights among the Quakers who worshipped the "idol of inward impulse" and allowed their "Luxuriance of imagination" to spread unchecked? Woods could just

---

13. George W. Lavington, *The Enthusiasm of Methodists and Papists Compared* (2nd ed.; 1749) II, 72; James Robe, *A Faithful Narrative of the Extraordinary Work of God, at Kilsyth* (Glasgow, 1742) 52-54; Anti-enthusiasticus, *The Wonderful Narrative* (Glasgow, 1742); E.S. Gaustad, "Charles Chauncy and the Great Awakening: A Survey and Bibliography," *Papers of the Bibliographical Society of America* 45 (1951) 125-35; William Wale, ed., *George Whitefield's Journals 1737-1741* (Gainesville, 1969) Journal 8, 8/13/1740; *Boston Evening Post*, No. 165 (Oct. 9, 1738); Jonathan Edwards, *Some Thoughts Concerning the present Revival of Religion in New-England*, ed. C.G. Goen (New Haven, 1972 [1742]) 313, 330, 341.

14. Robert C. Hoare, *The Ancient History of South Wiltshire* (1812) 210-11; Peter Annet, *Supernaturals Examined in Four Dissertations On Three Treatises* (1749) 104-13; Joseph Moser, *Anecdotes of Richard Brothers* (1795) 10.

remember a remnant of the French Prophets invading the Gracechurch Street (London) Meeting dressed in sackcloth and covered with ashes.[15]

The appearance of other millenarian groups stirred up memories of the French Prophets throughout the early 1800s. The Scottish preacher Edward Irving brought to London a prophetic and millenarian Christianity so popular in the 1820s that a writer for *The Congregational Magazine* sketched again the analogy between the pretences of the French Prophets and those of lively revivals.[16] The onset of the Second Great Awakening in America prompted others to turn to the works of John Lacy, either for enlightenment or for ammunition against the sudden conversions and nocturnal assemblies of the camp meetings.[17]

The significance of the French Prophets was horizontal: they mirrored the sweep of religious impulses in their own era, from the prophetic chiliasm of the mid-seventeenth century to the pietism of the mid-eighteenth, from alchemy and astrology to a science of minute particles ordered by divine providence. They attracted people from most of the social strata in England, they had enclaves in seven countries, their works were printed in four languages.

Their ebullience and appeal rankled a society that after civil war and political upheaval had all the more respect for stability and hierarchy. They were evidence of a continuity of religious beliefs that many would just as well have seen broken. The orthodox were tempted, as historians are tempted, to regard the Restoration as a tollbooth in English history beyond which earlier millenarian attitudes could not pass. The French Prophets were proof of the enduring attractions of millennial imagery,

15. On Pickworth, see his *A Charge of Error* (1716); John Burtt, "Brief Memorials of William and Alice Burtt," *Journal of the Friends Historical Society* 29 (1932) 83-84; Friends' House Library, MSS portfolio 32. 69-71. On Story, see John Kendall, ed., *The Life of Thomas Story* (1786) 371. On Whitehead, Bristol Archives Office, Thomas Whitehead will, proved January 1748/49 and record of burial in Quaker register (information supplied by city archivist, Mary E. Williams). On Woods, Friends' House Library, Matthews MSS 95, letter of 6/26/1804.

16. "On the Pretended Inspirations of the French Prophets," *The Congregational Magazine*, new ser., 7 (1831) 737, article signed β.

17. See flyleaf inscriptions dated 1812 in copies of the *Cry from the Desart*, Lacy's *Relation of Dealings* and *Letter to Woodward*, at the Library Company of Philadelphia; Amariah Brigham, *Observations on the Influence of Religion upon the Health and Physical Welfare of Mankind* (Boston, 1835) 243-46; Hannah Adams, *A View of Religions* (2nd ed.; Boston, 1791) 82-84. In Amos Bronson Alcott's library at Fruitlands (from the library of the English mystic J.P. Greaves) in the 1840s were Lacy's *The General Delusion of Christians* and Richard Roach's *The Great Crisis* and *The Imperial Standard*: Houghton Library (Cambridge, Mass.), Amos Bronson Alcott catalogue in typescript, *59A-329 and MS list in R.W. Emerson deposit.

proof too of a surviving impulse toward experimental religion. What has been interpreted as an age of decline for English dissent and Anglicanism may also be interpreted as a time when the devout chose the freedom of their prayer closets over church pews or meetinghouse benches.[18]

The status of inspired women among the French Prophets in the 1730s was a sign of this rejection of the hierarchy and organization of Christian church life, a life dominated by male authorities. In the patriarchal society of eighteenth-century England, the woman's ambit of action was generally greater when social interplay was modelled upon the relationships of companions or siblings, rather than upon parental or tribal (military) obligation. Powerful women were prophets of pentecost and New Jerusalem, rarely of judgment and cataclysm.[19]

The New Jerusalems imagined by Mme. Guyon at Blois, by Mrs. Keith at Montrose, by Hannah Wharton at Birmingham, were part of an urban image of the ideal gentle country estate. It was an image for the literate and leisured. The last French Prophets were not workers in collieries but gentlemen like Isaac Hollis and Benjamin Du Plan, rich merchants like Thomas Whitehead and Francis Wynantz. This drift away from the laborers in an industrializing English society may be a final explanation for the disappearance of the French Prophets.[20]

18. For the classic statement of the thesis of decline, see Mark Pattison, "Tendencies of Religious Thought in England 1688-1750," in his *Essays and Reviews* (1860) 254-329. Cf. Elie Halévy, *The Birth of Methodism in England*, trans. and ed. Bernard Semmel (Chicago, 1971); John Walsh, "Elie Halévy and the Birth of Methodism," *Transactions of the Royal Historical Society*, 5th ser., 25 (1975) 1-20; Geoffrey F.A. Best, *Temporal Pillars* (Cambridge, 1964); Norman Sykes, *From Sheldon to Secker* (Cambridge, 1959); Arthur Warne, *Church and Society in Eighteenth-Century Devon* (Newton Abbot, 1969); Russell E. Richey, "Effects of Toleration on Eighteenth-Century Dissent," *Journal of Religious History* 8 (1975) 350-63; Alan D. Gilbert, *Religion and Society in Industrial England: Church, Chapel and Social Change 1740-1914* (New York, 1976); Geoffrey F. Nuttall, "George Whitefield's 'Curate': Gloucestershire Dissent and the Revival," *Journal of Ecclesiastical History* 27 (1976) 369-86; Vann, *Social Development of English Quakerism*, 158-208; Davie, "Old Dissent, 1700-1740," 1491-92; Michael R. Watts, *The Dissenters* (Oxford, 1978) I, 267-89, 382-93.

19. On lateral and vertical groups in Christianity, see John Bossy, "Holiness and Society," *Past and Present* 75 (1977) 136-37; Natalie Zemon Davis, "Ghosts, Kin, and Progeny: Some Features of Family Life in Early Modern Europe," *Daedalus* 106 (Spring 1977) 87-114. Cf. Lawrence Stone, *The Family, Sex and Marriage In England 1500-1800* (New York, 1977) 115, 241, 325-35.

20. For evidence on the social and geographical appeal of Methodism and "New" Dissent, see Watts, *The Dissenters*, I, 408; Judith J. Hurwich, "Dissent and Catholicism in English Society: A Study of Warwickshire, 1660-1720," *Journal of British Studies* 16 (1976) 24-58; Clive D. Field, "The Social Structure of English Methodism. Eighteenth-Twentieth Centuries," *British Journal of Sociology* 28 (1977) 199-225; Alan Everitt, "Nonconformity in Country Parishes," *Agricultural History Review* 18 (1970) supplement, 178-99; Gilbert, *Religion and Society in Industrial England*, 34-36 *et passim*; cf. Christopher Hill, "Plebeian

To disappear . . . the historian's misleading infinitive. Rather, the French Prophets were no longer *placed*. The Camisard millennium had been rooted to the very specific geography of the Desert. In England the millennium was at first bi-local and then increasingly diffuse, bound to a vaguely international New Jerusalem. The group transformed Camisard laws of trespass into the signposts for a public garden. In the midst of the transformation, the personal placement of believers became a residual problem. Disobedience (acting out of one's place), false prophecy (speaking out of place), sexual misconduct (impurity, entering a wrong place), and upsetting social programs (levelling, violating the laws of placement) arose within the group as it tried to situate the Camisard millennium in the streets of London.[21] The fit was never good enough. By the 1730s, French followers held to their millenarian beliefs through their memories of the Desert, while English followers knew only the promise of the universal church. The French Prophets themselves had then no real location. They lived on in a Cévenol past and the wide millennial kingdom of the future. When the last French Prophet died, a certain world did end.

Irreligion in 17th Century England," in Manfred Kossok, ed., *Studien Uber die Revolution* (Berlin, 1969) 46-61. Henri Desroche describes Ann Lee's prophetic stance as a reaction to industrialization, and "The millenarian vision of the French Prophets inspired her with a kind of metaphysical Luddism." The suggestion of a parallel between production and reproduction is quite interesting, but the role of the French Prophets in shaping Shaker attitudes toward the new economic system is hardly proven. See Henri Desroche, *The American Shakers From Neo-Christianity to Presocialism*, ed. and trans. John K. Savacool (Amherst, 1971 [1955]) 39-43, 292-93.

21. On the importance of the experience of place and on millenarianism as a spatial reconstruction, see Desroche, *American Shakers*, 86-87, 108; Mircea Eliade, *Cosmos and History: The Myth of the Eternal Return,* trans. Willard R. Trask (New York, 1954); David Lowenthal, "Past Time, Present Place: Landscape and Memory," *Geographical Review* 65 (1975) 1-36; Yi-Fu Tuan, *Topophilia: A Study of Environmental Perception, Attitudes, and Values* (Englewood Cliffs, 1974) 129-40.

Appendices

I.	Chronological Profile of All French Prophets	297
II.	New Membership by Periods, 1706-1708	316
III.	Running Totals of Membership, 1706-1715	317
IV.	Occupations of Male Believers	318
V.	Religious Affiliations of the French Prophets	321
VI.	Chronological Profile of the Inspired	322
VII.	Running Totals of the Inspired, 1706-1714	326
VIII.	Ages of the French Prophets, 1706-1714	327
IX.	French Prophets with University Educations	328
X.	Types of Millenarian Ethos	329
XI.	Millenarianism and the French Prophets	330

Abbreviations and Symbols

- M: Male
- F: Female
- T: Total
- *: apostasy or exclusion from group
- Entry: Date of first appearance as a French Prophet in extant records
- DOB: Date of Birth (a = ante, c = circa, p = post). If exact year is unknown, I follow these rules in assigning general age categories: if married, born twenty years before marriage or entry; if parent, born twenty years before birth of eldest child. Demographic data suggest that average age at first marriage during this era was above 24, so these are minimum figures.
- POB: Place of Birth (E = England, Fr = France, Ge = Germany, Ho = Holland, Ir = Ireland, NE = New England, Sc = Scotland, Sw = Switzerland). England includes Wales.
- Rel: Religion (A = Anglican, B = Baptist, C = nonsectarian Protestant, J = Jew, M = Methodist/Moravian, P = Presbyterian, (P) = Swiss Protestant, Ph = Philadelphian, Pi = Pietist, Q = Quaker, (Q) = Quaker claimant, Qt = Quietist, RC = Roman Catholic, H = Huguenot and includes children born in England of Huguenot parents). If more than one affiliation, listed in chronological order of affiliation; affiliations after leaving the group are not listed.
- Role: (P = Prophet, m = missionary, s = scribe, h = host, c = receives cure, a = has agitations but does not speak, ? = possibly not a believer but a sympathizer or casual observer)
- Tribe: Tribe assignment, tribes numbered in the chronological order in which they were named and completed (1 = Levi, 2 = Benjamin, 3 = Issachar, 4 = Naphtali, 5 = Zebulon, 6 = Simeon, 7 = Judah, 8 = Gad, 9 = Ruben, 10 = Osser, 11 = Manasseh, 12 = Joseph; @ = appointed apostle to that tribe).
- Connections: intragroup relationships, as follows:
  = married to

     + nuclear relationship (brother, sister, father, mother, son, daughter)
     & other kinship relations
     [ ] friend, business or religious associate or employer

Occupation: when unknown or for women whose spouses are not believers, occasional references to occupations of h: (husband), f: (father), u: (uncle). These are not entered in Appendix IV.

APPENDIX 1. *Chronological Profile of All French Prophets*

No.	Entry	Name	DOB/POB	Rel.	Occupation	Role	Tribe	Connections
	1706							
1	6-	Durand Fage	1681 Fr	H	soldier	Pm	1	[10,4]
2	6-	Jean Daudé	1651 Fr	H	lawyer	msh		=35
3	6-	Charles Portales	1676 Fr	H	secretary, merchant	ms	1	=231,+198,&22 [8]
4	8-10	*Jean Cavalier	1686 Fr	H	weaver	Pm		=31,&5 [1]
5	8-15	Jean Allut	1682 Fr	H	cabinetmaker	Pmh		=29,&4 [9]
6	8-15	Richard Bulkeley	1660 Ir	A	baronet	csh	3	[15,63,220]
7	8-15	*Thomas Cotton	1653 E	P	minister	h		=311 [9?15?]
8	8-20	Armand de Bourbon	1656 Fr	H	marquis	h		[3,22]
9	8-30	Nicolas Fatio de Dullier	1664 Sw	(P)	tutor, mathematician	msh	1	[7?85,146,201,299]
10	9-16	Elie Marion	1678 Fr	H	clerk	Pm	1	[1,22]
11	9-	Jean Rouvière	a1683 Fr	H	innkeeper			+58
12	10-1	Matthieu Boissier	a1685 Fr	H	woolcarder			
13	11-	F.-M. Misson	a1660 Fr	H	writer	s	@2	+201,+164,+371...
14	11-23	Sara Dalgone	a1680 Fr	H	h:surgeon	?		
15	12-	John Lacy	1664 E	P	gentleman	Pm	1	[6,7?],=25
16	12-	Rebecca Critchlow	a1675 E	Ph		h		&46,&89,&115
	1707							
17	1-4	Jérémie Majou	1645 Fr	H	minister	?		
18	1-14	*Claude Arnassan	a1685 Fr	H				
19	1-14	John Philipps	c1666 E	A	baronet			+385
20	2-	*Ann d'Huisseau	a1688 Fr	H		?		
21	2-	*Abraham Verduron	a1668 Fr	H	silkweaver		5	=84,+31
22	3-1	David Flotard	1670 Fr	H	agent for 8		7	[3,8,10]
23	3-5	Elisabeth Charras	a1670 Fr	H	h:gunsmith	Pm	1	

297

Appendix I contd.

No.	Entry	Name	DOB/POB	Rel.	Occupation	Role	Tribe	Connections
24	3-7	Richard Roach	1662 E	A,Ph	minister	h	9	[many]
25	4-1	Elizabeth Gray	1692 E	A?	u:candlesnuffer	Pm	6	=15
26	4-1	James Keith	a1684 Sc	Qt	physician			=355
27	4-1	*Jean Lions	a1675 Fr		minister			&364?
28	4-1	Robert Roger	a1660 Fr	H	printer			
29	4-7	Henriette Allut	a1685 Fr	H		Pm	8	=5
30	4-11	Susanne des Brousses	Fr	H		P	11	
31	4-11	*Jeanne Cavalier	a1685 Fr	H		Pm		=4,+31,+84
32	4-11	Anne Voyer	?1637 Fr	H		P	3	
33	4-11	*Isaac Havy	a1680 Fr	H	weaver	Pm	@2	
34	4-13	*Daniel Le Tellier	a1670 Fr	H	weaver	P	@1	=73,+257,+258
35	4-13	Antoine Prade	a1680 Fr	H	innkeeper	h	1	=390,+263,+264
36	4-28	Mme. Daudé	c1650 Fr	H		sh		=2
37	4-29	Mr. Knight	E	Ph		?		[24]
38	5-28	Mr. Kemp	E	Ph	tallowchandler	s	5	&381 [24]
39	6-3	William King	a1680 E	Ph		?		+223,+229
40	6-3	Mrs. Wells	E	Ph	meatpacker?	Pm	4	[24]
41	6-6	John Potter	a1687 E	B	sergeant-at-law			=376 [65]
42	7-1	John Hooke	1655 Ir	A		h		[6?]
43	7-5	Marie Eyton	Fr	H		?		+44
44	7-5	Mme. Eyton	a1680 Fr	H		a		+43
45	7-5	Mary Tuckey	E		brasier	sh	2	+115
46	7-7	Sarah Critchlow	a1687 E	Ph	printer	Pm	10	+253,+120,+121
47	8-	William Draycott	a1685 E	B		h	10	+49,+50
48	8-	Mary Keimer	c1686 E	P,B	h:tailor			+48,+50
49	8-	*Samuel Keimer	1688 E	P,B	woolcomber	Pmh		+48,+49
50	8-	Mrs. Keimer	a1666 E	P,B		h		=53,+172,+173
51	8-6	Mme. Chanier	a1687 Fr	H				=52,+172,+173
52	8-10	*Abraham Whitrow	a1670 E	A?				[24]
53	8-10	*Deborah Whitrow	a1670 E	A?				
54	8-12	Mary Laughton	a1670 E	Ph				

Appendix I contd.

No.	Entry	Name	DOB/POB	Rel.	Occupation	Role	Tribe	Connections
55	8-16	James Craven	a1668 E	RC	chemist	h	1	=315 [146]
56	8-17	Timothy Byfield	c1650 E	A	physician			+296 [146]
57	8-17	Anne Watts	?1690 E		shopmaid	Pm	3	[25]
58	8-24	Anne Rouvière	Fr					+11 [99]
59	8-29	Mary Beer	1695 E	H		Pm	9	=511,+many
60	9-2	Ann Good	1697 E			P		+336
61	9-2	Sarah Wiltshire	c1680 E	Q,Ph		P		[24,165]
62	9-5	Thomas Emes	a1670 E	B,C	chemist	P		=122
63	9-5	Benjamin Jackson	a1670 E		inventor	s	1	[6] +461?
64	9-5	Beata Tovey	a1667 E	Q		h	9	=65 [500]
65	9-5	Joseph Tovey	a1667 E	Q	tallowchandler	h	1	=64,+193
66	9-11	Thomas Dutton	1679 E		lawyer	Pm	2	=437,+228
67	9-15	Mary Bullmore	E			P	10	=294
68	9-15	Edmund Everard	c1660 Fr?	Ph?	lawyer	a	1	[81,9?]
69	9-15	Mr. Hammond	E?			P		
70	9-21	Pierre Dubuc	Fr	H			4	
71	9-21	Jeanne Raoux	c1645 Fr	H		P	1	+72
72	9-21	Madeleine Raoux	1674 Fr	H			5	+71
73	9-27	Marie Le Tellier	a1675 Fr	H			9	=34,+257,+258
74	10-1	John Giles	a1670 E	Ph?	merchant	msh	1	
75	10-5	Rachel(?) East	E	Q	f:grocer	h		
76	10-5	Christian Steffkins	a1675		violplayer	s	5	[143,24?]
77	10-10	*Dinah Stoddart	E			P		
78	10-31	Jean Noual	c1693 Fr	H	apprentice	P		[116]
79	11-1	Mrs. Mosely	E			c		
80	11-1	Hugh Preston	1630 E	Q?		c	6	=391
81	11-10	Joseph Tiley	a1660 E	A	lawyer	ch		[68]
82	11-15	James Jackson	1636 E	I,Q	teacher	ch	6	[165]
83	12-14	Anna Maria King	1697 E			Pm	10	+39?
84	12-18	*Mme. Verduron	a1668 Fr	H			5	=21,+31
85	12-19	M. de Beaulieu	Sw?	(P)?				[9]

Appendix I contd.

No.	Entry	Name	DOB/POB	Rel.	Occupation	Role	Tribe	Connections
86	12-25	*Stephen Halford	1687 E	Q?	cutler	P		[87,88]
87	12-25	Jonathan Taylor	a1689 E		cabinetmaker	Pm		[86,88]
88	12-25	Richard Wharton	a1689 E		pattenmaker			=413,+many
89	12-31	Daniel Critchlow	a1680 E	Ph	chemist	a	3	=115,+46

1708

90	1-	Mary Clark	E			c	8	
91	1-	John Holloway	E			c		
92	1-	Mary Moore	E			c		
93	1-	John Moult	a1670 E	A?	apothecary	c	1	+231,+376
94	1-5	John Glover	1652 E	A?	victualler	Pm	6	=334
95	1-10	Mary Aspinal	a1688 E			Pm	11	=402
96	1-18	*John Parker	a1688 Ir?			Pm		=380

(Numbers 97-175, listed alphabetically, are first entered on a membership list – BPUG, MSS fr. 605 – dated January 19, 1707/08.)

97	1-19	*Anna Angibert	Fr	H		P		=99
98	1-19	Jeanne Audemar	c1662 Fr	H		h		=98 [57]
99	1-19	Pierre Audemar	1662 Fr	H	silkweaver	mch	1	=283
100	1-19	Mrs. Barker	E					=102?,+233
101	1-19	Elizabeth Bennet	a1680 E					=101?,+233
102	1-19	John Bennet	a1680 E		shoemaker			=104,+234
103	1-19	Esther Bernard	1671 Fr	H			7	=103,+234
104	1-19	Jaques Bernard	1657 Fr	H	engraver		2	=290
105	1-19	Mme. Boussac	a1688 Fr	H		h		
106	1-19	Margaret Brumston	E?					+114
107	1-19	James Carter	E?				10	=206
108	1-19	Elizabeth Charrier	1675 Fr	H			2	+217,+303
109	1-19	John Clark	p1690 E					+111,+112
110	1-19	John(?) Clere	p1700 E					=112,+110
111	1-19	William Clere	a1680 E	A?	minister		10	=112,+110
112	1-19	Mrs. Clere	a1680 E					=111,+110

300

Appendix I contd.

No.	Entry	Name	DOB/POB	Rel.	Occupation	Role	Tribe	Connections
113	1-19	William Cocq	a1670 E		upholsterer?			+107,&521?
114	1-19	Elizabeth Cooper	E					&14&45&89
115	1-19	Mary Critchlow	a1688 E	Ph		h	11	=117 [78]
116	1-19	John (Peter) Cuff	a1685 E	Ph	watchmaker	P	6	=116
117	1-19	Rebecca Cuff	a1685 E					=119
118	1-19	Olivier des Preaux	1662 Fr	H	gentleman		3	=118
119	1-19	René des Preaux	c1662 Fr	H			12	+121
120	1-19	Anna Draycott	a1675 E	B			10	+120
121	1-19	Sarah Draycott	E	B		P	10	=62
122	1-19	Mary Emes	a1675 E	B				=124
123	1-19	Mr. C. Gilman	a1688 E	Ph	f:physician?			=123
124	1-19	Mrs. Gilman	a1688 E					
125	1-19	Joseph Gladman	a1688 E					
126	1-19	Mr. Graissmit	E				5	
127	1-19	Isaac Guillemot	a1689 Fr	H		s	4	+128,+215
128	1-19	Susanna Guillemot	1659 Fr	H				=215,+127
129	1-19	Joseph Hodges	E					
130	1-19	William Humphreys	a1688 E	Ph?			8	[24]
131	1-19	Sarah Hunt	E					
132	1-19	George Jackson	a1688 E					
133	1-19	Jean Janson	Fr	H?				
134	1-19	Abraham Kell	a1675					
135	1-19	Joyce Kemp	E?					&38
136	1-19	Mme. La Jonquière	1666 Fr	H	h:weaver			
137	1-19	Jean Le Page	a1688 Fr	H			1	=360
138	1-19	Mary Maddox	E					
139	1-19	Abraham Mahieu	a1670 Fr	H	weaver	h		=140,+144
140	1-19	Susanne Mahieu	a1670 Fr	H		h		=139,+144
141	1-19	Elizabeth Marshall	E					
142	1-19	Thomas Middleton	Sc	Qt	principal?	a		[26?]
143	1-19	Mr. Monin	a1688 Fr	H				[76]

301

Appendix I contd.

No.	Entry	Name	DOB/POB	Rel.	Occupation	Role	Tribe	Connections
144	1-19	Jeanne Morel	a1689 Fr	H		P	9	+139,+140
145	1-19	Elias Moreton	p1696 E				8	+375
146	1-19	Francis Moult	a1675 E	A	apothecary	msh	1	+93,&147,&3 ...
147	1-19	John Moult	1694 E	A		Pm	@3	&146
148	1-19	Mr. Nait	Fr?	H?				
149	1-19	David Nolibet	a1680 Fr	H	f:minister	m	1	
150	1-19	Isaac Owen	p1679 E	P		ms	12	
151	1-19	Jaquette Perrot	1652 Fr	H	f:merchant		6	+262,&13
152	1-19	Marie Perrot	c1650 Fr	H			4	&262,&13
153	1-19	Edward Plass	a1685					=388
154	1-19	Elizabeth Pleuret	Fr	H				
155	1-19	Ann Ramsay	Sc?					
156	1-19	*Mary Rigby	a1695 E			a		+157,+158
157	1-19	Thomas Rigby	a1675 E		canemaker		12	=158,+156
158	1-19	Mrs. Rigby	a1675 E					=157,+156
159	1-19	Mrs. Rose	E?					
160	1-19	Susannah Sanger	E			Pm	12	=500
161	1-19	Thomas Seward	E					
162	1-19	Nathaniel Sheppard	p1690 E	A?	appr.chemist	ms	4	[473]
163	1-19	Susanne Soulet	Fr	H			8	+13,+238
164	1-19	Anne Southouse	a1680 Fr	H		Pm	7	[61,82,493]
165	1-19	Anne Steed	a1685 E	Q				[24]
166	1-19	*Marie Sterrill	a1650 Fr	H,Ph,Q			2	
167	1-19	Ann Topham	?1673 E	Q?		Pm	12	
168	1-19	Mary Turner	a1688 E	Q?		Pm	11	
169	1-19	Patrick Urquhart	a1688	RC?		ah	3	=407?
170	1-19	Pierre Valette	1644 Fr	H	merchant		1	
171	1-19	Pierre Vauloué	a1689 Fr	H	f:goldsmith?		1	
172	1-19	Ann Whitrow	p1696 E	A				+52,+53
173	1-19	Deborah Whitrow	p1696 E	A				+52,+53
174	1-19	Sarah Willson	E					

Appendix I contd.

No.	Entry	Name	DOB/POB	Rel.	Occupation	Role	Tribe	Connections
175	1-19	Mme. Yonge		E?				
176	1-24	Elizabeth Hughes	a1668 E		cookshop	h		+192
177	2-4	Mrs. Roberts	a1678 E			?		
178	2-4	Thomas Burbury	E					
179	2-4	*Samuel Cash	E					
180	2-7	Mr. Downing	E	Ph?				[24],&6?
181	2-23	Mrs. Plymore	a1688 E?	A,J		a	4	
182	3-11	François Pommier	a1675 Fr	H		c		
183	3-22	Mr. Rayner	E	B?		c	3	=398
184	3-29	William Spong	a1646 E	Ph	clogmaker	P	@6	
185	3-30	John Moore	a1688 E		minister	P		
186	4-1	John Moore	1642 E	A,B	student	c		[6]
187	4-6	*Timothy Plass	p1690 Ir	A?	teacher	h		=383
188	4-14	Mrs. Rustback	E		victualler	c		
189	4-17	Jean Pellet	c1672 Fr	H				
190	4-29	James Byworth	c1678 E	Q				
191	5-5	Mary Willis	a1651 E	B?		Pm	11	+176
192	5-23	Elizabeth Hughes	a1689 E	Ph		h	12	[65]
193	5-25	Elizabeth Blandford	a1688 E	A	apothecary	ms	3	
194	6-	Thomas Lardner	a1679 E	A	student	a		
195	6-	*Henry Nicholson	1683 Ir	A	waterman	c		[6]
196	6-23	Richard Cheney	a1678 E		gentleman	P		
197	7-25	Benjamin Rawson	E		gentleman	ms	1	+3
198	8-25	Jaques Portales	p1676 Fr	H	printer		6	
199	8-28	William Rogers	a1678 E?		gentleman		1	+13,+371
200	9-1	Jaques Misson	a1660 Fr	H	Sieur de Voutron		1	=460 [9]
201	9-7	Louis Henri de Mazières	1665 Fr	H			1	
202	9-14	Jean Grenier	Fr	H			1	[139]
203	9-21	Jaques Soulier	Fr	H	sawyer	P		
204	10-5	*Robert Wise	1688 E			P	1	

Appendix I contd.

No.	Entry	Name	DOB/POB	Rel.	Occupation	Role	Tribe	Connections
205	10-10	Marie Bouët	1674 Fr	H			2	=108
206	10-10	Jaques Charrier	1673 Fr	H			2	=241
207	10-10	François Gerald	a1688 Fr	H			2	=374
208	10-10	Jean Mony	a1688 Fr	H			2	=245 [13]
209	10-10	Thomas Thibault	a1679 Fr	H	goldsmith		2	
210	10-17	Mr. Mayn	a1688 Fr?	H?				
211	10-17	Mr. Oliver	a1688 Fr?	H?				
212	10-17	Mr. Geipin	a1688 Fr?	H?				
213	10-17	David Ducros	Fr	H			3	
214	10-17	Susan Eastman	E	Ph?			3	[24]
215	10-17	Jean Guillemot	1642 Fr	H	"incommode"	sh	3	=128,+127
216	10-18	Henry Pickworth	1673 E	Q	tanner		3	[65,426]
217	10-31	John Adam Clark	a1680 E		merchant		4	=303,+251
218	10-31	Robert Douglas	a1678 Sc		merchant		4	
219	10-31	Elizabeth Small	a1688 E				4	=237
220	11-	Benjamin Furly	1636 E	Q,C	merchant	sh	5	[6]
221	11-7	John Bagnal	E				5	+249,=279?
222	11-7	Marie Devaux	Fr	H			5	+261
223	11-7	Emma King	a1680 E				5	=39?,+83?
224	11-7	Mlle. Le Page	Fr	H			5	
225	11-7	Samuel Noble	a1680 E		bookseller	ms	5	=378
226	11-7	Jean Payn	Fr?	H?			5	
227	11-7	Hal Reason	1683 E	A?		s	5	
228	11-14	John Dutton	E		tailor		6	+66
229	11-14	William King jr.	p1700 E				6	+39,+223?
230	11-14	Pierre Langtuit	a1664 Fr	H	merchant		6	&224,&360
231	11-14	Mary Moult	1690 E	A			6	=3,+93,+374
232	11-23	Thomas Arpwood	a1688 Sc			P	7	
233	11-23	Stephen Bennet	p1700 E	A?		P	7	+101,+102?
234	11-23	Joseph Bernard	1702 E	H			7	+103,+104
235	11-23	John Cock	a1680 E	A?	clockmaker	h	7	

Appendix I contd.

No.	Entry	Name	DOB/POB	Rel.	Occupation	Role	Tribe	Connections
236	11-23	Mary Foster	E				7	=457?
237	11-23	Thomas Small	a1688 E				7	=219
238	11-23	Filmore Southouse	p1695 E	H			7	+164,&13
239	11-23	Louise Vergnon	a1682 Fr	H			7	+409,+240
240	11-23	Samuel Vergnon jr.	p1700 E	H			7	+239,+409
241	11-28	Anne Gerald	a1688 Fr				8	=207
242	11-28	Elizabeth Hubbard	E				8	
243	11-28	Guy Nutt	a1685 E	(Q)		Pm	8	=379
244	11-28	Jaques Paris	a1665 Fr	H	tradesman?		8	[13]
245	11-28	Marie Thibault	a1679 Fr	H			8	=209
246	11-28	Edward Wharton	E				8	+88,+413?
247	11-28	Isaac Wharton	E				8	+88,+413?
248	12-3	Thomas Alderidge	E				9	+221
249	12-3	George Bagnal					9	&266,&267
250	12-3	Harmond Beer	E				9	+216,+303
251	12-3	John Clark jr.	E				9	+254
252	12-3	Anne Finkley	a1668 E				9	
253	12-3	Ebenezer Draycott	E				10	&47,&120,&121
254	12-3	Nathan Finkley	E				10	+252
255	12-3	Sarah Harling	E	Q	furrier?		10	+343?
256	12-3	*John Hartland	E			P	@10	
257	12-3	Daniel Le Tellier jr.	1703 E	H			9	+34,+73
258	12-3	Jaques Le Tellier	1705 E	H			9	+34,+73
259	12-7	Handrior Beer	E			ms	11	+260?
260	12-7	John Barr	E				11	+259?
261	12-7	Suzanne Devaux	Fr	H			11	+222
262	12-7	Marguerite Perrot	1653 Fr	H	f:merchant		11	+151,+152
263	12-7	Jean Prade	c1705 E	H			11	+35,+390
264	12-7	Josué Prade	c1705 E	H			11	+35,+390
265	12-7	Peter Rochfort	. a1688 E?		mime,inventor		11	
266	12-12	Beata Beer	E				12	+267...

305

Appendix I contd.

No.	Entry	Name	DOB/POB	Rel.	Occupation	Role	Tribe	Connections
267	12-12	Sarah Beer	E				12	+266...
268	12-12	William Llewellyn	E?				12	
269	12-12	Robert Low	E				12	
270	12-12	Robert Richardson	a1691 E	Ph		P	12	[24]
271	12-12	John Spragg	E				12	
272	12-15	*Pierre Artaud	a1688 Fr	H				=275

(Numbers 273-417, listed alphabetically, are first entered on a list probably compiled at the end of 1708 – BPUG, MSS fr. 605, list with tribal markings – and may include some people who were only spectators.)

c. 1708

273		Pierre Allix	1641 Fr	H	minister	?		=274
274		Mme. Allix	c1650 Fr	H		?		=273
275		*Catherine Artaud	a1688 Fr	H				=272
276		Mr. Ash						=277
277		Mrs. Ash						=276
278		Elizabeth Ashey						
279		Mary Bagnal	c1688 E					=221?
280		John Balbing	E					
281		Mr. Barber	E					=282
282		Mrs. Barber	E					=281
283		Mr. Barker	E					=100
284		Mr. Basin	Fr					
285		George Bennet	E	H				+102
286		David Billard	a1685 Fr	H	soldier			[3?,22?]
287		Mrs. Bishop	E					&12?
288		Abraham Boissier	Fr	H				[13]
289		Marie Bouhault	1658 Fr	H	bourgeoise			=105
290		Moïse Boussac	a1688 Fr	H		h		

306

Appendix I contd.

No.	Entry	Name	DOB/POB	Rel.	Occupation	Role	Tribe	Connections
291		Mr. Bridges	E	Ph				[24]
292		Elizabeth Brousse	Fr	H		P		[24]
293		Mr. Bull	E	Ph?				=67
294		Mr. Bullmore	E					
295		Rebecca Burroughs	E					
296		Dorothy Byfield	a1675 E					=56
297		Mary Calverly	E		f:merchant			
298		Mrs. Case	E	Ph?				[24]
299		John Caswell	1655 E	A	astronomer			[9]
300		Martha Child	E					
301		Mr. Cholmondley	a1688 E					=302
302		Mrs. Cholmondley	a1688 E					=301
303		Mrs. Clark	a1680 E					=217,+109
304		Mrs. Collison	a1688 E					
305		Joan Comb	a1700 E		servant			[166]
306		Mr. Conway	E?					&412
307		Thomas Cook	a1673 E	Q				=308
308		Mrs. Cook	a1673					=307
309		Mrs. Coot	E					
310		Joseph Corbyn				s		
311		Mrs. Cotton	a1670 NE	P?				=7
312		Mr. Coughen	a1680 E	Ph	physician			[24]
313		Mlle.(?) Coulon	Fr	H				
314		Jenny Courtney	a1700 E		servant			[64]
315		Elizabeth Craven	a1678 E	Ph				=55
316		Joan Cream	E					
317		Mr. Creed	E					
318		Mlle. Croissac	Fr	H				
319		Mr. Darby	E?					
320		William Davies	E					
321		Hannah Dawson	E					

Appendix I contd.

No. Entry	Name	DOB/POB	Rel.	Occupation	Role	Tribe	Connections
322	Antoine Du Pont	a1685 Fr	H	secretary	?		[286]
323	Mr. Durand	a1688 Fr	H				=475(bigamy)
324	Mme. Durand	Fr	H				+323?
325	Mrs. Easton	a1688 E					
326	Daniel Eyres	a1692 E	Ph				+327 [24]
327	Robert Eyres	E					+326
328	Mr. Forester	E	Ph	oilman?	?		[24]
329	Edward Fowler	1632 E	A	bishop	?		[457]
330	Mrs. Fox	E					
331	William(?) Freak	1662 E	A	gentleman	?		
332	P.(?) de Gaujac	1655 Fr	H	minister	?		
333	Mlle. Gentil	Fr					
334	Constance Glover	1658 E					=94
335	Mr. Godfry	E					
336	Mrs. Good	a1677 E					+60
337	Anna Green	?a1675 E					[165?]
338	Joan Groves	a1688 E					
339	Martha Hall	E					
340	William Halloway	E					
341	Mrs. Hammond	?1664 E	Ph?				[24]
342	Edward Harley	a1668 E	A	lawyer?	?		[9?]
343	Mrs. Harling	E					+255,+425?
344	Timothy Harrys	E					
345	John Hartman	E					
346	Mary Headley	E					
347	John Hide	E					
348	Elizabeth Hodgkins	E					
349	Mr. Hoffman	E	Ph				[24]
350	Susannah Howe	E					
351	Elizabeth Johnson	E					
352	George Johnson	E			a		

Appendix I contd.

No.	Entry	Name	DOB/POB	Rel.	Occupation	Role	Tribe	Connections
353		Israel Juif	Fr?	J?				=354
354		Mme. Juif	Fr?	J?				=353
355		Mrs. Keith	a1685 Sc					=26
356		Mrs. Kinnady						
357		Pierre(?) Ladore	Fr?	H?	joiner?			
358		Bulfinch Lamb	E					
359		Jaques La Touche	Fr	H				[13]
360		Catherine Le Page	a1688 Fr	H				=137
361		Mr. Le Roi	Fr	H				
362		Jaques Levi	a1670 Fr	H	bookseller			
363		Mrs. Levit						
364		Susannah Lion	Fr?	H?				&27?
365		Mrs. Lockart	E					
366		Mr. Magpeth						
367		Susannah Martin	Sc?					=368
368		Mr. Martin	Sc?					=367
369		Mr. Mazarguille	Fr	H				=370
370		Mme. Mazarguille	Fr	H				=369
371		Mr. Messenger	E?					=372
372		Mrs. Messenger	E?					=371
373		Judith Misson	a1640 Fr	H	h:minister			+13,+200
374		Mme. Mony	Fr	H				=208
375		Mrs. Moreton	a1678 E		printer	h		+145
376		Margaret Moult	a1700 E	A		?		=41,+93
377		Mr. Neville						
378		Mrs. Noble	E					=225
379		Mrs. Nutt	E					=243
380		Mrs. Parker	Ir?	A?				=96
381		Ann Paterson	E?					&38
382		Mrs. Pearson	E					
383		Judith Pellet	a1663 Fr	H		h		=189

309

Appendix I contd.

No.	Entry	Name	DOB/POB	Rel.	Occupation	Role	Tribe	Connections
384		Mrs. Penny	E	Ph				[24]
385		Mrs. Philipps	E					+19
386		Mary Piggott	E					
387		Mary Pikes	E					
388		Mrs. Plass	a1680					=153
389		Mlle. Pontin	Fr					
390		Jeanne Prade	a1680 Fr	H				=35,+263,+264
391		Mrs. Preston	a1680 E	H				=80
392		Humphrey Price	E					=393
393		Mrs. Price	E					=392
394		Andrew M. Ramsay	1686 Sc	Qt	tutor, secretary			[420,428]
395		Mme. Saunier	Fr	H				
396		Richard Shepherd	E	A				
397		Mrs. Shovel	E		h:admiral			[3?]
398		Mary Spaven	E					
399		Rebecca Spong	a1646 E	Ph?				=184
400		Sarah Stample	E					
401		Benjamin Steele	a1680 E		watchmaker	s		[9]
402		Joseph Steel	a1688 E		staymaker			=95
403		Mr. Stevenson	a1688 E	Ph?				=404
404		Mrs. Stevenson	a1688 E	Ph?				=403
405		Mary Suttle	E					
406		Joshua Tilby	E					
407		Mrs. Urquhart						=169?
408		Marthe Vergnon	1702 E	H		P		+239,+409,+240
409		Samuel Vergnon	a1682 Fr	H				=239,+240,+408
410		Mr. Wall	E		physician			
411		Catharine Ward	E	Ph?				[24]
412		Mrs. Webster						&306
413		Hannah Wharton	a1688 E					=88,+many
414		Joseph Wharton	E					+88,+413

Appendix I contd.

No.	Entry	Name	DOB/POB	Rel.	Occupation	Role	Tribe	Connections
415		Thomas Whitehead	a1680 E	Q	merchant	h		
416		Betty Willson	c1695 E					[16]
417		Mary Willson	c1688 E					
	1709							
418	early	Hélène Jurieu	a1650 Fr	H	scholar	h		=429
419	early	Pierre Jurieu	1637 Fr	H	minister	h		=418 [220]
420	6-	James Cuninghame	c1665 Sc	Qt	"laird"	Pmh		[394,26,429]
421	6-	Kennet Gordon	a1688 Sc	Qt		sh		+422
422	7-14	Clara Gordon	a1688 Sc	Qt	"Lady"	Pm		+421
423	7-25	*(Mrs.) Abden	a1680 Sc	Qt	"Lady"	P		
424	7-25	Katharine Orme	Sc	Qt		P		
425	7-27	*Dorothy Harling	a1679 E	B		P		+431
426	8-1	Samuel Shaw	a1689 E	Q		P		[216]
427	8-29	Mr. Green	E			?		&333?
428	9-11	Thomas Hope	1633 Sc	Qt	baronet	?		[394,420]
429	10-1	David Spence	a1669 Sc	E	lawyer?	?		[420]
430	12-6	Jane Cameron	Sc	Qt		s		
431	12-	John Harling	a1699 E		barber?	Pm		+425?
432	12-	Mr. Newson	E			a		
	1710							
433	1-3	James Hogg	Sc			a		[394]
434	5-2	Mr. Carnegy	Sc			?		
435	5-2	Mr. Ferguson	Sc			?		
436	7-3	Margaret Mackenzie	a1688 Sc			Pm		
437	9-10	Mary Dutton	a1680 E	A?				=66,+228
438	12-24	Jonathan du Laurier	Fr	H				+439,+440
439	12-24	Marie du Laurier	Fr	H		h		+438,+440
440	12-24	Mme. du Laurier	Fr	H				+438,+439
441	12-25	Louis Gervaise	Fr	H		s		

311

Appendix I contd.

No.	Entry	Name	DOB/POB	Rel.	Occupation	Role	Tribe	Connections
442	12-27	Louis Joyneau	1648 Fr	H	leatherworker	P		
443	12-27	Mary Waller	?1689 E	A		P		
444	12-	Alexander Falconar	a1689 Sc	Qt	lawyer			[420]
	1711							
445	1-2	Jeanne Perrot	Fr	H		h		+259,+152,+153
446	1-2	Hannah Eversden	E	B	f:baker	P		&450
447	1-8	Liddy Carriage	E			P		
448	2-	Nathaniel Hicks	a1684 E	B				[449]
449	2-	Samuel Todd	a1684 E	B				[448]
450	3-1	Thomas Gardner	E			a		&446
451	3-12	John Mill	Sc			Pm		
452	3-16	John Forbes of Pitfichie	1680 Sc	Qt	f:baronet	P		&454
453	4-26	Mme. Petitmaitre	Sw	(P)		P		
454	5-2	John Forbes of Pitsligo	a1689 Sc	Qt	laird?			&452
455	5-2	*Christina Pickering	a1680 E	A		P		
456	5-2	Mr. Rigg	Ir	A?	gentleman			=236?
457	5-23	John Foster	1657 E	A	minister	ash		[216]
458	6-	Timothy Burgis	E	Q		P?		[216]
459	6-	Mary Parks	E	Q		P		=201
460	6-6	Mme. de Voutron	Fr	H				&63
461	6-17	(Miss) Jackson	E			s		
462	6-21	Mme. Broucktof	Sw	(P)				
463	6-21	Mr.(?) Marsh						
464	6-29	Judith Valentin	Fr?	H?		P		
465	8-8	Jean Forbes	a1664 Sc	Qt	"Lady"	Pm		[420],&452
466	8-8	Henrietta Irvine	Sc			Pm		
467	9-18	George Swan	a1681 Sc	Q	hammerman	h		
468	9-26	James Ogilvie	a1687 Sc	Qt	Lord Deskford	?		[420]
469	10-10	Mrs. Keith	a1684 Sc	Qt	"of Caddom"	h		+472
470	10-10	Daniel Sharp	Sc					

312

Appendix I contd.

No.	Entry	Name	DOB/POB	Rel.	Occupation	Role	Tribe	Connections
471	11-5	Mark Salter	a1689 E	B		Pm		[448,449]
472	12-12	Mr. Keith	a1689 Sc	Qt		a		+469
473	12-	Mr. Boulter	E					[162]
	1712							
474	3-19	Mr. Andrew	E					[5,9]
475	3-21	Anne Brunelle	Fr	H		P		=323
476	5-4	Mr.(?) M. C. Bouché	Fr?	H?		Ph		
477	6-6	William Phillips	a1680 E	A?	weaver			
478	6-27	Mrs. Harris	E	B				&497
479	7-3	Joseph Bundy	a1680 E	B				
480	?	Mr.(?) N. Browne	E					[146]
481	?	Mrs. Manwayring	E		housekeeper			
	1713							
482	3-20	*Paul Hanet	a1680 Fr	H	goldsmith			
483	6-3	Mary Wall	E?			?		+410?
484	6-13	Marie Hélène de Ridder	Ho	B?		P		
485	6-15	Etienne Jamets	Fr	H		P		
486	6-15	Sarah Webster	Ir			Pm		
487	7-6	Richard Gardiner	E			P		
488	11-13	J.-J. Doladille	1671 Fr	H		Pm		
	1714							
489	8-3	Mr. Boucher	Fr?					
490	9-5	Ann Petersen		H		P		
491	9-30	François Pagez	Fr	H		Pm		
492	10-20	Daniel Roussière	a1694 Fr	H		Pm		
493	?	Samuel Tomlinson	E	(Q)	butcher	a		[165]
494	*1718*	Mme. Pigrin	Fr?	H?				[48]

313

Appendix I contd

No.	Entry	Name	DOB/POB	Rel.	Occupation	Role	Tribe	Connections
	1719							
495	2-5	Robert Eaton	a1696 E		physician			[146]
496	3-1	Mrs. Hatton	a1699 E			h		
497	7-23	Robert Harris	E	B				
	1720							
498	11-10	Ann Baber	E	B				[499]
499	11-10	Mary Evans	E	B				[498]
500	*1726*	William Wilkins	a1690 E		printer			=161,&65
	1730							
501	3-25	George Wharton	E					&88,&413
502	4-26	Mr. Clay	E		watchmaker			
503	5-1	William Weintraub		Pi?				[146]
504	9-27	Timothy Ireland						
505	?	Johanna C. Zeidig	a1700 Ge	Pi	f:minister	s		
	1732							
506	early	Mary Wharton	E					+88,+413
507	early	Sarah Wharton	E					+88,+413
508	early	Francis Wynantz	a1700 Ge	Pi	merchant			&3
509	9-12	Susannah Haines	a1712 E					
510	10-3	Isaac Hollis	1699 E	B,Ph	gentleman	a		[24]
	1736							
511	early	George Stubbes	a1706 E					=59,&65
512	3-	Mme. Delbose	Fr?	H?	h:merchant?	h		
513	3-	Simon Saudignan	Fr?	H		P		
514	6-	Joseph Whitehead	E					&415?

Appendix I contd.

No.	Entry	Name	DOB/POB	Rel.	Occupation	Role	Tribe	Connections
	1739							
515	1-28	Mary Plewit	E?			P		
516	1-28	Lydia Sellers	E	M		m		[518]
517	4-17	Mr. Shaw	E	M				[518]
518	4-20	*John Bray	E	M				[516,517]
519	4-28	*Mr. Bowers	E	M				[518]
520	5-16	William Fish	E	M				[518]
521	6-7	Mrs. Cooper	E			P		
522	6-7	(Ms.) Lavington	E			P		[523]
523	6-7	Mr. Wise	E					[522]
524	6-13	Shepherd Wolf	E	M				
	1746							
525	2-18	Benjamin Du Plan	a1700 Fr	H	gentleman	h		

Major sources of biographical data:

Manuscripts: BPUG, Fatio Papers; Dutton-Cuninghame Corr.; Fatio Notebooks; Friends' House Library typescript Dictionary of Quaker Biography and Meetings minutes; HAL church registers; HSL church registers; PRO wills; Roach Diary; Stack MSS.

Printed Sources: David C. A. Agnew, *Protestant Exiles from France, Chiefly in the Reign of Louis XIV* (3rd ed.; 2 vols., 1886); *Brand*; Edgerton Brydges, *Collins's Peerage of England* (9 vols., 1812); G. E. Cockayne, *Complete Baronetage* (5 vols., Exeter, 1904); *DNB*; Joseph Foster, *Alumni Oxonienses 1500-1714*, early series (4 vols., Oxford, 1891-92); D. V. Glass, *London Inhabitants Within the Walls 1695*, London Record Society (1966); E. and E. Haag, *La France protestante, ou vies des Protestants français* (10 vols., Paris, 1846-58); *Harleian Society Publications, Register Series* (88 vols., 1877–); *Huguenot Society of London Publications, Registers, Letters of Denization and Acts of Naturalization, Témoignages, conversions et reconnaissances*; George D. Henderson, *Mystics of the North-East* (Aberdeen, 1934); *MMM*; William Munk, *Roll of the Royal College of Physicians of London* (2nd ed.; 3 vols., 1878); Henry R. Plomer et al., *A Dictionary of the Printers and Booksellers Who Were at Work in England, Scotland and Ireland from 1668 to 1725*, ed. A. Esdaile (1922); J. and J. A. Venn, *Alumni Cantabrigienses. Part I. From the Earliest Times to 1751* (4 vols., Cambridge, 1922-27).

APPENDIX II. *New Membership by Periods, 1706-1708*

Periods	Huguenot				English				Other-Unknown				Totals		
	M	F	T	%	M	F	T	%	M	F	T	%	M	F	All
1. June-Dec. 1706	10	1	11	69	2	1	3	19	2	–	2	12	14	2	16
2. Jan.-May, 1707	9	7	16	76	3	1	4	19	1	–	1	5	13	8	21
3. June-Dec. 1707	2	8	10	19	21	17	38	73	4	–	4	8	27	25	52
4. January 1708	12	16	28	32	22	30	52	60	6	1	7	8	40	47	87
5. Feb.-May 1708	2	–	2	11	8	7	15	83	1	–	1	6	11	7	18
6. June-Dec. 1708	25	8	33	42	31	11	42	56	4	–	4	3	60	19	79
7. circa 1708	14	18	32	22	38	54	92	64	8	13	21	14	60	85	145

Periods correspond to epochs in group development:

1. Huguenots cluster around *inspirés*
2. First contact with English and first publications
3. First English prophets and ascendance of the English
4. Membership list compiled (for Christmas communion?)
5. Awaiting the resurrection of Dr. Emes, defending the integrity of the *Théâtre sacré*
6. The Reunion of the Alliances, naming of tribes
7. Membership list (Christmas communion, Feast of the Lamb of the Lord's Supper?)

% column is percentage of the total new membership per period

APPENDIX III.

Running Totals of Membership, 1706-1715

End of Year	Huguenot	English	Other-Unknown	Totals M	F	All
1706	11	3	2	14	2	16
1707	65	89	12	87	79	166
1708	129	237	38	214	190	404
1709	125	240	45	217	193	410
1710	126	242	47	220	195	415
1711	129	253	61	235	208	443
1712	131	257	60	237	211	448
1713	131	259	61	237	214	451
1714	132	259	62	239	214	453
1715	132	257	61	236	214	450

All departures from the group—due to death, apostasy, or exclusion—have been subtracted from yearly totals. The totals and the proportions would not be significantly different if all those in Appendix I with question marks entered under their role were omitted.

APPENDIX IV. Occupations of Male Believers

Status or Occupation	Huguenots No.	% Range	English No.	% Range	Other-Unknown No.	% Range	All No.	% Range
Gentleman	6	7-15	4	3-6	7	16-37	17	6-14
Professional	12	13-29	17	11-27	9	20-47	38	13-31
clergy	5		5		–			
"inventors"	–		2		–			
lawyers	2		3		3			
musicians	–		–		1			
physicians	–		5		–			
secretaries	4		–		–			
students	–		–		2			
tutors	1		2		3			
Wholesale Traders	2	2-5	5	3-7	2	4-10	9	3-7
merchants	2		3		2			
tanners	–		1		–			
meatpackers	–		1		–			
Retail Traders	5	6-12	24	15-38	–		29	10-23
barbers	–		1		–			
booksellers	2		5		–			
butchers	–		1		–			
canemakers	–		1		–			
chemists and apothecaries	–		6		1			
innkeepers and victuallers	2		2		–			
furriers	–		1		–			

Appendix IV contd.

Status or Occupation	Huguenots No.	% Range	English No.	% Range	Other-Unknown No.	% Range	All No.	% Range
oilmen	—		1		—			
shoemakers	—		2		—			
staymakers	—		1		—			
tailors	—		1		—			
tallowchandlers	—		2		—			
"tradesman"	1		—		—			
Woolcombers	1	1-2	1	1-2	—	—	2	1-2
Artisans and Laborers		17-37		8-20		2-5	29	10-23
apprentices	15		13		1			
brasiers	1		1		—			
cabinetmakers	—		1		—			
cutlers	1		1		—			
engravers	1		—		—			
goldsmiths	2		—		—			
hammermen	—		—		1			
joiners	1		—		—			
leatherworkers	1		—		—			
pattenmakers	—		1		—			
sawyers	1		1		—			
soldiers	2		—		—			
upholsterers	—		1		—			
watermen	—		1		—			
watchmakers	—		4		—			
weavers	6		1		—			
Total Known	41 of 87		64 of 156		19 of 45		124 of 288	

Appendix IV contd.

Appendix IV is designed to correspond to Table 4 in Richard T. Vann, *The Social Development of English Quakerism 1655-1755* (Cambridge, Mass., 1969) 59-60. The column for % Range gives two percentages, the first of all males of that nationality, the second of all for whom occupations are know. "Secretaries" includes clerks and agents, "tutors" includes teachers. I have tried to distinguish between physicians and apothecaries (chemists) who assumed the title of "Dr." "Booksellers" includes printers; the two occupations were becoming distinct during this era, but the French Prophets who were printers were usually also booksellers. There are four men for whom two occupations have been given; in this chart Charles Portales (No. 3) is accounted a secretary, Fatio (No. 9) is accounted a tutor, Peter Rochfort (No. 265) an inventor, and A. M. Ramsay (No. 394) a tutor.

APPENDIX V.

Religious Affiliations of the French Prophets

Religious Connection	All Believers			Prophets			% inspired
	M	F	T	M	F	T	
[English]							
Anglicans[a]	26	12	38	3	4	7	18
Other Protestants	55	35	90	9	11	20	22
Baptists	12	10	22	3	6	9	41
Methodist/Moravian	5	1	6	—	—	—	—
Philadelphians[b]	21	13	34	1	—	1	3
Presbyterians	3	1	4	1	—	1	25
Quakers[c]	12	10	22	3	5	8	36
nonsectarian	2	—	2	1	—	1	50
Roman Catholics	2	—	2	—	—	—	—
Subtotal	83	47	130	12	15	27	21
[French]							
Huguenots	87	67	154	15	12	27	18
Jews	1	1	2	—	—	—	—
[Scottish]							
Quietists[d]	14	6	20	3	5	8	40
[Other]							
Pietists	2	1	3	—	—	—	—
Swiss Protestant	2	2	4	—	1	1	25
Total Known	189	124	313	30	33	63	20
Unknown	100	112	212	10	19	29	14
Total	289	236	525	40	52	92	18
% known	65	53	60	75	63	68	

This list is for affiliations at time of entry into group.

[a] — The French Prophets claimed that the majority of followers were Anglicans. If one assumes that all unknowns were Anglican, the percentage of inspired Anglicans is 13.

[b] — Most Philadelphians were also Anglicans; listing includes one French person.

[c] — Includes Quaker claimants and one Scottish person.

[d] — Most Quietists were also Episcopalians.

APPENDIX VI. *Chronological Profile of the Inspired*

(by date of first inspiration)

Date	Name	Nation	Rel.	Apostasy	Exclusion	Last Note	Death
1706							
6-	Durand Fage	Fr	H			1719	
8-10	Jean Cavalier	Fr	H	1710			
9-16	Elie Marion	Fr	H				1713
1707							
4-11	Susanne des Brousses	Fr	H			1711	
4-11	Jeanne Cavalier	Fr	H	1710			
4-11	Anne Voyer	Fr	H			1711	
4-13	Isaac Havy	Fr	H		1714		
4-13	Daniel Le Tellier	Fr	H		1713		
4-15	Jean Allut	Fr	H				a1740
4-16	Henriette Allut	Fr	H			1716	
6-13	John Lacy	E	P				1730
6-28	Elizabeth Gray	E	A?			1713	
8-	Anne Watts	E	B			1718	
8-24	Mary Keimer	E	B			1718	
8-29	Mary Beer	E	B				a1737
9-2	Ann Good	E	Q			11-1707	
9-2	Sarah Wiltshire	E	B,C			1723	
9-5	Thomas Emes	E				1740	12-1707
9-11	Thomas Dutton	E				12-1708	
9-15	Mary Bullmore[a]	E				9-1707	
9-15	Mr. Hammond[a]	E					
10-31	Jean Noual	Fr	H			1711	
12-2	Isabeau Charras	Fr	H			1719	
12-14	Anna Maria King	E				1710	

322

Appendix VI contd.

Date	Name	Nation	Rel.	Apostasy	Exclusion	Last Note	Death
12-25	John Potter	E	B				1740
?	Marthe Vergnon	Fr	H			1709	
1708							
1-	Stephen Halford[b]	E	Q?	1708			
1-10	Mary Aspinal	E				1709	
1-12	Abraham Whitrow	E	A?		7-1708		
1-18	John Parker	Ir?			1713		
2-	Jeanne Raoux	Fr	H			1709	
2-	Jonathan Taylor	E					
2-3	Deborah Whitrow	E	A?		7-1708		1733
3-30	John Moore (185)	E				6-1708	
4-8	Mary Turner	E	Q?			1710	
4-30	John Moult (147)	E	A			1709	
5-13	John Glover	E	A?				
5-23	Anne Steed	E	Q			1726	
7-23	Sarah Draycott	E	B			7-1708?	a1736
7-25	Benjamin Rawson[a]	E				7-1'08	
8-	Robert Wise	E			11-1708		
8-19	Elizabeth Hughes (192)	E	B?			1709	
9-30	Anna Angibert	Fr	H		1709		
12-4	Dinah Stoddart	E			12-1708		
1709							
1-1	Anne Topham	E	Q?			1711	
1-	John Hartland[c]	E		1709			
1-	Hannah Wharton	E				1740	
2-7	Guy Nutt	E	(Q)			1737	
5-28	Thomas Arpwood	Sc				1711	
7-27	Dorothy Harling[b]	E		1709			
7-31	[Lady] Abden	Sc	Qt	1710			

323

Appendix VI contd.

Date	Name	Nation	Rel.	Apostasy	Exclusion	Last Note	Death
?	Stephen Bennet	E	A?			1711?	
1710							
early	James Cuninghame	Sc	Qt				1716
1-14	Katharine Orme	Sc	Qt			1710	
1-14	Jane Cameron	Sc	Qt			1710?	
2-3	Margaret Mackenzie	Sc				1711	
12-24	Jeanne Morel	Fr	H			1714	
12-27	Mary Waller						1722
1711							
1-1	Robert Richardson	E	Ph			1719	
1-18	Liddy Carriage	E				1712	
3-3	Jaques Soulier	Fr	H			1732	
3-12	John Mill	Sc	Qt			1711	
3-16	John Forbes (452)	Sc	Qt				1715
4-26	Mme. Petitmaitre	Sw	(P)				
5-	Christina Pickering	E	A	1711		1711	
5-23	Rebecca Cuff	E				1711	
6-	Samuel Shaw[a]	E	Q			1711	
6-	Mary Parks[a]	E	Q			1711	
8-8	Jean Forbes	Sc	Qt			1712	
8-8	Henrietta Irvine	Sc				1712	
1712							
early	Mark Salter	E	B			1726	
1-21	Clara Gordon	Sc	Qt			1740	
3-21	Anne Brunelle	Fr	H			1719	
5-5	John Moore (186)	E	B			1719	
12-	Susannah Sanger	E					c1730

Appendix VI contd.

Date	Name	Nation	Rel.	Apostasy	Exclusion	Last Note	Death
1713							
early	J.J. Doladille	Fr	H				1761
5-7	Judith Valentin[a]	Fr	H?			1713	
6-13	Marie H. de Ridder	Ho	B?			1715	
6-15	Hannah Eversden	E	B			1714	
6-15	Etienne Jamets	Fr	H			1716	
6-15	Louis Joyneau	Fr	H			1732	
6-15	Sarah Webster	Ir				1713	
7-6	Elizabeth Brousse	Fr	H			1714	
7-6	Richard Gardiner	E				1713	
1714							
6-5	(Mr.?) M. C. Bouché	Fr	H?			1714	
9-5	Ann Peterson[a]					1714	
9-30	François Pagez	Fr	H			1718	
10-20	Daniel Roussière	Fr	H			1718	
1736							
	Simon Saudignan	Fr	H			1736	
1739							
1-28	Mary Plewit	E				1739	
6-7	[Mrs.] Cooper	E				1739	
6-7	[Ms.] Lavington	E				1739	

a – Only one recorded instance of prophecy.
b – Never recognized by the London group as a prophet.
c – John Hartland may have been inspired in 1708.
Dates for the first prophecies of Fage, Cavalier and Marion are of course for their first inspirations in England.

325

APPENDIX VII.
Running Totals of the Inspired, 1706-1714

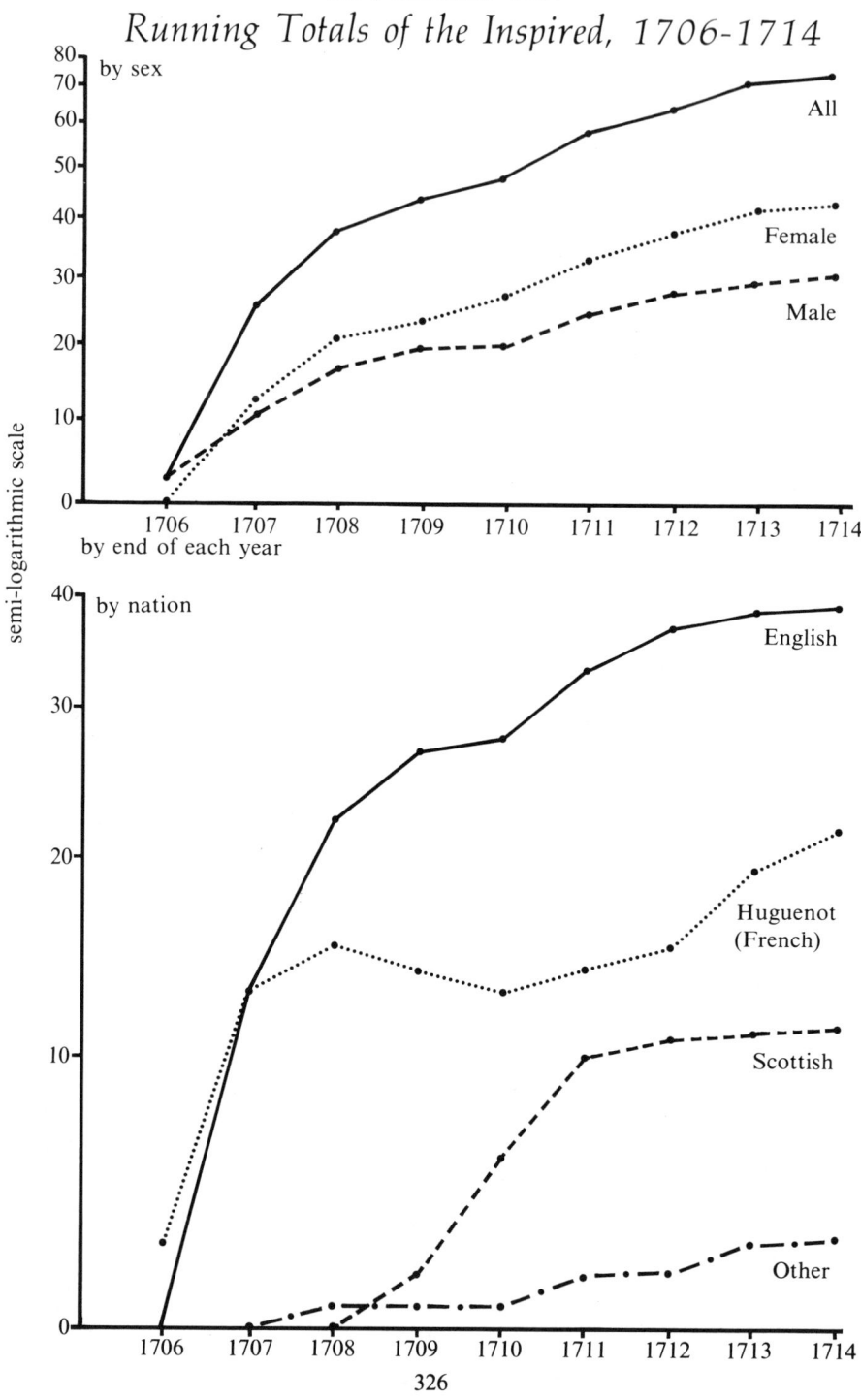

APPENDIX VIII.

Ages of the French Prophets, 1706-1714

Born no later than	% of all Inspired	% of Uninspired	% All	Cumulative Percentages		
				Inspired	Uninspired	All
1659	8.5	16.3	15	8.5	16.3	15
1660-64	3.3	6.1	6	11.8	22.4	21
1665-69	11.7	8.8	10	23.5	31.2	31
1670-74	3.3	10.5	9	26.8	41.7	40
1675-79	10.0	18.0	16	37.8	59.7	56
1680-84	15.0	8.3	10	51.8	68.0	66
1685-89	30.0	21.5	23	81.8	89.5	89
1690-94	8.3	3.0	4	90.1	92.5	92
1695-99	6.7	3.5	4	96.8	96.0	96
after 1699	3.3	3.5	3	100.0	100.0	100

Percentages are only of those for whom ages can be estimated, which is 58 percent of the entire group, 1706-1714 (287 out of 493). Ages for the inspired are generally more precise than for the uninspired, and there is a general bias toward the underestimation of ages in my methods of assigning general age-ranges. The difference in ages between the uninspired and the inspired is therefore likely to be greater than shown here.

APPENDIX IX.

French Prophets with University Educations

No.	Name	Institutions	Years
6	Richard Bulkeley	Trinity College, Dublin	1680-81
		Christ Church, Oxford	1680
7	Thomas Cotton	University of Edinburgh	1677
9	Nicolas Fatio	Academy of Geneva	1678-80
		University of Paris?	1680s
13	F.-M. Misson	Academy of Geneva	1675-78
19	John Philipps	Trinity College, Cambridge	1682-84
24	Richard Roach	St. John's, Oxford	1681-89
26	James Keith	University of Aberdeen	1704
41	John Hooke	Trinity College, Dublin	1672
		Gray's Inn, London	1674-
56	Timothy Byfield	Trinity College, Dublin	a1670
66	Thomas Dutton	Middle Temple(?), London	1690s?
81	Joseph Tiley	Middle Temple, London	1693
194	Thomas Lardner	Cambridge	1705
		Oxford	1707
195	Henry Nicholson	Trinity College, Dublin	1705
		University College, Oxford	1706
		Cambridge	1714
		Middle Temple, London	1715
200	Jaques Misson	Academy of Geneva	1675-77
227	Hal Reason	Lincoln College, Oxford	1701-02
268	Pierre Allix	Prot. Academies, Saumur and Sedan	1660s
295	John Caswell	Wadham College, Oxford	1671-77
329	Edward Fowler	Oxford	-1656
419	Pierre Jurieu	Prot. Academies, Saumur and Sedan	1650s-60s
457	John Foster	Wadham College, Oxford	1677-83
458	Robert Eaton	Avignon (medical school)	-1715

APPENDIX X.

Types of Millenarian Ethos

SHARED SYSTEM OF CLASSIFICATION

Cataclysm
1. Apostolic church as model
2. Personal election
3. Worshipper as refugee
4. Prayer and praise for rescue
5. Interventional behavior (war)
6. Prophet as martyr and warrior
7. Defensive prophecy
8. Miracle saves
9. Emphasis on time

Judgment
1. Present church as guardian
2. Collective faith
3. Worshipper as pilgrim
4. Obedience and confession
5. Preservative behavior (ritual)
6. Prophet as preacher, celebrant
7. Prophecy as moral imperative
8. Miracle ratifies
9. Emphasis on place as grid

SELF IN CONTROL  STRONG GROUP

Pentecost
1. No need for church
2. Personal faith
3. Worshipper as contemplative
4. Surrender
5. Expressive behavior (trance)
6. Prophet as oracle, codebreaker
7. Prophecy as key to secrets
8. Miracle innovates
9. Emphasis on timelessness

New Jerusalem
1. Universal church as reality
2. Collective works
3. Worshipper as evangelist
4. Social communion
5. Preparatory behavior (mission)
6. Prophet as healer, administrator
7. Prophecy as ethical guideline
8. Miracle renews, delineates
9. Emphasis on place as center

PERSONAL SYSTEM OF CLASSIFICATION

Key to categories:
1. Role of church in millennium
2. Means of redemption
3. Character of worshipper
4. Nature of worship
5. Characteristic behavior
6. Role of prophet
7. Nature of prophecy
8. Function of miracle
9. Primary eschatological concern

APPENDIX XI.
Millenarianism and the French Prophets

SHARED SYSTEM OF CLASSIFICATION

Cataclysm (Camisards)
1. The Desert/The Mountains
2. Tribe
3. The elect remnant
4. Home vs. exile
5. Battle
6. Warning, attack and reward
7. Prediction, tears of blood, walking through fire
8. Betrayal

Judgment (petits prophètes)
1. The Court/The Hearth
2. Family
3. The established church
4. Parent vs. child
5. Rule-making
6. Purification and instruction
7. Exegesis, power to curse, power to detect evil spirits
8. Immorality and insubordination

SELF IN CONTROL　　　　　　＋　　　　　　STRONG GROUP

Pentecost
1. The Fertile Field
2. Companionship
3. The person
4. Learned vs. unlearned
5. Trance and meditation
6. Blessing
7. Levitation, fasting, feats of strength
8. Inauthenticity

New Jerusalem
1. The Orchard/The Walled City
2. Brotherhood/Sisterhood
3. The world
4. City vs. country
5. Missions and publication
6. Communion
7. Eloquence, tongues and healing, raising the dead
8. Insincerity and exclusiveness

PERSONAL SYSTEM OF CLASSIFICATION

Key to categories:
1. Prophetic arena
2. Model of group relationships
3. Soteriological emphasis
4. Primary tension within the ethos
5. Primary character of activity
6. Type of prophetic action
7. Characteristic prophetic gifts and miracles
8. Nature of impurity (sin)

Bibliography of Manuscript Sources

Note: All manuscripts concern the group activities of the Camisards and the French Prophets, unless otherwise indicated or obvious. No printed manuscript collections are included.

France

Montpellier. Archives Départementales de l'Hérault. Archives Civiles, Intendance de Languedoc, MSS C. 180 (1700-1701), "Pièces judiciaires de l'Intendance de Languedoc."
    MSS C. 181, "Sur les phanatiques."
    MSS C. 191, ff. 354-355, 418-421, Letter from Lachaux to Claude Brousson and interrogation of Brousson, 1698.
Nîmes. Archives Départementales du Gard. MSS B. 2819, liasse "Pujolas 1703," *re* Col. Jean Cavalier.
    MSS B. 2820, "Grand criminel Procédures contre les Camisards, 1699-1703."
Nîmes. Bibliothèque municipale [Bibliothèque Séguier]. MSS 57(6), ff. 249-253, "Relation de ce qui s'est passé à Calvisson pendant le séjour que les Camisards y ont fait [en 1704]."
    MSS 186(15), "Lettre sans date adressée à un correspondant inconnu sur les prophètes et prophétesses des Cévennes par le prêtre Mongé."
    MSS 198, No. 22 (*sic* for 23), "Mémoire de tout ce qui a été fait pour et contre les Nouveaux Prophètes tant en François qu'en Anglois."
Paris. Archives des Affaires Etrangères. Correspondance Politique, Angleterre, MSS vols. 223-225, Letters from England, July, 1707—December, 1708, by l'abbé François Gaultier.
Paris. Archives Nationales. 154 A P II 120, microfilmed as 177 mi 171, Fonds Lamoignon de Basville.
Paris. Bibliothèque de la Société pour l'Histoire du Protestantisme français. MSS

966, "Mémoires de Jean Cavalier,1700-1704," copy of mss. at Bibliothèque Wallonne, Leiden.

Papiers Coquerel, MS 302, ff.3-5, Letter from Charles Portales to David Flotard, 4/22/1709, with list of tribe names and members.

Papiers Coquerel, MS 302, ff. 6-7, Letter from Charles Portales and Elie Marion to David Flotard, 9/26/1709.

Paris. Bibliothèque Nationale. MSS f.f. 24190, "Mémoires concernant la nouvelle secte des Piétistes ou Quiétistes ou société philadelphique, répandue dans les Cantons suisses."

Great Britain

Aylesbury. Buckinghamshire Record Office. D/LO/3, Drafts and abstracts concerning the farm late of Joshua Geary at Bellingdon, *re* estate of Greencroft supposedly purchased by Abraham Whitrow and Sir Richard Bulkeley.

Beckenham (Kent). Archives of Bethlem Royal Hospital and Maudsley Hospital. Bethlem Royal Hospital Admissions Book, 1702-1715, p. 159, *re* Mary Heath, later involved in controversial healing by Richard Roach and Sarah Wiltshire.

BSC 1, Bethlem Subcommittee Book, 1709-1717, pp. 3, 43, *re* Mary Heath.

Bedford. Bedfordshire County Record Office. MSS MO 607, Memoir of Thomas Pierson, *re* John Mason.

How Papers, HW 87/7, Letter of J. Padley to Richard How, 7/22/1707, *re Cry from the Desart.*

Birmingham. Central Reference Library. Joseph Hill MSS 244501, Parish of Birmingham [Poor Relief] Levy Book for 1736-45, *re* Richard Wharton (?), Thomas Halford (?).

MSS 570748, Pedigree of the Taylor Family of Birmingham and Strensham Court, co. Worcester, c. 1870, *re* Jonathan Taylor (the prophet?).

Bristol. Archives Office. Thomas Whitehead will, proved January, 1748-49, and register of burial, 1748.

Bristol. Baptist College Library. MSS "A[ndrew] & E[mmanuel] Gifford Remains," vol I.

Bristol. Broadmead Free Baptist Church. MSS, Church Records 1655-1784, pp. 171-177, 186.

Cambridge. Cambridge University Library. Add. MSS 5, ff. 160-160v., Letter from Jane Bonnell to J. Strype, 10/25/1709.

Add. MSS 2608.XII, Pierre Allix, Treatise on Anti-christ, 1710.

Cambridge. King's College, Keynes MSS 96 (microfilm, Add. MSS 4007, Cambridge University Library), Letters from Nicolas Fatio to Isaac Newton and John Conduit.

Keynes MSS 99 (microfilm), Letter from John Caswell to John Flamsteed, 10/14/1694.

Chester, County and Diocesan Record Office. MSS EDB/97, Bishop's Transcripts of the Great Budsworth Parish Church Register, *re* Thomas and Mary Dutton.

Colchester. Archives of the Eld Lane Baptist Church. Church Book 1707-1731, *re* Mark Salter, Nathaniel Hicks, Samuel Todd.

Colchester. Quaker Meeting House, Shewall Road. Colchester Friends Monthly Meeting Minutes 1672-1756 *re* Furly family.

Colchester Men's Two-Weeks Meetings 1705-1725, *re* Furly family and Samuel Ennew, who counterfeited inspirations in order to deceive the French Prophets.

Quarterly Meeting of Essex, Births, Marriages and Burials, with Supplement, 1660-1756, *re* Ennew.

Edinburgh. National Library of Scotland. Adv. MSS 29.1.1.(iii), ff. 24-27, Letters from James Cuninghame to Sir Alexander Murray, 12/11/1715 and 1/30/1716.

MS/493/73, Letters to Andrew Michael Ramsay from Dr. James Keith, James Cuninghame and others, 1709-1710.

MSS 2686, James Cuninghame of Barns, A volume of religious poetry, 1710-1712.

MSS 5166, James Cuninghame, A volume of religious verse and sermons, 1710-1711.

Wodrow MSS, Letters II, No. 114. Rev. James Webster to Rev. Robert Wodrow, 9/20/1710.

Edinburgh. Scottish Episcopal Theological College. Jolly Kist, MSS Quarto 12, Mary Baird commonplace book, introduction to and copy of three letters from James Cuninghame to George Garden, 1709-10, entry c. 1730?

Old Catalogue, Forbes MSS, Letter in Latin from Pierre Poiret [to James Cuninghame?], 1710.

Edinburgh. Scottish Record Office. MSS B10/2/2, p. 344, Register of Seasings of the burgh of Crail, land transaction involving James Cuninghame, 3/21/1706-07.

MSS CC8/8/86, Testament of James Cuningham [*sic*] of Barns, registered 1/1/1718.

MSS CC8/8/97, Testament of George Swan, 2/25/1735.

Edinburgh. University of Edinburgh Library. MSS La. III. 708, James Cuninghame, 248 religious hymns and prophetic poems, 1710-1714.

Gregory MSS, Folio c. DC. 1. 61, f. 707, entry for 1/29/1706-07. [Supplied by Prof. M.C. Jacob.]

Ewell (Surrey). Bourne Hall. Glyn Documents 3, 40, 66, 106, 423-429, Leases, bonds, indentures and mortgages by Sir Richard Bulkeley, 1705-1709.

Glasgow. Mitchell Library. Slains Collection 562590, Correspondence between James Cuninghame and Thomas Dutton, 1709-1740, copied by Alexander Falconar.

Guildford (Surrey). Guildford Muniment Room. PSH/EWL/1/2, St. Mary's Parish Register, Ewell, 1669-1723, *re* Sir Richard Bulkeley and Lucy Bulkeley, both deceased 1710.

Kingston-upon-Thames. Surrey Record Office. MSS Somers L/16, Nos. 342-343, Letter from Sir Richard Bulkeley to Lord Somers, 11/27/1695.

MSS 86/1/3.4 and 86/1/4.1, conveyance and release of rectory at Ewell, by Sir Richard Bulkeley, 1705-1709.

Lichfield (Staffordshire). Joint Record Office/Public Library. Will of Jonathan Taylor (the prophet?), 5/19/1733.

London. Baptist Church House Archives. MSS 090, Maze-Pond (Southwark) Baptist Church Book, 1713-22, re Lacy (the prophet?).

London. British Museum. Add. Ch. 46950, Medical Diploma of Robert Eaton, 1715.

Add. MSS 22,911, f. 51, Letter from Sir Richard Bulkeley to Dr. John Covell, 1/26/1706.

Add MSS 24,869, f. 146, Letter from John Hollis, 1816, re Isaac Hollis.

Add. MSS 28,536, f. 238, Letter from Nicolas Facio to Francis Hauksbee, 9/12/1731 [misdated in catalogue, 1737].

Add. MSS 28,883, f. 143, Letter from Benjamin Steele to John Ellis, 9/7/1698.

Add. MSS 28,916, f. 196, Letter from Pierre Jurieu to John Ellis, 3/2/1705 (N.S.).

Add. MSS 32,533, f. 171, "The Musicall Grammarian," re Steffkins family.

Add. MSS 32,799, ff. 33, 105, 335; 32,804, f. 127; 32,810, ff. 226, 228; 32,803, ff. 247-247v., Letters from Benjamin Du Plan to King George II, Newcastle and others.

Add. MSS 34,274 0_6, Letter from Mary Holms to Cosen Ives, 4/29/1694, re John Mason.

Add. MSS 34,274 0_7, Letter from W.C. to Mr. Mellefont (?), 5/20/1694, re John Mason.

Add. MSS 36,123, ff. 18-19, Copy of warrant for patent for Dr. Robert Eaton, signed by Carteret, 3/10/1722.

Add. MSS 39,794.GG.2, Rubbing of memorial inscription, for Richard Byfield, Mortlake, Surrey, re Timothy Byfield.

Add. MSS 41,812, ff. 226-227, 235, 246; 41,813, ff. 19, 203; 41,818, *passim;* 41,819, ff. 13-272, *passim*, Letters and reports from Edmond Everard, 1685-1686.

Add. MSS 41,813, f. 202; 41,819, ff. 121-126, 169-189, 190, 204-205, Letters from Joseph Tiley, 1686.

Harleian MSS 3777, ff. 282-285, Letters from Sir Richard Bulkeley to Humphrey Wanley, 1704.

Sloane MSS 2717, f. 47, Letter from Mr. Butler, 1695, re Joseph Tiley.

Sloane MSS 4043, f. 307, Letter from Nicolas Fatio (to Sir Hans Sloane?), 10/26/1714.

Sloane MSS 4045, ff. 126, 277; 4047, ff. 20, 159, 180; 4058, ff. 291, 293, Letters from Dr. Eaton to Hans Sloane, 1718-1723.

Sloane MSS 4047, f. 9, Letter from Benjamin Habakkuk Jackson to Hans Sloane, 6/21/1723.

Sloane MSS 4055, f. 27, Letter from Nicolas Facio to Hans Sloane, 12/28/1736.

Sloane MSS 4285, f. 145, Letter from F.-M. Mission to M. des Maizeaux, ("Lund. 5 du l'an 1718/19.")

Sloane MSS 4811, f. 45, Copy of a letter from Sir Richard Bulkeley to Mr. St. George Ash, 8/17/1685, from the minutes of the Philosophical Society of Dublin.

Stowe MSS 748, f. 63, Letter from John Lacy to Edmund Calamy, 9/3/1701? (note at bottom dated 1707). [This is the only extant manuscript in Lacy's hand that I have found.]

Stowe MSS Fr. 223, f. 345, Leaf from Nicolas Facio's memorandum book dated Rotterdam, July 18-19, 1710.

London. Dr. Williams's Library. MSS 24.33-34, Notes on the French Prophets by Nicolas Facio, in 2 vols. Second volume entitled "Avertissemens et Prieres de l'Esprit Eternel; Recueillis par moi Nicolas Facio, du 10 juin 1711 Stil Vieux, jusqu'au 22 may 1712."

MSS 24.278(a), C. Gilman, "Some most Deep and Profound Mysteries of the Invisible World disclosed At Sundry Times, and on various Subjects," written 1732.

MSS 24.109(8), Letters from Henry Dodwell to William and Francis Lee, 1698, *re* Philadelphians.

MSS 28.4, Diary of Elias Pledger, 1665-1725, *re* John Mason.

MSS 186.18(2), Francis Lee epistles to Peter Poiret in Holland, 1701-1703, and to some German associates of the Philadelphian Society, upon the decease of Mrs. Jane Lead, c. 1704.

MSS 533.B.1, Minutes of the Mill-Yard or Seventh-Day General Baptist Congregation, 1673-1840, *re* Mary Beer. [A photocopy; originals in possession of the Seventh Day Baptist Congregation, Plainfield, New Jersey.]

Walton MSS I.1.44, Autobiography of Charles Hector de St. George, Marquis de Marsay (trans. by J.P.?).

London. French Protestant Church, Soho. MS 187, Eglise de l'Artillerie, Registre des Actes du Consistoire 1695-1709.

Misc. Papers 105, Eglise de l'Artillerie.

MS 8, Threadneedle Street Church, Livre des actes de 1692/3 à 1708.

London. Friends' House Library. Typescript Dictionary of Quaker Biography, *re* Pickworth, Tovey, Steed, James Jackson, etc. [Copy also at Haverford College, Haverford, PA.]

Typed Register Extract, 11-vi-70, The Halford Family of Warwickshire, Leicestershire and Rutland Quarterly Meeting.

MSS Portfolio 32.68 through 32.71. Letters from Henry Pickworth, 1708-1711.

Matthews MSS 95, Letter from Joseph Woods to William Matthews, 6/26/1804.

London and Middlesex Two Weeks Meetings Minutes, I-IV, *re* Henry Pickworth, James Jackson, Joseph Tovey.

St. Albans Monthly Meeting Minutes, 1703-1724, *re* Marie Sterrill.

Wandsworth Monthly Meeting Minutes, 1695-1789, vol. 1, *re* Sterrill.

London. Greater London Record Office (Middlesex). Acc. 188/35-36, Deeds relating to property of Isaac Hollis, 1746, 1777.

Acc. 1017/2, Diary of Peter Briggins, 1706-1709.

MSP 1707 July/74, Middlesex Sessions Papers, July, 1707, Certificate of registration for Rebecca Critchlow's house as a place of religious worship for Independents.

London. Guildhall. MSS 6176, 1-18, Company of Tallow-Chandlers Search Books, 1672-1707, re William King, Joseph Tovey.

MSS 8201/8, Society of Apothecaries, Court book, November 1715-May 1721, re Francis Moult, James Craven.

MSS 8208/2, Society of Apothecaries quarterage accounts, 1703-1717, re Francis Moult.

London. House of Lords Record Office. Committee Book, Minutes, October 24, 1704-April 5, 1710, re John Lacy.

MSS 2519, Lacy's Estate Act.

London. Huguenot Society of London Library. MSS, Regitre des Acts En Consistoire de L'Eglise De Leicesterfields, 1693 Jusquà 1729.

MSS, Registre des Actes du Consistoire dans L'Eglise dans West Street St. Giles 1690 Jusquà 1741.

London. Lambeth Palace Archiepiscopal Library. MSS 931, f. 14, Letter from William Lloyd to Archbishop Tenison, 11/19/1712, re Bishop Fell and prophecies.

MSS 931, f. 22, Letter from Josiah Woodward, 3/11/1709.

MSS 934, f. 52, Preciz du Discours de Mr. Durand Fage d'Aubaye prononcé sous l'opération de l'Esprit: A Londres, le 3e septembre 1706, à 8 ou 9 Heures du matin. S.V., [and] Preciz du Discours de Mr. Jean Cavalier de Sauve, prononcé sous l'Opération de l'Esprit quelques Momens apres le Discours precedent.

MSS 942, f. 171, Letter from Sir Richard Bulkeley, 8/9/1701.

MSS 953, f. 124, Prophecies of Barbara Cadell, c. 1694.

MSS 1559, Copies of letters of Francis Lee, 1704, re Philadelphians.

London. Moravian Church House Archives. MSS Extracts from the London Archives of the United Brethren, re Jean Pellet.

MSS Diary of the English [Provincial] Pilgrim House, for July 27, 1743-October 30, 1748, copied from original and translated from the original German when necessary, by Miss E. Klesel, 1905-06.

MSS Fetter Lane Diaries, I, Oct. 31, 1742-July 12, 1743, and II, July 13, 1743-Jan. 27, 1744.

MSS Fetter Lane, Minutes of "Elders and Wardens," I.A. Jan. 26, 1743-May 1, 1744.

MSS EC 1, Fetter Lane Elders Conference Minutes, Aug. 18, 1743-April 3, 1744.

John Cennick, "Memorable passages relating to the Awakening in Wiltshire which began in the year 1740." [Parts pub. in *Moravian Messenger* (1874) 10-18, 335-45, 372-79.]

London. Public Record Office. MSS C10/525/71, Chancery Case involving John Lacy, November 4, 1700.

MSS C33.290, ff. 197, 390, 530, 664, Chancery Case involving Joseph Tiley, 1697.

MSS C66/3445, Patent to Nicolas Fatio, Peter and Jacob Debauffre, May 1, 1704.

MSS C66/3480, Patent to Timothy Byfield, October 22, 1711.

MSS K.B. 8/66, Part 1, p. 38, A List of the prisoners Rebells at Wiggin, re James Cuninghame.

MSS PROB 6/97, ff. 2v-4, Administration of will of Hélène du Moulin, 1721.
MSS PROB 6/108, Administration of will of Anna Southouse, 1732.
MSS PROB 11/584, No. 78, Will of Maximilien Misson, 1/3/1721.
MSS PROB 11/594, No. 253, Will of Timothy Byfield, 11/8/1715.
MSS PROB 11/622, No. 158, Will of Jane Perrott, 1728.
MSS PROB 11/633, S. 308, Will of Pierre Jurieu, 1728.
MSS PROB 11/659, No. 157, Will of Francis Moult, 4/20/1733.
MSS PROB 11/684, No. 171, Will of Joseph Tovey, 6/20/1737.
MSS PROB 11/793, No. 64, Will of Catherine Fatio de Duilliers, made 6/14/1749, entered 3/1752.
MSS PROB 11/917, No. 113, Will of Jaques Portales, 3/3/1766.
MSS PROB 11/1000, No. 288, Will of Francis Wynantz, 7/28/1774.

London. Royal Society Library. L.B.C. 10, ff. 162-163, 142-149; 11(1), ff. 317-319, Letters from Sir Richard Bulkeley, 1685, 1694.

R.B.C.9, ff. 77-78, "Mr. Furley's Account of a person who can neither Read nor write, yet will reckon Sums to a great exactness Communicated by Mr. Locke," 3/25/1701 (N.S.)

Gregory MS 247, f. 63, Memorandum, 10/26/1706 [Supplied by Prof. M.C. Jacob.]

London. Sion College Theological Library. MSS bound in collection of printed pamphlets, 47-B-5, Letter from Joseph Field to Sir Richard Bulkeley, 11/4/1707, and Bulkeley's reply, 11/15/1707, copied by George Hickes(?).

MS letter, bound in collection of printed works, A.22.4, As.6, Letter from Dr. John Moor to Dr. George Hickes, 4/12/1713.

London. S.P.C.K. Archives, MSS Minute Book, IV.

London. Stack Manuscripts [Private Collection of Mr. T. Lindsay Stack] including:

Stack MSS 1c, Notes by Charles Portales entered into the blank pages of an almanac, *Etrennes mignones curieuses et utiles augmentées pour l'Anne Bissextile de 1736* (Paris).

Stack MSS 1e, "A Short Historical Account of the Message of the Spirit of the Lord to His People in Germany in the Year 1711." [Pub. by T.S. Penny, "French Prophets of 1711," *Baptist Quarterly* (Oct. 1924) 169-79.]

Stack MSS 1g, "Recit Abregé des Persécutions et oppositions faites par les pretendus Ministres de Christ de la Nation Françoise contre Le Message de l'Eternel, Et contre ses Serviteurs, Qu'Il a envoyez au Roiaume d'Angleterre, Mais prémierement à La Ville de Londres, Capitale du Roiaume," 1709.

Stack MSS 1j, "A Historical Relation of the workings and operations of the Holy Spirit concerning the everlasting Covenant which Jesus Christ comes to establish upon the Earth with his People. To be left as a memorial for ever unto his universall Church upon the Earth, 1710." [Also in typescript prepared by Mrs. Shirley Stack.]

Stack MSS 1l, Charles Portales Notebook and Commonplace Book.

Stack MSS 2a, Letters from Francis Moult, 1726, copied into commonplace book of Charles Portales's daughter, Frances Belchier.

Stack MSS 12g, Bound notebook with divers enclosures compiled by F.M.E. Kennedy, includes copy of the will of Charles Portales (P.C.C. Simpson 363-364), proven 9/18/1764.

Maidstone. Kent County Archives Office. Sackville MSS U269 067/1-3, Lists of musicians, 1689-1694, re Steffkins family.

Manchester. Public Library, Archives Dept. MSS M9/40/2/12 and M9/40/2/16, Manchester Poor Rates Assessments, 1733-1755, and Manchester Township Lamp Tax, 1765, re Shakers.

Manchester. John Rylands Library. Eng. MS 897, Letter from R. Cruttenden to Mr. Godwin, 9/6/1742. [Supplied by Prof. John Walsh.]

Oxford. Bodleian Library. MSS Ashmole 1810-1813, Minutes of the Philosophical [Royal] Society of Oxford, re John Caswell, Sir Richard Bulkeley.

MSS Ashmole 1814, Letter from Sir Richard Bulkeley to Ed. Lhuyd, 4/30/1700.

Ballard MSS 12, ff. 189-190, 196, Letters from George Hickes to Arthur Charlett, 7/24/1711 and 1/21/1711-12.

Ballard MSS 13, ff. 43-44, Letter from Edward Thwaites to Arthur Charlett, 8/18/1709.

MSS Eng. Misc. d. 164, ff. 292-295, Letters from John Hollis to Rev. Mark Noble, 1819, re Isaac Hollis.

MSS Lister 3, ff. 35-54; MSS Lister 35, ff. 116-123v.; MSS Lister 36, ff. 43-47v., 55-57v., 61-63, 182-183, 213-214, Letters from Sir Richard Bulkeley to Dr. Martin Lister, 1686-1700.

MSS Locke c. 8, ff. 93-100, Letters from Nicolas Fatio to John Locke, 1691/92-1695.

Montagu MSS 1864, f. 285, Dedication from Sir Richard Bulkeley to John Lacy, 7/6/1709.

Rawlinson Letters 25, f. 44, Letter from Henry Dodwell to Thomas Hearne, 9/1/1709.

Rawlinson Letters 109, ff. 28-29, Letter from Nicolas Fatio to Mr. Thornton, 5/6/1696.

Rawlinson MSS B. 492, f. 8v., [copy of(?)] Letter conferring Baronetcy on Sir Richard Bulkeley, 9/24/1672, signed, Arlington.

Rawlinson MSS C. 847, ff. 41-92, Nathaniel Spinckes, "The Spirit of the New Pretenders to Prophecy, shewn to be not a Divine, but an Evil and a Wicked Spirit," c. 1710.

Rawlinson MSS C. 984, ff. 152, 242, 246-249, Account of interviews with the French Prophets, and declaration against them, by the French Protestant Church[es] in London, to the Bishop of London, Henry Compton, 1706.

Rawlinson MSS D. 832-833, Papers of Richard Roach.

Rawlinson MSS D. 1152-1157, Diary of Richard Roach, six volumes, 12/8/1706-6/8/1730 (last four volumes written primarily in shorthand).

Rawlinson MSS D. 1263, Ann Bathurst writings, vol. II, 1693-1696, re Philadelphians.

Rawlinson MSS D. 1312, ff. 2-18, A 1694 list of 265 tradesmen in London supporting the Reform societies.

Rawlinson MSS D. 1318, ff. 52-54, Elias Marion, "The Explanation of the

Figure of David: Shewing in what sence, He was a Type of Christ and of his Church, at this Day."

Rawlinson MSS D. 1318, ff. 55-66, "POLEMICA SACRO-Prophetica Anti-ROACHiana-WILTSHIREiana," 6/4/1710-6/15/1712.

Rawlinson MSS D. 1318, ff. 67-68, "Polemica Sacro-Prophetica Anti-ROACHiana-WHITE-ORIGENiana," 11/21/1712.

Rawlinson MSS D. 1341, "Mr. Freher's Remonstrance, at Mr. [Mrs.?] Leads, where Pitkin and his party [were?] also," re Philadelphians.

Oxford. Regents Park College, Angus Library. Berkhamsted Baptist Church Book January, 1712-June, 1781 [on loan], re Isaac Hollis. [Supplied by G. Reid Doster, III.]

Cripplegate (London) Baptist Congregation Church Book, 1699-1724, re Thomas and Mary Emes, Draycott family.

Witley (Surrey). King Edwards School, Archives of the Bridewell and Bethlem Hospitals. Court Books, August, 1695-August, 1722, re arts-masters William Phillips and John Bennett.

Worcester. Worcestershire Record Office. Microfilm of Lloyd Papers, BA 5230, Reference 970.5: 523 (originals at Gloucester Record Office). Appendix II. 14, Miscellaneous, Letter from Abraham Whitrow to Mr. [John] Moore, April or May, 1708, with prophetic discourse, March 29, 1708 (paginated 2026-2029).

Lloyd Papers, BA 5230, Appendix II. 14, Miscellaneous, Copy of a letter from William Lloyd to Sir Richard Bulkeley, 2/10/1707-08 (paginated 2030-2031).

Lloyd Papers, BA 5230, Appendix II. 14, Miscellaneous, Some Considerations by Sir Richard Bulkeley [on] the Following Passage in the Bishop of Worcester's Letter to Sir Richard Bulkeley (paginated 2032-2039).

Bishops Transcripts, 2015/297/83, Record of burial of Nicolas Fatio, April 28, 1753.

Ireland

Dublin. Genealogical Office. MS 87, p. 113, Funeral Certificate of Sir Richard Bulkeley, 1st Bart., March 17, 1684, with pedigree.

Dublin. Land Registry Office. Memorials, VI, 111, No. 1519, A Memorial of a Will to be Registered, Sir Richard Bulkeley, 2nd Bart., signed July 26, 1706, and registered October 9, 1710.

Dublin Public Record Office. MSS D. 19916, 19920, 19922-19923, 19925-19927, Mortgages and leases by Sir Richard Bulkeley.

Dublin. Trinity College. General Registry from 1640, V Mun 5/2, pp. 208, 226, re Sir Richard Bulkeley.

Archbishop of Dublin's MSS 132 No. 1, The Lordship of Tallagh Latlie belonging to the Bishope of Dublin, map of Old Bawn, re estate of Sir Richard Bulkeley.

Depositions, 1641, Dublin, I, pp. 250, 254-255, re estate and ancestors of Sir Richard Bulkeley.

MSS 1489(1), William King Letterbook, 1699-1700, letters from Sir Richard Bulkeley.

MSS 2531, William King Letterbook, transcribed by T. Fischer, *re* Bulkeley.

Netherlands

Rotterdam. Gemeentearchief. Actes du Consistoire de l'Eglise Wallonne de Rotterdam (Inventaris archief Waalsche Kerk nr. 2, actes du consistoire) B, 1694-1715, ff. 337-339, 400, 407, 410, 411.

Bronnen en Geschriedschrijving, 590/1685.XL, notes on Benjamin Furly by H.C. Hazewinkel.

Notarial documents *re* Benjamin Furly, 1710-1720, esp. series 1509/82 for 1714.

Notarial documents *re* Pierre Jurieu, 1701-1718, esp. series 1506 for 1713.

Switzerland

Geneva. Bibliothèque publique et universitaire. Ba 1751, Réserve, volume of printed works by F.-M. Misson, with MSS notes by Misson and a "Mémoire anecdote touchant M. Misson" by George-Louis Le Sage, inside back cover.

Ba 1910, vol. 31, *Receuil de diverses pièces imprimées,* MSS bound inside: "Chose bien suprenante arrivée à Mlle. de Chastre," "Lettre écrite à S. Daniel Dumond, à Lausanne, par M. Combet de la Ville de Crest, du premier May 1688," and "Autre lettre du 13 juin 1688."

C.F. no. 2, liasse E, ff. 137-138, Letter from Jaques Serces [pseud. "Hidden"] to Ami Lullin, 2/28/1746.

MSS fr. 489, Collection J.-A. Turretini, Correspondance de J.-F. Ostervald, 1697-1712.

MSS fr. 601, Lettres adressées à Nicolas Fatio et à J.-C. Fatio.

MSS fr. 602, ff. 42-184, Copies et minutes de lettres de Nicolas Fatio, 1681-1745.

MSS fr. 602, ff. 199-210, "Notes sur les songes de N. F[atio], 1714-1732."

MSS fr. 602, ff. 262-263, Letter from A. Fantin La Tour to M. De Luc, 6/11/1773, *re* William Clare and Fatio.

MSS fr. 603, including Nicolas Fatio's manuscript of *Navigation Improved* (pub. 1728) and, ff. 33-61, his "Notes sur la cabale."

MS fr. 605, papers of Nicolas Fatio, including the following: Booklets III. Fr.-X.Fr., "Assemblées III-X, 13 juin 1713-26 septembre 1713"; Correspondance et méditations de Jean Allut; Documents concernant quelques "Inspirés" (Michaut, Saudignan); Lettres/46 côtés, 1718-1731; "Notes sur les assemblées des Inspirés, 1706-13," with Fatio Calendar, Membership lists; incomplete draft of the *Plan de la justice de Dieu sur la terre* (pub. 1714).

MSS fr. 609, Divers: Papiers Fatio, including letter from Benjamin Furly, 1709.

Papiers Court no. 9, pp. 236-243, Copie de la lettre de Du Sablon [i.e., Jaques Serces] à Lullin, 6/17/1748.

Papiers Court 17 B, ff. 119-144, "Memoir de ce qui s'est passé dans le vivares au Sujet de la Religion, 20 mars 1734," par Jean Paul Ebruy.

Lausanne. Bibliothèque cantonale et universitaire. MSS TH 1194 B, Lettres diverses à Magny.
  MSS T. P. 1155, Recueil de divers traits sur les dernières années de Madame Guyon, *re* quietism.

United States
Cambridge. Houghton Library, Harvard University. Amos Bronson Alcott Library catalogue in typescript, *59A-329, and MS List, R.W. Emerson Deposit, *re* Francis Moult.
New York City. New York Public Library. MSS, Angel Matthewson, Reminiscences in the form of a series of 39 letters to his brother Jeffrey, Letter III, 1782, *re* Shakers.
Philadelphia. Historical Society of Pennsylvania. Martha Morris Lawrence Collection, Benjamin Furly papers. [Some printed in the *Pennsylvania Magazine of History and Biography* 27 (1903) 376-377.]
  Logan Papers, V. 10, p. 44, statement of account between Thomas Lawrence and Samuel Keimer.
Providence. John Hay Library, Brown University. MSS PR 1191/S3, James Cuninghame et al., Sacred Poems, 1712-1713.

Index

Note: after the name of each French Prophet appears a number in parentheses. This refers to the chronological number of his or her profile in Appendix I.

Abden, Lady (423): reprimanded, 140-41; heard by Cuninghame, 158; judgment on Edinburgh, 160; as inspired woman, 168; profile as prophet, 323; mentioned, 149
Aberdeen: French Prophets at, 156; monstrous children born at, 233; University of, 328
Accomplishment of Scripture Prophecies, 16
acids and alkalis, 250
"Acte Noir," 80, 81
Act of Settlement, 54
Act of Uniformity, 39
Adams, Mary, 52
Addison, Joseph, 265-66
Admirable Treatise of Solid Virtue, An, 204
adolescence: and prophecy, 230; and intimacy, 259; and Fatio's iconography, 270. *See also* apprentices; generations
adultery: of Lacy and Gray, 144-46, 285; of other believers, 146n; and Doladille, 186; and wilderness within walls, 277. *See also* bigamy
aging: middle age, 230-31; and intimacy, 259; and domestic roles, 259n. *See also* mortality
agitations: of *inspirés*, 17-19, 29-30; in London, 73-74; without prophecy, 78; condemned by Savoy consistory, 80; described, 92, 93n; of Lacy and Gray, 97; of Gray, 135; and false prophecy, 152; and quietists, 156, 158, 159, 164-66, 168, 185; and pietists, 182, 185; of Hollis, 205; of Plewit, 205; and John Wesley, 206-07; among Moravians, 208; importance to French Prophets, 211, 228; of Shakers, 212; as exercise, 229; and medicine, 241; as kinaesthetic message, 255-56; and laughter, 257; and hymnsinging, 260n; as illness, 268; and symbolic context, 284; and Great Awakening, 289
agriculture, 262. *See also* gardens; horticulture
alchemy: and Pordage, 45-46; and Jane Lead, 47; and mysticism, 165; and Boehme, 244; and Christianity, 244-46; and salt, 246-47; mentioned, 233, 242, 250, 290
Alcott, Amos Bronson: his library at Fruitlands, 249n; and works by French Prophets, 290n
Aldersgate Street: Moravian society at, 203; John Wesley at, 205
Alès (Alais), 268n
Allen, William, 37
Allix, Mme. (274), 220
Allix, Pierre (273): millenarianism of, 55n, 234; urban experience, 220; education, 328
All Souls' College, Oxford, 47n

Allut, Henriette (29): goes on retreats, 82-84, 96-98, 103; mission to Holland, 173-75; inspirations, 192, 241; moves to Worcester, 193, 222-23; status of, 211; children of, 279; profile as prophet, 322

Allut, Jean (5): host to *inspirés*, 72; chased by mob, 82; goes on retreats, 82-84, 96-98, 103; prophecies of, 98, 179, 269-71; administers sacrament, 129; dreams of, 131, 192; in tribes, 134*n*; continental missions, 173-75, 176, 179, 188; dispute with Wharton, 193, 198-200; moves to Worcester, 193, 222-23; on progress of French Prophets, 194; and Fatio, 199, 236, 240; and Portales, 199; and progressive revelation, 201; death of, 208; and female leadership, 211; and astronomy, 240; agitations of, 255-56; children of, 278; loyalty to Desert tradition, 285, 286; profile as prophet, 322

Almanza: English defeat at, 85; "Colonel" Cavalier at, 125

alms-giving: and popular religion, 67*n*; to French Prophets, 119*n*; Bulkeley's, 132; to Arnould, 199. *See also* charity

Alsted, Johann Heinrich: his eschatology, 7; millennial speculations, 38, 44; read by Mason, 43; mentioned, 40

Amana Society, 198*n*

Amélie, Princess, 209

America: Huguenots transported to, 16, 33; pietists in, 182, 204; hymns in, 198*n*; Shakers go to, 214, 279; crops from, 262; revivalism in, 288-89, 290. *See also* Connecticut Valley; Fruitlands; Georgia; Pennsylvania; South Carolina

ammonium carbonate, 247, 248*n*

Amsterdam: French Prophets in, 172; prophets from, 181; Roach letters to, 197

Amyraut, Moise, 12, 15

anatomy, 234

androgyneity: in Boehme's theosophy, 46, 48*n*; in mystical tradition, 213-14; in Shaker theology, 214

Angibert, Anna (97): expelled as false prophet, 140; and autonomy, 152; and Sterrill, 217; profile as prophet, 323

Anglicans: and Mason's hymns, 43; and Philadelphians, 45; and millenarianism, 51; responses to French Prophets, 53-54, 70, 86, 86*n*, 92*n*, 116, 135-36, 154-55, 232, 232*n*, 321; and reform, 63-65, 71, 210; suspicion of women prophets, 135-36; and New Jerusalem ethos, 151; in Ireland, 154-55; and Shakers, 212; and Whigs, 232*n*; and revivalism, 288. *See also* Church of England; high churchmen; latitudinarianism

Anne of England: abandons father, 41; succeeds to throne, 54, 68; parties during reign of, 56*n*; and Occasional Conformity Bill, 64*n*; death of, 71, 166; meets Abigail Hill, 84; and French Prophets, 88, 106, 109, 139; mentioned, 9, 65

Annet, Peter, 289

Anonymity: of early *inspirés*, 32; in London, 220-21

anticatholicism: of Restoration Parliament, 40-41; and Huguenot citizenship, 56; in England, 66, 69, 191; and response to French Prophets, 70, 122

Antichrist: mentioned by Jurieu, 16, 170; identified with Papacy, 37; John Robins as, 51; and Roman Catholics, 66; destruction prophesied, 76, 211

antinomianism, 39

antiquarianism, 45

Anti-Scripturists, 89. *See also* deism; scepticism

apocalypse: and time, 6; gradual, 168; in Hanoverian England, 192; and science, 250; scenery of, 252

Apocalypse. *See* Revelation, Book of

apostasy: of *Nouveaux Convertis*, 18, 19; of English Christians, 64-65; defined by French Prophets, 90; of women among the French Prophets, 113*n*; of various believers, 115, 133, 140, 144, 172, 193, 206. *See also* schism

apostles: among French Prophets, 135, 144; French Prophets compared to, 164; their miraculous gifts, 207

apostolic church: in ethos of pentecost, 4; as model for Camisards, 36; and faith of Philadelphians, 49; miracles and prophecy since, 63; Lacy on, 64; and French Prophets, 70, 91; and Primitive Christianity, 155, 184

apothecaries, chemists, 113, 124, 138, 193, 223, 228*n*, 237, 250, 318. *See also* salt

apprentices: and French Prophets, 229; Lacy-Gray relationship, 230; at spas, 253; living situation, 259; noted, 319. *See also* adolescence

Approaching Judgments of God upon the [Holy] Roman Empire, The, 175-176
Arch, Susannah, 69
architecture: of London churches, 2, 71; eighteenth-century domestic, 259; of country houses, 265; and iconography, 269-70; of Old Bawn, 273; of Giant's Causeway, 276; of Methodist chapels, 287; baroque, 288
Argenteuil, Charles Charlot, called d', 103
Arianism, 63-64
Ark of the Alliance of the Holy Spirit, 176
Arminianism: in Netherlands, 12; of Laudian bishops, 38
Arnassan, Claude (18), 78*n*
Arndt, Johann Jakob, 169-70
Arnold, Gottfried, 204
Arnould, Jean Philippe, 198-99
Arpwood, Thomas (232): prophecy of, 163; profile as prophet, 323
Arran, Charles Butler, earl of, 110
Artillery Church, The, 103
Ashmole, Elias: friend of Pordage, 45; friend of Lloyd, 46*n*
Aspinal, Mary (95), 323
Asseburg, Rosamunde von, 198, 211
Astell, Mary, 139
astrology, 45, 233, 242, 250, 290
astronomy: and divine intervention, 235-36; and the French Prophets, 240-41; and astrology, 242; and fruit trees, 269; mentioned, 234
atheism, atheists: and deism, 64; Camisard miracles as evidence against, 69; French Prophets accused of, 89; Emes as, 113; and London, 263
atonement. *See* repentance
Audemar, Pierre (99): wounded, 128; mission to Cévennes, 136*n*
audience: and prophecy, 134
Augsburg, League of: and Huguenot hopes, 20; and English plans for Languedoc, 68. *See also* Ryswick, Treaty of
Aurora Borealis, 243
autobiographies, 215*n*
automatic writing: by Lacy, 95; by Joanna Southcott, 278
autonomy: in each millenarian ethos, 3-5; and false prophecy, 152; and communalism, 190; mentioned, 251
Avertissemens: prepared for publication, 81; published, 82; translation published,
84; accused of inaccuracy, 91; denounced and defended, 94; translated by Furly, 171; function as scripture, 281; mentioned, 97
Avignon, 328
Axholme, Isle of, 65
Ayguesvives, 22

Babylon: destruction prophesied, 76, 199
Baker, Augustine, 157
Baker's Coffee House, 198
Baldwins Gardens: and Philadelphians, 47; Critchlow's home in, 87*n*; and pastoralism of French Prophets, 222
Baltic Sea, 85
Bank of England: Huguenot stock in, 60; and urban desert, 263; as symbol, 284
baptism: among Camisards, 29, 61; French Prophets' problems with, 103, 104*n*; by French Prophets, 135, 279; among Multipliants, 188; and children, 281. *See also* children
Baptists: and millenarianism, 37; miracle cures among, 69 and *n*; and early French Prophets, 87; Lacy speaks to, 116; and New Jerusalem ethos, 151; as French Prophets, 155, 199, 217, 321; and Whigs, 232*n*; and hymns, 260*n*; and Lacy's daughter, 280*n*; mentioned, 53, 71
Barbican: as French Prophet meetingplace, 87, 95, 105, 107, 112, 115, 116; as a theater, 252, 255
Barebones Parliament, 38-39
Barns, 157
barometer, 241
baroque: reason and sentiment in, 287; architecture, 288
Bartholomew Fair, 65
Bas-Languedoc. *See* Languedoc
Basnage de Beauval, Jacques: and Furly, 171; and Jurieu, 172*n*
Bath: Cuninghame healed at, 157, 162, 219; as marriage arena, 253
Bathurst, Ann: and stages of revelation, 47-48; death of, 51; and female leadership, 142
Bâville, Nicolas Lamoignon de: and millenarianism, 15; fears of revolt, 16, 23*n*; punishes prophets, 22; Camisard letter to, 23; devastation of Cévennes, 26; on royalism of *inspirés*, 27; on female *fanatiques*, 33
Bayle, Pierre, 171

Beast of Revelation: its reign, 15, 20; identified with the Pope, 15; its number, 39n; illustration of, 186-87
Beaux' Stratagem, The, 277n
Bedlam Hospital. *See* Bethlem Hospital
Beer, Mary (59): appears as prophet, 95; prophecies of, 108, 115, 120-21; dispute with Wharton, 193; death of, 202; prophetic status, 211; profile as prophet, 322
bees, 233
Behmenism: and Kabbala, 48n, 243-44; and Freher, 51; and "true Rosicrucians," 204. *See also* Boehme, Jakob
Beissel, Johann Konrad, 213n
Belchier, Frances: and French Prophet archives, 209; her wealth, 223n
Belchier, William: and Charles Portales, 210; member of urban patriciate, 223n
Belgrade, 180
belladonna, 242n
Bennet, Stephen (233), 324
Berger, Demoiselle, 182
Berkeley, George, 132
Berkshire, 45
Berlin, 176, 180
Berwick, James Fitz-James, duc de, 27
Bethlem Hospital, 254
Beverly, Thomas: millenarian speculations, 37, 42; and Philadelphians, 50n
Bible, the: Huguenots and, 12, 33, 69; textual criticism, 62; deist interpretation of, 63; its comprehensibility, 64; disseminated, 65; popular sense of, 66, 67n; as source of religious revival, 70; Old and New Testaments, 126, 178; pietist study of, 169, 203; and Kabbalism, 243
—citations from: Joshua, 244; Nehemiah, 273; Psalms, 13; Ezekiel, 243; Daniel, 176n, 270; Joel, 18; John, 132; Acts, 18; I Corinthians, 33, 135n; Revelation, 3n, 15, 18, 38, 42, 43, 44, 126, 140, 280. *See also* Ten Commandments
Bickerstaff, Isaac, 123
bigamy, 146n. *See also* adultery
Birmingham: French Prophets at, 105, 114-15, 149, 154, 196-97, 200, 214, 291; and London believers, 199; and Bristol believers, 203
Blackall, Offspring, 106
Blandford, Mrs. (193), 231
blasphemy: Marion's prophecy on, 80; charge against prophets, 84, 94; by Christina Pickering, 141
Blenheim, 26, 27n
blessings: by Marion, 84, 129; role of, 84-85, 85n, 103, 129; considered indiscriminate, 89; of Taylor, 105; and pollution, 111n; by male prophets, 135; by Mary Keimer, 162; and privacy, 255; and children, 281
blindness: in prophetic acts, 18-19, 99; of Jane Lead, 50; of Elizabeth Gray, 99, 242; of James Jackson, 108; healing of, prophesied, 113; and enthusiasm, 123
Blois, 156, 291
Böhler, Peter: and Wynantz, 198; and John Wesley, 198, 205
Boehme, Jakob: popularity in England, 8; theosophy of, 46; millenarianism of, 46; influence of ideas on Lead, 47; on androgyneity, 48n; and quietists, 155; and language of nature, 164; style of English translations of, 196, 211; and "true Rosicrucians," 204; published in Manchester, 213; read by Cheyne, 235; and inverse square law, 242; and Kabbalism, 243; on the sun standing still, 244; and Paracelsian element theory, 246. *See also* Behmenism
Bohemia, 203
Boissier, Matthieu (12), 20, 78n
Boîteuse, Marie, 21
Bolton, 211
Bonnisolle, Jeanne, 21, 117n
Book of Martyrs, 66
books. *See* printing; publication; *and individual titles*
Bossuet, Jacques-Bénigne, 156
Boston Evening Post, 289
Bouché, M. C. (476), 325
Bourbon, Armand de. *See* Miremont
Bourignon, Antoinette: and quietists, 8, 155-56, 183; her teachings, 155-56; and Cuninghame, 157; opposition to French Prophets, 157n; and Rosehearty coterie, 163; as model of female leader, 167-68, 210; read in Switzerland, 183, 185; read by Pellet, 204; Roach on, 211; on androgyneity, 213
Boussac, Mme. (105), 231
Boussac, Moïse (290), 147
Bowers, Mr. (519), 206, 206n
Boyle, Robert: millenarianism of, 8; theological treatises of, 233; his

experiments, 234; on clockwork universe, 239
Boyle sermon, 106
Bradfield, 45
Brandenburg: Huguenot connections with, 57; mission to, 176; von Knyphausen at, 197
Brandt, Louisa, 186
Bray, John (518): as French Prophet, 205-06; his apostasy, 206; as Moravian, 206n
Brice, Edmund: follower of Pordage, 47n; on salt, 246
Bridges, Mr. (291), 45n
Brightman, Thomas, 7, 38
Bristol: Quaker prophesying at, 52; French Prophets in, 146, 148, 154, 157, 202-03, 222; Quaker meeting at, 202-03, 289; John Wesley at, 203, 206-07; and the Evangelical Revival, 210; Huguenots in, 220; adulteries in, 277
Brittany, 221n
Bromley, Thomas, 47n
Brossard des Preaux. *See* Preaux
Brothers, Richard, 289
Brousse, Elizabeth (292), 325
Brousses, Susanne des (30), 322
Brousson, Claude, 35
Brunelle, Anne (475), 324
Buckingham: John Mason in, 43-45; Whitrow and Bulkeley in, 131
Bude, 180
Büdingen, 182
Bulkeley, Lancelot, 218n
Bulkeley, Lucy, 280
Bulkeley, Richard, second Baronet (6): attraction to French Prophets, 53, 70, 79; overzealous religious reformer, 65; and riots, 82, 83; legal actions, 83, 87, 87n, 92; and ethos of New Jerusalem, 86, 107; letter to Chamberlayne, 93; goes on retreats, 96-98, 103; promises 10,000 inspired, 112; letter to Lloyd, 115-16; money spent on group, 119; on Emes's resurrection, 120, 123; adherence to Whitrow, 131-33, 224, 275-77; and tribes, 131; his death, 132-133n; and Furly, 171-72; as a seeker, 218; his illnesses, 218, 272, 276; and healing gifts, 219; and horticulture, 222, 273; source of wealth, 223; his education, 228, 328; and Whigs, 232; on vacuum, 233; as Scientist and inventor, 237, 240, 276; and scripture, 241; and miracles, 241; and the public domain, 257 and n; and London, 263; Old Bawn estate, 273-75; childless, 280; mentioned, 154, 200, 214
Bulkeley, William, 218n
Bullmore, Mary (67), 322
Bundy, Joseph (479), 146n
Bunhill Fields: Emes buried at, 112; crowd at, 121-22; mentioned, 2
Burnet, Gilbert: friend of Allix, 55n; mentioned, 109
Burnet, Thomas, 42
Burridge, Kenelm, 2
Bushy, 96-98
business: and women, 138
Byfield, Dorothy (298), 280
Byfield, Richard, 86n
Byfield, Timothy (56): and ethos of New Jerusalem, 86; his *Sal volatile oleosum*, 99, 122, 237, 247-48, 257, 277; on healing of Gray, 99-100, 120; and inner meaning of events, 112; satirized, 122; and tribes, 134n-135n; dispute with Moult and Critchlow, 193; religious lineage, 218n; his wealth, 225n; troubles as Scientist, 237; on healing, 241, 257, 277; and alchemy, 247-48; extols alkali, 250; and the public domain, 257; and wildness, 277; childless, 280; his education, 328

cabbala. *See* Kabbala
Cabanel, Jean, 126
Cadell, Barbara: Jesus appears to her, 37; her illness, 218
Calamy, Edmund: preaches against French Prophets, 105, 117; debates with Moult, 120
calculus, the, 237, 258
Caliph, the: Daut on, 176; prophecy for, 180
Calvin, Jean, 12
Calvinism: in Languedoc, 11-12, 17; mercy and judgment, 30; and Camisards, 35, 90n; and Huguenot churches in England, 55, 71; and French Prophets, 89; in Holy Roman Empire, 169; condemned by Daut, 175; of Multipliants, 188; Calvinist Methodists, 207; of *inspirés*, 210
Cambridge: missions to, 136, 229; French Prophets at, 154
Cambridge Platonists: and androgyneity, 213n; and science, 233; and vacuum in nature, 234

Cambridge University: expels Whiston, 64*n*; and French Prophets, 228, 328. *See also* Trinity College, Cambridge
Cambuslang, 288
Cameron, Jane (430), 324
Cameron, John, 12
Camisards: and tourists, 1; tavern sign, 1; favorite psalm, 13; revolt, 22-27, 154; name, 23*n*; political radicalism, 27-28; prophecy among, 29-30, 34-36; and purification, 30-31; attitude toward defeat, 31; role of women among, 34-36; English attitude toward, 68-72; and ethos of cataclysm, 32-36, 54, 76, 98, 189-90, 200, 262, 268*n*, 282-84; and printing, 81 and *n*; and male leadership, 84; soteriology, 90*n*, 201; martyrdom and miracle among, 92; and resurrection ideas, 117; imitated in England, 128-29; their dress, 128*n*; Jean Pellet and, 204; descendants at Congénies, 210; and public territory, 258; and mountains, 268*n*; publicity and secrecy of, 283; their millennium, 292; mentioned, 51, 188 *et passim*. *See also* Desert, the; Huguenots
camp meetings, 290
Canterbury, 220
capitalism: and inspired women, 232*n*; agrarian, 266
Carriage, Liddy (447), 324
carriages, coaches: designed by Bulkeley, 240, 276; patrician, 252; on springs, 262; in illustration, 269-70
Cartesianism, 233
Cary, Mary, 36
Casaubon, Meric, 54
castration, 22, 30
Caswell, John (299): at Oxford University, 228; and perpetual motion, 239*n*; and astronomy, 240-41; his education, 328
cataclysm, ethos of: defined, 4-5; in the Desert, 32-36; among the Camisards, 54, 76, 98, 189-90, 200, 262, 268*n*, 282-84; in England after Restoration, 40, 53, 150; among English believers, 86-87, 96; transformed by French Prophets, 101, 103, 104, 107, 125, 149, 190, 215; among French believers, 107, 198, 200, 285; impurity in, 141-42; and inspired women, 189-90, 291; and initiative, 261*n*; and mountains, 268*n*; diagram of, 329-30
Catholicism. *See* Gallicanism; Roman Catholics
Cavalier, Jean, of Sauve (4): as Camisard, 23; on *ordure*, 30; early life, 72-73; prophecies, 75, 77, 91, 113, 117, 120; meeting with Testas, 76; chased by mobs, 82, 83; retreat to Northfleet, 82-84; receives sign, 84; on miracle and martyrdom, 92; not put on trial, 93; reprimands Dutton, 102; appears in Roach's dream, 112; receives alms, 119*n*; commanded to go to Bunhill Fields, 121; condemned by French Prophets, 133, 134; association with Emes's resurrection, 133; and impurity, 142; and autonomy, 152; mission to Holland, 170-72; his apostasy, 172; testifies at The Hague, 174; education, 228; and age, 229; as jester, 257*n*; agitations of, 284; and ethos of judgment, 285; profile as prophet, 322; mentioned, 71, 189, 226
Cavalier, "Colonel" Jean: as Camisard, 23, 26; regiment in Holland, 72; fights at Almanza, 125; denounces *TS*, 125-26, 174, 284; later exchanges with French Prophets, 126*n*, 200
Cavalier, Jeanne (31): goes on retreat, 82-84; mission to Holland, 133, 136, 170-72; profile as prophet, 322
celibacy: of Shakers, 212-14; in American religious groups, 213*n*; and French Prophets, 280; and millenarianism, 280
Cennick, John, 208
censorship: of book by French Prophets, 115; of d'Urfey's play, 139*n*
ceremony: Huguenot, 12; deist attack on, 63; among French Prophets, 84, 104, 129, 147, 255. *See also* baptism; blessings; communion; confession; death; mourning; rituals; worship
Cévennes, the: at present, 1; Protestantism in, 11; peace in, 11; revolt feared in, 16, 68; prophets in, 20, 22, 27, 185, 188; Camisards and, 22-36; maps of, 24-25; devastated, 26; taxes in, 27, 28*n*; differences between London and, 54, 282; expedition to relieve, 73; miracles in, 78-79, 126; independence of French Prophets from, 82; continuity between England and, 101; Mazel returns to, 128; mission to, 136*n*; final revolt in, 154; allied agents sent to, 170; Antoine Court in, 174; and literacy, 225-27; and children, 230; and mountains, 268*n*; mentioned, 107, 126. *See also* Desert, the
Chamberlayne, John, 92, 93
Chambers, William, 265

Chantagrel, Pierre, 21
chapel: Lacy's vision of, 98; image of, 104; as model for New Jerusalem, 151; Methodist architecture for, 287
Charbonet, Mlle., 177
Charing Cross: Sign of the Camisards at, 1; French Prophets on scaffold at, 109-10; as theater, 252; mentioned, 112
charity: for Huguenot refugees, 60-61; among French Prophets, 118n, 119; Whitrow's, 131; Bulkeley's, 131-32, 277; and Saudignan, 200. *See also* alms-giving
charity schools, 131, 252
Charles I of England, 38
Charles II of England: restored to throne, 7, 39; religious settlement of, 39; Roman Catholic sympathies, 40; and Savoy Church in London, 55; and Huguenot refugee relief, 60
Charles XII of Sweden: his millennial role, 175-76; flees to Turkey, 176n; French Prophet message for, 180
Charleston, 288
Charras, Elisabeth, Isabeau (23): TS witness, 78n; retreat to Northfleet, 83-84; prophesies, 112; a Levite, 134; mission to Holland, 173-75; her status, 211; profile as prophet, 322
Chayla, François de Langlade, Abbé du: supervisor of roads, 1; killed by Camisards, 22
chemistry: and divinity, 236; and alchemy, 242; mentioned, 234
Cheney, Richard (196), 124
Chesham, 131
Chester Castle, 167
Chester Circuit, 212n
Cheyne, George, 235
children: Huguenot, 12; as prophets, 17-22, 30, 31, 183, 230, 259; rescue *inspiré*, 21; howl for repentance, 21; thrown in pigsty, 22; as carriers of faith, 23; *Enfants de Dieu*, 26-27; and ritual, 30; and innocence, 31; millennial role, 31; part of family cult, 32; in Silesia, 170; at Halle orphanage, 170; and confession, 214, 283; monstrous, 233; and Desert secrets, 237; saved by *Sal volatile oleosum*, 248; processions of, 252; position among French Prophets, 279-81. *See also* baptism; infants; *petits prophètes*
chiliasm: and mortality, 129; tempered, 166; and deprivation, 225; mentioned, 290. *See also* millenarianism
China, 62
Christ Church, Manchester, 213
Christ Church College, Oxford, 228, 328
Christianity. *See* apostolic church; cataclysm, ethos of; judgment, ethos of; New Jerusalem, ethos of; pentecost, ethos of; *and specific churches, denominations, and theological positions, e.g.,* Arianism; Arminianism; Baptists; Church of England; *etc.*
Christianity not Mysterious, 63
chronology, millennial: in each millenarian ethos, 4-5; of du Moulin, 15; of Jurieu, 20; of French Prophets, 89-91, 130, 215, 281; of Roach, 194-95; of churchmen, 268; mentioned, 241. *See also* Two Witnesses
church: in each millenarian ethos, 4-5. *See also* True Church
churches: burned by Camisards, 23; Anglican, 67; Huguenot, in London, 54-55, 67n; controversy over, 70
Churchill. *See* Marlborough
"Church in Danger," 71
Church of England: and Restoration policies, 39; millennial role, 40, 42; Philadelphians conform to, 49; millenarianism within, 53; dispute with Savoy Church, 55; Occasional Conformity Bills, 64-65n, 191; churches in London, 67; and Cuninghame, 167; state of, in Hanoverian England, 191-92, 291; and the Wesleys, 206. *See also* Anglicans; high churchmen; latitudinarianism
citizenship: for Huguenot refugees, 57, 71
Civil War, the English: and millenarianism, 7, 38; victory of Parliament, 38; chiliasts during, 39; theosophy during, 45; Independents during, 51; and martyrdom, 66; fear of plots, 122
Claris, Pierre: walks through fire, 24, 30; denounces traitors, 30
Clarkson, Laurence, 53
Clay, Mr. (502), 239
Clerkenwell, 209
climate: Great Storm of 1703, 50; Little Ice Age, 191; sunspots, 240; cold weather, 269
clockmaking, clocks. *See* watches and clocks
clothing. *See* dress

coaches. *See* carriages
Coburg, 177
coffeehouses: as information centers, 71, 232; social role of, 253. *See also* Baker's Coffee House; Whitehall Coffee House
cohesion, social: in millenarian groups, 3; in each millenarian ethos, 4-5; of French Prophets, 100-01, 127, 133; and pietist communities, 190; and English believers, 286
Colchester: miracle cure at, 69*n*; mission to, 116-17, 119; French Prophets in, 154; Furly connection to, 171
Collection of Warnings, 124
comets: and millennium, 235; illustrated, 269-71
Commonwealth, the, 7, 39
communalism: of Mason's followers, 44; of pietists, 169; in ethos of pentecost, 190; in ethos of New Jerusalem, 190; among French Prophets, 279
communion: for *Nouveaux Convertis*, 14; among Camisards, 29; for French Prophets, 82; among French Prophets, 98-99, 103, 129, 135, 178
Community of True Inspiration, 182, 198*n*
companionship: *vs.* hierarchy, 20; and French Prophets, 251; in Hanoverian England, 259-60; for English believers, 286; for women, 291. *See also* sodality
Compton, Henry: and Huguenot ministers, 56; informed about *inspirés*, 77*n*; and "Acte Noir," 80*n*
confession: in ethos of judgment, 3; in ethos of pentecost, 4; for *Nouveaux Convertis*, 14; in the Desert, 32; and persecution of French Prophets, 151; among Shakers, 212-14, 215*n*; among *petits prophètes*, 214, 283; among French Prophets, 214*n*-215*n*. *See also* repentance
conformity, religious: Presbyterian attitude toward, 39; of Philadelphians, 49; of Huguenot churches in England, 55, 77; occasional, of dissenters, 64*n*-65*n*; of Scottish Episcopalians, 155
Congénies: *Gonfleurs* at, 189; and Jean Pellet, 204; and Lucrèce, 210
Congregational Magazine, 290
Congreve, William, 256
Connecticut Valley, 210
Constantinople: Quaker mission to, 52; French Prophet mission to, 180

conversion, religious: and obscenity, 141*n*; French Prophet narratives of, 215*n*; and illness, 218; inspiration as, 281; during the Evangelical Revival, 287
convulsions. *See* agitations
Cooper, Mrs. (521): visited by John Wesley, 206; as part of Female Embassy, 210; profile as prophet, 325
Cooper, Anthony Ashley. *See* Shaftesbury
Copenhagen, 198
costume. *See* dress
Cotton, Thomas (7): on religious controversy, 65; and apostolic spirit of French Prophets, 70; hosts meetings, 73; and ethos of New Jerusalem, 86; his apostasy, 144; education of, 328; mentioned, 79
Couderc, Salomon, 30
country houses: and New Jerusalem, 222; and gardens, 264-65; in illustrations, 269-71, 275; and French Prophets, 291. *See also* Old Bawn
Country-Parson, 66
Court, Antoine: his synod in the Desert, 174; Huc and Vesson split with, 188; his campaign against *inspirés*, 189
Coventry, 124
Craig, John, 234
Craven, James (55): dispute with Moult, 193; and astrology, 244; and Boehme?, 244
"Creation of the World," 65
Cri d'alarme: published in French and German, 178; carried by Marie Huber, 184; Saudignan allusion to, 200
Critchlow, Daniel (89): business dispute with Byfield, 193; and perpetual motion, 239; manufactures *Sal volatile oleosum*, 248
Critchlow, Rebecca (16): letter to Roach, 51; host for French Prophets, 83, 83*n*, 85-86, 87*n*, 231; her house, 222
Critchlow, Sarah (46), 194
Cromwell, Oliver, 38-39
Cruviers, 21
Cry from the Desart, A: published, 79 81; and pastoralism, 222; as transformation of the *TS*, 262, 268, 277. *See also* *Théâtre sacré des Cévennes*
Cuff, John (Peter) (116), 119
Cuff, Rebecca (117), 324
Cuninghame, James (420): on adultery, 145; on new prophets, 147; on the True

Church, 148; and Bourignon, 156; illnesses of, 157, 162, 218, 219; conversion of, 157-59; imprisoned in Edinburgh Tolbooth, 160; his despair, 161-62, 166; his hymns, 161, 260n; on novices, 165; as Jacobite, 166; his death, 167, 193; links to London, 168; anoints Allut and Marion, 178; his language, 196; Howell Harris impressed by, 207; as seeker, 218; and literacy, 227; his education, 228; his age, 230; and Cheyne, 235; his estate at Barns, 277; on education of children, 280; profile as prophet, 324; mentioned, 214, 233, 281
Cuper's Garden, 267
cures. See healing; miracles
curse, curses: Marion's prophecy about, 80; Lacy's power to, 107; political power and the power to, 111n

Dalgone, Sara (14), 78n
damnation, eternal: French Prophets on, 106n; Cuninghame on, 159; Marie Huber's arguments against, 287. See also hell; purgatory
dancing: at Mason's rectory, 44-45; of French Prophets, 114, 229; as religious role, 257n
Dantzig, 198
Daudé, Mme. (36), 83-84
Daudé, Jean (2): as scribe, 73, 74; participation in retreats, 82-84, 96; trial of, with Marion and Fatio, 84, 93-94, 105, 108-09; legal punishment of, 109-12; reports on the disobedient, 148; continental missions, 173, 178
Dauphiné: chamber of justice in, 14; *prédicants* in, 14; *inspirés* in, 17-20; identified as one of Two Witnesses, 42; geographical origin of French believers, 221; mentioned, 79
Dauphinenche, Isabeau, 21
Daut, Johann Maximilian: as pietist visionary, 175-76; and missions of French Prophets, 176
Davidic image: of William, Prince of Orange, 19, 36; of Charles XII, 175; in illustration, 195
Davis, Richard: and ecstatic religion, 52n; and hymns, 260n
death, deaths: and millenarianism, 113; and rituals, 113-14, 129-30; among French Prophets, 113, 180, 192-93, 194, 208; and missions, 202
De Bauffre, Jacob, 238-39
De Bauffre, Pierre, 238-39
Declarations of Indulgence, 40-41
Defoe, Daniel: on Emes's resurrection, 121, 123; on London, 263
deism, deists: defined, 62-65; Camisard miracles as evidence against, 69; and new prophets, 70; Emes and, 113; Furly and, 171; French Prophets and, 289; mentioned, 191
Delbose, Mme. (512), 200
Delft, 174
demography: sex ratios in Languedoc, 32n; population of England, 231n, 260, 263n; sex ratio in England, 231n; sex ratios and affective mysticism, 231n; sex ratio in London, 261n
denizenship, 57
deprivation theory, 28, 28n, 216, 225
Description of a New Blazing World, 243
desert: as wilderness, 262-63; as refuge, 264; meaning in England, 277
Desert, the: origin and meaning, 14; prophecy in, 17-36, 282-83; millenarianism in, 17-21, 28-29, 32, 34-36, 189, 282-83; and prophetic agitations, 30; sense of community in, 35; the Church of, 77; its image in England transformed, 79-81, 201, 221, 263-68; and law, 88; and idea of resurrection, 117; *TS* and, 126; Court's synod in, 174; and French believers, 200, 201, 221, 285-86, 292; and Shakers, 214; as opposed to London, 222, 229, 231; oral tradition in, 225-27; and children, 230; as both home and exile, 283; mentioned, 42, 54, 62, 75-76, 170, 220. See also Cévennes, the; Huguenots
Deverill-Longbridge, 144n, 148, 154
devil: and *ordure*, 30; as Lucifer in opera, 65-66; deceives Halford, 115; deludes French Prophets, 122; and Michaut, 199; and Charles Wesley, 205
Digby of Geashill, William, Lord, 266n-267n
Diggers, 7
Discernement des ténèbres d'avec la lumière, 173, 175
dissent, dissenters: at the Restoration, 39-40; Toleration Act for, 41; registered meetinghouses, 42n; and millenarian

tradition, 51; attraction to French Prophets, 54; occasional conformity of, 64n-65n, 191; in London, 71; and French Prophets, 87, 92n, 93n; decline, 192, 291; and sense of exile, 221; ejection of dissenting ministers, 230
dissonance, cognitive, 6. See also false prophecy
divine monarchy, 260n
Dodwell, Henry, 49
Doladille, Jean-Jacques (488): as prophet, 183, 185-86, 192; and sex, 185-86; and inspired women, 189; profile as prophet, 325; mentioned, 216n
Double-Dealer, The, 256
Douglas, Mary, 2, 3n
dragonnades, 14, 16, 35, 283
drama. See theater
Draycott, Sarah (121), 323
dreams: prophecy of Joel, 18; Roach's, 112; Allut's prophetic, 131, 192; Fatio's, 270-71
dress: of Camisards, 23n, 128n; and Gray, 135; and inspired women, 139; and agitations, 229; of the patriciate, 252; for hangings, 252
Drury Lane Theater, 254
dualism, 46
Dublin: and Bulkeley, 132, 273; French Prophets in, 154
Dubuc, Pierre (70), 103n
Duillier, Nicolas Fatio de. See Fatio de Duillier
Duke Street, 108
Dunkards, 204
Dunlavan, 274
Du Plan, Benjamin (525): as Multipliant, 188; as French Prophet, 209-10; as a gentleman, 291
Durkheim, Emile, 2
Dutton, Mary (437): missions in Scotland, 160; children of, 279, 280
Dutton, Thomas (66): forces the Spirit, 102; on the millennium, 106; his missions, 116-17, 154, 160-61; money spent on group, 119; on irregularities in God's work, 120; named into tribe, 134n; a lawyer, 138; on Lady Abden, 140, 149; opposes Roach and Wiltshire, 143; on Lacy-Gray adultery, 144-45; on patience, 149, 202-03; sceptical of mystics, 158, 165, 286; seizes Keimer's effects, 193; letter from Francis Moult, 194; letters to Scottish friends, 202-03; source of his wealth, 223; repudiates Whitrow, 224; attitude toward formal education, 228; on reason, 238; children of, 279, 280; profile as prophet, 322; education of, 328

East, Mrs. (75), 231
East India Company, 193n
Eaton, Robert (495): scientific correspondence, 193; his styptic, 248-49; education of, 328
Eclaircissement sur l'Apocalypse de St. Jean, 15
Eclair de lumière: Furly preface to, 175; read by Magny, 182; read by Swiss, 185
eclipses: and the millennium, 234
economic situation: and ethos of pentecost, 4; in Languedoc, 28; of Huguenot refugees in London, 60-61; of London, 71, 75, 85; of prophets among French Prophets, 118, 118n; of believers, 125, 223-25; in 1720, 191. See also levelling
ecstatic religion, 3n, 52, 52n. See also trance
ecumenism: in ethos of New Jerusalem, 5; of latitudinarians, 40, 53; of Bourignon, 155; and French Prophets, 286. See also universal church; universal salvation
Edict of Nantes, Revocation of: related to Two Witnesses, 15-16; related to William and Mary, 20; mentioned, 11, 14, 32, 55, 57, 61, 230, 282, 283
Edinburgh: French Prophets at, 138, 149, 156, 157; Lady Abden in, 140-41, 168; judgments on, 160, 167n; warning to French Prophets in, 165; University of, 328; mentioned, 162
Edinburgh Castle, 166
education; Ann Bathurst on learning, 47; of novice prophets, 165; and Hannah Wharton's teaching dispensation, 197, 201, 285; and millenarianism, 215; of French Prophets, 228, 328; of children of French Prophets, 280-81
Edwards, Jonathan: and the Evangelical Revival, 210; on the French Prophets, 289
election, doctrine of: in ethos of pentecost, 4; among Languedoc Huguenots, 12; Camisards and, 36, 90n; and French Prophet deaths, 194
Emes, Mary (122), 279
Emes, Thomas (62): his home, 2; on

religiosity, 62; attracted to French Prophets, 70; on retreat to Hoxton, 103; prophesies judgments on London, 104; his death, 113; as Scientist, 237; extols alkali, 250; children, 279; profile as prophet, 322
—his resurrection: prophesied, 113-15; French Prophets' understanding of, 120-21; failure of, 122-23; social function of, 126, 146; and Whitrow, 130-31; and Cavalier, 133; impact of failure, 150-53, 177, *et passim*
enclosure, 262, 265
encounter groups, 215n
endogamy, 194, 198, 219, 219n
Enfield: missions to, 116, 118, 138; French Prophets at, 154
Enfield Chase, 116
England: millenarianism in, 7, 8, 37-53; and William and Mary, 19-20; enters League of Augsburg, 20, 68; and War of Spanish Succession, 22, 71, 179; supports Camisards, 24, 27, 170; prophecy in, 37-53; identified with New Jerusalem, 38; Civil War, 38-39, 45, 51, 66, 122; the Commonwealth, 39; the Restoration settlement, 39-41; the Glorious Revolution, 41, 43, 56 and *n*, 66, 68n; reign of Anne, 54, 56n, 64n, 68, 71, 166; Huguenots in, 54-62, 220-21; popular religion in, 62-67; miraculous cures in, 69; union with Scotland, 85-86; map of, 137; distribution of French Prophets in, 137, 154; befriends France, 191; succession of George I, 191; Evangelical Revival in, 210; agricultural improvement in, 262; estate management in, 262-63, 265-66. *See also individual towns and counties, e.g.*, Longbridge-Deverill; Manchester; Wiltshire, *etc.*
Ennew, Samuel: imitates and deceives French Prophets, 333
Enochian time: defined by Boehme, 46; referred to by Lead, 47, 48
enthusiasm: Philadelphians accused of, 49; Casaubon on, 54; and politics, 122; and "regenerative gradualism," 164n; John Wesley on, 207; Henry More on, 233; and hymnsinging, 260n; of Methodists, 288-289; mentioned, 21n
Ephesus: Council of, 3n; church state, 195
Ephrata order, 213n
episcopacy: abolished in England, 38; restored in England, 39; and Huguenot churches in England, 54; abolished in Scotland, 155
Episcopalians: in Scotland, 155-57, 221; response to Bourignon, 156; response to Guyon, 156-57; and Evangelical Revival, 210; as French Prophets, 321
Epsom salt, 248. *See also* salt
Epworth, 65n
Erfurt, 177n, 204
Erikson, Erik H.: on intimacy, 259; on stages of psychological development, 261n-262n
Erlang, 177
Erroll, Mary, countess of, 167n
eschatology: of Independents, 51; of Quakers, 52; of French Prophets, 90, 150, 166, 180, 201; and confession, 215n. *See also* millenarianism
Essex, 222
Eternal Gospel of Heaven, Celebration for the Proclaiming of the, 178, 178n
ether: Fatio on, 235-36; and friction, 239
ethos, millenarian: defined, 2; four kinds, 3-5; tensions of, 6; appeal of, 8; transformations in, 9, 282-86; of the *Orders*, 150; changes among French Prophets, 150-53, 201; and stages of psychological development, 261; of individual believers, 278; axes of, 286; diagrams of, 329-30. *See also* cataclysm, ethos of; judgment, ethos of; New Jerusalem, ethos of; pentecost, ethos of; millenarianism
Evangelical Revival, the: described, 202-10; geography of, 210; prophecy and preaching in, 287; miracle and conversion in, 287; millenarianism of, 287; mentioned, 168, 185
evangelism. *See* missions
Evans, Valentine, 44
Everard, Edmund (68): his politics, 232n; as English informant, 258
Eversden, Hannah (446), 325
Ewell, 132
Exclusion Crisis, 128
exegesis: by *prédicants*, 14; as divine gift, 103, 255
exercise, physical: and agitations, 251
Exeter, 232n
exhibitionism, 141
exile: at Revocation of Edict of Nantes, 14; of Camisards, 27; of Huguenots in

England, 54, 61, 62, 76, 284; meaning to Huguenot clergy, 61, 76; prophecy concerning, 81; and legal punishment of Marion, Fatio and Daudé, 109n; of Jacobite quietists, 168; missions to continental Huguenots in, 172; and ethos of New Jerusalem, 200; and appeal of French Prophets, 220; Scottish quietists' sense of, 221; tourism and, 258; vision of return from, 282; mentioned, 277. *See also* Refuge, the; refugees
exorcism, 133, 205
Eye, 154

Facio, Nicolas. *See* Fatio de Duillier
Facio, Pierre, 272
Fage, Durand (1): as Camisard, 23, 72; prophecies, 73, 77, 80, 117; arrival noted by Fatio, 74; visited by Misson, 78; on retreat, 82-84; not prosecuted, 93; receives alms, 119n; a Levite, 133; missions to Switzerland, 183, 186; age, 229; profile as prophet, 322
fairs: Bartholomew Fair, 65; as theater, 252
faith: in ethos of pentecost, 4; in ethos of New Jerusalem, 5; importance to French Prophets, 92, 100, 149; attempt to explain, 216-17, 278
Falconar, Alexander (444): and Montrose meetings, 163; and spiritual novices, 165; as Jacobite, 167 and *n*
Falkner, Daniel, 204
false prophecy: Huguenot response to, 20; Mason's followers' response to, 45; among French Prophets, 91, 99-102, 119-20, 121, 152, 164, 166, 202, 215n, 281, 285; and quietists, 162-64; as problem of placement, 292. *See also* dissonance, cognitive; language; prophecy
false prophets; appearance among French Prophets, 130-35; women as, 140-41; group response to, 146-48; attachment to social network, 220. *See also* prophecy; schism; women
family: cult, 12, 14, 155, 282; in Desert, 32; role of Huguenot women in, 33; model for *inspirés*, 34-35; as model of community, 98-99; French Prophets as, 104, 130; and millenarian ethos, 107; and French Prophet meetings, 127, 147, 150; and missionaries, 138; and ethos of judgment, 151; in eighteenth-century England, 192, 259-61; and endogamy of French Prophets, 194; and Shakers, 214; performances in, 255; rejected as model by Camisards, 284
famine: expected by French prophets, 118, 119, 123, 284
fanatiques, fanatisme: definition, 21 and *n*; and taxation, 27; women and children as, 33; "systematic," 186
Farquhar, George, 277n
fasts: by Marion, 78, 83-84; by Portales, 83-84; of French Prophets, 99, 182; of Multipliants, 188; as private performance, 255
Fatio de Duillier, Jean Christophe: letters from his brother Nicolas, 89n, 110n-111n; letter to brother Nicolas, 272
Fatio de Duillier, Nicolas (9): as scribe, 73, 258, 272; his calendar, 74, 133; meeting with Testas, 76; and David Gregory, 77; on retreats, 82-84, 96-98, 103; trial of, with Marion and Daudé, 84, 88, 93-94, 105, 108-09; on the Trinity, 89n; on deferred miracle, 100; his legal punishment, 109-12, 258, 272; on tribes, 126; on assemblies by seven, 127, 146-47; suspicions of Stoddart, 134; edits *Orders*, 148; continental missions, 172, 173-75, 176-80; and Swiss pietists, 182; and Huber family, 183-85, 186-87; moves to Worcester, 193; as Scientist, 235-40, 245, 249, 258, 269, 278; letter from Moult, 194; reception of European prophets, 199; union with Portales and Allut, 199, 200; his enduring faith, 209; as seeker, 218; illness of, 218, 249; social networks, 220, 224; and fruit trees, 222, 268-69, 272; and Whigs, 232n; on providence, 235-36; on ether, 235-36; and Cheyne, 235; friendship with Newton, 237, 269; invention of jewelled watches, 237-39, 241; and perpetual motion, 239; and astronomy, 240; and scripture, 241; and medicine, 242, 249; and Kabbala, 243; and alchemy, 245, 249; and the calculus, 258; ambivalence about publicity, 258, 268-72, 277; and shame, 270-72, 277; on motion, 278; as a bachelor, 280; on prophetic novitiate, 281; and German pietists, 286; occupation, 320; education of, 328

Feast of Tabernacles, 273, 275-76
Feast of the Lamb of the Lord's Supper, Sign of the, 129, 316
Fell, John, 53
Female Embassy, the, 201-15. *See also* prophecy; women
Female Tatler, The, 256
Fetter Lane religious society: interest in French Prophets, 203, 205; Jean Pellet in, 204; argument over French Prophets, 205-06; Mrs. Inks of, 208; mission to, 208
Field, Joseph, 119*n*
Fielding, Henry, 263
Fife, 157
Fifth Monarchists: and Mary Cary, 37; role in 1660s, 39; and John Mason, 45*n*; and Philadelphians, 49; later history, 286; mentioned, 7
Fischer, Loth, 197
Fish, William (520), 206
Fisher, Mary, 52
Fleming, Robert, 69
Flotard, David (22): on "*fanatique*," 21*n*; promises allied help, 24; *TS* witness, 78*n*; on retreat, 83-84
flying ants, 95
Forbes, Jane (Jean) (465): Guyon, French Prophets, and, 157; as Jacobite, 167; her illness, 218; profile as prophet, 324
Forbes of Pitfichie, John (452): his conversion, 156; prophecy of, 159; death as Jacobite, 167; profile as prophet, 324
Forbes of Pitsligo, John (454): as Jacobite?, 167*n*
fossils, 258
Foster, John (457): as French Prophet, 53; Sanger prophesies to his congregation, 144*n*; education of, 328
Fowler, Edward (329): suspends Foster, 144*n*; education of, 328
Fox, George: miracle cures, 52; and Furly, 171
Foxe, John: his eschatology, 7; his *Book of Martyrs*, 66
France: Reformation in, 11; religious wars in, 11; persecution of Huguenots, 12, 14, 16, 35, 73 *et passim*; and War of the League of Augsburg, 20, 35, 68; and Treaty of Ryswick, 20, 35, 179*n*; and War of the Spanish Succession, 22, 26, 27*n*, 35, 71, 75, 179; defeat at Blenheim, 26-27*n*; Charles I's policy toward, 38; James II escapes to, 41; declaration against, by Huguenots in England, 56; Huguenot refugee origins in, 61; English attitude toward, 68, 190; defeat at Ramillies, 75; victory at Almanza, 85, 125; Bourignon's persecution in, 155; Mme. Guyon in, 156; and Peace of Utrecht, 179 and *n*; and Peace of Rastatt, 179; national bankruptcy, 188. *See also* Camisards; *and individual towns and provinces, e.g.*, Languedoc; Lyon; Pont-de-Montvert, *etc.*
Francke, August Hermann: and pietism, 169; his orphanage, 170, 177; meets with French Prophets, 177, 179; his support for other prophets, 177*n*; changes mind, 180
Frankfurt-am-Main, 169, 175
free will, 12
Freher, Dionysius Andreas, 51
Freke, William, 218
French Committee, 60
French Prophets: their name, 2*n*; political involvements, 7, 122, 155, 166-67, 177-78, 179; history of themselves, 11, 16, 19-20, 101-04, 112; occupations, 118, 138, 231*n*, 291, 318-19
—appeal of: 8, 45, 53-54, 62, 68-71, 73, 79-80, 86, 89, 112, 129, 154-59, 170-71, 175, 177, 179, 181-90, 205, 207-08, 211, 216-31, 241-42, 244, 250-51, 272, 276-77, 287-88
—composition and membership: 72-73, 79-80, 82-83, 85, 86-87, 89, 98, 105, 112, 126-29, 133, 134, 154, 192-94, 208, 210, 216-20, 223, 231, 232, 251, 279, 294-325
—ecclesiology and sacerdotal roles: 55, 77, 98-112, 117, 135, 146, 148-50, 165-66, 183, 193, 196-97, 199-200, 201-02, 210-15, 242, 244, 247, 251, 261, 271-72, 279
—eschatology: 77, 78, 89-91, 101, 106-07, 119-21, 125, 129, 149-50, 161-62, 166, 180, 186, 194-97, 201, 214-15, 230, 234-36, 278, 281
—generations and age groups: 61, 148-49, 193, 210, 229-31, 279-81, 327
—millenarian ethos of: 3, 8, 9, 54, 75-76, 79, 87, 89, 97, 104, 106-07, 118, 125, 141-42, 149-53, 156, 159-60, 168, 189-90, 194-95, 197, 199, 200-04, 214-15, 247, 250-51, 261*n*-262*n*, 263, 278, 282-86, 291, 330

—missions and evangelism: 75, 78-79, 104, 108, 110, 115, 116-17, 119, 124 and *n*, 126, 136-37, 147, 154, 156, 157, 170-81, 201-03, 207-08, 219, 221, 258
—nations, nationalities, problems between believers of different: 83-84, 85, 87-88, 102, 106-07, 117-18, 119-20, 123, 125-30, 133, 147, 172, 178, 198-202, 209, 210-11, 215, 221, 227, 282-86, 292
—opposition to: 61, 69-71, 76-77, 81-85, 91-95, 100, 106-07, 110-12, 116-17, 122-23, 173-74, 176-77, 186
—pietist and quietist influences on: 8, 162-69, 170, 177, 185, 193, 196-215, 285
—ritual and ceremony: 83, 84, 85 and *n*, 98-99, 103-05, 111*n*, 113-14, 126-28, 129-30, 147, 148, 151, 153, 177, 178, 203, 214*n*-215*n*, 241-42, 255, 281, 284-85
—sexes, problems between the: 83-84, 134-46, 150, 152, 162, 167-68, 189-90, 210-15, 221, 231, 259-61, 291
—sexuality and: 111*n*, 135, 139, 141-46, 152, 185-86, 213-15
—social hierarchy: 96-98, 131-32, 139-40, 152, 220, 225, 276-77, 291
—soteriology: 77, 90 and *n*, 106-07, 159, 179, 206, 234, 245, 246-48
—theatricality: 219, 251-63, 267
—theology: 89-90, 94, 106-07, 159, 175, 197, 201, 211-15, 238
—worship and liturgy: 72-75, 78, 84-85, 87, 87*n*, 91-92, 93, 95, 96-97, 98-99, 105, 113-14, 127-28, 129-30, 143, 147, 162, 163-66, 180-81, 183, 193, 196-97, 211-12, 215*n*, 253, 255, 281
—*See also individual believers*, e.g., Allut, Jean; Bulkeley, Richard; *etc*.
French Revolution, 184*n*
Friary Yearly Meeting, Bristol, 202
friction: and the decay of the world, 236-37; Fatio, watches, and, 238-39; and perpetual motion, 239
Friends, Society of. *See* Quakers
Frugières, 22
Fruitlands, 249*n*, 290*n*
Fruit-Walls Improved by Inclining Them to the Horizon, 240, 268-70
functionalism, 6, 251
funerals. *See* death
Furly, Arent, 171
Furly, Benjamin (220): and van Helmont, 48*n*; position in Rotterdam, 170-71; aids the English, 171; letter to French Prophets, 172; prefaces to books by French Prophets, 175; on Francke, 177*n*; corresponds with Swiss pietists, 183; death of, 193; Pennsylvania contacts, 204; mentioned, 216*n*

G . . . ton, Mr., 92*n*
galleys: Huguenots sentenced to, 16, 282; prophets condemned to, 22; prophecy concerning, 91
Gallicanism: of Louis XIV, 14; threatened by Vincent, 18; distrust of female leadership, 33; and Guyon, 156
Garden, George: translates Bourignon, 157; argues with Cuninghame, 158; European exile of, 168; scientific reports, 233
gardens: and True Church, 222; social role of, 253; Pope, Bulkeley, and, 257*n*; and Misson, 258; and friendship, 260; and sentiment, 260; of country houses, 265; and wildernesses, 265-66; their theatricality, 266; and scene design, 266*n*; in Lacy's prophecy, 267; and Fatio, 269; at Old Bawn, 273, 275; of English believers, 292; mentioned, 1, 262, 263
Gardiner, Richard (487), 325
Garland of Paradise, The, 170
Garret, Walter, 42
General Delusion of Christians, The, 7
generations: in ethos of pentecost, 4; of prophets in Languedoc, 21, 31; of Huguenot clergy and *inspirés*, 61; of French and English believers, 130; of male and female believers, 138; women as second generation, 210; and ages of prophets, 229-31; of believers, 280; and millenarianism, 287*n*; and ages of all believers, 327. *See also* adolescence
Geneva: Calvinism at, 12; responses to false prophecy, 20; exilic home for Camisards, 27; Cavalier and Fage in, 72; and Fatio, 73, 104, 182; and Huber family, 183-84; prophetic assemblies in, 185-86; landscape of, 269; motto of, 270*n*; Pierre Facio in, 272; academy of, 328
gentry: Scottish, 155; their decline, 223; and French Prophets, 224
geology, 234, 267*n*
geometry, 265, 269
George I of England, 191
George II of England: receives Fatio book, 241*n*; Fatio petitions, 271*n*

Georgia: founded, 191; Moravian mission to, 196, 203; John Wesley in, 198; and Evangelical Revival, 210
German Baptist Brethren. *See* Dunkards; Ephrata order
Germantown, 204
Germany: Philadelphians in, 47*n*, 50, 168, 197-98, 204; Beverly's *Indiction* circulating in, 50*n*; pietism in, 169-70, 183, 185; Furly in, 171; Huguenots in, 174, 177; prophets in, 177*n*, 181-82, 185, 198; princes of, 178; and quietism, 189; perpetual motion machines in, 239
Gervaise, Louis (441): reports on the disobedient, 148; communion for mission, 178
Giant's Causeway, 276
Gichtel, Johann Georg, 213
Giles, John (74): and tribes, 134-135*n*; missions, 136, 154, 172; merchant, 138
Gilman, Dr., 51
Glasgow: mission to, 160; *Wonderful Narrative* published in, 288
glassmaker myth, 18-19
Glauber, Johann: sodium sulphate, 247; Sign of Glauber's Head, 248
Glorious Revolution of 1688-89: and millenarianism, 7, 41, 43; and Huguenot refugee citizenship, 56; Whig and Tory attitudes toward, 56*n*; popular fears about, 66; and Camisards, 68*n*; mentioned, 230
glossolalia. *See* language; tongues, speaking in
Gloucester, 206
Glover, John (94): prophecy by, 121; face burned, 135; victualler, 138; death, 202; bankruptcy of, 225*n*; profile as prophet, 323
Gonfleurs: and ethos of pentecost, 189-90; and Jean Pellet, 204
Good, Ann (60): prophecy of, 259; profile as prophet, 322
Gordon, Clara (422): mention by Dutton, 202; profile as prophet, 324
Gordon, Kennet (421): as scribe, 160; on opposition to French Prophets, 161
Gospel's Glory, 86
Goudimel, Claude, 12
grace: Amyraut on, 12; Roach on, 195; among French Prophets, 215*n*; and science, 234; and the Wesleys, 287
Gracechurch Street, London, 290

grasshoppers, 15
gravity: and providence, 235-36; and prophecy, 241
Gravesend, 82
Gray, Elizabeth (25): and retreats, 83, 96-98, 103; and ethos of New Jerusalem, 86; her mime, 97, 99-100, 107, 120, 135; and miracle cures, 99-100, 108, 241-42; struck dumb by Lacy, 107; prophecies of, 103, 112, 116-17; missions, 124; as Whore of Babylon, 135; satirized as Betty Plotwell, 139; her adultery with Lacy, 144-46, 225, 261; and Ann Lee, 214; her education, 228; as apprentice, 230; and Drury Lane Theater, 254; as an adolescent, 259; profile as prophet, 322
Gray's Inn, 328
Great Awakenings, 288-90
Great Crisis, The: published, 195; and Female Embassy, 211; and androgyneity, 213
Great Storm of 1703, 50
Great Yarmouth, 154
Greaves, J. P., 290*n*
Greek: Lacy prophesies in, 95
Greek Orthodox Church, 270-71
Greeks, The: church near Allut's house, 73; denounces French Prophets, 80
green: significance of, 128-29, 128*n*
Greencroft, 131
Green Ribbon Club, 128*n*
Gregory, David, 77-78
Grew, Nehemiah: science as worship, 233; and Epsom salt, 248
Gribelin, Simon, 269*n*, 270
Groteste de la Mothe. *See* Mothe
Gruber, Eberhard Ludwig: as prophet, 182; and Amana Society, 198*n*
guerillas: Camisards as, 23; *inspirés* as, 70; French Prophets imitate pattern of, 78
Guienne: chamber of justice in, 14; refugees from, 221*n*
Guildhall: trial at, 93; Roach's dream about, 112
Guillemot, Jean (215), 60
Guillemot, Susanne (128), 60
Guyon, Mme., Jeanne Marie Bouvier de la Mothe: and Scottish quietists, 8, 155; opposes French Prophets, 156-57; as model of female leader, 167-68, 210, 211; works read in Geneva, 185; her image of New Jerusalem, 291

Hackney Marsh, 128-29, 285
Hague, The: "Colonel" Cavalier at, 125; mission to, 172, 174; Fatio imprisoned at, 174; Alliance of, 176n
Halford, Stephen (86): prophetic group in Birmingham, 114-15; profile as prophet, 322
Halford, Thomas, 115
Halle: university at, 169; orphanage at, 170; French Prophets at, 177, 179, 180; role of women at, 189; Spangenberg leaves, 198; mentioned, 174
Halley, Edmond: on providence, 234; on comets, 235
Hamburg, 155
Hammond, Mr. (69), 322
Hanoverian succession, 166
Harley, Edward, 56
Harling, Dorothy (425): expelled by French Prophets, 140; accused of sadism and exhibitionism, 141; autonomy, 152; profile as prophet, 323
Harris, Howell, 207
Harrop, Joseph, 213
Hartland, John (256): his apostasy, 144; profile as prophet, 323, 325
Hatton Gardens: French Prophets meet at, 115, 209; and pastoralism, 222
Hauksbee, Francis, 249
Hautes Cévennes, 1
Havy, Isaac (33): suspended by church, 103n; action at Hackney Marsh, 128; baptizes children, 129; expelled by French Prophets, 148; profile as prophet, 148
healing: by Quakers, 52; among Huguenot refugees, 69; by Baptists, 69, 116; Cavalier's prophecy concerning, 75; gift of, prophesied, 95, 96, 113; linked to miracle, 96; miracle cures among French Prophets, 99-100, 108, 110, 124, 142, 219, 241-42; and missionary impulse, 110, 219; by men, 135; by women, 142; and the Scientists, 246-51, 257; and privacy, 268; and wildness, 277. *See also* medicine; miracles; physicians; salt; *Sal volatile oleosum*
Heath, Mary, 142
Hebrew: used by Multipliants, 188
hell, 89, 145. *See also* damnation, eternal; purgatory
Helmont, Francis Mercurius van, 37, 48n

heresy: defined by French Prophets, 90. *See also* antinomianism; Arianism; deism; dualism; pantheism; scepticism; Socinianism; Unitarians
hermetic tradition: and science, 233-34; and the Scientists, 242-46
Hermitage, René Saunier de l', 125-26
Herrnhut: Moravian colony at, 198, 203; John Wesley at, 205; and Evangelical Revival, 285
Hickes, George: nonjuring bishop, 41n; opposed to Camisards, 68n
Hicks, Nathaniel (448), 69n
high churchmen: Laudian bishops, 38; and Huguenot refugee citizenship, 57; Charles Wesley, 206; Sacheverell, 252
High Wickham, 205
Hill, Abigail, 85
Himbach, 182
Historical Relation, 16, 19-20, 136, 225
history, history-writing: imperfect, 1; by French Prophets, 11, 101-02, 104, 105, 112, 215, 281; on Camisards, 31; and group identity, 104; and millenarianism, 105; and literacy, 225; meaning to Huguenot refugees, 231; unpublished, 255; Camisards and context, 282
Hitchin, 69
Hobbes, Thomas, 8
Hocknell, John, 212n
Hocknell, Mary, 212n
Hodges, Mr., 92n
Hoffman, Mr. (349), 45n
Hoffman, Francis, 195
Holland. *See* Netherlands, the
Hollis, Isaac (510): defends Arnould, 198-99; friend of Roach, 199; meets the Wesleys, 205, 207; meets Howell Harris, 207; meets with Moravians, 208; a seeker, 217; death, 278; meets Thomas Story, 289; a gentleman, 291; mentioned, 209
Holloway, 114-15
Holmes, Thomas, 52
Holms, Margaret, 44-45
Holt, John: warrant from, 83; trial of French Prophets, 84, 88, 94, 105n; and *nolle prosequi* incident, 88; on sedition, 88n
Holy Roman Empire: religious conflicts in, 169; judgments on, 176; Diet of, 177; and Peace of Rastatt, 179

Holy Spirit, Holy Ghost: role in Christian teaching, 77; and perpetual motion, 239. *See also* prophecy
homosexuality, 97*n*
Hooke, John (42): and ethos of New Jerusalem, 86; lawyer for French Prophets?, 94; education of, 328
Hope, Thomas (428), 280
horticulture: Bulkeley and, 222, 273-74; Fatio's fruit trees, 269-70
hosts: early reception of *inspirés*, 73; expenses of, 119; function of, 220; economic position of, 223; women as, 263
House of Lords, 88
Hoxton: Philadelphians in, 47, 50; retreat to, 102-03; mineral waters at, 247; view of London from, 264; mentioned, 2
Huber family, 285
Huber, Deborah: has agitations, 183-84
Huber, Jean: as novice, 183, 281; Fatio's advice to, 192
Huber, Marie: mission to Geneva, 184; drawing of Beast of Revelation, 186-87; and universal salvation, 287
Huber, Marthe: on pietism in France and Switzerland, 184; her eclecticism, 184
Huc, Jean, 188
Hughes, Elizabeth (176): as missionary, 138, 172; owns cook's shop, 138; illiterate, 225
Hughes, Elizabeth (192): missions, 138, 172, 229; profile as prophet, 323
Huguenots: statistics on, as believers, 316-21, 326
—in France: persecution of, 11-12, 14-22, 26, 28-31, 42; forms of worship, 12; family cult, 12, 14, 33; theology, 12; millenarianism, 15-21, 28-29, 31-32, 34-36, 189; and prophecy, 17-36, 78; and Treaty of Ryswick, 20, 35, 179*n*, 283; royalism, 27, 30; pacifism, 30; women's roles, 33-34; and Peace of Utrecht, 179*n*; French Prophets' missions to, 183, 186-87, 188*n*; and Swiss pietists, 186-87; and Multipliants, 188; and introspective religion, 189; and secrecy, 282
—in England: clergy, 54-56, 61, 76-77, 80-81, 82, 94, 103, 105*n*, 109*n*, 117, 126; and Whigs, 56-57, 60 232*n*; and citizenship, 56-57; weavers, 57; socioeconomic tensions, 57, 60; miracle cures among, 69; responses to *inspirés*, 69-71, 76-78, 80-83, 128-29, 220-21; as French Prophets, 83-84, 103 and *n*, 123, 125-30, 133, 147, 172, 174, 198-202, 209, 215, 220-21, 282-86, 292; their irenism, 90*n*; sense of exile, 258
—on continent, in exile: political position, 68*n*, 171, 172*n*; refugee troops, 125; clergy, 173-74, 177, 180, 189; *inspirés* in Schwabach, 177; meaning of missions to, 285. *See also* Camisards; Desert, the; Nouveaux Convertis
Humours of a Coffee House, 87
Humphreys, William (130), 115
Hungerford Market, 48, 49
Hunt, Jeremiah?, 92*n*
Hutton, James, 186
Hyde Park, 2
hymns, hymnsinging: and John Mason, 43-45, 45*n*, 260*n*; and Philadelphians, 45 and *n*, 260*n*; of Isaac Watts, 192, 260*n*; of Johann Petersen and Amana Society, 198*n*; of Charles Wesley, 205, 260*n*; of Shakers, 212; and sentiment, 260; of Richard Davis, 260*n*; of Benjamin Keach, 260*n*; of Cuninghame, 260*n*; of Moravians, 260*n*; and Methodism, 260*n*-261*n*. *See also* psalms
hypochondria, 218, 257. *See also* illness
hysteria, 33*n*

iatrochemistry, 250
iconoclasm: of Camisards, 21, 22, 30
iconography: of Fatio, 269-72; of Bulkeley, 273-74
illness: and religious conversion, 157, 218, 277. *See also* healing; miracles
immorality: of Restoration period, 62; attacked by reformers, 65, 70, 263; accusation against French Prophets, 98, 186; in ethos of judgment, 142. *See also* sexuality
Impartial Account of the Prophets: and scripture secrets, 238; and agitations, 241; reprinted in connection with Richard Brothers, 289
Imperial Standard of Messiah Triumphant, The, 195, 198
impurity. *See* purity; sexuality
Independents: position defined, 38-39; ejected, 39; and ecstatic religion, 52*n*; and Laurence Clarkson, 53;

meetinghouses of, 87n; in Colchester, 116; and New Jerusalem ethos, 151; among French Prophets, 217, 321; and hymnsinging, 260n
Indians, American, 65
industrialization: and French Prophets, 291; and Shakers, 292n
infants: precocious speech of, 21; prophesy in Desert, 31. *See also* baptism; children
information theory: and prophecy, 152n, 281n
initiation: and obscenity, 141n; and French Prophets, 220, 281
Inks, Mrs., 208
inns, innkeepers: named for Camisards, 1; at Ipswich, 117; as French Prophet occupation, 223, 318; social function, 253. *See also* Three Foxes Inn
insanity: and millenarians, 7; of Bulkeley, 132; and French Prophets, 161, 254; and John Wesley's audience, 207
inspiration. *See* prophecy
inspirés, inspirées: appear in Languedoc, 18; in public, 18; their agitations, 18-19; rescued, 21; imprisoned, 22; thrown in pigsty, 22-23; their youth, 31, 230; their anonymity, 32; role in Camisard revolt, 33-36; Philadelphians and, 53; English response to, 54, 69-71, 72-76, 79-98, 104-12, 228, 282, 284, 288; Huguenot refugee response to, 60-62, 70, 72-79, 80, 82-84, 94, 103-04, 105n, 109n, 125-26, 128-29, 173, 186, 258, 282, 284; millenarian ethos of, 107, 283-84; new, in France and Switzerland, 184, 188, 189-90, 192, 209, 211; and literacy, 227; in historical tradition, 287; mentioned, 133, 177, 185. See also *petits prophètes*; prophets
intimacy: Bulkeley and wife, 257; and the city, 259; and wildernesses, 266; and *petits prophètes*, 283
inventions and discoveries: jewelled watches, 237, 238-39; *Sal volatile oleosum*, 237, 247-49; perpetual motion machine, 239-40; air pump, 240; carriage, 240, 276; swimming machine, 240n; mock-trumpet, 240n; society for, 240n; tin separation process, 245; *sal mirabile*, 247; Epsom salt, 248; styptic, 248-49
Ipswich, 117
Ireland, Timothy (504), 199
Ireland, marvels in, 69; Bulkeley and, 79, 132, 222; Whitrow in, 132; missions to, 136, 154-55, 172; novices sent to, 165; Giant's Causeway, 276. *See also* Dublin; Old Bawn
irenism, 90n
Irish Sea, 136
irreligion: in England, 62, 64, 70
Irvine, Henrietta (466): prophecy, 145; tears up letters, 159-60; and Cuninghame, 168, 230; profile as prophet, 324
Irving, Edward, 290
Islington, 264

Jackson, Benjamin Habakkuk (63): on retreat, 103; scientific correspondence, 193, 237; on perpetual motion, 239; his inventions, 240

Jackson, James (82): as Quaker, 52, 117; style of argument, 88; sight restored, 108, 219; a seeker, 217
Jacobites: English fears of, 66, 122; rebellions, 118-19, 166-68; Scottish believers as, 155, 166-68; and death of Louis XIV, 191
Jacobs, Joseph, 217
James II of England: flight from England, 19, 41; issues Declarations of Indulgence, 40-41; his Catholicism, 41; and Act of Settlement, 54; and Huguenot relief, 60
James Frances Edward, Prince of Wales, Old Pretender: born, 41; invasions of Scotland, 118-19, 166-67
Jamets, Etienne (485), 325
jeremiads, 62
Jerusalem: rebuilding of, 273, 275-76. *See also* New Jerusalem; New Jerusalem, ethos of
Jesuits, 70
Jesus: appears to Barbara Cadell, 37; appears to Mason, 37, 44; and John Robins, 51; his divinity argued, 63; Emes confused with, 114; green his color, 128; as an adept, 243; as a laborer, 276. *See also* Second Coming
Jews: union with Gentiles, 104; tribes as a sign to, 127; in Ireland, 154; and Feast of Tabernacles, 275-76; among French Prophets, 321. *See also* Kabbala
Joachim of Fiore, 184n
Joan, Pope, 258

Johnson, Samuel, 263
Johnston, James, 109
Jones, Griffith, 70*n*
Joyneau, Louis (442): pummels Sarah Wiltshire, 143; disputes with Michaut and Allut, 198; profile as prophet, 325
judgment: in Huguenot theology, 12; in Desert sermons, 18; among Philadelphians, 50; dispute between French Prophets and Philadelphians, 142, 159; and quietists, 185-86. *See also* judgment, ethos of; Judgment Day; judgments
judgment, ethos of: defined, 3-4; in Desert, 32-36; in England, 40, 53, 54; for English believers, 107, 284-85; and New Jerusalem ethos, 125; and tribes, 127; impurity in, 142; and the True Church, 149-50; among the French Prophets, 151-53; and Scottish quietists, 159-60, 168; transformed, 190; among French believers, 200; among Shakers, 214; and trust, 261*n*; regularity, publicity, and, 278; and *petits prophètes*, 283; and inspired women, 291; diagram of, 329-30
Judgment Day: defined, 3*n*; Desert expectations of, 19, 20, 36; not dated by Mason, 43; imminence, for *inspirés*, 90, 119; Lacy on, 106; and death of believers, 113; prophesied, 170; in illustration, 195; and Aurora Borealis, 243
judgments: as stage of prophecy, 29; on London, 44, 52, 78, 90-91, 95, 104, 105*n*, 110, 118, 119, 120, 222, 263-64; and Philadelphians, 50, 195; on Colchester, 117; and ribbons, 128; on Edinburgh, 160, 167*n*; on Vienna, 176, 178; on Rome, 180; of Michaut, 199; of Saudignan, 200; and Huguenots, 201; and Hannah Wharton, 197, 201
Jurieu, Hélène (418): as French Prophet, 170-71, 173; death, 193; as English spy, 258; mentioned, 216*n*
Jurieu, Pierre (419): millenarianism of, 16, 19, 20, 42; and William of Orange, 19; antiroyalist rhetoric, 27*n*; as French Prophet, 170-71; his vision of exile, 172*n*; death, 193; as English spy, 258; education of, 328; mentioned, 216*n*

Kabbala: van Helmont and, 37, 48*n*; Philadelphians and, 48, 48*n*, 243, 257; androgyneity and, 48*n*; and Multipliants, 188; and science, 233, 243; and wildness, 277
Keach, Benjamin, 260*n*
Keimer, Mrs. (50), 114
Keimer, Mary (48): appears as prophet, 95; prophecies of, 105, 114, 141; shopmaid, 138; opposes Roach and Wiltshire, 143; on Lacy's adultery, 145; sexual activity of, 146*n*; role in assemblies of the inspired, 148-49; and Cuninghame, 161-62, 230; goes to Pennsylvania, 193, 204; her status among believers, 211; profile as prophet, 322
Keimer, Samuel (49): goes to French Prophet meeting, 114; to be "Minister Extraordinary," 124; his ribbon and new name, 128; belief in purgatory, 129*n*; on Lacy's adultery, 145; his apostasy, 193; on Francis Moult, 223; his education, 228; mentioned, 135
Keith of Caddam, Mrs.: leads Montrose group, 163, 210; Cuninghame writes to, 167; her vision of New Jerusalem, 291
Keith, George: meets French Prophets?, 92*n*, 93*n*; and Furly, 171
Keith, James (26), 328
Kelpius, Johannes, 213*n*
Kemp, Mr. (38), 86
Kennet, White: meets French Prophets, 92*n*; letter from Woodward, 95
Kensington Garden, 267-68
Kent, 260*n*
Kentish Town, 209
Kilsyth, 288
King, Anna Maria (83): turned out of meeting, 141; and university missions, 229; profile as prophet, 322
King, William (39), 86
Kingston Gravel Pits, 115
Knauth, Theodor, 179, 181
Knyphausen, Dodo von, 197-98
Kock, André, 177

Lacy, John (15): prophecies of, 1, 92, 95-97, 101-02, 104, 113, 152, 159, 237-38, 267; on history and history-writing, 1, 101-02; jeremiad, 64; becomes French Prophet, 70; translates *TS*, 79; mobs and riots, 82-83, 88, 123; begins to prophesy, 86; and New Jerusalem ethos, 86, 98, 267; litigation, 88*n*; on matters of doctrine, 90, 106, 106*n*-107*n*; speaks in tongues, 93, 95; retreat to Bushy, 96-98; acts of healing, 99, 108, 110, 241-42; vision of True Church, 98; and gift of exegesis, 103; on Emes's resurrection, 104, 112, 113, 123; judgment on London, 104; on the millennium, 106; his public promise, 109-10, 121, 125; mission to Colchester, 116; on regular church membership, 117 and *n*; money spent on French Prophets, 119; on failed prophecy, 120, 121, 123; opposes Whitrow, 131, 224; letter from Stoddart, 134; opposes Abden, 140; opposes Roach and Wiltshire, 143; adultery with Gray, 144-46, 225, 259, 261; on social hierarchy, 152; on universal salvation, 159; and ethos of judgment, 159; on reason, 164, 287-88; on Silesia, 170; death, 194; defends Montanists, 207; and Shakers, 214; his illness, 218; source of his wealth, 223; on formal education, 228; his age, 230; on science, 237-38; and the Kabbala, 243*n*; agitation described, 255-56; wife and intimacy, 261; on London, 263, 264, 267; his *Warnings* as scripture, 281; books circulating during Great Awakenings, 288, 290; referred to by deist, 289; profile as prophet, 322; mentioned, 227, 285

Lake Country, 262

Lancashire, 146 and *n*

landscape: of London, 263, 264; of country estate, 265; in Fatio iconography, 269-70

language: in each millenarian ethos, 3-5; prophetic speech, 31-32, 256-57; and clear discourse, 53; of Camisards, 54, 78, 199; theological jargon, 64; legal rhetoric, 88; elegance of speech, promised, 97; "mixtures" of human and divine, 125, 134, 140, 147, 163, 164, 192, 199; obscenity, 141 and *n*; of nature, 164; quietist syntax, 165-66, 196-97; role of multilingual believers, 172; of Wharton, 196-97; of later French Prophets, 211; and pastoralism, 226; of Cavalier, 228; and science, 233; and the city, 253; public speech, 256; and laughter, 256-57; and hymns, 260*n*-261*n*; of *petits prophètes*, 283; mystical, 286; French Prophet works printed, 290; speaking out of place, 292. *See also* exegesis; oral tradition; prayer; prophecy; sermons; tongues, speaking in

Languedoc, Bas-Languedoc: and chestnuts, 1; and the Reformation, 11; Huguenot theology in, 12; chambers of justice in, 14; *prédicants* in, 14, 61; millenarian poem in, 15; *inspirés* in, 18-23, 31-36, 184, 188-90; Camisards in, 22-36; plans for invasion of, 24, 24*n*, 26*n*, 68; manuscript prophecy in, 184; drought in, 188; Desert tradition in, 189; and Evangelical Revival, 210; believers from, 221; mentioned, 42, 70, 71, 79, 81, 170, *et passim*. *See also* Cévennes, the; Desert, the; *and individual towns, e.g.*, Alès; Montpellier; Nîmes

Lardner, Thomas (194): becomes believer, 124; apothecary, 138; death, 202; on formal education, 228; education of, 328

La Rochelle, 12

Latin: Lacy speaks in, 93; *Plan* translated into, 179; used by Multipliants, 188; prophet speaks in, 207

latitudinarianism, latitudinarians: and millenarianism, 8, 42, 53, 268; efforts toward a comprehensive church, 40-41; and Glorious Revolution, 41; millenarian ethos of, 54; support Huguenot refugees, 54; friendship with Allix, 55*n*; and Huguenot refugee citizenship, 57; and new prophets, 70-71; and Bulkeley, 79; and Whigs, 232 and *n*. *See also* Burnet, Gilbert; Lloyd, William; Woodward, Josiah

Laud, William, 38, 39

laughter: of French Prophets, 107, 229, 255-57; and wilderness, 277

Lausanne, 75, 182

Lavington, Ms. (520): cohabits with Mr. Wise, 206; as part of Female Embassy, 210; profile as prophet, 325

Lavington, George, 288

Law, John, 188

Law, William: his *Serious Call*, 192; on Newton, 242

law: in ethos of judgment, 3, 142, 151, 153, 200; Philadelphian warrant, 50; French Prophets' legal actions, 83, 87, 88; England, the Desert, and, 88; prosecution of French Prophets, 84, 88, 93-94, 104-12, 112*n*, 138, 173; French Prophets' attitude toward, 93; legal expenses of Huguenot consistories, 112*n*

Lawrence, Ann, 208

Lazarus, 66, 114

Lead, Jane: studies with Pordage, 46, 233; guides Philadelphians, 47-50; death, 50; her spirit visits to Roach and Oxenbridge, 51; as model of female leader, 142, 210-11; her books translated, 197; on androgyneity, 213; and Shakers, 214; mentioned, 85
Lee, Ann: becomes Mother of Shakers, 212; her theology, 213-15; sails to America, 214, 278; production and reproduction, 292*n*; mentioned, 211, 229
Lee, Francis: and Philadelphians, 48-51; letter from Dodwell, 49; contact with women prophets, 142; and Kabbala, 243; and Boehme, 244
Leeuwenhoek, Antony van: microscope of, 234; examines *Sal volatile oleosum*, 248*n*
Leghorn, Livorno, 180
Leibniz, Gottfried Wilhelm, 258
Leipzig, 177
Le Tellier, Daniel (34): baptism of children, 103, 129-30; expelled by French Prophets, 148; mission, 176; children of, 279; profile as prophet, 322
Le Tellier, Daniel, Jr. (257)?, 103, 129-30
Le Tellier, Elizabeth, 129-30
Le Tellier, Marie (73): her children, 103, 129-30, 279
Levellers: and Camisards, 27; and green, 128; mentioned, 7
levelling: of Camisards, 27; of Ranters and Fifth Monarchists, 39; of Mason's followers, 44 and *n*; association with French Prophets, 122; of Whitrow and Bulkeley, 131-32; of Lady Abden, 140; and sexual accusations, 140; and millenarian ethos, 152; and Bulkeley, 274, 277
levitation: by John Lacy, 9*n*, 95, 96
Levites: French Prophets' tribe named, 127, 128; omit Cavalier, 133; men and women in, 134; some expelled, 148
libertinism: of Restoration monarchy, 62; and London, 263
light: in Boehme's system, 46; of Quakers, 49, 207; of Episcopalians in Scotland, 155
Lignitz, duchy of, 170
Lincoln College, Oxford, 328
Lincolnshire, 65*n*, 154
Lions, Jean (27): defends French Prophets, 94*n*; advocate for Le Telliers, 103; on resurrection, 104-05; apostasy, 144

Lister, Martin, 218-19, 273
literacy: of *inspirés*, 31; in England, 67; of English believers, 80-81; among French Prophets, 151, 225-29, 232; and Camisard tradition, 282. *See also* oral tradition
Little Ice Age, 191
Little Savoy, the, 80
liturgy: of French Prophets, 180; and Moravians, 208. *See also* hymns; rituals
Lloyd, William: millenarianism of, 37, 42, 234, 268; presented living by Ashmole, 46*n*; friend of Bulkeley, 53, 79; friend of Allix, 55; shocked by prophecies, 115-16
Locke, John, 171
London: fire of 1666, 1, 2, 39, 230; reconstruction of, 2, 263; Mason's judgment on, 44; "true Rosicrucians" in, 47*n*, 204; Quaker judgments on, 52; Huguenot refugees in, 54-62; maps of, 58-59; Anglican churches in, 67; as financial center, 71; commercial prosperity in, 75; as replica of the Desert, 81, 284; French Prophets' judgments on, 78, 90-91, 104, 105*n*, 110, 118, 119, 120, 222, 263-64; flying ants in, 95; identified as New Jerusalem, 102, 264, 267; panic in, 118; French Prophet core group in, 149, 193; Cuninghame in, 160; Moravians in, 203; Du Plan in, 209; sense of exile in, 220-21; centrality in England, 221; English believers born in, 222; patriciate of, 223; literacy in, 225*n*; mineral springs in, 249*n*; public theatricality in, 252, 259, 260, 267, 278; strangers in, 253; forums in, 253; and intimacy, 259; surplus of women in, 261*n*; as a desert, 263, 268, 284; prisons in, 263; as a country estate, 267-68; adulteries in, 277; freedom of women in, 277; and *inspirés*, 284*n*; and the Camisard ethos, 292; mentioned, 11, 77, 78, 82, 105 *et passim*
Longbridge-Deverill, 144, 148
longitude, 241
Lorimer's Hall, 50
lotteries: French Prophets and, 193; women, time, and, 232*n*
Louis XIV of France, the Sun King: campaign against Huguenots, 14; sends Villars to Languedoc, 26; Camisard attitude to, 27; his death, 190; mentioned, 68

Louis XV of France, 191
Loutz, Samuel. *See* Lutz, Samuel
Love, John, 52
love feasts: among French Prophets, 127, 135, 285; as male ceremony, 135; among Moravians, 203
Lucius, Samuel. *See* Lutz, Samuel
Lucrèce, the prophet: leads *Gonfleurs*, 189, 210; early *inspirée?*, 189n; as inspired woman, 190
Luddism, 292n
Lundie, George, 156
Lutherans: in Holy Roman Empire, 169; revival among children, 170; condemned by Daut, 175; French Prophets' judgments on Swedish, 178; ministers become prophets, 182; and Evangelical Revival, 210; in illustration, 270-71
Lutz, Samuel: pietist minister, 183; and Huber family, 184, 186-87; influence on Genevan prophetic group, 185
Lyon, 183, 285

Mace, William, 105n
Mackenzie, Margaret (436): missions, 160, 168, 230; and Cuninghame, 168, 230; profile as prophet, 324
madness. *See* insanity
Madrid, 75
magic, 233
Magny, François: translates Tennhardt, 175; on French Prophets, 182-83; leads group in Geneva, 185
Mahieu, Abraham (139): mission to Cévennes, 136n; embraces Michaut, 199
Maillard, Mary: lameness cured, 69
Manchester: French Prophets at, 141, 154, 211; Shakers at, 211-14; Boehme's works printed in, 213
Manchester Mercury, 213
Marienborn, 182
Marion, Elie (10): as Camisard, 23, 26, 27; weeps blood, 30; arrives in London, 37, 71, 72; inspired to go to England, 75; his prophecies, 75-76, 77, 78, 90-91, 104n, 115, 149; 284; fasts, 78, 83-84; agitations without speech, 78; on retreats, 82-84, 96-97, 103; and mob, 83; trial of, with Fatio and Daudé, 84, 93-94, 105, 108-09; gives blessings, 84; and Philadelphians, 85; confronts sceptics, 92; legal punishment of, 109-12; receives alms, 119n; Whitrow's command to, 121;

names tribes, 126-27, 285; commands the wearing of ribbons, 128; gives sacrament, 129; a Levite, 133; refutes Abden, 140; continental missions, 176-80, 271; his death, 180; impact of his death, 193; present with Saudignan, 200; memoirs of, 225; age, 229; as a bachelor, 280; profile as prophet, 322; mentioned, 189, 198, 226
Marlborough, John Churchill, 1st Duke of: victory at Blenheim, 26; and War of the Spanish Succession, 71; victory at Ramillies, 75
Marlborough, Sarah Churchill, Duchess of, 85
Marot, Clément, 12, 15
Marseille, 188
martyrdom: meaning in England, 54; in English popular religion, 66; in the Desert, 70, 283; prophesied by Fage, 80; believers' attitude toward, 91; linked to miracle, 92; linked to missions, 96, 104, 108; redefined by English believers, 107; of Marion, Fatio and Daudé, 108; linked to New Jerusalem, 112; publicity of, 114; and law, 138; mentioned, 252. *See also* persecution
Mary II of England: crowned joint sovereign, 20, 41; oath of allegiance to, 41; Huguenot relief, 60
Masham, Mrs. *See* Hill, Abigail
Mason, John: Jesus appears to, 37, 44; his hymns, 43, 260 and n; millenarian visions, 43-44; his prophesied resurrection, 44, 118; his illness, 44, 218; his death, 44; his followers, 45, 286; millenarian ethos of, 53
mathematics: and Fatio, 73, 193, 236, 258; and probability, 193; calculus, 237, 258; and the millennium, 234; and fruit trees, 269
Mathes, Maria Elisabeth, 181
Maurice, Henry, 44
Mazel, Abraham: prophecies of, 22, 26, 30; as Camisard, 22-23, 26, 27, 30; memoirs of, 128, 133, 225; in England, 128; death, 154n; mentioned, 94n, 284
Mazel, James, 94n
Meath Street, Dublin, 155
mechanics: celestial, 238; physical, 239, 242
Mede, Joseph, 7, 38, 40
medicine: ideas on hysteria, 33n; Pordage and, 45-46; Byfield's, 112, 237, 247-48,

277; and the Scientists, 234, 241-42, 246-51; and miracle, 241; and salt, 243-51; universal medicines, 245*n*, 246-51; acids and alkalis, 250; and the millennium, 250. *See also* healing; miracles; physicians; salt

Mediterranean Sea, 15

meetinghouses: registered by dissenters, 42*n*; registered by Philadelphians, 48; in London, 71; registered by French Prophets, 87 and *n*, 89, 116; importance to French Prophets, 93; mentioned, 129. *See also* chapel

memory: and Huguenot children, 12; of *inspirés*, 31, 134; function of scribes, 75; during prophecy, 134; and oral tradition, 225; importance to French believers, 286, 292. *See also* history

men, males: as Camisard leaders, 84; sacerdotal function, 143, 146, 149, 291; fears of inspired women, 146; and schism, 144; and Christian church life, 291

mercury: in Paracelsian system, 46, 246

mercy: in Huguenot theology, 12; in Desert sermons, 18; and French Prophets, 116, 200; publicity and prophecy of, 181; and pietism, 185; Roach on, 196

Messiah: awaited by Multipliants, 188

meteors, 244

Methodists: and French Prophets, 8, 70*n*, 203-07, 210, 286-88, 321; and Mason's hymns, 43, 260*n*-261*n*; and Sir John Philipps, 70*n*; Moravian connection, 203-05, 205*n*; and Shakers, 212*n*; and confession, 215*n*; architecture of, 287; Huguenots among, 287*n*

Michaut, Jean: prophet of Camisard tradition, 199-200, 285

microscope, 234, 242, 248*n*, 288

Middle Temple, 328

Middleton, Thomas (142), 157

Midnight Cry, 43

Mill, John (451), 324

millenarianism, millennialism: kinds of millenarian ethos, 2-5; and time, 4-6, 36, 38, 232*n*; theories about, 5-6, 216; in 17th-century England, 6-9, 37-54, 289-90; and politics, 6-8, 39, 287*n*; in the Desert, 15-36, 77, 174; and children, 31, 280; and sexual equality, 34; and social equality, 34, 96, 98; of quietists, 156, 161; in illustration, 195; and exile, 225; and prophecy, 230, 240; and science, 234-36, 239; and mathematics, 234; and perpetual motion, 239; and medicine, 250; and privacy, 268; and celibacy, 280; and missions, 287
—of the French Prophets: and the true ministry, 77; chronology for the millennium, 89-91, 91*n*; and history, 101, 286; refined by the group, 104, 106-07; and prophecy, 119-20, 230, 240, 288; and quietists, 156; and Shakers, 214-15; and individual believers, 278; and childrearing, 280; and evangelical religion, 287; diagram, 330
—and responses to delay: history-writing, 101; deaths of believers, 129, 150; correlation to personal life, 161; progressive revelation, 201; Shaker solution, 214-15; waiting, 285-86
—*See also* cataclysm, ethos of; chiliasm; ethos, millenarian; false prophecy; *inspirés*; judgment, ethos of; millennium; New Jerusalem, ethos of; pentecost, ethos of; prophecy; *and individual religious groups, e.g.*, Philadelphians; Quakers; *etc.*

Millennial Christian Church. *See* Shakers

millennium, the: defined, 3*n*; expected by French Prophets, 91*n*, 119-20; and internal events, 215. *See also* millenarianism; prophecy; premillennialism; postmillennialism; Second Coming

Millery, 183

Milliet, pastor, 144

Mills, Lydia, 69

mime: of Lacy and Gray, 97, 99-100, 107, 120, 135; and quietists, 168; and theater, 252; and prostitutes, 253; and publicity, 268

mineral waters and spas: and French Prophets, 247-49, 249*n*; social role of, 253

ministry: *prédicants* as lay, 14; Isabeau Vincent as minister, 18; absent from Desert, 21; mythical role in Desert, 29; Huguenot, in exile, 54-55, 61, 76, 77, 105*n*, 176, 177, 180; of *inspirés*, 77; witness agitations of French Prophets, 92-93; and baptism, 103; among French Prophets, 104, 130, 149-50; and schisms, 144; Court's Desert synod, 174; Wesleys oppose lay, 206. *See also* rituals miracles: in ethos of New Jerusalem, 5, 125; walking over burning coals, 21; precocious speech, 21; tears of blood, 21, 30; walking through flames, 24; role among Camisards, 32; miraculous cures, 52, 69, 96, 99-100, 108, 110, 116, 124, 142, 219, 241-42; and science, 62, 241; since apostolic times, 63; appeal in England, 68, 70; to validate prophecy, 76-77, 114, 119-20; and *TS*, 78, 126, 282; linked to martyrdom, 92; importance to French Prophets, 91-92, 104, 114, 119-20; and Camisard tradition, 126; and Cuninghame, 157; and publicity, 255, 268; conversion process and, 287. *See also* healing; levitation; resurrection; tongues, speaking in

Miremont, Armand de Bourbon, marquis de (8): pushes for Languedoc expedition, 26n; sympathies for French Prophets, 70; hosts *inspirés*, 72-73; and Flotard, 83; and Fatio's sea watches, 241n

Miroir d'astrologie, 243

missions, evangelism: in ethos of New Jerusalem, 5, 86, 151; of Philadelphians, 50; of Quakers, 42; of the Society for the Propagation of the Gospel in Foreign Parts, 65; and *TS*, 79; linked to martyrdom, 96, 104, 108; Marion's sense of, 104n; to Sardinian chapel, 108; and healing, 110, 118, 219; and publicity, 117, 255; stimulated by death of Emes, 115-18; expense of, 119; and false prophecy, 124n, 133, 281; women as missionaries, 136-37; importance to French believers, 200-01, 285; and introspective religion, 202; of Methodists, 203; and millenarianism, 215; function of missionaries, 220; and urbanization, 221; and personal contact, 227; as affirmation of belief, 281; importance to English believers, 285; and ethos of pentecost, 285. *See also* French Prophets—missions and evangelism; universal church

Misson, Françoise, 280

Misson, François-Maximilien (13): on London air, 2; edits brother's book, 49n; editor of *TS*, 78-79; on "Acte Noir," 80; his home as refuge, 82; style of argument, 88; testifies for French Prophets, 94; on poverty of *inspirés*, 119n; "Colonel" Cavalier apologizes to, 126n; letters from Furly, 170; his will, 219n; and urban life, 220; his social connections, 224; and Whigs, 232n; and Kabbala, 243n; as tourist, 258; as a public man, 258; childless, 280; education of, 328

Misson, Henri, 48, 49n

Misson, Jaques (200), 328

mobs, riots: slogan of English, 71; in Soho, 82-83; as part of pattern, 83; legal action against rioters, 88, 93; at Colchester and Enfield, 116-17; at Bunhill Fields, 121-22; at Hackney Marsh, 128-29; in Scotland, 160; at St. Paul's Cathedral, 160; in Rotterdam, 173, 180; in Berlin, 176, 180; and anticatholicism, 191; at Bristol, 203; as customary force, 252

mock-trumpet, 240n

Modern Prophets, The: performance, 139; censored, 139n; and theatricality of French Prophets, 254

Monmouth, 138

monsters, 233, 252

Montanists, 207

Montet, M., 183

Montpellier, 188

Montrevel, Nicolas-Auguste de La Baume, marquis de, 26

Montrose: quietist congregation at, 163, 165; as New Jerusalem model, 291; mentioned, 174

Moore, John (185), 323

Moore, John (186), 324

Moorfields, 69

Moravia, 210

Moravians: and French Prophets, 8, 203-06, 208, 286; and Mason's hymns, 43; and Zinzendorf, 182, 198, 203; and Spangenberg, 198, 204; Jean Pellet and, 204; Zeidig and, 204, 217; the Wesleys and, 205; their hymns, 260n; on grace and perfection, 287; Huguenots among, 287n; as French Prophets, 321; mentioned, 186, 285

More, Henry, 233

Morel, Jeanne (144), 324

Moreton, Mrs. (375), 231

mortality: prophets' sense of, 231n; rates in England, 260; Bulkeley's sense of, 277; infant rates, 280

Mothe, Claude Groteste de la: Chamberlayne's friend, 92; on Emes's resurrection, 123n motion: and the Scientists, 233-42; and God, 235; and health, 250; of particles, 278

Moulin, Pierre du: opposes Amyraut, 12; millenarianism of, 12, 15; influence of, 15; grandfather of Pierre Jurieu, 16, 170; grandfather of Hélène Jurieu, 170; mentioned, 36

Moult, Francis (146): style of argument, 88; reshapes ethos of prophets, 107; bails the missionaries, 116; money spent on group, 119; on Emes's resurrection, 120; satirized, 122; missions, 124, 138; chemist, 138; communion service, 178; business disputes, 193; death of nieces, 194; friend of Roach, 196; follower of Wharton, 197; related to Wynantz, 198; gives property to Wharton, 199-200; death, 202; name scratched out of records, 210; will of, 219; his house, 222, 223; social connections, 224; wealth, 225n; portrait, 226; scripture reading, 238; and perpetual motion, 239; Fatio's chemical legacy to, 245; powder of projection, 245; mineral springs and salts, 248-49; Grand Elixir, 249; his city garden, 277; as a bachelor, 280

Moult, George, 248-49

Moult, John (93): missions, 124, 136, 154, 172; reprimands inspired women, 141; healed, 219; his prophecy, 259; profile as prophet, 323

Moult, Margaret (376): marries John Potter, 194; her death, 194; death of children, 280

Moult, Mary (231): marries Charles Portales, 194; her death, 194; mother of Marguerite, 198; death of children, 280

mountains: of Cévennes, 1, 11, 20, 23, 71, 103, 268n, 277; and London as New Jerusalem, 264; and ethos of cataclysm, 268n; and TS, 277

mourning: for Emes, 113-14; for Marion, 180; sackcloth prophesying, 202-03, 290. See also death; rituals

Mudd, Thomas, 52

Muggleton, Lodowick, 51

Muggletonians: founded, 51; and Clarkson, 53; French Prophets associated with, 89; and millennial delay, 286; mentioned, 71

Multipliants: their rituals and beliefs, 188-89; and the New Jerusalem ethos, 190

Munnings, Anne: her miracle cure, 69n, 116

museum: Roland's home as, 1; as paradigm of urban experience, 252-53; and Misson, 258; Bulkeley's proposal for, 274

music: for psalms, 12; angelic, 16; Isabeau Vincent's singing, 17; and laughter, 256. See also hymns; psalms

muteness, dumbness, 107

mysticism: and Cuninghame, 157-58; Dutton's scepticism of, 158, 165, 286; and Roach, 194; affective, 231n; and science, 242-45; and Byfield's *mistio*, 247-48; J. P. Greaves, 290n. See also Behmenism; Kabbala

nakedness: of Quaker prophet, 52; of French Prophet, 108, 135, 252; of Moult's statues, 223, 277. See also dress

names and naming: Camisard, 32; renaming by Lacy, 97; renaming by Marion and Raoux, 126-27, 129; Bulkeley and titles, 132; and millenarianism, 151; and children, 279, 281. See also baptism

naturalization, 56-57

Naylor, James, 52

Nehemiah, 273-75

Netherlands, the, Holland, United Provinces: support for Camisards, 24, 27; Philadelphians in, 47n, 168; Huguenot connections with, 57, 68n, 174; Fage and Cavalier in, 72; and Ramillies, 75; "Colonel" Cavalier in, 125; missions to, 133, 136, 170-78; Bourignon in, 155; Furly in, 171; Fatio in, 181; "true Rosicrucians" travel from, 205; Tiley and Everard in, 232

networks, social: of the French Prophets, 219-21

Newcastle, Margaret Cavendish, Duchess of, 243

Newcomen, Thomas, 71

New England: colonial millenarianism, 8n, 286, 287n

New Jerusalem: puritans identify with England, 38; Mason's visions of, 43; "true Rosicrucian" vision of, 47n; Lacy's image of, 106, 264, 267; Marion's image of, 102; linked to martyrdom, 112; pastoral image of, 222. See also London; Nehemiah; New Jerusalem, ethos of

New Jerusalem, ethos of: defined, 5; in

Restoration England, 40, 53, 54; and healing, 96; and speaking in tongues, 96; among French Prophets, 98, 100-01, 103, 104, 107, 118, 125-26, 149, 151-52, 201, 214, 284-85; and universal family, 127; impurity in, 142; among Huguenots in France, 190; and Arnould, 198; and French Prophet split, 200; and Hannah Wharton, 201, 214; and Shakers, 214; and alchemy, 246; and the Scientists, 251; and intimacy, 262n; and publicity, 278; among English believers, 284-85; and inspired women, 291; diagrams of, 329-30
New Model Army, 38
New Testament. See Bible
Newton, Isaac: millenarianism of, 8; friendship with Fatio, 73, 237, 258, 269; religious speculations of, 233-35, 241; on providence, 234-35; on Fatio's watches, 238-39; and scripture, 241; and alchemy, 242; and transmutation of metals, 244; and Fatio's medicines, 249; and the calculus, 258; and motion, 278
Newtonianism: and natural laws, 62, 278; the Scientists and, 233, 235; Fatio and, 236n; and time, 239
New Voyage to Italy, A, 78
Nicholson, Henry (195), 124, 133, 328
Nîmes: Camisards caught in, 27; new prophets near, 188; and *Gonfleurs*, 189
Noble, Mrs. (378), 138
Noble, Samuel (225), 138
Nolibet, David (149): mission to Cévennes, 136n; expelled from Rotterdam, 173
nolle prosequi, 88
nonconformists. See dissent
nonjurors: defined, 41n; Francis Lee, 48; Henry Dodwell, 49; on Camisards, 68n, at Cuninghame's death, 167
nonresistance, doctrine of: and nonjurors, 41n; disputed by Huguenots in exile, 68n. See also pacifism
Norfolk, 154, 222n
Normandy, 62, 221n
Northampton: missions to, 136; French Prophets at, 154; Cuninghame at, 160-61
Northfleet, 82-84
Norwich: missions to, 136; Huguenots in, 220
nostalgia, 258n
Noual, Jean (78), 322
Nourse, Timothy: on London, 263; on wildernesses, 266, 267
Nouveaux Convertis: defined, 14; remorse of, 16, 282; their spiritual conflict, 18; rituals of atonement, 30; and Huguenot refugee clergy, 61; and Multipliants, 188; secrecy of, 282
novices, novitiate: Lady Abden as, 140; conduct of, 148; defined by French Prophets, 165-66; Fatio on, 183; Jean Huber as, 192; and children, 281
Nuremberg, 175
Nutt, Guy (243): missions, 138, 154; death, 202; profile as prophet, 323

oaths: of allegiance, 41; and laughter, 256
obscenity, 141n
Observator, The, 95
Occasional Conformity Bills, 64-65n, 191
Ogilvie, James. See Seafield, James Ogilvie
Old Bawn: described, 273; its chimney piece, 273-74; groundplan, 274
Old Street Square, 2
Old Testament. See Bible
opera, 65
Opticks, 242
oral tradition: of French Prophets and Camisards, 225-27; and missions to universities, 229; admired by English believers, 282. See also hymns; literacy; memory
Orders for Assemblies: recorded, 148; edited, 148n; impose caution, 149; and ethos of judgment, 149-50, 152; Cuninghame's role in, 162; and quietist liturgy, 163; and agitations, 164; on novices, 165, 183; and women, 210; and millenarianism, 215; and children, 281; as codebook, 285
ordure, *ordure*: linked to the devil, 30; thrown at French Prophets, 80, 110-11; and pollution, 111n
Orme, Katharine (424): speaks in tongues, 164; profile as prophet, 324
Ormond, Ormonde, James Butler, 2nd Duke of, 110
Ottoman Empire, 180
Owen, Isaac (150): sells estate, 118; religious lineage, 218n
Owen, James, 218n
Oxenbridge, Joanna: hosts Philadelphians, 47; Lead's spirit visits her, 51
Oxford: missions to, 136, 229

Oxford University: and Philadelphians, 47n, 48; and French Prophets, 228, 240, 328. See also All Soul's College; Christ Church College; Lincoln College; St. John's College; University College; Wadham College

pacifism, 30. See also nonresistance
Pagez, François (491): and Huber family, 183, 186-87; in English assemblies, 192; profile as prophet, 325
Palladio, Andrea, 265
Pall Mall, 2
panacea. See medicine; Sal volatile oleosum
pantheism, 235
Paracelsus, Theophrastus Bombastus von Hohenheim, 46, 246
parallax: solar, 236
parents: in Desert, 18; Guyon as mother, 156; French Prophets as, 279-281, 280n; and petits prophètes, 283. See also children
Paris: Allix and Misson from, 220; Gribelin from, 269n; University of, 328
Parke, James, 52
Parker, John (96), 323
Parks, Mary (459), 324
parks. See country houses; gardens
Parliament, English: during Civil War and Restoration, 41; and Huguenot citizenship acts, 56-57; mentioned, 122n. See also House of Lords
Parsons, William, 204n
Partington, John, 212n
Pastoral Letters, Lettres pastorales, 16, 170
pastoralism: and appeal of French Prophets, 222-23, 224-25, 226; and women, 231; and wildernesses, 266; of London, 267-68, 278. See also rural society
patriarchy: and ethos of judgment, 142; among French Prophets, 143; and inspired women, 291
patriciate, the: urban, 223; costume and theater of, 252; friendship in, 259-61; marital obligations of, 259-61; and country estates, 265-66
Pearson, Susanna, 52
Peel Meeting, London, 117
Pellet, Jean (189): death of child, 126; tribes, 134n-135n; and Saudignan, 200;

spiritual odyssey of, 204; and universal church, 286
Pembroke, Herbert Philip, 2nd earl of, 47
Pennsylvania: "true Rosicrucians" go to, 47n, 204; Mary Keimer goes to, 193, 204; Moravians in, 203-04; Zeidig in, 204; Furly and, 204
pentecost, ethos of: described, 3n; defined, 4; in Restoration England, 40, 53, 54; Marion's vision of a new Pentecost, 81-82; among the French Prophets, 87, 149, 151-52, 201; and quietists, 168, 285; and the Gonfleurs, 190; and Wharton, 201; among Shakers, 214; and the Scientists, 251; and identity, 262n; and intimacy, 278; and petits prophètes, 283; and inspired women, 291; diagrams of, 329-30
perfection, doctrine of spiritual: prophet Lavington on, 206, 213n; and the Shakers, 212-14; the Wesleys on, 213n, 287
perpetual motion: machines, 239; and health, 250
Perrot, Jeanne (445), 223n
persecution: of Huguenots, 11-12, 14-22, 26, 28-31, 42; linked to millenarian ideas, 15-17, 42, 108; prophecy about, 17-18; of Philadelphians, 49-50; meaning to Huguenot ministers in exile, 61; meaning in popular English religion, 66; French Prophets' interpretation of, 100, 108, 151; of Scottish Episcopalians, 156; and quietists, 161; and prophecy, 180; and patience, 182; of Moravians, 203; and literacy, 225; in Desert, 282-83; of inspirés, 284. See also deprivation theory; martyrdom
Peter I of Russia, 176n
Peterborough, Charles Mordaunt, 3rd earl of, 171
Petersen, Johann: meets French Prophets, 198; his hymns, 198n
Petersen, Johanna, 198
Peterson, Ann (490), 325
Petitmaitre, Mme. (453), 324
petits prophètes: their millennial vision, 98; as model for English believers, 107; resurrection, sleep, and, 117; and Desert ethos, 127; and Shakers, 214; and confession, 214, 283; and secrecy, 283. See also children; inspirés; prophets
Philadelphia, church of: reign dated by van

Helmont, 37; Mason and, 43; state at birth of Christianity, 48; its history of persecution, 49-50. *See also* Philadelphians: origins and beliefs, 45-51, 233; and hymns, 45, 260*n*; and the "true Rosicrucians," 47*n*, 213*n*; public assemblies, 48-50; publications, 48-49, 194-97; and the Kabbala, 48, 48*n*, 243; and social conservatism, 49; persecution of, 49-50; schism among, 51; and universal redemption, 53; millenarian ethos of, 53, 159, 194-96; and early French Prophets, 85-87; martyrdom, miracle, and, 92; historical approach, 101, 282; role of women among, 135, 142-43, 168, 210; and Scottish quietists, 155, 159, 164; on mercy, 159, 194-96; and pietists, 169; schism with French Prophets, 142-43, 194-96, 285; and Hannah Wharton, 196-97; and androgyneity, 213; Hollis, Sterrill, and, 217; and alchemy, 245; as religious brokers, 286; as believers, 321; mentioned, 8

Philadelphus, 49

Philipps, John (19): SPCK, Methodists, and, 70*n*; as French Prophet, 80; and ethos of New Jerusalem, 86; education of, 328

philosopher's stone: in ethos of New Jerusalem, 5; and Boehme, 244; Moult and Portales on, 245; and Christianity, 246; and salt, 246; Byfield and, 247; mentioned, 243

physicians: examine Isabeau Vincent, 17; said to examine *fanatiques*, 21*n*; Francis Lee, 48; Martin Lister, 218-19; Byfield as, 248; Robert Eaton, 248-49. *See also* healing; medicine; Royal College of Physicians

physics: and the Scientists, 234-36; and providence, 235-36; and divinity, 236; and metaphysics, 242; and wildness, 277

Pia desideria, 169

Picardy, 221*n*

Pickering, Christina (455): her blasphemies and bawdiness, 141; autonomy, 152; profile as prophet, 324

Pickworth, Henry (216), 117*n*, 289

Pierre, François, 21

pietists: and quietists, 168; origins, 169-70; and Furly, 175, 183; in Berlin, 176-77; and millenarianism, 177*n*; French Prophets' ties to, 180-88, 196-99, 201, 203, 205, 209, 288; in Wetteravia, 185, 198*n*; and *Gonfleurs*, 189; and Spangenberg, 198; and Arnould, 198-99; and public ministry, 202; in Pennsylvania, 204, 217; influence on John Wesley, 205, 207; influence on Howell Harris, 207; and women, 210; and Zeidig, 217; and Methodists, 288; as believers, 321; mentioned, 8, 192, 290

pilgrimage: and prophecy, 284; and French believers, 285

pillory. *See* scaffold

Place, Daniel Chaise de la, 82 and *n*

place, placement: Camisards and, 35-36; sense of, 284; French Prophets and, 292

Plan de la justice de Dieu sur la terre, 178-79, 180, 200

Pledger, Elias, 44, 69

Plewit, Mary (515): visited by John Wesley, 205-06; part of Female Embassy, 210; profile as prophet, 325

Pliny the Younger, 260

poetry: in Desert, 15; on Emes's resurrection, 122; by Cuninghame, 161-62, 165, 166; by Roach, 225; by Moult, 245. *See also* hymns; psalms

Poiret, Pierre: and Bourignon, 155; and alchemy, 244

Poitiers, 73

Poland, 179-80

politics: and millenarian prophecy, 6-7, 39, 122, 287*n*; and prophets in Desert, 27-28, 30; in England, 38-42, 78, 85, 94, 122*n*; and Philadelphians, 49; republicans, 171; of individual believers, 232 and *n*. *See also* nonresistance; Tories; Whigs

pollution, 30, 111*n*. *See also* ordure; sexuality

Pont-de-Montvert: prophecy at, 15; Huguenots imprisoned at, 16; start of Camisard revolt, 16, 17*n*; and Multipliants, 188

Pool, William, 52

Pope, Alexander: letter from Wycherly, 139*n*-140*n*; and the public domain, 257; and gardens, 257*n*, 260; and friendship, 260

population. *See* demography; mortality

Pordage, John: and Philadelphians, 45-46; and alchemy, 45-46, 233

Portales, Charles (3): expedition to Languedoc, 25*n*-26*n*; as scribe, 73-75; on

retreats, 82, 96, 103; and mob, 83; fasts, 83-84; at trial, 93-94; continental missions, 176-80; on silence of French Prophets, 192; as Scientist, 193, 240, 243-44, 245, 246; marries Mary Moult, 194; father-in-law to Wynantz, 198; union with Fatio, Allut, 199; suspicion of Moult and Wharton, 200; his archive, 209-10; his will, 219n; social network, 220, 224; house of, 222; wealth of, 223n, 225n; portrait of, 227; on astrology, 243-44; occupation, 320
Portales, Jaques (198), 173, 209
Portales, Marguerite, 198
Portugal, 72, 75
postmillennialism, 6n, 38
Pott, the brothers, 180
Potter, John (41): appears as prophet, 95; prophesies resurrection, 113-14, 117; interpretation of prophecies, 120; exorcises, 133; in tribes, 134n; as missionary, 136; excludes false prophets, 140; rebukes Mary Keimer, 141; defines assemblies, 147-48; importance to *Orders*, 148; on passivity, 163-64; on novices, 165; on silence, 193; seizes Samuel Keimer's effects, 193; marries Margaret Moult, 194; death of, 208; death of children, 280; a son?, 280n; profile as prophet, 323
powder of projection, 245
Powell, Martin, 254
prayer: Huguenot, 12; as a stage of prophecy, 29; of *Nouveaux Convertis*, 30; among Philadelphians, 47; Camisard, printed, 68; as sacerdotal function, 103, 129; and oral tradition, 225; written, 227n; and privacy, 257
preaching: of Isabeau Vincent, 17; of *inspirés*, 18; and prophecy, 18, 29, 287-88; of young boy, 22; extempore, 43; as gift among French Prophets, 103; lay, 206; kerygmatic, 260n-261n; charismatic, 287-88; in fields, 288. *See also* exegesis; language; *prédicants*; sermons
Preaux, Olivier de Brossard des (118), 60
Preaux, Renée de Brossard des (119), 60
prédicants: arise in Languedoc, Dauphiné, 14; not prophets, 29; Brousson, 35; woman among, 35n; attitude of Huguenot clergy toward, 61; and Camisards, 283
prediction: as stage of prophesy, 29; time-specific, 90-91, 95, 99, 104. *See also* false prophecy; prophecy
Predictions Concerning the Raising the Dead Body of Dr. Thomas Emes, 115
prefiguration: in ethos of judgment, 4
premillennialism: defined, 5n-6n, 38; Restoration attitude toward, 39; Lacy's, 106
Presbyterians: during Comonwealth and Protectorate, 38-39; ejected, 39; Clarkson as, 53; Lacy as, 64n, 117n; Cotton as, 65; and early French Prophets, 86-87; clergy witness agitations, 92n; and New Jerusalem ethos, 151; in Scotland, 155-56; Keimer as, 217; and Byfield and Owen, 232n; as believers, 321
Preston, Hugh (80) 2, 110, 219
Preston, 167
Pretender, Old. *See* James Francis Edward
printers, 114, 138, 318, 320
printing: religious books in England, 67; edition sizes, 81n; costs, of French Prophets, 81n, 119; and literacy in England, 225, 226. *See also* publication
prism, 234
privacy: of symbolic systems, 3n, 4; and Huguenot worship, 14; of Philadelphian meetings, 47, 50, 142; Marion and Portales fast, 83; mob, miracle, and, 123; of French Prophet assemblies, 127, 195; of women's opposition to French Prophets, 139n; of quietists, 163, 185; of missionaries, 180, 255; and French Prophets' performances, 255; and companionship, 260; and divine monarchy, 260n. *See also* intimacy; publicity; shame
processions, 252
progress: in ethos of cataclysm, 4-5; idea of, in England, 7, 192
prophecy: and ethos of pentecost, 4; and preaching, 18, 29, 287-88; stages of, 29; as a vocation, 31-33; in 17th-century England, 37-54; and Mason, 43-45, 53; among Philadelphians, 49; among Quakers, 52-53; and latitudinarians, 53, 115-16; since apostolic times, 63; English response to, 70-71; Cévenol tradition of, 77; *TS* record of, 78-79; as center of French Prophets' beliefs, 89-91, 281; process of, 133-34; scale and density of, 150; and quietism, 156-59, 189-90, 285;

and continental pietism, 181-90; its decline among the French Prophets, 192-94, 208; and Shakers, 211-13; appeal of, 217, 225; and oral tradition, 225-27; written and printed, 227, 227n; and the ether, 236n; and alchemy, 244; and salt, 246; and adolescents, 259; and conversion experiences, 281; generations of, 281n; and millennial errand, 286n-287n; and charismatic preaching, 287-88. *See also* false prophecy; *inspirés*; language; prophets

prophecies. *See individual prophets and publications, e.g., Collection of Warnings*; Keimer, Mary; Lacy, John

prophets: orthography in this book, 2n; in the Desert, 17-36; as figures for Desert anxiety, 18; as dramatists, 28; ranks of, 29; and community, 29; as ministers, 30, 103, 148; generations of, 31, 210; women as, 32-36, 102, 134-36, 140-43, 146, 162, 167-68, 204, 210-11, 214, 231, 232n, 291; Quakers, 52-53; role among French Prophets, 78-79, 81, 82, 84-85, 89-91, 96, 98, 103-04, 106-07, 112, 113-15, 119-20, 126-130, 143, 147-50, 150-153, 200-02; and logic, 92; hierarchy of, 148, 164-66: in Scotland, 155-69; pietists, 181-90; Moravian, 208; and rural imagery, 224-30; ages, 229, 327; profiles, 322-25; statistics, 326, 327. See also *inspirés*; women; *and individual prophets, e.g., Potter, John; Turner, Mary*

prostitution, 1, 65, 253

Protectorate, 39

Protestants, Protestantism: 3n, 11-12, 37, 40, 41, 70, 168, 321. *See also individual churches and denominations*

providence: and prophecy, 99; Lacy on, 121; and French Prophets' eschatology, 150; Cuninghame on, 157; Fatio on, 209, 235-36; Bulkeley and, 218, 219, 274; and healing, 219; and inspired women, 232n; Newton on, 235; mentioned, 290

Prussia, Polish, 179

psalms: sung by Huguenots, 12, 61; Psalm LXVIII, 13; in the Desert, 14, 15, 16, 17, 22; and Mason, 43

publication: *TS* and, 79, 81, 84n, 107, 151, 225, 284; Marion's *Warnings*, 81-82, 84, 94; part of French Prophet pattern, 83, 180; function of, 85; advertisements, 87, 96; Lacy's *Warnings*, 96, 97, 102, 109-10, 181; against French Prophets, 106; on Emes, 115; Whitrow's warnings, 116, 117; costs, 119; Whitrow's *Warnings*, 132; Lady Abden's book, 168; and continental missions, 172, 175, 178, 179, 180; and literacy, 225-27; and membership, 316. *See also* printing; *and individual titles, e.g., Avertissemens; Cri d'alarme, etc.*

publicity: and symbolic systems, 3n; of *inspirés* in 1689, 18; of Desert assemblies, 19, 283; of repentance in Desert, 21; of confession in Desert, 32; of Philadelphians, 48-49; and scribes, 75; and commitment of believers, 79, 84, 116, 202, 284; controlled environment and, 87n; and social awareness, 107; of martyrdom, 114; from English missions, 117; around Emes's resurrection, 121, 124-25; and ethos of French Prophets, 151; and Cuninghame's prophecies, 160-61; mercy, judgment, and, 180; pietists, quietists, and, 185; and evangelism, 202; and the millennium, 215; believers' ambivalence toward, 255-62; and wilderness, 266; and Fatio, 269-72; and Bulkeley, 275-77. *See also* intimacy; secrecy; shame

puer aeternus, 243n

Pulham: missions to, 136; French Prophets jailed in, 138; false prophet in, 140; French Prophets at, 149, 154

pump, air, 240

puppet shows, 66n, 254

purgatory, 129n. *See also* sleeping in Jesus

puritans: their forms of worship, 12; their eschatology, 38; centers of, 155; and believers, 218n; in New England, 286, 287n

purity, purification: among Camisards, 29, 30; youth as sign of, 31; illiteracy as sign of, 31, 226; and attack on *inspirées*, 34; retreats and, 99; and charity, 132; and women, 141; prophetic, 143; in French Prophets' assemblies, 148; and ethos of judgment, 200; and French believers, 201; and Ann Lee, 214; and language, 226; and alchemy, 244; as problem of placement, 292. *See also* ordure; pollution; sexuality

Quakers, Society of Friends: and van Helmont, 37; silent worship, 47, 189;

doctrine of inner revelation, 48; and Philadelphians, 48, 49; and Furly, 48n, 171; prophecy and millenarianism, 52, 286; identified with French Prophets, 53, 89; millenarian ethos of, 54; women among, 83n, 135; in Birmingham, 115; in Colchester, 116, 171; expel French Prophets, 117; and resurrection attempts, 117-18; Sarah Wiltshire, 142; and New Jerusalem ethos, 151; in Ireland, 154; as French Prophets, 155, 217, 289, 321; and *Gonfleurs*, 189; meeting interrupted in Bristol, 202-03; and Shakers, 211-13, 212n; and Whigs, 232n; and trance, 254; and historical context, 282; and revivalists, 288; memories of French Prophets, 289-90; New Lights, 289-90

Quand vous aurez saccagé, vous serez saccagés: published, 179-80; carried by Marie Huber, 184; frontispiece of, 271
Quedlinburg, 204
Queen's Bench Court, 84, 93, 252
quietists: in Scotland, 155-69; as French Prophets, 155-69, 321; women among, 167-68, 210, 291; European contacts, 168-69; and pietists, 169, 174, 189; and liturgy and eschatology of French Prophets, 180, 285; in Switzerland, 185; and *Gonfleurs*, 189; and Hannah Wharton, 196; and French Prophets' missions, 201; and public ministry, 202; and last French Prophets, 203, 215; feeling of exile, 221; as religious brokers, 286

Ramillies, 75
Ramsay, Andrew Michael (394): on Bourignon, 156; on education, 280; occupation, 320
Ranc, Jacquette, 19
Ranters: radicalism of, 7, 39; and John Robins, 51; and Clarkson, 53; identified with French Prophets, 89; Roach accused of Ranterism, 143; passivity of, 286; revivalists and, 288
Raoux, Daniel, 20-21
Raoux, Jeanne (71): suspended by Huguenot church, 103n; hears celestial voice, 126; names tribes, 126-27, 285; vision, 133; Levite, 134; in Rotterdam, 173; profile as prophet, 323
Raoux, Madeleine (72), 103n, 173
Rastatt, Peace of, 179

Ratisbon, 177
Rawson, Benjamin (197), 323
Reason, Hal (227), 328
reason: in Huguenot theology, 12; and deism, 63-64; and orthodoxy, 64; in religious publications, 67; controversies over, 70; French Prophet attitude toward, 92; Lacy on, 164; and the Scientists, 236; and prophets, 238; and sentiment, 287; and revelation, 288
reciprocity, theory of, 4
redemption. *See* soteriology; universalism; universal salvation
Red Lion Square, 87n
Red Sea, 165
Reeve, John, 51
reform societies: in London, 64-65, 71; and early French Prophets, 86. *See also* Societies for the Reformation of Manners; Society for Promoting Christian Knowledge; Society for the Propagation of the Gospel in Foreign Parts
Reformation, the: 11, 37
refuge: as part of French Prophet pattern, 83, 180; and French believers, 285
Refuge, the, 172n
refugees, Huguenot: in England, 55-62, 67n, 220-21 and n; and Cotton, 73; and English politics, 85; irenism of, 90n; on doctrine of election, 90n; and isolation, 220; attitude toward London, 263; and symbolic context, 284
religion: popular, in England, 62, 65-70. *See also* anticatholicism; Antichrist; Anti-Scripturists; apostolic church; Beast of Revelation; Bible; blasphemy; blessings; Boyle sermon; camp meetings; cataclysm, ethos of; ceremony; chapel; chiliasm; chronology, millennial; church; churches; communion; confession; conversion; curse; damnation; death; devil; divine monarchy; ecstatic religion; election; enthusiasm; eschatology; ethos, millenarian; exegesis; exorcism; faith; false prophecy; fasts; Feast of Tabernacles; fossils; free will; grace; healing; hell; heresy; hermetic tradition; hymns; initiation; irreligion; jeremiads; judgment, ethos of; Judgment Day; judgments; light; love feasts; martyrdom; mercy; millenarianism; millennium; ministry; missions; mourning; mysticism;

New Jerusalem, ethos of; novices; pentecost, ethos of; perfection; persecution; pilgrimage; postmillennialism; prayer; preaching; prefiguration; premillennialism; prophecy; providence; purgatory; purity; reason; repentance; resurrection; revelation; Revelation, Book of; revivalism; rituals; sect-church typology; seekers; sermons; sin; soteriology; syncretism; theosophy; time; trance; True Church; Two Witnesses; universal church; universalism; universal salvation; visions; Whore of Babylon; worship; *and specific churches, denominations, and theological positions, e.g.,* Arianism; Baptists; deism; *etc.*

Religion Prétendue Réformée, 14

repentance: psalms and, 16; physical act of, 19; by *Nouveaux Convertis*, 30, 31; and prophecy, 105 and *n*; conversion and, 107*n*; French Prophets' call to, 175; drama of, 202-03, 205. *See also* confession

republicans, 171

Restitution of the Great Scepter, 84

Restoration, the: and millenarianism, 7-8, 40, 51, 287*n*, 290; and martyrdom, 66; and ethos of cataclysm, 150; theater during, 256; mentioned, 55, 230

resurrection: promised by Bonnisolle, 21, 117*n*; promised by Mason, 44-45; attempts by Quakers, 52, 117-18; in opera, 66; by French Prophets, 104-05, 112, 113-15, 120-24, 284; attempts in England, 117-18; and healing, 118; importance to French Prophets, 120-21, 124; and Cuninghame, 162. *See also* Emes, Thomas

retreats: part of pattern, 78, 180; to Northfleet, 82-84; function of, 85; to Bushy, 96-98; to Hoxton, 102-03; as private performances, 255; and group cohesion, 284

Reunion of the Two Alliances, Sign of the, 126-27, 316

revelation: and symbolic systems, 3*n*; and prophecy, 7; for Philadelphians, 47-48; stages of, 47, 164, 197, 215, 285; for Quakers, 48, 52; religious books favor, 67; controversy over, 70; and French Prophets, 147; progressive, 201; science and, 236-37, 244. *See also* prophecy

Revelation, Book of: and the millennium, 3*n*; and Judgment Day, 3*n*; decoded, 4; cited by du Moulin, 15; in prophecy of Vincent, 18; Camisard use of, 27; and number of the Beast, 39*n*; read by Mason, 43; and French Prophets, 90; and Kabbala, 243; cited or mentioned, 38, 42, 44, 91, 112, 126, 140, 252, 268, 280. *See also* Bible, the; Beast of Revelation; Judgment Day; Second Coming; Two Witnesses; Whore of Babylon

revivalism, revivalists, 288-89, 290

Revocation of the Edict of Nantes. *See* Edict of Nantes

Revolution Settlement, 155

rhetoric. *See* language; names and naming

Rhône River, 27*n*

ribbons: worn by French Prophets, 128 and *n*, 285; used by Multipliants, 188; and publicity, 255

Richardson, Robert (270), 197*n*, 324

Ridder, Marie Hélène de (484), 192, 325

Rigby, Thomas (157), 118

riot, riots. *See* mobs

rites of passage, 150

rituals: baptism, 29, 61, 103, 104*n*, 129-30, 135, 279; communion, 29, 61, 98, 129-30, 172, 178; prophetic redirection of, 30; of purification, 30, 99, 148; atonement, 30-31; Laudian attitude toward, 38; of Huguenot churches in England, 55; blessings, 84, 85, 85*n*, 105, 111*n*, 129, 135, 162; and legalism, 88; naming, 96-97, 126-27; mourning, 113-14, 129-30; as response to false prophecy, 147; and healing, 150; and children, 281. *See also* baptism; blessings; communion; confession; death; exorcism; healing; repentance; worship

Rivière, Jean Brutel de la, 173

Roach, Richard (24): and Mason's hymns, 45; and *Theosophical Transactions*, 48, 243, 257; leads Philadelphians, 51, 194-98; appeal of French Prophets, 80; meets French Prophets, 85-86; restores Gray's voice, 108; dreams, 112, 257; on Emes's resurrection, 120; on millenarian ethos of French Prophets, 142, 150*n*, 159, 195-96; on assemblies, 147; compared to Cuninghame, 159; letters torn up, 160; death, 194; European contacts, 194-98;

friend of Hollis, 199; on split among French Prophets, 200; on the Female Embassy, 211-13; and multiple religious allegiances, 220; habitation, 222; satiric poem, 225; his education, 228, 328; and Cheyne, 235; and Hermetic tradition, 242; and Kabbala, 243; and astrology, 244; and doubling of gold, 245; and publicity, 257; as a bachelor, 280
roads, 1, 262
Roberts, Mrs. (177), 115
Robins, John, 51
Rochfort, Peter (265), 240n, 320
Rock, Johann Friedrich, 182, 185
Roland, the Camisard, 1
Roman Catholics: on the millennium, 3n; on Judgment Day, 3n; debate over faith and grace, 12; and Laudians, 38; and Charles I, 38; and Restoration monarchs, 40-42, 62; among French Prophets, 87n, 321; identified with French Prophets, 89; prophecy at chapel of, 108; Lloyd project to convert, 115; and New Jerusalem ethos, 151; Bourignon, 155; in Holy Roman Empire, 169; condemned by Daut, 175; in Berlin, 176; Allut judgments against, 178; Keimer, 217; mentioned, 230. *See also* anticatholicism
romanticism: and confession, 215n; and women prophets, 232n; and friendship, 260
Rome: destruction prophesied, 78, 180; mission to, 179-80
Rosehearty, 163
"Rosicrucians, true": contact with Philadelphians, 47n, 204; and celibacy, 213n
Rothwell, 52, 260n
Rotterdam: Pierre Jurieu at, 16, 20, 170, 193; Furly at, 48n, 171, 193; French Prophets' missions to, 170-73, 178; Hélène Jurieu at, 170-71; French Prophets expelled from, 173
Rosseau, Jean-Jacques, 287
Roussière, Daniel (492): prophecy in Languedoc, 184; prophecy in Switzerland, 188; in English assemblies, 192; profile as prophet, 325
Royal College of Physicians, 228n
Royal Exchange, 109, 111
royalism: of Huguenots, 12, 30; of Camisards, 27, 68n; and Jurieu, 27n

royalists, 39, 218n
Royal Society of Ireland, 80
Royal Society of London, of Oxford: letters to, 233; French Prophets as fellows of, 73, 240-41; its desiderata, 244n-245n; George Moult a fellow, 248
rural society: *inspirés* and, 31, 282; Huguenot weavers, 60; and appeal of French Prophets, 220-22, 226, 229, 230; and science, 237; and country houses, 265-67. *See also* pastoralism; urban culture
Russell family, 73
Rye House Plot, 232n
Ryswick, Treaty of, Peace of: disappoints Huguenots, 20, 35, 179n, 283; and Philadelphians, 50

Sacheverell, Henry, 252
sacraments. *See* baptism; communion; ministry; rituals
sadism, 141
Saffron Walden, 222
sages, 5, 62
St. Albans, 96-98
St. John of the Cross, 158
St. John's College, Oxford, 328
St. Paul's Cathedral, 160
sal armoniac, sal ammoniac, 249, 250n
Salisbury, 144n, 148, 154, 289
Salisbury Cathedral, 53, 144n
sal mirabile, 247
salt: and the Scientists, 246-51; and wildness, 277. *See also* Epsom salt; *sal armoniac; sal mirabile; Sal volatile oleosum*
Salter, Mark (471), 324
Sal volatile oleosum: satirized, 122; its discovery, 237, 247-48; and the public domain, 237, 257; and wildness, 277
Sancta Sophia, 157
Sanger, Susannah (160), 144n, 324
Sardinian Chapel, 108, 252
satan. *See* devil
Saturn, 240, 243
Saudignan, Simon (513): prophesies against Wharton, 200; astronomical dream, 238; and clockwork, 239; importance of Camisard tradition, 285; profile as prophet, 325
Saumur, 12, 73, 328
Savage, Elizabeth, 69, 70
Savoy, Victor Amadeus, Duke of, 42

Savoy: allied against France, 26; as one of Two Witnesses, 42; agents to, 170
Savoy Church: conformist, 55; its annex, 73; consistory meets with *inspirés*, 77; denounces French Prophets, 80, 173; banishes Cavalier, Marion, Fage, 82; legal prosecution of French Prophets, 84, 94, 105n, 109n; "Colonel" Cavalier deposition for, 126
Saxony, 198, 203
scaffold: Marion, Fatio and Daude stand on, 109-12, 109n, 113; as a stage, 252; and public humiliation, 258; in contrast to pillory, 272, 272n
scatology, 141. *See also* obscenity; ordure
Scene of Delusions, By the Reverend Mr. OWEN . . . Confuted, The, 194, 288
scepticism: in France, 56; of Fatio, 218
schism: among Philadelphians, 51; among French Prophets, 93, 127, 133, 135, 140-43, 144, 148, 200-01; with Whitrow and Bulkeley, 133, 158, 171-72, 200; and inspired women, 135, 140-141, 144; with Philadelphians, 142-43, 194-96, 285; and ministers, 144; and *Orders*, 147-49; and True Church, 148; and group boundaries, 281. *See also* apostasy; false prophets
Schuchart, Anna Maria, 177n, 204
Schwabach, 177
Schwarzenau: inspired community at, 182, 285; Arnould from, 199-200; and American settlements, 204, 213n
science: in ethos of New Jerusalem, 5; and miracles, 62, 241; and millenarianism, 233-51, 282; and the hermetic tradition, 242-46; and prophecy, 282
scientific method, 241, 287
Scientists, the: and millenarianism, 40, 234, 239, 245, 250-51; and sense of exile, 221; and prophecy, 233-51; and motion, 233-42; and salt, 242-51; as spiritual mediums, 244; and space, 288
Scotland: union with England, 85, 86; prophecies of Emes's resurrection in, 123; missions to, 136, 172; French Prophets in, 155-69, 223; religious settlement in, 155; quietists in, 155-69; Jacobite rebellion in, 165-68, 191; Dutton's letters to believers in, 202; King of, 209; Evangelical Revival in, 210, 288; mentioned, 207, 227 *et passim*. *See also individual towns and counties, e.g.,* Barns; Edinburgh; Fife; *etc*.
scribes: for Isabeau Vincent, 17; their procedures, 73-74; declaration by, 74-75; on retreats, 82, 83; functions, 101, 124, 220; and women, 136; males, missions, and, 138; and publication, 175; economic status, 223; and literacy, 226
scripture. *See* Bible
scriptures, new, 116
Seafield, James Ogilvie, 2nd earl of, 157
Second Christian Church. *See* Shakers
Second Coming: in ethos of pentecost, 4; oppression and prophecies of, 6; dated by du Moulin, 15; predicted in England, 37; and Church of Philadelphia, 37, 43; English ideas on, 37-38, 43, 70; French Prophets' ideas on, 90-91; Lacy on, 106; Wardley visions of, 211; and passive waiting, 286
secrecy: Marion and, 78; Lacy and, 96; problems with, 97; of Multipliants, 188; and science, 236-37; and Scientists, 241; as Christian mystery, 244; and Desert Huguenots, 282
sect-church typology, 6
Sedan, 12, 328
sedition: French Prophets accused of, 84, 94; Holt on, 88n
Seeker, 53
seekers: French Prophets as, 217-19
Sellers, Lydia (516): exposure to French Prophets, 204; and lay preaching, 206; mission to Moravians, 208; as part of Female Embassy, 210
seniority: asserted among French Prophets, 149
sentiment, 287, 288
Separatists, German Protestant, 47n, 180, 180n, 204, 210, 213n, 285
Serious Call to a Devout and Holy Life, 192
sermons: by *prédicants*, 14; by *inspirés*, 18; published by Societies for the Reformation of Manners, 65; and oral tradition, 225. *See also* preaching
Seven Bishops, 41
sexes, problems between the. *See* sexuality; women
sexuality: in ethos of pentecost, 4; and Camisards, 23n, 35; and Catholic innuendo, 34; and millenarianism, 34; of Restoration period, 62; attacked by reformers, 65; and popular religion, 67n;

innuendo against Lacy and Gray, 97; homosexuality, 97*n*; and pollution, 111*n*; among French Prophets, 135-36, 185-86, 214; innuendo against French Prophets, 139; in small groups, 141; fears of, 152; of Lavington, 206; and isolation, 259; as problem of placement, 292. *See also* adultery; bigamy; homosexuality

Shaftesbury, Anthony Ashley Cooper, 3rd earl of: meets French Prophets, 93*n*; attacked by Mary Astell, 139*n*; and Furly, 171

Shakers: origins and history, 211-15; connections with French Prophets, 211-12, 214; and dance, 212, 229; and celibacy, 214, 280; and industrialization, 292; mentioned, 279

shame: in Desert, 18; and sexuality, 111*n*; and Fatio, 270-72; and believers' roles, 277

Shaw, Mr. (517), 206

Shaw, Samuel (426), 117*n*, 324

Shechina, 48*n*

Sheppard, Nathaniel (162): promised gift of healing, 124; as missionary, 136; apothecary, 138; illness of, 141

Shovel, Cloudesly, 24

Shrewsbury, Charles Talbot, 12th earl and Duke of, 232*n*

Sidney, Algernon, 171

silence: in ethos of pentecost, 4; and Marion, 26; and Philadelphians, 47; in French Prophet meetings, 147, 192; and agitations, 157; and Abden's inspirations, 158; at Montrose, 163; and Scottish quietists, 167; in pietist worship, 170; and *Gonfleurs*, 189; of the French Prophets, 191-94, 201-02

Silesia, 170, 210

sin: in ethos of judgment, 3; as plot, 66; Shakers on, 212-14; French Prophets on, 214*n*-215*n*. *See also* perfection

Sinai, 165, 275

Sleaford, 154

sleeping in Jesus, 106, 107*n*

Smyrna, 180

Societies for the Reformation of Manners: Philadelphians as one, 45; origin and activity, 64-65; and Bulkeley, 79-80; view of London, 263

Society for Promoting Christian Knowledge: prints Bibles, 65; and Sir John Philipps, 84*n*; and John Hooke, 86; and John Chamberlayne, 92

Society for the Propagation of the Gospel in Foreign Parts, 65

Socinianism: Huguenot declaration against, 56; deists accused of, 63-64; and French Prophets, 89; Emes and, 89*n*

sodality, 260-61 and *n*. *See also* women

sodomy, 111*n*

Soho: refugees in, 55, 57; economic tensions in, 60; Allut's house in, 72; mob in, 82; mentioned, 62, 76, 77

Somerset House, 72

Sophia: Pordage's image of wisdom, 46; likened to Shechina, 48*n*; and Ann Lee, 214

soteriology: of Camisards, 90*n*, 201; of Lacy, 106; of French Prophets, 107, 215*n*. *See also* universalism; universal salvation; and specific denominations

Soulier, Jaques (203), 324

South Carolina, 288

Southcott, Joanna: and androgyneity, 213*n*; identifies herself as the second Eve, 279; and Richard Brothers, 289

South Sea Company, 191

Southwark, 114, 115, 223*n*

space: war and male, 36; open, 223; for play, 229; in universe, 234-35; in cities, churches, 288

Spademan, John, 92*n*

Spain, 85, 125, 171

Spangenberg, August: in London, 198; at Herrnhut, 198, 203; to Georgia, 198; in Pennsylvania, 204

Spanish Succession, War of the: and Camisard revolt, 22; and Philadelphians, 50; in 1706, 71; ends, 179. *See also* Blenheim; Ramillies; Turin; Utrecht, Peace of

spas. *See* mineral waters and spas

Spence, David (429), 202

Spener, Philipp Jakob, 8, 169, 182

spies, spying: missionaries arrested as, 179; French Prophets as, 258

Spinckes, Nathaniel: opposition to Camisards, 68*n*; on failure of Emes's resurrection, 123

spirit mediums, 45

spirits, discerning of: gift promised Fatio, 97*n*; method of, 148. *See also* false prophecy; language

Spiritual Songs, 43, 45*n*

Spitalfields: Huguenot refugees in, 55, 57,

62, 221; weavers in, 57, 62; economic tensions in, 60; Fatio teaches in, 237; mentioned, 77
Spong, William (184), 219
spontaneity: in ethos of pentecost, 4; feared, 152; and generations of prophecy, 281*n*
sports, pastimes, 229
Spring Gardens, 265
Sprogel, Johann Heinrich, 204
steam engine, 71
Steed, Anne (165): as Quaker prophet, 52; problems as Quaker, 117*n*, 289; sexual activity of, 146*n*; religious connections of, 224; profile as prophet, 323
Steele, Benjamin (401): as Scientist, 193, 239, 241*n*; admires Wharton, 197; and perpetual motion, 239; and sea watches, 241*n*
Steele, Elizabeth, 197
Steele, Richard, 260
Steffkins, Christian (76), 118
Sterrill, Marie (166), 217
Stirling, 160
Stockholm, 178-79
stock market, 191, 193 and *n*
Stoddard, Dinah (77), 134, 323
Story, Thomas, 289
Strand, the, 72
Stratford, 124
Street-Light Club, 171
structuralism, 251
stuttering, 255. *See also* language
Suffolk, 154, 222*n*
sulphur, sulfur: defined by Paracelsus, 46, 246; and Byfield, 247-48
Sultan, the: Quaker mission to, 52
sunspots, 240
Superville, Daniel de, 173
Surrey, 79, 132, 222
Sweden: Daut on, 175; mission to, 176; possessions in Germany, 176*n*. *See also* Charles XII of Sweden
Swift, Jonathan: on the French Prophets, 123; and Moult, 245; on London, 263
swimming machine, 240
Switzerland: Philadelphians in, 47; Fage and Cavalier in, 72; pietists in, 182-84, 186-87, 189; prophets in, 185-86, 188. *See also* Geneva; Lausanne; Vaud; Vevey
symbolic system: in each millenarian ethos, 3-5, 329-30; and false prophecy, 152; of Scientists, 251; of *inspirés* and French Prophets, 284
syncretism, 189

Tabernacles, Feast of. *See* Feast of Tabernacles
taxation: and Camisards, 27-28
Taylor, Jonathan (87): visits French Prophets, 105; his prophetic group in Birmingham, 114-15; on Lacy-Gray adultery, 144-45; dispute with Beer and Allut, 193; follower of Wharton, 196*n*; letter from Allut, 198; age, 230; son?, 280; profile as prophet, 323
telescope, 234, 241
Ten Commandments: sung by Vincent, 17
tenements, 2, 226
Tennhardt, Johann: cited by Furly, 175; French Prophets compared to, 182; works studied in Switzerland, 185
Test Act, 41
Testas, Pierre, 76
Thames River, 122
theater, theaters: drama of Restoration period, 62, 256; Emes's resurrection as, 121; d'Urfey's play, 139, 254; repentance as drama, 202-03, 205; healing as drama, 219; French Prophets and, 251-78; playhouses, 252, 253; London as place of public theater, 252-54; spas and, 253; Elizabeth Grey as actress, 254; pastoral, 266-67. *See also* publicity; puppet shows; scaffold.
Théâtre sacré des Cévennes: prepared, 78-79, 81, 84*n*; translated, 84*n*, 107, 170, 262, 268, 277; controversy over, 125-26, 284; shapes millenarian ethos, 151; function of, 189, 258, 284; and literacy, 225-26; theater simile in, 252; as public drama, 255; and membership, 316
Theologia Christianae Principia Mathematica, 234
theology: of French Prophets, 89, 220. *See also* French Prophets; millenarianism; soteriology; *and specific churches, denominations and doctrines, e.g.*, election; Philadelphians; Socinianism; *etc.*
Theosophical Transactions: and Philadelphians, 48; on orderly prophecy, 49; language of, 196; and Kabbala, 243
theosophy, 8, 45, 46, 195
third age, 184 and *n*

Thirty Years' War: and apocalypse, 8; as fourth vial of Revelation, 38; and pietism, 169
Threadneedle Street Church: Calvinist, 55; consistory interviews *inspirés*, 76; alerts Savoy Church, 77; suspends French Prophets, 103; challenges *TS*, 126
Three Foxes Inn, 114
Tiley, Joseph (81): chambers in Whitehall, 1-2; illness of, 218*n*; healed, 219; and politics, 232*n*; as spy, 258; education of, 328
time: in each millenarian ethos, 4-5; monochronic and polychronic, 5*n*; and apocalypse, 6; for Camisards, 35, 283; millennial, 36; feminized, 232*n*; and Newtonian mechanics, 239; and longitude, 241; and agitations, 241-42; and the Desert, 285; and the French Prophets, 292. *See also* watches and clocks
tin, 245
Todd, Samuel (449), 69*n*
Toland, John, 63, 64
Toleration Act, 41, 48
Tomlinson, Samuel (493), 146*n*
Tong, William, 92*n* (for T . . . g, Mr.)
tongues, speaking in: Lacy's gift of, 93, 95, 146; Bulkeley on, 93; promised to Gray, 97*n*; by Orme, 164; missing in Stockholm, 178-79; prophet, 207; as part of theater, 255. *See also* language; prophecy
Topham, Ann (167), 141, 323
Tories: and Huguenot churches, 56; problems of definition, 56*n*; opposition to Huguenot citizenship, 57; and Occasional Conformity Bill, 64*n*; and Abigail Hill, 85; pamphlets attributed to Lacy, 167*n*; and French Prophets, 232 and *n*
tourism, 1, 258
Tovey, Beata (64): death, 202; childless, 280; as Quaker, 289
Tovey, Joseph (65): death, 202; will, 219; childless, 280; as Quaker, 289
Tower Guns: prophecy by Lacy, 95, 97, 99, 120, 264; timing, 97; failure of, explained, 99; and London as Desert, 264
Tower of Constance, 188
Tower Street, 78
Townley, John, 211-12

trance: among Shakers, 214; of *petits prophètes*, 283
Transcendent Spiritual Treatise, 51
translation: by Philadelphians, 51*n*, 197-98, 213; of works by French Prophets, 81, 84*n*, 85, 107, 170, 171, 179, 181, 262, 268, 277, 291; of Daut's work, 175; as transformation, 262, 268, 277
transmutation of metals, 244-45
treason: inspired discernment of traitors, 29, 30; and pollution, 30; and Jean Cavalier, 72; French Prophets accused of, 117; in ethos of cataclysm, 142
tribes: Desert image, 32; sexuality and, 35; role of women in, 35; as models for Camisards, 36, 98, 284; and chapel, 104; French Prophets named into, 126-27, 164, 279, 281, 285; and Bulkeley, 131; and Jean Cavalier, 133; men and women in, 135; and millenarian ethos of French Prophets, 151; and inspired women, 210; and social models for women, 291
Trinity, the: John Robins as one of, 51; Huguenot churches on, 56; Fatio on, 89*n*
Trinity College, Cambridge, 328
Trinity College, Dublin, 228, 328
True Church: French Prophets as, 6*n*, 54, 98-104, 108, 112, 148; in the Desert, 17, 29, 30, 32; and millenarianism, 149; reconstrued, 150; as a garden, 222; in illustration, 269-70; and publicity, 272
Trumbull, William, 109
Turin, 76
Turkey, Turks: philosophers of, 62; Daut on, 175; missions to, 176; Charles XII in, 176*n*; prophecy about, 178
Turner, Mr., 92*n*
Turner, Mary (168): accused of false prophecy, 133; reprimanded, 141; missions to university towns, 229; mission to Quakers, 289; profile as prophet, 323
Turner, Victor, 2
Twickenham, 260
Two Treatises, 175
Two Witnesses, of Revelation: their resurrection dated, 15-16; as metaphor, 17, 91; and Desert Huguenots, 17, 42, 68, 117; among Mason's followers, 44; and Muggleton, 51; Camisards as one of, 68; in illustration, 195
Tyburn, 252

Unitarians, 89*n*
Unitas Fratrum. *See* Moravians
United Provinces. *See* Netherlands
universal church: as prophetic theme, 86, 98, 104, 201, 284, 292; Lacy's vision of, 98; Bourignon on, 155; and English believers, 284, 292. *See also* ecumenism; New Jerusalem, ethos of
universalism, 90*n*. *See also* universal salvation
universal salvation: Jane Lead on, 47; Philadelphians on, 49, 53, 90*n*, 159; Quakers and, 52-53; and French Prophets, 152, 159, 198; Marie Huber on, 184, 287; Petersen on, 198; and alchemy, 245-46. *See also* damnation; election; soteriology; universalism
universities: James II's appointments, 41; French Prophets' education at, 124, 228, 328; French Prophets' attitudes toward, 228-29
University College, Oxford, 328
urban culture: and Huguenot refugees, 60, 220-22; of London, 71, 222, 225-27, 253-54, 263; and English believers, 80, 221-33, 282; religious movements and, 185; and the young, 229-30; and the Whigs, 232*n*; and science, 237; its theatricality, 252-54; contemporary attitudes toward, 263; and millenarian transformation, 282
Urfey, Thomas d', 139, 254
Ussher, James: eschatology of, 38; foresees persecution in France, 42; read by Mason, 43
utopianism: of Ranters and Fifth Monarchists, 39. *See also* New Jerusalem; New Jerusalem, ethos of
Utrecht, Peace of, 179 and *n*, 191

vacuum, 234
Valentin, Judith (464), 325
Valérargues, 21
Valette, Pierre (170), 225*n*
Vaud, canton of, 185
Vaudois, the, 42
Verchand, Mme., 188, 189
Verduron, Abraham (21), 121*n*
Vergnon, Louise (239), 173
Vergnon, Marthe (408), 173, 323
Vergnon, Samuel (409), 173
Versailles, 265
Vesson, Jean, 188

Vevey: pietist colony at, 183, 185, 189, 210, 250*n*, 285
Vienna: missions to, 176, 178, 180; mineral spring near, 247
Villars, Charles Louis Hector, duc de: replaces Montrevel, 26; his strategies, 26; departure from Languedoc, 27; significance of victory, 27*n*; on Camisard youth, 31*n*; treaty with "Colonel" Cavalier, 125
Vincent, Isabeau: her prophecies, 17-19; imprisoned, 18; as a child, 34; mentioned, 150
Vincent, Nathaniel, 122*n*
Virginia, 273
virtuosi: their two traditions, 233-34; perpetual motion and, 239; and the hermetic tradition, 242-46; hunt for antiquities, 262
visions: of army, 19; of golden bird, 95; of True Church, 98; of New Jerusalem, 102, 267; of porcelain cup, 133; and Richard Roach, 257
Vivarais, the: prophets in, 20, 21; revolt in, 26
Voyer, Anne (32), 83-84, 322

Wadham College, Oxford, 228, 328
waiting: and eschatology, 153, 166, 201; at Montrose, 163; importance to Wharton, 196-97, 215; as root metaphor, 215; and religious experience, 285
Wales: and Sir John Philipps, 70; missions to, 136, 154; Howell Harris, 207
Waller, Mary (443), 324
Walpole, Robert, 191
Waltham Abbey, 52*n*
Ward, Thomas, 44
Wardley, James, 211-12
Wardley, Jane, 211-12
Warens, Ursule de: Magny's student, 183; her Vevey colony, 185, 189, 210; attitude toward French Prophets, 186; and alchemy, 250*n*; and Rousseau, 287
Warnings: Elie Marion's, 81, 82, 84, 91, 94, 171, 281; John Lacy's, 96, 97, 102, 109-10, 181, 207, 227, 281; Abraham Whitrow's, 132. *See also Avertissemens*
watches and clocks: Huguenot watchmakers, 57; Fatio's; jewelled, 237, 238-39; and French Prophets, 241; and Caswell, 241; and prophecy, 241-42;

ornaments for, 269*n*; occupations, 319
Water Stratford, 37, 43-45, 53, 118
Watling Street, 248
Watts, Anne (57): as Levite, 134; as pie vendor, 138; profile as prophet, 322
Watts, Isaac, 192, 260 and *n*
Way to Christ Discovered, The, 213
weather. *See* climate; Great Storm of 1703; Little Ice Age
weavers: among Camisards, 27; Huguenots in London, 57, 60, 70, 89; among French Prophets, 62, 221, 224, 319; Cavalier as, 72; and green ribbons, 128*n*; and Whitrow's charity, 132
Weavers Company, 57
Weavers' Hall, Bristol, 206
Weber, Max, 2
Webster, Sarah (486), 325
Weintraub, William (503), 198
Wells, Mrs. (40), 86
Wesley, Charles: his conversion, 205; hymns, 205, 260, 260*n*-261*n*; battles with French Prophets, 206; on perfectionism, 213*n*
Wesley, John: and the Moravians, 8, 198, 205; birthplace, 65*n*; and French Prophets, 198, 205-07, 210; on perfectionism, 213*n*; hymns, 260*n*-261*n*; Methodist circuit, 279; on personal sanctification, 286; on grace, 287; on reason, 287-88
Wesley, Samuel, 65*n*
Westminster, 105
Westmoreland House, 48, 49
Wetteravia: religious toleration in, 181; pietists in, 185, 198*n*, 210
Wharton, George (501), 199
Wharton, Hannah (413): and quietism, 165-66, 196, 201; dispute with Allut and Beer, 193; her rhetoric, 196, 201; her control of property, 199, 200, 203*n*; and progressive revelation, 201, 215; and evangelism, 202, 203; and Wynantz and Wesley, 205; prophetic status, 211; and Shakers, 214; her age, 230; and intimacy, 261; her children, 279; and waiting, 285; and the New Jerusalem, 291; mentioned, 115, 210, 249; profile as prophet, 323
Wharton, Joseph (414), 279*n*
Wharton, Mary (506), 279*n*
Wharton, Richard (88), 114-15
Wharton, Sarah (507), 279*n*

Whigs: and Huguenots, 56, 232*n*; problems of definition, 56*n*; and citizenship acts, 57; and Huguenot nobility, 60; and Abigail Hill, 85; Junto, 122*n*; Green Ribbon Club, 128*n*; Lacy's vision, 167*n*; and Hanoverian government, 191; French Prophets as, 232 and *n*
Whiston, William: millenarianism of, 37, 192; Arianism of, 64*n*; sermon against French Prophets, 106; on providence, 234; on comets, 235; science, scripture, and, 241
Whitefield, George, 206, 288
Whitehall, 2
Whitehall Coffee House, 112
Whitehead, Thomas (415): host to French Prophets, 202; baptized by Whitefield, 206; as French Prophet, 289; merchant, 291
Whitrow, Abraham (52): appears as prophet, 95; blessings at Enfield, 116; his wealth, 119; on Emes's resurrection, 120-21, 123; heals waterman, 124; expelled by French Prophets, 130-31, 134; his levelling, 131-32, 152; and Bulkeley's will, 133*n*; on female prophets, 135*n*; and impurity, 142; and autonomy, 152; Furly on, 171-72; residence, 222; and literacy, 228; image for Bulkeley, 275; agricultural images, 276; and ethos of judgment, 285; profile as prophet, 323; mentioned, 140, 144, 154, 158, 200, 257
Whitrow, Deborah (53): mission, 116; rebuked, 131; profile as prophet, 323
Whore of Babylon, 32, 97, 135
wilderness: in Languedoc and Dauphiné, 14; cries in the, 195; and the Desert, 189, 283; defined, 262, 265-66, 268; London as, 263 and *n*; as a stage, 266; publicity, intimacy, and, 266, 277; and French Prophets, 266*n*; and restoration of nature, 267; and Feast of Tabernacles, 275-76
William III of England, Prince of Orange: seen in vision, 19; crowned, 19-20; oath of allegiance to, 41; parties during reign of, 56*n*; Huguenot relief, 60; mentioned, 36
Willis, Francis, 249
Willis, Mary (191), 117*n*
wills: and popular religion, 67*n*; of French Prophets, 219*n*

Wiltshire, Sarah (61): and ethos of New Jerusalem, 142-43; heals Mary Heath, 142; on Elizabeth Gray, 146; and mercy, 159; last prophecies, 195; as female leader, 210-11; on education of youth, 281; profile as prophet, 322
Wiltshire: French Prophets in, 144, 222*n*; Moravian prophecy in, 208
Wimbledon, 265
Wise, Mr. (523), 206
Wise, Robert (204), 323
Wissahickon River, 47*n*
wit, 256
Wittgenstein, 182
Wodrow, Robert, 167*n*
Wolf, Shepherd (524), 206
women: rescue *inspiré*, 21; childrearing role in Desert, 32-33; "character" of, 33, 33*n*, 231*n*; as prophets, 32-36, 102, 134, 136, 140-44, 146, 210-11, 214, 231, 232*n*, 291, 326; among French Prophets, 83, 85*n*, 135, 143, 316-17, 321; and early Quakers, 83*n*; blessing men, 85*n*, 136; their sacerdotal powers, 135; latitude as French Prophets, 135-36; mobility of, 136; as missionaries, 136-38, 229; in business, 138; opposition to French Prophets from, 139*n*; sexual suspicions of, 139, 141; and dress, 139, 229; and ethos of judgment, 142, 291; and ethos of pentecost, 142, 291; as healers, 142; and schisms, 144; omitted from *Orders*, 148*n*; and quietists, 167-68, 170; as religious leaders, 167-68, 170, 189-90, 210-14; new spiritual woman, 213; fear of inspired women, 214; and androgyneity, 214; their agitations, 229; as English citizens, 231; as hosts, 231, 261, 277; surplus of, 231*n*, 261*n*; and friendships, 259-61; in the city, 277*n*; and the model of companionship, 291. *See also* demography; false prophets; sexuality; sodality
Wonderful Narrative, 288
Woodcock, Mr., 92*n*, 93*n*
Woods, Joseph, 289-90
Woodward, Josiah: meets French Prophets, 92*n*; on the gift of tongues, 95; on Silesian children, 170
Worcester, 193, 197, 199, 222-23
worship: in ethos of New Jerusalem, 5; of Huguenot refugees, 61; redefined for French Prophets, 107; quietist model of, 163; French Prophets and Shakers compared, 211-12; and science, 233. *See also* French Prophets; ritual
Wotton, William. *See* Astell, Mary
Wren, Christopher, 2, 71
Wright, David, 69
Wycherly, William, 139
Wynantz, Francis (508): host to Spangenberg, 198; brings together Wesley and Böhler, 205; inherits archives, 209-10; merchant, 291

Yates, Mr., 92*n*, 93*n*
York, 161
York Buildings Company, 193
Yverdon: quietist community at, 183; prophets near, 186

Zeidig, Johanna Christina (505): as French Prophet, 204; a seeker, 217; mentioned, 213*n*, 216*n*
Zimmerman, Johann, 47*n*, 204
Zinzendorf, Nicolaus Ludwig, Count von: sees Rock prophesying, 182; Spangenberg and, 198; Moravians and, 203
zodiacal light, 240

Designer:	Barbara Llewellyn
Compositor:	U.C. Press
Printer:	Braun-Brumfield
Binder:	Braun-Brumfield
Text:	Compset Times Roman
Display:	Compset Andover
Cloth:	Arrestox B 56668 and Elephant Hide Paper
Paper:	50 lb. P & S Offset